The Designer's Guide to TEXT TYPE

The Designer's Guide to TEXT TYPE

Jean Callan King and Tony Esposito

VNR VAN NOSTRAND REINHOLD COMPANY
New York

Library of Congress Catalog Card Number 80-23722
ISBN 0-442-25425-3

Printed in the United States of America.

Published by Van Nostrand Reinhold Company Inc.
115 Fifth Avenue, New York, New York 10003

Van Nostrand Reinhold Australia Pty. Ltd.
480 La Trobe Street
Melbourne, Victoria 3000, Australia

Van Nostrand Reinhold Company Limited
Molly Millars Lane
Wokingham, Berkshire, RG11 2PY England

Macmillan of Canada
Division of Canada Publishing Corporation
164 Commander Boulevard
Agincourt, Ontario M1S 3C7, Canada

16 15 14 13 12 10 9 8 7 6 5

Library of Congress Cataloging in Publication Data

King, Jean Callan.
The designer's guide to text type.

1. Printing—Specimens. 2. Type and type-founding.
I. Esposito, Tony, 1942– joint author. II. Title
Z250.K49 686.2'24 80-23722
ISBN 0-442-25425-3 (pbk.)

To the craftsmen of Volk & Huxley

with thanks for their efforts in producing this book.

CONTENTS

® Registered in U.S. Patent & TM. Off.

INTRODUCTION

Most type books emphasize display typefaces, giving short shrift to their less showy companions, the text faces. Two- and three-line samples of a text type face are insufficient material for most designers and type specifiers. Hence, *A Designer's Guide to Text Type,* which is devoted entirely to providing a substantial block of text type for each typeface shown.

Legibility, color, and the character of each face may be thoroughly examined and compared with other faces. We chose the fifty-one most frequently specified text typefaces based on our experience.

Typefaces with extensive ranges of weights are shown with the selected combinations we felt would prove most useful. However, this is not meant to imply that the weights may be set only in these combinations.

These leaded samples provide a long needed tool and visual aid for designers, art directors, type directors, production personnel, and students of graphic design.

FACTS ABOUT THE VIP

- The VIP (Variable Input Processor), is a computer-aided photo-typesetting system with an output of positive film or reproduction quality paper.
- Type sizes of 6 through 72 point may be set from the 12 point grid shown at the right.
- Maximum line length is 45 picas.
- Leading increments range from zero (no advance) to 99 points.
- Film advance may increase or decrease in ½ point increments. Minus leading is also available. (Example: 12 point type size on an 11½ point film advance.)
- Justification is automatic between words only.
- Standard word spacing is 4 units.*
- Plus or minus letterspacing for any type size may be specified for manuscript copy, a single word or a group of characters.
- All typefaces in all sizes are base-aligned.
- The VIP holds eighteen fonts at once, allowing a wide choice when mixing typefaces, weights or sizes on the same line.

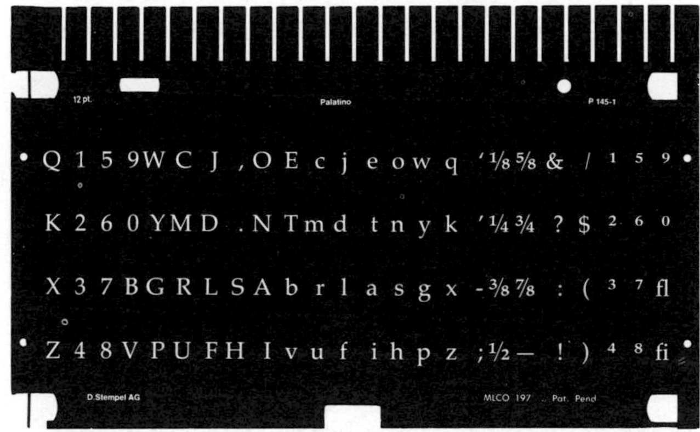

ACTUAL SIZE

A few notes:

- When specifying letterspacing consider each typeface individually since basic character fit differs. Letter-spacing is described as normal, minus ½ unit, or minus 1 unit. A complete overlap of characters is also available on the VIP.
- The typefaces in this book are set to a uniform character space for ease of comparison. Normal letterspacing for 6 through 9 point showings, and minus ½ unit for 10 through 14 point.
- A complete showing of each font in its corresponding size appears with the leaded samples.
- All of the sample settings are set in the same copy for convenient copy casting. This use of the same copy also affords helpful comparison between different type sizes.

*A unit is a varying measure of space relative to type size.

Copyfitting determines the amount of space that typewritten copy will occupy when it is typeset.

There are many ways to copyfit as well as numerous devices available to assist the designer. The copyfitting method described below has been somewhat simplified by the use of the gauge shown at the right. However, it is entirely possible to copyfit from these instructions without the gauge.

Procedure:

1. Determine the total number of characters in your copy. To do this multiply the number of characters per line in your typewritten copy by the total number of lines. *This will give you the total number of characters.* Note that each letter, punctuation mark, and space between words must be counted as a character.

2. Select a typeface.

3. Determine the width in picas to which the copy will be set.

4. Determine the number of typeset characters per pica by placing a pica (12-point) gauge on the first line showing of the chosen typeface and size. Begin measuring at the first word on the left, noting the last character where your pica width ends on the right.

The type gauge at the right gives the same copy in a typewritten line as the first line of copy used throughout the book. Find the last (right hand) character on the typed part of the gauge. Each character is numbered and the number directly below will give you the number of characters per line at the width you have chosen. (If your setting width exceeds the width of the samples shown in this book, then measure only one-half of the line width, find the number of characters using the gauge, then double this figure to give you the character count per line.) Without the gauge at the right, simply count the number of characters in the first line of type to obtain the number of characters per typeset line.

5. Divide your total character count (from step 1) by the number of typeset characters per line (step 4). This will give you the total number of typeset lines.

CHARACTER COUNT RULE

Based on 10 pt. Typewriter

6 pt. | 7 pt. | 8 pt. | 9 pt. | 12 pt.

ABCDEFGHIJKLMNOPQRSTUVWXYZ

The main purpose of letters is the practical one of making thoughts visi

volk&huxley

TYPOGRAPHERS

228 E. 45 STREET/NEW YORK NY 10017/682-1800

6. Determine the depth you want your typeset copy to be. You may need to decrease or increase point size or amount of planned leading at this point to make your copy fit a predetermined layout.

If the depth of the type is not critical then choose the visual sample you prefer, noting the bottom part of the fraction above the copy. Look on the gauge and find the scale with the corresponding number. Find the number of lines on this scale, showing you the final depth of the typeset copy.

Or, add the number of points of space you want between each line to the point size of the typeface. Then look at the gauge and find the scale with the corresponding number. Find the number of lines on the scale, showing you the final depth of the typeset copy.

Character count rules are available on request from Volk & Huxley, 228 East 45 Street, New York, New York 10017.

The Designer's Guide to TEXT TYPE

ITC AMERICAN TYPEWRITER 6 & 7 POINT SET NORMAL

LIGHT, MEDIUM, BOLD

ABCDEFGHIJKLMNOPQRSTUVWXYZ 1234567890 abcdefghijklmnopqrstuvwxyz

ABCDEFGHIJKLMNOPQRSTUVWXYZ 1234567890 abcdefghijklmnopqrstuvwxyz

ABCDEFGHIJKLMNOPQRSTUVWXYZ 1234567890 abcdefghijklmnopqrstuvwxyz

6/6

The main purpose of letters is the practical one of making thoughts visible. Ruskin says th at all letters are frightful things and to be endured only on occasion, that is to say, in places where the sense of the inscription is of more importance than external ornament. This is a sweeping statement, from which we need not suffer unduly; yet it is doubtful whether ther e is art in individual letters. Letters in combination may be satisfying and in a well compose d page even beautiful as a whole, but art in letters consists rather in the art of arranging a nd composing them in a pleasing and appropriate manner. The main purpose of letters is t he practical one of making thoughts visible. Ruskin says that all letters are frightful thing s and to be endured only on occasion, that is to say, in places where the sense of the inscript ion is of more importance than external ornament. This is a sweeping statement, from whi ch we need not suffer unduly; yet it is doubtful whether there is art in individual letters. Let ters in combination may be satisfying and in a well composed page even beautiful as a who le, but art in letters consists rather in the art of arranging and composing them in a pleasi
The main purpose of letters is the practical one of making thoughts visible. Ruskin sa ys that all letters are frightful things and to be endured only on occasion, that is to say,
The main purpose of letters is the practical one of making thoughts visible. R uskin says that all letters are frightful things and to be endured only on occa

6/7

The main purpose of letters is the practical one of making thoughts visible. Ruskin says th at all letters are frightful things and to be endured only on occasion, that is to say, in places where the sense of the inscription is of more importance than external ornament. This is a sweeping statement, from which we need not suffer unduly; yet it is doubtful whether ther e is art in individual letters. Letters in combination may be satisfying and in a well compose d page even beautiful as a whole, but art in letters consists rather in the art of arranging a nd composing them in a pleasing and appropriate manner. The main purpose of letters is t he practical one of making thoughts visible. Ruskin says that all letters are frightful thing s and to be endured only on occasion, that is to say, in places where the sense of the inscript ion is of more importance than external ornament. This is a sweeping statement, from whi ch we need not suffer unduly; yet it is doubtful whether there is art in individual letters. Let
The main purpose of letters is the practical one of making thoughts visible. Ruskin sa ys that all letters are frightful things and to be endured only on occasion, that is to say,
The main purpose of letters is the practical one of making thoughts visible. R uskin says that all letters are frightful things and to be endured only on occa

6/8

The main purpose of letters is the practical one of making thoughts visible. Ruskin says th at all letters are frightful things and to be endured only on occasion, that is to say, in places where the sense of the inscription is of more importance than external ornament. This is a sweeping statement, from which we need not suffer unduly; yet it is doubtful whether ther e is art in individual letters. Letters in combination may be satisfying and in a well compose d page even beautiful as a whole, but art in letters consists rather in the art of arranging a nd composing them in a pleasing and appropriate manner. The main purpose of letters is t he practical one of making thoughts visible. Ruskin says that all letters are frightful thing s and to be endured only on occasion, that is to say, in places where the sense of the inscript
The main purpose of letters is the practical one of making thoughts visible. Ruskin sa ys that all letters are frightful things and to be endured only on occasion, that is to say,
The main purpose of letters is the practical one of making thoughts visible. R uskin says that all letters are frightful things and to be endured only on occa

6/9

The main purpose of letters is the practical one of making thoughts visible. Ruskin says th at all letters are frightful things and to be endured only on occasion, that is to say, in places where the sense of the inscription is of more importance than external ornament. This is a sweeping statement, from which we need not suffer unduly; yet it is doubtful whether ther e is art in individual letters. Letters in combination may be satisfying and in a well compose d page even beautiful as a whole, but art in letters consists rather in the art of arranging a nd composing them in a pleasing and appropriate manner. The main purpose of letters is t he practical one of making thoughts visible. Ruskin says that all letters are frightful thing
The main purpose of letters is the practical one of making thoughts visible. Ruskin sa ys that all letters are frightful things and to be endured only on occasion, that is to say,
The main purpose of letters is the practical one of making thoughts visible. R uskin says that all letters are frightful things and to be endured only on occa

---

ABCDEFGHIJKLMNOPQRSTUVWXYZ 1234567890 abcdefghijklmnopqrstuvwxyz

ABCDEFGHIJKLMNOPQRSTUVWXYZ 1234567890 abcdefghijklmnopqrstuvwxyz

ABCDEFGHIJKLMNOPQRSTUVWXYZ 1234567890 abcdefghijklmnopqrstuvwxyz

7/7

The main purpose of letters is the practical one of making thoughts visible. R uskin says that all letters are frightful things and to be endured only on occas ion, that is to say, in places where the sense of the inscription is of more impor tance than external ornament. This is a sweeping statement, from which we need not suffer unduly; yet it is doubtful whether there is art in individual lett ers. Letters in combination may be satisfying and in a well composed page eve n beautiful as a whole, but art in letters consists rather in the art of arranging and composing them in a pleasing and appropriate manner. The main purpo se of letters is the practical one of making thoughts visible. Ruskin says that a ll letters are frightful things and to be endured only on occasion, that is to say, in places where the sense of the inscription is of more importance than exter
The main purpose of letters is the practical one of making thoughts visibl e. Ruskin says that all letters are frightful things and to be endured only o
The main purpose of letters is the practical one of making thought s visible. Ruskin says that all letters are frightful things and to be

7/8

The main purpose of letters is the practical one of making thoughts visible. R uskin says that all letters are frightful things and to be endured only on occas ion, that is to say, in places where the sense of the inscription is of more impor tance than external ornament. This is a sweeping statement, from which we need not suffer unduly; yet it is doubtful whether there is art in individual lett ers. Letters in combination may be satisfying and in a well composed page eve n beautiful as a whole, but art in letters consists rather in the art of arranging and composing them in a pleasing and appropriate manner. The main purpo se of letters is the practical one of making thoughts visible. Ruskin says that a ll letters are frightful things and to be endured only on occasion, that is to say,
The main purpose of letters is the practical one of making thoughts visibl e. Ruskin says that all letters are frightful things and to be endured only o
The main purpose of letters is the practical one of making thought s visible. Ruskin says that all letters are frightful things and to be

7/9

The main purpose of letters is the practical one of making thoughts visible. R uskin says that all letters are frightful things and to be endured only on occas ion, that is to say, in places where the sense of the inscription is of more impor tance than external ornament. This is a sweeping statement, from which we need not suffer unduly; yet it is doubtful whether there is art in individual lett ers. Letters in combination may be satisfying and in a well composed page eve n beautiful as a whole, but art in letters consists rather in the art of arranging and composing them in a pleasing and appropriate manner. The main purpo se of letters is the practical one of making thoughts visible. Ruskin says that a ll letters are frightful things and to be endured only on occasion, that is to say,
The main purpose of letters is the practical one of making thoughts visibl e. Ruskin says that all letters are frightful things and to be endured only o
The main purpose of letters is the practical one of making thought s visible. Ruskin says that all letters are frightful things and to be

7/10

The main purpose of letters is the practical one of making thoughts visible. R uskin says that all letters are frightful things and to be endured only on occas ion, that is to say, in places where the sense of the inscription is of more impor tance than external ornament. This is a sweeping statement, from which we need not suffer unduly; yet it is doubtful whether there is art in individual lett ers. Letters in combination may be satisfying and in a well composed page eve n beautiful as a whole, but art in letters consists rather in the art of arranging and composing them in a pleasing and appropriate manner. The main purpo se of letters is the practical one of making thoughts visible. Ruskin says that a
The main purpose of letters is the practical one of making thoughts visibl e. Ruskin says that all letters are frightful things and to be endured only o
The main purpose of letters is the practical one of making thought s visible. Ruskin says that all letters are frightful things and to be

ITC AMERICAN TYPEWRITER 8 & 9 POINT SET NORMAL

LIGHT, MEDIUM, BOLD

ABCDEFGHIJKLMNOPQRSTUVWXYZ 1234567890 abcdefghijklmnopqrstuvwxyz

ABCDEFGHIJKLMNOPQRSTUVWXYZ 1234567890 abcdefghijklmnopqrstuvwxyz

ABCDEFGHIJKLMNOPQRSTUVWXYZ 1234567890 abcdefghijklmnopqrstuvwxyz

8/8

The main purpose of letters is the practical one of making thoughts visible. Ruskin says that all letters are frightful things and to be end ured only on occasion, that is to say, in places where the sense of the inscription is of more importance than external ornament. This is a sweeping statement, from which we need not suffer unduly; yet it is doubtful whether there is art in individual letters. Letters in combin ation may be satisfying and in a well composed page even beautiful as a whole, but art in letters consists rather in the art of arranging a nd composing them in a pleasing and appropriate manner. The ma

The main purpose of letters is the practical one of making thoug hts visible. Ruskin says that all letters are frightful things and to

The main purpose of letters is the practical one of making thoughts visible. Ruskin says that all letters are frightful

8/9

The main purpose of letters is the practical one of making thoughts visible. Ruskin says that all letters are frightful things and to be end ured only on occasion, that is to say, in places where the sense of the inscription is of more importance than external ornament. This is a sweeping statement, from which we need not suffer unduly; yet it is doubtful whether there is art in individual letters. Letters in combin ation may be satisfying and in a well composed page even beautiful as a whole, but art in letters consists rather in the art of arranging a

The main purpose of letters is the practical one of making thoug hts visible. Ruskin says that all letters are frightful things and to

The main purpose of letters is the practical one of making thoughts visible. Ruskin says that all letters are frightful

8/10

The main purpose of letters is the practical one of making thoughts visible. Ruskin says that all letters are frightful things and to be end ured only on occasion, that is to say, in places where the sense of the inscription is of more importance than external ornament. This is a sweeping statement, from which we need not suffer unduly; yet it is doubtful whether there is art in individual letters. Letters in combin ation may be satisfying and in a well composed page even beautiful

The main purpose of letters is the practical one of making thoug hts visible. Ruskin says that all letters are frightful things and to

The main purpose of letters is the practical one of making thoughts visible. Ruskin says that all letters are frightful

8/11

The main purpose of letters is the practical one of making thoughts visible. Ruskin says that all letters are frightful things and to be end ured only on occasion, that is to say, in places where the sense of the inscription is of more importance than external ornament. This is a sweeping statement, from which we need not suffer unduly; yet it is doubtful whether there is art in individual letters. Letters in combin ation may be satisfying and in a well composed page even beautiful

The main purpose of letters is the practical one of making thoug hts visible. Ruskin says that all letters are frightful things and to

The main purpose of letters is the practical one of making thoughts visible. Ruskin says that all letters are frightful

---

ABCDEFGHIJKLMNOPQRSTUVWXYZ 1234567890 abcdefghijklmnopqrstuvwxyz

ABCDEFGHIJKLMNOPQRSTUVWXYZ 1234567890 abcdefghijklmnopqrstuvwxyz

ABCDEFGHIJKLMNOPQRSTUVWXYZ 1234567890 abcdefghijklmnopqrstuvwxyz

9/9

The main purpose of letters is the practical one of making th oughts visible. Ruskin says that all letters are frightful thing s and to be endured only on occasion, that is to say, in places where the sense of the inscription is of more importance tha n external ornament. This is a sweeping statement, from wh ich we need not suffer unduly; yet it is doubtful whether ther e is art in individual letters. Letters in combination may be s atisfying and in a well composed page even beautiful as a wh

The main purpose of letters is the practical one of makin g thoughts visible. Ruskin says that all letters are frightf

The main purpose of letters is the practical one of making thoughts visible. Ruskin says that all lette

9/10

The main purpose of letters is the practical one of making th oughts visible. Ruskin says that all letters are frightful thing s and to be endured only on occasion, that is to say, in places where the sense of the inscription is of more importance tha n external ornament. This is a sweeping statement, from wh ich we need not suffer unduly; yet it is doubtful whether ther e is art in individual letters. Letters in combination may be s

The main purpose of letters is the practical one of makin g thoughts visible. Ruskin says that all letters are frightf

The main purpose of letters is the practical one of making thoughts visible. Ruskin says that all lette

9/11

The main purpose of letters is the practical one of making th oughts visible. Ruskin says that all letters are frightful thing s and to be endured only on occasion, that is to say, in places where the sense of the inscription is of more importance tha n external ornament. This is a sweeping statement, from wh ich we need not suffer unduly; yet it is doubtful whether ther e is art in individual letters. Letters in combination may be s

The main purpose of letters is the practical one of makin g thoughts visible. Ruskin says that all letters are frightf

The main purpose of letters is the practical one of making thoughts visible. Ruskin says that all lette

9/12

The main purpose of letters is the practical one of making th oughts visible. Ruskin says that all letters are frightful thing s and to be endured only on occasion, that is to say, in places where the sense of the inscription is of more importance tha n external ornament. This is a sweeping statement, from wh ich we need not suffer unduly; yet it is doubtful whether ther e is art in individual letters. Letters in combination may be s

The main purpose of letters is the practical one of makin g thoughts visible. Ruskin says that all letters are frightf

The main purpose of letters is the practical one of making thoughts visible. Ruskin says that all lette

ITC AMERICAN TYPEWRITER 10 POINT SET MINUS ½ UNIT

LIGHT, MEDIUM, BOLD

abcdefghijklmnopqrstuvwxyz – 1 UNIT
abcdefghijklmnopqrstuvwxyz – ½ UNIT
abcdefghijklmnopqrstuvwxyz NORMAL

ABCDEFGHIJKLMNOPQRSTUVWXYZ 1234567890 abcdefghijklmnopqrstuvwxyz
ABCDEFGHIJKLMNOPQRSTUVWXYZ 1234567890 abcdefghijklmnopqrstuvwxyz
ABCDEFGHIJKLMNOPQRSTUVWXYZ 1234567890 abcdefghijklmnopqrstuvwxyz

10/10

The main purpose of letters is the practical one of makin g thoughts visible. Ruskin says that all letters are frightf ul things and to be endured only on occasion, that is to sa y, in places where the sense of the inscription is of more i mportance than external ornament. This is a sweeping statement, from which we need not suffer unduly; yet it is doubtful whether there is art in individual letters. Lette rs in combination may be satisfying and in a well compo sed page even beautiful as a whole, but art in letters cons ists rather in the art of arranging and composing them in a pleasing and appropriate manner. The main purpo se of letters is the practical one of making thoughts visib le. Ruskin says that all letters are frightful things and to b e endured only on occasion, that is to say, in places where the sense of the inscription is of more importance than external ornament. This is a sweeping statement, from which we need not suffer unduly; yet it is doubtful wheth er there is art in individual letters. Letters in combinatio n may be satisfying and in a well composed page even be autiful as a whole, but art in letters consists rather in the art of arranging and composing them in a pleasing and appropriate manner. The main purpose of letters is the

The main purpose of letters is the practical one of ma king thoughts visible. Ruskin says that all letters are

The main purpose of letters is the practical one of making thoughts visible. Ruskin says that all

10/11

The main purpose of letters is the practical one of makin g thoughts visible. Ruskin says that all letters are frightf ul things and to be endured only on occasion, that is to sa y, in places where the sense of the inscription is of more i mportance than external ornament. This is a sweeping statement, from which we need not suffer unduly; yet it is doubtful whether there is art in individual letters. Lette rs in combination may be satisfying and in a well compo sed page even beautiful as a whole, but art in letters cons ists rather in the art of arranging and composing them in a pleasing and appropriate manner. The main purpo se of letters is the practical one of making thoughts visib le. Ruskin says that all letters are frightful things and to b e endured only on occasion, that is to say, in places where the sense of the inscription is of more importance than external ornament. This is a sweeping statement, from which we need not suffer unduly; yet it is doubtful wheth er there is art in individual letters. Letters in combinatio n may be satisfying and in a well composed page even be autiful as a whole, but art in letters consists rather in the

The main purpose of letters is the practical one of ma king thoughts visible. Ruskin says that all letters are

The main purpose of letters is the practical one of making thoughts visible. Ruskin says that all

10/12

The main purpose of letters is the practical one of makin g thoughts visible. Ruskin says that all letters are frightf ul things and to be endured only on occasion, that is to sa y, in places where the sense of the inscription is of more i mportance than external ornament. This is a sweeping statement, from which we need not suffer unduly; yet it is doubtful whether there is art in individual letters. Lette rs in combination may be satisfying and in a well compo sed page even beautiful as a whole, but art in letters cons ists rather in the art of arranging and composing them in a pleasing and appropriate manner. The main purpo se of letters is the practical one of making thoughts visib le. Ruskin says that all letters are frightful things and to b e endured only on occasion, that is to say, in places where the sense of the inscription is of more importance than external ornament. This is a sweeping statement, from which we need not suffer unduly; yet it is doubtful wheth er there is art in individual letters. Letters in combinatio

The main purpose of letters is the practical one of ma king thoughts visible. Ruskin says that all letters are

The main purpose of letters is the practical one of making thoughts visible. Ruskin says that all

10/13

The main purpose of letters is the practical one of makin g thoughts visible. Ruskin says that all letters are frightf ul things and to be endured only on occasion, that is to sa y, in places where the sense of the inscription is of more i mportance than external ornament. This is a sweeping statement, from which we need not suffer unduly; yet it is doubtful whether there is art in individual letters. Lette rs in combination may be satisfying and in a well compo sed page even beautiful as a whole, but art in letters cons ists rather in the art of arranging and composing them in a pleasing and appropriate manner. The main purpo se of letters is the practical one of making thoughts visib le. Ruskin says that all letters are frightful things and to b e endured only on occasion, that is to say, in places where the sense of the inscription is of more importance than external ornament. This is a sweeping statement, from which we need not suffer unduly; yet it is doubtful wheth

The main purpose of letters is the practical one of ma king thoughts visible. Ruskin says that all letters are

The main purpose of letters is the practical one of making thoughts visible. Ruskin says that all

ITC AMERICAN TYPEWRITER 11 POINT SET MINUS ½ UNIT

LIGHT, MEDIUM, BOLD

abcdefghijklmnopqrstuvwxyz – 1 UNIT
abcdefghijklmnopqrstuvwxyz – ½ UNIT
abcdefghijklmnopqrstuvwxyz NORMAL

ABCDEFGHIJKLMNOPQRSTUVWXYZ 1234567890 abcdefghijklmnopqrstuvwxyz
ABCDEFGHIJKLMNOPQRSTUVWXYZ 1234567890 abcdefghijklmnopqrstuvwxyz
ABCDEFGHIJKLMNOPQRSTUVWXYZ 1234567890 abcdefghijklmnopqrstuvwxyz

11/11

The main purpose of letters is the practical one of making thoughts visible. Ruskin says that all letter s are frightful things and to be endured only on occ asion, that is to say, in places where the sense of the inscription is of more importance than external or nament. This is a sweeping statement, from which we need not suffer unduly; yet it is doubtful whethe r there is art in individual letters. Letters in combin ation may be satisfying and in a well composed pa ge even beautiful as a whole, but art in letters consi sts rather in the art of arranging and composing th em in a pleasing and appropriate manner. The ma in purpose of letters is the practical one of making thoughts visible. Ruskin says that all letters are fri ghtful things and to be endured only on occasion, that is to say, in places where the sense of the inscr iption is of more importance than external orname nt. This is a sweeping statement, from which we ne ed not suffer unduly; yet it is doubtful whether there
The main purpose of letters is the practical one o f making thoughts visible. Ruskin says that all le
The main purpose of letters is the practical one of making thoughts visible. Ruskin say

11/12

The main purpose of letters is the practical one of making thoughts visible. Ruskin says that all letter s are frightful things and to be endured only on occ asion, that is to say, in places where the sense of the inscription is of more importance than external or nament. This is a sweeping statement, from which we need not suffer unduly; yet it is doubtful whethe r there is art in individual letters. Letters in combin ation may be satisfying and in a well composed pa ge even beautiful as a whole, but art in letters consi sts rather in the art of arranging and composing th em in a pleasing and appropriate manner. The ma in purpose of letters is the practical one of making thoughts visible. Ruskin says that all letters are fri ghtful things and to be endured only on occasion, that is to say, in places where the sense of the inscr iption is of more importance than external orname nt. This is a sweeping statement, from which we ne
The main purpose of letters is the practical one o f making thoughts visible. Ruskin says that all le
The main purpose of letters is the practical one of making thoughts visible. Ruskin say

11/13

The main purpose of letters is the practical one of making thoughts visible. Ruskin says that all letter s are frightful things and to be endured only on occ asion, that is to say, in places where the sense of the inscription is of more importance than external or nament. This is a sweeping statement, from which we need not suffer unduly; yet it is doubtful whethe r there is art in individual letters. Letters in combin ation may be satisfying and in a well composed pa ge even beautiful as a whole, but art in letters consi sts rather in the art of arranging and composing th em in a pleasing and appropriate manner. The ma in purpose of letters is the practical one of making thoughts visible. Ruskin says that all letters are fri ghtful things and to be endured only on occasion, that is to say, in places where the sense of the inscr iption is of more importance than external orname
The main purpose of letters is the practical one o f making thoughts visible. Ruskin says that all le
The main purpose of letters is the practical one of making thoughts visible. Ruskin say

11/14

The main purpose of letters is the practical one of making thoughts visible. Ruskin says that all letter s are frightful things and to be endured only on occ asion, that is to say, in places where the sense of the inscription is of more importance than external or nament. This is a sweeping statement, from which we need not suffer unduly; yet it is doubtful whethe r there is art in individual letters. Letters in combin ation may be satisfying and in a well composed pa ge even beautiful as a whole, but art in letters consi sts rather in the art of arranging and composing th em in a pleasing and appropriate manner. The ma in purpose of letters is the practical one of making thoughts visible. Ruskin says that all letters are fri ghtful things and to be endured only on occasion, that is to say, in places where the sense of the inscr
The main purpose of letters is the practical one o f making thoughts visible. Ruskin says that all le
The main purpose of letters is the practical one of making thoughts visible. Ruskin say

ITC AMERICAN TYPEWRITER 12 POINT SET MINUS ½ UNIT

LIGHT, MEDIUM, BOLD

abcdefghijklmnopqrstuvwxyz – 1 UNIT
abcdefghijklmnopqrstuvwxyz – ½ UNIT
abcdefghijklmnopqrstuvwxyz NORMAL

ABCDEFGHIJKLMNOPQRSTUVWXYZ 1234567890 abcdefghijklmnopqrstuvwxyz
ABCDEFGHIJKLMNOPQRSTUVWXYZ 1234567890 abcdefghijklmnopqrstuvwxyz
ABCDEFGHIJKLMNOPQRSTUVWXYZ 1234567890 abcdefghijklmnopqrstuv

12/12

The main purpose of letters is the practical one of making thoughts visible. Ruskin says that all letters are frightful things and to be endured on ly on occasion, that is to say, in places where the sense of the inscription is of more importance t han external ornament. This is a sweeping stat ement, from which we need not suffer unduly; yet it is doubtful whether there is art in individu al letters. Letters in combination may be satisfyi ng and in a well composed page even beautiful as a whole, but art in letters consists rather in t he art of arranging and composing them in a pl easing and appropriate manner. The main pur pose of letters is the practical one of making tho ughts visible. Ruskin says that all letters are frig
The main purpose of letters is the practical one of making thoughts visible. Ruskin says
The main purpose of letters is the practi cal one of making thoughts visible. Rus

12/13

The main purpose of letters is the practical one of making thoughts visible. Ruskin says that all letters are frightful things and to be endured on ly on occasion, that is to say, in places where the sense of the inscription is of more importance t han external ornament. This is a sweeping stat ement, from which we need not suffer unduly; yet it is doubtful whether there is art in individu al letters. Letters in combination may be satisfyi ng and in a well composed page even beautiful as a whole, but art in letters consists rather in t he art of arranging and composing them in a pl easing and appropriate manner. The main pur pose of letters is the practical one of making tho
The main purpose of letters is the practical one of making thoughts visible. Ruskin says
The main purpose of letters is the practi cal one of making thoughts visible. Rus

12/14

The main purpose of letters is the practical one of making thoughts visible. Ruskin says that all letters are frightful things and to be endured on ly on occasion, that is to say, in places where the sense of the inscription is of more importance t han external ornament. This is a sweeping stat ement, from which we need not suffer unduly; yet it is doubtful whether there is art in individu al letters. Letters in combination may be satisfyi ng and in a well composed page even beautiful as a whole, but art in letters consists rather in t he art of arranging and composing them in a pl easing and appropriate manner. The main pur pose of letters is the practical one of making tho ughts visible. Ruskin says that all letters are frig
The main purpose of letters is the practical one of making thoughts visible. Ruskin says
The main purpose of letters is the practi cal one of making thoughts visible. Rus

12/15

The main purpose of letters is the practical one of making thoughts visible. Ruskin says that all letters are frightful things and to be endured on ly on occasion, that is to say, in places where the sense of the inscription is of more importance t han external ornament. This is a sweeping stat ement, from which we need not suffer unduly; yet it is doubtful whether there is art in individu al letters. Letters in combination may be satisfyi ng and in a well composed page even beautiful as a whole, but art in letters consists rather in t he art of arranging and composing them in a pl easing and appropriate manner. The main pur pose of letters is the practical one of making tho
The main purpose of letters is the practical one of making thoughts visible. Ruskin says
The main purpose of letters is the practi cal one of making thoughts visible. Rus

ITC AMERICAN TYPEWRITER 14 POINT SET MINUS ½ UNIT

LIGHT, MEDIUM, BOLD

abcdefghijklmnopqrstuvwxyz – 1 UNIT
abcdefghijklmnopqrstuvwxyz – ½ UNIT
abcdefghijklmnopqrstuvwxyz NORMAL

ABCDEFGHIJKLMNOPQRSTUVWXYZ abcdefghijklmnopqrstuvwxyz
ABCDEFGHIJKLMNOPQRSTUVWXYZ abcdefghijklmnopqrstuvwxyz
ABCDEFGHIJKLMNOPQRSTUVWXYZ abcdefghijklmnopqrstuvwxyz

14/14

The main purpose of letters is the practic al one of making thoughts visible. Ruski n says that all letters are frightful things and to be endured only on occasion, that is to say, in places where the sense of the inscription is of more importance than e xternal ornament. This is a sweeping sta tement, from which we need not suffer unduly; yet it is doubtful whether there i s art in individual letters. Letters in comb ination may be satisfying and in a well c omposed page even beautiful as a whole, but art in letters consists rather in the ar

The main purpose of letters is the prac tical one of making thoughts visible. R

The main purpose of letters is the practical one of making thoughts

14/15

The main purpose of letters is the practic al one of making thoughts visible. Ruski n says that all letters are frightful things and to be endured only on occasion, that is to say, in places where the sense of the inscription is of more importance than e xternal ornament. This is a sweeping sta tement, from which we need not suffer unduly; yet it is doubtful whether there i s art in individual letters. Letters in comb ination may be satisfying and in a well c omposed page even beautiful as a whole,

The main purpose of letters is the prac tical one of making thoughts visible. R

The main purpose of letters is the practical one of making thoughts

14/16

The main purpose of letters is the practic al one of making thoughts visible. Ruski n says that all letters are frightful things and to be endured only on occasion, that is to say, in places where the sense of the inscription is of more importance than e xternal ornament. This is a sweeping sta tement, from which we need not suffer unduly; yet it is doubtful whether there i s art in individual letters. Letters in comb ination may be satisfying and in a well c omposed page even beautiful as a whole, but art in letters consists rather in the ar

The main purpose of letters is the prac tical one of making thoughts visible. R

The main purpose of letters is the practical one of making thoughts

14/17

The main purpose of letters is the practic al one of making thoughts visible. Ruski n says that all letters are frightful things and to be endured only on occasion, that is to say, in places where the sense of the inscription is of more importance than e xternal ornament. This is a sweeping sta tement, from which we need not suffer unduly; yet it is doubtful whether there i s art in individual letters. Letters in comb ination may be satisfying and in a well c omposed page even beautiful as a whole,

The main purpose of letters is the prac tical one of making thoughts visible. R

The main purpose of letters is the practical one of making thoughts

ASTER 6 & 7 POINT SET NORMAL

ROMAN, ITALIC, BOLD

ABCDEFGHIJKLMNOPQRSTUVWXYZ 1234567890 abcdefghijklmnopqrstuvwxyz

ABCDEFGHIJKLMNOPQRSTUVWXYZ 1234567890 abcdefghijklmnopqrstuvwxyz

ABCDEFGHIJKLMNOPQRSTUVWXYZ 1234567890 abcdefghijklmnopqrstuvwxyz

6/6

The main purpose of letters is the practical one of making thoughts visible. Ruskin says that all letters are frightful things and to be endured only on occasion, that is to say, in p laces where the sense of the inscription is of more importance than external ornament. This is a sweeping statement, from which we need not suffer unduly; yet it is doubtful w hether there is art in individual letters. Letters in combination may be satisfying and in a well composed page even beautiful as a whole, but art in letters consists rather in the art of arranging and composing them in a pleasing and appropriate manner. The main purpose of letters is the practical one of making thoughts visible. Ruskin says that all let ters are frightful things and to be endured only on occasion, that is to say, in places wher e the sense of the inscription is of more importance than external ornament. This is a sw eeping statement, from which we need not suffer unduly; yet it is doubtful whether ther e is art in individual letters. Letters in combination may be satisfying and in a well com posed page even beautiful as a whole, but art in letters consists rather in the art of arran
The main purpose of letters is the practical one of making thoughts visible. Ruskin says that all letters are frightful things and to be endured only on occasion, that is to say, in places wh
The main purpose of letters is the practical one of making thoughts visible. Ruskin says that all letters are frightful things and to be endured only on occasion, that is to say, in p

6/7

The main purpose of letters is the practical one of making thoughts visible. Ruskin says that all letters are frightful things and to be endured only on occasion, that is to say, in p laces where the sense of the inscription is of more importance than external ornament. This is a sweeping statement, from which we need not suffer unduly; yet it is doubtful w hether there is art in individual letters. Letters in combination may be satisfying and in a well composed page even beautiful as a whole, but art in letters consists rather in the art of arranging and composing them in a pleasing and appropriate manner. The main purpose of letters is the practical one of making thoughts visible. Ruskin says that all let ters are frightful things and to be endured only on occasion, that is to say, in places wher e the sense of the inscription is of more importance than external ornament. This is a sw eeping statement, from which we need not suffer unduly; yet it is doubtful whether ther
The main purpose of letters is the practical one of making thoughts visible. Ruskin says that all letters are frightful things and to be endured only on occasion, that is to say, in places wh
The main purpose of letters is the practical one of making thoughts visible. Ruskin says that all letters are frightful things and to be endured only on occasion, that is to say, in p

6/8

The main purpose of letters is the practical one of making thoughts visible. Ruskin says that all letters are frightful things and to be endured only on occasion, that is to say, in p laces where the sense of the inscription is of more importance than external ornament. This is a sweeping statement, from which we need not suffer unduly; yet it is doubtful w hether there is art in individual letters. Letters in combination may be satisfying and in a well composed page even beautiful as a whole, but art in letters consists rather in the art of arranging and composing them in a pleasing and appropriate manner. The main purpose of letters is the practical one of making thoughts visible. Ruskin says that all let ters are frightful things and to be endured only on occasion, that is to say, in places wher
The main purpose of letters is the practical one of making thoughts visible. Ruskin says that all letters are frightful things and to be endured only on occasion, that is to say, in places wh
The main purpose of letters is the practical one of making thoughts visible. Ruskin says that all letters are frightful things and to be endured only on occasion, that is to say, in p

6/9

The main purpose of letters is the practical one of making thoughts visible. Ruskin says that all letters are frightful things and to be endured only on occasion, that is to say, in p laces where the sense of the inscription is of more importance than external ornament. This is a sweeping statement, from which we need not suffer unduly; yet it is doubtful w hether there is art in individual letters. Letters in combination may be satisfying and in a well composed page even beautiful as a whole, but art in letters consists rather in the art of arranging and composing them in a pleasing and appropriate manner. The main purpose of letters is the practical one of making thoughts visible. Ruskin says that all let
The main purpose of letters is the practical one of making thoughts visible. Ruskin says that all letters are frightful things and to be endured only on occasion, that is to say, in places wh
The main purpose of letters is the practical one of making thoughts visible. Ruskin says that all letters are frightful things and to be endured only on occasion, that is to say, in p

---

ABCDEFGHIJKLMNOPQRSTUVWXYZ 1234567890 abcdefghijklmnopqrstuvwxyz

ABCDEFGHIJKLMNOPQRSTUVWXYZ 1234567890 abcdefghijklmnopqrstuvwxyz

ABCDEFGHIJKLMNOPQRSTUVWXYZ 1234567890 abcdefghijklmnopqrstuvwxyz

7/7

The main purpose of letters is the practical one of making thoughts visible. Ruskin says that all letters are frightful things and to be endured only on oc casion, that is to say, in places where the sense of the inscription is of more i mportance than external ornament. This is a sweeping statement, from wh ich we need not suffer unduly; yet it is doubtful whether there is art in indiv idual letters. Letters in combination may be satisfying and in a well compo sed page even beautiful as a whole, but art in letters consists rather in the a rt of arranging and composing them in a pleasing and appropriate manner. The main purpose of letters is the practical one of making thoughts visible. Ruskin says that all letters are frightful things and to be endured only on oc casion, that is to say, in places where the sense of the inscription is of more i
The main purpose of letters is the practical one of making thoughts visible. Rus kin says that all letters are frightful things and to be endured only on occasion,
The main purpose of letters is the practical one of making thoughts visible. Ruskin says that all letters are frightful things and to be endured only on o

7/8

The main purpose of letters is the practical one of making thoughts visible. Ruskin says that all letters are frightful things and to be endured only on oc casion, that is to say, in places where the sense of the inscription is of more i mportance than external ornament. This is a sweeping statement, from wh ich we need not suffer unduly; yet it is doubtful whether there is art in indiv idual letters. Letters in combination may be satisfying and in a well compo sed page even beautiful as a whole, but art in letters consists rather in the a rt of arranging and composing them in a pleasing and appropriate manner. The main purpose of letters is the practical one of making thoughts visible. Ruskin says that all letters are frightful things and to be endured only on oc
The main purpose of letters is the practical one of making thoughts visible. Rus kin says that all letters are frightful things and to be endured only on occasion,
The main purpose of letters is the practical one of making thoughts visible. Ruskin says that all letters are frightful things and to be endured only on o

7/9

The main purpose of letters is the practical one of making thoughts visible. Ruskin says that all letters are frightful things and to be endured only on oc casion, that is to say, in places where the sense of the inscription is of more i mportance than external ornament. This is a sweeping statement, from wh ich we need not suffer unduly; yet it is doubtful whether there is art in indiv idual letters. Letters in combination may be satisfying and in a well compo sed page even beautiful as a whole, but art in letters consists rather in the a rt of arranging and composing them in a pleasing and appropriate manner. The main purpose of letters is the practical one of making thoughts visible. Ruskin says that all letters are frightful things and to be endured only on oc
The main purpose of letters is the practical one of making thoughts visible. Rus kin says that all letters are frightful things and to be endured only on occasion,
The main purpose of letters is the practical one of making thoughts visible. Ruskin says that all letters are frightful things and to be endured only on o

7/10

The main purpose of letters is the practical one of making thoughts visible. Ruskin says that all letters are frightful things and to be endured only on oc casion, that is to say, in places where the sense of the inscription is of more i mportance than external ornament. This is a sweeping statement, from wh ich we need not suffer unduly; yet it is doubtful whether there is art in indiv idual letters. Letters in combination may be satisfying and in a well compo sed page even beautiful as a whole, but art in letters consists rather in the a rt of arranging and composing them in a pleasing and appropriate manner. The main purpose of letters is the practical one of making thoughts visible.
The main purpose of letters is the practical one of making thoughts visible. Rus kin says that all letters are frightful things and to be endured only on occasion,
The main purpose of letters is the practical one of making thoughts visible. Ruskin says that all letters are frightful things and to be endured only on o

ASTER 8 & 9 POINT SET NORMAL

ROMAN, ITALIC, BOLD

ABCDEFGHIJKLMNOPQRSTUVWXYZ 1234567890 abcdefghijklmnopqrstuvwxyz

ABCDEFGHIJKLMNOPQRSTUVWXYZ 1234567890 abcdefghijklmnopqrstuvwxyz

ABCDEFGHIJKLMNOPQRSTUVWXYZ 1234567890 abcdefghijklmnopqrstuvwxyz

8/8

The main purpose of letters is the practical one of making thought s visible. Ruskin says that all letters are frightful things and to be endured only on occasion, that is to say, in places where the sense of the inscription is of more importance than external ornament. This is a sweeping statement, from which we need not suffer undu ly; yet it is doubtful whether there is art in individual letters. Lett ers in combination may be satisfying and in a well composed pag e even beautiful as a whole, but art in letters consists rather in the art of arranging and composing them in a pleasing and appropria

The main purpose of letters is the practical one of making thoughts vi sible. Ruskin says that all letters are frightful things and to be endure

The main purpose of letters is the practical one of making though ts visible. Ruskin says that all letters are frightful things and to b

8/9

The main purpose of letters is the practical one of making thought s visible. Ruskin says that all letters are frightful things and to be endured only on occasion, that is to say, in places where the sense of the inscription is of more importance than external ornament. This is a sweeping statement, from which we need not suffer undu ly; yet it is doubtful whether there is art in individual letters. Lett ers in combination may be satisfying and in a well composed pag e even beautiful as a whole, but art in letters consists rather in the

The main purpose of letters is the practical one of making thoughts vi sible. Ruskin says that all letters are frightful things and to be endure

The main purpose of letters is the practical one of making though ts visible. Ruskin says that all letters are frightful things and to b

8/10

The main purpose of letters is the practical one of making thought s visible. Ruskin says that all letters are frightful things and to be endured only on occasion, that is to say, in places where the sense of the inscription is of more importance than external ornament. This is a sweeping statement, from which we need not suffer undu ly; yet it is doubtful whether there is art in individual letters. Lett ers in combination may be satisfying and in a well composed pag

The main purpose of letters is the practical one of making thoughts vi sible. Ruskin says that all letters are frightful things and to be endure

The main purpose of letters is the practical one of making though ts visible. Ruskin says that all letters are frightful things and to b

8/11

The main purpose of letters is the practical one of making thought s visible. Ruskin says that all letters are frightful things and to be endured only on occasion, that is to say, in places where the sense of the inscription is of more importance than external ornament. This is a sweeping statement, from which we need not suffer undu ly; yet it is doubtful whether there is art in individual letters. Lett ers in combination may be satisfying and in a well composed pag

The main purpose of letters is the practical one of making thoughts vi sible. Ruskin says that all letters are frightful things and to be endure

The main purpose of letters is the practical one of making though ts visible. Ruskin says that all letters are frightful things and to b

---

ABCDEFGHIJKLMNOPQRSTUVWXYZ 1234567890 abcdefghijklmnopqrstuvwxyz

ABCDEFGHIJKLMNOPQRSTUVWXYZ 1234567890 abcdefghijklmnopqrstuvwxyz

ABCDEFGHIJKLMNOPQRSTUVWXYZ 1234567890 abcdefghijklmnopqrstuvwxyz

9/9

The main purpose of letters is the practical one of making t houghts visible. Ruskin says that all letters are frightful th ings and to be endured only on occasion, that is to say, in pl aces where the sense of the inscription is of more importan ce than external ornament. This is a sweeping statement, f rom which we need not suffer unduly; yet it is doubtful wh ether there is art in individual letters. Letters in combinat ion may be satisfying and in a well composed page even be

The main purpose of letters is the practical one of making tho ughts visible. Ruskin says that all letters are frightful things a

The main purpose of letters is the practical one of making thoughts visible. Ruskin says that all letters are frightful t

9/10

The main purpose of letters is the practical one of making t houghts visible. Ruskin says that all letters are frightful th ings and to be endured only on occasion, that is to say, in pl aces where the sense of the inscription is of more importan ce than external ornament. This is a sweeping statement, f rom which we need not suffer unduly; yet it is doubtful wh ether there is art in individual letters. Letters in combinat

The main purpose of letters is the practical one of making tho ughts visible. Ruskin says that all letters are frightful things a

The main purpose of letters is the practical one of making thoughts visible. Ruskin says that all letters are frightful t

9/11

The main purpose of letters is the practical one of making t houghts visible. Ruskin says that all letters are frightful th ings and to be endured only on occasion, that is to say, in pl aces where the sense of the inscription is of more importan ce than external ornament. This is a sweeping statement, f rom which we need not suffer unduly; yet it is doubtful wh ether there is art in individual letters. Letters in combinat

The main purpose of letters is the practical one of making tho ughts visible. Ruskin says that all letters are frightful things a

The main purpose of letters is the practical one of making thoughts visible. Ruskin says that all letters are frightful t

9/12

The main purpose of letters is the practical one of making t houghts visible. Ruskin says that all letters are frightful th ings and to be endured only on occasion, that is to say, in pl aces where the sense of the inscription is of more importan ce than external ornament. This is a sweeping statement, f rom which we need not suffer unduly; yet it is doubtful wh ether there is art in individual letters. Letters in combinat

The main purpose of letters is the practical one of making tho ughts visible. Ruskin says that all letters are frightful things a

The main purpose of letters is the practical one of making thoughts visible. Ruskin says that all letters are frightful t

10 POINT SET MINUS ½ UNIT

ROMAN, ITALIC, BOLD

abcdefghijklmnopqrstuvwxyz – 1 UNIT
abcdefghijklmnopqrstuvwxyz – ½ UNIT
abcdefghijklmnopqrstuvwxyz NORMAL

ABCDEFGHIJKLMNOPQRSTUVWXYZ 1234567890 abcdefghijklmnopqrstuvwxyz
ABCDEFGHIJKLMNOPQRSTUVWXYZ 1234567890 abcdefghijklmnopqrstuvwxyz
ABCDEFGHIJKLMNOPQRSTUVWXYZ 1234567890 abcdefghijklmnopqrstuvwxyz

10/10

The main purpose of letters is the practical one of maki
ng thoughts visible. Ruskin says that all letters are frig
htful things and to be endured only on occasion, that is
to say, in places where the sense of the inscription is of
more importance than external ornament. This is a sw
eeping statement, from which we need not suffer undu
ly; yet it is doubtful whether there is art in individual l
etters. Letters in combination may be satisfying and in
a well composed page even beautiful as a whole, but ar
t in letters consists rather in the art of arranging and co
mposing them in a pleasing and appropriate manner.
The main purpose of letters is the practical one of maki
ng thoughts visible. Ruskin says that all letters are frig
htful things and to be endured only on occasion, that is
to say, in places where the sense of the inscription is of
more importance than external ornament. This is a sw
eeping statement, from which we need not suffer undu
ly; yet it is doubtful whether there is art in individual l
etters. Letters in combination may be satisfying and in
a well composed page even beautiful as a whole, but ar
t in letters consists rather in the art of arranging and co
mposing them in a pleasing and appropriate manner.
The main purpose of letters is the practical one of making
thoughts visible. Ruskin says that all letters are frightful t
The main purpose of letters is the practical one of mak
ing thoughts visible. Ruskin says that all letters are fri

10/11

The main purpose of letters is the practical one of maki
ng thoughts visible. Ruskin says that all letters are frig
htful things and to be endured only on occasion, that is
to say, in places where the sense of the inscription is of
more importance than external ornament. This is a sw
eeping statement, from which we need not suffer undu
ly; yet it is doubtful whether there is art in individual l
etters. Letters in combination may be satisfying and in
a well composed page even beautiful as a whole, but ar
t in letters consists rather in the art of arranging and co
mposing them in a pleasing and appropriate manner.
The main purpose of letters is the practical one of maki
ng thoughts visible. Ruskin says that all letters are frig
htful things and to be endured only on occasion, that is
to say, in places where the sense of the inscription is of
more importance than external ornament. This is a sw
eeping statement, from which we need not suffer undu
ly; yet it is doubtful whether there is art in individual l
etters. Letters in combination may be satisfying and in
a well composed page even beautiful as a whole, but ar
The main purpose of letters is the practical one of making
thoughts visible. Ruskin says that all letters are frightful t
The main purpose of letters is the practical one of mak
ing thoughts visible. Ruskin says that all letters are fri

10/12

The main purpose of letters is the practical one of maki
ng thoughts visible. Ruskin says that all letters are frig
htful things and to be endured only on occasion, that is
to say, in places where the sense of the inscription is of
more importance than external ornament. This is a sw
eeping statement, from which we need not suffer undu
ly; yet it is doubtful whether there is art in individual l
etters. Letters in combination may be satisfying and in
a well composed page even beautiful as a whole, but ar
t in letters consists rather in the art of arranging and co
mposing them in a pleasing and appropriate manner.
The main purpose of letters is the practical one of maki
ng thoughts visible. Ruskin says that all letters are frig
htful things and to be endured only on occasion, that is
to say, in places where the sense of the inscription is of
more importance than external ornament. This is a sw
eeping statement, from which we need not suffer undu
ly; yet it is doubtful whether there is art in individual l
The main purpose of letters is the practical one of making
thoughts visible. Ruskin says that all letters are frightful t
The main purpose of letters is the practical one of mak
ing thoughts visible. Ruskin says that all letters are fri

10/13

The main purpose of letters is the practical one of maki
ng thoughts visible. Ruskin says that all letters are frig
htful things and to be endured only on occasion, that is
to say, in places where the sense of the inscription is of
more importance than external ornament. This is a sw
eeping statement, from which we need not suffer undu
ly; yet it is doubtful whether there is art in individual l
etters. Letters in combination may be satisfying and in
a well composed page even beautiful as a whole, but ar
t in letters consists rather in the art of arranging and co
mposing them in a pleasing and appropriate manner.
The main purpose of letters is the practical one of maki
ng thoughts visible. Ruskin says that all letters are frig
htful things and to be endured only on occasion, that is
to say, in places where the sense of the inscription is of
more importance than external ornament. This is a sw
eeping statement, from which we need not suffer undu
The main purpose of letters is the practical one of making
thoughts visible. Ruskin says that all letters are frightful t
The main purpose of letters is the practical one of mak
ing thoughts visible. Ruskin says that all letters are fri

ASTER 11 POINT SET MINUS ½ UNIT

ROMAN, ITALIC, BOLD

abcdefghijklmnopqrstuvwxyz – 1 UNIT
abcdefghijklmnopqrstuvwxyz – ½ UNIT
abcdefghijklmnopqrstuvwxyz NORMAL

ABCDEFGHIJKLMNOPQRSTUVWXYZ 1234567890 abcdefghijklmnopqrstuvwxyz
ABCDEFGHIJKLMNOPQRSTUVWXYZ 1234567890 abcdefghijklmnopqrstuvwxyz
ABCDEFGHIJKLMNOPQRSTUVWXYZ 1234567890 abcdefghijklmnopqrstuvwxyz

11/11

The main purpose of letters is the practical one of making thoughts visible. Ruskin says that all lett ers are frightful things and to be endured only on occasion, that is to say, in places where the sense o f the inscription is of more importance than exter nal ornament. This is a sweeping statement, from which we need not suffer unduly; yet it is doubtfu l whether there is art in individual letters. Letters in combination may be satisfying and in a well co mposed page even beautiful as a whole, but art in letters consists rather in the art of arranging and composing them in a pleasing and appropriate m anner. The main purpose of letters is the practica l one of making thoughts visible. Ruskin says tha t all letters are frightful things and to be endured only on occasion, that is to say, in places where th e sense of the inscription is of more importance tha n external ornament. This is a sweeping stateme nt, from which we need not suffer unduly; yet it is
The main purpose of letters is the practical one of m aking thoughts visible. Ruskin says that all letters ar
The main purpose of letters is the practical one of making thoughts visible. Ruskin says that all lett

11/12

The main purpose of letters is the practical one of making thoughts visible. Ruskin says that all lett ers are frightful things and to be endured only on occasion, that is to say, in places where the sense o f the inscription is of more importance than exter nal ornament. This is a sweeping statement, from which we need not suffer unduly; yet it is doubtfu l whether there is art in individual letters. Letters in combination may be satisfying and in a well co mposed page even beautiful as a whole, but art in letters consists rather in the art of arranging and composing them in a pleasing and appropriate m anner. The main purpose of letters is the practica l one of making thoughts visible. Ruskin says tha t all letters are frightful things and to be endured only on occasion, that is to say, in places where th e sense of the inscription is of more importance tha n external ornament. This is a sweeping stateme
The main purpose of letters is the practical one of m aking thoughts visible. Ruskin says that all letters ar
The main purpose of letters is the practical one of making thoughts visible. Ruskin says that all lett

11/13

The main purpose of letters is the practical one of making thoughts visible. Ruskin says that all lett ers are frightful things and to be endured only on occasion, that is to say, in places where the sense o f the inscription is of more importance than exter nal ornament. This is a sweeping statement, from which we need not suffer unduly; yet it is doubtfu l whether there is art in individual letters. Letters in combination may be satisfying and in a well co mposed page even beautiful as a whole, but art in letters consists rather in the art of arranging and composing them in a pleasing and appropriate m anner. The main purpose of letters is the practica l one of making thoughts visible. Ruskin says tha t all letters are frightful things and to be endured only on occasion, that is to say, in places where th e sense of the inscription is of more importance tha
The main purpose of letters is the practical one of m aking thoughts visible. Ruskin says that all letters ar
The main purpose of letters is the practical one of making thoughts visible. Ruskin says that all lett

11/14

The main purpose of letters is the practical one of making thoughts visible. Ruskin says that all lett ers are frightful things and to be endured only on occasion, that is to say, in places where the sense o f the inscription is of more importance than exter nal ornament. This is a sweeping statement, from which we need not suffer unduly; yet it is doubtfu l whether there is art in individual letters. Letters in combination may be satisfying and in a well co mposed page even beautiful as a whole, but art in letters consists rather in the art of arranging and composing them in a pleasing and appropriate m anner. The main purpose of letters is the practica l one of making thoughts visible. Ruskin says tha t all letters are frightful things and to be endured only on occasion, that is to say, in places where th
The main purpose of letters is the practical one of m aking thoughts visible. Ruskin says that all letters ar
The main purpose of letters is the practical one of making thoughts visible. Ruskin says that all lett

ASTER 12 POINT SET MINUS ½ UNIT

ROMAN, ITALIC, BOLD

abcdefghijklmnopqrstuvwxyz – 1 UNIT
abcdefghijklmnopqrstuvwxyz – ½ UNIT
abcdefghijklmnopqrstuvwxyz NORMAL

ABCDEFGHIJKLMNOPQRSTUVWXYZ 1234567890 abcdefghijklmnopqrstuvwxyz
ABCDEFGHIJKLMNOPQRSTUVWXYZ 1234567890 abcdefghijklmnopqrstuvwxyz
ABCDEFGHIJKLMNOPQRSTUVWXYZ 1234567890 abcdefghijklmnopqrstuvwxyz

12/12

The main purpose of letters is the practical on e of making thoughts visible. Ruskin says that all letters are frightful things and to be endure d only on occasion, that is to say, in places whe re the sense of the inscription is of more impor tance than external ornament. This is a sweep ing statement, from which we need not suffer unduly; yet it is doubtful whether there is art i n individual letters. Letters in combination m ay be satisfying and in a well composed page e ven beautiful as a whole, but art in letters con sists rather in the art of arranging and compo sing them in a pleasing and appropriate man ner. The main purpose of letters is the practica l one of making thoughts visible. Ruskin says t
The main purpose of letters is the practical one o f making thoughts visible. Ruskin says that all le
The main purpose of letters is the practical on e of making thoughts visible. Ruskin says that

12/13

The main purpose of letters is the practical on e of making thoughts visible. Ruskin says that all letters are frightful things and to be endure d only on occasion, that is to say, in places whe re the sense of the inscription is of more impor tance than external ornament. This is a sweep ing statement, from which we need not suffer unduly; yet it is doubtful whether there is art i n individual letters. Letters in combination m ay be satisfying and in a well composed page e ven beautiful as a whole, but art in letters con sists rather in the art of arranging and compo sing them in a pleasing and appropriate man ner. The main purpose of letters is the practica
The main purpose of letters is the practical one o f making thoughts visible. Ruskin says that all le
The main purpose of letters is the practical on e of making thoughts visible. Ruskin says that

12/14

The main purpose of letters is the practical on e of making thoughts visible. Ruskin says that all letters are frightful things and to be endure d only on occasion, that is to say, in places whe re the sense of the inscription is of more impor tance than external ornament. This is a sweep ing statement, from which we need not suffer unduly; yet it is doubtful whether there is art i n individual letters. Letters in combination m ay be satisfying and in a well composed page e ven beautiful as a whole, but art in letters con sists rather in the art of arranging and compo sing them in a pleasing and appropriate man ner. The main purpose of letters is the practica l one of making thoughts visible. Ruskin says t
The main purpose of letters is the practical one o f making thoughts visible. Ruskin says that all le
The main purpose of letters is the practical on e of making thoughts visible. Ruskin says that

12/15

The main purpose of letters is the practical on e of making thoughts visible. Ruskin says that all letters are frightful things and to be endure d only on occasion, that is to say, in places whe re the sense of the inscription is of more impor tance than external ornament. This is a sweep ing statement, from which we need not suffer unduly; yet it is doubtful whether there is art i n individual letters. Letters in combination m ay be satisfying and in a well composed page e ven beautiful as a whole, but art in letters con sists rather in the art of arranging and compo sing them in a pleasing and appropriate man ner. The main purpose of letters is the practica
The main purpose of letters is the practical one o f making thoughts visible. Ruskin says that all le
The main purpose of letters is the practical on e of making thoughts visible. Ruskin says that

ASTER 14 POINT SET MINUS ½ UNIT

ROMAN, ITALIC, BOLD

abcdefghijklmnopqrstuvwxyz – 1 UNIT
abcdefghijklmnopqrstuvwxyz – ½ UNIT
abcdefghijklmnopqrstuvwxyz NORMAL

ABCDEFGHIJKLMNOPQRSTUVWXYZ abcdefghijklmnopqrstuvwxyz
ABCDEFGHIJKLMNOPQRSTUVWXYZ abcdefghijklmnopqrstuvwxyz
ABCDEFGHIJKLMNOPQRSTUVWXYZ abcdefghijklmnopqrstuvwxyz

14/14

The main purpose of letters is the pract ical one of making thoughts visible. Ru skin says that all letters are frightful thi ngs and to be endured only on occasion, that is to say, in places where the sense of the inscription is of more importanc e than external ornament. This is a swe eping statement, from which we need not suffer unduly; yet it is doubtful whe ther there is art in individual letters. Le tters in combination may be satisfying and in a well composed page even beau tiful as a whole, but art in letters consis
The main purpose of letters is the practic al one of making thoughts visible. Ruski
The main purpose of letters is the pract ical one of making thoughts visible. Ru

14/15

The main purpose of letters is the pract ical one of making thoughts visible. Ru skin says that all letters are frightful thi ngs and to be endured only on occasion, that is to say, in places where the sense of the inscription is of more importanc e than external ornament. This is a swe eping statement, from which we need not suffer unduly; yet it is doubtful whe ther there is art in individual letters. Le tters in combination may be satisfying and in a well composed page even beau
The main purpose of letters is the practic al one of making thoughts visible. Ruski
The main purpose of letters is the pract ical one of making thoughts visible. Ru

14/16

The main purpose of letters is the pract ical one of making thoughts visible. Ru skin says that all letters are frightful thi ngs and to be endured only on occasion, that is to say, in places where the sense of the inscription is of more importanc e than external ornament. This is a swe eping statement, from which we need not suffer unduly; yet it is doubtful whe ther there is art in individual letters. Le tters in combination may be satisfying and in a well composed page even beau tiful as a whole, but art in letters consis
The main purpose of letters is the practic al one of making thoughts visible. Ruski
The main purpose of letters is the pract ical one of making thoughts visible. Ru

14/17

The main purpose of letters is the pract ical one of making thoughts visible. Ru skin says that all letters are frightful thi ngs and to be endured only on occasion, that is to say, in places where the sense of the inscription is of more importanc e than external ornament. This is a swe eping statement, from which we need not suffer unduly; yet it is doubtful whe ther there is art in individual letters. Le tters in combination may be satisfying and in a well composed page even beau
The main purpose of letters is the practic al one of making thoughts visible. Ruski
The main purpose of letters is the pract ical one of making thoughts visible. Ru

ITC AVANT GARDE 6 & 7 POINT SET NORMAL

BOOK. ITALIC. DEMI. DEMI ITALIC

ABCDEFGHIJKLMNOPQRSTUVWXYZ 1234567890 abcdefghijklmnopqrstuvwxyz

ABCDEFGHIJKLMNOPQRSTUVWXYZ 1234567890 abcdefghijklmnopqrstuvwxyz

ABCDEFGHIJKLMNOPQRSTUVWXYZ 1234567890 abcdefghijklmnopqrstuvwxyz

ABCDEFGHIJKLMNOPQRSTUVWXYZ 1234567890 abcdefghijklmnopqrstuvwxyz

6/6

The main purpose of letters is the practical one of making thoughts visible. Ruskin says that all
letters are frightful things and to be endured only on occasion, that is to say, in places where t
he sense of the inscription is of more importance than external ornament. This is a sweeping
statement, from which we need not suffer unduly; yet it is doubtful whether there is art in indiv
idual letters. Letters in combination may be satisfying and in a well composed page even b
eautiful as a whole, but art in letters consists rather in the art of arranging and composing th
em in a pleasing and appropriate manner. The main purpose of letters is the practical one
of making thoughts visible. Ruskin says that all letters are frightful things and to be endured o
nly on occasion, that is to say, in places where the sense of the inscription is of more importa
nce than external ornament. This is a sweeping statement, from which we need not suffer un
duly; yet it is doubtful whether there is art in individual letters. Letters in combination may be
satisfying and in a well composed page even beautiful as a whole, but art in letters consists
rather in the art of arranging and composing them in a pleasing and appropriate manner.
The main purpose of letters is the practical one of making thoughts visible. Ruskin says that
all letters are frightful things and to be endured only on occasion, that is to say, in places wh
The main purpose of letters is the practical one of making thoughts visible. Ruskin says th
at all letters are frightful things and to be endured only on occasion, that is to say, in place

6/7

The main purpose of letters is the practical one of making thoughts visible. Ruskin says that all
letters are frightful things and to be endured only on occasion, that is to say, in places where t
he sense of the inscription is of more importance than external ornament. This is a sweeping
statement, from which we need not suffer unduly; yet it is doubtful whether there is art in indiv
idual letters. Letters in combination may be satisfying and in a well composed page even b
eautiful as a whole, but art in letters consists rather in the art of arranging and composing th
em in a pleasing and appropriate manner. The main purpose of letters is the practical one
of making thoughts visible. Ruskin says that all letters are frightful things and to be endured o
nly on occasion, that is to say, in places where the sense of the inscription is of more importa
nce than external ornament. This is a sweeping statement, from which we need not suffer un
duly; yet it is doubtful whether there is art in individual letters. Letters in combination may be
The main purpose of letters is the practical one of making thoughts visible. Ruskin says that
all letters are frightful things and to be endured only on occasion, that is to say, in places wh
The main purpose of letters is the practical one of making thoughts visible. Ruskin says th
at all letters are frightful things and to be endured only on occasion, that is to say, in place

6/8

The main purpose of letters is the practical one of making thoughts visible. Ruskin says that all
letters are frightful things and to be endured only on occasion, that is to say, in places where t
he sense of the inscription is of more importance than external ornament. This is a sweeping
statement, from which we need not suffer unduly; yet it is doubtful whether there is art in indiv
idual letters. Letters in combination may be satisfying and in a well composed page even b
eautiful as a whole, but art in letters consists rather in the art of arranging and composing th
em in a pleasing and appropriate manner. The main purpose of letters is the practical one
of making thoughts visible. Ruskin says that all letters are frightful things and to be endured o
nly on occasion, that is to say, in places where the sense of the inscription is of more importa
The main purpose of letters is the practical one of making thoughts visible. Ruskin says that
all letters are frightful things and to be endured only on occasion, that is to say, in places wh
The main purpose of letters is the practical one of making thoughts visible. Ruskin says th
at all letters are frightful things and to be endured only on occasion, that is to say, in place

6/9

The main purpose of letters is the practical one of making thoughts visible. Ruskin says that all
letters are frightful things and to be endured only on occasion, that is to say, in places where t
he sense of the inscription is of more importance than external ornament. This is a sweeping
statement, from which we need not suffer unduly; yet it is doubtful whether there is art in indiv
idual letters. Letters in combination may be satisfying and in a well composed page even b
eautiful as a whole, but art in letters consists rather in the art of arranging and composing th
em in a pleasing and appropriate manner. The main purpose of letters is the practical one
of making thoughts visible. Ruskin says that all letters are frightful things and to be endured o
The main purpose of letters is the practical one of making thoughts visible. Ruskin says that
all letters are frightful things and to be endured only on occasion, that is to say, in places wh
The main purpose of letters is the practical one of making thoughts visible. Ruskin says th
at all letters are frightful things and to be endured only on occasion, that is to say, in place

---

ABCDEFGHIJKLMNOPQRSTUVWXYZ 1234567890 abcdefghijklmnopqrstuvwxyz

ABCDEFGHIJKLMNOPQRSTUVWXYZ 1234567890 abcdefghijklmnopqrstuvwxyz

ABCDEFGHIJKLMNOPQRSTUVWXYZ 1234567890 abcdefghijklmnopqrstuvwxyz

ABCDEFGHIJKLMNOPQRSTUVWXYZ 1234567890 abcdefghijklmnopqrstuvwxyz

7/7

The main purpose of letters is the practical one of making thoughts visible. Rus
kin says that all letters are frightful things and to be endured only on occasion,
that is to say, in places where the sense of the inscription is of more importance
than external ornament. This is a sweeping statement, from which we need not
suffer unduly; yet it is doubtful whether there is art in individual letters. Letters in
combination may be satisfying and in a well composed page even beautiful
as a whole, but art in letters consists rather in the art of arranging and composin
g them in a pleasing and appropriate manner. The main purpose of letters is
the practical one of making thoughts visible. Ruskin says that all letters are fright
ful things and to be endured only on occasion, that is to say, in places where th
e sense of the inscription is of more importance than external ornament. This is
The main purpose of letters is the practical one of making thoughts visible. Rus
kin says that all letters are frightful things and to be endured only on occasion,
The main purpose of letters is the practical one of making thoughts visible. R
uskin says that all letters are frightful things and to be endured only on occas

7/8

The main purpose of letters is the practical one of making thoughts visible. Rus
kin says that all letters are frightful things and to be endured only on occasion,
that is to say, in places where the sense of the inscription is of more importance
than external ornament. This is a sweeping statement, from which we need not
suffer unduly; yet it is doubtful whether there is art in individual letters. Letters in
combination may be satisfying and in a well composed page even beautiful
as a whole, but art in letters consists rather in the art of arranging and composin
g them in a pleasing and appropriate manner. The main purpose of letters is
the practical one of making thoughts visible. Ruskin says that all letters are fright
ful things and to be endured only on occasion, that is to say, in places where th
The main purpose of letters is the practical one of making thoughts visible. Rus
kin says that all letters are frightful things and to be endured only on occasion,
The main purpose of letters is the practical one of making thoughts visible. R
uskin says that all letters are frightful things and to be endured only on occas

7/9

The main purpose of letters is the practical one of making thoughts visible. Rus
kin says that all letters are frightful things and to be endured only on occasion,
that is to say, in places where the sense of the inscription is of more importance
than external ornament. This is a sweeping statement, from which we need not
suffer unduly; yet it is doubtful whether there is art in individual letters. Letters in
combination may be satisfying and in a well composed page even beautiful
as a whole, but art in letters consists rather in the art of arranging and composin
g them in a pleasing and appropriate manner. The main purpose of letters is
the practical one of making thoughts visible. Ruskin says that all letters are fright
ful things and to be endured only on occasion, that is to say, in places where th
The main purpose of letters is the practical one of making thoughts visible. Rus
kin says that all letters are frightful things and to be endured only on occasion,
The main purpose of letters is the practical one of making thoughts visible. R
uskin says that all letters are frightful things and to be endured only on occas

7/10

The main purpose of letters is the practical one of making thoughts visible. Rus
kin says that all letters are frightful things and to be endured only on occasion,
that is to say, in places where the sense of the inscription is of more importance
than external ornament. This is a sweeping statement, from which we need not
suffer unduly; yet it is doubtful whether there is art in individual letters. Letters in
combination may be satisfying and in a well composed page even beautiful
as a whole, but art in letters consists rather in the art of arranging and composin
g them in a pleasing and appropriate manner. The main purpose of letters is
the practical one of making thoughts visible. Ruskin says that all letters are fright
The main purpose of letters is the practical one of making thoughts visible. Rus
kin says that all letters are frightful things and to be endured only on occasion,
The main purpose of letters is the practical one of making thoughts visible. R
uskin says that all letters are frightful things and to be endured only on occas

ITC AVANT GARDE 8 & 9 POINT SET NORMAL

BOOK, ITALIC, DEMI, DEMI ITALIC

ABCDEFGHIJKLMNOPQRSTUVWXYZ 1234567890 abcdefghijklmnopqrstuvwxyz

ABCDEFGHIJKLMNOPQRSTUVWXYZ 1234567890 abcdefghijklmnopqrstuvwxyz

ABCDEFGHIJKLMNOPQRSTUVWXYZ 1234567890 abcdefghijklmnopqrstuvwxyz

ABCDEFGHIJKLMNOPQRSTUVWXYZ 1234567890 abcdefghijklmnopqrstuvwxyz

8/8

The main purpose of letters is the practical one of making thoughts vi sible. Ruskin says that all letters are frightful things and to be endured only on occasion, that is to say, in places where the sense of the inscri ption is of more importance than external ornament. This is a sweepi ng statement, from which we need not suffer unduly; yet it is doubtful whether there is art in individual letters. Letters in combination may b e satisfying and in a well composed page even beautiful as a whole, but art in letters consists rather in the art of arranging and composing them in a pleasing and appropriate manner. The main purpose of le

The main purpose of letters is the practical one of making thoughts v isible. Ruskin says that all letters are frightful things and to be endure

The main purpose of letters is the practical one of making thoughts visible. Ruskin says that all letters are frightful things and to be end

8/9

The main purpose of letters is the practical one of making thoughts vi sible. Ruskin says that all letters are frightful things and to be endured only on occasion, that is to say, in places where the sense of the inscri ption is of more importance than external ornament. This is a sweepi ng statement, from which we need not suffer unduly; yet it is doubtful whether there is art in individual letters. Letters in combination may b e satisfying and in a well composed page even beautiful as a whole, but art in letters consists rather in the art of arranging and composing

The main purpose of letters is the practical one of making thoughts v isible. Ruskin says that all letters are frightful things and to be endure

The main purpose of letters is the practical one of making thoughts visible. Ruskin says that all letters are frightful things and to be end

8/10

The main purpose of letters is the practical one of making thoughts vi sible. Ruskin says that all letters are frightful things and to be endured only on occasion, that is to say, in places where the sense of the inscri ption is of more importance than external ornament. This is a sweepi ng statement, from which we need not suffer unduly; yet it is doubtful whether there is art in individual letters. Letters in combination may b e satisfying and in a well composed page even beautiful as a whole,

The main purpose of letters is the practical one of making thoughts v isible. Ruskin says that all letters are frightful things and to be endure

The main purpose of letters is the practical one of making thoughts visible. Ruskin says that all letters are frightful things and to be end

8/11

The main purpose of letters is the practical one of making thoughts vi sible. Ruskin says that all letters are frightful things and to be endured only on occasion, that is to say, in places where the sense of the inscri ption is of more importance than external ornament. This is a sweepi ng statement, from which we need not suffer unduly; yet it is doubtful whether there is art in individual letters. Letters in combination may b e satisfying and in a well composed page even beautiful as a whole,

The main purpose of letters is the practical one of making thoughts v isible. Ruskin says that all letters are frightful things and to be endure

The main purpose of letters is the practical one of making thoughts visible. Ruskin says that all letters are frightful things and to be end

---

ABCDEFGHIJKLMNOPQRSTUVWXYZ 1234567890 abcdefghijklmnopqrstuvwxyz

ABCDEFGHIJKLMNOPQRSTUVWXYZ 1234567890 abcdefghijklmnopqrstuvwxyz

ABCDEFGHIJKLMNOPQRSTUVWXYZ 1234567890 abcdefghijklmnopqrstuvwxyz

ABCDEFGHIJKLMNOPQRSTUVWXYZ 1234567890 abcdefghijklmnopqrstuvwxyz

9/9

The main purpose of letters is the practical one of making tho ughts visible. Ruskin says that all letters are frightful things and t o be endured only on occasion, that is to say, in places where the sense of the inscription is of more importance than extern al ornament. This is a sweeping statement, from which we ne ed not suffer unduly; yet it is doubtful whether there is art in ind ividual letters. Letters in combination may be satisfying and in a well composed page even beautiful as a whole, but art in l

The main purpose of letters is the practical one of making th oughts visible. Ruskin says that all letters are frightful things a

The main purpose of letters is the practical one of making t houghts visible. Ruskin says that all letters are frightful thing

9/10

The main purpose of letters is the practical one of making tho ughts visible. Ruskin says that all letters are frightful things and t o be endured only on occasion, that is to say, in places where the sense of the inscription is of more importance than extern al ornament. This is a sweeping statement, from which we ne ed not suffer unduly; yet it is doubtful whether there is art in ind ividual letters. Letters in combination may be satisfying and in

The main purpose of letters is the practical one of making th oughts visible. Ruskin says that all letters are frightful things a

The main purpose of letters is the practical one of making t houghts visible. Ruskin says that all letters are frightful thing

9/11

The main purpose of letters is the practical one of making tho ughts visible. Ruskin says that all letters are frightful things and t o be endured only on occasion, that is to say, in places where the sense of the inscription is of more importance than extern al ornament. This is a sweeping statement, from which we ne ed not suffer unduly; yet it is doubtful whether there is art in ind ividual letters. Letters in combination may be satisfying and in

The main purpose of letters is the practical one of making th oughts visible. Ruskin says that all letters are frightful things a

The main purpose of letters is the practical one of making t houghts visible. Ruskin says that all letters are frightful thing

9/12

The main purpose of letters is the practical one of making tho ughts visible. Ruskin says that all letters are frightful things and t o be endured only on occasion, that is to say, in places where the sense of the inscription is of more importance than extern al ornament. This is a sweeping statement, from which we ne ed not suffer unduly; yet it is doubtful whether there is art in ind ividual letters. Letters in combination may be satisfying and in

The main purpose of letters is the practical one of making th oughts visible. Ruskin says that all letters are frightful things a

The main purpose of letters is the practical one of making t houghts visible. Ruskin says that all letters are frightful thing

ITC AVANT GARDE 10 POINT SET MINUS ½ UNIT

BOOK, ITALIC, DEMI, DEMI ITALIC

abcdefghijklmnopqrstuvwxyz – 1 UNIT
abcdefghijklmnopqrstuvwxyz – ½ UNIT
abcdefghijklmnopqrstuvwxyz NORMAL

ABCDEFGHIJKLMNOPQRSTUVWXYZ 1234567890 abcdefghijklmnopqrstuvwxyz
ABCDEFGHIJKLMNOPQRSTUVWXYZ 1234567890 abcdefghijklmnopqrstuvwxyz
ABCDEFGHIJKLMNOPQRSTUVWXYZ 1234567890 abcdefghijklmnopqrstuvwxyz
ABCDEFGHIJKLMNOPQRSTUVWXYZ 1234567890 abcdefghijklmnopqrstuvwxyz

10/10

The main purpose of letters is the practical one of making thoughts visible. Ruskin says that all letters are frightful thing s and to be endured only on occasion, that is to say, in pla ces where the sense of the inscription is of more importan ce than external ornament. This is a sweeping statement, from which we need not suffer unduly; yet it is doubtful wh ether there is art in individual letters. Letters in combinatio n may be satisfying and in a well composed page even b eautiful as a whole, but art in letters consists rather in the ar t of arranging and composing them in a pleasing and ap propriate manner. The main purpose of letters is the pract ical one of making thoughts visible. Ruskin says that all lett ers are frightful things and to be endured only on occasio n, that is to say, in places where the sense of the inscription is of more importance than external ornament. This is a s weeping statement, from which we need not suffer undul y; yet it is doubtful whether there is art in individual letters. L etters in combination may be satisfying and in a well com posed page even beautiful as a whole, but art in letters c onsists rather in the art of arranging and composing the m in a pleasing and appropriate manner. The main purp ose of letters is the practical one of making thoughts visibl
The main purpose of letters is the practical one of makin g thoughts visible. Ruskin says that all letters are frightful t
The main purpose of letters is the practical one of maki ng thoughts visible. Ruskin says that all letters are frightf

10/11

The main purpose of letters is the practical one of making thoughts visible. Ruskin says that all letters are frightful thing s and to be endured only on occasion, that is to say, in pla ces where the sense of the inscription is of more importan ce than external ornament. This is a sweeping statement, from which we need not suffer unduly; yet it is doubtful wh ether there is art in individual letters. Letters in combinatio n may be satisfying and in a well composed page even b eautiful as a whole, but art in letters consists rather in the ar t of arranging and composing them in a pleasing and ap propriate manner. The main purpose of letters is the pract ical one of making thoughts visible. Ruskin says that all lett ers are frightful things and to be endured only on occasio n, that is to say, in places where the sense of the inscription is of more importance than external ornament. This is a s weeping statement, from which we need not suffer undul y; yet it is doubtful whether there is art in individual letters. L etters in combination may be satisfying and in a well com posed page even beautiful as a whole, but art in letters c onsists rather in the art of arranging and composing the
The main purpose of letters is the practical one of makin g thoughts visible. Ruskin says that all letters are frightful t
The main purpose of letters is the practical one of maki ng thoughts visible. Ruskin says that all letters are frightf

10/12

The main purpose of letters is the practical one of making thoughts visible. Ruskin says that all letters are frightful thing s and to be endured only on occasion, that is to say, in pla ces where the sense of the inscription is of more importan ce than external ornament. This is a sweeping statement, from which we need not suffer unduly; yet it is doubtful wh ether there is art in individual letters. Letters in combinatio n may be satisfying and in a well composed page even b eautiful as a whole, but art in letters consists rather in the ar t of arranging and composing them in a pleasing and ap propriate manner. The main purpose of letters is the pract ical one of making thoughts visible. Ruskin says that all lett ers are frightful things and to be endured only on occasio n, that is to say, in places where the sense of the inscription is of more importance than external ornament. This is a s weeping statement, from which we need not suffer undul y; yet it is doubtful whether there is art in individual letters. L etters in combination may be satisfying and in a well com
The main purpose of letters is the practical one of makin g thoughts visible. Ruskin says that all letters are frightful t
The main purpose of letters is the practical one of maki ng thoughts visible. Ruskin says that all letters are frightf

10/13

The main purpose of letters is the practical one of making thoughts visible. Ruskin says that all letters are frightful thing s and to be endured only on occasion, that is to say, in pla ces where the sense of the inscription is of more importan ce than external ornament. This is a sweeping statement, from which we need not suffer unduly; yet it is doubtful wh ether there is art in individual letters. Letters in combinatio n may be satisfying and in a well composed page even b eautiful as a whole, but art in letters consists rather in the ar t of arranging and composing them in a pleasing and ap propriate manner. The main purpose of letters is the pract ical one of making thoughts visible. Ruskin says that all lett ers are frightful things and to be endured only on occasio n, that is to say, in places where the sense of the inscription is of more importance than external ornament. This is a s weeping statement, from which we need not suffer undul y; yet it is doubtful whether there is art in individual letters. L
The main purpose of letters is the practical one of makin g thoughts visible. Ruskin says that all letters are frightful t
The main purpose of letters is the practical one of maki ng thoughts visible. Ruskin says that all letters are frightf

ITC AVANT GARDE 11 POINT SET MINUS ½ UNIT

BOOK. ITALIC. DEMI. DEMI ITALIC

abcdefghijklmnopqrstuvwxyz – 1 UNIT
abcdefghijklmnopqrstuvwxyz – ½ UNIT
abcdefghijklmnopqrstuvwxyz NORMAL

ABCDEFGHIJKLMNOPQRSTUVWXYZ 1234567890 abcdefghijklmnopqrstuvwxyz
ABCDEFGHIJKLMNOPQRSTUVWXYZ 1234567890 abcdefghijklmnopqrstuvwxyz
ABCDEFGHIJKLMNOPQRSTUVWXYZ 1234567890 abcdefghijklmnopqrstuvwxyz
ABCDEFGHIJKLMNOPQRSTUVWXYZ 1234567890 abcdefghijklmnopqrstuvwxyz

11/11

The main purpose of letters is the practical one of m aking thoughts visible. Ruskin says that all letters are fr ightful things and to be endured only on occasion, t hat is to say, in places where the sense of the inscripti on is of more importance than external ornament. T his is a sweeping statement, from which we need no t suffer unduly; yet it is doubtful whether there is art in i ndividual letters. Letters in combination may be satis fying and in a well composed page even beautiful as a whole, but art in letters consists rather in the art of arranging and composing them in a pleasing an d appropriate manner. The main purpose of letters i s the practical one of making thoughts visible. Ruskin says that all letters are frightful things and to be endu red only on occasion, that is to say, in places where t he sense of the inscription is of more importance th an external ornament. This is a sweeping statement, from which we need not suffer unduly; yet it is doubtf ul whether there is art in individual letters. Letters in c

The main purpose of letters is the practical one of m aking thoughts visible. Ruskin says that all letters are

The main purpose of letters is the practical one of making thoughts visible. Ruskin says that all letters

11/12

The main purpose of letters is the practical one of m aking thoughts visible. Ruskin says that all letters are fr ightful things and to be endured only on occasion, t hat is to say, in places where the sense of the inscripti on is of more importance than external ornament. T his is a sweeping statement, from which we need no t suffer unduly; yet it is doubtful whether there is art in i ndividual letters. Letters in combination may be satis fying and in a well composed page even beautiful as a whole, but art in letters consists rather in the art of arranging and composing them in a pleasing an d appropriate manner. The main purpose of letters i s the practical one of making thoughts visible. Ruskin says that all letters are frightful things and to be endu red only on occasion, that is to say, in places where t he sense of the inscription is of more importance th an external ornament. This is a sweeping statement, from which we need not suffer unduly; yet it is doubtf

The main purpose of letters is the practical one of m aking thoughts visible. Ruskin says that all letters are

The main purpose of letters is the practical one of making thoughts visible. Ruskin says that all letters

11/13

The main purpose of letters is the practical one of m aking thoughts visible. Ruskin says that all letters are fr ightful things and to be endured only on occasion, t hat is to say, in places where the sense of the inscripti on is of more importance than external ornament. T his is a sweeping statement, from which we need no t suffer unduly; yet it is doubtful whether there is art in i ndividual letters. Letters in combination may be satis fying and in a well composed page even beautiful as a whole, but art in letters consists rather in the art of arranging and composing them in a pleasing an d appropriate manner. The main purpose of letters i s the practical one of making thoughts visible. Ruskin says that all letters are frightful things and to be endu red only on occasion, that is to say, in places where t he sense of the inscription is of more importance th an external ornament. This is a sweeping statement,

The main purpose of letters is the practical one of m aking thoughts visible. Ruskin says that all letters are

The main purpose of letters is the practical one of making thoughts visible. Ruskin says that all letters

11/14

The main purpose of letters is the practical one of m aking thoughts visible. Ruskin says that all letters are fr ightful things and to be endured only on occasion, t hat is to say, in places where the sense of the inscripti on is of more importance than external ornament. T his is a sweeping statement, from which we need no t suffer unduly; yet it is doubtful whether there is art in i ndividual letters. Letters in combination may be satis fying and in a well composed page even beautiful as a whole, but art in letters consists rather in the art of arranging and composing them in a pleasing an d appropriate manner. The main purpose of letters i s the practical one of making thoughts visible. Ruskin says that all letters are frightful things and to be endu red only on occasion, that is to say, in places where t he sense of the inscription is of more importance th

The main purpose of letters is the practical one of m aking thoughts visible. Ruskin says that all letters are

The main purpose of letters is the practical one of making thoughts visible. Ruskin says that all letters

ITC AVANT GARDE 12 POINT SET MINUS ½ UNIT

BOOK, ITALIC, DEMI, DEMI ITALIC

abcdefghijklmnopqrstuvwxyz – 1 UNIT
abcdefghijklmnopqrstuvwxyz – ½ UNIT
abcdefghijklmnopqrstuvwxyz NORMAL

ABCDEFGHIJKLMNOPQRSTUVWXYZ 1234567890 abcdefghijklmnopqrstuvwxyz
ABCDEFGHIJKLMNOPQRSTUVWXYZ 1234567890 abcdefghijklmnopqrstuvwxyz
ABCDEFGHIJKLMNOPQRSTUVWXYZ 1234567890 abcdefghijklmnopqrstuvwxyz
ABCDEFGHIJKLMNOPQRSTUVWXYZ 1234567890 abcdefghijklmnopqrstuvwxyz

12/12

The main purpose of letters is the practical one o f making thoughts visible. Ruskin says that all lette rs are frightful things and to be endured only on occasion, that is to say, in places where the sens e of the inscription is of more importance than e xternal ornament. This is a sweeping statement, f rom which we need not suffer unduly; yet it is dou btful whether there is art in individual letters. Lette rs in combination may be satisfying and in a well composed page even beautiful as a whole, but art in letters consists rather in the art of arranging and composing them in a pleasing and appro priate manner. The main purpose of letters is the practical one of making thoughts visible. Ruskin s ays that all letters are frightful things and to be en

The main purpose of letters is the practical one of making thoughts visible. Ruskin says that all let

The main purpose of letters is the practical one of making thoughts visible. Ruskin says that all l

12/13

The main purpose of letters is the practical one o f making thoughts visible. Ruskin says that all lette rs are frightful things and to be endured only on occasion, that is to say, in places where the sens e of the inscription is of more importance than e xternal ornament. This is a sweeping statement, f rom which we need not suffer unduly; yet it is dou btful whether there is art in individual letters. Lette rs in combination may be satisfying and in a well composed page even beautiful as a whole, but art in letters consists rather in the art of arranging and composing them in a pleasing and appro priate manner. The main purpose of letters is the practical one of making thoughts visible. Ruskin s

The main purpose of letters is the practical one of making thoughts visible. Ruskin says that all let

The main purpose of letters is the practical one of making thoughts visible. Ruskin says that all l

12/14

The main purpose of letters is the practical one o f making thoughts visible. Ruskin says that all lette rs are frightful things and to be endured only on occasion, that is to say, in places where the sens e of the inscription is of more importance than e xternal ornament. This is a sweeping statement, f rom which we need not suffer unduly; yet it is dou btful whether there is art in individual letters. Lette rs in combination may be satisfying and in a well composed page even beautiful as a whole, but art in letters consists rather in the art of arranging and composing them in a pleasing and appro priate manner. The main purpose of letters is the practical one of making thoughts visible. Ruskin s ays that all letters are frightful things and to be en

The main purpose of letters is the practical one of making thoughts visible. Ruskin says that all let

The main purpose of letters is the practical one of making thoughts visible. Ruskin says that all l

12/15

The main purpose of letters is the practical one o f making thoughts visible. Ruskin says that all lette rs are frightful things and to be endured only on occasion, that is to say, in places where the sens e of the inscription is of more importance than e xternal ornament. This is a sweeping statement, f rom which we need not suffer unduly; yet it is dou btful whether there is art in individual letters. Lette rs in combination may be satisfying and in a well composed page even beautiful as a whole, but art in letters consists rather in the art of arranging and composing them in a pleasing and appro priate manner. The main purpose of letters is the practical one of making thoughts visible. Ruskin s

The main purpose of letters is the practical one of making thoughts visible. Ruskin says that all let

The main purpose of letters is the practical one of making thoughts visible. Ruskin says that all l

ITC AVANT GARDE 14 POINT SET MINUS ½ UNIT

BOOK, ITALIC, DEMI, DEMI ITALIC

abcdefghijklmnopqrstuvwxyz – 1 UNIT
abcdefghijklmnopqrstuvwxyz – ½ UNIT
abcdefghijklmnopqrstuvwxyz NORMAL

ABCDEFGHIJKLMNOPQRSTUVWXYZ abcdefghijklmnopqrstuvwxyz
ABCDEFGHIJKLMNOPQRSTUVWXYZ abcdefghijklmnopqrstuvwxyz
ABCDEFGHIJKLMNOPQRSTUVWXYZ abcdefghijklmnopqrstuvwxyz
ABCDEFGHIJKLMNOPQRSTUVWXYZ abcdefghijklmnopqrstuvwxyz

14/14

The main purpose of letters is the practic al one of making thoughts visible. Ruskin s ays that all letters are frightful things and t o be endured only on occasion, that is to say, in places where the sense of the inscr iption is of more importance than extern al ornament. This is a sweeping statemen t, from which we need not suffer unduly; y et it is doubtful whether there is art in indiv idual letters. Letters in combination may be satisfying and in a well composed pa ge even beautiful as a whole, but art in le tters consists rather in the art of arranging
The main purpose of letters is the practic al one of making thoughts visible. Ruskin
The main purpose of letters is the practi cal one of making thoughts visible. Rusk

14/15

The main purpose of letters is the practic al one of making thoughts visible. Ruskin s ays that all letters are frightful things and t o be endured only on occasion, that is to say, in places where the sense of the inscr iption is of more importance than extern al ornament. This is a sweeping statemen t, from which we need not suffer unduly; y et it is doubtful whether there is art in indiv idual letters. Letters in combination may be satisfying and in a well composed pa ge even beautiful as a whole, but art in le
The main purpose of letters is the practic al one of making thoughts visible. Ruskin
The main purpose of letters is the practi cal one of making thoughts visible. Rusk

14/16

The main purpose of letters is the practic al one of making thoughts visible. Ruskin s ays that all letters are frightful things and t o be endured only on occasion, that is to say, in places where the sense of the inscr iption is of more importance than extern al ornament. This is a sweeping statemen t, from which we need not suffer unduly; y et it is doubtful whether there is art in indiv idual letters. Letters in combination may be satisfying and in a well composed pa ge even beautiful as a whole, but art in le tters consists rather in the art of arranging
The main purpose of letters is the practic al one of making thoughts visible. Ruskin
The main purpose of letters is the practi cal one of making thoughts visible. Rusk

14/17

The main purpose of letters is the practic al one of making thoughts visible. Ruskin s ays that all letters are frightful things and t o be endured only on occasion, that is to say, in places where the sense of the inscr iption is of more importance than extern al ornament. This is a sweeping statemen t, from which we need not suffer unduly; y et it is doubtful whether there is art in indiv idual letters. Letters in combination may be satisfying and in a well composed pa ge even beautiful as a whole, but art in le
The main purpose of letters is the practic al one of making thoughts visible. Ruskin
The main purpose of letters is the practi cal one of making thoughts visible. Rusk

ITC AVANT GARDE 6 & 7 POINT SET NORMAL

MEDIUM, ITALIC, BOLD, BOLD ITALIC

ABCDEFGHIJKLMNOPQRSTUVWXYZ 1234567890 abcdefghijklmnopqrstuvwxyz

ABCDEFGHIJKLMNOPQRSTUVWXYZ 1234567890 abcdefghijklmnopqrstuvwxyz

ABCDEFGHIJKLMNOPQRSTUVWXYZ 1234567890 abcdefghijklmnopqrstuvwxyz

ABCDEFGHIJKLMNOPQRSTUVWXYZ 1234567890 abcdefghijklmnopqrstuvwxyz

6/6

The main purpose of letters is the practical one of making thoughts visible. Ruskin says that all letters are frightful things and to be endured only on occasion, that is to say, in places w here the sense of the inscription is of more importance than external ornament. This is a sw eeping statement, from which we need not suffer unduly; yet it is doubtful whether there is art in individual letters. Letters in combination may be satisfying and in a well composed p age even beautiful as a whole, but art in letters consists rather in the art of arranging and c omposing them in a pleasing and appropriate manner. The main purpose of letters is the practical one of making thoughts visible. Ruskin says that all letters are frightful things and t o be endured only on occasion, that is to say, in places where the sense of the inscription is of more importance than external ornament. This is a sweeping statement, from which we need not suffer unduly; yet it is doubtful whether there is art in individual letters. Letters in co mbination may be satisfying and in a well composed page even beautiful as a whole, but art in letters consists rather in the art of arranging and composing them in a pleasing and *The main purpose of letters is the practical one of making thoughts visible. Ruskin says tha t all letters are frightful things and to be endured only on occasion, that is to say, in places* **The main purpose of letters is the practical one of making thoughts visible. Ruskin says t hat all letters are frightful things and to be endured only on occasion, that is to say, in pl**

6/7

The main purpose of letters is the practical one of making thoughts visible. Ruskin says that all letters are frightful things and to be endured only on occasion, that is to say, in places w here the sense of the inscription is of more importance than external ornament. This is a sw eeping statement, from which we need not suffer unduly; yet it is doubtful whether there is art in individual letters. Letters in combination may be satisfying and in a well composed p age even beautiful as a whole, but art in letters consists rather in the art of arranging and c omposing them in a pleasing and appropriate manner. The main purpose of letters is the practical one of making thoughts visible. Ruskin says that all letters are frightful things and t o be endured only on occasion, that is to say, in places where the sense of the inscription is of more importance than external ornament. This is a sweeping statement, from which we need not suffer unduly; yet it is doubtful whether there is art in individual letters. Letters in co *The main purpose of letters is the practical one of making thoughts visible. Ruskin says tha t all letters are frightful things and to be endured only on occasion, that is to say, in places* **The main purpose of letters is the practical one of making thoughts visible. Ruskin says t hat all letters are frightful things and to be endured only on occasion, that is to say, in pl**

6/8

The main purpose of letters is the practical one of making thoughts visible. Ruskin says that all letters are frightful things and to be endured only on occasion, that is to say, in places w here the sense of the inscription is of more importance than external ornament. This is a sw eeping statement, from which we need not suffer unduly; yet it is doubtful whether there is art in individual letters. Letters in combination may be satisfying and in a well composed p age even beautiful as a whole, but art in letters consists rather in the art of arranging and c omposing them in a pleasing and appropriate manner. The main purpose of letters is the practical one of making thoughts visible. Ruskin says that all letters are frightful things and t o be endured only on occasion, that is to say, in places where the sense of the inscription is *The main purpose of letters is the practical one of making thoughts visible. Ruskin says tha t all letters are frightful things and to be endured only on occasion, that is to say, in places* **The main purpose of letters is the practical one of making thoughts visible. Ruskin says t hat all letters are frightful things and to be endured only on occasion, that is to say, in pl**

6/9

The main purpose of letters is the practical one of making thoughts visible. Ruskin says that all letters are frightful things and to be endured only on occasion, that is to say, in places w here the sense of the inscription is of more importance than external ornament. This is a sw eeping statement, from which we need not suffer unduly; yet it is doubtful whether there is art in individual letters. Letters in combination may be satisfying and in a well composed p age even beautiful as a whole, but art in letters consists rather in the art of arranging and c omposing them in a pleasing and appropriate manner. The main purpose of letters is the practical one of making thoughts visible. Ruskin says that all letters are frightful things and t *The main purpose of letters is the practical one of making thoughts visible. Ruskin says tha t all letters are frightful things and to be endured only on occasion, that is to say, in places* **The main purpose of letters is the practical one of making thoughts visible. Ruskin says t hat all letters are frightful things and to be endured only on occasion, that is to say, in pl**

ABCDEFGHIJKLMNOPQRSTUVWXYZ 1234567890 abcdefghijklmnopqrstuvwxyz

ABCDEFGHIJKLMNOPQRSTUVWXYZ 1234567890 abcdefghijklmnopqrstuvwxyz

ABCDEFGHIJKLMNOPQRSTUVWXYZ 1234567890 abcdefghijklmnopqrstuvwxyz

ABCDEFGHIJKLMNOPQRSTUVWXYZ 1234567890 abcdefghijklmnopqrstuvwxyz

7/7

The main purpose of letters is the practical one of making thoughts visible. Ru skin says that all letters are frightful things and to be endured only on occasio n, that is to say, in places where the sense of the inscription is of more importa nce than external ornament. This is a sweeping statement, from which we nee d not suffer unduly; yet it is doubtful whether there is art in individual letters. Let ters in combination may be satisfying and in a well composed page even be autiful as a whole, but art in letters consists rather in the art of arranging and c omposing them in a pleasing and appropriate manner. The main purpose of letters is the practical one of making thoughts visible. Ruskin says that all letter s are frightful things and to be endured only on occasion, that is to say, in plac es where the sense of the inscription is of more importance than external orn *The main purpose of letters is the practical one of making thoughts visible. R uskin says that all letters are frightful things and to be endured only on occasi* **The main purpose of letters is the practical one of making thoughts visible. Ruskin says that all letters are frightful things and to be endured only on oc**

7/8

The main purpose of letters is the practical one of making thoughts visible. Ru skin says that all letters are frightful things and to be endured only on occasio n, that is to say, in places where the sense of the inscription is of more importa nce than external ornament. This is a sweeping statement, from which we nee d not suffer unduly; yet it is doubtful whether there is art in individual letters. Let ters in combination may be satisfying and in a well composed page even be autiful as a whole, but art in letters consists rather in the art of arranging and c omposing them in a pleasing and appropriate manner. The main purpose of letters is the practical one of making thoughts visible. Ruskin says that all letter s are frightful things and to be endured only on occasion, that is to say, in plac *The main purpose of letters is the practical one of making thoughts visible. R uskin says that all letters are frightful things and to be endured only on occasi* **The main purpose of letters is the practical one of making thoughts visible. Ruskin says that all letters are frightful things and to be endured only on oc**

7/9

The main purpose of letters is the practical one of making thoughts visible. Ru skin says that all letters are frightful things and to be endured only on occasio n, that is to say, in places where the sense of the inscription is of more importa nce than external ornament. This is a sweeping statement, from which we nee d not suffer unduly; yet it is doubtful whether there is art in individual letters. Let ters in combination may be satisfying and in a well composed page even be autiful as a whole, but art in letters consists rather in the art of arranging and c omposing them in a pleasing and appropriate manner. The main purpose of letters is the practical one of making thoughts visible. Ruskin says that all letter s are frightful things and to be endured only on occasion, that is to say, in plac *The main purpose of letters is the practical one of making thoughts visible. R uskin says that all letters are frightful things and to be endured only on occasi* **The main purpose of letters is the practical one of making thoughts visible. Ruskin says that all letters are frightful things and to be endured only on oc**

7/10

The main purpose of letters is the practical one of making thoughts visible. Ru skin says that all letters are frightful things and to be endured only on occasio n, that is to say, in places where the sense of the inscription is of more importa nce than external ornament. This is a sweeping statement, from which we nee d not suffer unduly; yet it is doubtful whether there is art in individual letters. Let ters in combination may be satisfying and in a well composed page even be autiful as a whole, but art in letters consists rather in the art of arranging and c omposing them in a pleasing and appropriate manner. The main purpose of letters is the practical one of making thoughts visible. Ruskin says that all letter *The main purpose of letters is the practical one of making thoughts visible. R uskin says that all letters are frightful things and to be endured only on occasi* **The main purpose of letters is the practical one of making thoughts visible. Ruskin says that all letters are frightful things and to be endured only on oc**

ITC AVANT GARDE 8 & 9 POINT SET NORMAL

MEDIUM, ITALIC, BOLD, BOLD ITALIC

ABCDEFGHIJKLMNOPQRSTUVWXYZ 1234567890 abcdefghijklmnopqrstuvwxyz

ABCDEFGHIJKLMNOPQRSTUVWXYZ 1234567890 abcdefghijklmnopqrstuvwxyz

ABCDEFGHIJKLMNOPQRSTUVWXYZ 1234567890 abcdefghijklmnopqrstuvwxyz

ABCDEFGHIJKLMNOPQRSTUVWXYZ 1234567890 abcdefghijklmnopqrstuvwxyz

8/8

The main purpose of letters is the practical one of making thoughts visible. Ruskin says that all letters are frightful things and to be endur ed only on occasion, that is to say, in places where the sense of the inscription is of more importance than external ornament. This is a sweeping statement, from which we need not suffer unduly; yet it is doubtful whether there is art in individual letters. Letters in combina tion may be satisfying and in a well composed page even beautif ul as a whole, but art in letters consists rather in the art of arranging and composing them in a pleasing and appropriate manner. The
The main purpose of letters is the practical one of making thoughts visible. Ruskin says that all letters are frightful things and to be endu
The main purpose of letters is the practical one of making though ts visible. Ruskin says that all letters are frightful things and to be

8/9

The main purpose of letters is the practical one of making thoughts visible. Ruskin says that all letters are frightful things and to be endur ed only on occasion, that is to say, in places where the sense of the inscription is of more importance than external ornament. This is a sweeping statement, from which we need not suffer unduly; yet it is doubtful whether there is art in individual letters. Letters in combina tion may be satisfying and in a well composed page even beautif ul as a whole, but art in letters consists rather in the art of arranging
The main purpose of letters is the practical one of making thoughts visible. Ruskin says that all letters are frightful things and to be endu
The main purpose of letters is the practical one of making though ts visible. Ruskin says that all letters are frightful things and to be

8/10

The main purpose of letters is the practical one of making thoughts visible. Ruskin says that all letters are frightful things and to be endur ed only on occasion, that is to say, in places where the sense of the inscription is of more importance than external ornament. This is a sweeping statement, from which we need not suffer unduly; yet it is doubtful whether there is art in individual letters. Letters in combina tion may be satisfying and in a well composed page even beautif
The main purpose of letters is the practical one of making thoughts visible. Ruskin says that all letters are frightful things and to be endu
The main purpose of letters is the practical one of making though ts visible. Ruskin says that all letters are frightful things and to be

8/11

The main purpose of letters is the practical one of making thoughts visible. Ruskin says that all letters are frightful things and to be endur ed only on occasion, that is to say, in places where the sense of the inscription is of more importance than external ornament. This is a sweeping statement, from which we need not suffer unduly; yet it is doubtful whether there is art in individual letters. Letters in combina tion may be satisfying and in a well composed page even beautif
The main purpose of letters is the practical one of making thoughts visible. Ruskin says that all letters are frightful things and to be endu
The main purpose of letters is the practical one of making though ts visible. Ruskin says that all letters are frightful things and to be

---

ABCDEFGHIJKLMNOPQRSTUVWXYZ 1234567890 abcdefghijklmnopqrstuvwxyz

ABCDEFGHIJKLMNOPQRSTUVWXYZ 1234567890 abcdefghijklmnopqrstuvwxyz

ABCDEFGHIJKLMNOPQRSTUVWXYZ 1234567890 abcdefghijklmnopqrstuvwxyz

ABCDEFGHIJKLMNOPQRSTUVWXYZ 1234567890 abcdefghijklmnopqrstuvwxyz

9/9

The main purpose of letters is the practical one of making th oughts visible. Ruskin says that all letters are frightful things a nd to be endured only on occasion, that is to say, in places where the sense of the inscription is of more importance tha n external ornament. This is a sweeping statement, from whi ch we need not suffer unduly; yet it is doubtful whether there is art in individual letters. Letters in combination may be satis fying and in a well composed page even beautiful as a wh
The main purpose of letters is the practical one of making t houghts visible. Ruskin says that all letters are frightful things
The main purpose of letters is the practical one of making thoughts visible. Ruskin says that all letters are frightful thi

9/10

The main purpose of letters is the practical one of making th oughts visible. Ruskin says that all letters are frightful things a nd to be endured only on occasion, that is to say, in places where the sense of the inscription is of more importance tha n external ornament. This is a sweeping statement, from whi ch we need not suffer unduly; yet it is doubtful whether there is art in individual letters. Letters in combination may be satis
The main purpose of letters is the practical one of making t houghts visible. Ruskin says that all letters are frightful things
The main purpose of letters is the practical one of making thoughts visible. Ruskin says that all letters are frightful thi

9/11

The main purpose of letters is the practical one of making th oughts visible. Ruskin says that all letters are frightful things a nd to be endured only on occasion, that is to say, in places where the sense of the inscription is of more importance tha n external ornament. This is a sweeping statement, from whi ch we need not suffer unduly; yet it is doubtful whether there is art in individual letters. Letters in combination may be satis
The main purpose of letters is the practical one of making t houghts visible. Ruskin says that all letters are frightful things
The main purpose of letters is the practical one of making thoughts visible. Ruskin says that all letters are frightful thi

9/12

The main purpose of letters is the practical one of making th oughts visible. Ruskin says that all letters are frightful things a nd to be endured only on occasion, that is to say, in places where the sense of the inscription is of more importance tha n external ornament. This is a sweeping statement, from whi ch we need not suffer unduly; yet it is doubtful whether there is art in individual letters. Letters in combination may be satis
The main purpose of letters is the practical one of making t houghts visible. Ruskin says that all letters are frightful things
The main purpose of letters is the practical one of making thoughts visible. Ruskin says that all letters are frightful thi

ITC AVANT GARDE 10 POINT SET MINUS ½ UNIT

MEDIUM, ITALIC, BOLD, BOLD ITALIC

abcdefghijklmnopqrstuvwxyz – 1 UNIT
abcdefghijklmnopqrstuvwxyz – ½ UNIT
abcdefghijklmnopqrstuvwxyz NORMAL

ABCDEFGHIJKLMNOPQRSTUVWXYZ 1234567890 abcdefghijklmnopqrstuvwxyz
ABCDEFGHIJKLMNOPQRSTUVWXYZ 1234567890 abcdefghijklmnopqrstuvwxyz
ABCDEFGHIJKLMNOPQRSTUVWXYZ 1234567890 abcdefghijklmnopqrstuvwxyz
ABCDEFGHIJKLMNOPQRSTUVWXYZ 1234567890 abcdefghijklmnopqrstuvwxyz

10/10

The main purpose of letters is the practical one of makin g thoughts visible. Ruskin says that all letters are frightful t hings and to be endured only on occasion, that is to say, in places where the sense of the inscription is of more im portance than external ornament. This is a sweeping sta tement, from which we need not suffer unduly; yet it is do ubtful whether there is art in individual letters. Letters in c ombination may be satisfying and in a well composed page even beautiful as a whole, but art in letters consis ts rather in the art of arranging and composing them in a pleasing and appropriate manner. The main purpose of letters is the practical one of making thoughts visible. Ruskin says that all letters are frightful things and to be en dured only on occasion, that is to say, in places where t he sense of the inscription is of more importance than ex ternal ornament. This is a sweeping statement, from whi ch we need not suffer unduly; yet it is doubtful whether there is art in individual letters. Letters in combination ma y be satisfying and in a well composed page even bea utiful as a whole, but art in letters consists rather in the ar t of arranging and composing them in a pleasing and a ppropriate manner. The main purpose of letters is the pr
The main purpose of letters is the practical one of maki ng thoughts visible. Ruskin says that all letters are frightful
The main purpose of letters is the practical one of mak ing thoughts visible. Ruskin says that all letters are frig

10/11

The main purpose of letters is the practical one of makin g thoughts visible. Ruskin says that all letters are frightful t hings and to be endured only on occasion, that is to say, in places where the sense of the inscription is of more im portance than external ornament. This is a sweeping sta tement, from which we need not suffer unduly; yet it is do ubtful whether there is art in individual letters. Letters in c ombination may be satisfying and in a well composed page even beautiful as a whole, but art in letters consis ts rather in the art of arranging and composing them in a pleasing and appropriate manner. The main purpose of letters is the practical one of making thoughts visible. Ruskin says that all letters are frightful things and to be en dured only on occasion, that is to say, in places where t he sense of the inscription is of more importance than ex ternal ornament. This is a sweeping statement, from whi ch we need not suffer unduly; yet it is doubtful whether there is art in individual letters. Letters in combination ma y be satisfying and in a well composed page even bea utiful as a whole, but art in letters consists rather in the ar
The main purpose of letters is the practical one of maki ng thoughts visible. Ruskin says that all letters are frightful
The main purpose of letters is the practical one of mak ing thoughts visible. Ruskin says that all letters are frig

10/12

The main purpose of letters is the practical one of makin g thoughts visible. Ruskin says that all letters are frightful t hings and to be endured only on occasion, that is to say, in places where the sense of the inscription is of more im portance than external ornament. This is a sweeping sta tement, from which we need not suffer unduly; yet it is do ubtful whether there is art in individual letters. Letters in c ombination may be satisfying and in a well composed page even beautiful as a whole, but art in letters consis ts rather in the art of arranging and composing them in a pleasing and appropriate manner. The main purpose of letters is the practical one of making thoughts visible. Ruskin says that all letters are frightful things and to be en dured only on occasion, that is to say, in places where t he sense of the inscription is of more importance than ex ternal ornament. This is a sweeping statement, from whi ch we need not suffer unduly; yet it is doubtful whether there is art in individual letters. Letters in combination ma
The main purpose of letters is the practical one of maki ng thoughts visible. Ruskin says that all letters are frightful
The main purpose of letters is the practical one of mak ing thoughts visible. Ruskin says that all letters are frig

10/13

The main purpose of letters is the practical one of makin g thoughts visible. Ruskin says that all letters are frightful t hings and to be endured only on occasion, that is to say, in places where the sense of the inscription is of more im portance than external ornament. This is a sweeping sta tement, from which we need not suffer unduly; yet it is do ubtful whether there is art in individual letters. Letters in c ombination may be satisfying and in a well composed page even beautiful as a whole, but art in letters consis ts rather in the art of arranging and composing them in a pleasing and appropriate manner. The main purpose of letters is the practical one of making thoughts visible. Ruskin says that all letters are frightful things and to be en dured only on occasion, that is to say, in places where t he sense of the inscription is of more importance than ex ternal ornament. This is a sweeping statement, from whi ch we need not suffer unduly; yet it is doubtful whether
The main purpose of letters is the practical one of maki ng thoughts visible. Ruskin says that all letters are frightful
The main purpose of letters is the practical one of mak ing thoughts visible. Ruskin says that all letters are frig

ITC AVANT GARDE 11 POINT SET MINUS ½ UNIT

MEDIUM, ITALIC, BOLD, BOLD ITALIC

abcdefghijklmnopqrstuvwxyz – 1 UNIT
abcdefghijklmnopqrstuvwxyz ½ UNIT
abcdefghijklmnopqrstuvwxyz NORMAL

ABCDEFGHIJKLMNOPQRSTUVWXYZ 1234567890 abcdefghijklmnopqrstuvwxyz
ABCDEFGHIJKLMNOPQRSTUVWXYZ 1234567890 abcdefghijklmnopqrstuvwxyz
ABCDEFGHIJKLMNOPQRSTUVWXYZ 1234567890 abcdefghijklmnopqrstuvwxyz
ABCDEFGHIJKLMNOPQRSTUVWXYZ 1234567890 abcdefghijklmnopqrstuvwxyz

11/11

The main purpose of letters is the practical one of making thoughts visible. Ruskin says that all letters a re frightful things and to be endured only on occas ion, that is to say, in places where the sense of the in scription is of more importance than external orna ment. This is a sweeping statement, from which we need not suffer unduly; yet it is doubtful whether th ere is art in individual letters. Letters in combination may be satisfying and in a well composed page e ven beautiful as a whole, but art in letters consists ra ther in the art of arranging and composing them in a pleasing and appropriate manner. The main pur pose of letters is the practical one of making thoug hts visible. Ruskin says that all letters are frightful thin gs and to be endured only on occasion, that is to s ay, in places where the sense of the inscription is of more importance than external ornament. This is a sweeping statement, from which we need not suffe r unduly; yet it is doubtful whether there is art in indiv
The main purpose of letters is the practical one of making thoughts visible. Ruskin says that all letters
The main purpose of letters is the practical one of making thoughts visible. Ruskin says that all lette

11/12

The main purpose of letters is the practical one of making thoughts visible. Ruskin says that all letters a re frightful things and to be endured only on occas ion, that is to say, in places where the sense of the in scription is of more importance than external orna ment. This is a sweeping statement, from which we need not suffer unduly; yet it is doubtful whether th ere is art in individual letters. Letters in combination may be satisfying and in a well composed page e ven beautiful as a whole, but art in letters consists ra ther in the art of arranging and composing them in a pleasing and appropriate manner. The main pur pose of letters is the practical one of making thoug hts visible. Ruskin says that all letters are frightful thin gs and to be endured only on occasion, that is to s ay, in places where the sense of the inscription is of more importance than external ornament. This is a sweeping statement, from which we need not suffe
The main purpose of letters is the practical one of making thoughts visible. Ruskin says that all letters
The main purpose of letters is the practical one of making thoughts visible. Ruskin says that all lette

11/13

The main purpose of letters is the practical one of making thoughts visible. Ruskin says that all letters a re frightful things and to be endured only on occas ion, that is to say, in places where the sense of the in scription is of more importance than external orna ment. This is a sweeping statement, from which we need not suffer unduly; yet it is doubtful whether th ere is art in individual letters. Letters in combination may be satisfying and in a well composed page e ven beautiful as a whole, but art in letters consists ra ther in the art of arranging and composing them in a pleasing and appropriate manner. The main pur pose of letters is the practical one of making thoug hts visible. Ruskin says that all letters are frightful thin gs and to be endured only on occasion, that is to s ay, in places where the sense of the inscription is of more importance than external ornament. This is a
The main purpose of letters is the practical one of making thoughts visible. Ruskin says that all letters
The main purpose of letters is the practical one of making thoughts visible. Ruskin says that all lette

11/14

The main purpose of letters is the practical one of making thoughts visible. Ruskin says that all letters a re frightful things and to be endured only on occas ion, that is to say, in places where the sense of the in scription is of more importance than external orna ment. This is a sweeping statement, from which we need not suffer unduly; yet it is doubtful whether th ere is art in individual letters. Letters in combination may be satisfying and in a well composed page e ven beautiful as a whole, but art in letters consists ra ther in the art of arranging and composing them in a pleasing and appropriate manner. The main pur pose of letters is the practical one of making thoug hts visible. Ruskin says that all letters are frightful thin gs and to be endured only on occasion, that is to s ay, in places where the sense of the inscription is of
The main purpose of letters is the practical one of making thoughts visible. Ruskin says that all letters
The main purpose of letters is the practical one of making thoughts visible. Ruskin says that all lette

ITC AVANT GARDE 12 POINT SET MINUS ½ UNIT

MEDIUM, ITALIC, BOLD, BOLD ITALIC

abcdefghijklmnopqrstuvwxyz – 1 UNIT
abcdefghijklmnopqrstuvwxyz – ½ UNIT
abcdefghijklmnopqrstuvwxyz NORMAL

ABCDEFGHIJKLMNOPQRSTUVWXYZ 1234567890 abcdefghijklmnopqrstuvwxyz
ABCDEFGHIJKLMNOPQRSTUVWXYZ 1234567890 abcdefghijklmnopqrstuvwxyz
ABCDEFGHIJKLMNOPQRSTUVWXYZ 1234567890 abcdefghijklmnopqrstuvwxyz
ABCDEFGHIJKLMNOPQRSTUVWXYZ 1234567890 abcdefghijklmnopqrstuvwxyz

12/12

The main purpose of letters is the practical one of making thoughts visible. Ruskin says that all le tters are frightful things and to be endured only on occasion, that is to say, in places where the s ense of the inscription is of more importance th an external ornament. This is a sweeping state ment, from which we need not suffer unduly; yet it is doubtful whether there is art in individual lett ers. Letters in combination may be satisfying an d in a well composed page even beautiful as a whole, but art in letters consists rather in the art of arranging and composing them in a pleasi ng and appropriate manner. The main purpos e of letters is the practical one of making thoug hts visible. Ruskin says that all letters are frightful
The main purpose of letters is the practical one of making thoughts visible. Ruskin says that all l
The main purpose of letters is the practical on e of making thoughts visible. Ruskin says that

12/13

The main purpose of letters is the practical one of making thoughts visible. Ruskin says that all le tters are frightful things and to be endured only on occasion, that is to say, in places where the s ense of the inscription is of more importance th an external ornament. This is a sweeping state ment, from which we need not suffer unduly; yet it is doubtful whether there is art in individual lett ers. Letters in combination may be satisfying an d in a well composed page even beautiful as a whole, but art in letters consists rather in the art of arranging and composing them in a pleasi ng and appropriate manner. The main purpos e of letters is the practical one of making thoug
The main purpose of letters is the practical one of making thoughts visible. Ruskin says that all l
The main purpose of letters is the practical on e of making thoughts visible. Ruskin says that

12/14

The main purpose of letters is the practical one of making thoughts visible. Ruskin says that all le tters are frightful things and to be endured only on occasion, that is to say, in places where the s ense of the inscription is of more importance th an external ornament. This is a sweeping state ment, from which we need not suffer unduly; yet it is doubtful whether there is art in individual lett ers. Letters in combination may be satisfying an d in a well composed page even beautiful as a whole, but art in letters consists rather in the art of arranging and composing them in a pleasi ng and appropriate manner. The main purpos e of letters is the practical one of making thoug hts visible. Ruskin says that all letters are frightful
The main purpose of letters is the practical one of making thoughts visible. Ruskin says that all l
The main purpose of letters is the practical on e of making thoughts visible. Ruskin says that

12/15

The main purpose of letters is the practical one of making thoughts visible. Ruskin says that all le tters are frightful things and to be endured only on occasion, that is to say, in places where the s ense of the inscription is of more importance th an external ornament. This is a sweeping state ment, from which we need not suffer unduly; yet it is doubtful whether there is art in individual lett ers. Letters in combination may be satisfying an d in a well composed page even beautiful as a whole, but art in letters consists rather in the art of arranging and composing them in a pleasi ng and appropriate manner. The main purpos e of letters is the practical one of making thoug
The main purpose of letters is the practical one of making thoughts visible. Ruskin says that all l
The main purpose of letters is the practical on e of making thoughts visible. Ruskin says that

ITC AVANT GARDE 14 POINT SET MINUS ½ UNIT

MEDIUM, ITALIC, BOLD, BOLD ITALIC

abcdefghijklmnopqrstuvwxyz – 1 UNIT

abcdefghijklmnopqrstuvwxyz – ½ UNIT

abcdefghijklmnopqrstuvwxyz NORMAL

ABCDEFGHIJKLMNOPQRSTUVWXYZ abcdefghijklmnopqrstuvwxyz

ABCDEFGHIJKLMNOPQRSTUVWXYZ abcdefghijklmnopqrstuvwxyz

ABCDEFGHIJKLMNOPQRSTUVWXYZ abcdefghijklmnopqrstuvwxyz

ABCDEFGHIJKLMNOPQRSTUVWXYZ abcdefghijklmnopqrstuvwxyz

14/14

The main purpose of letters is the practic al one of making thoughts visible. Ruskin says that all letters are frightful things an d to be endured only on occasion, that i s to say, in places where the sense of the inscription is of more importance than e xternal ornament. This is a sweeping stat ement, from which we need not suffer u nduly; yet it is doubtful whether there is a rt in individual letters. Letters in combinat ion may be satisfying and in a well com posed page even beautiful as a whole, but art in letters consists rather in the art

The main purpose of letters is the practi cal one of making thoughts visible. Ruski

The main purpose of letters is the pract ical one of making thoughts visible. Ru

14/15

The main purpose of letters is the practic al one of making thoughts visible. Ruskin says that all letters are frightful things an d to be endured only on occasion, that i s to say, in places where the sense of the inscription is of more importance than e xternal ornament. This is a sweeping stat ement, from which we need not suffer u nduly; yet it is doubtful whether there is a rt in individual letters. Letters in combinat ion may be satisfying and in a well com posed page even beautiful as a whole,

The main purpose of letters is the practi cal one of making thoughts visible. Ruski

The main purpose of letters is the pract ical one of making thoughts visible. Ru

14/16

The main purpose of letters is the practic al one of making thoughts visible. Ruskin says that all letters are frightful things an d to be endured only on occasion, that i s to say, in places where the sense of the inscription is of more importance than e xternal ornament. This is a sweeping stat ement, from which we need not suffer u nduly; yet it is doubtful whether there is a rt in individual letters. Letters in combinat ion may be satisfying and in a well com posed page even beautiful as a whole, but art in letters consists rather in the art

The main purpose of letters is the practi cal one of making thoughts visible. Ruski

The main purpose of letters is the pract ical one of making thoughts visible. Ru

14/17

The main purpose of letters is the practic al one of making thoughts visible. Ruskin says that all letters are frightful things an d to be endured only on occasion, that i s to say, in places where the sense of the inscription is of more importance than e xternal ornament. This is a sweeping stat ement, from which we need not suffer u nduly; yet it is doubtful whether there is a rt in individual letters. Letters in combinat ion may be satisfying and in a well com posed page even beautiful as a whole,

The main purpose of letters is the practi cal one of making thoughts visible. Ruski

The main purpose of letters is the pract ical one of making thoughts visible. Ru

BASKERVILLE 6 & 7 POINT SET NORMAL

ROMAN, ITALIC, BOLD, BOLD ITALIC

ABCDEFGHIJKLMNOPQRSTUVWXYZ 1234567890 abcdefghijklmnopqrstuvwxyz

ABCDEFGHIJKLMNOPQRSTUVWXYZ 1234567890 abcdefghijklmnopqrstuvwxyz

ABCDEFGHIJKLMNOPQRSTUVWXYZ 1234567890 abcdefghijklmnopqrstuvwxyz

ABCDEFGHIJKLMNOPQRSTUVWXYZ 1234567890 abcdefghijklmnopqrstuvwxyz

6/6

The main purpose of letters is the practical one of making thoughts visible. Ruskin says that
all letters are frightful things and to be endured only on occasion, that is to say, in places whe
re the sense of the inscription is of more importance than external ornament. This is a swee
ping statement, from which we need not suffer unduly; yet it is doubtful whether there is ar
t in individual letters. Letters in combination may be satisfying and in a well composed page
even beautiful as a whole, but art in letters consists rather in the art of arranging and compo
sing them in a pleasing and appropriate manner. The main purpose of letters is the practica
l one of making thoughts visible. Ruskin says that all letters are frightful things and to be en
dured only on occasion, that is to say, in places where the sense of the inscription is of more i
mportance than external ornament. This is a sweeping statement, from which we need not s
uffer unduly; yet it is doubtful whether there is art in individual letters. Letters in combinati
on may be satisfying and in a well composed page even beautiful as a whole, but art in letters
consists rather in the art of arranging and composing them in a pleasing and appropriate m
The main purpose of letters is the practical one of making thoughts visible. Ruskin says that all letters ar
e frightful things and to be endured only on occasion, that is to say, in places where the sense of the inscri
The main purpose of letters is the practical one of making thoughts visible. Ruskin says t
hat all letters are frightful things and to be endured only on occasion, that is to say, in plac

6/7

The main purpose of letters is the practical one of making thoughts visible. Ruskin says that
all letters are frightful things and to be endured only on occasion, that is to say, in places whe
re the sense of the inscription is of more importance than external ornament. This is a swee
ping statement, from which we need not suffer unduly; yet it is doubtful whether there is ar
t in individual letters. Letters in combination may be satisfying and in a well composed page
even beautiful as a whole, but art in letters consists rather in the art of arranging and compo
sing them in a pleasing and appropriate manner. The main purpose of letters is the practica
l one of making thoughts visible. Ruskin says that all letters are frightful things and to be en
dured only on occasion, that is to say, in places where the sense of the inscription is of more i
mportance than external ornament. This is a sweeping statement, from which we need not s
uffer unduly; yet it is doubtful whether there is art in individual letters. Letters in combinati
The main purpose of letters is the practical one of making thoughts visible. Ruskin says that all letters ar
e frightful things and to be endured only on occasion, that is to say, in places where the sense of the inscri
The main purpose of letters is the practical one of making thoughts visible. Ruskin says t
hat all letters are frightful things and to be endured only on occasion, that is to say, in plac

6/8

The main purpose of letters is the practical one of making thoughts visible. Ruskin says that
all letters are frightful things and to be endured only on occasion, that is to say, in places whe
re the sense of the inscription is of more importance than external ornament. This is a swee
ping statement, from which we need not suffer unduly; yet it is doubtful whether there is ar
t in individual letters. Letters in combination may be satisfying and in a well composed page
even beautiful as a whole, but art in letters consists rather in the art of arranging and compo
sing them in a pleasing and appropriate manner. The main purpose of letters is the practica
l one of making thoughts visible. Ruskin says that all letters are frightful things and to be en
dured only on occasion, that is to say, in places where the sense of the inscription is of more i
The main purpose of letters is the practical one of making thoughts visible. Ruskin says that all letters ar
e frightful things and to be endured only on occasion, that is to say, in places where the sense of the inscri
The main purpose of letters is the practical one of making thoughts visible. Ruskin says t
hat all letters are frightful things and to be endured only on occasion, that is to say, in plac

6/9

The main purpose of letters is the practical one of making thoughts visible. Ruskin says that
all letters are frightful things and to be endured only on occasion, that is to say, in places whe
re the sense of the inscription is of more importance than external ornament. This is a swee
ping statement, from which we need not suffer unduly; yet it is doubtful whether there is ar
t in individual letters. Letters in combination may be satisfying and in a well composed page
even beautiful as a whole, but art in letters consists rather in the art of arranging and compo
sing them in a pleasing and appropriate manner. The main purpose of letters is the practica
l one of making thoughts visible. Ruskin says that all letters are frightful things and to be en
The main purpose of letters is the practical one of making thoughts visible. Ruskin says that all letters ar
e frightful things and to be endured only on occasion, that is to say, in places where the sense of the inscri
The main purpose of letters is the practical one of making thoughts visible. Ruskin says t
hat all letters are frightful things and to be endured only on occasion, that is to say, in plac

---

ABCDEFGHIJKLMNOPQRSTUVWXYZ 1234567890 abcdefghijklmnopqrstuvwxyz

ABCDEFGHIJKLMNOPQRSTUVWXYZ 1234567890 abcdefghijklmnopqrstuvwxyz

ABCDEFGHIJKLMNOPQRSTUVWXYZ 1234567890 abcdefghijklmnopqrstuvwxyz

ABCDEFGHIJKLMNOPQRSTUVWXYZ 1234567890 abcdefghijklmnopqrstuvwxyz

7/7

The main purpose of letters is the practical one of making thoughts visible. Ru
skin says that all letters are frightful things and to be endured only on occasion,
that is to say, in places where the sense of the inscription is of more importanc
e than external ornament. This is a sweeping statement, from which we need n
ot suffer unduly; yet it is doubtful whether there is art in individual letters. Let
ters in combination may be satisfying and in a well composed page even beauti
ful as a whole, but art in letters consists rather in the art of arranging and comp
osing them in a pleasing and appropriate manner. The main purpose of letters
is the practical one of making thoughts visible. Ruskin says that all letters are fr
ightful things and to be endured only on occasion, that is to say, in places where
the sense of the inscription is of more importance than external ornament. Thi
The main purpose of letters is the practical one of making thoughts visible. Ruskin says th
at all letters are frightful things and to be endured only on occasion, that is to say, in place
The main purpose of letters is the practical one of making thoughts visible.
Ruskin says that all letters are frightful things and to be endured only on occ

7/8

The main purpose of letters is the practical one of making thoughts visible. Ru
skin says that all letters are frightful things and to be endured only on occasion,
that is to say, in places where the sense of the inscription is of more importanc
e than external ornament. This is a sweeping statement, from which we need n
ot suffer unduly; yet it is doubtful whether there is art in individual letters. Let
ters in combination may be satisfying and in a well composed page even beauti
ful as a whole, but art in letters consists rather in the art of arranging and comp
osing them in a pleasing and appropriate manner. The main purpose of letters
is the practical one of making thoughts visible. Ruskin says that all letters are fr
ightful things and to be endured only on occasion, that is to say, in places where
The main purpose of letters is the practical one of making thoughts visible. Ruskin says th
at all letters are frightful things and to be endured only on occasion, that is to say, in place
The main purpose of letters is the practical one of making thoughts visible.
Ruskin says that all letters are frightful things and to be endured only on occ

7/9

The main purpose of letters is the practical one of making thoughts visible. Ru
skin says that all letters are frightful things and to be endured only on occasion,
that is to say, in places where the sense of the inscription is of more importanc
e than external ornament. This is a sweeping statement, from which we need n
ot suffer unduly; yet it is doubtful whether there is art in individual letters. Let
ters in combination may be satisfying and in a well composed page even beauti
ful as a whole, but art in letters consists rather in the art of arranging and comp
osing them in a pleasing and appropriate manner. The main purpose of letters
is the practical one of making thoughts visible. Ruskin says that all letters are fr
ightful things and to be endured only on occasion, that is to say, in places where
The main purpose of letters is the practical one of making thoughts visible. Ruskin says th
at all letters are frightful things and to be endured only on occasion, that is to say, in place
The main purpose of letters is the practical one of making thoughts visible.
Ruskin says that all letters are frightful things and to be endured only on occ

7/10

The main purpose of letters is the practical one of making thoughts visible. Ru
skin says that all letters are frightful things and to be endured only on occasion,
that is to say, in places where the sense of the inscription is of more importanc
e than external ornament. This is a sweeping statement, from which we need n
ot suffer unduly; yet it is doubtful whether there is art in individual letters. Let
ters in combination may be satisfying and in a well composed page even beauti
ful as a whole, but art in letters consists rather in the art of arranging and comp
osing them in a pleasing and appropriate manner. The main purpose of letters
is the practical one of making thoughts visible. Ruskin says that all letters are fr
The main purpose of letters is the practical one of making thoughts visible. Ruskin says th
at all letters are frightful things and to be endured only on occasion, that is to say, in place
The main purpose of letters is the practical one of making thoughts visible.
Ruskin says that all letters are frightful things and to be endured only on occ

BASKERVILLE 8 & 9 POINT SET NORMAL

ROMAN, ITALIC, BOLD, BOLD ITALIC

ABCDEFGHIJKLMNOPQRSTUVWXYZ 1234567890 abcdefghijklmnopqrstuvwxyz
ABCDEFGHIJKLMNOPQRSTUVWXYZ 1234567890 abcdefghijklmnopqrstuvwxyz
ABCDEFGHIJKLMNOPQRSTUVWXYZ 1234567890 abcdefghijklmnopqrstuvwxyz
ABCDEFGHIJKLMNOPQRSTUVWXYZ 1234567890 abcdefghijklmnopqrstuvwxyz

8/8

The main purpose of letters is the practical one of making thoughts v isible. Ruskin says that all letters are frightful things and to be endur ed only on occasion, that is to say, in places where the sense of the insc ription is of more importance than external ornament. This is a swee ping statement, from which we need not suffer unduly; yet it is doub tful whether there is art in individual letters. Letters in combination may be satisfying and in a well composed page even beautiful as a wh ole, but art in letters consists rather in the art of arranging and comp osing them in a pleasing and appropriate manner. The main purpos
The main purpose of letters is the practical one of making thoughts visible. Ru skin says that all letters are frightful things and to be endured only on occasion
The main purpose of letters is the practical one of making thoughts visible. Ruskin says that all letters are frightful things and to be en

8/9

The main purpose of letters is the practical one of making thoughts v isible. Ruskin says that all letters are frightful things and to be endur ed only on occasion, that is to say, in places where the sense of the insc ription is of more importance than external ornament. This is a swee ping statement, from which we need not suffer unduly; yet it is doub tful whether there is art in individual letters. Letters in combination may be satisfying and in a well composed page even beautiful as a wh ole, but art in letters consists rather in the art of arranging and comp
The main purpose of letters is the practical one of making thoughts visible. Ru skin says that all letters are frightful things and to be endured only on occasion
The main purpose of letters is the practical one of making thoughts visible. Ruskin says that all letters are frightful things and to be en

8/10

The main purpose of letters is the practical one of making thoughts v isible. Ruskin says that all letters are frightful things and to be endur ed only on occasion, that is to say, in places where the sense of the insc ription is of more importance than external ornament. This is a swee ping statement, from which we need not suffer unduly; yet it is doub tful whether there is art in individual letters. Letters in combination may be satisfying and in a well composed page even beautiful as a wh
The main purpose of letters is the practical one of making thoughts visible. Ru skin says that all letters are frightful things and to be endured only on occasion
The main purpose of letters is the practical one of making thoughts visible. Ruskin says that all letters are frightful things and to be en

8/11

The main purpose of letters is the practical one of making thoughts v isible. Ruskin says that all letters are frightful things and to be endur ed only on occasion, that is to say, in places where the sense of the insc ription is of more importance than external ornament. This is a swee ping statement, from which we need not suffer unduly; yet it is doub tful whether there is art in individual letters. Letters in combination may be satisfying and in a well composed page even beautiful as a wh
The main purpose of letters is the practical one of making thoughts visible. Ru skin says that all letters are frightful things and to be endured only on occasion
The main purpose of letters is the practical one of making thoughts visible. Ruskin says that all letters are frightful things and to be en

---

ABCDEFGHIJKLMNOPQRSTUVWXYZ 1234567890 abcdefghijklmnopqrstuvwxyz
ABCDEFGHIJKLMNOPQRSTUVWXYZ 1234567890 abcdefghijklmnopqrstuvwxyz
ABCDEFGHIJKLMNOPQRSTUVWXYZ 1234567890 abcdefghijklmnopqrstuvwxyz
ABCDEFGHIJKLMNOPQRSTUVWXYZ 1234567890 abcdefghijklmnopqrstuvwxyz

9/9

The main purpose of letters is the practical one of making th oughts visible. Ruskin says that all letters are frightful things and to be endured only on occasion, that is to say, in places wh ere the sense of the inscription is of more importance than ex ternal ornament. This is a sweeping statement, from which w e need not suffer unduly; yet it is doubtful whether there is a rt in individual letters. Letters in combination may be satisfyi ng and in a well composed page even beautiful as a whole, bu
The main purpose of letters is the practical one of making thoughts vi sible. Ruskin says that all letters are frightful things and to be endure
The main purpose of letters is the practical one of making t houghts visible. Ruskin says that all letters are frightful thi

9/10

The main purpose of letters is the practical one of making th oughts visible. Ruskin says that all letters are frightful things and to be endured only on occasion, that is to say, in places wh ere the sense of the inscription is of more importance than ex ternal ornament. This is a sweeping statement, from which w e need not suffer unduly; yet it is doubtful whether there is a rt in individual letters. Letters in combination may be satisfyi
The main purpose of letters is the practical one of making thoughts vi sible. Ruskin says that all letters are frightful things and to be endure
The main purpose of letters is the practical one of making t houghts visible. Ruskin says that all letters are frightful thi

9/11

The main purpose of letters is the practical one of making th oughts visible. Ruskin says that all letters are frightful things and to be endured only on occasion, that is to say, in places wh ere the sense of the inscription is of more importance than ex ternal ornament. This is a sweeping statement, from which w e need not suffer unduly; yet it is doubtful whether there is a rt in individual letters. Letters in combination may be satisfyi
The main purpose of letters is the practical one of making thoughts vi sible. Ruskin says that all letters are frightful things and to be endure
The main purpose of letters is the practical one of making t houghts visible. Ruskin says that all letters are frightful thi

9/12

The main purpose of letters is the practical one of making th oughts visible. Ruskin says that all letters are frightful things and to be endured only on occasion, that is to say, in places wh ere the sense of the inscription is of more importance than ex ternal ornament. This is a sweeping statement, from which w e need not suffer unduly; yet it is doubtful whether there is a rt in individual letters. Letters in combination may be satisfyi
The main purpose of letters is the practical one of making thoughts vi sible. Ruskin says that all letters are frightful things and to be endure
The main purpose of letters is the practical one of making t houghts visible. Ruskin says that all letters are frightful thi

BASKERVILLE 10 POINT SET MINUS ½ UNIT

ROMAN, ITALIC, BOLD, BOLD ITALIC

abcdefghijklmnopqrstuvwxyz – 1 UNIT
abcdefghijklmnopqrstuvwxyz – ½ UNIT
abcdefghijklmnopqrstuvwxyz NORMAL

ABCDEFGHIJKLMNOPQRSTUVWXYZ 1234567890 abcdefghijklmnopqrstuvwxyz
ABCDEFGHIJKLMNOPQRSTUVWXYZ 1234567890 abcdefghijklmnopqrstuvwxyz
ABCDEFGHIJKLMNOPQRSTUVWXYZ 1234567890 abcdefghijklmnopqrstuvwxyz
ABCDEFGHIJKLMNOPQRSTUVWXYZ 1234567890 abcdefghijklmnopqrstuvwxyz

10/10

The main purpose of letters is the practical one of makin g thoughts visible. Ruskin says that all letters are frightful things and to be endured only on occasion, that is to say, i n places where the sense of the inscription is of more imp ortance than external ornament. This is a sweeping state ment, from which we need not suffer unduly; yet it is dou btful whether there is art in individual letters. Letters in c ombination may be satisfying and in a well composed pag e even beautiful as a whole, but art in letters consists rather in the art of arranging and composing them in a pleasing and appropriate manner. The main purpose of letters is the practical one of making thoughts visible. Ruskin says that all letters are frightful things and to be endured only on occasion, that is to say, in places where the sense of the inscription is of more importance than external orname nt. This is a sweeping statement, from which we need not suffer unduly; yet it is doubtful whether there is art in in dividual letters. Letters in combination may be satisfying and in a well composed page even beautiful as a whole, b ut art in letters consists rather in the art of arranging and composing them in a pleasing and appropriate manner. The main purpose of letters is the practical one of makin
The main purpose of letters is the practical one of making thought s visible. Ruskin says that all letters are frightful things and to be e
The main purpose of letters is the practical one of maki ng thoughts visible. Ruskin says that all letters are frigh

10/11

The main purpose of letters is the practical one of makin g thoughts visible. Ruskin says that all letters are frightful things and to be endured only on occasion, that is to say, i n places where the sense of the inscription is of more imp ortance than external ornament. This is a sweeping state ment, from which we need not suffer unduly; yet it is dou btful whether there is art in individual letters. Letters in c ombination may be satisfying and in a well composed pag e even beautiful as a whole, but art in letters consists rather in the art of arranging and composing them in a pleasing and appropriate manner. The main purpose of letters is the practical one of making thoughts visible. Ruskin says that all letters are frightful things and to be endured only on occasion, that is to say, in places where the sense of the inscription is of more importance than external orname nt. This is a sweeping statement, from which we need not suffer unduly; yet it is doubtful whether there is art in in dividual letters. Letters in combination may be satisfying and in a well composed page even beautiful as a whole, b ut art in letters consists rather in the art of arranging and
The main purpose of letters is the practical one of making thought s visible. Ruskin says that all letters are frightful things and to be e
The main purpose of letters is the practical one of maki ng thoughts visible. Ruskin says that all letters are frigh

10/12

The main purpose of letters is the practical one of makin g thoughts visible. Ruskin says that all letters are frightful things and to be endured only on occasion, that is to say, i n places where the sense of the inscription is of more imp ortance than external ornament. This is a sweeping state ment, from which we need not suffer unduly; yet it is dou btful whether there is art in individual letters. Letters in c ombination may be satisfying and in a well composed pag e even beautiful as a whole, but art in letters consists rather in the art of arranging and composing them in a pleasing and appropriate manner. The main purpose of letters is the practical one of making thoughts visible. Ruskin says that all letters are frightful things and to be endured only on occasion, that is to say, in places where the sense of the inscription is of more importance than external orname nt. This is a sweeping statement, from which we need not suffer unduly; yet it is doubtful whether there is art in in dividual letters. Letters in combination may be satisfying
The main purpose of letters is the practical one of making thought s visible. Ruskin says that all letters are frightful things and to be e
The main purpose of letters is the practical one of maki ng thoughts visible. Ruskin says that all letters are frigh

10/13

The main purpose of letters is the practical one of makin g thoughts visible. Ruskin says that all letters are frightful things and to be endured only on occasion, that is to say, i n places where the sense of the inscription is of more imp ortance than external ornament. This is a sweeping state ment, from which we need not suffer unduly; yet it is dou btful whether there is art in individual letters. Letters in c ombination may be satisfying and in a well composed pag e even beautiful as a whole, but art in letters consists rather in the art of arranging and composing them in a pleasing and appropriate manner. The main purpose of letters is the practical one of making thoughts visible. Ruskin says that all letters are frightful things and to be endured only on occasion, that is to say, in places where the sense of the inscription is of more importance than external orname nt. This is a sweeping statement, from which we need not suffer unduly; yet it is doubtful whether there is art in in
The main purpose of letters is the practical one of making thought s visible. Ruskin says that all letters are frightful things and to be e
The main purpose of letters is the practical one of maki ng thoughts visible. Ruskin says that all letters are frigh

BASKERVILLE 11 POINT SET MINUS ½ UNIT

ROMAN, ITALIC, BOLD, BOLD ITALIC

abcdefghijklmnopqrstuvwxyz – 1 UNIT
abcdefghijklmnopqrstuvwxyz – ½ UNIT
abcdefghijklmnopqrstuvwxyz NORMAL

ABCDEFGHIJKLMNOPQRSTUVWXYZ 1234567890 abcdefghijklmnopqrstuvwxyz
ABCDEFGHIJKLMNOPQRSTUVWXYZ 1234567890 abcdefghijklmnopqrstuvwxyz
ABCDEFGHIJKLMNOPQRSTUVWXYZ 1234567890 abcdefghijklmnopqrstuvwxyz
ABCDEFGHIJKLMNOPQRSTUVWXYZ 1234567890 abcdefghijklmnopqrstuvwxyz

11/11

The main purpose of letters is the practical one of m aking thoughts visible. Ruskin says that all letters ar e frightful things and to be endured only on occasio n, that is to say, in places where the sense of the inscr iption is of more importance than external orname nt. This is a sweeping statement, from which we nee d not suffer unduly; yet it is doubtful whether there is art in individual letters. Letters in combination m ay be satisfying and in a well composed page even b eautiful as a whole, but art in letters consists rather i n the art of arranging and composing them in a plea sing and appropriate manner. The main purpose of letters is the practical one of making thoughts visibl e. Ruskin says that all letters are frightful things and to be endured only on occasion, that is to say, in plac es where the sense of the inscription is of more impo rtance than external ornament. This is a sweeping st atement, from which we need not suffer unduly; ye t it is doubtful whether there is art in individual lette
The main purpose of letters is the practical one of making t houghts visible. Ruskin says that all letters are frightful thi
The main purpose of letters is the practical one of making thoughts visible. Ruskin says that all letter

11/12

The main purpose of letters is the practical one of m aking thoughts visible. Ruskin says that all letters ar e frightful things and to be endured only on occasio n, that is to say, in places where the sense of the inscr iption is of more importance than external orname nt. This is a sweeping statement, from which we nee d not suffer unduly; yet it is doubtful whether there is art in individual letters. Letters in combination m ay be satisfying and in a well composed page even b eautiful as a whole, but art in letters consists rather i n the art of arranging and composing them in a plea sing and appropriate manner. The main purpose of letters is the practical one of making thoughts visibl e. Ruskin says that all letters are frightful things and to be endured only on occasion, that is to say, in plac es where the sense of the inscription is of more impo rtance than external ornament. This is a sweeping st atement, from which we need not suffer unduly; ye
The main purpose of letters is the practical one of making t houghts visible. Ruskin says that all letters are frightful thi
The main purpose of letters is the practical one of making thoughts visible. Ruskin says that all letter

11/13

The main purpose of letters is the practical one of m aking thoughts visible. Ruskin says that all letters ar e frightful things and to be endured only on occasio n, that is to say, in places where the sense of the inscr iption is of more importance than external orname nt. This is a sweeping statement, from which we nee d not suffer unduly; yet it is doubtful whether there is art in individual letters. Letters in combination m ay be satisfying and in a well composed page even b eautiful as a whole, but art in letters consists rather i n the art of arranging and composing them in a plea sing and appropriate manner. The main purpose of letters is the practical one of making thoughts visibl e. Ruskin says that all letters are frightful things and to be endured only on occasion, that is to say, in plac es where the sense of the inscription is of more impo rtance than external ornament. This is a sweeping st
The main purpose of letters is the practical one of making t houghts visible. Ruskin says that all letters are frightful thi
The main purpose of letters is the practical one of making thoughts visible. Ruskin says that all letter

11/14

The main purpose of letters is the practical one of m aking thoughts visible. Ruskin says that all letters ar e frightful things and to be endured only on occasio n, that is to say, in places where the sense of the inscr iption is of more importance than external orname nt. This is a sweeping statement, from which we nee d not suffer unduly; yet it is doubtful whether there is art in individual letters. Letters in combination m ay be satisfying and in a well composed page even b eautiful as a whole, but art in letters consists rather i n the art of arranging and composing them in a plea sing and appropriate manner. The main purpose of letters is the practical one of making thoughts visibl e. Ruskin says that all letters are frightful things and to be endured only on occasion, that is to say, in plac es where the sense of the inscription is of more impo
The main purpose of letters is the practical one of making t houghts visible. Ruskin says that all letters are frightful thi
The main purpose of letters is the practical one of making thoughts visible. Ruskin says that all letter

BASKERVILLE 12 POINT SET MINUS ½ UNIT

ROMAN, ITALIC, BOLD, BOLD ITALIC

abcdefghijklmnopqrstuvwxyz – 1 UNIT
abcdefghijklmnopqrstuvwxyz – ½ UNIT
abcdefghijklmnopqrstuvwxyz NORMAL

ABCDEFGHIJKLMNOPQRSTUVWXYZ 1234567890 abcdefghijklmnopqrstuvwxyz
ABCDEFGHIJKLMNOPQRSTUVWXYZ 1234567890 abcdefghijklmnopqrstuvwxyz
ABCDEFGHIJKLMNOPQRSTUVWXYZ 1234567890 abcdefghijklmnopqrstuvwxyz
ABCDEFGHIJKLMNOPQRSTUVWXYZ 1234567890 abcdefghijklmnopqrstuvwxyz

12/12

The main purpose of letters is the practical one of making thoughts visible. Ruskin says that all l etters are frightful things and to be endured onl y on occasion, that is to say, in places where the se nse of the inscription is of more importance tha n external ornament. This is a sweeping stateme nt, from which we need not suffer unduly; yet it is doubtful whether there is art in individual lett ers. Letters in combination may be satisfying an d in a well composed page even beautiful as a wh ole, but art in letters consists rather in the art of a rranging and composing them in a pleasing and appropriate manner. The main purpose of lette ers is the practical one of making thoughts visible. Ruskin says that all letters are frightful things an
The main purpose of letters is the practical one of maki ng thoughts visible. Ruskin says that all letters are frigh
The main purpose of letters is the practical one of making thoughts visible. Ruskin says that all

12/13

The main purpose of letters is the practical one of making thoughts visible. Ruskin says that all l etters are frightful things and to be endured onl y on occasion, that is to say, in places where the se nse of the inscription is of more importance tha n external ornament. This is a sweeping stateme nt, from which we need not suffer unduly; yet it is doubtful whether there is art in individual lett ers. Letters in combination may be satisfying an d in a well composed page even beautiful as a wh ole, but art in letters consists rather in the art of a rranging and composing them in a pleasing and appropriate manner. The main purpose of lette ers is the practical one of making thoughts visible.
The main purpose of letters is the practical one of maki ng thoughts visible. Ruskin says that all letters are frigh
The main purpose of letters is the practical one of making thoughts visible. Ruskin says that all

12/14

The main purpose of letters is the practical one of making thoughts visible. Ruskin says that all l etters are frightful things and to be endured onl y on occasion, that is to say, in places where the se nse of the inscription is of more importance tha n external ornament. This is a sweeping stateme nt, from which we need not suffer unduly; yet it is doubtful whether there is art in individual lett ers. Letters in combination may be satisfying an d in a well composed page even beautiful as a wh ole, but art in letters consists rather in the art of a rranging and composing them in a pleasing and appropriate manner. The main purpose of lette ers is the practical one of making thoughts visible. Ruskin says that all letters are frightful things an
The main purpose of letters is the practical one of maki ng thoughts visible. Ruskin says that all letters are frigh
The main purpose of letters is the practical one of making thoughts visible. Ruskin says that all

12/15

The main purpose of letters is the practical one of making thoughts visible. Ruskin says that all l etters are frightful things and to be endured onl y on occasion, that is to say, in places where the se nse of the inscription is of more importance tha n external ornament. This is a sweeping stateme nt, from which we need not suffer unduly; yet it is doubtful whether there is art in individual lett ers. Letters in combination may be satisfying an d in a well composed page even beautiful as a wh ole, but art in letters consists rather in the art of a rranging and composing them in a pleasing and appropriate manner. The main purpose of lette ers is the practical one of making thoughts visible.
The main purpose of letters is the practical one of maki ng thoughts visible. Ruskin says that all letters are frigh
The main purpose of letters is the practical one of making thoughts visible. Ruskin says that all

BASKERVILLE 14 POINT SET MINUS ½ UNIT

ROMAN, ITALIC, BOLD, BOLD ITALIC

abcdefghijklmnopqrstuvwxyz – 1 UNIT
abcdefghijklmnopqrstuvwxyz – ½ UNIT
abcdefghijklmnopqrstuvwxyz NORMAL

ABCDEFGHIJKLMNOPQRSTUVWXYZ abcdefghijklmnopqrstuvwxyz
ABCDEFGHIJKLMNOPQRSTUVWXYZ abcdefghijklmnopqrstuvwxyz
ABCDEFGHIJKLMNOPQRSTUVWXYZ abcdefghijklmnopqrstuvwxyz
ABCDEFGHIJKLMNOPQRSTUVWXYZ abcdefghijklmnopqrstuvwxyz

14/14

The main purpose of letters is the practic al one of making thoughts visible. Ruskin says that all letters are frightful things an d to be endured only on occasion, that is t o say, in places where the sense of the insc ription is of more importance than exter nal ornament. This is a sweeping stateme nt, from which we need not suffer undul y; yet it is doubtful whether there is art in individual letters. Letters in combination may be satisfying and in a well composed page even beautiful as a whole, but art in letters consists rather in the art of arrangi
The main purpose of letters is the practical one of making thoughts visible. Ruskin says that al
The main purpose of letters is the practi cal one of making thoughts visible. Rus

14/15

The main purpose of letters is the practic al one of making thoughts visible. Ruskin says that all letters are frightful things an d to be endured only on occasion, that is t o say, in places where the sense of the insc ription is of more importance than exter nal ornament. This is a sweeping stateme nt, from which we need not suffer undul y; yet it is doubtful whether there is art in individual letters. Letters in combination may be satisfying and in a well composed page even beautiful as a whole, but art in
The main purpose of letters is the practical one of making thoughts visible. Ruskin says that al
The main purpose of letters is the practi cal one of making thoughts visible. Rus

14/16

The main purpose of letters is the practic al one of making thoughts visible. Ruskin says that all letters are frightful things an d to be endured only on occasion, that is t o say, in places where the sense of the insc ription is of more importance than exter nal ornament. This is a sweeping stateme nt, from which we need not suffer undul y; yet it is doubtful whether there is art in individual letters. Letters in combination may be satisfying and in a well composed page even beautiful as a whole, but art in letters consists rather in the art of arrangi
The main purpose of letters is the practical one of making thoughts visible. Ruskin says that al
The main purpose of letters is the practi cal one of making thoughts visible. Rus

14/17

The main purpose of letters is the practic al one of making thoughts visible. Ruskin says that all letters are frightful things an d to be endured only on occasion, that is t o say, in places where the sense of the insc ription is of more importance than exter nal ornament. This is a sweeping stateme nt, from which we need not suffer undul y; yet it is doubtful whether there is art in individual letters. Letters in combination may be satisfying and in a well composed page even beautiful as a whole, but art in
The main purpose of letters is the practical one of making thoughts visible. Ruskin says that al
The main purpose of letters is the practi cal one of making thoughts visable. Rus

BEMBO 6 & 7 POINT SET NORMAL

ROMAN, ITALIC, BOLD, BOLD ITALIC

ABCDEFGHIJKLMNOPQRSTUVWXYZ 1234567890 abcdefghijklmnopqrstuvwxyz

ABCDEFGHIJKLMNOPQRSTUVWXYZ 1234567890 abcdefghijklmnopqrstuvwxyz

ABCDEFGHIJKLMNOPQRSTUVWXYZ 1234567890 abcdefghijklmnopqrstuvwxyz

ABCDEFGHIJKLMNOPQRSTUVWXYZ 1234567890 abcdefghijklmnopqrstuvwxyz

6/6

The main purpose of letters is the practical one of making thoughts visible. Ruskin says that all l etters are frightful things and to be endured only on occasion, that is to say, in places where the s ense of the inscription is of more importance than external ornament. This is a sweeping statem ent, from which we need not suffer unduly; yet it is doubtful whether there is art in individual let ters. Letters in combination may be satisfying and in a well composed page even beautiful as a w hole, but art in letters consists rather in the art of arranging and composing them in a pleasing an d appropriate manner. The main purpose of letters is the practical one of making thoughts visibl e. Ruskin says that all letters are frightful things and to be endured only on occasion, that is to sa y, in places where the sense of the inscription is of more importance than external ornament. This is a sweeping statement, from which we need not suffer unduly; yet it is doubtful whether there is art in individual letters. Letters in combination may be satisfying and in a well composed page even beautiful as a whole, but art in letters consists rather in the art of arranging and composing them in a pleasing and appropriate manner. The main purpose of letters is the practical one of
The main purpose of letters is the practical one of making thoughts visible. Ruskin says that all letters are fr ightful things and to be endured only on occasion, that is to say, in places where the sense of the inscription is
The main purpose of letters is the practical one of making thoughts visible. Ruskin says that all letters are frightful things and to be endured only on occasion, that is to say, in p

6/7

The main purpose of letters is the practical one of making thoughts visible. Ruskin says that all l etters are frightful things and to be endured only on occasion, that is to say, in places where the s ense of the inscription is of more importance than external ornament. This is a sweeping statem ent, from which we need not suffer unduly; yet it is doubtful whether there is art in individual let ters. Letters in combination may be satisfying and in a well composed page even beautiful as a w hole, but art in letters consists rather in the art of arranging and composing them in a pleasing an d appropriate manner. The main purpose of letters is the practical one of making thoughts visibl e. Ruskin says that all letters are frightful things and to be endured only on occasion, that is to sa y, in places where the sense of the inscription is of more importance than external ornament. This is a sweeping statement, from which we need not suffer unduly; yet it is doubtful whether there is art in individual letters. Letters in combination may be satisfying and in a well composed page
The main purpose of letters is the practical one of making thoughts visible. Ruskin says that all letters are fr ightful things and to be endured only on occasion, that is to say, in places where the sense of the inscription is
The main purpose of letters is the practical one of making thoughts visible. Ruskin says that all letters are frightful things and to be endured only on occasion, that is to say, in p

6/8

The main purpose of letters is the practical one of making thoughts visible. Ruskin says that all l etters are frightful things and to be endured only on occasion, that is to say, in places where the s ense of the inscription is of more importance than external ornament. This is a sweeping statem ent, from which we need not suffer unduly; yet it is doubtful whether there is art in individual let ters. Letters in combination may be satisfying and in a well composed page even beautiful as a w hole, but art in letters consists rather in the art of arranging and composing them in a pleasing an d appropriate manner. The main purpose of letters is the practical one of making thoughts visibl e. Ruskin says that all letters are frightful things and to be endured only on occasion, that is to sa y, in places where the sense of the inscription is of more importance than external ornament. This
The main purpose of letters is the practical one of making thoughts visible. Ruskin says that all letters are fr ightful things and to be endured only on occasion, that is to say, in places where the sense of the inscription is
The main purpose of letters is the practical one of making thoughts visible. Ruskin says that all letters are frightful things and to be endured only on occasion, that is to say, in p

6/9

The main purpose of letters is the practical one of making thoughts visible. Ruskin says that all l etters are frightful things and to be endured only on occasion, that is to say, in places where the s ense of the inscription is of more importance than external ornament. This is a sweeping statem ent, from which we need not suffer unduly; yet it is doubtful whether there is art in individual let ters. Letters in combination may be satisfying and in a well composed page even beautiful as a w hole, but art in letters consists rather in the art of arranging and composing them in a pleasing an d appropriate manner. The main purpose of letters is the practical one of making thoughts visibl e. Ruskin says that all letters are frightful things and to be endured only on occasion, that is to sa
The main purpose of letters is the practical one of making thoughts visible. Ruskin says that all letters are fr ightful things and to be endured only on occasion, that is to say, in places where the sense of the inscription is
The main purpose of letters is the practical one of making thoughts visible. Ruskin says that all letters are frightful things and to be endured only on occasion, that is to say, in p

---

ABCDEFGHIJKLMNOPQRSTUVWXYZ 1234567890 abcdefghijklmnopqrstuvwxyz

ABCDEFGHIJKLMNOPQRSTUVWXYZ 1234567890 abcdefghijklmnopqrstuvwxyz

ABCDEFGHIJKLMNOPQRSTUVWXYZ 1234567890 abcdefghijklmnopqrstuvwxyz

ABCDEFGHIJKLMNOPQRSTUVWXYZ 1234567890 abcdefghijklmnopqrstuvwxyz

7/7

The main purpose of letters is the practical one of making thoughts visible. Ruskin says that all letters are frightful things and to be endured only on occasion, that is t o say, in places where the sense of the inscription is of more importance than exter nal ornament. This is a sweeping statement, from which we need not suffer undul y; yet it is doubtful whether there is art in individual letters. Letters in combinatio n may be satisfying and in a well composed page even beautiful as a whole, but art i n letters consists rather in the art of arranging and composing them in a pleasing an d appropriate manner. The main purpose of letters is the practical one of making t houghts visible. Ruskin says that all letters are frightful things and to be endured o nly on occasion, that is to say, in places where the sense of the inscription is of mor e importance than external ornament. This is a sweeping statement, from which
The main purpose of letters is the practical one of making thoughts visible. Ruskin says that all letters are frightful things and to be endured only on occasion, that is to say, in places wher
The main purpose of letters is the practical one of making thoughts visible. Ruskin says that all letters are frightful things and to be endured only on o

7/8

The main purpose of letters is the practical one of making thoughts visible. Ruskin says that all letters are frightful things and to be endured only on occasion, that is t o say, in places where the sense of the inscription is of more importance than exter nal ornament. This is a sweeping statement, from which we need not suffer undul y; yet it is doubtful whether there is art in individual letters. Letters in combinatio n may be satisfying and in a well composed page even beautiful as a whole, but art i n letters consists rather in the art of arranging and composing them in a pleasing an d appropriate manner. The main purpose of letters is the practical one of making t houghts visible. Ruskin says that all letters are frightful things and to be endured o nly on occasion, that is to say, in places where the sense of the inscription is of mor
The main purpose of letters is the practical one of making thoughts visible. Ruskin says that all letters are frightful things and to be endured only on occasion, that is to say, in places wher
The main purpose of letters is the practical one of making thoughts visible. Ruskin says that all letters are frightful things and to be endured only on o

7/9

The main purpose of letters is the practical one of making thoughts visible. Ruskin says that all letters are frightful things and to be endured only on occasion, that is t o say, in places where the sense of the inscription is of more importance than exter nal ornament. This is a sweeping statement, from which we need not suffer undul y; yet it is doubtful whether there is art in individual letters. Letters in combinatio n may be satisfying and in a well composed page even beautiful as a whole, but art i n letters consists rather in the art of arranging and composing them in a pleasing an d appropriate manner. The main purpose of letters is the practical one of making t houghts visible. Ruskin says that all letters are frightful things and to be endured o nly on occasion, that is to say, in places where the sense of the inscription is of mor
The main purpose of letters is the practical one of making thoughts visible. Ruskin says that all letters are frightful things and to be endured only on occasion, that is to say, in places wher
The main purpose of letters is the practical one of making thoughts visible. Ruskin says that all letters are frightful things and to be endured only on o

7/10

The main purpose of letters is the practical one of making thoughts visible. Ruskin says that all letters are frightful things and to be endured only on occasion, that is t o say, in places where the sense of the inscription is of more importance than exter nal ornament. This is a sweeping statement, from which we need not suffer undul y; yet it is doubtful whether there is art in individual letters. Letters in combinatio n may be satisfying and in a well composed page even beautiful as a whole, but art i n letters consists rather in the art of arranging and composing them in a pleasing an d appropriate manner. The main purpose of letters is the practical one of making t houghts visible. Ruskin says that all letters are frightful things and to be endured o
The main purpose of letters is the practical one of making thoughts visible. Ruskin says that all letters are frightful things and to be endured only on occasion, that is to say, in places wher
The main purpose of letters is the practical one of making thoughts visible. Ruskin says that all letters are frightful things and to be endured only on o

BEMBO 8 & 9 POINT SET NORMAL

ROMAN, ITALIC, BOLD, BOLD ITALIC

ABCDEFGHIJKLMNOPQRSTUVWXYZ 1234567890 abcdefghijklmnopqrstuvwxyz

ABCDEFGHIJKLMNOPQRSTUVWXYZ 1234567890 abcdefghijklmnopqrstuvwxyz

ABCDEFGHIJKLMNOPQRSTUVWXYZ 1234567890 abcdefghijklmnopqrstuvwxyz

ABCDEFGHIJKLMNOPQRSTUVWXYZ 1234567890 abcdefghijklmnopqrstuvwxyz

8/8

The main purpose of letters is the practical one of making thoughts visib le. Ruskin says that all letters are frightful things and to be endured only on occasion, that is to say, in places where the sense of the inscription is of more importance than external ornament. This is a sweeping stateme nt, from which we need not suffer unduly; yet it is doubtful whether the re is art in individual letters. Letters in combination may be satisfying an d in a well composed page even beautiful as a whole, but art in letters co nsists rather in the art of arranging and composing them in a pleasing an d appropriate manner. The main purpose of letters is the practical one of
The main purpose of letters is the practical one of making thoughts visible. Rusk in says that all letters are frightful things and to be endured only on occasion, that
The main purpose of letters is the practical one of making though ts visible. Ruskin says that all letters are frightful things and to be

8/9

The main purpose of letters is the practical one of making thoughts visib le. Ruskin says that all letters are frightful things and to be endured only on occasion, that is to say, in places where the sense of the inscription is of more importance than external ornament. This is a sweeping stateme nt, from which we need not suffer unduly; yet it is doubtful whether the re is art in individual letters. Letters in combination may be satisfying an d in a well composed page even beautiful as a whole, but art in letters co nsists rather in the art of arranging and composing them in a pleasing an
The main purpose of letters is the practical one of making thoughts visible. Rusk in says that all letters are frightful things and to be endured only on occasion, that
The main purpose of letters is the practical one of making though ts visible. Ruskin says that all letters are frightful things and to be

8/10

The main purpose of letters is the practical one of making thoughts visib le. Ruskin says that all letters are frightful things and to be endured only on occasion, that is to say, in places where the sense of the inscription is of more importance than external ornament. This is a sweeping stateme nt, from which we need not suffer unduly; yet it is doubtful whether the re is art in individual letters. Letters in combination may be satisfying an d in a well composed page even beautiful as a whole, but art in letters co
The main purpose of letters is the practical one of making thoughts visible. Rusk in says that all letters are frightful things and to be endured only on occasion, that
The main purpose of letters is the practical one of making though ts visible. Ruskin says that all letters are frightful things and to be

8/11

The main purpose of letters is the practical one of making thoughts visib le. Ruskin says that all letters are frightful things and to be endured only on occasion, that is to say, in places where the sense of the inscription is of more importance than external ornament. This is a sweeping stateme nt, from which we need not suffer unduly; yet it is doubtful whether the re is art in individual letters. Letters in combination may be satisfying an d in a well composed page even beautiful as a whole, but art in letters co
The main purpose of letters is the practical one of making thoughts visible. Rusk in says that all letters are frightful things and to be endured only on occasion, that
The main purpose of letters is the practical one of making though ts visible. Ruskin says that all letters are frightful things and to be

---

ABCDEFGHIJKLMNOPQRSTUVWXYZ 1234567890 abcdefghijklmnopqrstuvwxyz

ABCDEFGHIJKLMNOPQRSTUVWXYZ 1234567890 abcdefghijklmnopqrstuvwxyz

ABCDEFGHIJKLMNOPQRSTUVWXYZ 1234567890 abcdefghijklmnopqrstuvwxyz

ABCDEFGHIJKLMNOPQRSTUVWXYZ 1234567890 abcdefghijklmnopqrstuvwxyz

9/9

The main purpose of letters is the practical one of making thoug hts visible. Ruskin says that all letters are frightful things and to be endured only on occasion, that is to say, in places where the s ense of the inscription is of more importance than external orna ment. This is a sweeping statement, from which we need not su ffer unduly; yet it is doubtful whether there is art in individual le tters. Letters in combination may be satisfying and in a well co mposed page even beautiful as a whole, but art in letters consists
The main purpose of letters is the practical one of making thoughts visib le. Ruskin says that all letters are frightful things and to be endured only
The main purpose of letters is the practical one of making thoughts visible. Ruskin says that all letters are frightful t

9/10

The main purpose of letters is the practical one of making thoug hts visible. Ruskin says that all letters are frightful things and to be endured only on occasion, that is to say, in places where the s ense of the inscription is of more importance than external orna ment. This is a sweeping statement, from which we need not su ffer unduly; yet it is doubtful whether there is art in individual le tters. Letters in combination may be satisfying and in a well co
The main purpose of letters is the practical one of making thoughts visib le. Ruskin says that all letters are frightful things and to be endured only
The main purpose of letters is the practical one of making thoughts visible. Ruskin says that all letters are frightful t

9/11

The main purpose of letters is the practical one of making thoug hts visible. Ruskin says that all letters are frightful things and to be endured only on occasion, that is to say, in places where the s ense of the inscription is of more importance than external orna ment. This is a sweeping statement, from which we need not su ffer unduly; yet it is doubtful whether there is art in individual le tters. Letters in combination may be satisfying and in a well co
The main purpose of letters is the practical one of making thoughts visib le. Ruskin says that all letters are frightful things and to be endured only
The main purpose of letters is the practical one of making thoughts visible. Ruskin says that all letters are frightful t

9/12

The main purpose of letters is the practical one of making thoug hts visible. Ruskin says that all letters are frightful things and to be endure only on occasion, that is to say, in places where the s ense of the inscription is of more importance than external orna ment. This is a sweeping statement, from which we need not su ffer unduly; yet it is doubtful whether there is art in individual le tters. Letters in combination may be satisfying and in a well co
The main purpose of letters is the practical one of making thoughts visib le. Ruskin says that all letters are frightful things and to be endured only
The main purpose of letters is the practical one of making thoughts visible. Ruskin says that all letters are frightful t

BEMBO 10 POINT SET MINUS ½ UNIT

ROMAN, ITALIC, BOLD, BOLD ITALIC

abcdefghijklmnopqrstuvwxyz – 1 UNIT
abcdefghijklmnopqrstuvwxyz – ½ UNIT
abcdefghijklmnopqrstuvwxyz NORMAL

ABCDEFGHIJKLMNOPQRSTUVWXYZ 1234567890 abcdefghijklmnopqrstuvwxyz
ABCDEFGHIJKLMNOPQRSTUVWXYZ 1234567890 abcdefghijklmnopqrstuvwxyz
ABCDEFGHIJKLMNOPQRSTUVWXYZ 1234567890 abcdefghijklmnopqrstuvwxyz
ABCDEFGHIJKLMNOPQRSTUVWXYZ 1234567890 abcdefghijklmnopqrstuvwxyz

10/10

The main purpose of letters is the practical one of making th oughts visible. Ruskin says that all letters are frightful things and to be endured only on occasion, that is to say, in places where the sense of the inscription is of more importance tha n external ornament. This is a sweeping statement, from w hich we need not suffer unduly; yet it is doubtful whether th ere is art in individual letters. Letters in combination may be satisfying and in a well composed page even beautiful as a w hole, but art in letters consists rather in the art of arranging a nd composing them in a pleasing and appropriate manner. The main purpose of letters is the practical one of making th oughts visible. Ruskin says that all letters are frightful things and to be endured only on occasion, that is to say, in places where the sense of the inscription is of more importance tha n external ornament. This is a sweeping statement, from w hich we need not suffer unduly; yet it is doubtful whether th ere is art in individual letters. Letters in combination may be satisfying and in a well composed page even beautiful as a w hole, but art in letters consists rather in the art of arranging a nd composing them in a pleasing and appropriate manner. The main purpose of letters is the practical one of making th oughts visible. Ruskin says that all letters are frightful things
The main purpose of letters is the practical one of making thoughts visible. Ruskin says that all letters are frightful things and to be end
The main purpose of letters is the practical one of mak ing thoughts visible. Ruskin says that all letters are fri

10/11

The main purpose of letters is the practical one of making th oughts visible. Ruskin says that all letters are frightful things and to be endured only on occasion, that is to say, in places where the sense of the inscription is of more importance tha n external ornament. This is a sweeping statement, from w hich we need not suffer unduly; yet it is doubtful whether th ere is art in individual letters. Letters in combination may be satisfying and in a well composed page even beautiful as a w hole, but art in letters consists rather in the art of arranging a nd composing them in a pleasing and appropriate manner. The main purpose of letters is the practical one of making th oughts visible. Ruskin says that all letters are frightful things and to be endured only on occasion, that is to say, in places where the sense of the inscription is of more importance tha n external ornament. This is a sweeping statement, from w hich we need not suffer unduly; yet it is doubtful whether th ere is art in individual letters. Letters in combination may be satisfying and in a well composed page even beautiful as a w hole, but art in letters consists rather in the art of arranging a nd composing them in a pleasing and appropriate manner.
The main purpose of letters is the practical one of making thoughts visible. Ruskin says that all letters are frightful things and to be end
The main purpose of letters is the practical one of mak ing thoughts visible. Ruskin says that all letters are fri

10/12

The main purpose of letters is the practical one of making th oughts visible. Ruskin says that all letters are frightful things and to be endured only on occasion, that is to say, in places where the sense of the inscription is of more importance tha n external ornament. This is a sweeping statement, from w hich we need not suffer unduly; yet it is doubtful whether th ere is art in individual letters. Letters in combination may be satisfying and in a well composed page even beautiful as a w hole, but art in letters consists rather in the art of arranging a nd composing them in a pleasing and appropriate manner. The main purpose of letters is the practical one of making th oughts visible. Ruskin says that all letters are frightful things and to be endured only on occasion, that is to say, in places where the sense of the inscription is of more importance tha n external ornament. This is a sweeping statement, from w hich we need not suffer unduly; yet it is doubtful whether th ere is art in individual letters. Letters in combination may be satisfying and in a well composed page even beautiful as a w
The main purpose of letters is the practical one of making thoughts visible. Ruskin says that all letters are frightful things and to be end
The main purpose of letters is the practical one of mak ing thoughts visible. Ruskin says that all letters are fri

10/13

The main purpose of letters is the practical one of making th oughts visible. Ruskin says that all letters are frightful things and to be endured only on occasion, that is to say, in places where the sense of the inscription is of more importance tha n external ornament. This is a sweeping statement, from w hich we need not suffer unduly; yet it is doubtful whether th ere is art in individual letters. Letters in combination may be satisfying and in a well composed page even beautiful as a w hole, but art in letters consists rather in the art of arranging a nd composing them in a pleasing and appropriate manner. The main purpose of letters is the practical one of making th oughts visible. Ruskin says that all letters are frightful things and to be endured only on occasion, that is to say, in places where the sense of the inscription is of more importance tha n external ornament. This is a sweeping statement, from w hich we need not suffer unduly; yet it is doubtful whether th ere is art in individual letters. Letters in combination may be
The main purpose of letters is the practical one of making thoughts visible. Ruskin says that all letters are frightful things and to be end
The main purpose of letters is the practical one of mak ing thoughts visible. Ruskin says that all letters are fri

BEMBO 11 POINT SET MINUS ½ UNIT

ROMAN, ITALIC, BOLD, BOLD ITALIC

abcdefghijklmnopqrstuvwxyz – 1 UNIT
abcdefghijklmnopqrstuvwxyz – ½ UNIT
abcdefghijklmnopqrstuvwxyz NORMAL

ABCDEFGHIJKLMNOPQRSTUVWXYZ 1234567890 abcdefghijklmnopqrstuvwxyz
ABCDEFGHIJKLMNOPQRSTUVWXYZ 1234567890 abcdefghijklmnopqrstuvwxyz
ABCDEFGHIJKLMNOPQRSTUVWXYZ 1234567890 abcdefghijklmnopqrstuvwxyz
ABCDEFGHIJKLMNOPQRSTUVWXYZ 1234567890 abcdefghijklmnopqrstuvwxyz

11/11

The main purpose of letters is the practical one of maki ng thoughts visible. Ruskin says that all letters are frig htful things and to be endured only on occasion, that is to say, in places where the sense of the inscription is of more importance than external ornament. This is a sw eeping statement, from which we need not suffer und uly; yet it is doubtful whether there is art in individual l etters. Letters in combination may be satisfying and in a well composed page even beautiful as a whole, but ar t in letters consists rather in the art of arranging and co mposing them in a pleasing and appropriate manner. The main purpose of letters is the practical one of maki ng thoughts visible. Ruskin says that all letters are frig htful things and to be endured only on occasion, that is to say, in places where the sense of the inscription is of more importance than external ornament. This is a sw eeping statement, from which we need not suffer und uly; yet it is doubtful whether there is art in individual l etters. Letters in combination may be satisfying and in
The main purpose of letters is the practical one of making tho ughts visible. Ruskin says that all letters are frightful things a
The main purpose of letters is the practical one of making thoughts visible. Ruskin says that all lett

11/12

The main purpose of letters is the practical one of maki ng thoughts visible. Ruskin says that all letters are frig htful things and to be endured only on occasion, that is to say, in places where the sense of the inscription is of more importance than external ornament. This is a sw eeping statement, from which we need not suffer und uly; yet it is doubtful whether there is art in individual l etters. Letters in combination may be satisfying and in a well composed page even beautiful as a whole, but ar t in letters consists rather in the art of arranging and co mposing them in a pleasing and appropriate manner. The main purpose of letters is the practical one of maki ng thoughts visible. Ruskin says that all letters are frig htful things and to be endured only on occasion, that is to say, in places where the sense of the inscription is of more importance than external ornament. This is a sw eeping statement, from which we need not suffer und uly; yet it is doubtful whether there is art in individual l
The main purpose of letters is the practical one of making tho ughts visible. Ruskin says that all letters are frightful things a
The main purpose of letters is the practical one of making thoughts visible. Ruskin says that all lett

11/13

The main purpose of letters is the practical one of maki ng thoughts visible. Ruskin says that all letters are frig htful things and to be endured only on occasion, that is to say, in places where the sense of the inscription is of more importance than external ornament. This is a sw eeping statement, from which we need not suffer und uly; yet it is doubtful whether there is art in individual l etters. Letters in combination may be satisfying and in a well composed page even beautiful as a whole, but ar t in letters consists rather in the art of arranging and co mposing them in a pleasing and appropriate manner. The main purpose of letters is the practical one of maki ng thoughts visible. Ruskin says that all letters are frig htful things and to be endured only on occasion, that is to say, in places where the sense of the inscription is of more importance than external ornament. This is a sw eeping statement, from which we need not suffer und
The main purpose of letters is the practical one of making tho ughts visible. Ruskin says that all letters are frightful things a
The main purpose of letters is the practical one of making thoughts visible. Ruskin says that all lett

11/14

The main purpose of letters is the practical one of maki ng thoughts visible. Ruskin says that all letters are frig htful things and to be endured only on occasion, that is to say, in places where the sense of the inscription is of more importance than external ornament. This is a sw eeping statement, from which we need not suffer und uly; yet it is doubtful whether there is art in individual l etters. Letters in combination may be satisfying and in a well composed page even beautiful as a whole, but ar t in letters consists rather in the art of arranging and co mposing them in a pleasing and appropriate manner. The main purpose of letters is the practical one of maki ng thoughts visible. Ruskin says that all letters are frig htful things and to be endured only on occasion, that is to say, in places where the sense of the inscription is of more importance than external ornament. This is a sw
The main purpose of letters is the practical one of making tho ughts visible. Ruskin says that all letters are frightful things a
The main purpose of letters is the practical one of making thoughts visible. Ruskin says that all lett

BEMBO 12 POINT SET MINUS ½ UNIT

ROMAN, ITALIC, BOLD, BOLD ITALIC

abcdefghijklmnopqrstuvwxyz – 1 UNIT
abcdefghijklmnopqrstuvwxyz – ½ UNIT
abcdefghijklmnopqrstuvwxyz NORMAL

ABCDEFGHIJKLMNOPQRSTUVWXYZ 1234567890 abcdefghijklmnopqrstuvwxyz
ABCDEFGHIJKLMNOPQRSTUVWXYZ 1234567890 abcdefghijklmnopqrstuvwxyz
ABCDEFGHIJKLMNOPQRSTUVWXYZ 1234567890 abcdefghijklmnopqrstuvwxyz
ABCDEFGHIJKLMNOPQRSTUVWXYZ 1234567890 abcdefghijklmnopqrstuvwxyz

12/12

The main purpose of letters is the practical one of making thoughts visible. Ruskin says that all letter s are frightful things and to be endured only on occ asion, that is to say, in places where the sense of the inscription is of more importance than external or nament. This is a sweeping statement, from which we need not suffer unduly; yet it is doubtful wheth er there is art in individual letters. Letters in combi nation may be satisfying and in a well composed p age even beautiful as a whole, but art in letters cons ists rather in the art of arranging and composing th em in a pleasing and appropriate manner. The mai n purpose of letters is the practical one of making t houghts visible. Ruskin says that all letters are frig htful things and to be endured only on occasion, th
The main purpose of letters is the practical one of making thoughts visible. Ruskin says that all letters are frightful t
The main purpose of letters is the practical on e of making thoughts visible. Ruskin says that

12/13

The main purpose of letters is the practical one of making thoughts visible. Ruskin says that all letter s are frightful things and to be endured only on occ asion, that is to say, in places where the sense of the inscription is of more importance than external or nament. This is a sweeping statement, from which we need not suffer unduly; yet it is doubtful wheth er there is art in individual letters. Letters in combi nation may be satisfying and in a well composed p age even beautiful as a whole, but art in letters cons ists rather in the art of arranging and composing th em in a pleasing and appropriate manner. The mai n purpose of letters is the practical one of making t houghts visible. Ruskin says that all letters are frig
The main purpose of letters is the practical one of making thoughts visible. Ruskin says that all letters are frightful t
The main purpose of letters is the practical on e of making thoughts visible. Ruskin says that

12/14

The main purpose of letters is the practical one of making thoughts visible. Ruskin says that all letter s are frightful things and to be endured only on occ asion, that is to say, in places where the sense of the inscription is of more importance than external or nament. This is a sweeping statement, from which we need not suffer unduly; yet it is doubtful wheth er there is art in individual letters. Letters in combi nation may be satisfying and in a well composed p age even beautiful as a whole, but art in letters cons ists rather in the art of arranging and composing th em in a pleasing and appropriate manner. The mai n purpose of letters is the practical one of making t houghts visible. Ruskin says that all letters are frig htful things and to be endured only on occasion, th
The main purpose of letters is the practical one of making thoughts visible. Ruskin says that all letters are frightful t
The main purpose of letters is the practical on e of making thoughts visible. Ruskin says that

12/15

The main purpose of letters is the practical one of making thoughts visible. Ruskin says that all letter s are frightful things and to be endured only on occ asion, that is to say, in places where the sense of the inscription is of more importance than external or nament. This is a sweeping statement, from which we need not suffer unduly; yet it is doubtful wheth er there is art in individual letters. Letters in combi nation may be satisfying and in a well composed p age even beautiful as a whole, but art in letters cons ists rather in the art of arranging and composing th em in a pleasing and appropriate manner. The mai n purpose of letters is the practical one of making t houghts visible. Ruskin says that all letters are frig
The main purpose of letters is the practical one of making thoughts visible. Ruskin says that all letters are frightful t
The main purpose of letters is the practical on e of making thoughts visible. Ruskin says that

BEMBO 14 POINT SET MINUS ½ UNIT

ROMAN, ITALIC, BOLD, BOLD ITALIC

abcdefghijklmnopqrstuvwxyz – 1 UNIT
abcdefghijklmnopqrstuvwxyz – ½ UNIT
abcdefghijklmnopqrstuvwxyz NORMAL

ABCDEFGHIJKLMNOPQRSTUVWXYZ abcdefghijklmnopqrstuvwxyz
ABCDEFGHIJKLMNOPQRSTUVWXYZ abcdefghijklmnopqrstuvwxyz
ABCDEFGHIJKLMNOPQRSTUVWXYZ abcdefghijklmnopqrstuvwxyz
ABCDEFGHIJKLMNOPQRSTUVWXYZ abcdefghijklmnopqrstuvwxyz

14/14

The main purpose of letters is the practical one of making thoughts visible. Ruskin sa ys that all letters are frightful things and to be endured only on occasion, that is to say, in places where the sense of the inscription i s of more importance than external ornam ent. This is a sweeping statement, from wh ich we need not suffer unduly; yet it is dou btful whether there is art in individual lette rs. Letters in combination may be satisfyin g and in a well composed page even beautif ul as a whole, but art in letters consists rath er in the art of arranging and composing th
The main purpose of letters is the practical one of making thoughts visible. Ruskin says that all let
The main purpose of letters is the pract ical one of making thoughts visible. R

14/15

The main purpose of letters is the practical one of making thoughts visible. Ruskin sa ys that all letters are frightful things and to be endured only on occasion, that is to say, in places where the sense of the inscription i s of more importance than external ornam ent. This is a sweeping statement, from wh ich we need not suffer unduly; yet it is dou btful whether there is art in individual lette rs. Letters in combination may be satisfyin g and in a well composed page even beautif ul as a whole, but art in letters consists rath
The main purpose of letters is the practical one of making thoughts visible. Ruskin says that all let
The main purpose of letters is the pract ical one of making thoughts visible. R

14/16

The main purpose of letters is the practical one of making thoughts visible. Ruskin sa ys that all letters are frightful things and to be endured only on occasion, that is to say, in places where the sense of the inscription i s of more importance than external ornam ent. This is a sweeping statement, from wh ich we need not suffer unduly; yet it is dou btful whether there is art in individual lette rs. Letters in combination may be satisfyin g and in a well composed page even beautif ul as a whole, but art in letters consists rath er in the art of arranging and composing th
The main purpose of letters is the practical one of making thoughts visible. Ruskin says that all let
The main purpose of letters is the pract ical one of making thoughts visible. R

14/17

The main purpose of letters is the practical one of making thoughts visible. Ruskin sa ys that all letters are frightful things and to be endured only on occasion, that is to say, in places where the sense of the inscription i s of more importance than external ornam ent. This is a sweeping statement, from wh ich we need not suffer unduly; yet it is dou btful whether there is art in individual lette rs. Letters in combination may be satisfyin g and in a well composed page even beautif ul as a whole, but art in letters consists rath
The main purpose of letters is the practical one of making thoughts visible. Ruskin says that all let
The main purpose of letters is the pract ical one of making thoughts visible. R

ITC BENGUIAT 6 & 7 POINT SET NORMAL

BOOK, ITALIC, BOLD, BOLD ITALIC

ABCDEFGHIJKLMNOPQRSTUVWXYZ 1234567890 abcdefghijklmnopqrstuvwxyz

ABCDEFGHIJKLMNOPQRSTUVWXYZ 1234567890 abcdefghijklmnopqrstuvwxyz

ABCDEFGHIJKLMNOPQRSTUVWXYZ 1234567890 abcdefghijklmnopqrstuvwxyz

ABCDEFGHIJKLMNOPQRSTUVWXYZ 1234567890 abcdefghijklmnopqrstuvwxyz

6/6

The main purpose of letters is the practical one of making thoughts visible. Ruskin says that all letters are frightful things and to be endured only on occasion, that is to say, in pl aces where the sense of the inscription is of more importance than external ornament. T his is a sweeping statement, from which we need not suffer unduly; yet it is doubtful whe ther there is art in individual letters. Letters in combination may be satisfying and in a we ll composed page even beautiful as a whole, but art in letters consists rather in the art of arranging and composing them in a pleasing and appropriate manner. The main purpo se of letters is the practical one of making thoughts visible. Ruskin says that all letters ar e frightful things and to be endured only on occasion, that is to say, in places where the s ense of the inscription is of more importance than external ornament. This is a sweepin g statement, from which we need not suffer unduly; yet it is doubtful whether there is art in individual letters. Letters in combination may be satisfying and in a well composed pa ge even beautiful as a whole, but art in letters consists rather in the art of arranging and *The main purpose of letters is the practical one of making thoughts visible. Ruskin says that all letters are frightful things and to be endured only on occasion, that is to say, in p* **The main purpose of letters is the practical one of making thoughts visible. Rus kin says that all letters are frightful things and to be endured only on occasion,**

6/7

The main purpose of letters is the practical one of making thoughts visible. Ruskin says that all letters are frightful things and to be endured only on occasion, that is to say, in pl aces where the sense of the inscription is of more importance than external ornament. T his is a sweeping statement, from which we need not suffer unduly; yet it is doubtful whe ther there is art in individual letters. Letters in combination may be satisfying and in a we ll composed page even beautiful as a whole, but art in letters consists rather in the art of arranging and composing them in a pleasing and appropriate manner. The main purpo se of letters is the practical one of making thoughts visible. Ruskin says that all letters ar e frightful things and to be endured only on occasion, that is to say, in places where the s ense of the inscription is of more importance than external ornament. This is a sweepin g statement, from which we need not suffer unduly; yet it is doubtful whether there is art *The main purpose of letters is the practical one of making thoughts visible. Ruskin says that all letters are frightful things and to be endured only on occasion, that is to say, in p* **The main purpose of letters is the practical one of making thoughts visible. Rus kin says that all letters are frightful things and to be endured only on occasion,**

6/8

The main purpose of letters is the practical one of making thoughts visible. Ruskin says that all letters are frightful things and to be endured only on occasion, that is to say, in pl aces where the sense of the inscription is of more importance than external ornament. T his is a sweeping statement, from which we need not suffer unduly; yet it is doubtful whe ther there is art in individual letters. Letters in combination may be satisfying and in a we ll composed page even beautiful as a whole, but art in letters consists rather in the art of arranging and composing them in a pleasing and appropriate manner. The main purpo se of letters is the practical one of making thoughts visible. Ruskin says that all letters ar e frightful things and to be endured only on occasion, that is to say, in places where the s *The main purpose of letters is the practical one of making thoughts visible. Ruskin says that all letters are frightful things and to be endured only on occasion, that is to say, in p* **The main purpose of letters is the practical one of making thoughts visible. Rus kin says that all letters are frightful things and to be endured only on occasion,**

6/9

The main purpose of letters is the practical one of making thoughts visible. Ruskin says that all letters are frightful things and to be endured only on occasion, that is to say, in pl aces where the sense of the inscription is of more importance than external ornament. T his is a sweeping statement, from which we need not suffer unduly; yet it is doubtful whe ther there is art in individual letters. Letters in combination may be satisfying and in a we ll composed page even beautiful as a whole, but art in letters consists rather in the art of arranging and composing them in a pleasing and appropriate manner. The main purpo se of letters is the practical one of making thoughts visible. Ruskin says that all letters ar *The main purpose of letters is the practical one of making thoughts visible. Ruskin says that all letters are frightful things and to be endured only on occasion, that is to say, in p* **The main purpose of letters is the practical one of making thoughts visible. Rus kin says that all letters are frightful things and to be endured only on occasion,**

ABCDEFGHIJKLMNOPQRSTUVWXYZ 1234567890 abcdefghijklmnopqrstuvwxyz

ABCDEFGHIJKLMNOPQRSTUVWXYZ 1234567890 abcdefghijklmnopqrstuvwxyz

ABCDEFGHIJKLMNOPQRSTUVWXYZ 1234567890 abcdefghijklmnopqrstuvwxyz

ABCDEFGHIJKLMNOPQRSTUVWXYZ 1234567890 abcdefghijklmnopqrstuvwxyz

7/7

The main purpose of letters is the practical one of making thoughts visible. Ruskin says that all letters are frightful things and to be endured only on occ asion, that is to say, in places where the sense of the inscription is of more i mportance than external ornament. This is a sweeping statement, from wh ich we need not suffer unduly; yet it is doubtful whether there is art in individ ual letters. Letters in combination may be satisfying and in a well compose d page even beautiful as a whole, but art in letters consists rather in the art o f arranging and composing them in a pleasing and appropriate manner. Th e main purpose of letters is the practical one of making thoughts visible. Ru skin says that all letters are frightful things and to be endured only on occas ion, that is to say, in places where the sense of the inscription is of more imp *The main purpose of letters is the practical one of making thoughts visible. Ruskin says that all letters are frightful things and to be endured only on oc* **The main purpose of letters is the practical one of making thoughts visible. Ruskin says that all letters are frightful things and to be end**

7/8

The main purpose of letters is the practical one of making thoughts visible. Ruskin says that all letters are frightful things and to be endured only on occ asion, that is to say, in places where the sense of the inscription is of more i mportance than external ornament. This is a sweeping statement, from wh ich we need not suffer unduly; yet it is doubtful whether there is art in individ ual letters. Letters in combination may be satisfying and in a well compose d page even beautiful as a whole, but art in letters consists rather in the art o f arranging and composing them in a pleasing and appropriate manner. Th e main purpose of letters is the practical one of making thoughts visible. Ru skin says that all letters are frightful things and to be endured only on occas *The main purpose of letters is the practical one of making thoughts visible. Ruskin says that all letters are frightful things and to be endured only on oc* **The main purpose of letters is the practical one of making thoughts visible. Ruskin says that all letters are frightful things and to be end**

7/9

The main purpose of letters is the practical one of making thoughts visible. Ruskin says that all letters are frightful things and to be endured only on occ asion, that is to say, in places where the sense of the inscription is of more i mportance than external ornament. This is a sweeping statement, from wh ich we need not suffer unduly; yet it is doubtful whether there is art in individ ual letters. Letters in combination may be satisfying and in a well compose d page even beautiful as a whole, but art in letters consists rather in the art o f arranging and composing them in a pleasing and appropriate manner. Th e main purpose of letters is the practical one of making thoughts visible. Ru skin says that all letters are frightful things and to be endured only on occas *The main purpose of letters is the practical one of making thoughts visible. Ruskin says that all letters are frightful things and to be endured only on oc* **The main purpose of letters is the practical one of making thoughts visible. Ruskin says that all letters are frightful things and to be end**

7/10

The main purpose of letters is the practical one of making thoughts visible. Ruskin says that all letters are frightful things and to be endured only on occ asion, that is to say, in places where the sense of the inscription is of more i mportance than external ornament. This is a sweeping statement, from wh ich we need not suffer unduly; yet it is doubtful whether there is art in individ ual letters. Letters in combination may be satisfying and in a well compose d page even beautiful as a whole, but art in letters consists rather in the art o f arranging and composing them in a pleasing and appropriate manner. Th e main purpose of letters is the practical one of making thoughts visible. Ru *The main purpose of letters is the practical one of making thoughts visible. Ruskin says that all letters are frightful things and to be endured only on oc* **The main purpose of letters is the practical one of making thoughts visible. Ruskin says that all letters are frightful things and to be end**

ITC BENGUIAT 8 & 9 POINT SET NORMAL

BOOK, ITALIC, BOLD, BOLD ITALIC

ABCDEFGHIJKLMNOPQRSTUVWXYZ 1234567890 abcdefghijklmnopqrstuvwxyz

ABCDEFGHIJKLMNOPQRSTUVWXYZ 1234567890 abcdefghijklmnopqrstuvwxyz

ABCDEFGHIJKLMNOPQRSTUVWXYZ 1234567890 abcdefghijklmnopqrstuvwxyz

ABCDEFGHIJKLMNOPQRSTUVWXYZ 1234567890 abcdefghijklmnopqrstuvwxyz

8/8

The main purpose of letters is the practical one of making thought s visible. Ruskin says that all letters are frightful things and to be e ndured only on occasion, that is to say, in places where the sense of the inscription is of more importance than external ornament. This is a sweeping statement, from which we need not suffer undu ly; yet it is doubtful whether there is art in individual letters. Letter s in combination may be satisfying and in a well composed page e ven beautiful as a whole, but art in letters consists rather in the art of arranging and composing them in a pleasing and appropriate

The main purpose of letters is the practical one of making thought s visible. Ruskin says that all letters are frightful things and to be e

The main purpose of letters is the practical one of making t houghts visible. Ruskin says that all letters are frightful thi

8/9

The main purpose of letters is the practical one of making thought s visible. Ruskin says that all letters are frightful things and to be e ndured only on occasion, that is to say, in places where the sense of the inscription is of more importance than external ornament. This is a sweeping statement, from which we need not suffer undu ly; yet it is doubtful whether there is art in individual letters. Letter s in combination may be satisfying and in a well composed page e ven beautiful as a whole, but art in letters consists rather in the art

The main purpose of letters is the practical one of making thought s visible. Ruskin says that all letters are frightful things and to be e

The main purpose of letters is the practical one of making t houghts visible. Ruskin says that all letters are frightful thi

8/10

The main purpose of letters is the practical one of making thought s visible. Ruskin says that all letters are frightful things and to be e ndured only on occasion, that is to say, in places where the sense of the inscription is of more importance than external ornament. This is a sweeping statement, from which we need not suffer undu ly; yet it is doubtful whether there is art in individual letters. Letter s in combination may be satisfying and in a well composed page e

The main purpose of letters is the practical one of making thought s visible. Ruskin says that all letters are frightful things and to be en

The main purpose of letters is the practical one of making t houghts visible. Ruskin says that all letters are frightful thi

8/11

The main purpose of letters is the practical one of making thought s visible. Ruskin says that all letters are frightful things and to be e ndured only on occasion, that is to say, in places where the sense of the inscription is of more importance than external ornament. This is a sweeping statement, from which we need not suffer undu ly; yet it is doubtful whether there is art in individual letters. Letter s in combination may be satisfying and in a well composed page e

The main purpose of letters is the practical one of making thought s visible. Ruskin says that all letters are frightful things and to be en

The main purpose of letters is the practical one of making t houghts visible. Ruskin says that all letters are frightful thi

---

ABCDEFGHIJKLMNOPQRSTUVWXYZ 1234567890 abcdefghijklmnopqrstuvwxyz

ABCDEFGHIJKLMNOPQRSTUVWXYZ 1234567890 abcdefghijklmnopqrstuvwxyz

ABCDEFGHIJKLMNOPQRSTUVWXYZ 1234567890 abcdefghijklmnopqrstuvwxyz

ABCDEFGHIJKLMNOPQRSTUVWXYZ 1234567890 abcdefghijklmnopqrstuvwxyz

9/9

The main purpose of letters is the practical one of making t houghts visible. Ruskin says that all letters are frightful thi ngs and to be endured only on occasion, that is to say, in pl aces where the sense of the inscription is of more importa nce than external ornament. This is a sweeping statement, from which we need not suffer unduly; yet it is doubtful wh ether there is art in individual letters. Letters in combinatio n may be satisfying and in a well composed page even bea

The main purpose of letters is the practical one of making t houghts visible. Ruskin says that all letters are frightful thi

The main purpose of letters is the practical one of ma king thoughts visible. Ruskin says that all letters are

9/10

The main purpose of letters is the practical one of making t houghts visible. Ruskin says that all letters are frightful thi ngs and to be endured only on occasion, that is to say, in pl aces where the sense of the inscription is of more importa nce than external ornament. This is a sweeping statement, from which we need not suffer unduly; yet it is doubtful wh ether there is art in individual letters. Letters in combinatio

The main purpose of letters is the practical one of making t houghts visible. Ruskin says that all letters are frightful thi

The main purpose of letters is the practical one of ma king thoughts visible. Ruskin says that all letters are

9/11

The main purpose of letters is the practical one of making t houghts visible. Ruskin says that all letters are frightful thi ngs and to be endured only on occasion, that is to say, in pl aces where the sense of the inscription is of more importa nce than external ornament. This is a sweeping statement, from which we need not suffer unduly; yet it is doubtful wh ether there is art in individual letters. Letters in combinatio

The main purpose of letters is the practical one of making t houghts visible. Ruskin says that all letters are frightful thi

The main purpose of letters is the practical one of ma king thoughts visible. Ruskin says that all letters are

9/12

The main purpose of letters is the practical one of making t houghts visible. Ruskin says that all letters are frightful thi ngs and to be endured only on occasion, that is to say, in pl aces where the sense of the inscription is of more importa nce than external ornament. This is a sweeping statement, from which we need not suffer unduly; yet it is doubtful wh ether there is art in individual letters. Letters in combinatio

The main purpose of letters is the practical one of making t houghts visible. Ruskin says that all letters are frightful thi

The main purpose of letters is the practical one of ma king thoughts visible. Ruskin says that all letters are

ITC BENGUIAT 10 POINT SET MINUS ½ UNIT

BOOK, ITALIC, BOLD, BOLD ITALIC

abcdefghijklmnopqrstuvwxyz – 1 UNIT
abcdefghijklmnopqrstuvwxyz – ½ UNIT
abcdefghijklmnopqrstuvwxyz NORMAL

ABCDEFGHIJKLMNOPQRSTUVWXYZ 1234567890 abcdefghijklmnopqrstuvwxyz
ABCDEFGHIJKLMNOPQRSTUVWXYZ 1234567890 abcdefghijklmnopqrstuvwxyz
ABCDEFGHIJKLMNOPQRSTUVWXYZ 1234567890 abcdefghijklmnopqrstuvwxyz
ABCDEFGHIJKLMNOPQRSTUVWXYZ 1234567890 abcdefghijklmnopqrstuvwxyz

10/10

The main purpose of letters is the practical one of maki ing thoughts visible. Ruskin says that all letters are frigh tful things and to be endured only on occasion, that is t o say, in places where the sense of the inscription is of more importance than external ornament. This is a sw eeping statement, from which we need not suffer undu ly; yet it is doubtful whether there is art in individual lett ers. Letters in combination may be satisfying and in a well composed page even beautiful as a whole, but art i n letters consists rather in the art of arranging and com posing them in a pleasing and appropriate manner. Th e main purpose of letters is the practical one of making thoughts visible. Ruskin says that all letters are frightfu l things and to be endured only on occasion, that is to s ay, in places where the sense of the inscription is of mo re importance than external ornament. This is a sweep ing statement, from which we need not suffer unduly; y et it is doubtful whether there is art in individual letters. Letters in combination may be satisfying and in a well c omposed page even beautiful as a whole, but art in lett ers consists rather in the art of arranging and composi ng them in a pleasing and appropriate manner. The m

The main purpose of letters is the practical one of maki ng thoughts visible. Ruskin says that all letters are frig

The main purpose of letters is the practical one of making thoughts visible. Ruskin says that all lett

10/11

The main purpose of letters is the practical one of maki ing thoughts visible. Ruskin says that all letters are frigh tful things and to be endured only on occasion, that is t o say, in places where the sense of the inscription is of more importance than external ornament. This is a sw eeping statement, from which we need not suffer undu ly; yet it is doubtful whether there is art in individual lett ers. Letters in combination may be satisfying and in a well composed page even beautiful as a whole, but art i n letters consists rather in the art of arranging and com posing them in a pleasing and appropriate manner. Th e main purpose of letters is the practical one of making thoughts visible. Ruskin says that all letters are frightfu l things and to be endured only on occasion, that is to s ay, in places where the sense of the inscription is of mo re importance than external ornament. This is a sweep ing statement, from which we need not suffer unduly; y et it is doubtful whether there is art in individual letters. Letters in combination may be satisfying and in a well c omposed page even beautiful as a whole, but art in lett

The main purpose of letters is the practical one of maki ng thoughts visible. Ruskin says that all letters are frig

The main purpose of letters is the practical one of making thoughts visible. Ruskin says that all lett

10/12

The main purpose of letters is the practical one of maki ing thoughts visible. Ruskin says that all letters are frigh tful things and to be endured only on occasion, that is t o say, in places where the sense of the inscription is of more importance than external ornament. This is a sw eeping statement, from which we need not suffer undu ly; yet it is doubtful whether there is art in individual lett ers. Letters in combination may be satisfying and in a well composed page even beautiful as a whole, but art i n letters consists rather in the art of arranging and com posing them in a pleasing and appropriate manner. Th e main purpose of letters is the practical one of making thoughts visible. Ruskin says that all letters are frightfu l things and to be endured only on occasion, that is to s ay, in places where the sense of the inscription is of mo re importance than external ornament. This is a sweep ing statement, from which we need not suffer unduly; y et it is doubtful whether there is art in individual letters.

The main purpose of letters is the practical one of maki ng thoughts visible. Ruskin says that all letters are frig

The main purpose of letters is the practical one of making thoughts visible. Ruskin says that all lett

10/13

The main purpose of letters is the practical one of maki ing thoughts visible. Ruskin says that all letters are frigh tful things and to be endured only on occasion, that is t o say, in places where the sense of the inscription is of more importance than external ornament. This is a sw eeping statement, from which we need not suffer undu ly; yet it is doubtful whether there is art in individual lett ers. Letters in combination may be satisfying and in a well composed page even beautiful as a whole, but art i n letters consists rather in the art of arranging and com posing them in a pleasing and appropriate manner. Th e main purpose of letters is the practical one of making thoughts visible. Ruskin says that all letters are frightfu l things and to be endured only on occasion, that is to s ay, in places where the sense of the inscription is of mo re importance than external ornament. This is a sweep ing statement, from which we need not suffer unduly; y

The main purpose of letters is the practical one of maki ng thoughts visible. Ruskin says that all letters are frig

The main purpose of letters is the practical one of making thoughts visible. Ruskin says that all lett

ITC BENGUIAT 11 POINT SET MINUS ½ UNIT

BOOK, ITALIC, BOLD, BOLD ITALIC

abcdefghijklmnopqrstuvwxyz – 1 UNIT
abcdefghijklmnopqrstuvwxyz – ½ UNIT
abcdefghijklmnopqrstuvwxyz NORMAL

ABCDEFGHIJKLMNOPQRSTUVWXYZ 1234567890 abcdefghijklmnopqrstuvwxyz
ABCDEFGHIJKLMNOPQRSTUVWXYZ 1234567890 abcdefghijklmnopqrstuvwxyz
ABCDEFGHIJKLMNOPQRSTUVWXYZ 1234567890 abcdefghijklmnopqrstuvwxyz
ABCDEFGHIJKLMNOPQRSTUVWXYZ 1234567890 abcdefghijklmnopqrstuvwxyz

11/11

The main purpose of letters is the practical one of
making thoughts visible. Ruskin says that all lette
rs are frightful things and to be endured only o
n occasion, that is to say, in places where the sense o
f the inscription is of more importance than exter
nal ornament. This is a sweeping statement, fro
m which we need not suffer unduly; yet it is doubtf
ul whether there is art in individual letters. Letters
in combination may be satisfying and in a well co
mposed page even beautiful as a whole, but art in
letters consists rather in the art of arranging and c
omposing them in a pleasing and appropriate ma
nner. The main purpose of letters is the practical o
ne of making thoughts visible. Ruskin says that all
letters are frightful things and to be endured only
on occasion, that is to say, in places where the sen
se of the inscription is of more importance than e
xternal ornament. This is a sweeping statement, f
rom which we need not suffer unduly; yet it is dou
The main purpose of letters is the practical one of
making thoughts visible. Ruskin says that all lette
The main purpose of letters is the practical o
ne of making thoughts visible. Ruskin says t

11/12

The main purpose of letters is the practical one of
making thoughts visible. Ruskin says that all lette
rs are frightful things and to be endured only on o
ccasion, that is to say, in places where the sense o
f the inscription is of more importance than exter
nal ornament. This is a sweeping statement, fro
m which we need not suffer unduly; yet it is doubtf
ul whether there is art in individual letters. Letters
in combination may be satisfying and in a well co
mposed page even beautiful as a whole, but art in
letters consists rather in the art of arranging and c
omposing them in a pleasing and appropriate ma
nner. The main purpose of letters is the practical o
ne of making thoughts visible. Ruskin says that all
letters are frightful things and to be endured only
on occasion, that is to say, in places where the sen
se of the inscription is of more importance than e
xternal ornament. This is a sweeping statement, f
The main purpose of letters is the practical one of
making thoughts visible. Ruskin says that all lette
The main purpose of letters is the practical o
ne of making thoughts visible. Ruskin says t

11/13

The main purpose of letters is the practical one of
making thoughts visible. Ruskin says that all lette
rs are frightful things and to be endured only on o
ccasion, that is to say, in places where the sense o
f the inscription is of more importance than exter
nal ornament. This is a sweeping statement, fro
m which we need not suffer unduly; yet it is doubtf
ul whether there is art in individual letters. Letters
in combination may be satisfying and in a well co
mposed page even beautiful as a whole, but art in
letters consists rather in the art of arranging and c
omposing them in a pleasing and appropriate ma
nner. The main purpose of letters is the practical o
ne of making thoughts visible. Ruskin says that all
letters are frightful things and to be endured only
on occasion, that is to say, in places where the sen
se of the inscription is of more importance than e
The main purpose of letters is the practical one of
making thoughts visible. Ruskin says that all lette
The main purpose of letters is the practical o
ne of making thoughts visible. Ruskin says t

11/14

The main purpose of letters is the practical one of
making thoughts visible. Ruskin says that all lette
rs are frightful things and to be endured only on o
ccasion, that is to say, in places where the sense o
f the inscription is of more importance than exter
nal ornament. This is a sweeping statement, fro
m which we need not suffer unduly; yet it is doubtf
ul whether there is art in individual letters. Letters
in combination may be satisfying and in a well co
mposed page even beautiful as a whole, but art in
letters consists rather in the art of arranging and c
omposing them in a pleasing and appropriate ma
nner. The main purpose of letters is the practical o
ne of making thoughts visible. Ruskin says that all
letters are frightful things and to be endured only
on occasion, that is to say, in places where the sen
The main purpose of letters is the practical one of
making thoughts visible. Ruskin says that all lette
The main purpose of letters is the practical o
ne of making thoughts visible. Ruskin says t

ITC BENGUIAT 12 POINT SET MINUS ½ UNIT

BOOK, ITALIC, BOLD, BOLD ITALIC

abcdefghijklmnopqrstuvwxyz – 1 UNIT
abcdefghijklmnopqrstuvwxyz – ½ UNIT
abcdefghijklmnopqrstuvwxyz NORMAL

ABCDEFGHIJKLMNOPQRSTUVWXYZ 1234567890 abcdefghijklmnopqrstuvwxyz
ABCDEFGHIJKLMNOPQRSTUVWXYZ 1234567890 abcdefghijklmnopqrstuvwxyz
ABCDEFGHIJKLMNOPQRSTUVWXYZ 1234567890 abcdefghijklmnopqrstuvwxyz
ABCDEFGHIJKLMNOPQRSTUVWXYZ 1234567890 abcdefghijklmnopqrstuvwxy

12/12

The main purpose of letters is the practical on e of making thoughts visible. Ruskin says that all letters are frightful things and to be endure d only on occasion, that is to say, in places whe re the sense of the inscription is of more impo rtance than external ornament. This is a swee ping statement, from which we need not suffe r unduly; yet it is doubtful whether there is art i n individual letters. Letters in combination ma y be satisfying and in a well composed page ev en beautiful as a whole, but art in letters consi sts rather in the art of arranging and composi ng them in a pleasing and appropriate manne r. The main purpose of letters is the practical o ne of making thoughts visible. Ruskin says tha
The main purpose of letters is the practical on e of making thoughts visible. Ruskin says that
The main purpose of letters is the practic al one of making thoughts visible. Ruskin

12/13

The main purpose of letters is the practical on e of making thoughts visible. Ruskin says that all letters are frightful things and to be endure d only on occasion, that is to say, in places whe re the sense of the inscription is of more impo rtance than external ornament. This is a swee ping statement, from which we need not suffe r unduly; yet it is doubtful whether there is art i n individual letters. Letters in combination ma y be satisfying and in a well composed page ev en beautiful as a whole, but art in letters consi sts rather in the art of arranging and composi ng them in a pleasing and appropriate manne r. The main purpose of letters is the practical o
The main purpose of letters is the practical on e of making thoughts visible. Ruskin says that
The main purpose of letters is the practic al one of making thoughts visible. Ruskin

12/14

The main purpose of letters is the practical on e of making thoughts visible. Ruskin says that all letters are frightful things and to be endure d only on occasion, that is to say, in places whe re the sense of the inscription is of more impo rtance than external ornament. This is a swee ping statement, from which we need not suffe r unduly; yet it is doubtful whether there is art i n individual letters. Letters in combination ma y be satisfying and in a well composed page ev en beautiful as a whole, but art in letters consi sts rather in the art of arranging and composi ng them in a pleasing and appropriate manne r. The main purpose of letters is the practical o ne of making thoughts visible. Ruskin says tha
The main purpose of letters is the practical on e of making thoughts visible. Ruskin says that
The main purpose of letters is the practic al one of making thoughts visible. Ruskin

12/15

The main purpose of letters is the practical on e of making thoughts visible. Ruskin says that all letters are frightful things and to be endure d only on occasion, that is to say, in places whe re the sense of the inscription is of more impo rtance than external ornament. This is a swee ping statement, from which we need not suffe r unduly; yet it is doubtful whether there is art i n individual letters. Letters in combination ma y be satisfying and in a well composed page ev en beautiful as a whole, but art in letters consi sts rather in the art of arranging and composi ng them in a pleasing and appropriate manne r. The main purpose of letters is the practical o
The main purpose of letters is the practical on e of making thoughts visible. Ruskin says that
The main purpose of letters is the practic al one of making thoughts visible. Ruskin

ITC BENGUIAT 14 POINT SET MINUS ½ UNIT

BOOK, ITALIC, BOLD, BOLD ITALIC

abcdefghijklmnopqrstuvwxyz – 1 UNIT
abcdefghijklmnopqrstuvwxyz – ½ UNIT
abcdefghijklmnopqrstuvwxyz NORMAL

ABCDEFGHIJKLMNOPQRSTUVWXYZ abcdefghijklmnopqrstuvwxyz
ABCDEFGHIJKLMNOPQRSTUVWXYZ abcdefghijklmnopqrstuvwxyz
ABCDEFGHIJKLMNOPQRSTUVWXYZ abcdefghijklmnopqrstuvwxyz
ABCDEFGHIJKLMNOPQRSTUVWXYZ abcdefghijklmnopqrstuvwxyz

14/14

The main purpose of letters is the pract ical one of making thoughts visible. Ru skin says that all letters are frightful thi ngs and to be endured only on occasio n, that is to say, in places where the sen se of the inscription is of more importa nce than external ornament. This is a s weeping statement, from which we nee d not suffer unduly; yet it is doubtful wh ether there is art in individual letters. Le tters in combination may be satisfying and in a well composed page even bea utiful as a whole, but art in letters consi
The main purpose of letters is the pract ical one of making thoughts visible. Ru
The main purpose of letters is the p ractical one of making thoughts vis

14/15

The main purpose of letters is the pract ical one of making thoughts visible. Ru skin says that all letters are frightful thi ngs and to be endured only on occasio n, that is to say, in places where the sen se of the inscription is of more importa nce than external ornament. This is a s weeping statement, from which we nee d not suffer unduly; yet it is doubtful wh ether there is art in individual letters. Le tters in combination may be satisfying and in a well composed page even bea
The main purpose of letters is the pract ical one of making thoughts visible. Ru
The main purpose of letters is the p ractical one of making thoughts vis

14/16

The main purpose of letters is the pract ical one of making thoughts visible. Ru skin says that all letters are frightful thi ngs and to be endured only on occasio n, that is to say, in places where the sen se of the inscription is of more importa nce than external ornament. This is a s weeping statement, from which we nee d not suffer unduly; yet it is doubtful wh ether there is art in individual letters. Le tters in combination may be satisfying and in a well composed page even bea utiful as a whole, but art in letters consi
The main purpose of letters is the pract ical one of making thoughts visible. Ru
The main purpose of letters is the p ractical one of making thoughts vis

14/17

The main purpose of letters is the pract ical one of making thoughts visible. Ru skin says that all letters are frightful thi ngs and to be endured only on occasio n, that is to say, in places where the sen se of the inscription is of more importa nce than external ornament. This is a s weeping statement, from which we nee d not suffer unduly; yet it is doubtful wh ether there is art in individual letters. Le tters in combination may be satisfying and in a well composed page even bea
The main purpose of letters is the pract ical one of making thoughts visible. Ru
The main purpose of letters is the p ractical one of making thoughts vis

BODONI BOOK 6 & 7 POINT SET NORMAL

ROMAN, ITALIC, BOLD, BOLD ITALIC

ABCDEFGHIJKLMNOPQRSTUVWXYZ 1234567890 abcdefghijklmnopqrstuvwxyz

ABCDEFGHIJKLMNOPQRSTUVWXYZ 1234567890 abcdefghijklmnopqrstuvwxyz

ABCDEFGHIJKLMNOPQRSTUVWXYZ 1234567890 abcdefghijklmnopqrstuvwxyz

ABCDEFGHIJKLMNOPQRSTUVWXYZ 1234567890 abcdefghijklmnopqrstuvwxyz

6/6

The main purpose of letters is the practical one of making thoughts visible. Ruskin says that all letters are frightful things and to be endured only on occasion, that is to say, in places where the sense of the inscript ion is of more importance than external ornament. This is a sweeping statement, from which we need not s uffer unduly; yet it is doubtful whether there is art in individual letters. Letters in combination may be sat isfying and in a well composed page even beautiful as a whole, but art in letters consists rather in the art o f arranging and composing them in a pleasing and appropriate manner. The main purpose of letters is the practical one of making thoughts visible. Ruskin says that all letters are frightful things and to be endured only on occasion, that is to say, in places where the sense of the inscription is of more importance than ext ernal ornament. This is a sweeping statement, from which we need not suffer unduly; yet it is doubtful wh ether there is art in individual letters. Letters in combination may be satisfying and in a well composed pa ge even beautiful as a whole, but art in letters consists rather in the art of arranging and composing them i n a pleasing and appropriate manner. The main purpose of letters is the practical one of making thoughts visible. Ruskin says that all letters are frightful things and to be endured only on occasion, that is to say, i
The main purpose of letters is the practical one of making thoughts visible. Ruskin says that all letters are fri ghtful things and to be endured only on occasion, that is to say, in places where the sense of the inscription is
The main purpose of letters is the practical one of making thoughts visible. Ruskin says that all letters are frightful things and to be endured only on occasion, that is to say, in places where th

6/7

The main purpose of letters is the practical one of making thoughts visible. Ruskin says that all letters are frightful things and to be endured only on occasion, that is to say, in places where the sense of the inscript ion is of more importance than external ornament. This is a sweeping statement, from which we need not s uffer unduly; yet it is doubtful whether there is art in individual letters. Letters in combination may be sat isfying and in a well composed page even beautiful as a whole, but art in letters consists rather in the art o f arranging and composing them in a pleasing and appropriate manner. The main purpose of letters is the practical one of making thoughts visible. Ruskin says that all letters are frightful things and to be endured only on occasion, that is to say, in places where the sense of the inscription is of more importance than ext ernal ornament. This is a sweeping statement, from which we need not suffer unduly; yet it is doubtful wh ether there is art in individual letters. Letters in combination may be satisfying and in a well composed pa ge even beautiful as a whole, but art in letters consists rather in the art of arranging and composing them i
The main purpose of letters is the practical one of making thoughts visible. Ruskin says that all letters are fri ghtful things and to be endured only on occasion, that is to say, in places where the sense of the inscription is
The main purpose of letters is the practical one of making thoughts visible. Ruskin says that all letters are frightful things and to be endured only on occasion, that is to say, in places where th

6/8

The main purpose of letters is the practical one of making thoughts visible. Ruskin says that all letters are frightful things and to be endured only on occasion, that is to say, in places where the sense of the inscript ion is of more importance than external ornament. This is a sweeping statement, from which we need not s uffer unduly; yet it is doubtful whether there is art in individual letters. Letters in combination may be sat isfying and in a well composed page even beautiful as a whole, but art in letters consists rather in the art o f arranging and composing them in a pleasing and appropriate manner. The main purpose of letters is the practical one of making thoughts visible. Ruskin says that all letters are frightful things and to be endured only on occasion, that is to say, in places where the sense of the inscription is of more importance than ext ernal ornament. This is a sweeping statement, from which we need not suffer unduly; yet it is doubtful wh
The main purpose of letters is the practical one of making thoughts visible. Ruskin says that all letters are fri ghtful things and to be endured only on occasion, that is to say, in places where the sense of the inscription is
The main purpose of letters is the practical one of making thoughts visible. Ruskin says that all letters are frightful things and to be endured only on occasion, that is to say, in places where th

6/9

The main purpose of letters is the practical one of making thoughts visible. Ruskin says that all letters are frightful things and to be endured only on occasion, that is to say, in places where the sense of the inscript ion is of more importance than external ornament. This is a sweeping statement, from which we need not s uffer unduly; yet it is doubtful whether there is art in individual letters. Letters in combination may be sat isfying and in a well composed page even beautiful as a whole, but art in letters consists rather in the art o f arranging and composing them in a pleasing and appropriate manner. The main purpose of letters is the practical one of making thoughts visible. Ruskin says that all letters are frightful things and to be endured only on occasion, that is to say, in places where the sense of the inscription is of more importance than ext
The main purpose of letters is the practical one of making thoughts visible. Ruskin says that all letters are fri ghtful things and to be endured only on occasion, that is to say, in places where the sense of the inscription is
The main purpose of letters is the practical one of making thoughts visible. Ruskin says that all letters are frightful things and to be endured only on occasion, that is to say, in places where th

ABCDEFGHIJKLMNOPQRSTUVWXYZ 1234567890 abcdefghijklmnopqrstuvwxyz

ABCDEFGHIJKLMNOPQRSTUVWXYZ 1234567890 abcdefghijklmnopqrstuvwxyz

ABCDEFGHIJKLMNOPQRSTUVWXYZ 1234567890 abcdefghijklmnopqrstuvwxyz

ABCDEFGHIJKLMNOPQRSTUVWXYZ 1234567890 abcdefghijklmnopqrstuvwxyz

7/7

The main purpose of letters is the practical one of making thoughts visible. Ruskin says th at all letters are frightful things and to be endured only on occasion, that is to say, in places where the sense of the inscription is of more importance than external ornament. This is a s weeping statement, from which we need not suffer unduly; yet it is doubtful whether there i s art in individual letters. Letters in combination may be satisfying and in a well composed page even beautiful as a whole, but art in letters consists rather in the art of arranging and composing them in a pleasing and appropriate manner. The main purpose of letters is the p ractical one of making thoughts visible. Ruskin says that all letters are frightful things and to be endured only on occasion, that is to say, in places where the sense of the inscription i s of more importance than external ornament. This is a sweeping statment, from which we need not suffer unduly; yet it is doubtful whether there is art in individual letters. Letters i
The main purpose of letters is the practical one of making thoughts visible. Ruskin says that all letters are frightful things and to be endured only on occasion, that is to say, in places wh
The main purpose of letters is the practical one of making thoughts visible. Ruski n says that all letters are frightful things and to be endured only on occasion, that

7/8

The main purpose of letters is the practical one of making thoughts visible. Ruskin says th at all letters are frightful things and to be endured only on occasion, that is to say, in places where the sense of the inscription is of more importance than external ornament. This is a s weeping statement, from which we need not suffer unduly; yet it is doubtful whether there i s art in individual letters. Letters in combination may be satisfying and in a well composed page even beautiful as a whole, but art in letters consists rather in the art of arranging and composing them in a pleasing and appropriate manner. The main purpose of letters is the p ractical one of making thoughts visible. Ruskin says that all letters are frightful things and to be endured only on occasion, that is to say, in places where the sense of the inscription i s of more importance than external ornament. This is a sweeping statment, from which we
The main purpose of letters is the practical one of making thoughts visible. Ruskin says that all letters are frightful things and to be endured only on occasion, that is to say, in places wh
The main purpose of letters is the practical one of making thoughts visible. Ruski n says that all letters are frightful things and to be endured only on occasion, that

7/9

The main purpose of letters is the practical one of making thoughts visible. Ruskin says th at all letters are frightful things and to be endured only on occasion, that is to say, in places where the sense of the inscription is of more importance than external ornament. This is a s weeping statement, from which we need not suffer unduly; yet it is doubtful whether there i s art in individual letters. Letters in combination may be satisfying and in a well composed page even beautiful as a whole, but art in letters consists rather in the art of arranging and composing them in a pleasing and appropriate manner. The main purpose of letters is the p ractical one of making thoughts visible. Ruskin says that all letters are frightful things and to be endured only on occasion, that is to say, in places where the sense of the inscription i s of more importance than external ornament. This is a sweeping statement, from which we
The main purpose of letters is the practical one of making thoughts visible. Ruskin says that all letters are frightful things and to be endured only on occasion, that is to say, in places wh
The main purpose of letters is the practical one of making thoughts visible. Ruski n says that all letters are frightful things and to be endured only on occasion, that

7/10

The main purpose of letters is the practical one of making thoughts visible. Ruskin says th at all letters are frightful things and to be endured only on occasion, that is to say, in places where the sense of the inscription is of more importance than external ornament. This is a s weeping statement, from which we need not suffer unduly; yet it is doubtful whether there i s art in individual letters. Letters in combination may be satisfying and in a well composed page even beautiful as a whole, but art in letters consists rather in the art of arranging and composing them in a pleasing and appropriate manner. The main purpose of letters is the p ractical one of making thoughts visible. Ruskin says that all letters are frightful things and to be endured only on occasion, that is to say, in places where the sense of the inscription i
The main purpose of letters is the practical one of making thoughts visible. Ruskin says that all letters are frightful things and to be endured only on occasion, that is to say, in places wh
The main purpose of letters is the practical one of making thoughts visible. Ruski n says that all letters are frightful things and to be endured only on occasion, that

BODONI BOOK 8 & 9 POINT SET NORMAL

ROMAN, ITALIC, BOLD, BOLD ITALIC

ABCDEFGHIJKLMNOPQRSTUVWXYZ 1234567890 abcdefghijklmnopqrstuvwxyz

ABCDEFGHIJKLMNOPQRSTUVWXYZ 1234567890 abcdefghijklmnopqrstuvwxyz

ABCDEFGHIJKLMNOPQRSTUVWXYZ 1234567890 abcdefghijklmnopqrstuvwxyz

ABCDEFGHIJKLMNOPQRSTUVWXYZ 1234567890 abcdefghijklmnopqrstuvwxyz

8/8

The main purpose of letters is the practical one of making thoughts visible. Rus kin says that all letters are frightful things and to be endured only on occasion, t hat is to say, in places where the sense of the inscription is of more importance t han external ornament. This is a sweeping statement, from which we need not s uffer unduly; yet it is doubtful whether there is art in individual letters. Letters in combination may be satisfying and in a well composed page even beautiful a s a whole, but art in letters consists rather in the art of arranging and composing them in a pleasing and appropriate manner. The main purpose of letters is the p ractical one of making thoughts visible. Ruskin says that all letters are frightful
The main purpose of letters is the practical one of making thoughts visible. Ruski n says that all letters are frightful things and to be endured only on occasion, tha
The main purpose of letters is the practical one of making thoughts visi ble. Ruskin says that all letters are frightful things and to be endured o

8/9

The main purpose of letters is the practical one of making thoughts visible. Rus kin says that all letters are frightful things and to be endured only on occasion, t hat is to say, in places where the sense of the inscription is of more importance t han external ornament. This is a sweeping statement, from which we need not s uffer unduly; yet it is doubtful whether there is art in individual letters. Letters in combination may be satisfying and in a well composed page even beautiful a s a whole, but art in letters consists rather in the art of arranging and composing them in a pleasing and appropriate manner. The main purpose of letters is the p
The main purpose of letters is the practical one of making thoughts visible. Ruski n says that all letters are frightful things and to be endured only on occasion, tha
The main purpose of letters is the practical one of making thoughts visi ble. Ruskin says that all letters are frightful things and to be endured o

8/10

The main purpose of letters is the practical one of making thoughts visible. Rus kin says that all letters are frightful things and to be endured only on occasion, t hat is to say, in places where the sense of the inscription is of more importance t han external ornament. This is a sweeping statement, from which we need not s uffer unduly; yet it is doubtful whether there is art in individual letters. Letters in combination may be satisfying and in a well composed page even beautiful a s a whole, but art in letters consists rather in the art of arranging and composing
The main purpose of letters is the practical one of making thoughts visible. Ruski n says that all letters are frightful things and to be endured only on occasion, tha
The main purpose of letters is the practical one of making thoughts visi ble. Ruskin says that all letters are frightful things and to be endured o

8/11

The main purpose of letters is the practical one of making thoughts visible. Rus kin says that all letters are frightful things and to be endured only on occasion, t hat is to say, in places where the sense of the inscription is of more importance t han external ornament. This is a sweeping statement, from which we need not s uffer unduly; yet it is doubtful whether there is art in individual letters. Letters in combination may be satisfying and in a well composed page even beautiful a s a whole, but art in letters consists rather in the art of arranging and composing
The main purpose of letters is the practical one of making thoughts visible. Ruski n says that all letters are frightful things and to be endured only on occasion, tha
The main purpose of letters is the practical one of making thoughts visi ble. Ruskin says that all letters are frightful things and to be endured o

---

ABCDEFGHIJKLMNOPQRSTUVWXYZ 1234567890 abcdefghijklmnopqrstuvwxyz

ABCDEFGHIJKLMNOPQRSTUVWXYZ 1234567890 abcdefghijklmnopqrstuvwxyz

ABCDEFGHIJKLMNOPQRSTUVWXYZ 1234567890 abcdefghijklmnopqrstuvwxyz

ABCDEFGHIJKLMNOPQRSTUVWXYZ 1234567890 abcdefghijklmnopqrstuvwxyz

9/9

The main purpose of letters is the practical one of making thoughts vis ible. Ruskin says that all letters are frightful things and to be endured only on occasion, that is to say, in places where the sense of the inscrip tion is of more importance than external ornament. This is a sweeping statement, from which we need not suffer unduly; yet it is doubtful wh ether there is art in individual letters. Letters in combination may be s atisfying and in a well composed page even beautiful as a whole, but a rt in letters consists rather in the art of arranging and composing them
The main purpose of letters is the practical one of making thoughts visib le. Ruskin says that all letters are frightful things and to be endured onl
The main purpose of letters is the practical one of making thou ghts visible. Ruskin says that all letters are frightful things and t

9/10

The main purpose of letters is the practical one of making thoughts vis ible. Ruskin says that all letters are frightful things and to be endured only on occasion, that is to say, in places where the sense of the inscrip tion is of more importance than external ornament. This is a sweeping statement, from which we need not suffer unduly; yet it is doubtful wh ether there is art in individual letters. Letters in combination may be s atisfying and in a well composed page even beautiful as a whole, but a
The main purpose of letters is the practical one of making thoughts visib le. Ruskin says that all letters are frightful things and to be endured onl
The main purpose of letters is the practical one of making thou ghts visible. Ruskin says that all letters are frightful things and t

9/11

The main purpose of letters is the practical one of making thoughts vis ible. Ruskin says that all letters are frightful things and to be endured only on occasion, that is to say, in places where the sense of the inscrip tion is of more importance than external ornament. This is a sweeping statement, from which we need not suffer unduly; yet it is doubtful wh ether there is art in individual letters. Letters in combination may be s atisfying and in a well composed page even beautiful as a whole, but a
The main purpose of letters is the practical one of making thoughts visib le. Ruskin says that all letters are frightful things and to be endured onl
The main purpose of letters is the practical one of making thou ghts visible. Ruskin says that all letters are frightful things and t

9/12

The main purpose of letters is the practical one of making thoughts vis ible. Ruskin says that all letters are frightful things and to be endured only on occasion, that is to say, in places where the sense of the inscrip tion is of more importance than external ornament. This is a sweeping statement, from which we need not suffer unduly; yet it is doubtful wh ether there is art in individual letters. Letters in combination may be s atisfying and in a well composed page even beautiful as a whole, but a
The main purpose of letters is the practical one of making thoughts visib le. Ruskin says that all letters are frightful things and to be endured onl
The main purpose of letters is the practical one of making thou ghts visible. Ruskin says that all letters are frightful things and t

BODONI BOOK 10 POINT SET MINUS ½ UNIT

ROMAN, ITALIC, BOLD, BOLD ITALIC

abcdefghijklmnopqrstuvwxyz – 1 UNIT
abcdefghijklmnopqrstuvwxyz – ½ UNIT
abcdefghijklmnopqrstuvwxyz NORMAL

ABCDEFGHIJKLMNOPQRSTUVWXYZ 1234567890 abcdefghijklmnopqrstuvwxyz
ABCDEFGHIJKLMNOPQRSTUVWXYZ 1234567890 abcdefghijklmnopqrstuvwxyz
ABCDEFGHIJKLMNOPQRSTUVWXYZ 1234567890 abcdefghijklmnopqrstuvwxyz
ABCDEFGHIJKLMNOPQRSTUVWXYZ 1234567890 abcdefghijklmnopqrstuvwxyz

10/10

The main purpose of letters is the practical one of making thoughts visible. Ruskin says that all letters are frightful things and to be en dured only on occasion, that is to say, in places where the sense of t he inscription is of more importance than external ornament. This is a sweeping statement, from which we need not suffer unduly; ye t it is doubtful whether there is art in individual letters. Letters in c ombination may be satisfying and in a well composed page even b eautiful as a whole, but art in letters consists rather in the art of arr anging and composing them in a pleasing and appropriate manne r. The main purpose of letters is the practical one of making though ts visible. Ruskin says that all letters are frightful things and to be endured only on occasion, that is to say, in places where the sense of the inscription is of more importance than external ornament. T his is a sweeping statement, from which we need not suffer unduly; yet it is doubtful whether there is art in individual letters. Letters in combination may be satisfying and in a well composed page eve n beautiful as a whole, but art in letters consists rather in the art of arranging and composing them in a pleasing and appropriate man ner. The main purpose of letters is the practical one of making tho ughts visible. Ruskin says that all letters are frightful things and to be endured only on occasion, that is to say, in places where the sen se of the inscription is of more importance than external ornament.
The main purpose of letters is the practical one of making thoughts v isible. Ruskin says that all letters are frightful things and to be endu
The main purpose of letters is the practical one of making t houghts visible. Ruskin says that all letters are frightful thin

10/11

The main purpose of letters is the practical one of making thoughts visible. Ruskin says that all letters are frightful things and to be en dured only on occasion, that is to say, in places where the sense of t he inscription is of more importance than external ornament. This is a sweeping statement, from which we need not suffer unduly; ye t it is doubtful whether there is art in individual letters. Letters in c ombination may be satisfying and in a well composed page even b eautiful as a whole, but art in letters consists rather in the art of arr anging and composing them in a pleasing and appropriate manne r. The main purpose of letters is the practical one of making though ts visible. Ruskin says that all letters are frightful things and to be endured only on occasion, that is to say, in places where the sense of the inscription is of more importance than external ornament. T his is a sweeping statement, from which we need not suffer unduly; yet it is doubtful whether there is art in individual letters. Letters in combination may be satisfying and in a well composed page eve n beautiful as a whole, but art in letters consists rather in the art of arranging and composing them in a pleasing and appropriate man ner. The main purpose of letters is the practical one of making tho ughts visible. Ruskin says that all letters are frightful things and to
The main purpose of letters is the practical one of making thoughts v isible. Ruskin says that all letters are frightful things and to be endu
The main purpose of letters is the practical one of making t houghts visible. Ruskin says that all letters are frightful thin

10/12

The main purpose of letters is the practical one of making thoughts visible. Ruskin says that all letters are frightful things and to be en dured only on occasion, that is to say, in places where the sense of t he inscription is of more importance than external ornament. This is a sweeping statement, from which we need not suffer unduly; ye t it is doubtful whether there is art in individual letters. Letters in c ombination may be satisfying and in a well composed page even b eautiful as a whole, but art in letters consists rather in the art of arr anging and composing them in a pleasing and appropriate manne r. The main purpose of letters is the practical one of making though ts visible. Ruskin says that all letters are frightful things and to be endured only on occasion, that is to say, in places where the sense of the inscription is of more importance than external ornament. T his is a sweeping statement, from which we need not suffer unduly; yet it is doubtful whether there is art in individual letters. Letters in combination may be satisfying and in a well composed page eve n beautiful as a whole, but art in letters consists rather in the art of arranging and composing them in a pleasing and appropriate man
The main purpose of letters is the practical one of making thoughts v isible. Ruskin says that all letters are frightful things and to be endu
The main purpose of letters is the practical one of making t houghts visible. Ruskin says that all letters are frightful thin

10/13

The main purpose of letters is the practical one of making thoughts visible. Ruskin says that all letters are frightful things and to be en dured only on occasion, that is to say, in places where the sense of t he inscription is of more importance than external ornament. This is a sweeping statement, from which we need not suffer unduly; ye t it is doubtful whether there is art in individual letters. Letters in c ombination may be satisfying and in a well composed page even b eautiful as a whole, but art in letters consists rather in the art of arr anging and composing them in a pleasing and appropriate manne r. The main purpose of letters is the practical one of making though ts visible. Ruskin says that all letters are frightful things and to be endured only on occasion, that is to say, in places where the sense of the inscription is of more importance than external ornament. T his is a sweeping statement, from which we need not suffer unduly; yet it is doubtful whether there is art in individual letters. Letters in combination may be satisfying and in a well composed page eve n beautiful as a whole, but art in letters consists rather in the art of
The main purpose of letters is the practical one of making thoughts v isible. Ruskin says that all letters are frightful things and to be endu
The main purpose of letters is the practical one of making t houghts visible. Ruskin says that all letters are frightful thin

BODONI BOOK 11 POINT SET MINUS ½ UNIT

ROMAN, ITALIC, BOLD, BOLD ITALIC

abcdefghijklmnopqrstuvwxyz − 1 UNIT
abcdefghijklmnopqrstuvwxyz − ½ UNIT
abcdefghijklmnopqrstuvwxyz NORMAL

ABCDEFGHIJKLMNOPQRSTUVWXYZ 1234567890 abcdefghijklmnopqrstuvwxyz
ABCDEFGHIJKLMNOPQRSTUVWXYZ 1234567890 abcdefghijklmnopqrstuvwxyz
ABCDEFGHIJKLMNOPQRSTUVWXYZ 1234567890 abcdefghijklmnopqrstuvwxyz
ABCDEFGHIJKLMNOPQRSTUVWXYZ 1234567890 abcdefghijklmnopqrstuvwxyz

11/11

The main purpose of letters is the practical one of making th oughts visible. Ruskin says that all letters are frightful thing s and to be endured only on occasion, that is to say, in places where the sense of the inscription is of more importance tha n external ornament. This is a sweeping statement, from whi ch we need not suffer unduly; yet it is doubtful whether there is art in individual letters. Letters in combination may be sa tisfying and in a well composed page even beautiful as a wh ole, but art in letters consists rather in the art of arranging an d composing them in a pleasing and appropriate manner. Th e main purpose of letters is the practical one of making thou ghts visible. Ruskin says that all letters are frightful things a nd to be endured only on occasion, that is to say, in places w here the sense of the inscription is of more importance than external ornament. This is a sweeping statement, from whic h we need not suffer unduly; yet it is doubtful whether there i s art in individual letters. Letters in combination may be sat isfying and in a well composed page even beautiful as a who le, but art in letters consists rather in the art of arranging an
The main purpose of letters is the practical one of making tho ughts visible. Ruskin says that all letters are frightful things a
The main purpose of letters is the practical one of ma king thoughts visible. Ruskin says that all letters are f

11/12

The main purpose of letters is the practical one of making th oughts visible. Ruskin says that all letters are frightful thing s and to be endured only on occasion, that is to say, in places where the sense of the inscription is of more importance tha n external ornament. This is a sweeping statement, from whi ch we need not suffer unduly; yet it is doubtful whether there is art in individual letters. Letters in combination may be sa tisfying and in a well composed page even beautiful as a wh ole, but art in letters consists rather in the art of arranging an d composing them in a pleasing and appropriate manner. Th e main purpose of letters is the practical one of making thou ghts visible. Ruskin says that all letters are frightful things a nd to be endured only on occasion, that is to say, in places w here the sense of the inscription is of more importance than external ornament. This is a sweeping statement, from whic h we need not suffer unduly; yet it is doubtful whether there i s art in individual letters. Letters in combination may be sat isfying and in a well composed page even beautiful as a who
The main purpose of letters is the practical one of making tho ughts visible. Ruskin says that all letters are frightful things a
The main purpose of letters is the practical one of ma king thoughts visible. Ruskin says that all letters are f

11/13

The main purpose of letters is the practical one of making th oughts visible. Ruskin says that all letters are frightful thing s and to be endured only on occasion, that is to say, in places where the sense of the inscription is of more importance tha n external ornament. This is a sweeping statement, from whi ch we need not suffer unduly; yet it is doubtful whether there is art in individual letters. Letters in combination may be sa tisfying and in a well composed page even beautiful as a wh ole, but art in letters consists rather in the art of arranging an d composing them in a pleasing and appropriate manner. Th e main purpose of letters is the practical one of making thou ghts visible. Ruskin says that all letters are frightful things a nd to be endured only on occasion, that is to say, in places w here the sense of the inscription is of more importance than external ornament. This is a sweeping statement, from whic h we need not suffer unduly; yet it is doubtful whether there i s art in individual letters. Letters in combination may be sat
The main purpose of letters is the practical one of making tho ughts visible. Ruskin says that all letters are frightful things a
The main purpose of letters is the practical one of ma king thoughts visible. Ruskin says that all letters are f

11/14

The main purpose of letters is the practical one of making th oughts visible. Ruskin says that all letters are frightful thing s and to be endured only on occasion, that is to say, in places where the sense of the inscription is of more importance tha n external ornament. This is a sweeping statement, from whi ch we need not suffer unduly; yet it is doubtful whether there is art in individual letters. Letters in combination may be sa tisfying and in a well composed page even beautiful as a wh ole, but art in letters consists rather in the art of arranging an d composing them in a pleasing and appropriate manner. Th e main purpose of letters is the practical one of making thou ghts visible. Ruskin says that all letters are frightful things a nd to be endured only on occasion, that is to say, in places w here the sense of the inscription is of more importance than external ornament. This is a sweeping statement, from whic h we need not suffer unduly; yet it is doubtful whether there i
The main purpose of letters is the practical one of making tho ughts visible. Ruskin says that all letters are frightful things a
The main purpose of letters is the practical one of ma king thoughts visible. Ruskin says that all letters are f

BODONI BOOK 12 POINT SET MINUS ½ UNIT

ROMAN, ITALIC, BOLD, BOLD ITALIC

abcdefghijklmnopqrstuvwxyz – 1 UNIT
abcdefghijklmnopqrstuvwxyz – ½ UNIT
abcdefghijklmnopqrstuvwxyz NORMAL

ABCDEFGHIJKLMNOPQRSTUVWXYZ 1234567890 abcdefghijklmnopqrstuvwxyz
ABCDEFGHIJKLMNOPQRSTUVWXYZ 1234567890 abcdefghijklmnopqrstuvwxyz
ABCDEFGHIJKLMNOPQRSTUVWXYZ 1234567890 abcdefghijklmnopqrstuvwxyz
ABCDEFGHIJKLMNOPQRSTUVWXYZ 1234567890 abcdefghijklmnopqrstuvwxyz

12/12

The main purpose of letters is the practical one of makin g thoughts visible. Ruskin says that all letters are frightf ul things and to be endured only on occasion, that is to s ay, in places where the sense of the inscription is of mor e importance than external ornament. This is a sweepin g statement, from which we need not suffer unduly; yet i t is doubtful whether there is art in individual letters. Le tters in combination may be satisfying and in a well com posed page even beautiful as a whole, but art in letters c onsists rather in the art of arranging and composing the m in a pleasing and appropriate manner. The main purp ose of letters is the practical one of making thoughts visi ble. Ruskin says that all letters are frightful things and t o be endured only on occasion, that is to say, in places w here the sense of the inscription is of more importance t
The main purpose of letters is the practical one of making thoughts visible. Ruskin says that all letters are frightful t
The main purpose of letters is the practical one of making thoughts visible. Ruskin says that all letter

12/13

The main purpose of letters is the practical one of makin g thoughts visible. Ruskin says that all letters are frightf ul things and to be endured only on occasion, that is to s ay, in places where the sense of the inscription is of mor e importance than external ornament. This is a sweepin g statement, from which we need not suffer unduly; yet i t is doubtful whether there is art in individual letters. Le tters in combination may be satisfying and in a well com posed page even beautiful as a whole, but art in letters c onsists rather in the art of arranging and composing the m in a pleasing and appropriate manner. The main purp ose of letters is the practical one of making thoughts visi ble. Ruskin says that all letters are frightful things and t o be endured only on occasion, that is to say, in places w
The main purpose of letters is the practical one of making thoughts visible. Ruskin says that all letters are frightful t
The main purpose of letters is the practical one of making thoughts visible. Ruskin says that all letter

12/14

The main purpose of letters is the practical one of makin g thoughts visible. Ruskin says that all letters are frightf ul things and to be endured only on occasion, that is to s ay, in places where the sense of the inscription is of mor e importance than external ornament. This is a sweepin g statement, from which we need not suffer unduly; yet i t is doubtful whether there is art in individual letters. Le tters in combination may be satisfying and in a well com posed page even beautiful as a whole, but art in letters c onsists rather in the art of arranging and composing the m in a pleasing and appropriate manner. The main purp ose of letters is the practical one of making thoughts visi ble. Ruskin says that all letters are frightful things and t o be endured only on occasion, that is to say, in places w here the sense of the inscription is of more importance t
The main purpose of letters is the practical one of making thoughts visible. Ruskin says that all letters are frightful t
The main purpose of letters is the practical one of making thoughts visible. Ruskin says that all letter

12/15

The main purpose of letters is the practical one of makin g thoughts visible. Ruskin says that all letters are frightf ul things and to be endured only on occasion, that is to s ay, in places where the sense of the inscription is of mor e importance than external ornament. This is a sweepin g statement, from which we need not suffer unduly; yet i t is doubtful whether there is art in individual letters. Le tters in combination may be satisfying and in a well com posed page even beautiful as a whole, but art in letters c onsists rather in the art of arranging and composing the m in a pleasing and appropriate manner. The main purp ose of letters is the practical one of making thoughts visi ble. Ruskin says that all letters are frightful things and t o be endured only on occasion, that is to say, in places w
The main purpose of letters is the practical one of making thoughts visible. Ruskin says that all letters are frightful t
The main purpose of letters is the practical one of making thoughts visible. Ruskin says that all letter

BODONI BOOK 14 POINT SET MINUS ½ UNIT

ROMAN, ITALIC, BOLD, BOLD ITALIC

abcdefghijklmnopqrstuvwxyz – 1 UNIT
abcdefghijklmnopqrstuvwxyz – ½ UNIT
abcdefghijklmnopqrstuvwxyz NORMAL

ABCDEFGHIJKLMNOPQRSTUVWXYZ abcdefghijklmnopqrstuvwxyz
ABCDEFGHIJKLMNOPQRSTUVWXYZ abcdefghijklmnopqrstuvwxyz
ABCDEFGHIJKLMNOPQRSTUVWXYZ abcdefghijklmnopqrstuvwxyz
ABCDEFGHIJKLMNOPQRSTUVWXYZ abcdefghijklmnopqrstuvwxyz

14/14

The main purpose of letters is the practical one of making thoughts visible. Ruskin says that all letters are frightful things and to be endured onl y on occasion, that is to say, in places where the sense of the inscription is of more importance th an external ornament. This is a sweeping state ment, from which we need not suffer unduly; ye t it is doubtful whether there is art in individual letters. Letters in combination may be satisfyin g and in a well composed page even beautiful a s a whole, but art in letters consists rather in the art of arranging and composing them in a pleasi ng and appropriate manner. The main purpose
The main purpose of letters is the practical one o f making thoughts visible. Ruskin says that all let
The main purpose of letters is the practica l one of making thoughts visible. Ruskin sa

14/15

The main purpose of letters is the practical one of making thoughts visible. Ruskin says that all letters are frightful things and to be endured onl y on occasion, that is to say, in places where the sense of the inscription is of more importance th an external ornament. This is a sweeping state ment, from which we need not suffer unduly; ye t it is doubtful whether there is art in individual letters. Letters in combination may be satisfyin g and in a well composed page even beautiful a s a whole, but art in letters consists rather in the art of arranging and composing them in a pleasi
The main purpose of letters is the practical one o f making thoughts visible. Ruskin says that all let
The main purpose of letters is the practica l one of making thoughts visible. Ruskin sa

14/16

The main purpose of letters is the practical one of making thoughts visible. Ruskin says that all letters are frightful things and to be endured onl y on occasion, that is to say, in places where the sense of the inscription is of more importance th an external ornament. This is a sweeping state ment, from which we need not suffer unduly; ye t it is doubtful whether there is art in individual letters. Letters in combination may be satisfyin g and in a well composed page even beautiful a s a whole, but art in letters consists rather in the art of arranging and composing them in a pleasi ng and appropriate manner. The main purpose
The main purpose of letters is the practical one o f making thoughts visible. Ruskin says that all let
The main purpose of letters is the practica l one of making thoughts visible. Ruskin sa

14/17

The main purpose of letters is the practical one of making thoughts visible. Ruskin says that all letters are frightful things and to be endured onl y on occasion, that is to say, in places where the sense of the inscription is of more importance th an external ornament. This is a sweeping state ment, from which we need not suffer unduly; ye t it is doubtful whether there is art in individual letters. Letters in combination may be satisfyin g and in a well composed page even beautiful a s a whole, but art in letters consists rather in the art of arranging and composing them in a pleasi
The main purpose of letters is the practical one o f making thoughts visible. Ruskin says that all let
The main purpose of letters is the practica l one of making thoughts visible. Ruskin sa

ITC BOOKMAN 6 & 7 POINT SET NORMAL

LIGHT, ITALIC, DEMI, DEMI ITALIC

ABCDEFGHIJKLMNOPQRSTUVWXYZ 1234567890 abcdefghijklmnopqrstuvwxyz

ABCDEFGHIJKLMNOPQRSTUVWXYZ 1234567890 abcdefghijklmnopqrstuvwxyz

ABCDEFGHIJKLMNOPQRSTUVWXYZ 1234567890 abcdefghijklmnopqrstuvwxyz

ABCDEFGHIJKLMNOPQRSTUVWXYZ 1234567890 abcdefghijklmnopqrstuvwxyz

6/6

The main purpose of letters is the practical one of making thoughts visible. Ruskin sa ys that all letters are frightful things and to be endured only on occasion, that is to say, in places where the sense of the inscription is of more importance than external orna ment. This is a sweeping statement, from which we need not suffer unduly; yet it is do ubtful whether there is art in individual letters. Letters in combination may be satisfyi ng and in a well composed page even beautiful as a whole, but art in letters consists ra ther in the art of arranging and composing them in a pleasing and appropriate manner. The main purpose of letters is the practical one of making thoughts visible. Ruskin s ays that all letters are frightful things and to be endured only on occasion, that is to say, in places where the sense of the inscription is of more importance than external orna ment. This is a sweeping statement, from which we need not suffer unduly; yet it is do ubtful whether there is art in individual letters. Letters in combination may be satisfyi ng and in a well composed page even beautiful as a whole, but art in letters consists ra
The main purpose of letters is the practical one of making thoughts visible. Ruskin s ays that all letters are frightful things and to be endured only on occasion, that is to s
The main purpose of letters is the practical one of making thoughts visible. Ruskin says that all letters are frightful things and to be endured only on occasion, that is to

6/7

The main purpose of letters is the practical one of making thoughts visible. Ruskin sa ys that all letters are frightful things and to be endured only on occasion, that is to say, in places where the sense of the inscription is of more importance than external orna ment. This is a sweeping statement, from which we need not suffer unduly; yet it is do ubtful whether there is art in individual letters. Letters in combination may be satisfyi ng and in a well composed page even beautiful as a whole, but art in letters consists ra ther in the art of arranging and composing them in a pleasing and appropriate manner. The main purpose of letters is the practical one of making thoughts visible. Ruskin s ays that all letters are frightful things and to be endured only on occasion, that is to say, in places where the sense of the inscription is of more importance than external orna ment. This is a sweeping statement, from which we need not suffer unduly; yet it is do
The main purpose of letters is the practical one of making thoughts visible. Ruskin s ays that all letters are frightful things and to be endured only on occasion, that is to s
The main purpose of letters is the practical one of making thoughts visible. Ruskin says that all letters are frightful things and to be endured only on occasion, that is to

6/8

The main purpose of letters is the practical one of making thoughts visible. Ruskin sa ys that all letters are frightful things and to be endured only on occasion, that is to say, in places where the sense of the inscription is of more importance than external orna ment. This is a sweeping statement, from which we need not suffer unduly; yet it is do ubtful whether there is art in individual letters. Letters in combination may be satisfyi ng and in a well composed page even beautiful as a whole, but art in letters consists ra ther in the art of arranging and composing them in a pleasing and appropriate manner. The main purpose of letters is the practical one of making thoughts visible. Ruskin s ays that all letters are frightful things and to be endured only on occasion, that is to say,
The main purpose of letters is the practical one of making thoughts visible. Ruskin s ays that all letters are frightful things and to be endured only on occasion, that is to s
The main purpose of letters is the practical one of making thoughts visible. Ruskin says that all letters are frightful things and to be endured only on occasion, that is to

6/9

The main purpose of letters is the practical one of making thoughts visible. Ruskin sa ys that all letters are frightful things and to be endured only on occasion, that is to say, in places where the sense of the inscription is of more importance than external orna ment. This is a sweeping statement, from which we need not suffer unduly; yet it is do ubtful whether there is art in individual letters. Letters in combination may be satisfyi ng and in a well composed page even beautiful as a whole, but art in letters consists ra ther in the art of arranging and composing them in a pleasing and appropriate manner. The main purpose of letters is the practical one of making thoughts visible. Ruskin s
The main purpose of letters is the practical one of making thoughts visible. Ruskin s ays that all letters are frightful things and to be endured only on occasion, that is to s
The main purpose of letters is the practical one of making thoughts visible. Ruskin says that all letters are frightful things and to be endured only on occasion, that is to

---

ABCDEFGHIJKLMNOPQRSTUVWXYZ 1234567890 abcdefghijklmnopqrstuvwxyz

ABCDEFGHIJKLMNOPQRSTUVWXYZ 1234567890 abcdefghijklmnopqrstuvwxyz

ABCDEFGHIJKLMNOPQRSTUVWXYZ 1234567890 abcdefghijklmnopqrstuvwxyz

ABCDEFGHIJKLMNOPQRSTUVWXYZ 1234567890 abcdefghijklmnopqrstuvwxyz

7/7

The main purpose of letters is the practical one of making thoughts visibl e. Ruskin says that all letters are frightful things and to be endured only o n occasion, that is to say, in places where the sense of the inscription is of more importance than external ornament. This is a sweeping statement, f rom which we need not suffer unduly; yet it is doubtful whether there is ar t in individual letters. Letters in combination may be satisfying and in a w ell composed page even beautiful as a whole, but art in letters consists rat her in the art of arranging and composing them in a pleasing and appropr iate manner. The main purpose of letters is the practical one of making th oughts visible. Ruskin says that all letters are frightful things and to be en dured only on occasion, that is to say, in places where the sense of the insc
The main purpose of letters is the practical one of making thoughts visib le. Ruskin says that all letters are frightful things and to be endured onl
The main purpose of letters is the practical one of making thoughts visi ble. Ruskin says that all letters are frightful things and to be endured on

7/8

The main purpose of letters is the practical one of making thoughts visibl e. Ruskin says that all letters are frightful things and to be endured only o n occasion, that is to say, in places where the sense of the inscription is of more importance than external ornament. This is a sweeping statement, f rom which we need not suffer unduly; yet it is doubtful whether there is ar t in individual letters. Letters in combination may be satisfying and in a w ell composed page even beautiful as a whole, but art in letters consists rat her in the art of arranging and composing them in a pleasing and appropr iate manner. The main purpose of letters is the practical one of making th oughts visible. Ruskin says that all letters are frightful things and to be en
The main purpose of letters is the practical one of making thoughts visib le. Ruskin says that all letters are frightful things and to be endured onl
The main purpose of letters is the practical one of making thoughts visi ble. Ruskin says that all letters are frightful things and to be endured on

7/9

The main purpose of letters is the practical one of making thoughts visibl e. Ruskin says that all letters are frightful things and to be endured only o n occasion, that is to say, in places where the sense of the inscription is of more importance than external ornament. This is a sweeping statement, f rom which we need not suffer unduly; yet it is doubtful whether there is ar t in individual letters. Letters in combination may be satisfying and in a w ell composed page even beautiful as a whole, but art in letters consists rat her in the art of arranging and composing them in a pleasing and appropr iate manner. The main purpose of letters is the practical one of making th oughts visible. Ruskin says that all letters are frightful things and to be en
The main purpose of letters is the practical one of making thoughts visib le. Ruskin says that all letters are frightful things and to be endured onl
The main purpose of letters is the practical one of making thoughts visi ble. Ruskin says that all letters are frightful things and to be endured on

7/10

The main purpose of letters is the practical one of making thoughts visibl e. Ruskin says that all letters are frightful things and to be endured only o n occasion, that is to say, in places where the sense of the inscription is of more importance than external ornament. This is a sweeping statement, f rom which we need not suffer unduly; yet it is doubtful whether there is ar t in individual letters. Letters in combination may be satisfying and in a w ell composed page even beautiful as a whole, but art in letters consists rat her in the art of arranging and composing them in a pleasing and appropr iate manner. The main purpose of letters is the practical one of making th
The main purpose of letters is the practical one of making thoughts visib le. Ruskin says that all letters are frightful things and to be endured onl
The main purpose of letters is the practical one of making thoughts visi ble. Ruskin says that all letters are frightful things and to be endured on

ITC BOOKMAN 8 & 9 POINT SET NORMAL

LIGHT, ITALIC, DEMI, DEMI ITALIC

ABCDEFGHIJKLMNOPQRSTUVWXYZ 1234567890 abcdefghijklmnopqrstuvwxyz

ABCDEFGHIJKLMNOPQRSTUVWXYZ 1234567890 abcdefghijklmnopqrstuvwxyz

ABCDEFGHIJKLMNOPQRSTUVWXYZ 1234567890 abcdefghijklmnopqrstuvwxyz

ABCDEFGHIJKLMNOPQRSTUVWXYZ 1234567890 abcdefghijklmnopqrstuvwxyz

8/8

The main purpose of letters is the practical one of making thoug hts visible. Ruskin says that all letters are frightful things and to be endured only on occasion, that is to say, in places where the se nse of the inscription is of more importance than external orna ment. This is a sweeping statement, from which we need not suff er unduly; yet it is doubtful whether there is art in individual let ters. Letters in combination may be satisfying and in a well comp osed page even beautiful as a whole, but art in letters consists rat her in the art of arranging and composing them in a pleasing an
The main purpose of letters is the practical one of making thoug hts visible. Ruskin says that all letters are frightful things and t
The main purpose of letters is the practical one of making thou ghts visible. Ruskin says that all letters are frightful things and

8/9

The main purpose of letters is the practical one of making thoug hts visible. Ruskin says that all letters are frightful things and to be endured only on occasion, that is to say, in places where the se nse of the inscription is of more importance than external orna ment. This is a sweeping statement, from which we need not suff er unduly; yet it is doubtful whether there is art in individual let ters. Letters in combination may be satisfying and in a well comp osed page even beautiful as a whole, but art in letters consists rat
The main purpose of letters is the practical one of making thoug hts visible. Ruskin says that all letters are frightful things and t
The main purpose of letters is the practical one of making thou ghts visible. Ruskin says that all letters are frightful things and

8/10

The main purpose of letters is the practical one of making thoug hts visible. Ruskin says that all letters are frightful things and to be endured only on occasion, that is to say, in places where the se nse of the inscription is of more importance than external orna ment. This is a sweeping statement, from which we need not suff er unduly; yet it is doubtful whether there is art in individual let ters. Letters in combination may be satisfying and in a well comp
The main purpose of letters is the practical one of making thoug hts visible. Ruskin says that all letters are frightful things and t
The main purpose of letters is the practical one of making thou ghts visible. Ruskin says that all letters are frightful things and

8/11

The main purpose of letters is the practical one of making thoug hts visible. Ruskin says that all letters are frightful things and to be endured only on occasion, that is to say, in places where the se nse of the inscription is of more importance than external orna ment. This is a sweeping statement, from which we need not suff er unduly; yet it is doubtful whether there is art in individual let ters. Letters in combination may be satisfying and in a well comp
The main purpose of letters is the practical one of making thoug hts visible. Ruskin says that all letters are frightful things and t
The main purpose of letters is the practical one of making thou ghts visible. Ruskin says that all letters are frightful things and

---

ABCDEFGHIJKLMNOPQRSTUVWXYZ 1234567890 abcdefghijklmnopqrstuvxyz

ABCDEFGHIJKLMNOPQRSTUVWXYZ 1234567890 abcdefghijklmnopqrstuvwxyz

ABCDEFGHIJKLMNOPQRSTUVWXYZ 1234567890 abcdefghijklmnopqrstuvwxyz

ABCDEFGHIJKLMNOPQRSTUVWXYZ 1234567890 abcdefghijklmnopqrstuvwxyz

9/9

The main purpose of letters is the practical one of making thoughts visible. Ruskin says that all letters are frightful things and to be endured only on occasion, that is to say, i n places where the sense of the inscription is of more imp ortance than external ornament. This is a sweeping state ment, from which we need not suffer unduly; yet it is dou btful whether there is art in individual letters. Letters in c ombination may be satisfying and in a well composed pag
The main purpose of letters is the practical one of makin g thoughts visible. Ruskin says that all letters are fright
The main purpose of letters is the practical one of maki ng thoughts visible. Ruskin says that all letters are frigh

9/10

The main purpose of letters is the practical one of making thoughts visible. Ruskin says that all letters are frightful things and to be endured only on occasion, that is to say, i n places where the sense of the inscription is of more imp ortance than external ornament. This is a sweeping state ment, from which we need not suffer unduly; yet it is dou btful whether there is art in individual letters. Letters in c
The main purpose of letters is the practical one of makin g thoughts visible. Ruskin says that all letters are fright
The main purpose of letters is the practical one of maki ng thoughts visible. Ruskin says that all letters are frigh

9/11

The main purpose of letters is the practical one of making thoughts visible. Ruskin says that all letters are frightful things and to be endured only on occasion, that is to say, i n places where the sense of the inscription is of more imp ortance than external ornament. This is a sweeping state ment, from which we need not suffer unduly; yet it is dou btful whether there is art in individual letters. Letters in c
The main purpose of letters is the practical one of makin g thoughts visible. Ruskin says that all letters are fright
The main purpose of letters is the practical one of maki ng thoughts visible. Ruskin says that all letters are frigh

9/12

The main purpose of letters is the practical one of making thoughts visible. Ruskin says that all letters are frightful things and to be endured only on occasion, that is to say, i n places where the sense of the inscription is of more imp ortance than external ornament. This is a sweeping state ment, from which we need not suffer unduly; yet it is dou btful whether there is art in individual letters. Letters in c
The main purpose of letters is the practical one of makin g thoughts visible. Ruskin says that all letters are fright
The main purpose of letters is the practical one of maki ng thoughts visible. Ruskin says that all letters are frigh

ITC BOOKMAN 10 POINT SET MINUS ½ UNIT

LIGHT, ITALIC, DEMI, DEMI ITALIC

abcdefghijklmnopqrstuvwxyz – 1 UNIT
abcdefghijklmnopqrstuvwxyz – ½ UNIT
abcdefghijklmnopqrstuvwxyz NORMAL

ABCDEFGHIJKLMNOPQRSTUVWXYZ 1234567890 abcdefghijklmnopqrstuvwxyz
ABCDEFGHIJKLMNOPQRSTUVWXYZ 1234567890 abcdefghijklmnopqrstuvwxyz
ABCDEFGHIJKLMNOPQRSTUVWXYZ 1234567890 abcdefghijklmnopqrstuvwxyz
ABCDEFGHIJKLMNOPQRSTUVWXYZ 1234567890 abcdefghijklmnopqrstuvwxyz

10/10

The main purpose of letters is the practical one of ma
king thoughts visible. Ruskin says that all letters are f
rightful things and to be endured only on occasion, th
at is to say, in places where the sense of the inscriptio
n is of more importance than external ornament. Th
is is a sweeping statement, from which we need not su
ffer unduly; yet it is doubtful whether there is art in in
dividual letters. Letters in combination may be satisfy
ing and in a well composed page even beautiful as a w
hole, but art in letters consists rather in the art of arra
nging and composing them in a pleasing and appropr
iate manner. The main purpose of letters is the practi
cal one of making thoughts visible. Ruskin says that a
ll letters are frightful things and to be endured only on
occasion, that is to say, in places where the sense of th
e inscription is of more importance than external orn
ament. This is a sweeping statement, from which we
need not suffer unduly; yet it is doubtful whether ther
e is art in individual letters. Letters in combination m
ay be satisfying and in a well composed page even bea
utiful as a whole, but art in letters consists rather in t
he art of arranging and composing them in a pleasing
The main purpose of letters is the practical one of ma
king thoughts visible. Ruskin says that all letters are
The main purpose of letters is the practical one of m
aking thoughts visible. Ruskin says that all letters a

10/11

The main purpose of letters is the practical one of ma
king thoughts visible. Ruskin says that all letters are f
rightful things and to be endured only on occasion, th
at is to say, in places where the sense of the inscriptio
n is of more importance than external ornament. Th
is is a sweeping statement, from which we need not su
ffer unduly; yet it is doubtful whether there is art in in
dividual letters. Letters in combination may be satisfy
ing and in a well composed page even beautiful as a w
hole, but art in letters consists rather in the art of arra
nging and composing them in a pleasing and appropr
iate manner. The main purpose of letters is the practi
cal one of making thoughts visible. Ruskin says that a
ll letters are frightful things and to be endured only on
occasion, that is to say, in places where the sense of th
e inscription is of more importance than external orn
ament. This is a sweeping statement, from which we
need not suffer unduly; yet it is doubtful whether ther
e is art in individual letters. Letters in combination m
ay be satisfying and in a well composed page even bea
The main purpose of letters is the practical one of ma
king thoughts visible. Ruskin says that all letters are
The main purpose of letters is the practical one of m
aking thoughts visible. Ruskin says that all letters a

10/12

The main purpose of letters is the practical one of ma
king thoughts visible. Ruskin says that all letters are f
rightful things and to be endured only on occasion, th
at is to say, in places where the sense of the inscriptio
n is of more importance than external ornament. Th
is is a sweeping statement, from which we need not su
ffer unduly; yet it is doubtful whether there is art in in
dividual letters. Letters in combination may be satisfy
ing and in a well composed page even beautiful as a w
hole, but art in letters consists rather in the art of arra
nging and composing them in a pleasing and appropr
iate manner. The main purpose of letters is the practi
cal one of making thoughts visible. Ruskin says that a
ll letters are frightful things and to be endured only on
occasion, that is to say, in places where the sense of th
e inscription is of more importance than external orn
ament. This is a sweeping statement, from which we
need not suffer unduly; yet it is doubtful whether ther
The main purpose of letters is the practical one of ma
king thoughts visible. Ruskin says that all letters are
The main purpose of letters is the practical one of m
aking thoughts visible. Ruskin says that all letters a

10/13

The main purpose of letters is the practical one of ma
king thoughts visible. Ruskin says that all letters are f
rightful things and to be endured only on occasion, th
at is to say, in places where the sense of the inscriptio
n is of more importance than external ornament. Th
is is a sweeping statement, from which we need not su
ffer unduly; yet it is doubtful whether there is art in in
dividual letters. Letters in combination may be satisfy
ing and in a well composed page even beautiful as a w
hole, but art in letters consists rather in the art of arra
nging and composing them in a pleasing and appropr
iate manner. The main purpose of letters is the practi
cal one of making thoughts visible. Ruskin says that a
ll letters are frightful things and to be endured only on
occasion, that is to say, in places where the sense of th
e inscription is of more importance than external orn
ament. This is a sweeping statement, from which we
The main purpose of letters is the practical one of ma
king thoughts visible. Ruskin says that all letters are
The main purpose of letters is the practical one of m
aking thoughts visible. Ruskin says that all letters a

ITC BOOKMAN 11 POINT SET MINUS ½ UNIT

LIGHT, ITALIC, DEMI, DEMI ITALIC

abcdefghijklmnopqrstuvwxyz – 1 UNIT
abcdefghijklmnopqrstuvwxyz – ½ UNIT
abcdefghijklmnopqrstuvwxyz NORMAL

ABCDEFGHIJKLMNOPQRSTUVWXYZ 1234567890 abcdefghijklmnopqrstuvwxyz
ABCDEFGHIJKLMNOPQRSTUVWXYZ 1234567890 abcdefghijklmnopqrstuvwxyz
ABCDEFGHIJKLMNOPQRSTUVWXYZ 1234567890 abcdefghijklmnopqrstuvwxyz
ABCDEFGHIJKLMNOPQRSTUVWXYZ 1234567890 abcdefghijklmnopqrstuvwxyz

11/11

The main purpose of letters is the practical one o f making thoughts visible. Ruskin says that all le tters are frightful things and to be endured only on occasion, that is to say, in places where the se nse of the inscription is of more importance tha n external ornament. This is a sweeping stateme nt, from which we need not suffer unduly; yet it i s doubtful whether there is art in individual lette rs. Letters in combination may be satisfying and in a well composed page even beautiful as a whol e, but art in letters consists rather in the art of ar ranging and composing them in a pleasing and a ppropriate manner. The main purpose of letters is the practical one of making thoughts visible. R uskin says that all letters are frightful things and to be endured only on occasion, that is to say, in places where the sense of the inscription is of mo re importance than external ornament. This is a sweeping statement, from which we need not suf
The main purpose of letters is the practical one of making thoughts visible. Ruskin says that al
The main purpose of letters is the practical one of making thoughts visible. Ruskin says that al

11/12

The main purpose of letters is the practical one o f making thoughts visible. Ruskin says that all le tters are frightful things and to be endured only on occasion, that is to say, in places where the se nse of the inscription is of more importance tha n external ornament. This is a sweeping stateme nt, from which we need not suffer unduly; yet it i s doubtful whether there is art in individual lette rs. Letters in combination may be satisfying and in a well composed page even beautiful as a whol e, but art in letters consists rather in the art of ar ranging and composing them in a pleasing and a ppropriate manner. The main purpose of letters is the practical one of making thoughts visible. R uskin says that all letters are frightful things and to be endured only on occasion, that is to say, in places where the sense of the inscription is of mo re importance than external ornament. This is a
The main purpose of letters is the practical one of making thoughts visible. Ruskin says that al
The main purpose of letters is the practical one of making thoughts visible. Ruskin says that al

11/13

The main purpose of letters is the practical one o f making thoughts visible. Ruskin says that all le tters are frightful things and to be endured only on occasion, that is to say, in places where the se nse of the inscription is of more importance tha n external ornament. This is a sweeping stateme nt, from which we need not suffer unduly; yet it i s doubtful whether there is art in individual lette rs. Letters in combination may be satisfying and in a well composed page even beautiful as a whol e, but art in letters consists rather in the art of ar ranging and composing them in a pleasing and a ppropriate manner. The main purpose of letters is the practical one of making thoughts visible. R uskin says that all letters are frightful things and to be endured only on occasion, that is to say, in places where the sense of the inscription is of mo
The main purpose of letters is the practical one of making thoughts visible. Ruskin says that al
The main purpose of letters is the practical one of making thoughts visible. Ruskin says that al

11/14

The main purpose of letters is the practical one o f making thoughts visible. Ruskin says that all le tters are frightful things and to be endured only on occasion, that is to say, in places where the se nse of the inscription is of more importance tha n external ornament. This is a sweeping stateme nt, from which we need not suffer unduly; yet it i s doubtful whether there is art in individual lette rs. Letters in combination may be satisfying and in a well composed page even beautiful as a whol e, but art in letters consists rather in the art of ar ranging and composing them in a pleasing and a ppropriate manner. The main purpose of letters is the practical one of making thoughts visible. R uskin says that all letters are frightful things and to be endured only on occasion, that is to say, in
The main purpose of letters is the practical one of making thoughts visible. Ruskin says that al
The main purpose of letters is the practical one of making thoughts visible. Ruskin says that al

ITC BOOKMAN 12 POINT SET MINUS ½ UNIT

LIGHT, ITALIC, DEMI, DEMI BOLD ITALIC

abcdefghijklmnopqrstuvwxyz – 1 UNIT
abcdefghijklmnopqrstuvwxyz – ½ UNIT
abcdefghijklmnopqrstuvwxyz NORMAL

ABCDEFGHIJKLMNOPQRSTUVWXYZ 1234567890 abcdefghijklmnopqrstuvwxyz
ABCDEFGHIJKLMNOPQRSTUVWXYZ 1234567890 abcdefghijklmnopqrstuvwxyz
ABCDEFGHIJKLMNOPQRSTUVWXYZ 1234567890 abcdefghijklmnopqrstuvwxy
ABCDEFGHIJKLMNOPQRSTUVWXYZ 1234567890 abcdefghijklmnopqrstuvwx

12/12

The main purpose of letters is the practical o ne of making thoughts visible. Ruskin says t hat all letters are frightful things and to be en dured only on occasion, that is to say, in place s where the sense of the inscription is of more importance than external ornament. This is a sweeping statement, from which we need n ot suffer unduly; yet it is doubtful whether th ere is art in individual letters. Letters in comb ination may be satisfying and in a well compo sed page even beautiful as a whole, but art in l etters consists rather in the art of arranging and composing them in a pleasing and appro priate manner. The main purpose of letters is the practical one of making thoughts visible.
The main purpose of letters is the practical o ne of making thoughts visible. Ruskin says t
The main purpose of letters is the practical one of making thoughts visible. Ruskin say

12/13

The main purpose of letters is the practical o ne of making thoughts visible. Ruskin says t hat all letters are frightful things and to be en dured only on occasion, that is to say, in place s where the sense of the inscription is of more importance than external ornament. This is a sweeping statement, from which we need n ot suffer unduly; yet it is doubtful whether th ere is art in individual letters. Letters in comb ination may be satisfying and in a well compo sed page even beautiful as a whole, but art in l etters consists rather in the art of arranging and composing them in a pleasing and appro priate manner. The main purpose of letters is
The main purpose of letters is the practical o ne of making thoughts visible. Ruskin says t
The main purpose of letters is the practical one of making thoughts visible. Ruskin say

12/14

The main purpose of letters is the practical o ne of making thoughts visible. Ruskin says t hat all letters are frightful things and to be en dured only on occasion, that is to say, in place s where the sense of the inscription is of more importance than external ornament. This is a sweeping statement, from which we need n ot suffer unduly; yet it is doubtful whether th ere is art in individual letters. Letters in comb ination may be satisfying and in a well compo sed page even beautiful as a whole, but art in l etters consists rather in the art of arranging and composing them in a pleasing and appro priate manner. The main purpose of letters is the practical one of making thoughts visible.
The main purpose of letters is the practical o ne of making thoughts visible. Ruskin says t
The main purpose of letters is the practical one of making thoughts visible. Ruskin say

12/15

The main purpose of letters is the practical o ne of making thoughts visible. Ruskin says t hat all letters are frightful things and to be en dured only on occasion, that is to say, in place s where the sense of the inscription is of more importance than external ornament. This is a sweeping statement, from which we need n ot suffer unduly; yet it is doubtful whether th ere is art in individual letters. Letters in comb ination may be satisfying and in a well compo sed page even beautiful as a whole, but art in l etters consists rather in the art of arranging and composing them in a pleasing and appro priate manner. The main purpose of letters is
The main purpose of letters is the practical o ne of making thoughts visible. Ruskin says t
The main purpose of letters is the practical one of making thoughts visible. Ruskin say

ITC BOOKMAN 14 POINT SET MINUS ½ UNIT

LIGHT, ITALIC, DEMI, DEMI ITALIC

abcdefghijklmnopqrstuvwxyz – 1 UNIT
abcdefghijklmnopqrstuvwxyz – ½ UNIT
abcdefghijklmnopqrstuvwxyz NORMAL

ABCDEFGHIJKLMNOPQRSTUVWXYZ abcdefghijklmnopqrstuvwxyz
ABCDEFGHIJKLMNOPQRSTUVWXYZ abcdefghijklmnopqrstuvwxyz
ABCDEFGHIJKLMNOPQRSTUVWXYZ abcdefghijklmnopqrstuvwxyz
ABCDEFGHIJKLMNOPQRSTUVWXYZ abcdefghijklmnopqrstuvwxyz

14/14

The main purpose of letters is the prac tical one of making thoughts visible. R uskin says that all letters are frightful t hings and to be endured only on occas ion, that is to say, in places where the s ense of the inscription is of more impo rtance than external ornament. This i s a sweeping statement, from which w e need not suffer unduly; yet it is doub tful whether there is art in individual l etters. Letters in combination may be satisfying and in a well composed page even beautiful as a whole, but art in let
The main purpose of letters is the pra ctical one of making thoughts visible.
The main purpose of letters is the pra ctical one of making thoughts visible.

14/15

The main purpose of letters is the prac tical one of making thoughts visible. R uskin says that all letters are frightful t hings and to be endured only on occas ion, that is to say, in places where the s ense of the inscription is of more impo rtance than external ornament. This i s a sweeping statement, from which w e need not suffer unduly; yet it is doub tful whether there is art in individual l etters. Letters in combination may be satisfying and in a well composed page
The main purpose of letters is the pra ctical one of making thoughts visible.
The main purpose of letters is the pra ctical one of making thoughts visible.

14/16

The main purpose of letters is the prac tical one of making thoughts visible. R uskin says that all letters are frightful t hings and to be endured only on occas ion, that is to say, in places where the s ense of the inscription is of more impo rtance than external ornament. This i s a sweeping statement, from which w e need not suffer unduly; yet it is doub tful whether there is art in individual l etters. Letters in combination may be satisfying and in a well composed page even beautiful as a whole, but art in let
The main purpose of letters is the pra ctical one of making thoughts visible.
The main purpose of letters is the pra ctical one of making thoughts visible.

14/17

The main purpose of letters is the prac tical one of making thoughts visible. R uskin says that all letters are frightful t hings and to be endured only on occas ion, that is to say, in places where the s ense of the inscription is of more impo rtance than external ornament. This i s a sweeping statement, from which w e need not suffer unduly; yet it is doub tful whether there is art in individual l etters. Letters in combination may be satisfying and in a well composed page
The main purpose of letters is the pra ctical one of making thoughts visible.
The main purpose of letters is the pra ctical one of making thoughts visible.

ITC BOOKMAN 6 & 7 POINT SET NORMAL

MEDIUM, ITALIC, BOLD, BOLD ITALIC

ABCDEFGHIJKLMNOPQRSTUVWXYZ 1234567890 abcdefghijklmnopqrstuvwxyz

ABCDEFGHIJKLMNOPQRSTUVWXYZ 1234567890 abcdefghijklmnopqrstuvwxyz

ABCDEFGHIJKLMNOPQRSTUVWXYZ 1234567890 abcdefghijklmnopqrstuvwxyz

ABCDEFGHIJKLMNOPQRSTUVWXYZ 1234567890 abcdefghijklmnopqrstuvwxyz

6/6

The main purpose of letters is the practical one of making thoughts visible. Ruskin
says that all letters are frightful things and to be endured only on occasion, that is t
o say, in places where the sense of the inscription is of more importance than exter
nal ornament. This is a sweeping statement, from which we need not suffer unduly;
yet it is doubtful whether there is art in individual letters. Letters in combination m
ay be satisfying and in a well composed page even beautiful as a whole, but art in lett
ers consists rather in the art of arranging and composing them in a pleasing and ap
propriate manner. The main purpose of letters is the practical one of making thoug
hts visible. Ruskin says that all letters are frightful things and to be endured only o
n occasion, that is to say, in places where the sense of the inscription is of more imp
ortance than external ornament. This is a sweeping statement, from which we need
not suffer unduly; yet it is doubtful whether there is art in individual letters. Letters
in combination may be satisfying and in a well composed page even beautiful as a w
The main purpose of letters is the practical one of making thoughts visible. Ruski
n says that all letters are frightful things and to be endured only on occasion, that
The main purpose of letters is the practical one of making thoughts visible. Rus
kin says that all letters are frightful things and to be endured only on occasion, t

6/7

The main purpose of letters is the practical one of making thoughts visible. Ruskin
says that all letters are frightful things and to be endured only on occasion, that is t
o say, in places where the sense of the inscription is of more importance than exter
nal ornament. This is a sweeping statement, from which we need not suffer unduly;
yet it is doubtful whether there is art in individual letters. Letters in combination m
ay be satisfying and in a well composed page even beautiful as a whole, but art in lett
ers consists rather in the art of arranging and composing them in a pleasing and ap
propriate manner. The main purpose of letters is the practical one of making thoug
hts visible. Ruskin says that all letters are frightful things and to be endured only o
n occasion, that is to say, in places where the sense of the inscription is of more imp
ortance than external ornament. This is a sweeping statement, from which we need
The main purpose of letters is the practical one of making thoughts visible. Ruski
n says that all letters are frightful things and to be endured only on occasion, that
The main purpose of letters is the practical one of making thoughts visible. Rus
kin says that all letters are frightful things and to be endured only on occasion, t

6/8

The main purpose of letters is the practical one of making thoughts visible. Ruskin
says that all letters are frightful things and to be endured only on occasion, that is t
o say, in places where the sense of the inscription is of more importance than exter
nal ornament. This is a sweeping statement, from which we need not suffer unduly;
yet it is doubtful whether there is art in individual letters. Letters in combination m
ay be satisfying and in a well composed page even beautiful as a whole, but art in lett
ers consists rather in the art of arranging and composing them in a pleasing and ap
propriate manner. The main purpose of letters is the practical one of making thoug
hts visible. Ruskin says that all letters are frightful things and to be endured only o
The main purpose of letters is the practical one of making thoughts visible. Ruski
n says that all letters are frightful things and to be endured only on occasion, that
The main purpose of letters is the practical one of making thoughts visible. Rus
kin says that all letters are frightful things and to be endured only on occasion, t

6/9

The main purpose of letters is the practical one of making thoughts visible. Ruskin
says that all letters are frightful things and to be endured only on occasion, that is t
o say, in places where the sense of the inscription is of more importance than exter
nal ornament. This is a sweeping statement, from which we need not suffer unduly;
yet it is doubtful whether there is art in individual letters. Letters in combination m
ay be satisfying and in a well composed page even beautiful as a whole, but art in lett
ers consists rather in the art of arranging and composing them in a pleasing and ap
propriate manner. The main purpose of letters is the practical one of making thoug
The main purpose of letters is the practical one of making thoughts visible. Ruski
n says that all letters are frightful things and to be endured only on occasion, that
The main purpose of letters is the practical one of making thoughts visible. Rus
kin says that all letters are frightful things and to be endured only on occasion, t

---

ABCDEFGHIJKLMNOPQRSTUVWXYZ 1234567890 abcdefghijklmnopqrstuvwxyz

ABCDEFGHIJKLMNOPQRSTUVWXYZ 1234567890 abcdefghijklmnopqrstuvwxyz

ABCDEFGHIJKLMNOPQRSTUVWXYZ 1234567890 abcdefghijklmnopqrstuvwxyz

ABCDEFGHIJKLMNOPQRSTUVWXYZ 1234567890 abcdefghijklmnopqrstuvwxyz

7/7

The main purpose of letters is the practical one of making thoughts visi
ble. Ruskin says that all letters are frightful things and to be endured on
ly on occasion, that is to say, in places where the sense of the inscriptio
n is of more importance than external ornament. This is a sweeping stat
ement, from which we need not suffer unduly; yet it is doubtful whether
there is art in individual letters. Letters in combination may be satisfyi
ng and in a well composed page even beautiful as a whole, but art in lette
rs consists rather in the art of arranging and composing them in a pleas
ing and appropriate manner. The main purpose of letters is the practica
l one of making thoughts visible. Ruskin says that all letters are frightfu
l things and to be endured only on occasion, that is to say, in places whe
The main purpose of letters is the practical one of making thoughts vi
sible. Ruskin says that all letters are frightful things and to be endure
The main purpose of letters is the practical one of making thoughts
visible. Ruskin says that all letters are frightful things and to be end

7/8

The main purpose of letters is the practical one of making thoughts visi
ble. Ruskin says that all letters are frightful things and to be endured on
ly on occasion, that is to say, in places where the sense of the inscriptio
n is of more importance than external ornament. This is a sweeping stat
ement, from which we need not suffer unduly; yet it is doubtful whether
there is art in individual letters. Letters in combination may be satisfyi
ng and in a well composed page even beautiful as a whole, but art in lette
rs consists rather in the art of arranging and composing them in a pleas
ing and appropriate manner. The main purpose of letters is the practica
l one of making thoughts visible. Ruskin says that all letters are frightfu
The main purpose of letters is the practical one of making thoughts vi
sible. Ruskin says that all letters are frightful things and to be endure
The main purpose of letters is the practical one of making thoughts
visible. Ruskin says that all letters are frightful things and to be end

7/9

The main purpose of letters is the practical one of making thoughts visi
ble. Ruskin says that all letters are frightful things and to be endured on
ly on occasion, that is to say, in places where the sense of the inscriptio
n is of more importance than external ornament. This is a sweeping stat
ement, from which we need not suffer unduly; yet it is doubtful whether
there is art in individual letters. Letters in combination may be satisfyi
ng and in a well composed page even beautiful as a whole, but art in lette
rs consists rather in the art of arranging and composing them in a pleas
ing and appropriate manner. The main purpose of letters is the practica
l one of making thoughts visible. Ruskin says that all letters are frightfu
The main purpose of letters is the practical one of making thoughts vi
sible. Ruskin says that all letters are frightful things and to be endure
The main purpose of letters is the practical one of making thoughts
visible. Ruskin says that all letters are frightful things and to be end

7/10

The main purpose of letters is the practical one of making thoughts visi
ble. Ruskin says that all letters are frightful things and to be endured on
ly on occasion, that is to say, in places where the sense of the inscriptio
n is of more importance than external ornament. This is a sweeping stat
ement, from which we need not suffer unduly; yet it is doubtful whether
there is art in individual letters. Letters in combination may be satisfyi
ng and in a well composed page even beautiful as a whole, but art in lette
rs consists rather in the art of arranging and composing them in a pleas
ing and appropriate manner. The main purpose of letters is the practica
The main purpose of letters is the practical one of making thoughts vi
sible. Ruskin says that all letters are frightful things and to be endure
The main purpose of letters is the practical one of making thoughts
visible. Ruskin says that all letters are frightful things and to be end

ITC BOOKMAN 8 & 9 POINT SET NORMAL

MEDIUM, ITALIC, BOLD, BOLD ITALIC

ABCDEFGHIJKLMNOPQRSTUVWXYZ 1234567890 abcdefghijklmnopqrstuvwxyz

ABCDEFGHIJKLMNOPQRSTUVWXYZ 1234567890 abcdefghijklmnopqrstuvwxyz

ABCDEFGHIJKLMNOPQRSTUVWXYZ 1234567890 abcdefghijklmnopqrstuvwxyz

ABCDEFGHIJKLMNOPQRSTUVWXYZ 1234567890 abcdefghijklmnopqrstuvwxyz

8/8

The main purpose of letters is the practical one of making thou ghts visible. Ruskin says that all letters are frightful things an d to be endured only on occasion, that is to say, in places wher e the sense of the inscription is of more importance than exter nal ornament. This is a sweeping statement, from which we ne ed not suffer unduly; yet it is doubtful whether there is art in in dividual letters. Letters in combination may be satisfying and i n a well composed page even beautiful as a whole, but art in lett ers consists rather in the art of arranging and composing them
The main purpose of letters is the practical one of making tho ughts visible. Ruskin says that all letters are frightful things
The main purpose of letters is the practical one of making t houghts visible. Ruskin says that all letters are frightful thi

8/9

The main purpose of letters is the practical one of making thou ghts visible. Ruskin says that all letters are frightful things an d to be endured only on occasion, that is to say, in places wher e the sense of the inscription is of more importance than exter nal ornament. This is a sweeping statement, from which we ne ed not suffer unduly; yet it is doubtful whether there is art in in dividual letters. Letters in combination may be satisfying and i n a well composed page even beautiful as a whole, but art in lett
The main purpose of letters is the practical one of making tho ughts visible. Ruskin says that all letters are frightful things
The main purpose of letters is the practical one of making t houghts visible. Ruskin says that all letters are frightful thi

8/10

The main purpose of letters is the practical one of making thou ghts visible. Ruskin says that all letters are frightful things an d to be endured only on occasion, that is to say, in places wher e the sense of the inscription is of more importance than exter nal ornament. This is a sweeping statement, from which we ne ed not suffer unduly; yet it is doubtful whether there is art in in dividual letters. Letters in combination may be satisfying and i
The main purpose of letters is the practical one of making tho ughts visible. Ruskin says that all letters are frightful things
The main purpose of letters is the practical one of making t houghts visible. Ruskin says that all letters are frightful thi

8/11

The main purpose of letters is the practical one of making thou ghts visible. Ruskin says that all letters are frightful things an d to be endured only on occasion, that is to say, in places wher e the sense of the inscription is of more importance than exter nal ornament. This is a sweeping statement, from which we ne ed not suffer unduly; yet it is doubtful whether there is art in in dividual letters. Letters in combination may be satisfying and i
The main purpose of letters is the practical one of making tho ughts visible. Ruskin says that all letters are frightful things
The main purpose of letters is the practical one of making t houghts visible. Ruskin says that all letters are frightful thi

---

ABCDEFGHIJKLMNOPQRSTUVWXYZ 1234567890 abcdefghijklmnopqrstuvwxyz

ABCDEFGHIJKLMNOPQRSTUVWXYZ 1234567890 abcdefghijklmnopqrstuvwxyz

ABCDEFGHIJKLMNOPQRSTUVWXYZ 1234567890 abcdefghijklmnopqrstuvwxyz

ABCDEFGHIJKLMNOPQRSTUVWXYZ 1234567890 abcdefghijklmnopqrstuvwxyz

9/9

The main purpose of letters is the practical one of maki ng thoughts visible. Ruskin says that all letters are frig htful things and to be endured only on occasion, that is to say, in places where the sense of the inscription is of more importance than external ornament. This is a swe eping statement, from which we need not suffer unduly; yet it is doubtful whether there is art in individual letter s. Letters in combination may be satisfying and in a wel
The main purpose of letters is the practical one of mak ing thoughts visible. Ruskin says that all letters are fri
The main purpose of letters is the practical one of ma king thoughts visible. Ruskin says that all letters are

9/10

The main purpose of letters is the practical one of maki ng thoughts visible. Ruskin says that all letters are frig htful things and to be endured only on occasion, that is to say, in places where the sense of the inscription is of more importance than external ornament. This is a swe eping statement, from which we need not suffer unduly; yet it is doubtful whether there is art in individual letter
The main purpose of letters is the practical one of mak ing thoughts visible. Ruskin says that all letters are fri
The main purpose of letters is the practical one of ma king thoughts visible. Ruskin says that all letters are

9/11

The main purpose of letters is the practical one of maki ng thoughts visible. Ruskin says that all letters are frig htful things and to be endured only on occasion, that is to say, in places where the sense of the inscription is of more importance than external ornament. This is a swe eping statement, from which we need not suffer unduly; yet it is doubtful whether there is art in individual letter
The main purpose of letters is the practical one of mak ing thoughts visible. Ruskin says that all letters are fri
The main purpose of letters is the practical one of ma king thoughts visible. Ruskin says that all letters are

9/12

The main purpose of letters is the practical one of maki ng thoughts visible. Ruskin says that all letters are frig htful things and to be endured only on occasion, that is to say, in places where the sense of the inscription is of more importance than external ornament. This is a swe eping statement, from which we need not suffer unduly; yet it is doubtful whether there is art in individual letter
The main purpose of letters is the practical one of mak ing thoughts visible. Ruskin says that all letters are fri
The main purpose of letters is the practical one of ma king thoughts visible. Ruskin says that all letters are

ITC BOOKMAN 10 POINT SET MINUS ½ UNIT

MEDIUM, ITALIC, BOLD, BOLD ITALIC

abcdefghijklmnopqrstuvwxyz – 1 UNIT
abcdefghijklmnopqrstuvwxyz – ½ UNIT
abcdefghijklmnopqrstuvwxyz NORMAL

ABCDEFGHIJKLMNOPQRSTUVWXYZ 1234567890 abcdefghijklmnopqrstuvwxyz
ABCDEFGHIJKLMNOPQRSTUVWXYZ 1234567890 abcdefghijklmnopqrstuvwxyz
ABCDEFGHIJKLMNOPQRSTUVWXYZ 1234567890 abcdefghijklmnopqrstuvwxyz
ABCDEFGHIJKLMNOPQRSTUVWXYZ 1234567890 abcdefghijklmnopqrstuvwxyz

10/10

The main purpose of letters is the practical one of m aking thoughts visible. Ruskin says that all letters a re frightful things and to be endured only on occasi on, that is to say, in places where the sense of the in scription is of more importance than external orna ment. This is a sweeping statement, from which we need not suffer unduly; yet it is doubtful whether th ere is art in individual letters. Letters in combinatio n may be satisfying and in a well composed page eve n beautiful as a whole, but art in letters consists rat her in the art of arranging and composing them in a pleasing and appropriate manner. The main purpos e of letters is the practical one of making thoughts vi sible. Ruskin says that all letters are frightful things and to be endured only on occasion, that is to say, in places where the sense of the inscription is of more importance than external ornament. This is a sweep ing statement, from which we need not suffer undul y; yet it is doubtful whether there is art in individual letters. Letters in combination may be satisfying an d in a well composed page even beautiful as a whole, but art in letters consists rather in the art of arrangi

The main purpose of letters is the practical one of making thoughts visible. Ruskin says that all lette

The main purpose of letters is the practical one of making thoughts visible. Ruskin says that all let

10/11

The main purpose of letters is the practical one of m aking thoughts visible. Ruskin says that all letters a re frightful things and to be endured only on occasi on, that is to say, in places where the sense of the in scription is of more importance than external orna ment. This is a sweeping statement, from which we need not suffer unduly; yet it is doubtful whether th ere is art in individual letters. Letters in combinatio n may be satisfying and in a well composed page eve n beautiful as a whole, but art in letters consists rat her in the art of arranging and composing them in a pleasing and appropriate manner. The main purpos e of letters is the practical one of making thoughts vi sible. Ruskin says that all letters are frightful things and to be endured only on occasion, that is to say, in places where the sense of the inscription is of more importance than external ornament. This is a sweep ing statement, from which we need not suffer undul y; yet it is doubtful whether there is art in individual letters. Letters in combination may be satisfying an

The main purpose of letters is the practical one of making thoughts visible. Ruskin says that all lette

The main purpose of letters is the practical one of making thoughts visible. Ruskin says that all let

10/12

The main purpose of letters is the practical one of m aking thoughts visible. Ruskin says that all letters a re frightful things and to be endured only on occasi on, that is to say, in places where the sense of the in scription is of more importance than external orna ment. This is a sweeping statement, from which we need not suffer unduly; yet it is doubtful whether th ere is art in individual letters. Letters in combinatio n may be satisfying and in a well composed page eve n beautiful as a whole, but art in letters consists rat her in the art of arranging and composing them in a pleasing and appropriate manner. The main purpos e of letters is the practical one of making thoughts vi sible. Ruskin says that all letters are frightful things and to be endured only on occasion, that is to say, in places where the sense of the inscription is of more importance than external ornament. This is a sweep ing statement, from which we need not suffer undul

The main purpose of letters is the practical one of making thoughts visible. Ruskin says that all lette

The main purpose of letters is the practical one of making thoughts visible. Ruskin says that all let

10/13

The main purpose of letters is the practical one of m aking thoughts visible. Ruskin says that all letters a re frightful things and to be endured only on occasi on, that is to say, in places where the sense of the in scription is of more importance than external orna ment. This is a sweeping statement, from which we need not suffer unduly; yet it is doubtful whether th ere is art in individual letters. Letters in combinatio n may be satisfying and in a well composed page eve n beautiful as a whole, but art in letters consists rat her in the art of arranging and composing them in a pleasing and appropriate manner. The main purpos e of letters is the practical one of making thoughts vi sible. Ruskin says that all letters are frightful things and to be endured only on occasion, that is to say, in places where the sense of the inscription is of more importance than external ornament. This is a sweep

The main purpose of letters is the practical one of making thoughts visible. Ruskin says that all lette

The main purpose of letters is the practical one of making thoughts visible. Ruskin says that all let

ITC BOOKMAN 11 POINT SET MINUS ½ UNIT

MEDIUM, ITALIC, BOLD, BOLD ITALIC

abcdefghijklmnopqrstuvwxyz – 1 UNIT
abcdefghijklmnopqrstuvwxyz – ½ UNIT
abcdefghijklmnopqrstuvwxyz NORMAL

ABCDEFGHIJKLMNOPQRSTUVWXYZ 1234567890 abcdefghijklmnopqrstuvwxyz
ABCDEFGHIJKLMNOPQRSTUVWXYZ 1234567890 abcdefghijklmnopqrstuvwxyz
ABCDEFGHIJKLMNOPQRSTUVWXYZ 1234567890 abcdefghijklmnopqrstuvwxyz
ABCDEFGHIJKLMNOPQRSTUVWXYZ 1234567890 abcdefghijklmnopqrstuvwxyz

11/11

The main purpose of letters is the practical one of making thoughts visible. Ruskin says that al l letters are frightful things and to be endured o nly on occasion, that is to say, in places where t he sense of the inscription is of more importan ce than external ornament. This is a sweeping statement, from which we need not suffer und uly; yet it is doubtful whether there is art in indi vidual letters. Letters in combination may be s atisfying and in a well composed page even bea utiful as a whole, but art in letters consists rath er in the art of arranging and composing them i n a pleasing and appropriate manner. The main purpose of letters is the practical one of makin g thoughts visible. Ruskin says that all letters a re frightful things and to be endured only on oc casion, that is to say, in places where the sense of the inscription is of more importance than e xternal ornament. This is a sweeping statemen
The main purpose of letters is the practical on e of making thoughts visible. Ruskin says tha
The main purpose of letters is the practical o ne of making thoughts visible. Ruskin says t

11/12

The main purpose of letters is the practical one of making thoughts visible. Ruskin says that al l letters are frightful things and to be endured o nly on occasion, that is to say, in places where t he sense of the inscription is of more importan ce than external ornament. This is a sweeping statement, from which we need not suffer und uly; yet it is doubtful whether there is art in indi vidual letters. Letters in combination may be s atisfying and in a well composed page even bea utiful as a whole, but art in letters consists rath er in the art of arranging and composing them i n a pleasing and appropriate manner. The main purpose of letters is the practical one of makin g thoughts visible. Ruskin says that all letters a re frightful things and to be endured only on oc casion, that is to say, in places where the sense of the inscription is of more importance than e
The main purpose of letters is the practical on e of making thoughts visible. Ruskin says tha
The main purpose of letters is the practical o ne of making thoughts visible. Ruskin says t

11/13

The main purpose of letters is the practical one of making thoughts visible. Ruskin says that al l letters are frightful things and to be endured o nly on occasion, that is to say, in places where t he sense of the inscription is of more importan ce than external ornament. This is a sweeping statement, from which we need not suffer und uly; yet it is doubtful whether there is art in indi vidual letters. Letters in combination may be s atisfying and in a well composed page even bea utiful as a whole, but art in letters consists rath er in the art of arranging and composing them i n a pleasing and appropriate manner. The main purpose of letters is the practical one of makin g thoughts visible. Ruskin says that all letters a re frightful things and to be endured only on oc casion, that is to say, in places where the sense
The main purpose of letters is the practical on e of making thoughts visible. Ruskin says tha
The main purpose of letters is the practical o ne of making thoughts visible. Ruskin says t

11/14

The main purpose of letters is the practical one of making thoughts visible. Ruskin says that al l letters are frightful things and to be endured o nly on occasion, that is to say, in places where t he sense of the inscription is of more importan ce than external ornament. This is a sweeping statement, from which we need not suffer und uly; yet it is doubtful whether there is art in indi vidual letters. Letters in combination may be s atisfying and in a well composed page even bea utiful as a whole, but art in letters consists rath er in the art of arranging and composing them i n a pleasing and appropriate manner. The main purpose of letters is the practical one of makin g thoughts visible. Ruskin says that all letters a re frightful things and to be endured only on oc
The main purpose of letters is the practical on e of making thoughts visible. Ruskin says tha
The main purpose of letters is the practical o ne of making thoughts visible. Ruskin says t

ITC BOOKMAN 12 POINT SET MINUS ½ UNIT

MEDIUM, ITALIC, BOLD, BOLD ITALIC

abcdefghijklmnopqrstuvwxyz – 1 UNIT
abcdefghijklmnopqrstuvwxyz – ½ UNIT
abcdefghijklmnopqrstuvwxyz NORMAL

ABCDEFGHIJKLMNOPQRSTUVWXYZ 1234567890 abcdefghijklmnopqrstuvwxyz
ABCDEFGHIJKLMNOPQRSTUVWXYZ 1234567890 abcdefghijklmnopqrstuvwxyz
ABCDEFGHIJKLMNOPQRSTUVWXYZ 1234567890 abcdefghijklmnopqrstuv
ABCDEFGHIJKLMNOPQRSTUVWXYZ 1234567890 abcdefghijklmnopqrstu

12/12

The main purpose of letters is the practical one of making thoughts visible. Ruskin say s that all letters are frightful things and to b e endured only on occasion, that is to say, in places where the sense of the inscription is of more importance than external ornamen t. This is a sweeping statement, from which we need not suffer unduly; yet it is doubtful whether there is art in individual letters. Le tters in combination may be satisfying and i n a well composed page even beautiful as a whole, but art in letters consists rather in t he art of arranging and composing them in a pleasing and appropriate manner. The mai n purpose of letters is the practical one of m
The main purpose of letters is the practical one of making thoughts visible. Ruskin sa
The main purpose of letters is the practic al one of making thoughts visible. Ruskin

12/13

The main purpose of letters is the practical one of making thoughts visible. Ruskin say s that all letters are frightful things and to b e endured only on occasion, that is to say, in places where the sense of the inscription is of more importance than external ornamen t. This is a sweeping statement, from which we need not suffer unduly; yet it is doubtful whether there is art in individual letters. Le tters in combination may be satisfying and i n a well composed page even beautiful as a whole, but art in letters consists rather in t he art of arranging and composing them in a pleasing and appropriate manner. The mai
The main purpose of letters is the practical one of making thoughts visible. Ruskin sa
The main purpose of letters is the practic al one of making thoughts visible. Ruskin

12/14

The main purpose of letters is the practical one of making thoughts visible. Ruskin say s that all letters are frightful things and to b e endured only on occasion, that is to say, in places where the sense of the inscription is of more importance than external ornamen t. This is a sweeping statement, from which we need not suffer unduly; yet it is doubtful whether there is art in individual letters. Le tters in combination may be satisfying and i n a well composed page even beautiful as a whole, but art in letters consists rather in t he art of arranging and composing them in a pleasing and appropriate manner. The mai n purpose of letters is the practical one of m
The main purpose of letters is the practical one of making thoughts visible. Ruskin sa
The main purpose of letters is the practic al one of making thoughts visible. Ruskin

12/15

The main purpose of letters is the practical one of making thoughts visible. Ruskin say s that all letters are frightful things and to b e endured only on occasion, that is to say, in places where the sense of the inscription is of more importance than external ornamen t. This is a sweeping statement, from which we need not suffer unduly; yet it is doubtful whether there is art in individual letters. Le tters in combination may be satisfying and i n a well composed page even beautiful as a whole, but art in letters consists rather in t he art of arranging and composing them in a pleasing and appropriate manner. The mai
The main purpose of letters is the practical one of making thoughts visible. Ruskin sa
The main purpose of letters is the practic al one of making thoughts visible. Ruskin

ITC BOOKMAN 14 POINT SET MINUS ½ UNIT

MEDIUM, ITALIC, BOLD, BOLD ITALIC

abcdefghijklmnopqrstuvwxyz – 1 UNIT
abcdefghijklmnopqrstuvwxyz – ½ UNIT
abcdefghijklmnopqrstuvwxyz NORMAL

ABCDEFGHIJKLMNOPQRSTUVWXYZ abcdefghijklmnopqrstuvwxyz
ABCDEFGHIJKLMNOPQRSTUVWXYZ abcdefghijklmnopqrstuvwxyz
ABCDEFGHIJKLMNOPQRSTUVWXYZ abcdefghijklmnopqrstuvwxyz
ABCDEFGHIJKLMNOPQRSTUVWXYZ abcdefghijklmnopqrstuvwxy

14/14

The main purpose of letters is the pra ctical one of making thoughts visible. Ruskin says that all letters are fright ful things and to be endured only on occasion, that is to say, in places whe re the sense of the inscription is of m ore importance than external ornam ent. This is a sweeping statement, fro m which we need not suffer unduly; y et it is doubtful whether there is art i n individual letters. Letters in combi nation may be satisfying and in a well composed page even beautiful as a w
The main purpose of letters is the pr actical one of making thoughts visib
The main purpose of letters is the p ractical one of making thoughts vis

14/15

The main purpose of letters is the pra ctical one of making thoughts visible. Ruskin says that all letters are fright ful things and to be endured only on occasion, that is to say, in places whe re the sense of the inscription is of m ore importance than external ornam ent. This is a sweeping statement, fro m which we need not suffer unduly; y et it is doubtful whether there is art i n individual letters. Letters in combi nation may be satisfying and in a well
The main purpose of letters is the pr actical one of making thoughts visib
The main purpose of letters is the p ractical one of making thoughts vis

14/16

The main purpose of letters is the pra ctical one of making thoughts visible. Ruskin says that all letters are fright ful things and to be endured only on occasion, that is to say, in places whe re the sense of the inscription is of m ore importance than external ornam ent. This is a sweeping statement, fro m which we need not suffer unduly; y et it is doubtful whether there is art i n individual letters. Letters in combi nation may be satisfying and in a well composed page even beautiful as a w
The main purpose of letters is the pr actical one of making thoughts visib
The main purpose of letters is the p ractical one of making thoughts vis

14/17

The main purpose of letters is the pra ctical one of making thoughts visible. Ruskin says that all letters are fright ful things and to be endured only on occasion, that is to say, in places whe re the sense of the inscription is of m ore importance than external ornam ent. This is a sweeping statement, fro m which we need not suffer unduly; y et it is doubtful whether there is art i n individual letters. Letters in combi nation may be satisfying and in a well
The main purpose of letters is the pr actical one of making thoughts visib
The main purpose of letters is the p ractical one of making thoughts vis

CALEDONIA 6 &7 POINT SET NORMAL

ROMAN, ITALIC, BOLD, BOLD ITALIC

ABCDEFGHIJKLMNOPQRSTUVWXYZ 1234567890 abcdefghijklmnopqrstuvwxyz

ABCDEFGHIJKLMNOPQRSTUVWXYZ 1234567890 abcdefghijklmnopqrstuvwxyz

ABCDEFGHIJKLMNOPQRSTUVWXYZ 1234567890 abcdefghijklmnopqrstuvwxyz

ABCDEFGHIJKLMNOPQRSTUVWXYZ 1234567890 abcdefghijklmnopqrstuvwxyz

6/6

The main purpose of letters is the practical one of making thoughts visible. Ruskin says that all let
ters are frightful things and to be endured only on occasion, that is to say, in places where the sens
e of the inscription is of more importance than external ornament. This is a sweeping statement, f
rom which we need not suffer unduly; yet it is doubtful whether there is art in individual letters.
Letters in combination may be satisfying and in a well composed page even beautiful as a whole,
but art in letters consists rather in the art of arranging and composing them in a pleasing and appr
opriate manner. The main purpose of letters is the practical one of making thoughts visible. Ruski
n says that all letters are frightful things and to be endured only on occasion, that is to say, in place
s where the sense of the inscription is of more importance than external ornament. This is a swee
ping statement, from which we need not suffer unduly; yet it is doubtful whether there is art in in
dividual letters. Letters in combination may be satisfying and in a well composed page even beau
tiful as a whole, but art in letters consists rather in the art of arranging and composing them in a pl
easing and appropriate manner. The main purpose of letters is the practical one of making though
The main purpose of letters is the practical one of making thoughts visible. Ruskin says that all let
ters are frightful things and to be endured only on occasion, that is to say, in places where the sen
The main purpose of letters is the practical one of making thoughts visible. Ruskin says that all
letters are frightful things and to be endured only on occasion, that is to say, in places where the

6/7

The main purpose of letters is the practical one of making thoughts visible. Ruskin says that all let
ters are frightful things and to be endured only on occasion, that is to say, in places where the sens
e of the inscription is of more importance than external ornament. This is a sweeping statement, f
rom which we need not suffer unduly; yet it is doubtful whether there is art in individual letters.
Letters in combination may be satisfying and in a well composed page even beautiful as a whole,
but art in letters consists rather in the art of arranging and composing them in a pleasing and appr
opriate manner. The main purpose of letters is the practical one of making thoughts visible. Ruski
n says that all letters are frightful things and to be endured only on occasion, that is to say, in place
s where the sense of the inscription is of more importance than external ornament. This is a swee
ping statement, from which we need not suffer unduly; yet it is doubtful whether there is art in in
dividual letters. Letters in combination may be satisfying and in a well composed page even beau
The main purpose of letters is the practical one of making thoughts visible. Ruskin says that all let
ters are frightful things and to be endured only on occasion, that is to say, in places where the sen
The main purpose of letters is the practical one of making thoughts visible. Ruskin says that all
letters are frightful things and to be endured only on occasion, that is to say, in places where the

6/8

The main purpose of letters is the practical one of making thoughts visible. Ruskin says that all let
ters are frightful things and to be endured only on occasion, that is to say, in places where the sens
e of the inscription is of more importance than external ornament. This is a sweeping statement, f
rom which we need not suffer unduly; yet it is doubtful whether there is art in individual letters.
Letters in combination may be satisfying and in a well composed page even beautiful as a whole,
but art in letters consists rather in the art of arranging and composing them in a pleasing and appr
opriate manner. The main purpose of letters is the practical one of making thoughts visible. Ruski
n says that all letters are frightful things and to be endured only on occasion, that is to say, in place
s where the sense of the inscription is of more importance than external ornament. This is a swee
The main purpose of letters is the practical one of making thoughts visible. Ruskin says that all let
ters are frightful things and to be endured only on occasion, that is to say, in places where the sen
The main purpose of letters is the practical one of making thoughts visible. Ruskin says that all
letters are frightful things and to be endured only on occasion, that is to say, in places where the

6/9

The main purpose of letters is the practical one of making thoughts visible. Ruskin says that all let
ters are frightful things and to be endured only on occasion, that is to say, in places where the sens
e of the inscription is of more importance than external ornament. This is a sweeping statement, f
rom which we need not suffer unduly; yet it is doubtful whether there is art in individual letters.
Letters in combination may be satisfying and in a well composed page even beautiful as a whole,
but art in letters consists rather in the art of arranging and composing them in a pleasing and appr
opriate manner. The main purpose of letters is the practical one of making thoughts visible. Ruski
n says that all letters are frightful things and to be endured only on occasion, that is to say, in place
The main purpose of letters is the practical one of making thoughts visible. Ruskin says that all let
ters are frightful things and to be endured only on occasion, that is to say, in places where the sen
The main purpose of letters is the practical one of making thoughts visible. Ruskin says that all
letters are frightful things and to be endured only on occasion, that is to say, in places where the

---

ABCDEFGHIJKLMNOPQRSTUVWXYZ 1234567890 abcdefghijklmnopqrstuvwxyz

ABCDEFGHIJKLMNOPQRSTUVWXYZ 1234567890 abcdefghijklmnopqrstuvwxyz

ABCDEFGHIJKLMNOPQRSTUVWXYZ 1234567890 abcdefghijklmnopqrstuvwxyz

ABCDEFGHIJKLMNOPQRSTUVWXYZ 1234567890 abcdefghijklmnopqrstuvwxyz

7/7

The main purpose of letters is the practical one of making thoughts visible. Ruskin s
ays that all letters are frightful things and to be endured only on occasion, that is to s
ay, in places where the sense of the inscription is of more importance than external
ornament. This is a sweeping statement, from which we need not suffer unduly; ye
t it is doubtful whether there is art in individual letters. Letters in combination ma
y be satisfying and in a well composed page even beautiful as a whole, but art in lett
ers consists rather in the art of arranging and composing them in a pleasing and app
ropriate manner. The main purpose of letters is the practical one of making thought
s visible. Ruskin says that all letters are frightful things and to be endured only on o
ccasion, that is to say, in places where the sense of the inscription is of more importa
nce than external ornament. This is a sweeping statement, from which we need not
The main purpose of letters is the practical one of making thoughts visible. Ruskin s
ays that all letters are frightful things and to be endured only on occasion, that is to
The main purpose of letters is the practical one of making thoughts visible. Ruski
n says that all letters are frightful things and to be endured only on occasion, that i

7/8

The main purpose of letters is the practical one of making thoughts visible. Ruskin s
ays that all letters are frightful things and to be endured only on occasion, that is to s
ay, in places where the sense of the inscription is of more importance than external
ornament. This is a sweeping statement, from which we need not suffer unduly; ye
t it is doubtful whether there is art in individual letters. Letters in combination ma
y be satisfying and in a well composed page even beautiful as a whole, but art in lett
ers consists rather in the art of arranging and composing them in a pleasing and app
ropriate manner. The main purpose of letters is the practical one of making thought
s visible. Ruskin says that all letters are frightful things and to be endured only on o
ccasion, that is to say, in places where the sense of the inscription is of more importa
The main purpose of letters is the practical one of making thoughts visible. Ruskin s
ays that all letters are frightful things and to be endured only on occasion, that is to
The main purpose of letters is the practical one of making thoughts visible. Ruski
n says that all letters are frightful things and to be endured only on occasion, that i

7/9

The main purpose of letters is the practical one of making thoughts visible. Ruskin s
ays that all letters are frightful things and to be endured only on occasion, that is to s
ay, in places where the sense of the inscription is of more importance than external
ornament. This is a sweeping statement, from which we need not suffer unduly; ye
t it is doubtful whether there is art in individual letters. Letters in combination ma
y be satisfying and in a well composed page even beautiful as a whole, but art in lett
ers consists rather in the art of arranging and composing them in a pleasing and app
ropriate manner. The main purpose of letters is the practical one of making thought
s visible. Ruskin says that all letters are frightful things and to be endured only on o
ccasion, that is to say, in places where the sense of the inscription is of more importa
The main purpose of letters is the practical one of making thoughts visible. Ruskin s
ays that all letters are frightful things and to be endured only on occasion, that is to
The main purpose of letters is the practical one of making thoughts visible. Ruski
n says that all letters are frightful things and to be endured only on occasion, that i

7/10

The main purpose of letters is the practical one of making thoughts visible. Ruskin s
ays that all letters are frightful things and to be endured only on occasion, that is to s
ay, in places where the sense of the inscription is of more importance than external
ornament. This is a sweeping statement, from which we need not suffer unduly; ye
t it is doubtful whether there is art in individual letters. Letters in combination ma
y be satisfying and in a well composed page even beautiful as a whole, but art in lett
ers consists rather in the art of arranging and composing them in a pleasing and app
ropriate manner. The main purpose of letters is the practical one of making thought
s visible. Ruskin says that all letters are frightful things and to be endured only on o
The main purpose of letters is the practical one of making thoughts visible. Ruskin s
ays that all letters are frightful things and to be endured only on occasion, that is to
The main purpose of letters is the practical one of making thoughts visible. Ruski
n says that all letters are frightful things and to be endured only on occasion, that i

CALEDONIA 8 & 9 POINT SET NORMAL

ROMAN, ITALIC, BOLD, BOLD ITALIC

ABCDEFGHIJKLMNOPQRSTUVWXYZ 1234567890 abcdefghijklmnopqrstuvwxyz

ABCDEFGHIJKLMNOPQRSTUVWXYZ 1234567890 abcdefghijklmnopqrstuvwxyz

ABCDEFGHIJKLMNOPQRSTUVWXYZ 1234567890 abcdefghijklmnopqrstuvwxyz

ABCDEFGHIJKLMNOPQRSTUVWXYZ 1234567890 abcdefghijklmnopqrstuvwxyz

8/8

The main purpose of letters is the practical one of making thoughts visibl e. Ruskin says that all letters are frightful things and to be endured only o n occasion, that is to say, in places where the sense of the inscription is of more importance than external ornament. This is a sweeping statement, from which we need not suffer unduly; yet it is doubtful whether there is art in individual letters. Letters in combination may be satisfying and in a well composed page even beautiful as a whole, but art in letters consist s rather in the art of arranging and composing them in a pleasing and app ropriate manner. The main purpose of letters is the practical one of maki

The main purpose of letters is the practical one of making thoughts visibl e. Ruskin says that all letters are frightful things and to be endured only

The main purpose of letters is the practical one of making thoughts visi ble. Ruskin says that all letters are frightful things and to be endured on

8/9

The main purpose of letters is the practical one of making thoughts visibl e. Ruskin says that all letters are frightful things and to be endured only o n occasion, that is to say, in places where the sense of the inscription is of more importance than external ornament. This is a sweeping statement, from which we need not suffer unduly; yet it is doubtful whether there is art in individual letters. Letters in combination may be satisfying and in a well composed page even beautiful as a whole, but art in letters consist s rather in the art of arranging and composing them in a pleasing and app

The main purpose of letters is the practical one of making thoughts visibl e. Ruskin says that all letters are frightful things and to be endured only

The main purpose of letters is the practical one of making thoughts visi ble. Ruskin says that all letters are frightful things and to be endured on

8/10

The main purpose of letters is the practical one of making thoughts visibl e. Ruskin says that all letters are frightful things and to be endured only o n occasion, that is to say, in places where the sense of the inscription is of more importance than external ornament. This is a sweeping statement, from which we need not suffer unduly; yet it is doubtful whether there is art in individual letters. Letters in combination may be satisfying and in a well composed page even beautiful as a whole, but art in letters consist

The main purpose of letters is the practical one of making thoughts visibl e. Ruskin says that all letters are frightful things and to be endured only

The main purpose of letters is the practical one of making thoughts visi ble. Ruskin says that all letters are frightful things and to be endured on

8/11

The main purpose of letters is the practical one of making thoughts visibl e. Ruskin says that all letters are frightful things and to be endured only o n occasion, that is to say, in places where the sense of the inscription is of more importance than external ornament. This is a sweeping statement, from which we need not suffer unduly; yet it is doubtful whether there is art in individual letters. Letters in combination may be satisfying and in a well composed page even beautiful as a whole, but art in letters consist

The main purpose of letters is the practical one of making thoughts visibl e. Ruskin says that all letters are frightful things and to be endured only

The main purpose of letters is the practical one of making thoughts visi ble. Ruskin says that all letters are frightful things and to be endured on

ABCDEFGHIJKLMNOPQRSTUVWXYZ 1234567890 abcdefghijklmnopqrstuvxyz

ABCDEFGHIJKLMNOPQRSTUVWXYZ 1234567890 abcdefghijklmnopqrstuvwxyz

ABCDEFGHIJKLMNOPQRSTUVWXYZ 1234567890 abcdefghijklmnopqrstuvwxyz

ABCDEFGHIJKLMNOPQRSTUVWXYZ 1234567890 abcdefghijklmnopqrstuvwxyz

9/9

The main purpose of letters is the practical one of making though ts visible. Ruskin says that all letters are frightful things and to be endured only on occasion, that is to say, in places where the sens e of the inscription is of more importance than external ornamen t. This is a sweeping statement, from which we need not suffer u nduly; yet it is doubtful whether there is art in individual letters. Letters in combination may be satisfying and in a well composed page even beautiful as a whole, but art in letters consists rather i

The main purpose of letters is the practical one of making though ts vsible. Ruskin says that all letters are frightful things and to b

The main purpose of letters is the practical one of making thoug hts visible. Ruskin says that all letters are frightful things and to

9/10

The main purpose of letters is the practical one of making though ts visible. Ruskin says that all letters are frightful things and to be endured only on occasion, that is to say, in places where the sens e of the inscription is of more importance than external ornamen t. This is a sweeping statement, from which we need not suffer u nduly; yet it is doubtful whether there is art in individual letters. Letters in combination may be satisfying and in a well composed

The main purpose of letters is the practical one of making though ts vsible. Ruskin says that all letters are frightful things and to b

The main purpose of letters is the practical one of making thoug hts visible. Ruskin says that all letters are frightful things and to

9/11

The main purpose of letters is the practical one of making though ts visible. Ruskin says that all letters are frightful things and to be endured only on occasion, that is to say, in places where the sens e of the inscription is of more importance than external ornamen t. This is a sweeping statement, from which we need not suffer u nduly; yet it is doubtful whether there is art in individual letters. Letters in combination may be satisfying and in a well composed

The main purpose of letters is the practical one of making though ts vsible. Ruskin says that all letters are frightful things and to b

The main purpose of letters is the practical one of making thoug hts visible. Ruskin says that all letters are frightful things and to

9/12

The main purpose of letters is the practical one of making though ts visible. Ruskin says that all letters are frightful things and to be endured only on occasion, that is to say, in places where the sens e of the inscription is of more importance than external ornamen t. This is a sweeping statement, from which we need not suffer u nduly; yet it is doubtful whether there is art in individual letters. Letters in combination may be satisfying and in a well composed

The main purpose of letters is the practical one of making though ts vsible. Ruskin says that all letters are frightful things and to b

The main purpose of letters is the practical one of making thoug hts visible. Ruskin says that all letters are frightful things and to

CALEDONIA 10 POINT SET MINUS ½ UNIT

ROMAN, ITALIC, BOLD, BOLD ITALIC

abcdefghijklmnopqrstuvwxyz – 1 UNIT
abcdefghijklmnopqrstuvwxyz – ½ UNIT
abcdefghijklmnopqrstuvwxyz NORMAL

ABCDEFGHIJKLMNOPQRSTUVWXYZ 1234567890 abcdefghijklmnopqrstuvwxyz
ABCDEFGHIJKLMNOPQRSTUVWXYZ 1234567890 abcdefghijklmnopqrstuvwxyz
ABCDEFGHIJKLMNOPQRSTUVWXYZ 1234567890 abcdefghijklmnopqrstuvwxyz
ABCDEFGHIJKLMNOPQRSTUVWXYZ 1234567890 abcdefghijklmnopqrstuvwxyz

10/10

The main purpose of letters is the practical one of making tho ghts visible. Ruskin says that all letters are frightful things a nd to be endured only on occasion, that is to say, in places wh ere the sense of the inscription is of more importance than ex ternal ornament. This is a sweeping statement, from which we need not suffer unduly; yet it is doubtful whether there is art in individual letters. Letters in combination may be satisf ying and in a well composed page even beautiful as a whole, but art in letters consists rather in the art of arranging and co mposing them in a pleasing and appropriate manner. The ma in purpose of letters is the practical one of making thoughts v isible. Ruskin says that all letters are frightful things and to b e endured only on occasion, that is to say, in places where the sense of the inscription is of more importance than external o rnament. This is a sweeping statement, from which we need not suffer unduly; yet it is doubtful whether there is art in ind ividual letters. Letters in combination may be satisfying and in a well composed page even beautiful as a whole, but art in letters consists rather in the art of arranging and composing t hem in a pleasing and appropriate manner. The main purpos e of letters is the practical one of making thoughts visible. Ru skin says that all letters are frightful things and to be endured
The main purpose of letters is the practical one of making tho ughts visible. Ruskin says that all letters are frightful things
The main purpose of letters is the practical one of making th oughts visible. Ruskin says that all letters are frightful thing

10/11

The main purpose of letters is the practical one of making tho ughts visible. Ruskin says that all letters are frightful things a nd to be endured only on occasion, that is to say, in places wh ere the sense of the inscription is of more importance than ex ternal ornament. This is a sweeping statement, from which we need not suffer unduly; yet it is doubtful whether there is art in individual letters. Letters in combination may be satisf ying and in a well composed page even beautiful as a whole, but art in letters consists rather in the art of arranging and co mposing them in a pleasing and appropriate manner. The ma in purpose of letters is the practical one of making thoughts v isible. Ruskin says that all letters are frightful things and to b e endured only on occasion, that is to say, in places where the sense of the inscription is of more importance than external o rnament. This is a sweeping statement, from which we need not suffer unduly; yet it is doubtful whether there is art in ind ividual letters. Letters in combination may be satisfying and in a well composed page even beautiful as a whole, but art in letters consists rather in the art of arranging and composing t hem in a pleasing and appropriate manner. The main purpos
The main purpose of letters is the practical one of making tho ughts visible. Ruskin says that all letters are frightful things
The main purpose of letters is the practical one of making th oughts visible. Ruskin says that all letters are frightful thing

10/12

The main purpose of letters is the practical one of making tho ughts visible. Ruskin says that all letters are frightful things a nd to be endured only on occasion, that is to say, in places wh ere the sense of the inscription is of more importance than ex ternal ornament. This is a sweeping statement, from which we need not suffer unduly; yet it is doubtful whether there is art in individual letters. Letters in combination may be satisf ying and in a well composed page even beautiful as a whole, but art in letters consists rather in the art of arranging and co mposing them in a pleasing and appropriate manner. The ma in purpose of letters is the practical one of making thoughts v isible. Ruskin says that all letters are frightful things and to b e endured only on occasion, that is to say, in places where the sense of the inscription is of more importance than external o rnament. This is a sweeping statement, from which we need not suffer unduly; yet it is doubtful whether there is art in ind ividual letters. Letters in combination may be satisfying and in a well composed page even beautiful as a whole, but art in
The main purpose of letters is the practical one of making tho ughts visible. Ruskin says that all letters are frightful things
The main purpose of letters is the practical one of making th oughts visible. Ruskin says that all letters are frightful thing

10/13

The main purpose of letters is the practical one of making tho ughts visible. Ruskin says that all letters are frightful things a nd to be endured only on occasion, that is to say, in places wh ere the sense of the inscription is of more importance than ex ternal ornament. This is a sweeping statement, from which we need not suffer unduly; yet it is doubtful whether there is art in individual letters. Letters in combination may be satisf ying and in a well composed page even beautiful as a whole, but art in letters consists rather in the art of arranging and co mposing them in a pleasing and appropriate manner. The ma in purpose of letters is the practical one of making thoughts v isible. Ruskin says that all letters are frightful things and to b e endured only on occasion, that is to say, in places where the sense of the inscription is of more importance than external o rnament. This is a sweeping statement, from which we need not suffer unduly; yet it is doubtful whether there is art in ind ividual letters. Letters in combination may be satisfying and
The main purpose of letters is the practical one of making tho ughts visible. Ruskin says that all letters are frightful things
The main purpose of letters is the practical one of making th oughts visible. Ruskin says that all letters are frightful thing

CALEDONIA 11 POINT SET MINUS ½ UNIT

ROMAN, ITALIC, BOLD, BOLD ITALIC

abcdefghijklmnopqrstuvwxyz – 1 UNIT
abcdefghijklmnopqrstuvwxyz – ½ UNIT
abcdefghijklmnopqrstuvwxyz NORMAL

ABCDEFGHIJKLMNOPQRSTUVWXYZ 1234567890 abcdefghijklmnopqrstuvwxyz
ABCDEFGHIJKLMNOPQRSTUVWXYZ 1234567890 abcdefghijklmnopqrstuvwxyz
ABCDEFGHIJKLMNOPQRSTUVWXYZ 1234567890 abcdefghijklmnopqrstuvwxyz
ABCDEFGHIJKLMNOPQRSTUVWXYZ 1234567890 abcdefghijklmnopqrstuvwxyz

11/11

The main purpose of letters is the practical one of maki ng thoughts visible. Ruskin says that all letters are frigh tful things and to be endured only on occasion, that is t o say, in places where the sense of the inscription is of more importance than external ornament. This is a swe eping statement, from which we need not suffer undul y; yet it is doubtful whether there is art in individual let ters. Letters in combination may be satisfying and in a well composed page even beautiful as a whole, but art i n letters consists rather in the art of arranging and com posing them in a pleasing and appropriate manner. Th e main purpose of letters is the practical one of making thoughts visible. Ruskin says that all letters are frightfu l things and to be endured only on occasion, that is to sa y, in places where the sense of the inscription is of more importance than external ornament. This is a sweeping statement, from which we need not suffer unduly; yet i t is doubtful whether there is art in individual letters. L etters in combination may be satisfying and in a well co
The main purpose of letters is the practical one of maki ng thoughts visible. Ruskin says that all letters are frig
The main purpose of letters is the practical one of mak ing thoughts visible. Ruskin says that all letters are fri

11/12

The main purpose of letters is the practical one of maki ng thoughts visible. Ruskin says that all letters are frigh tful things and to be endured only on occasion, that is t o say, in places where the sense of the inscription is of more importance than external ornament. This is a swe eping statement, from which we need not suffer undul y; yet it is doubtful whether there is art in individual let ters. Letters in combination may be satisfying and in a well composed page even beautiful as a whole, but art i n letters consists rather in the art of arranging and com posing them in a pleasing and appropriate manner. Th e main purpose of letters is the practical one of making thoughts visible. Ruskin says that all letters are frightfu l things and to be endured only on occasion, that is to sa y, in places where the sense of the inscription is of more importance than external ornament. This is a sweeping statement, from which we need not suffer unduly; yet i t is doubtful whether there is art in individual letters. L
The main purpose of letters is the practical one of maki ng thoughts visible. Ruskin says that all letters are frig
The main purpose of letters is the practical one of mak ing thoughts visible. Ruskin says that all letters are fri

11/13

The main purpose of letters is the practical one of maki ng thoughts visible. Ruskin says that all letters are frigh tful things and to be endured only on occasion, that is t o say, in places where the sense of the inscription is of more importance than external ornament. This is a swe eping statement, from which we need not suffer undul y; yet it is doubtful whether there is art in individual let ters. Letters in combination may be satisfying and in a well composed page even beautiful as a whole, but art i n letters consists rather in the art of arranging and com posing them in a pleasing and appropriate manner. Th e main purpose of letters is the practical one of making thoughts visible. Ruskin says that all letters are frightfu l things and to be endured only on occasion, that is to sa y, in places where the sense of the inscription is of more importance than external ornament. This is a sweeping statement, from which we need not suffer unduly; yet i
The main purpose of letters is the practical one of maki ng thoughts visible. Ruskin says that all letters are frig
The main purpose of letters is the practical one of mak ing thoughts visible. Ruskin says that all letters are fri

11/14

The main purpose of letters is the practical one of maki ng thoughts visible. Ruskin says that all letters are frigh tful things and to be endured only on occasion, that is t o say, in places where the sense of the inscription is of more importance than external ornament. This is a swe eping statement, from which we need not suffer undul y; yet it is doubtful whether there is art in individual let ters. Letters in combination may be satisfying and in a well composed page even beautiful as a whole, but art i n letters consists rather in the art of arranging and com posing them in a pleasing and appropriate manner. Th e main purpose of letters is the practical one of making thoughts visible. Ruskin says that all letters are frightfu l things and to be endured only on occasion, that is to sa y, in places where the sense of the inscription is of more importance than external ornament. This is a sweeping
The main purpose of letters is the practical one of maki ng thoughts visible. Ruskin says that all letters are frig
The main purpose of letters is the practical one of mak ing thoughts visible. Ruskin says that all letters are fri

CALEDONIA 12 POINT SET MINUS ½ UNIT

ROMAN, ITALIC, BOLD, BOLD ITALIC

abcdefghijklmnopqrstuvwxyz – 1 UNIT
abcdefghijklmnopqrstuvwxyz – ½ UNIT
abcdefghijklmnopqrstuvwxyz NORMAL

ABCDEFGHIJKLMNOPQRSTUVWXYZ 1234567890 abcdefghijklmnopqrstuvwxyz
ABCDEFGHIJKLMNOPQRSTUVWXYZ 1234567890 abcdefghijklmnopqrstuvwxyz
ABCDEFGHIJKLMNOPQRSTUVWXYZ 1234567890 abcdefghijklmnopqrstuvwxyz
ABCDEFGHIJKLMNOPQRSTUVWXYZ 1234567890 abcdefghijklmnopqrstuvwxyz

12/12

The main purpose of letters is the practical one of m aking thoughts visible. Ruskin says that all letters ar e frightful things and to be endured only on occasio n, that is to say, in places where the sense of the insc ription is of more importance than external ornamе nt. This is a sweeping statement, from which we ne ed not suffer unduly; yet it is doubtful whether ther e is art in individual letters. Letters in combination may be satisfying and in a well composed page eve n beautiful as a whole, but art in letters consists rat her in the art of arranging and composing them in a pleasing and appropriate manner. The main purpo se of letters is the practical one of making thoughts visible. Ruskin says that all letters are frightful thin gs and to be endured only on occasion, that is to say,
The main purpose of letters is the practical one of m aking thoughts visible. Ruskin says that all letters a
The main purpose of letters is the practical one of making thoughts visible. Ruskin says that all letter

12/13

The main purpose of letters is the practical one of m aking thoughts visible. Ruskin says that all letters ar e frightful things and to be endured only on occasio n, that is to say, in places where the sense of the insc ription is of more importance than external orname nt. This is a sweeping statement, from which we ne ed not suffer unduly; yet it is doubtful whether ther e is art in individual letters. Letters in combination may be satisfying and in a well composed page eve n beautiful as a whole, but art in letters consists rat her in the art of arranging and composing them in a pleasing and appropriate manner. The main purpo se of letters is the practical one of making thoughts visible. Ruskin says that all letters are frightful thin
The main purpose of letters is the practical one of m aking thoughts visible. Ruskin says that all letters a
The main purpose of letters is the practical one of making thoughts visible. Ruskin says that all letter

12/14

The main purpose of letters is the practical one of m aking thoughts visible. Ruskin says that all letters ar e frightful things and to be endured only on occasio n, that is to say, in places where the sense of the insc ription is of more importance than external orname nt. This is a sweeping statement, from which we ne ed not suffer unduly; yet it is doubtful whether ther e is art in individual letters. Letters in combination may be satisfying and in a well composed page eve n beautiful as a whole, but art in letters consists rat her in the art of arranging and composing them in a pleasing and appropriate manner. The main purpo se of letters is the practical one of making thoughts visible. Ruskin says that all letters are frightful thin gs and to be endured only on occasion, that is to say,
The main purpose of letters is the practical one of m aking thoughts visible. Ruskin says that all letters a
The main purpose of letters is the practical one of making thoughts visible. Ruskin says that all letter

12/15

The main purpose of letters is the practical one of m aking thoughts visible. Ruskin says that all letters ar e frightful things and to be endured only on occasio n, that is to say, in places where the sense of the insc ription is of more importance than external orname nt. This is a sweeping statement, from which we ne ed not suffer unduly; yet it is doubtful whether ther e is art in individual letters. Letters in combination may be satisfying and in a well composed page eve n beautiful as a whole, but art in letters consists rat her in the art of arranging and composing them in a pleasing and appropriate manner. The main purpo se of letters is the practical one of making thoughts visible. Ruskin says that all letters are frightful thin
The main purpose of letters is the practical one of m aking thoughts visible. Ruskin says that all letters a
The main purpose of letters is the practical one of making thoughts visible. Ruskin says that all letter

CALEDONIA 14 POINT SET MINUS ½ UNIT

ROMAN, ITALIC, BOLD, BOLD ITALIC

abcdefghijklmnopqrstuvwxyz – 1 UNIT
abcdefghijklmnopqrstuvwxyz ½ UNIT
abcdefghijklmnopqrstuvwxyz NORMAL

ABCDEFGHIJKLMNOPQRSTUVWXYZ abcdefghijklmnopqrstuvwxyz
ABCDEFGHIJKLMNOPQRSTUVWXYZ abcdefghijklmnopqrstuvwxyz
ABCDEFGHIJKLMNOPQRSTUVWXYZ abcdefghijklmnopqrstuvwxyz
ABCDEFGHIJKLMNOPQRSTUVWXYZ abcdefghijklmnopqrstuvwxyz

14/14

The main purpose of letters is the practical one of making thoughts visible. Ruskin says that all letters are frightful things and to be endured only on occasion, that is to say, in p laces where the sense of the inscription is of more importance than external ornament. This is a sweeping statement, from which w e need not suffer unduly; yet it is doubtful whether there is art in individual letters. L etters in combination may be satisfying and in a well composed page even beautiful as a whole, but art in letters consists rather in th e art of arranging and composing them in a
The main purpose of letters is the practical one of making thoughts visible. Ruskin says
The main purpose of letters is the practical one of making thoughts visible. Ruskin say

14/15

The main purpose of letters is the practical one of making thoughts visible. Ruskin says that all letters are frightful things and to be endured only on occasion, that is to say, in p laces where the sense of the inscription is of more importance than external ornament. This is a sweeping statement, from which w e need not suffer unduly; yet it is doubtful whether there is art in individual letters. L etters in combination may be satisfying and in a well composed page even beautiful as a whole, but art in letters consists rather in th
The main purpose of letters is the practical one of making thoughts visible. Ruskin says
The main purpose of letters is the practical one of making thoughts visible. Ruskin say

14/16

The main purpose of letters is the practical one of making thoughts visible. Ruskin says that all letters are frightful things and to be endured only on occasion, that is to say, in p laces where the sense of the inscription is of more importance than external ornament. This is a sweeping statement, from which w e need not suffer unduly; yet it is doubtful whether there is art in individual letters. L etters in combination may be satisfying and in a well composed page even beautiful as a whole, but art in letters consists rather in th e art of arranging and composing them in a
The main purpose of letters is the practical one of making thoughts visible. Ruskin says
The main purpose of letters is the practical one of making thoughts visible. Ruskin say

14/17

The main purpose of letters is the practical one of making thoughts visible. Ruskin says that all letters are frightful things and to be endured only on occasion, that is to say, in p laces where the sense of the inscription is of more importance than external ornament. This is a sweeping statement, from which w e need not suffer unduly; yet it is doubtful whether there is art in individual letters. L etters in combination may be satisfying and in a well composed page even beautiful as a whole, but art in letters consists rather in th
The main purpose of letters is the practical one of making thoughts visible. Ruskin says
The main purpose of letters is the practical one of making thoughts visible. Ruskin say

CASLON 6 & 7 POINT SET NORMAL

540 ROMAN, ITALIC, #3 BOLD, BOLD ITALIC

ABCDEFGHIJKLMNOPQRSTUVWXYZ 1234567890 abcdefghijklmnopqrstuvwxyz

ABCDEFGHIJKLMNOPQRSTUVWXYZ 1234567890 abcdefghijklmnopqrstuvwxyz

ABCDEFGHIJKLMNOPQRSTUVWXYZ 1234567890 abcdefghijklmnopqrstuvwxyz

ABCDEFGHIJKLMNOPQRSTUVWXYZ 1234567890 abcdefghijklmnopqrstuvwxyz

6/6

The main purpose of letters is the practical one of making thoughts visible. Ruskin says that all le
tters are frightful things and to be endured only on occasion, that is to say, in places where the sen
se of the inscription is of more importance than external ornament. This is a sweeping statement,
from which we need not suffer unduly; yet it is doubtful whether there is art in individual letters.
Letters in combination may be satisfying and in a well composed page even beautiful as a whole,
but art in letters consists rather in the art of arranging and composing them in a pleasing and appro
priate manner. The main purpose of letters is the practical one of making thoughts visible. Rusk
in says that all letters are frightful things and to be endured only on occasion, that is to say, in place
s where the sense of the inscription is of more importance than external ornament. This is a swee
ping statement, from which we need not suffer unduly; yet it is doubtful whether there is art in in
dividual letters. Letters in combination may be satisfying and in a well composed page even beau
tiful as a whole, but art in letters consists rather in the art of arranging and composing them in a pl
easing and appropriate manner. The main purpose of letters is the practical one of making though
The main purpose of letters is the practical one of making thoughts visible. Ruskin says that all letters are frig
htful things and to be endured only on occasion, that is to say, in places where the sense of the inscription is of
The main purpose of letters is the practical one of making thoughts visible. Ruskin says th
at all letters are frightful things and to be endured only on occasion, that is to say, in places

6/7

The main purpose of letters is the practical one of making thoughts visible. Ruskin says that all le
tters are frightful things and to be endured only on occasion, that is to say, in places where the sen
se of the inscription is of more importance than external ornament. This is a sweeping statement,
from which we need not suffer unduly; yet it is doubtful whether there is art in individual letters.
Letters in combination may be satisfying and in a well composed page even beautiful as a whole,
but art in letters consists rather in the art of arranging and composing them in a pleasing and appro
priate manner. The main purpose of letters is the practical one of making thoughts visible. Rusk
in says that all letters are frightful things and to be endured only on occasion, that is to say, in place
s where the sense of the inscription is of more importance than external ornament. This is a swee
ping statement, from which we need not suffer unduly; yet it is doubtful whether there is art in in
dividual letters. Letters in combination may be satisfying and in a well composed page even beau
The main purpose of letters is the practical one of making thoughts visible. Ruskin says that all letters are frig
htful things and to be endured only on occasion, that is to say, in places where the sense of the inscription is of
The main purpose of letters is the practical one of making thoughts visible. Ruskin says th
at all letters are frightful things and to be endured only on occasion, that is to say, in places

6/8

The main purpose of letters is the practical one of making thoughts visible. Ruskin says that all le
tters are frightful things and to be endured only on occasion, that is to say, in places where the sen
se of the inscription is of more importance than external ornament. This is a sweeping statement,
from which we need not suffer unduly; yet it is doubtful whether there is art in individual letters.
Letters in combination may be satisfying and in a well composed page even beautiful as a whole,
but art in letters consists rather in the art of arranging and composing them in a pleasing and appro
priate manner. The main purpose of letters is the practical one of making thoughts visible. Rusk
in says that all letters are frightful things and to be endured only on occasion, that is to say, in place
s where the sense of the inscription is of more importance than external ornament. This is a swee
The main purpose of letters is the practical one of making thoughts visible. Ruskin says that all letters are frig
htful things and to be endured only on occasion, that is to say, in places where the sense of the inscription is of
The main purpose of letters is the practical one of making thoughts visible. Ruskin says th
at all letters are frightful things and to be endured only on occasion, that is to say, in places

6/9

The main purpose of letters is the practical one of making thoughts visible. Ruskin says that all le
tters are frightful things and to be endured only on occasion, that is to say, in places where the sen
se of the inscription is of more importance than external ornament. This is a sweeping statement,
from which we need not suffer unduly; yet it is doubtful whether there is art in individual letters.
Letters in combination may be satisfying and in a well composed page even beautiful as a whole,
but art in letters consists rather in the art of arranging and composing them in a pleasing and appro
priate manner. The main purpose of letters is the practical one of making thoughts visible. Rusk
in says that all letters are frightful things and to be endured only on occasion, that is to say, in place
The main purpose of letters is the practical one of making thoughts visible. Ruskin says that all letters are frig
htful things and to be endured only on occasion, that is to say, in places where the sense of the inscription is of
The main purpose of letters is the practical one of making thoughts visible. Ruskin says th
at all letters are frightful things and to be endured only on occasion, that is to say, in places

---

ABCDEFGHIJKLMNOPQRSTUVWXYZ 1234567890 abcdefghijklmnopqrstuvwxyz

ABCDEFGHIJKLMNOPQRSTUVWXYZ 1234567890 abcdefghijklmnopqrstuvwxyz

ABCDEFGHIJKLMNOPQRSTUVWXYZ 1234567890 abcdefghijklmnopqrstuvwxyz

ABCDEFGHIJKLMNOPQRSTUVWXYZ 1234567890 abcdefghijklmnopqrstuvwxyz

7/7

The main purpose of letters is the practical one of making thoughts visible. Ruskin
says that all letters are frightful things and to be endured only on occasion, that is to
say, in places where the sense of the inscription is of more importance than external
ornament. This is a sweeping statement, from which we need not suffer unduly; ye
t it is doubtful whether there is art in individual letters. Letters in combination may
be satisfying and in a well composed page even beautiful as a whole, but art in letter
s consists rather in the art of arranging and composing them in a pleasing and appro
priate manner. The main purpose of letters is the practical one of making thoughts
visible. Ruskin says that all letters are frightful things and to be endured only on oc
casion, that is to say, in places where the sense of the inscription is of more importan
ce than external ornament. This is a sweeping statement, from which we need not s
The main purpose of letters is the practical one of making thoughts visible. Ruskin says that al
l letters are frightful things and to be endured only on occasion, that is to say, in places where t
The main purpose of letters is the practical one of making thoughts visible. R
uskin says that all letters are frightful things and to be endured only on occasi

7/8

The main purpose of letters is the practical one of making thoughts visible. Ruskin
says that all letters are frightful things and to be endured only on occasion, that is to
say, in places where the sense of the inscription is of more importance than external
ornament. This is a sweeping statement, from which we need not suffer unduly; ye
t it is doubtful whether there is art in individual letters. Letters in combination may
be satisfying and in a well composed page even beautiful as a whole, but art in letter
s consists rather in the art of arranging and composing them in a pleasing and appro
priate manner. The main purpose of letters is the practical one of making thoughts
visible. Ruskin says that all letters are frightful things and to be endured only on oc
casion, that is to say, in places where the sense of the inscription is of more importan
The main purpose of letters is the practical one of making thoughts visible. Ruskin says that al
l letters are frightful things and to be endured only on occasion, that is to say, in places where t
The main purpose of letters is the practical one of making thoughts visible. R
uskin says that all letters are frightful things and to be endured only on occasi

7/9

The main purpose of letters is the practical one of making thoughts visible. Ruskin
says that all letters are frightful things and to be endured only on occasion, that is to
say, in places where the sense of the inscription is of more importance than external
ornament. This is a sweeping statement, from which we need not suffer unduly; ye
t it is doubtful whether there is art in individual letters. Letters in combination may
be satisfying and in a well composed page even beautiful as a whole, but art in letter
s consists rather in the art of arranging and composing them in a pleasing and appro
priate manner. The main purpose of letters is the practical one of making thoughts
visible. Ruskin says that all letters are frightful things and to be endured only on oc
casion, that is to say, in places where the sense of the inscription is of more importan
The main purpose of letters is the practical one of making thoughts visible. Ruskin says that al
l letters are frightful things and to be endured only on occasion, that is to say, in places where t
The main purpose of letters is the practical one of making thoughts visible. R
uskin says that all letters are frightful things and to be endured only on occasi

7/10

The main purpose of letters is the practical one of making thoughts visible. Ruskin
says that all letters are frightful things and to be endured only on occasion, that is to
say, in places where the sense of the inscription is of more importance than external
ornament. This is a sweeping statement, from which we need not suffer unduly; ye
t it is doubtful whether there is art in individual letters. Letters in combination may
be satisfying and in a well composed page even beautiful as a whole, but art in letter
s consists rather in the art of arranging and composing them in a pleasing and appro
priate manner. The main purpose of letters is the practical one of making thoughts
visible. Ruskin says that all letters are frightful things and to be endured only on oc
The main purpose of letters is the practical one of making thoughts visible. Ruskin says that al
l letters are frightful things and to be endured only on occasion, that is to say, in places where t
The main purpose of letters is the practical one of making thoughts visible. R
uskin says that all letters are frightful things and to be endured only on occasi

CASLON 8 & 9 POINT SET NORMAL

540 ROMAN, ITALIC, #3 BOLD, BOLD ITALIC

ABCDEFGHIJKLMNOPQRSTUVWXYZ 1234567890 abcdefghijklmnopqrstuvwxyz

ABCDEFGHIJKLMNOPQRSTUVWXYZ 1234567890 abcdefghijklmnopqrstuvwxyz

ABCDEFGHIJKLMNOPQRSTUVWXYZ 1234567890 abcdefghijklmnopqrstuvwxyz

ABCDEFGHIJKLMNOPQRSTUVWXYZ 1234567890 abcdefghijklmnopqrstuvwxyz

8/8

The main purpose of letters is the practical one of making thoughts visibl e. Ruskin says that all letters are frightful things and to be endured only o n occasion, that is to say, in places where the sense of the inscription is of more importance than external ornament. This is a sweeping statement, from which we need not suffer unduly; yet it is doubtful whether there is art in individual letters. Letters in combination may be satisfying and in a well composed page even beautiful as a whole, but art in letters consists rather in the art of arranging and composing them in a pleasing and appro priate manner. The main purpose of letters is the practical one of making
The main purpose of letters is the practical one of making thoughts visible. Ruskin says that all letters are frightful things and to be endured only on occasion, that is t
The main purpose of letters is the practical one of making thoughts visible. Ruskin says that all letters are frightful things and to be end

8/9

The main purpose of letters is the practical one of making thoughts visibl e. Ruskin says that all letters are frightful things and to be endured only o n occasion, that is to say, in places where the sense of the inscription is of more importance than external ornament. This is a sweeping statement, from which we need not suffer unduly; yet it is doubtful whether there is art in individual letters. Letters in combination may be satisfying and in a well composed page even beautiful as a whole, but art in letters consists rather in the art of arranging and composing them in a pleasing and appro
The main purpose of letters is the practical one of making thoughts visible. Ruskin says that all letters are frightful things and to be endured only on occasion, that is t
The main purpose of letters is the practical one of making thoughts visible. Ruskin says that all letters are frightful things and to be end

8/10

The main purpose of letters is the practical one of making thoughts visibl e. Ruskin says that all letters are frightful things and to be endured only o n occasion, that is to say, in places where the sense of the inscription is of more importance than external ornament. This is a sweeping statement, from which we need not suffer unduly; yet it is doubtful whether there is art in individual letters. Letters in combination may be satisfying and in a well composed page even beautiful as a whole, but art in letters consists
The main purpose of letters is the practical one of making thoughts visible. Ruskin says that all letters are frightful things and to be endured only on occasion, that is t
The main purpose of letters is the practical one of making thoughts visible. Ruskin says that all letters are frightful things and to be end

8/11

The main purpose of letters is the practical one of making thoughts visibl e. Ruskin says that all letters are frightful things and to be endured only o n occasion, that is to say, in places where the sense of the inscription is of more importance than external ornament. This is a sweeping statement, from which we need not suffer unduly; yet it is doubtful whether there is art in individual letters. Letters in combination may be satisfying and in a well composed page even beautiful as a whole, but art in letters consists
The main purpose of letters is the practical one of making thoughts visible. Ruskin says that all letters are frightful things and to be endured only on occasion, that is t
The main purpose of letters is the practical one of making thoughts visible. Ruskin says that all letters are frightful things and to be end

---

ABCDEFGHIJKLMNOPQRSTUVWXYZ 1234567890 abcdefghijklmnopqrstuvwxyz

ABCDEFGHIJKLMNOPQRSTUVWXYZ 1234567890 abcdefghijklmnopqrstuvwxyz

ABCDEFGHIJKLMNOPQRSTUVWXYZ 1234567890 abcdefghijklmnopqrstuvwxyz

ABCDEFGHIJKLMNOPQRSTUVWXYZ 1234567890 abcdefghijklmnopqrstuvwxyz

9/9

The main purpose of letters is the practical one of making thoug hts visible. Ruskin says that all letters are frightful things and to be endured only on occasion, that is to say, in places where the se nse of the inscription is of more importance than external ornam ent. This is a sweeping statement, from which we need not suffe r unduly; yet it is doubtful whether there is art in individual lette rs. Letters in combination may be satisfying and in a well compo sed page even beautiful as a whole, but art in letters consists rath
The main purpose of letters is the practical one of making thoughts vsibl e. Ruskin says that all letters are frightful things and to be endured only o
The main purpose of letters is the practical one of making th oughts visible. Ruskin says that all letters are frightful thing

9/10

The main purpose of letters is the practical one of making thoug hts visible. Ruskin says that all letters are frightful things and to be endured only on occasion, that is to say, in places where the se nse of the inscription is of more importance than external ornam ent. This is a sweeping statement, from which we need not suffe r unduly; yet it is doubtful whether there is art in individual lette rs. Letters in combination may be satisfying and in a well compo
The main purpose of letters is the practical one of making thoughts vsibl e. Ruskin says that all letters are frightful things and to be endured only o
The main purpose of letters is the practical one of making th oughts visible. Ruskin says that all letters are frightful thing

9/11

The main purpose of letters is the practical one of making thoug hts visible. Ruskin says that all letters are frightful things and to be endured only on occasion, that is to say, in places where the se nse of the inscription is of more importance than external ornam ent. This is a sweeping statement, from which we need not suffe r unduly; yet it is doubtful whether there is art in individual lette rs. Letters in combination may be satisfying and in a well compo
The main purpose of letters is the practical one of making thoughts vsibl e. Ruskin says that all letters are frightful things and to be endured only o
The main purpose of letters is the practical one of making th oughts visible. Ruskin says that all letters are frightful thing

9/12

The main purpose of letters is the practical one of making thoug hts visible. Ruskin says that all letters are frightful things and to be endured only on occasion, that is to say, in places where the se nse of the inscription is of more importance than external ornam ent. This is a sweeping statement, from which we need not suffe r unduly; yet it is doubtful whether there is art in individual lette rs. Letters in combination may be satisfying and in a well compo
The main purpose of letters is the practical one of making thoughts vsibl e. Ruskin says that all letters are frightful things and to be endured only o
The main purpose of letters is the practical one of making th oughts visible. Ruskin says that all letters are frightful thing

CASLON 10 POINT SET MINUS ½ UNIT

540 ROMAN, ITALIC, #3 BOLD, BOLD ITALIC

abcdefghijklmnopqrstuvwxyz – 1 UNIT
abcdefghijklmnopqrstuvwxyz – ½ UNIT
abcdefghijklmnopqrstuvwxyz NORMAL

ABCDEFGHIJKLMNOPQRSTUVWXYZ 1234567890 abcdefghijklmnopqrstuvwxyz
ABCDEFGHIJKLMNOPQRSTUVWXYZ 1234567890 abcdefghijklmnopqrstuvwxyz
ABCDEFGHIJKLMNOPQRSTUVWXYZ 1234567890 abcdefghijklmnopqrstuvwxyz
ABCDEFGHIJKLMNOPQRSTUVWXYZ 1234567890 abcdefghijklmnopqrstuvwxyz

10/10

The main purpose of letters is the practical one of making th oughts visible. Ruskin says that all letters are frightful things and to be endured only on occasion, that is to say, in places w here the sense of the inscription is of more importance than e xternal ornament. This is a sweeping statement, from which we need not suffer unduly; yet it is doubtful whether there is art in individual letters. Letters in combination may be satisf ying and in a well composed page even beautiful as a whole, but art in letters consists rather in the art of arranging and co mposing them in a pleasing and appropriate manner. The ma in purpose of letters is the practical one of making thoughts v isible. Ruskin says that all letters are frightful things and to b e endured only on occasion, that is to say, in places where the sense of the inscription is of more importance than external o rnament. This is a sweeping statement, from which we need not suffer unduly; yet it is doubtful whether there is art in ind ividual letters. Letters in combination may be satisfying and in a well composed page even beautiful as a whole, but art in l etters consists rather in the art of arranging and composing th em in a pleasing and appropriate manner. The main purpose of letters is the practical one of making thoughts visible. Rus kin says that all letters are frightful things and to be endured
The main purpose of letters is the practical one of making thoughts vi sible. Ruskin says that all letters are frightful things and to be endure
The main purpose of letters is the practical one of makin g thoughts visible. Ruskin says that all letters are frightf

10/11

The main purpose of letters is the practical one of making th oughts visible. Ruskin says that all letters are frightful things and to be endured only on occasion, that is to say, in places w here the sense of the inscription is of more importance than e xternal ornament. This is a sweeping statement, from which we need not suffer unduly; yet it is doubtful whether there is art in individual letters. Letters in combination may be satisf ying and in a well composed page even beautiful as a whole, but art in letters consists rather in the art of arranging and co mposing them in a pleasing and appropriate manner. The ma in purpose of letters is the practical one of making thoughts v isible. Ruskin says that all letters are frightful things and to b e endured only on occasion, that is to say, in places where the sense of the inscription is of more importance than external o rnament. This is a sweeping statement, from which we need not suffer unduly; yet it is doubtful whether there is art in ind ividual letters. Letters in combination may be satisfying and in a well composed page even beautiful as a whole, but art in l etters consists rather in the art of arranging and composing th em in a pleasing and appropriate manner. The main purpose
The main purpose of letters is the practical one of making thoughts vi sible. Ruskin says that all letters are frightful things and to be endure
The main purpose of letters is the practical one of makin g thoughts visible. Ruskin says that all letters are frightf

10/12

The main purpose of letters is the practical one of making th oughts visible. Ruskin says that all letters are frightful things and to be endured only on occasion, that is to say, in places w here the sense of the inscription is of more importance than e xternal ornament. This is a sweeping statement, from which we need not suffer unduly; yet it is doubtful whether there is art in individual letters. Letters in combination may be satisf ying and in a well composed page even beautiful as a whole, but art in letters consists rather in the art of arranging and co mposing them in a pleasing and appropriate manner. The ma in purpose of letters is the practical one of making thoughts v isible. Ruskin says that all letters are frightful things and to b e endured only on occasion, that is to say, in places where the sense of the inscription is of more importance than external o rnament. This is a sweeping statement, from which we need not suffer unduly; yet it is doubtful whether there is art in ind ividual letters. Letters in combination may be satisfying and in a well composed page even beautiful as a whole, but art in l
The main purpose of letters is the practical one of making thoughts vi sible. Ruskin says that all letters are frightful things and to be endure
The main purpose of letters is the practical one of makin g thoughts visible. Ruskin says that all letters are frightf

10/13

The main purpose of letters is the practical one of making th oughts visible. Ruskin says that all letters are frightful things and to be endured only on occasion, that is to say, in places w here the sense of the inscription is of more importance than e xternal ornament. This is a sweeping statement, from which we need not suffer unduly; yet it is doubtful whether there is art in individual letters. Letters in combination may be satisf ying and in a well composed page even beautiful as a whole, but art in letters consists rather in the art of arranging and co mposing them in a pleasing and appropriate manner. The ma in purpose of letters is the practical one of making thoughts v isible. Ruskin says that all letters are frightful things and to b e endured only on occasion, that is to say, in places where the sense of the inscription is of more importance than external o rnament. This is a sweeping statement, from which we need not suffer unduly; yet it is doubtful whether there is art in ind ividual letters. Letters in combination may be satisfying and
The main purpose of letters is the practical one of making thoughts vi sible. Ruskin says that all letters are frightful things and to be endure
The main purpose of letters is the practical one of makin g thoughts visible. Ruskin says that all letters are frightf

CASLON 11 POINT SET MINUS ½ UNIT

540 ROMAN, ITALIC, #3 BOLD, BOLD ITALIC

abcdefghijklmnopqrstuvwxyz – 1 UNIT
abcdefghijklmnopqrstuvwxyz – ½ UNIT
abcdefghijklmnopqrstuvwxyz NORMAL

ABCDEFGHIJKLMNOPQRSTUVWXYZ 1234567890 abcdefghijklmnopqrstuvwxyz
ABCDEFGHIJKLMNOPQRSTUVWXYZ 1234567890 abcdefghijklmnopqrstuvwxyz
ABCDEFGHIJKLMNOPQRSTUVWXYZ 1234567890 abcdefghijklmnopqrstuvwxyz
ABCDEFGHIJKLMNOPQRSTUVWXYZ 1234567890 abcdefghijklmnopqrstuvwxyz

11/11

The main purpose of letters is the practical one of maki ng thoughts visible. Ruskin says that all letters are frigh tful things and to be endured only on occasion, that is t o say, in places where the sense of the inscription is of more importance than external ornament. This is a swe eping statement, from which we need not suffer undul y; yet it is doubtful whether there is art in individual let ters. Letters in combination may be satisfying and in a well composed page even beautiful as a whole, but art i n letters consists rather in the art of arranging and comp osing them in a pleasing and appropriate manner. The main purpose of letters is the practical one of making th oughts visible. Ruskin says that all letters are frightful t hings and to be endured only on occasion, that is to say, in places where the sense of the inscription is of more i mportance than external ornament. This is a sweeping statement, from which we need not suffer unduly; yet it is doubtful whether there is art in individual letters. Le tters in combination may be satisfying and in a well co
The main purpose of letters is the practical one of making thou ghts visible. Ruskin says that all letters are frightful things and
The main purpose of letters is the practical one of making thoughts visible. Ruskin says that all letter

11/12

The main purpose of letters is the practical one of maki ng thoughts visible. Ruskin says that all letters are frigh tful things and to be endured only on occasion, that is t o say, in places where the sense of the inscription is of more importance than external ornament. This is a swe eping statement, from which we need not suffer undul y; yet it is doubtful whether there is art in individual let ters. Letters in combination may be satisfying and in a well composed page even beautiful as a whole, but art i n letters consists rather in the art of arranging and comp osing them in a pleasing and appropriate manner. The main purpose of letters is the practical one of making th oughts visible. Ruskin says that all letters are frightful t hings and to be endured only on occasion, that is to say, in places where the sense of the inscription is of more i mportance than external ornament. This is a sweeping statement, from which we need not suffer unduly; yet it is doubtful whether there is art in individual letters. Le
The main purpose of letters is the practical one of making thou ghts visible. Ruskin says that all letters are frightful things and
The main purpose of letters is the practical one of making thoughts visible. Ruskin says that all letter

11/13

The main purpose of letters is the practical one of maki ng thoughts visible. Ruskin says that all letters are frigh tful things and to be endured only on occasion, that is t o say, in places where the sense of the inscription is of more importance than external ornament. This is a swe eping statement, from which we need not suffer undul y; yet it is doubtful whether there is art in individual let ters. Letters in combination may be satisfying and in a well composed page even beautiful as a whole, but art i n letters consists rather in the art of arranging and comp osing them in a pleasing and appropriate manner. The main purpose of letters is the practical one of making th oughts visible. Ruskin says that all letters are frightful t hings and to be endured only on occasion, that is to say, in places where the sense of the inscription is of more i mportance than external ornament. This is a sweeping statement, from which we need not suffer unduly; yet it
The main purpose of letters is the practical one of making thou ghts visible. Ruskin says that all letters are frightful things and
The main purpose of letters is the practical one of making thoughts visible. Ruskin says that all letter

11/14

The main purpose of letters is the practical one of maki ng thoughts visible. Ruskin says that all letters are frigh tful things and to be endured only on occasion, that is t o say, in places where the sense of the inscription is of more importance than external ornament. This is a swe eping statement, from which we need not suffer undul y; yet it is doubtful whether there is art in individual let ters. Letters in combination may be satisfying and in a well composed page even beautiful as a whole, but art i n letters consists rather in the art of arranging and comp osing them in a pleasing and appropriate manner. The main purpose of letters is the practical one of making th oughts visible. Ruskin says that all letters are frightful t hings and to be endured only on occasion, that is to say, in places where the sense of the inscription is of more i mportance than external ornament. This is a sweeping
The main purpose of letters is the practical one of making thou ghts visible. Ruskin says that all letters are frightful things and
The main purpose of letters is the practical one of making thoughts visible. Ruskin says that all letter

CASLON 12 POINT SET MINUS ½ UNIT

540 ROMAN, ITALIC, #3 BOLD, BOLD ITALIC

abcdefghijklmnopqrstuvwxyz – 1 UNIT
abcdefghijklmnopqrstuvwxyz – ½ UNIT
abcdefghijklmnopqrstuvwxyz NORMAL

ABCDEFGHIJKLMNOPQRSTUVWXYZ 1234567890 abcdefghijklmnopqrstuvwxyz
ABCDEFGHIJKLMNOPQRSTUVWXYZ 1234567890 abcdefghijklmnopqrstuvwxyz
ABCDEFGHIJKLMNOPQRSTUVWXYZ 1234567890 abcdefghijklmnopqrstuvwxy
ABCDEFGHIJKLMNOPQRSTUVWXYZ 1234567890 abcdefghijklmnopqrstuvwxyz

12/12

The main purpose of letters is the practical one of making thoughts visible. Ruskin says that all letters are frightful things and to be endured only on occas ion, that is to say, in places where the sense of the in scription is of more importance than external orna ment. This is a sweeping statement, from which w e need not suffer unduly; yet it is doubtful whether there is art in individual letters. Letters in combinat ion may be satisfying and in a well composed page even beautiful as a whole, but art in letters consists r ather in the art of arranging and composing them in a pleasing and appropriate manner. The main purp ose of letters is the practical one of making thoughts visible. Ruskin says that all letters are frightful thin gs and to be endured only on occasion, that is to say,
The main purpose of letters is the practical one of making t houghts visible. Ruskin says that all letters are frightful thi
The main purpose of letters is the practical one of making thoughts visible. Ruskin says that all

12/13

The main purpose of letters is the practical one of making thoughts visible. Ruskin says that all letters are frightful things and to be endured only on occas ion, that is to say, in places where the sense of the in scription is of more importance than external orna ment. This is a sweeping statement, from which w e need not suffer unduly; yet it is doubtful whether there is art in individual letters. Letters in combinat ion may be satisfying and in a well composed page even beautiful as a whole, but art in letters consists r ather in the art of arranging and composing them in a pleasing and appropriate manner. The main purp ose of letters is the practical one of making thoughts visible. Ruskin says that all letters are frightful thin
The main purpose of letters is the practical one of making t houghts visible. Ruskin says that all letters are frightful thi
The main purpose of letters is the practical one of making thoughts visible. Ruskin says that all

12/14

The main purpose of letters is the practical one of making thoughts visible. Ruskin says that all letters are frightful things and to be endured only on occas ion, that is to say, in places where the sense of the in scription is of more importance than external orna ment. This is a sweeping statement, from which w e need not suffer unduly; yet it is doubtful whether there is art in individual letters. Letters in combinat ion may be satisfying and in a well composed page even beautiful as a whole, but art in letters consists r ather in the art of arranging and composing them in a pleasing and appropriate manner. The main purp ose of letters is the practical one of making thoughts visible. Ruskin says that all letters are frightful thin gs and to be endured only on occasion, that is to say,
The main purpose of letters is the practical one of making t houghts visible. Ruskin says that all letters are frightful thi
The main purpose of letters is the practical one of making thoughts visible. Ruskin says that all

12/15

The main purpose of letters is the practical one of making thoughts visible. Ruskin says that all letters are frightful things and to be endured only on occas ion, that is to say, in places where the sense of the in scription is of more importance than external orna ment. This is a sweeping statement, from which w e need not suffer unduly; yet it is doubtful whether there is art in individual letters. Letters in combinat ion may be satisfying and in a well composed page even beautiful as a whole, but art in letters consists r ather in the art of arranging and composing them in a pleasing and appropriate manner. The main purp ose of letters is the practical one of making thoughts visible. Ruskin says that all letters are frightful thin
The main purpose of letters is the practical one of making t houghts visible. Ruskin says that all letters are frightful thi
The main purpose of letters is the practical one of making thoughts visible. Ruskin says that all

CASLON 14 POINT SET MINUS ½ UNIT

540 ROMAN, ITALIC, #3 BOLD, BOLD ITALIC

abcdefghijklmnopqrstuvwxyz – 1 UNIT
abcdefghijklmnopqrstuvwxyz – ½ UNIT
abcdefghijklmnopqrstuvwxyz NORMAL

ABCDEFGHIJKLMNOPQRSTUVWXYZ abcdefghijklmnopqrstuvwxyz
ABCDEFGHIJKLMNOPQRSTUVWXYZ abcdefghijklmnopqrstuvwxyz
ABCDEFGHIJKLMNOPQRSTUVWXYZ abcdefghijklmnopqrstuvwxyz
ABCDEFGHIJKLMNOPQRSTUVWXYZ abcdefghijklmnopqrstuvwxyz

14/14

The main purpose of letters is the practical one of making thoughts visible. Ruskin say s that all letters are frightful things and to be endured only on occasion, that is to say, in p laces where the sense of the inscription is of more importance than external ornament. T his is a sweeping statement, from which we need not suffer unduly; yet it is doubtful w hether there is art in individual letters. Let ters in combination may be satisfying and in a well composed page even beautiful as a wh ole, but art in letters consists rather in the art of arranging and composing them in a ple
The main purpose of letters is the practical one of making thoughts visible. Ruskin says that all lette
The main purpose of letters is the practi cal one of making thoughts visible. Rus

14/15

The main purpose of letters is the practical one of making thoughts visible. Ruskin say s that all letters are frightful things and to be endured only on occasion, that is to say, in p laces where the sense of the inscription is of more importance than external ornament. T his is a sweeping statement, from which we need not suffer unduly; yet it is doubtful w hether there is art in individual letters. Let ters in combination may be satisfying and in a well composed page even beautiful as a wh ole, but art in letters consists rather in the
The main purpose of letters is the practical one of making thoughts visible. Ruskin says that all lette
The main purpose of letters is the practi cal one of making thoughts visible. Rus

14/16

The main purpose of letters is the practical one of making thoughts visible. Ruskin say s that all letters are frightful things and to be endured only on occasion, that is to say, in p laces where the sense of the inscription is of more importance than external ornament. T his is a sweeping statement, from which we need not suffer unduly; yet it is doubtful w hether there is art in individual letters. Let ters in combination may be satisfying and in a well composed page even beautiful as a wh ole, but art in letters consists rather in the art of arranging and composing them in a ple
The main purpose of letters is the practical one of making thoughts visible. Ruskin says that all lette
The main purpose of letters is the practi cal one of making thoughts visible. Rus

14/17

The main purpose of letters is the practical one of making thoughts visible. Ruskin say s that all letters are frightful things and to be endured only on occasion, that is to say, in p laces where the sense of the inscription is of more importance than external ornament. T his is a sweeping statement, from which we need not suffer unduly; yet it is doubtful w hether there is art in individual letters. Let ters in combination may be satisfying and in a well composed page even beautiful as a wh ole, but art in letters consists rather in the
The main purpose of letters is the practical one of making thoughts visible. Ruskin says that all lette
The main purpose of letters is the practi cal one of making thoughts visible. Rus

CENTURY EXPANDED 6 & 7 POINT SET NORMAL

ROMAN, ITALIC, BOLD, BOLD ITALIC

ABCDEFGHIJKLMNOPQRSTUVWXYZ 1234567890 abcdefghijklmnopqrstuvwxyz

ABCDEFGHIJKLMNOPQRSTUVWXYZ 1234567890 abcdefghijklmnopqrstuvwxyz

ABCDEFGHIJKLMNOPQRSTUVWXYZ 1234567890 abcdefghijklmnopqrstuvwxyz

ABCDEFGHIJKLMNOPQRSTUVWXYZ 1234567890 abcdefghijklmnopqrstuvwxyz

6/6

The main purpose of letters is the practical one of making thoughts visible. Ruskin says that all letters are frightful things and to be endured only on occasion, that is to say, in places whe re the sense of the inscription is of more importance than external ornament. This is a sweepi ng statement, from which we need not suffer unduly; yet it is doubtful whether there is art in individual letters. Letters in combination may be satisfying and in a well composed page eve n beautiful as a whole, but art in letters consists rather in the art of arranging and composing them in a pleasing and appropriate manner. The main purpose of letters is the practical one of making thoughts visible. Ruskin says that all letters are frightful things and to be endured o nly on occasion, that is to say, in places where the sense of the inscription is of more importan ce than external ornament. This is a sweeping statement, from which we need not suffer und uly; yet it is doubtful whether there is art in individual letters. Letters in combination may b e satisfying and in a well composed page even beautiful as a whole, but art in letters consists r ather in the art of arranging and composing them in a pleasing and appropriate manner. The
The main purpose of letters is the practical one of making thoughts visible. Ruskin says that all letters are frightful things and to be endured only on occasion, that is to say, in places wh
The main purpose of letters is the practical one of making thoughts visible. Ruskin says that all letters are frightful things and to be endured only on occasion, that is to say, in pl

6/7

The main purpose of letters is the practical one of making thoughts visible. Ruskin says that all letters are frightful things and to be endured only on occasion, that is to say, in places whe re the sense of the inscription is of more importance than external ornament. This is a sweepi ng statement, from which we need not suffer unduly; yet it is doubtful whether there is art in individual letters. Letters in combination may be satisfying and in a well composed page eve n beautiful as a whole, but art in letters consists rather in the art of arranging and composing them in a pleasing and appropriate manner. The main purpose of letters is the practical one of making thoughts visible. Ruskin says that all letters are frightful things and to be endured o nly on occasion, that is to say, in places where the sense of the inscription is of more importan ce than external ornament. This is a sweeping statement, from which we need not suffer und uly; yet it is doubtful whether there is art in individual letters. Letters in combination may b
The main purpose of letters is the practical one of making thoughts visible. Ruskin says that all letters are frightful things and to be endured only on occasion, that is to say, in places wh
The main purpose of letters is the practical one of making thoughts visible. Ruskin says that all letters are frightful things and to be endured only on occasion, that is to say, in pl

6/8

The main purpose of letters is the practical one of making thoughts visible. Ruskin says that all letters are frightful things and to be endured only on occasion, that is to say, in places whe re the sense of the inscription is of more importance than external ornament. This is a sweepi ng statement, from which we need not suffer unduly; yet it is doubtful whether there is art in individual letters. Letters in combination may be satisfying and in a well composed page eve n beautiful as a whole, but art in letters consists rather in the art of arranging and composing them in a pleasing and appropriate manner. The main purpose of letters is the practical one of making thoughts visible. Ruskin says that all letters are frightful things and to be endured o nly on occasion, that is to say, in places where the sense of the inscription is of more importan
The main purpose of letters is the practical one of making thoughts visible. Ruskin says that all letters are frightful things and to be endured only on occasion, that is to say, in places wh
The main purpose of letters is the practical one of making thoughts visible. Ruskin says that all letters are frightful things and to be endured only on occasion, that is to say, in pl

6/9

The main purpose of letters is the practical one of making thoughts visible. Ruskin says that all letters are frightful things and to be endured only on occasion, that is to say, in places whe re the sense of the inscription is of more importance than external ornament. This is a sweepi ng statement, from which we need not suffer unduly; yet it is doubtful whether there is art in individual letters. Letters in combination may be satisfying and in a well composed page eve n beautiful as a whole, but art in letters consists rather in the art of arranging and composing them in a pleasing and appropriate manner. The main purpose of letters is the practical one of making thoughts visible. Ruskin says that all letters are frightful things and to be endured o
The main purpose of letters is the practical one of making thoughts visible. Ruskin says that all letters are frightful things and to be endured only on occasion, that is to say, in places wh
The main purpose of letters is the practical one of making thoughts visible. Ruskin says that all letters are frightful things and to be endured only on occasion, that is to say, in pl

---

ABCDEFGHIJKLMNOPQRSTUVWXYZ 1234567890 abcdefghijklmnopqrstuvwxyz

ABCDEFGHIJKLMNOPQRSTUVWXYZ 1234567890 abcdefghijklmnopqrstuvwxyz

ABCDEFGHIJKLMNOPQRSTUVWXYZ 1234567890 abcdefghijklmnopqrstuvwxyz

ABCDEFGHIJKLMNOPQRSTUVWXYZ 1234567890 abcdefghijklmnopqrstuvwxyz

7/7

The main purpose of letters is the practical one of making thoughts visible. Rus kin says that all letters are frightful things and to be endured only on occasion, that is to say, in places where the sense of the inscription is of more importance than external ornament. This is a sweeping statement, from which we need not suffer unduly; yet it is doubtful whether there is art in individual letters. Lette rs in combination may be satisfying and in a well composed page even beautiful as a whole, but art in letters consists rather in the art of arranging and composi ng them in a pleasing and appropriate manner. The main purpose of letters is th e practical one of making thoughts visible. Ruskin says that all letters are fright ful things and to be endured only on occasion, that is to say, in places where the sense of the inscription is of more importance than external ornament. This is a
The main purpose of letters is the practical one of making thoughts visible. Rus kin says that all letters are frightful things and to be endured only on occasion,
The main purpose of letters is the practical one of making thoughts visible. Ruskin says that all letters are frightful things and to be endured only on oc

7/8

The main purpose of letters is the practical one of making thoughts visible. Rus kin says that all letters are frightful things and to be endured only on occasion, that is to say, in places where the sense of the inscription is of more importance than external ornament. This is a sweeping statement, from which we need not suffer unduly; yet it is doubtful whether there is art in individual letters. Lette rs in combination may be satisfying and in a well composed page even beautiful as a whole, but art in letters consists rather in the art of arranging and composi ng them in a pleasing and appropriate manner. The main purpose of letters is th e practical one of making thoughts visible. Ruskin says that all letters are fright ful things and to be endured only on occasion, that is to say, in places where the
The main purpose of letters is the practical one of making thoughts visible. Rus kin says that all letters are frightful things and to be endured only on occasion,
The main purpose of letters is the practical one of making thoughts visible. Ruskin says that all letters are frightful things and to be endured only on oc

7/9

The main purpose of letters is the practical one of making thoughts visible. Rus kin says that all letters are frightful things and to be endured only on occasion, that is to say, in places where the sense of the inscription is of more importance than external ornament. This is a sweeping statement, from which we need not suffer unduly; yet it is doubtful whether there is art in individual letters. Lette rs in combination may be satisfying and in a well composed page even beautiful as a whole, but art in letters consists rather in the art of arranging and composi ng them in a pleasing and appropriate manner. The main purpose of letters is th e practical one of making thoughts visible. Ruskin says that all letters are fright ful things and to be endured only on occasion, that is to say, in places where the
The main purpose of letters is the practical one of making thoughts visible. Rus kin says that all letters are frightful things and to be endured only on occasion,
The main purpose of letters is the practical one of making thoughts visible. Ruskin says that all letters are frightful things and to be endured only on oc

7/10

The main purpose of letters is the practical one of making thoughts visible. Rus kin says that all letters are frightful things and to be endured only on occasion, that is to say, in places where the sense of the inscription is of more importance than external ornament. This is a sweeping statement, from which we need not suffer unduly; yet it is doubtful whether there is art in individual letters. Lette rs in combination may be satisfying and in a well composed page even beautiful as a whole, but art in letters consists rather in the art of arranging and composi ng them in a pleasing and appropriate manner. The main purpose of letters is th e practical one of making thoughts visible. Ruskin says that all letters are fright
The main purpose of letters is the practical one of making thoughts visible. Rus kin says that all letters are frightful things and to be endured only on occasion,
The main purpose of letters is the practical one of making thoughts visible. Ruskin says that all letters are frightful things and to be endured only on oc

CENTURY EXPANDED 8 & 9 POINT SET NORMAL

ROMAN, ITALIC, BOLD, BOLD ITALIC

ABCDEFGHIJKLMNOPQRSTUVWXYZ 1234567890 abcdefghijklmnopqrstuvwxyz

ABCDEFGHIJKLMNOPQRSTUVWXYZ 1234567890 abcdefghijklmnopqrstuvwxyz

ABCDEFGHIJKLMNOPQRSTUVWXYZ 1234567890 abcdefghijklmnopqrstuvwxyz

ABCDEFGHIJKLMNOPQRSTUVWXYZ 1234567890 abcdefghijklmnopqrstuvwxyz

8/8

The main purpose of letters is the practical one of making thoughts vi sible. Ruskin says that all letters are frightful things and to be endure d only on occasion, that is to say, in places where the sense of the inscr iption is of more importance than external ornament. This is a sweepi ng statement, from which we need not suffer unduly; yet it is doubtful whether there is art in individual letters. Letters in combination may be satisfying and in a well composed page even beautiful as a whole, but art in letters consists rather in the art of arranging and composing them in a pleasing and appropriate manner. The main purpose of lette

The main purpose of letters is the practical one of making thoughts vi sible. Ruskin says that all letters are frightful things and to be endur

The main purpose of letters is the practical one of making thought s visible. Ruskin says that all letters are frightful things and to be

8/9

The main purpose of letters is the practical one of making thoughts vi sible. Ruskin says that all letters are frightful things and to be endure d only on occasion, that is to say, in places where the sense of the inscr iption is of more importance than external ornament. This is a sweepi ng statement, from which we need not suffer unduly; yet it is doubtful whether there is art in individual letters. Letters in combination may be satisfying and in a well composed page even beautiful as a whole, but art in letters consists rather in the art of arranging and composing

The main purpose of letters is the practical one of making thoughts vi sible. Ruskin says that all letters are frightful things and to be endur

The main purpose of letters is the practical one of making thought s visible. Ruskin says that all letters are frightful things and to be

8/10

The main purpose of letters is the practical one of making thoughts vi sible. Ruskin says that all letters are frightful things and to be endure d only on occasion, that is to say, in places where the sense of the inscr iption is of more importance than external ornament. This is a sweepi ng statement, from which we need not suffer unduly; yet it is doubtful whether there is art in individual letters. Letters in combination may be satisfying and in a well composed page even beautiful as a whole,

The main purpose of letters is the practical one of making thoughts vi sible. Ruskin says that all letters are frightful things and to be endur

The main purpose of letters is the practical one of making thought s visible. Ruskin says that all letters are frightful things and to be

8/11

The main purpose of letters is the practical one of making thoughts vi sible. Ruskin says that all letters are frightful things and to be endure d only on occasion, that is to say, in places where the sense of the inscr iption is of more importance than external ornament. This is a sweepi ng statement, from which we need not suffer unduly; yet it is doubtful whether there is art in individual letters. Letters in combination may be satisfying and in a well composed page even beautiful as a whole,

The main purpose of letters is the practical one of making thoughts vi sible. Ruskin says that all letters are frightful things and to be endur

The main purpose of letters is the practical one of making thought s visible. Ruskin says that all letters are frightful things and to be

---

ABCDEFGHIJKLMNOPQRSTUVWXYZ 1234567890 abcdefghijklmnopqrstuvwxyz

ABCDEFGHIJKLMNOPQRSTUVWXYZ 1234567890 abcdefghijklmnopqrstuvwxyz

ABCDEFGHIJKLMNOPQRSTUVWXYZ 1234567890 abcdefghijklmnopqrstuvwxyz

ABCDEFGHIJKLMNOPQRSTUVWXYZ 1234567890 abcdefghijklmnopqrstuvwxyz

9/9

The main purpose of letters is the practical one of making thou ghts visible. Ruskin says that all letters are frightful things a nd to be endured only on occasion, that is to say, in places whe re the sense of the inscription is of more importance than exte rnal ornament. This is a sweeping statement, from which we need not suffer unduly; yet it is doubtful whether there is art i n individual letters. Letters in combination may be satisfying and in a well composed page even beautiful as a whole, but art

The main purpose of letters is the practical one of making tho ughts visible. Ruskin says that all letters are frightful things

The main purpose of letters is the practical one of making t houghts visible. Ruskin says that all letters are frightful th

9/10

The main purpose of letters is the practical one of making thou ghts visible. Ruskin says that all letters are frightful things a nd to be endured only on occasion, that is to say, in places whe re the sense of the inscription is of more importance than exte rnal ornament. This is a sweeping statement, from which we need not suffer unduly; yet it is doubtful whether there is art i n individual letters. Letters in combination may be satisfying

The main purpose of letters is the practical one of making tho ughts visible. Ruskin says that all letters are frightful things

The main purpose of letters is the practical one of making t houghts visible. Ruskin says that all letters are frightful th

9/11

The main purpose of letters is the practical one of making thou ghts visible. Ruskin says that all letters are frightful things a nd to be endured only on occasion, that is to say, in places whe re the sense of the inscription is of more importance than exte rnal ornament. This is a sweeping statement, from which we need not suffer unduly; yet it is doubtful whether there is art i n individual letters. Letters in combination may be satisfying

The main purpose of letters is the practical one of making tho ughts visible. Ruskin says that all letters are frightful things

The main purpose of letters is the practical one of making t houghts visible. Ruskin says that all letters are frightful th

9/12

The main purpose of letters is the practical one of making thou ghts visible. Ruskin says that all letters are frightful things a nd to be endured only on occasion, that is to say, in places whe re the sense of the inscription is of more importance than exte rnal ornament. This is a sweeping statement, from which we need not suffer unduly; yet it is doubtful whether there is art i n individual letters. Letters in combination may be satisfying

The main purpose of letters is the practical one of making tho ughts visible. Ruskin says that all letters are frightful things

The main purpose of letters is the practical one of making t houghts visible. Ruskin says that all letters are frightful th

CENTURY EXPANDED 10 POINT SET MINUS ½ UNIT

ROMAN, ITALIC, BOLD, BOLD ITALIC

abcdefghijklmnopqrstuvwxyz – 1 UNIT
abcdefghijklmnopqrstuvwxyz – ½ UNIT
abcdefghijklmnopqrstuvwxyz NORMAL

ABCDEFGHIJKLMNOPQRSTUVWXYZ 1234567890 abcdefghijklmnopqrstuvwxyz
ABCDEFGHIJKLMNOPQRSTUVWXYZ 1234567890 abcdefghijklmnopqrstuvwxyz
ABCDEFGHIJKLMNOPQRSTUVWXYZ 1234567890 abcdefghijklmnopqrstuvwxyz
ABCDEFGHIJKLMNOPQRSTUVWXYZ 1234567890 abcdefghijklmnopqrstuvwxyz

10/10

The main purpose of letters is the practical one of making thoughts visible. Ruskin says that all letters are frightful things and to be endured only on occasion, that is to say, in places where the sense of the inscription is of more import ance than external ornament. This is a sweeping stateme nt, from which we need not suffer unduly; yet it is doubtfu l whether there is art in individual letters. Letters in comb ination may be satisfying and in a well composed page eve n beautiful as a whole, but art in letters consists rather in t he art of arranging and composing them in a pleasing and appropriate manner. The main purpose of letters is the pr actical one of making thoughts visible. Ruskin says that all letters are frightful things and to be endured only on occas ion, that is to say, in places where the sense of the inscripti on is of more importance than external ornament. This is a sweeping statement, from which we need not suffer undul y; yet it is doubtful whether there is art in individual lette rs. Letters in combination may be satisfying and in a well composed page even beautiful as a whole, but art in lette rs consists rather in the art of arranging and composing th em in a pleasing and appropriate manner. The main purpo se of letters is the practical one of making thoughts visible
The main purpose of letters is the practical one of making thoughts visible. Ruskin says that all letters are frightful
The main purpose of letters is the practical one of maki ng thoughts visible. Ruskin says that all letters are frig

10/11

The main purpose of letters is the practical one of making thoughts visible. Ruskin says that all letters are frightful things and to be endured only on occasion, that is to say, in places where the sense of the inscription is of more import ance than external ornament. This is a sweeping stateme nt, from which we need not suffer unduly; yet it is doubtfu l whether there is art in individual letters. Letters in comb ination may be satisfying and in a well composed page eve n beautiful as a whole, but art in letters consists rather in t he art of arranging and composing them in a pleasing and appropriate manner. The main purpose of letters is the pr actical one of making thoughts visible. Ruskin says that all letters are frightful things and to be endured only on occas ion, that is to say, in places where the sense of the inscripti on is of more importance than external ornament. This is a sweeping statement, from which we need not suffer undul y; yet it is doubtful whether there is art in individual lette rs. Letters in combination may be satisfying and in a well composed page even beautiful as a whole, but art in lette rs consists rather in the art of arranging and composing th
The main purpose of letters is the practical one of making thoughts visible. Ruskin says that all letters are frightful
The main purpose of letters is the practical one of maki ng thoughts visible. Ruskin says that all letters are frig

10/12

The main purpose of letters is the practical one of making thoughts visible. Ruskin says that all letters are frightful things and to be endured only on occasion, that is to say, in places where the sense of the inscription is of more import ance than external ornament. This is a sweeping stateme nt, from which we need not suffer unduly; yet it is doubtfu l whether there is art in individual letters. Letters in comb ination may be satisfying and in a well composed page eve n beautiful as a whole, but art in letters consists rather in t he art of arranging and composing them in a pleasing and appropriate manner. The main purpose of letters is the pr actical one of making thoughts visible. Ruskin says that all letters are frightful things and to be endured only on occas ion, that is to say, in places where the sense of the inscripti on is of more importance than external ornament. This is a sweeping statement, from which we need not suffer undul y; yet it is doubtful whether there is art in individual lette rs. Letters in combination may be satisfying and in a well
The main purpose of letters is the practical one of making thoughts visible. Ruskin says that all letters are frightful
The main purpose of letters is the practical one of maki ng thoughts visible. Ruskin says that all letters are frig

10/13

The main purpose of letters is the practical one of making thoughts visible. Ruskin says that all letters are frightful things and to be endured only on occasion, that is to say, in places where the sense of the inscription is of more import ance than external ornament. This is a sweeping stateme nt, from which we need not suffer unduly; yet it is doubtfu l whether there is art in individual letters. Letters in comb ination may be satisfying and in a well composed page eve n beautiful as a whole, but art in letters consists rather in t he art of arranging and composing them in a pleasing and appropriate manner. The main purpose of letters is the pr actical one of making thoughts visible. Ruskin says that all letters are frightful things and to be endured only on occas ion, that is to say, in places where the sense of the inscripti on is of more importance than external ornament. This is a sweeping statement, from which we need not suffer undul y; yet it is doubtful whether there is art in individual lette
The main purpose of letters is the practical one of making thoughts visible. Ruskin says that all letters are frightful
The main purpose of letters is the practical one of maki ng thoughts visible. Ruskin says that all letters are frig

CENTURY EXPANDED 11 POINT SET MINUS ½ UNIT

ROMAN, ITALIC, BOLD, BOLD ITALIC

abcdefghijklmnopqrstuvwxyz – 1 UNIT
abcdefghijklmnopqrstuvwxyz – ½ UNIT
abcdefghijklmnopqrstuvwxyz NORMAL

ABCDEFGHIJKLMNOPQRSTUVWXYZ 1234567890 abcdefghijklmnopqrstuvwxyz
ABCDEFGHIJKLMNOPQRSTUVWXYZ 1234567890 abcdefghijklmnopqrstuvwxyz
ABCDEFGHIJKLMNOPQRSTUVWXYZ 1234567890 abcdefghijklmnopqrstuvwxyz
ABCDEFGHIJKLMNOPQRSTUVWXYZ 1234567890 abcdefghijklmnopqrstuvwxyz

11/11

The main purpose of letters is the practical one of ma king thoughts visible. Ruskin says that all letters ar e frightful things and to be endured only on occasion, that is to say, in places where the sense of the inscrip tion is of more importance than external ornament. This is a sweeping statement, from which we need n ot suffer unduly; yet it is doubtful whether there is a rt in individual letters. Letters in combination may b e satisfying and in a well composed page even beauti ful as a whole, but art in letters consists rather in the art of arranging and composing them in a pleasing an d appropriate manner. The main purpose of letters is the practical one of making thoughts visible. Ruskin says that all letters are frightful things and to be end ured only on occasion, that is to say, in places where t he sense of the inscription is of more importance tha n external ornament. This is a sweeping statement, f rom which we need not suffer unduly; yet it is doubtf ul whether there is art in individual letters. Letters i

The main purpose of letters is the practical one of making thoughts visible. Ruskin says that all letter

The main purpose of letters is the practical one of making thoughts visible. Ruskin says that all lett

11/12

The main purpose of letters is the practical one of ma king thoughts visible. Ruskin says that all letters ar e frightful things and to be endured only on occasion, that is to say, in places where the sense of the inscrip tion is of more importance than external ornament. This is a sweeping statement, from which we need n ot suffer unduly; yet it is doubtful whether there is a rt in individual letters. Letters in combination may b e satisfying and in a well composed page even beauti ful as a whole, but art in letters consists rather in the art of arranging and composing them in a pleasing an d appropriate manner. The main purpose of letters is the practical one of making thoughts visible. Ruskin says that all letters are frightful things and to be end ured only on occasion, that is to say, in places where t he sense of the inscription is of more importance tha n external ornament. This is a sweeping statement, f rom which we need not suffer unduly; yet it is doubtf

The main purpose of letters is the practical one of making thoughts visible. Ruskin says that all letter

The main purpose of letters is the practical one of making thoughts visible. Ruskin says that all lett

11/13

The main purpose of letters is the practical one of ma king thoughts visible. Ruskin says that all letters ar e frightful things and to be endured only on occasion, that is to say, in places where the sense of the inscrip tion is of more importance than external ornament. This is a sweeping statement, from which we need n ot suffer unduly; yet it is doubtful whether there is a rt in individual letters. Letters in combination may b e satisfying and in a well composed page even beauti ful as a whole, but art in letters consists rather in the art of arranging and composing them in a pleasing an d appropriate manner. The main purpose of letters is the practical one of making thoughts visible. Ruskin says that all letters are frightful things and to be end ured only on occasion, that is to say, in places where t he sense of the inscription is of more importance tha n external ornament. This is a sweeping statement, f

The main purpose of letters is the practical one of making thoughts visible. Ruskin says that all letter

The main purpose of letters is the practical one of making thoughts visible. Ruskin says that all lett

11/14

The main purpose of letters is the practical one of ma king thoughts visible. Ruskin says that all letters ar e frightful things and to be endured only on occasion, that is to say, in places where the sense of the inscrip tion is of more importance than external ornament. This is a sweeping statement, from which we need n ot suffer unduly; yet it is doubtful whether there is a rt in individual letters. Letters in combination may b e satisfying and in a well composed page even beauti ful as a whole, but art in letters consists rather in the art of arranging and composing them in a pleasing an d appropriate manner. The main purpose of letters is the practical one of making thoughts visible. Ruskin says that all letters are frightful things and to be end ured only on occasion, that is to say, in places where t he sense of the inscription is of more importance tha

The main purpose of letters is the practical one of making thoughts visible. Ruskin says that all letter

The main purpose of letters is the practical one of making thoughts visible. Ruskin says that all lett

CENTURY EXPANDED 12 POINT SET MINUS ½ UNIT

ROMAN, ITALIC, BOLD, BOLD ITALIC

abcdefghijklmnopqrstuvwxyz – 1 UNIT
abcdefghijklmnopqrstuvwxyz – ½ UNIT
abcdefghijklmnopqrstuvwxyz NORMAL

ABCDEFGHIJKLMNOPQRSTUVWXYZ 1234567890 abcdefghijklmnopqrstuvwxyz
ABCDEFGHIJKLMNOPQRSTUVWXYZ 1234567890 abcdefghijklmnopqrstuvwxyz
ABCDEFGHIJKLMNOPQRSTUVWXYZ 1234567890 abcdefghijklmnopqrstuvwxyz
ABCDEFGHIJKLMNOPQRSTUVWXYZ 1234567890 abcdefghijklmnopqrstuvwxyz

12/12

The main purpose of letters is the practical one of making thoughts visible. Ruskin says that all lett ers are frightful things and to be endured only on occasion, that is to say, in places where the sense of the inscription is of more importance than exte rnal ornament. This is a sweeping statement, fro m which we need not suffer unduly; yet it is doub tful whether there is art in individual letters. Let ters in combination may be satisfying and in a we ll composed page even beautiful as a whole, but art in letters consists rather in the art of arrangi ng and composing them in a pleasing and approp riate manner. The main purpose of letters is the practical one of making thoughts visible. Ruskin says that all letters are frightful things and to be
The main purpose of letters is the practical one of making thoughts visible. Ruskin says that all
The main purpose of letters is the practical on e of making thoughts visible. Ruskin says that

12/13

The main purpose of letters is the practical one of making thoughts visible. Ruskin says that all lett ers are frightful things and to be endured only on occasion, that is to say, in places where the sense of the inscription is of more importance than exte rnal ornament. This is a sweeping statement, fro m which we need not suffer unduly; yet it is doub tful whether there is art in individual letters. Let ters in combination may be satisfying and in a we ll composed page even beautiful as a whole, but art in letters consists rather in the art of arrangi ng and composing them in a pleasing and approp riate manner. The main purpose of letters is the practical one of making thoughts visible. Ruskin
The main purpose of letters is the practical one of making thoughts visible. Ruskin says that all
The main purpose of letters is the practical on e of making thoughts visible. Ruskin says that

12/14

The main purpose of letters is the practical one of making thoughts visible. Ruskin says that all lett ers are frightful things and to be endured only on occasion, that is to say, in places where the sense of the inscription is of more importance than exte rnal ornament. This is a sweeping statement, fro m which we need not suffer unduly; yet it is doub tful whether there is art in individual letters. Let ters in combination may be satisfying and in a we ll composed page even beautiful as a whole, but art in letters consists rather in the art of arrangi ng and composing them in a pleasing and approp riate manner. The main purpose of letters is the practical one of making thoughts visible. Ruskin says that all letters are frightful things and to be
The main purpose of letters is the practical one of making thoughts visible. Ruskin says that all
The main purpose of letters is the practical on e of making thoughts visible. Ruskin says that

12/15

The main purpose of letters is the practical one of making thoughts visible. Ruskin says that all lett ers are frightful things and to be endured only on occasion, that is to say, in places where the sense of the inscription is of more importance than exte rnal ornament. This is a sweeping statement, fro m which we need not suffer unduly; yet it is doub tful whether there is art in individual letters. Let ters in combination may be satisfying and in a we ll composed page even beautiful as a whole, but art in letters consists rather in the art of arrangi ng and composing them in a pleasing and approp riate manner. The main purpose of letters is the practical one of making thoughts visible. Ruskin
The main purpose of letters is the practical one of making thoughts visible. Ruskin says that all
The main purpose of letters is the practical on e of making thoughts visible. Ruskin says that

CENTURY EXPANDED

14 POINT SET MINUS ½ UNIT

ROMAN, ITALIC, BOLD, BOLD ITALIC

abcdefghijklmnopqrstuvwxyz – 1 UNIT
abcdefghijklmnopqrstuvwxyz – ½ UNIT
abcdefghijklmnopqrstuvwxyz NORMAL

ABCDEFGHIJKLMNOPQRSTUVWXYZ abcdefghijklmnopqrstuvwxyz
ABCDEFGHIJKLMNOPQRSTUVWXYZ abcdefghijklmnopqrstuvwxyz
ABCDEFGHIJKLMNOPQRSTUVWXYZ abcdefghijklmnopqrstuvwxyz
ABCDEFGHIJKLMNOPQRSTUVWXYZ abcdefghijklmnopqrstuvwxyz

14/14

The main purpose of letters is the practic al one of making thoughts visible. Ruskin says that all letters are frightful things an d to be endured only on occasion, that is t o say, in places where the sense of the insc ription is of more importance than extern al ornament. This is a sweeping statemen t, from which we need not suffer unduly; yet it is doubtful whether there is art in individual letters. Letters in combination may be satisfying and in a well composed page even beautiful as a whole, but art in letters consists rather in the art of arrang
The main purpose of letters is the practic al one of making thoughts visible. Ruski
The main purpose of letters is the pract ical one of making thoughts visible. Ru

14/15

The main purpose of letters is the practic al one of making thoughts visible. Ruskin says that all letters are frightful things an d to be endured only on occasion, that is t o say, in places where the sense of the insc ription is of more importance than extern al ornament. This is a sweeping statemen t, from which we need not suffer unduly; yet it is doubtful whether there is art in individual letters. Letters in combination may be satisfying and in a well composed page even beautiful as a whole, but art in
The main purpose of letters is the practic al one of making thoughts visible. Ruski
The main purpose of letters is the pract ical one of making thoughts visible. Ru

14/16

The main purpose of letters is the practic al one of making thoughts visible. Ruskin says that all letters are frightful things an d to be endured only on occasion, that is t o say, in places where the sense of the insc ription is of more importance than extern al ornament. This is a sweeping statemen t, from which we need not suffer unduly; yet it is doubtful whether there is art in individual letters. Letters in combination may be satisfying and in a well composed page even beautiful as a whole, but art in letters consists rather in the art of arrang
The main purpose of letters is the practic al one of making thoughts visible. Ruski
The main purpose of letters is the pract ical one of making thoughts visible. Ru

14/17

The main purpose of letters is the practic al one of making thoughts visible. Ruskin says that all letters are frightful things an d to be endured only on occasion, that is t o say, in places where the sense of the insc ription is of more importance than extern al ornament. This is a sweeping statemen t, from which we need not suffer unduly; yet it is doubtful whether there is art in individual letters. Letters in combination may be satisfying and in a well composed page even beautiful as a whole, but art in
The main purpose of letters is the practic al one of making thoughts visible. Ruski
The main purpose of letters is the pract ical one of making thoughts visible. Ru

CENTURY OLDSTYLE 6 & 7 POINT SET NORMAL

ROMAN, ITALIC, BOLD, BOLD ITALIC

ABCDEFGHIJKLMNOPQRSTUVWXYZ 1234567890 abcdefghijklmnopqrstuvwxyz

ABCDEFGHIJKLMNOPQRSTUVWXYZ 1234567890 abcdefghijklmnopqrstuvwxyz

ABCDEFGHIJKLMNOPQRSTUVWXYZ 1234567890 abcdefghijklmnopqrstuvwxyz

6/6

The main purpose of letters is the practical one of making thoughts visible. Ruskin says that all letter
s are frightful things and to be endured only on occasion, that is to say, in places where the sense of t
he inscription is of more importance than external ornament. This is a sweeping statement, from wh
ich we need not suffer unduly; yet it is doubtful whether there is art in individual letters. Letters in co
mbination may be satisfying and in a well composed page even beautiful as a whole, but art in letters
consists rather in the art of arranging and composing them in a pleasing and appropriate manner. Th
e main purpose of letters is the practical one of making thoughts visible. Ruskin says that all letters a
re frightful things and to be endured only on occasion, that is to say, in places where the sense of the i
nscription is of more importance than external ornament. This is a sweeping statement, from which
we need not suffer unduly; yet it is doubtful whether there is art in individual letters. Letters in comb
ination may be satisfying and in a well composed page even beautiful as a whole, but art in letters con
sists rather in the art of arranging and composing them in a pleasing and appropriate manner. The ma
in purpose of letters is the practical one of making thoughts visible. Ruskin says that all letters are fri
The main purpose of letters is the practical one of making thoughts visible. Ruskin says that all letters ar
e frightful things and to be endured only on occasion, that is to say, in places where the sense of the inscri
The main purpose of letters is the practical one of making thoughts visible. Ruskin say
s that all letters are frightful things and to be endured only on occasion, that is to say, i

6/7

The main purpose of letters is the practical one of making thoughts visible. Ruskin says that all letter
s are frightful things and to be endured only on occasion, that is to say, in places where the sense of t
he inscription is of more importance than external ornament. This is a sweeping statement, from wh
ich we need not suffer unduly; yet it is doubtful whether there is art in individual letters. Letters in co
mbination may be satisfying and in a well composed page even beautiful as a whole, but art in letters
consists rather in the art of arranging and composing them in a pleasing and appropriate manner. Th
e main purpose of letters is the practical one of making thoughts visible. Ruskin says that all letters a
re frightful things and to be endured only on occasion, that is to say, in places where the sense of the i
nscription is of more importance than external ornament. This is a sweeping statement, from which
we need not suffer unduly; yet it is doubtful whether there is art in individual letters. Letters in comb
ination may be satisfying and in a well composed page even beautiful as a whole, but art in letters con
The main purpose of letters is the practical one of making thoughts visible. Ruskin says that all letters ar
e frightful things and to be endured only on occasion, that is to say, in places where the sense of the inscri
The main purpose of letters is the practical one of making thoughts visible. Ruskin say
s that all letters are frightful things and to be endured only on occasion, that is to say, i

6/8

The main purpose of letters is the practical one of making thoughts visible. Ruskin says that all letter
s are frightful things and to be endured only on occasion, that is to say, in places where the sense of t
he inscription is of more importance than external ornament. This is a sweeping statement, from wh
ich we need not suffer unduly; yet it is doubtful whether there is art in individual letters. Letters in co
mbination may be satisfying and in a well composed page even beautiful as a whole, but art in letters
consists rather in the art of arranging and composing them in a pleasing and appropriate manner. Th
e main purpose of letters is the practical one of making thoughts visible. Ruskin says that all letters a
re frightful things and to be endured only on occasion, that is to say, in places where the sense of the i
nscription is of more importance than external ornament. This is a sweeping statement, from which
The main purpose of letters is the practical one of making thoughts visible. Ruskin says that all letters ar
e frightful things and to be endured only on occasion, that is to say, in places where the sense of the inscri
The main purpose of letters is the practical one of making thoughts visible. Ruskin say
s that all letters are frightful things and to be endured only on occasion, that is to say, i

6/9

The main purpose of letters is the practical one of making thoughts visible. Ruskin says that all letter
s are frightful things and to be endured only on occasion, that is to say, in places where the sense of t
he inscription is of more importance than external ornament. This is a sweeping statement, from wh
ich we need not suffer unduly; yet it is doubtful whether there is art in individual letters. Letters in co
mbination may be satisfying and in a well composed page even beautiful as a whole, but art in letters
consists rather in the art of arranging and composing them in a pleasing and appropriate manner. Th
e main purpose of letters is the practical one of making thoughts visible. Ruskin says that all letters a
re frightful things and to be endured only on occasion, that is to say, in places where the sense of the i
The main purpose of letters is the practical one of making thoughts visible. Ruskin says that all letters ar
e frightful things and to be endured only on occasion, that is to say, in places where the sense of the inscri
The main purpose of letters is the practical one of making thoughts visible. Ruskin say
s that all letters are frightful things and to be endured only on occasion, that is to say, i

---

ABCDEFGHIJKLMNOPQRSTUVWXYZ 1234567890 abcdefghijklmnopqrstuvwxyz

ABCDEFGHIJKLMNOPQRSTUVWXYZ 1234567890 abcdefghijklmnopqrstuvwxyz

ABCDEFGHIJKLMNOPQRSTUVWXYZ 1234567890 abcdefghijklmnopqrstuvwxyz

7/7

The main purpose of letters is the practical one of making thoughts visible. Ruskin say
s that all letters are frightful things and to be endured only on occasion, that is to say, i
n places where the sense of the inscription is of more importance than external ornam
ent. This is a sweeping statement, from which we need not suffer unduly; yet it is dou
btful whether there is art in individual letters. Letters in combination may be satisfyin
g and in a well composed page even beautiful as a whole, but art in letters consists rath
er in the art of arranging and composing them in a pleasing and appropriate manner. T
he main purpose of letters is the practical one of making thoughts visible. Ruskin says
that all letters are frightful things and to be endured only on occasion, that is to say, in
places where the sense of the inscription is of more importance than external orname
nt. This is a sweeping statement, from which we need not suffer unduly; yet it is doubt
The main purpose of letters is the practical one of making thoughts visible. Ruskin says t
hat all letters are frightful things and to be endured only on occasion, that is to say, in pla
The main purpose of letters is the practical one of making thoughts visible.
Ruskin says that all letters are frightful things and to be endured only on

7/8

The main purpose of letters is the practical one of making thoughts visible. Ruskin say
s that all letters are frightful things and to be endured only on occasion, that is to say, i
n places where the sense of the inscription is of more importance than external ornam
ent. This is a sweeping statement, from which we need not suffer unduly; yet it is dou
btful whether there is art in individual letters. Letters in combination may be satisfyin
g and in a well composed page even beautiful as a whole, but art in letters consists rath
er in the art of arranging and composing them in a pleasing and appropriate manner. T
he main purpose of letters is the practical one of making thoughts visible. Ruskin says
that all letters are frightful things and to be endured only on occasion, that is to say, in
places where the sense of the inscription is of more importance than external orname
The main purpose of letters is the practical one of making thoughts visible. Ruskin says t
hat all letters are frightful things and to be endured only on occasion, that is to say, in pla
The main purpose of letters is the practical one of making thoughts visible.
Ruskin says that all letters are frightful things and to be endured only on

7/9

The main purpose of letters is the practical one of making thoughts visible. Ruskin say
s that all letters are frightful things and to be endured only on occasion, that is to say, i
n places where the sense of the inscription is of more importance than external ornam
ent. This is a sweeping statement, from which we need not suffer unduly; yet it is dou
btful whether there is art in individual letters. Letters in combination may be satisfyin
g and in a well composed page even beautiful as a whole, but art in letters consists rath
er in the art of arranging and composing them in a pleasing and appropriate manner. T
he main purpose of letters is the practical one of making thoughts visible. Ruskin says
that all letters are frightful things and to be endured only on occasion, that is to say, in
places where the sense of the inscription is of more importance than external orname
The main purpose of letters is the practical one of making thoughts visible. Ruskin says t
hat all letters are frightful things and to be endured only on occasion, that is to say, in pla
The main purpose of letters is the practical one of making thoughts visible.
Ruskin says that all letters are frightful things and to be endured only on

7/10

The main purpose of letters is the practical one of making thoughts visible. Ruskin say
s that all letters are frightful things and to be endured only on occasion, that is to say, i
n places where the sense of the inscription is of more importance than external ornam
ent. This is a sweeping statement, from which we need not suffer unduly; yet it is dou
btful whether there is art in individual letters. Letters in combination may be satisfyin
g and in a well composed page even beautiful as a whole, but art in letters consists rath
er in the art of arranging and composing them in a pleasing and appropriate manner. T
he main purpose of letters is the practical one of making thoughts visible. Ruskin says
that all letters are frightful things and to be endured only on occasion, that is to say, in
The main purpose of letters is the practical one of making thoughts visible. Ruskin says t
hat all letters are frightful things and to be endured only on occasion, that is to say, in pla
The main purpose of letters is the practical one of making thoughts visible.
Ruskin says that all letters are frightful things and to be endured only on

CENTURY OLDSTYLE 8 & 9 POINT SET NORMAL

ROMAN, ITALIC, BOLD, BOLD ITALIC

ABCDEFGHIJKLMNOPQRSTUVWXYZ 1234567890 abcdefghijklmnopqrstuvwxyz

ABCDEFGHIJKLMNOPQRSTUVWXYZ 1234567890 abcdefghijklmnopqrstuvwxyz

ABCDEFGHIJKLMNOPQRSTUVWXYZ 1234567890 abcdefghijklmnopqrstuvwxyz

8/8

The main purpose of letters is the practical one of making thoughts visible. Ruskin says that all letters are frightful things and to be endured only on occ asion, that is to say, in places where the sense of the inscription is of more i mportance than external ornament. This is a sweeping statement, from wh ich we need not suffer unduly; yet it is doubtful whether there is art in indivi dual letters. Letters in combination may be satisfying and in a well compose d page even beautiful as a whole, but art in letters consists rather in the art of arranging and composing them in a pleasing and appropriate manner. The main purpose of letters is the practical one of making thoughts visible. Ru

The main purpose of letters is the practical one of making thoughts visible. Ru skin says that all letters are frightful things and to be endured only on occasio

The main purpose of letters is the practical one of making though ts visible. Ruskin says that all letters are frightful things and to b

8/9

The main purpose of letters is the practical one of making thoughts visible. Ruskin says that all letters are frightful things and to be endured only on occ asion, that is to say, in places where the sense of the inscription is of more i mportance than external ornament. This is a sweeping statement, from wh ich we need not suffer unduly; yet it is doubtful whether there is art in indivi dual letters. Letters in combination may be satisfying and in a well compose d page even beautiful as a whole, but art in letters consists rather in the art of arranging and composing them in a pleasing and appropriate manner.

The main purpose of letters is the practical one of making thoughts visible. Ru skin says that all letters are frightful things and to be endured only on occasio

The main purpose of letters is the practical one of making though ts visible. Ruskin says that all letters are frightful things and to b

8/10

The main purpose of letters is the practical one of making thoughts visible. Ruskin says that all letters are frightful things and to be endured only on occ asion, that is to say, in places where the sense of the inscription is of more i mportance than external ornament. This is a sweeping statement, from wh ich we need not suffer unduly; yet it is doubtful whether there is art in indivi dual letters. Letters in combination may be satisfying and in a well compose d page even beautiful as a whole, but art in letters consists rather in the

The main purpose of letters is the practical one of making thoughts visible. Ru skin says that all letters are frightful things and to be endured only on occasio

The main purpose of letters is the practical one of making though ts visible. Ruskin says that all letters are frightful things and to b

8/11

The main purpose of letters is the practical one of making thoughts visible. Ruskin says that all letters are frightful things and to be endured only on occ asion, that is to say, in places where the sense of the inscription is of more i mportance than external ornament. This is a sweeping statement, from wh ich we need not suffer unduly; yet it is doubtful whether there is art in indivi dual letters. Letters in combination may be satisfying and in a well compose d page even beautiful as a whole, but art in letters consists rather in the

The main purpose of letters is the practical one of making thoughts visible. Ru skin says that all letters are frightful things and to be endured only on occasio

The main purpose of letters is the practical one of making though ts visible. Ruskin says that all letters are frightful things and to b

---

ABCDEFGHIJKLMNOPQRSTUVWXYZ 1234567890 abcdefghijklmnopqrstuvwxyz

ABCDEFGHIJKLMNOPQRSTUVWXYZ 1234567890 abcdefghijklmnopqrstuvwxyz

ABCDEFGHIJKLMNOPQRSTUVWXYZ 1234567890 abcdefghijklmnopqrstuvwxyz

9/9

The main purpose of letters is the practical one of making thoughts visible. Ruskin says that all letters are frightful things and to be end ured only on occasion, that is to say, in places where the sense of t he inscription is of more importance than external ornament. This i s a sweeping statement, from which we need not suffer unduly; yet it is doubtful whether there is art in individual letters. Letters in co mbination may be satisfying and in a well composed page even beau tiful as a whole, but art in letters consists rather in the art of arrangi

The main purpose of letters is the practical one of making thoughts vi sible. Ruskin says that all letters are frightful things and to be endure

The main purpose of letters is the practical one of making thoughts visible. Ruskin says that all letters are frightful

9/10

The main purpose of letters is the practical one of making thoughts visible. Ruskin says that all letters are frightful things and to be end ured only on occasion, that is to say, in places where the sense of t he inscription is of more importance than external ornament. This i s a sweeping statement, from which we need not suffer unduly; yet it is doubtful whether there is art in individual letters. Letters in co mbination may be satisfying and in a well composed page even beau

The main purpose of letters is the practical one of making thoughts vi sible. Ruskin says that all letters are frightful things and to be endure

The main purpose of letters is the practical one of making thoughts visible. Ruskin says that all letters are frightful

9/11

The main purpose of letters is the practical one of making thoughts visible. Ruskin says that all letters are frightful things and to be end ured only on occasion, that is to say, in places where the sense of t he inscription is of more importance than external ornament. This i s a sweeping statement, from which we need not suffer unduly; yet it is doubtful whether there is art in individual letters. Letters in co mbination may be satisfying and in a well composed page even beau

The main purpose of letters is the practical one of making thoughts vi sible. Ruskin says that all letters are frightful things and to be endure

The main purpose of letters is the practical one of making thoughts visible. Ruskin says that all letters are frightful

9/12

The main purpose of letters is the practical one of making thoughts visible. Ruskin says that all letters are frightful things and to be end ured only on occasion, that is to say, in places where the sense of t he inscription is of more importance than external ornament. This i s a sweeping statement, from which we need not suffer unduly; yet it is doubtful whether there is art in individual letters. Letters in co mbination may be satisfying and in a well composed page even beau

The main purpose of letters is the practical one of making thoughts vi sible. Ruskin says that all letters are frightful things and to be endure

The main purpose of letters is the practical one of making thoughts visible. Ruskin says that all letters are frightful

CENTURY OLDSTYLE 10 POINT SET MINUS ½ UNIT

ROMAN, ITALIC, BOLD, BOLD ITALIC

abcdefghijklmnopqrstuvwxyz – 1 UNIT
abcdefghijklmnopqrstuvwxyz – ½ UNIT
abcdefghijklmnopqrstuvwxyz NORMAL

ABCDEFGHIJKLMNOPQRSTUVWXYZ 1234567890 abcdefghijklmnopqrstuvwxyz
ABCDEFGHIJKLMNOPQRSTUVWXYZ 1234567890 abcdefghijklmnopqrstuvwxyz
ABCDEFGHIJKLMNOPQRSTUVWXYZ 1234567890 abcdefghijklmnopqrstuvwxyz

10/10

The main purpose of letters is the practical one of making thou
ghts visible. Ruskin says that all letters are frightful things and t
o be endured only on occasion, that is to say, in places where th
e sense of the inscription is of more importance than external o
rnament. This is a sweeping statement, from which we need n
ot suffer unduly; yet it is doubtful whether there is art in individ
ual letters. Letters in combination may be satisfying and in a w
ell composed page even beautiful as a whole, but art in letters c
onsists rather in the art of arranging and composing them in a pl
easing and appropriate manner. The main purpose of letters is
the practical one of making thoughts visible. Ruskin says that al
l letters are frightful things and to be endured only on occasion,
that is to say, in places where the sense of the inscription is of
more importance than external ornament. This is a sweeping s
tatement, from which we need not suffer unduly; yet it is doubt
ful whether there is art in individual letters. Letters in combina
tion may be satisfying and in a well composed page even beautif
ul as a whole, but art in letters consists rather in the art of arran
ging and composing them in a pleasing and appropriate manner.
The main purpose of letters is the practical one of making tho
ughts visible. Ruskin says that all letters are frightful things and
to be endured only on occasion, that is to say, in places where t
The main purpose of letters is the practical one of making thought
s visible. Ruskin says that all letters are frightful things and to be
The main purpose of letters is the practical one of mak
ing thoughts visible. Ruskin says that all letters are fr

10/11

The main purpose of letters is the practical one of making thou
ghts visible. Ruskin says that all letters are frightful things and t
o be endured only on occasion, that is to say, in places where th
e sense of the inscription is of more importance than external o
rnament. This is a sweeping statement, from which we need n
ot suffer unduly; yet it is doubtful whether there is art in individ
ual letters. Letters in combination may be satisfying and in a w
ell composed page even beautiful as a whole, but art in letters c
onsists rather in the art of arranging and composing them in a pl
easing and appropriate manner. The main purpose of letters is
the practical one of making thoughts visible. Ruskin says that al
l letters are frightful things and to be endured only on occasion,
that is to say, in places where the sense of the inscription is of
more importance than external ornament. This is a sweeping s
tatement, from which we need not suffer unduly; yet it is doubt
ful whether there is art in individual letters. Letters in combina
tion may be satisfying and in a well composed page even beautif
ul as a whole, but art in letters consists rather in the art of arran
ging and composing them in a pleasing and appropriate manner.
The main purpose of letters is the practical one of making tho
The main purpose of letters is the practical one of making thought
s visible. Ruskin says that all letters are frightful things and to be
The main purpose of letters is the practical one of mak
ing thoughts visible. Ruskin says that all letters are fr

10/12

The main purpose of letters is the practical one of making thou
ghts visible. Ruskin says that all letters are frightful things and t
o be endured only on occasion, that is to say, in places where th
e sense of the inscription is of more importance than external o
rnament. This is a sweeping statement, from which we need n
ot suffer unduly; yet it is doubtful whether there is art in individ
ual letters. Letters in combination may be satisfying and in a w
ell composed page even beautiful as a whole, but art in letters c
onsists rather in the art of arranging and composing them in a pl
easing and appropriate manner. The main purpose of letters is
the practical one of making thoughts visible. Ruskin says that al
l letters are frightful things and to be endured only on occasion,
that is to say, in places where the sense of the inscription is of
more importance than external ornament. This is a sweeping s
tatement, from which we need not suffer unduly; yet it is doubt
ful whether there is art in individual letters. Letters in combina
tion may be satisfying and in a well composed page even beautif
ul as a whole, but art in letters consists rather in the art of arran
The main purpose of letters is the practical one of making thought
s visible. Ruskin says that all letters are frightful things and to be
The main purpose of letters is the practical one of mak
ing thoughts visible. Ruskin says that all letters are fr

10/13

The main purpose of letters is the practical one of making thou
ghts visible. Ruskin says that all letters are frightful things and t
o be endured only on occasion, that is to say, in places where th
e sense of the inscription is of more importance than external o
rnament. This is a sweeping statement, from which we need n
ot suffer unduly; yet it is doubtful whether there is art in individ
ual letters. Letters in combination may be satisfying and in a w
ell composed page even beautiful as a whole, but art in letters c
onsists rather in the art of arranging and composing them in a pl
easing and appropriate manner. The main purpose of letters is
the practical one of making thoughts visible. Ruskin says that al
l letters are frightful things and to be endured only on occasion,
that is to say, in places where the sense of the inscription is of
more importance than external ornament. This is a sweeping s
tatement, from which we need not suffer unduly; yet it is doubt
ful whether there is art in individual letters. Letters in combina
tion may be satisfying and in a well composed page even beautif
The main purpose of letters is the practical one of making thought
s visible. Ruskin says that all letters are frightful things and to be
The main purpose of letters is the practical one of mak
ing thoughts visible. Ruskin says that all letters are fr

CENTURY OLDSTYLE 11 POINT SET MINUS ½ UNIT

ROMAN, ITALIC, BOLD, BOLD ITALIC

abcdefghijklmnopqrstuvwxyz – 1 UNIT
abcdefghijklmnopqrstuvwxyz – ½ UNIT
abcdefghijklmnopqrstuvwxyz NORMAL

ABCDEFGHIJKLMNOPQRSTUVWXYZ 1234567890 abcdefghijklmnopqrstuvwxyz
ABCDEFGHIJKLMNOPQRSTUVWXYZ 1234567890 abcdefghijklmnopqrstuvwxyz
ABCDEFGHIJKLMNOPQRSTUVWXYZ 1234567890 abcdefghijklmnopqrstuvwxyz

11/11

The main purpose of letters is the practical one of making thoughts visible. Ruskin says that all letters are frightful t hings and to be endured only on occasion, that is to say, i n places where the sense of the inscription is of more imp ortance than external ornament. This is a sweeping state ment, from which we need not suffer unduly; yet it is dou btful whether there is art in individual letters. Letters in c ombination may be satisfying and in a well composed pag e even beautiful as a whole, but art in letters consists rath er in the art of arranging and composing them in a pleasin g and appropriate manner. The main purpose of letters is the practical one of making thoughts visible. Ruskin says that all letters are frightful things and to be endured only on occasion, that is to say, in places where the sense of th e inscription is of more importance than external orname nt. This is a sweeping statement, from which we need no t suffer unduly; yet it is doubtful whether there is art in in dividual letters. Letters in combination may be satisfying and in a well composed page even beautiful as a whole, bu
The main purpose of letters is the practical one of making t houghts visible. Ruskin says that all letters are frightful thi
The main purpose of letters is the practical one o f making thoughts visible. Ruskin says that all le

11/12

The main purpose of letters is the practical one of making thoughts visible. Ruskin says that all letters are frightful t hings and to be endured only on occasion, that is to say, i n places where the sense of the inscription is of more imp ortance than external ornament. This is a sweeping state ment, from which we need not suffer unduly; yet it is dou btful whether there is art in individual letters. Letters in c ombination may be satisfying and in a well composed pag e even beautiful as a whole, but art in letters consists rath er in the art of arranging and composing them in a pleasin g and appropriate manner. The main purpose of letters is the practical one of making thoughts visible. Ruskin says that all letters are frightful things and to be endured only on occasion, that is to say, in places where the sense of th e inscription is of more importance than external orname nt. This is a sweeping statement, from which we need no t suffer unduly; yet it is doubtful whether there is art in in dividual letters. Letters in combination may be satisfying
The main purpose of letters is the practical one of making t houghts visible. Ruskin says that all letters are frightful thi
The main purpose of letters is the practical one o f making thoughts visible. Ruskin says that all le

11/13

The main purpose of letters is the practical one of making thoughts visible. Ruskin says that all letters are frightful t hings and to be endured only on occasion, that is to say, i n places where the sense of the inscription is of more imp ortance than external ornament. This is a sweeping state ment, from which we need not suffer unduly; yet it is dou btful whether there is art in individual letters. Letters in c ombination may be satisfying and in a well composed pag e even beautiful as a whole, but art in letters consists rath er in the art of arranging and composing them in a pleasin g and appropriate manner. The main purpose of letters is the practical one of making thoughts visible. Ruskin says that all letters are frightful things and to be endured only on occasion, that is to say, in places where the sense of th e inscription is of more importance than external orname nt. This is a sweeping statement, from which we need no t suffer unduly; yet it is doubtful whether there is art in in
The main purpose of letters is the practical one of making t houghts visible. Ruskin says that all letters are frightful thi
The main purpose of letters is the practical one o f making thoughts visible. Ruskin says that all le

11/14

The main purpose of letters is the practical one of making thoughts visible. Ruskin says that all letters are frightful t hings and to be endured only on occasion, that is to say, i n places where the sense of the inscription is of more imp ortance than external ornament. This is a sweeping state ment, from which we need not suffer unduly; yet it is dou btful whether there is art in individual letters. Letters in c ombination may be satisfying and in a well composed pag e even beautiful as a whole, but art in letters consists rath er in the art of arranging and composing them in a pleasin g and appropriate manner. The main purpose of letters is the practical one of making thoughts visible. Ruskin says that all letters are frightful things and to be endured only on occasion, that is to say, in places where the sense of th e inscription is of more importance than external orname nt. This is a sweeping statement, from which we need no
The main purpose of letters is the practical one of making t houghts visible. Ruskin says that all letters are frightful thi
The main purpose of letters is the practical one o f making thoughts visible. Ruskin says that all le

CENTURY OLDSTYLE 12 POINT SET MINUS ½ UNIT

ROMAN, ITALIC, BOLD, BOLD ITALIC

abcdefghijklmnopqrstuvwxyz – 1 UNIT
abcdefghijklmnopqrstuvwxyz – ½ UNIT
abcdefghijklmnopqrstuvwxyz NORMAL

ABCDEFGHIJKLMNOPQRSTUVWXYZ 1234567890 abcdefghijklmnopqrstuvwxyz
ABCDEFGHIJKLMNOPQRSTUVWXYZ 1234567890 abcdefghijklmnopqrstuvwxyz
ABCDEFGHIJKLMNOPQRSTUVWXYZ 1234567890 abcdefghijklmnopqrstuvwxyz

12/12

The main purpose of letters is the practical one of ma king thoughts visible. Ruskin says that all letters are f rightful things and to be endured only on occasion, th at is to say, in places where the sense of the inscriptio n is of more importance than external ornament. Thi s is a sweeping statement, from which we need not s uffer unduly; yet it is doubtful whether there is art in i ndividual letters. Letters in combination may be satis fying and in a well composed page even beautiful as a whole, but art in letters consists rather in the art of ar ranging and composing them in a pleasing and approp riate manner. The main purpose of letters is the prac tical one of making thoughts visible. Ruskin says that all letters are frightful things and to be endured only on occasion, that is to say, in places where the sense
The main purpose of letters is the practical one of maki ng thoughts visible. Ruskin says that all letters are frig
The main purpose of letters is the practical on e of making thoughts visible. Ruskin says tha

12/13

The main purpose of letters is the practical one of ma king thoughts visible. Ruskin says that all letters are f rightful things and to be endured only on occasion, th at is to say, in places where the sense of the inscriptio n is of more importance than external ornament. Thi s is a sweeping statement, from which we need not s uffer unduly; yet it is doubtful whether there is art in i ndividual letters. Letters in combination may be satis fying and in a well composed page even beautiful as a whole, but art in letters consists rather in the art of ar ranging and composing them in a pleasing and approp riate manner. The main purpose of letters is the prac tical one of making thoughts visible. Ruskin says that all letters are frightful things and to be endured only
The main purpose of letters is the practical one of maki ng thoughts visible. Ruskin says that all letters are frig
The main purpose of letters is the practical on e of making thoughts visible. Ruskin says tha

12/14

The main purpose of letters is the practical one of ma king thoughts visible. Ruskin says that all letters are f rightful things and to be endured only on occasion, th at is to say, in places where the sense of the inscriptio n is of more importance than external ornament. Thi s is a sweeping statement, from which we need not s uffer unduly; yet it is doubtful whether there is art in i ndividual letters. Letters in combination may be satis fying and in a well composed page even beautiful as a whole, but art in letters consists rather in the art of ar ranging and composing them in a pleasing and approp riate manner. The main purpose of letters is the prac tical one of making thoughts visible. Ruskin says that all letters are frightful things and to be endured only on occasion, that is to say, in places where the sense
The main purpose of letters is the practical one of maki ng thoughts visible. Ruskin says that all letters are frig
The main purpose of letters is the practical on e of making thoughts visible. Ruskin says tha

12/15

The main purpose of letters is the practical one of ma king thoughts visible. Ruskin says that all letters are f rightful things and to be endured only on occasion, th at is to say, in places where the sense of the inscriptio n is of more importance than external ornament. Thi s is a sweeping statement, from which we need not s uffer unduly; yet it is doubtful whether there is art in i ndividual letters. Letters in combination may be satis fying and in a well composed page even beautiful as a whole, but art in letters consists rather in the art of ar ranging and composing them in a pleasing and approp riate manner. The main purpose of letters is the prac tical one of making thoughts visible. Ruskin says that all letters are frightful things and to be endured only
The main purpose of letters is the practical one of maki ng thoughts visible. Ruskin says that all letters are frig
The main purpose of letters is the practical on e of making thoughts visible. Ruskin says tha

CENTURY OLDSTYLE 14 POINT SET MINUS ½ UNIT

ROMAN, ITALIC, BOLD, BOLD ITALIC

abcdefghijklmnopqrstuvwxyz – 1 UNIT
abcdefghijklmnopqrstuvwxyz – ½ UNIT
abcdefghijklmnopqrstuvwxyz NORMAL

ABCDEFGHIJKLMNOPQRSTUVWXYZ abcdefghijklmnopqrstuvwxyz
ABCDEFGHIJKLMNOPQRSTUVWXYZ abcdefghijklmnopqrstuvwxyz
ABCDEFGHIJKLMNOPQRSTUVWXYZ abcdefghijklmnopqrstuvwxyz

14/14

The main purpose of letters is the practical o ne of making thoughts visible. Ruskin says th at all letters are frightful things and to be end ured only on occasion, that is to say, in places where the sense of the inscription is of more i mportance than external ornament. This is a sweeping statement, from which we need no t suffer unduly; yet it is doubtful whether the re is art in individual letters. Letters in combi nation may be satisfying and in a well compos ed page even beautiful as a whole, but art in l etters consists rather in the art of arranging a nd composing them in a pleasing and appropri
The main purpose of letters is the practical one of making thoughts visible. Ruskin says that al
The main purpose of letters is the prac tical one of making thoughts visible. R

14/15

The main purpose of letters is the practical o ne of making thoughts visible. Ruskin says th at all letters are frightful things and to be end ured only on occasion, that is to say, in places where the sense of the inscription is of more i mportance than external ornament. This is a sweeping statement, from which we need no t suffer unduly; yet it is doubtful whether the re is art in individual letters. Letters in combi nation may be satisfying and in a well compos ed page even beautiful as a whole, but art in l etters consists rather in the art of arranging a
The main purpose of letters is the practical one of making thoughts visible. Ruskin says that al
The main purpose of letters is the prac tical one of making thoughts visible. R

14/16

The main purpose of letters is the practical o ne of making thoughts visible. Ruskin says th at all letters are frightful things and to be end ured only on occasion, that is to say, in places where the sense of the inscription is of more i mportance than external ornament. This is a sweeping statement, from which we need no t suffer unduly; yet it is doubtful whether the re is art in individual letters. Letters in combi nation may be satisfying and in a well compos ed page even beautiful as a whole, but art in l etters consists rather in the art of arranging a nd composing them in a pleasing and appropri
The main purpose of letters is the practical one of making thoughts visible. Ruskin says that al
The main purpose of letters is the prac tical one of making thoughts visible. R

14/17

The main purpose of letters is the practical o ne of making thoughts visible. Ruskin says th at all letters are frightful things and to be end ured only on occasion, that is to say, in places where the sense of the inscription is of more i mportance than external ornament. This is a sweeping statement, from which we need no t suffer unduly; yet it is doubtful whether the re is art in individual letters. Letters in combi nation may be satisfying and in a well compos ed page even beautiful as a whole, but art in l etters consists rather in the art of arranging a
The main purpose of letters is the practical one of making thoughts visible. Ruskin says that al
The main purpose of letters is the prac tical one of making thoughts visible. R

CENTURY SCHOOLBOOK 6 & 7 POINT SET NORMAL

ROMAN, ITALIC, BOLD

ABCDEFGHIJKLMNOPQRSTUVWXYZ 1234567890 abcdefghijklmnopqrstuvwxyz

ABCDEFGHIJKLMNOPQRSTUVWXYZ 1234567890 abcdefghijklmnopqrstuvwxyz

ABCDEFGHIJKLMNOPQRSTUVWXYZ 1234567890 abcdefghijklmnopqrstuvwxyz

6/6

The main purpose of letters is the practical one of making thoughts visible. Ruskin says t hat all letters are frightful things and to be endured only on occasion, that is to say, in plac es where the sense of the inscription is of more importance than external ornament. This i s a sweeping statement, from which we need not suffer unduly; yet it is doubtful whether t here is art in individual letters. Letters in combination may be satisfying and in a well co mposed page even beautiful as a whole, but art in letters consists rather in the art of arra nging and composing them in a pleasing and appropriate manner. The main purpose of let ters is the practical one of making thoughts visible. Ruskin says that all letters are frightf ul things and to be endured only on occasion, that is to say, in places where the sense of the inscription is of more importance than external ornament. This is a sweeping statement, from which we need not suffer unduly; yet it is doubtful whether there is art in individual letters. Letters in combination may be satisfying and in a well composed page even beauti ful as a whole, but art in letters consists rather in the art of arranging and composing the
The main purpose of letters is the practical one of making thoughts visible. Ruskin says tha t all letters are frightful things and to be endured only on occasion, that is to say, in places w
The main purpose of letters is the practical one of making thoughts visible. Ruski n says that all letters are frightful things and to be endured only on occasion, that

6/7

The main purpose of letters is the practical one of making thoughts visible. Ruskin says t hat all letters are frightful things and to be endured only on occasion, that is to say, in plac es where the sense of the inscription is of more importance than external ornament. This i s a sweeping statement, from which we need not suffer unduly; yet it is doubtful whether t here is art in individual letters. Letters in combination may be satisfying and in a well co mposed page even beautiful as a whole, but art in letters consists rather in the art of arra nging and composing them in a pleasing and appropriate manner. The main purpose of let ters is the practical one of making thoughts visible. Ruskin says that all letters are frightf ul things and to be endured only on occasion, that is to say, in places where the sense of the inscription is of more importance than external ornament. This is a sweeping statement, from which we need not suffer unduly; yet it is doubtful whether there is art in individual
The main purpose of letters is the practical one of making thoughts visible. Ruskin says tha t all letters are frightful things and to be endured only on occasion, that is to say, in places w
The main purpose of letters is the practical one of making thoughts visible. Ruski n says that all letters are frightful things and to be endured only on occasion, that

6/8

The main purpose of letters is the practical one of making thoughts visible. Ruskin says t hat all letters are frightful things and to be endured only on occasion, that is to say, in plac es where the sense of the inscription is of more importance than external ornament. This i s a sweeping statement, from which we need not suffer unduly; yet it is doubtful whether t here is art in individual letters. Letters in combination may be satisfying and in a well co mposed page even beautiful as a whole, but art in letters consists rather in the art of arra nging and composing them in a pleasing and appropriate manner. The main purpose of let ters is the practical one of making thoughts visible. Ruskin says that all letters are frightf ul things and to be endured only on occasion, that is to say, in places where the sense of the
The main purpose of letters is the practical one of making thoughts visible. Ruskin says tha t all letters are frightful things and to be endured only on occasion, that is to say, in places w
The main purpose of letters is the practical one of making thoughts visible. Ruski n says that all letters are frightful things and to be endured only on occasion, that

6/9

The main purpose of letters is the practical one of making thoughts visible. Ruskin says t hat all letters are frightful things and to be endured only on occasion, that is to say, in plac es where the sense of the inscription is of more importance than external ornament. This i s a sweeping statement, from which we need not suffer unduly; yet it is doubtful whether t here is art in individual letters. Letters in combination may be satisfying and in a well co mposed page even beautiful as a whole, but art in letters consists rather in the art of arra nging and composing them in a pleasing and appropriate manner. The main purpose of let ters is the practical one of making thoughts visible. Ruskin says that all letters are frightf
The main purpose of letters is the practical one of making thoughts visible. Ruskin says tha t all letters are frightful things and to be endured only on occasion, that is to say, in places w
The main purpose of letters is the practical one of making thoughts visible. Ruski n says that all letters are frightful things and to be endured only on occasion, that

---

ABCDEFGHIJKLMNOPQRSTUVWXYZ 1234567890 abcdefghijklmnopqrstuvwxyz

ABCDEFGHIJKLMNOPQRSTUVWXYZ 1234567890 abcdefghijklmnopqrstuvwxyz

ABCDEFGHIJKLMNOPQRSTUVWXYZ 1234567890 abcdefghijklmnopqrstuvwxyz

7/7

The main purpose of letters is the practical one of making thoughts visible. R uskin says that all letters are frightful things and to be endured only on occa sion, that is to say, in places where the sense of the inscription is of more impo rtance than external ornament. This is a sweeping statement, from which w e need not suffer unduly; yet it is doubtful whether there is art in individual l etters. Letters in combination may be satisfying and in a well composed page even beautiful as a whole, but art in letters consists rather in the art of arran ging and composing them in a pleasing and appropriate manner. The main p urpose of letters is the practical one of making thoughts visible. Ruskin says that all letters are frightful things and to be endured only on occasion, that is to say, in places where the sense of the inscription is of more importance than
The main purpose of letters is the practical one of making thoughts visible. Ru skin says that all letters are frightful things and to be endured only on occasio
The main purpose of letters is the practical one of making thoughts vi sible. Ruskin says that all letters are frightful things and to be endure

7/8

The main purpose of letters is the practical one of making thoughts visible. R uskin says that all letters are frightful things and to be endured only on occa sion, that is to say, in places where the sense of the inscription is of more impo rtance than external ornament. This is a sweeping statement, from which w e need not suffer unduly; yet it is doubtful whether there is art in individual l etters. Letters in combination may be satisfying and in a well composed page even beautiful as a whole, but art in letters consists rather in the art of arran ging and composing them in a pleasing and appropriate manner. The main p urpose of letters is the practical one of making thoughts visible. Ruskin says that all letters are frightful things and to be endured only on occasion, that is
The main purpose of letters is the practical one of making thoughts visible. Ru skin says that all letters are frightful things and to be endured only on occasio
The main purpose of letters is the practical one of making thoughts vi sible. Ruskin says that all letters are frightful things and to be endure

7/9

The main purpose of letters is the practical one of making thoughts visible. R uskin says that all letters are frightful things and to be endured only on occa sion, that is to say, in places where the sense of the inscription is of more impo rtance than external ornament. This is a sweeping statement, from which w e need not suffer unduly; yet it is doubtful whether there is art in individual l etters. Letters in combination may be satisfying and in a well composed page even beautiful as a whole, but art in letters consists rather in the art of arran ging and composing them in a pleasing and appropriate manner. The main p urpose of letters is the practical one of making thoughts visible. Ruskin says that all letters are frightful things and to be endured only on occasion, that is
The main purpose of letters is the practical one of making thoughts visible. Ru skin says that all letters are frightful things and to be endured only on occasio
The main purpose of letters is the practical one of making thoughts vi sible. Ruskin says that all letters are frightful things and to be endure

7/10

The main purpose of letters is the practical one of making thoughts visible. R uskin says that all letters are frightful things and to be endured only on occa sion, that is to say, in places where the sense of the inscription is of more impo rtance than external ornament. This is a sweeping statement, from which w e need not suffer unduly; yet it is doubtful whether there is art in individual l etters. Letters in combination may be satisfying and in a well composed page even beautiful as a whole, but art in letters consists rather in the art of arran ging and composing them in a pleasing and appropriate manner. The main p urpose of letters is the practical one of making thoughts visible. Ruskin says
The main purpose of letters is the practical one of making thoughts visible. Ru skin says that all letters are frightful things and to be endured only on occasio
The main purpose of letters is the practical one of making thoughts vi sible. Ruskin says that all letters are frightful things and to be endure

CENTURY SCHOOLBOOK
8 & 9 POINT SET NORMAL

ROMAN, ITALIC, BOLD

ABCDEFGHIJKLMNOPQRSTUVWXYZ 1234567890 abcdefghijklmnopqrstuvwxyz
ABCDEFGHIJKLMNOPQRSTUVWXYZ 1234567890 abcdefghijklmnopqrstuvwxyz
ABCDEFGHIJKLMNOPQRSTUVWXYZ 1234567890 abcdefghijklmnopqrstuvwxyz

8/8

The main purpose of letters is the practical one of making thoughts visible. Ruskin says that all letters are frightful things and to be en dured only on occasion, that is to say, in places where the sense of th e inscription is of more importance than external ornament. This is a sweeping statement, from which we need not suffer unduly; yet it is doubtful whether there is art in individual letters. Letters in com bination may be satisfying and in a well composed page even beaut iful as a whole, but art in letters consists rather in the art of arrang ing and composing them in a pleasing and appropriate manner. Th
The main purpose of letters is the practical one of making thoughts v isible. Ruskin says that all letters are frightful things and to be endu
The main purpose of letters is the practical one of making tho ughts visible. Ruskin says that all letters are frightful things

8/9

The main purpose of letters is the practical one of making thoughts visible. Ruskin says that all letters are frightful things and to be en dured only on occasion, that is to say, in places where the sense of th e inscription is of more importance than external ornament. This is a sweeping statement, from which we need not suffer unduly; yet it is doubtful whether there is art in individual letters. Letters in com bination may be satisfying and in a well composed page even beaut iful as a whole, but art in letters consists rather in the art of arrang
The main purpose of letters is the practical one of making thoughts v isible. Ruskin says that all letters are frightful things and to be endu
The main purpose of letters is the practical one of making tho ughts visible. Ruskin says that all letters are frightful things

8/10

The main purpose of letters is the practical one of making thoughts visible. Ruskin says that all letters are frightful things and to be en dured only on occasion, that is to say, in places where the sense of th e inscription is of more importance than external ornament. This is a sweeping statement, from which we need not suffer unduly; yet it is doubtful whether there is art in individual letters. Letters in com bination may be satisfying and in a well composed page even beaut
The main purpose of letters is the practical one of making thoughts v isible. Ruskin says that all letters are frightful things and to be endu
The main purpose of letters is the practical one of making tho ughts visible. Ruskin says that all letters are frightful things

8/11

The main purpose of letters is the practical one of making thoughts visible. Ruskin says that all letters are frightful things and to be en dured only on occasion, that is to say, in places where the sense of th e inscription is of more importance than external ornament. This is a sweeping statement, from which we need not suffer unduly; yet it is doubtful whether there is art in individual letters. Letters in com bination may be satisfying and in a well composed page even beaut
The main purpose of letters is the practical one of making thoughts v isible. Ruskin says that all letters are frightful things and to be endu
The main purpose of letters is the practical one of making tho ughts visible. Ruskin says that all letters are frightful things

---

ABCDEFGHIJKLMNOPQRSTUVWXYZ 1234567890 abcdefghijklmnopqrstuvwxyz
ABCDEFGHIJKLMNOPQRSTUVWXYZ 1234567890 abcdefghijklmnopqrstuvwxyz
ABCDEFGHIJKLMNOPQRSTUVWXYZ 1234567890 abcdefghijklmnopqrstuvwxyz

9/9

The main purpose of letters is the practical one of making t houghts visible. Ruskin says that all letters are frightful th ings and to be endured only on occasion, that is to say, in pla ces where the sense of the inscription is of more importance than external ornament. This is a sweeping statement, fro m which we need not suffer unduly; yet it is doubtful wheth er there is art in individual letters. Letters in combination may be satisfying and in a well composed page even beautif
The main purpose of letters is the practical one of making tho ughts visible. Ruskin says that all letters are frightful things
The main purpose of letters is the practical one of mak ing thoughts visible. Ruskin says that all letters are fri

9/10

The main purpose of letters is the practical one of making t houghts visible. Ruskin says that all letters are frightful th ings and to be endured only on occasion, that is to say, in pla ces where the sense of the inscription is of more importance than external ornament. This is a sweeping statement, fro m which we need not suffer unduly; yet it is doubtful wheth er there is art in individual letters. Letters in combination
The main purpose of letters is the practical one of making tho ughts visible. Ruskin says that all letters are frightful things
The main purpose of letters is the practical one of mak ing thoughts visible. Ruskin says that all letters are fri

9/11

The main purpose of letters is the practical one of making t houghts visible. Ruskin says that all letters are frightful th ings and to be endured only on occasion, that is to say, in pla ces where the sense of the inscription is of more importance than external ornament. This is a sweeping statement, fro m which we need not suffer unduly; yet it is doubtful wheth er there is art in individual letters. Letters in combination
The main purpose of letters is the practical one of making tho ughts visible. Ruskin says that all letters are frightful things
The main purpose of letters is the practical one of mak ing thoughts visible. Ruskin says that all letters are fri

9/12

The main purpose of letters is the practical one of making t houghts visible. Ruskin says that all letters are frightful th ings and to be endured only on occasion, that is to say, in pla ces where the sense of the inscription is of more importance than external ornament. This is a sweeping statement, fro m which we need not suffer unduly; yet it is doubtful wheth er there is art in individual letters. Letters in combination
The main purpose of letters is the practical one of making tho ughts visible. Ruskin says that all letters are frightful things
The main purpose of letters is the practical one of mak ing thoughts visible. Ruskin says that all letters are fri

CENTURY SCHOOLBOOK 10 POINT SET MINUS ½ UNIT

ROMAN, ITALIC, BOLD

abcdefghijklmnopqrstuvwxyz – 1 UNIT
abcdefghijklmnopqrstuvwxyz – ½ UNIT
abcdefghijklmnopqrstuvwxyz NORMAL

ABCDEFGHIJKLMNOPQRSTUVWXYZ 1234567890 abcdefghijklmnopqrstuvwxyz
ABCDEFGHIJKLMNOPQRSTUVWXYZ 1234567890 abcdefghijklmnopqrstuvwxyz
ABCDEFGHIJKLMNOPQRSTUVWXYZ 1234567890 abcdefghijklmnopqrstuvwxyz

10/10

The main purpose of letters is the practical one of makin g thoughts visible. Ruskin says that all letters are frigh tful things and to be endured only on occasion, that is to say, in places where the sense of the inscription is of mo re importance than external ornament. This is a sweepi ng statement, from which we need not suffer unduly; yet it is doubtful whether there is art in individual letters. L etters in combination may be satisfying and in a well co mposed page even beautiful as a whole, but art in letter s consists rather in the art of arranging and composing t hem in a pleasing and appropriate manner. The main p urpose of letters is the practical one of making thoughts visible. Ruskin says that all letters are frightful things and to be endured only on occasion, that is to say, in plac es where the sense of the inscription is of more importan ce than external ornament. This is a sweeping statemen t, from which we need not suffer unduly; yet it is doubtf ul whether there is art in individual letters. Letters in c ombination may be satisfying and in a well composed p age even beautiful as a whole, but art in letters consists rather in the art of arranging and composing them in a pleasing and appropriate manner. The main purpose of l
The main purpose of letters is the practical one of making thoughts visible. Ruskin says that all letters are frightful
The main purpose of letters is the practical one of making thoughts visible. Ruskin says that all lette

10/11

The main purpose of letters is the practical one of makin g thoughts visible. Ruskin says that all letters are frigh tful things and to be endured only on occasion, that is to say, in places where the sense of the inscription is of mo re importance than external ornament. This is a sweepi ng statement, from which we need not suffer unduly; yet it is doubtful whether there is art in individual letters. L etters in combination may be satisfying and in a well co mposed page even beautiful as a whole, but art in letter s consists rather in the art of arranging and composing t hem in a pleasing and appropriate manner. The main p urpose of letters is the practical one of making thoughts visible. Ruskin says that all letters are frightful things and to be endured only on occasion, that is to say, in plac es where the sense of the inscription is of more importan ce than external ornament. This is a sweeping statemen t, from which we need not suffer unduly; yet it is doubtf ul whether there is art in individual letters. Letters in c ombination may be satisfying and in a well composed p age even beautiful as a whole, but art in letters consists
The main purpose of letters is the practical one of making thoughts visible. Ruskin says that all letters are frightful
The main purpose of letters is the practical one of making thoughts visible. Ruskin says that all lette

10/12

The main purpose of letters is the practical one of makin g thoughts visible. Ruskin says that all letters are frigh tful things and to be endured only on occasion, that is to say, in places where the sense of the inscription is of mo re importance than external ornament. This is a sweepi ng statement, from which we need not suffer unduly; yet it is doubtful whether there is art in individual letters. L etters in combination may be satisfying and in a well co mposed page even beautiful as a whole, but art in letter s consists rather in the art of arranging and composing t hem in a pleasing and appropriate manner. The main p urpose of letters is the practical one of making thoughts visible. Ruskin says that all letters are frightful things and to be endured only on occasion, that is to say, in plac es where the sense of the inscription is of more importan ce than external ornament. This is a sweeping statemen t, from which we need not suffer unduly; yet it is doubtf ul whether there is art in individual letters. Letters in c
The main purpose of letters is the practical one of making thoughts visible. Ruskin says that all letters are frightful
The main purpose of letters is the practical one of making thoughts visible. Ruskin says that all lette

10/13

The main purpose of letters is the practical one of makin g thoughts visible. Ruskin says that all letters are frigh tful things and to be endured only on occasion, that is to say, in places where the sense of the inscription is of mo re importance than external ornament. This is a sweepi ng statement, from which we need not suffer unduly; yet it is doubtful whether there is art in individual letters. L etters in combination may be satisfying and in a well co mposed page even beautiful as a whole, but art in letter s consists rather in the art of arranging and composing t hem in a pleasing and appropriate manner. The main p urpose of letters is the practical one of making thoughts visible. Ruskin says that all letters are frightful things and to be endured only on occasion, that is to say, in plac es where the sense of the inscription is of more importan ce than external ornament. This is a sweeping statemen t, from which we need not suffer unduly; yet it is doubtf
The main purpose of letters is the practical one of making thoughts visible. Ruskin says that all letters are frightful
The main purpose of letters is the practical one of making thoughts visible. Ruskin says that all lette

CENTURY SCHOOLBOOK 11 POINT SET MINUS ½ UNIT

ROMAN, ITALIC, BOLD

abcdefghijklmnopqrstuvwxyz – 1 UNIT
abcdefghijklmnopqrstuvwxyz – ½ UNIT
abcdefghijklmnopqrstuvwxyz NORMAL

ABCDEFGHIJKLMNOPQRSTUVWXYZ 1234567890 abcdefghijklmnopqrstuvwxyz
ABCDEFGHIJKLMNOPQRSTUVWXYZ 1234567890 abcdefghijklmnopqrstuvwxyz
ABCDEFGHIJKLMNOPQRSTUVWXYZ 1234567890 abcdefghijklmnopqrstuvwxyz

11/11

The main purpose of letters is the practical one of making thoughts visible. Ruskin says that all lett ers are frightful things and to be endured only on o ccasion, that is to say, in places where the sense of t he inscription is of more importance than external ornament. This is a sweeping statement, from whi ch we need not suffer unduly; yet it is doubtful whe ther there is art in individual letters. Letters in co mbination may be satisfying and in a well compos ed page even beautiful as a whole, but art in letters consists rather in the art of arranging and composi ng them in a pleasing and appropriate manner. Th e main purpose of letters is the practical one of ma king thoughts visible. Ruskin says that all letters are frightful things and to be endured only on occa sion, that is to say, in places where the sense of the i nscription is of more importance than external orn ament. This is a sweeping statement, from which we need not suffer unduly; yet it is doubtful wheth
The main purpose of letters is the practical one of m aking thoughts visible. Ruskin says that all letters
The main purpose of letters is the practical on e of making thoughts visible. Ruskin says that

11/12

The main purpose of letters is the practical one of making thoughts visible. Ruskin says that all lett ers are frightful things and to be endured only on o ccasion, that is to say, in places where the sense of t he inscription is of more importance than external ornament. This is a sweeping statement, from whi ch we need not suffer unduly; yet it is doubtful whe ther there is art in individual letters. Letters in co mbination may be satisfying and in a well compos ed page even beautiful as a whole, but art in letters consists rather in the art of arranging and composi ng them in a pleasing and appropriate manner. Th e main purpose of letters is the practical one of ma king thoughts visible. Ruskin says that all letters are frightful things and to be endured only on occa sion, that is to say, in places where the sense of the i nscription is of more importance than external orn ament. This is a sweeping statement, from which
The main purpose of letters is the practical one of m aking thoughts visible. Ruskin says that all letters
The main purpose of letters is the practical on e of making thoughts visible. Ruskin says that

11/13

The main purpose of letters is the practical one of making thoughts visible. Ruskin says that all lett ers are frightful things and to be endured only on o ccasion, that is to say, in places where the sense of t he inscription is of more importance than external ornament. This is a sweeping statement, from whi ch we need not suffer unduly; yet it is doubtful whe ther there is art in individual letters. Letters in co mbination may be satisfying and in a well compos ed page even beautiful as a whole, but art in letters consists rather in the art of arranging and composi ng them in a pleasing and appropriate manner. Th e main purpose of letters is the practical one of ma king thoughts visible. Ruskin says that all letters are frightful things and to be endured only on occa sion, that is to say, in places where the sense of the i nscription is of more importance than external orn
The main purpose of letters is the practical one of m aking thoughts visible. Ruskin says that all letters
The main purpose of letters is the practical on e of making thoughts visible. Ruskin says that

11/14

The main purpose of letters is the practical one of making thoughts visible. Ruskin says that all lett ers are frightful things and to be endured only on o ccasion, that is to say, in places where the sense of t he inscription is of more importance than external ornament. This is a sweeping statement, from whi ch we need not suffer unduly; yet it is doubtful whe ther there is art in individual letters. Letters in co mbination may be satisfying and in a well compos ed page even beautiful as a whole, but art in letters consists rather in the art of arranging and composi ng them in a pleasing and appropriate manner. Th e main purpose of letters is the practical one of ma king thoughts visible. Ruskin says that all letters are frightful things and to be endured only on occa sion, that is to say, in places where the sense of the i
The main purpose of letters is the practical one of m aking thoughts visible. Ruskin says that all letters
The main purpose of letters is the practical on e of making thoughts visible. Ruskin says that

CENTURY SCHOOLBOOK 12 POINT SET MINUS ½ UNIT

ROMAN, ITALIC, BOLD

abcdefghijklmnopqrstuvwxyz – 1 UNIT
abcdefghijklmnopqrstuvwxyz – ½ UNIT
abcdefghijklmnopqrstuvwxyz NORMAL

ABCDEFGHIJKLMNOPQRSTUVWXYZ 1234567890 abcdefghijklmnopqrstuvwxyz
ABCDEFGHIJKLMNOPQRSTUVWXYZ 1234567890 abcdefghijklmnopqrstuvwxyz
ABCDEFGHIJKLMNOPQRSTUVWXYZ 1234567890 abcdefghijklmnopqrstuvwx

12/12

The main purpose of letters is the practical one of making thoughts visible. Ruskin says that a ll letters are frightful things and to be endured only on occasion, that is to say, in places where t he sense of the inscription is of more importanc e than external ornament. This is a sweeping s tatement, from which we need not suffer undul y; yet it is doubtful whether there is art in indiv idual letters. Letters in combination may be sa tisfying and in a well composed page even beau tiful as a whole, but art in letters consists rathe r in the art of arranging and composing them i n a pleasing and appropriate manner. The mai n purpose of letters is the practical one of maki ng thoughts visible. Ruskin says that all letter
The main purpose of letters is the practical one of making thoughts visible. Ruskin says that al
The main purpose of letters is the practical one of making thoughts visible. Ruskin sa

12/13

The main purpose of letters is the practical one of making thoughts visible. Ruskin says that a ll letters are frightful things and to be endured only on occasion, that is to say, in places where t he sense of the inscription is of more importanc e than external ornament. This is a sweeping s tatement, from which we need not suffer undul y; yet it is doubtful whether there is art in indiv idual letters. Letters in combination may be sa tisfying and in a well composed page even beau tiful as a whole, but art in letters consists rathe r in the art of arranging and composing them i n a pleasing and appropriate manner. The mai n purpose of letters is the practical one of maki
The main purpose of letters is the practical one of making thoughts visible. Ruskin says that al
The main purpose of letters is the practical one of making thoughts visible. Ruskin sa

12/14

The main purpose of letters is the practical one of making thoughts visible. Ruskin says that a ll letters are frightful things and to be endured only on occasion, that is to say, in places where t he sense of the inscription is of more importanc e than external ornament. This is a sweeping s tatement, from which we need not suffer undul y; yet it is doubtful whether there is art in indiv idual letters. Letters in combination may be sa tisfying and in a well composed page even beau tiful as a whole, but art in letters consists rathe r in the art of arranging and composing them i n a pleasing and appropriate manner. The mai n purpose of letters is the practical one of maki ng thoughts visible. Ruskin says that all letter
The main purpose of letters is the practical one of making thoughts visible. Ruskin says that al
The main purpose of letters is the practical one of making thoughts visible. Ruskin sa

12/15

The main purpose of letters is the practical one of making thoughts visible. Ruskin says that a ll letters are frightful things and to be endured only on occasion, that is to say, in places where t he sense of the inscription is of more importanc e than external ornament. This is a sweeping s tatement, from which we need not suffer undul y; yet it is doubtful whether there is art in indiv idual letters. Letters in combination may be sa tisfying and in a well composed page even beau tiful as a whole, but art in letters consists rathe r in the art of arranging and composing them i n a pleasing and appropriate manner. The mai n purpose of letters is the practical one of maki
The main purpose of letters is the practical one of making thoughts visible. Ruskin says that al
The main purpose of letters is the practical one of making thoughts visible. Ruskin sa

CENTURY SCHOOLBOOK 14 POINT SET MINUS ½ UNIT

ROMAN, ITALIC, BOLD

abcdefghijklmnopqrstuvwxyz – 1 UNIT
abcdefghijklmnopqrstuvwxyz – ½ UNIT
abcdefghijklmnopqrstuvwxyz NORMAL

ABCDEFGHIJKLMNOPQRSTUVWXYZ abcdefghijklmnopqrstuvwxyz
ABCDEFGHIJKLMNOPQRSTUVWXYZ abcdefghijklmnopqrstuvwxyz
ABCDEFGHIJKLMNOPQRSTUVWXYZ abcdefghijklmnopqrstuvwxyz

14/14

The main purpose of letters is the practi cal one of making thoughts visible. Rus kin says that all letters are frightful thi ngs and to be endured only on occasion, that is to say, in places where the sense o f the inscription is of more importance t han external ornament. This is a sweepi ng statement, from which we need not s uffer unduly; yet it is doubtful whether t here is art in individual letters. Letters i n combination may be satisfying and in a well composed page even beautiful as a whole, but art in letters consists rathe
The main purpose of letters is the practic al one of making thoughts visible. Ruski
The main purpose of letters is the pr actical one of making thoughts visib

14/15

The main purpose of letters is the practi cal one of making thoughts visible. Rus kin says that all letters are frightful thi ngs and to be endured only on occasion, that is to say, in places where the sense o f the inscription is of more importance t han external ornament. This is a sweepi ng statement, from which we need not s uffer unduly; yet it is doubtful whether t here is art in individual letters. Letters i n combination may be satisfying and in a well composed page even beautiful as
The main purpose of letters is the practic al one of making thoughts visible. Ruski
The main purpose of letters is the pr actical one of making thoughts visib

14/16

The main purpose of letters is the practi cal one of making thoughts visible. Rus kin says that all letters are frightful thi ngs and to be endured only on occasion, that is to say, in places where the sense o f the inscription is of more importance t han external ornament. This is a sweepi ng statement, from which we need not s uffer unduly; yet it is doubtful whether t here is art in individual letters. Letters i n combination may be satisfying and in a well composed page even beautiful as a whole, but art in letters consists rathe
The main purpose of letters is the practic al one of making thoughts visible. Ruski
The main purpose of letters is the pr actical one of making thoughts visib

14/17

The main purpose of letters is the practi cal one of making thoughts visible. Rus kin says that all letters are frightful thi ngs and to be endured only on occasion, that is to say, in places where the sense o f the inscription is of more importance t han external ornament. This is a sweepi ng statement, from which we need not s uffer unduly; yet it is doubtful whether t here is art in individual letters. Letters i n combination may be satisfying and in a well composed page even beautiful as
The main purpose of letters is the practic al one of making thoughts visible. Ruski
The main purpose of letters is the pr actical one of making thoughts visib

ITC CHELTENHAM 6 & 7 POINT SET NORMAL

LIGHT, ITALIC, BOLD, BOLD ITALIC

ABCDEFGHIJKLMNOPQRSTUVWXYZ 1234567890 abcdefghijklmnopqrstuvwxyz

ABCDEFGHIJKLMNOPQRSTUVWXYZ 1234567890 abcdefghijklmnopqrstuvwxyz

ABCDEFGHIJKLMNOPQRSTUVWXYZ 1234567890 abcdefghijklmnopqrstuvwxyz

ABCDEFGHIJKLMNOPQRSTUVWXYZ 1234567890 abcdefghijklmnopqrstuvwxyz

6/6

The main purpose of letters is the practical one of making thoughts visible. Ruskin says that all le tters are frightful things and to be endured only on occasion, that is to say, in places where the se nse of the inscription is of more importance than external ornament. This is a sweeping stateme nt, from which we need not suffer unduly; yet it is doubtful whether there is art in individual letter s. Letters in combination may be satisfying and in a well composed page even beautiful as a who le, but art in letters consists rather in the art of arranging and composing them in a pleasing and a ppropriate manner. The main purpose of letters is the practical one of making thoughts visible. R uskin says that all letters are frightful things and to be endured only on occasion, that is to say, in places where the sense of the inscription is of more importance than external ornament. This is a sweeping statement, from which we need not suffer unduly; yet it is doubtful whether there is art in individual letters. Letters in combination may be satisfying and in a well composed page eve n beautiful as a whole, but art in letters consists rather in the art of arranging and composing the m in a pleasing and appropriate manner. The main purpose of letters is the practical one of maki
The main purpose of letters is the practical one of making thoughts visible. Ruskin says that all letters are frightful things and to be endured only on occasion, that is to say, in places where the
The main purpose of letters is the practical one of making thoughts visible. Ruskin say s that all letters are frightful things and to be endured only on occasion, that is to say, i

6/7

The main purpose of letters is the practical one of making thoughts visible. Ruskin says that all le tters are frightful things and to be endured only on occasion, that is to say, in places where the se nse of the inscription is of more importance than external ornament. This is a sweeping stateme nt, from which we need not suffer unduly; yet it is doubtful whether there is art in individual letter s. Letters in combination may be satisfying and in a well composed page even beautiful as a who le, but art in letters consists rather in the art of arranging and composing them in a pleasing and a ppropriate manner. The main purpose of letters is the practical one of making thoughts visible. R uskin says that all letters are frightful things and to be endured only on occasion, that is to say, in places where the sense of the inscription is of more importance than external ornament. This is a sweeping statement, from which we need not suffer unduly; yet it is doubtful whether there is art in individual letters. Letters in combination may be satisfying and in a well composed page eve
The main purpose of letters is the practical one of making thoughts visible. Ruskin says that all letters are frightful things and to be endured only on occasion, that is to say, in places where the
The main purpose of letters is the practical one of making thoughts visible. Ruskin say s that all letters are frightful things and to be endured only on occasion, that is to say, i

6/8

The main purpose of letters is the practical one of making thoughts visible. Ruskin says that all le tters are frightful things and to be endured only on occasion, that is to say, in places where the se nse of the inscription is of more importance than external ornament. This is a sweeping stateme nt, from which we need not suffer unduly; yet it is doubtful whether there is art in individual letter s. Letters in combination may be satisfying and in a well composed page even beautiful as a who le, but art in letters consists rather in the art of arranging and composing them in a pleasing and a ppropriate manner. The main purpose of letters is the practical one of making thoughts visible. R uskin says that all letters are frightful things and to be endured only on occasion, that is to say, in places where the sense of the inscription is of more importance than external ornament. This is
The main purpose of letters is the practical one of making thoughts visible. Ruskin says that all letters are frightful things and to be endured only on occasion, that is to say, in places where the
The main purpose of letters is the practical one of making thoughts visible. Ruskin say s that all letters are frightful things and to be endured only on occasion, that is to say, i

6/9

The main purpose of letters is the practical one of making thoughts visible. Ruskin says that all le tters are frightful things and to be endured only on occasion, that is to say, in places where the se nse of the inscription is of more importance than external ornament. This is a sweeping stateme nt, from which we need not suffer unduly; yet it is doubtful whether there is art in individual letter s. Letters in combination may be satisfying and in a well composed page even beautiful as a who le, but art in letters consists rather in the art of arranging and composing them in a pleasing and a ppropriate manner. The main purpose of letters is the practical one of making thoughts visible. R uskin says that all letters are frightful things and to be endured only on occasion, that is to say, in
The main purpose of letters is the practical one of making thoughts visible. Ruskin says that all letters are frightful things and to be endured only on occasion, that is to say, in places where the
The main purpose of letters is the practical one of making thoughts visible. Ruskin say s that all letters are frightful things and to be endured only on occasion, that is to say, i

---

ABCDEFGHIJKLMNOPQRSTUVWXYZ 1234567890 abcdefghijklmnopqrstuvwxyz

ABCDEFGHIJKLMNOPQRSTUVWXYZ 1234567890 abcdefghijklmnopqrstuvwxyz

ABCDEFGHIJKLMNOPQRSTUVWXYZ 1234567890 abcdefghijklmnopqrstuvwxyz

ABCDEFGHIJKLMNOPQRSTUVWXYZ 1234567890 abcdefghijklmnopqrstuvwxyz

7/7

The main purpose of letters is the practical one of making thoughts visible. Ruskin says that all letters are frightful things and to be endured only on occasion, that is t o say, in places where the sense of the inscription is of more importance than exter nal ornament. This is a sweeping statement, from which we need not suffer unduly; yet it is doubtful whether there is art in individual letters. Letters in combination m ay be satisfying and in a well composed page even beautiful as a whole, but art in l etters consists rather in the art of arranging and composing them in a pleasing and appropriate manner. The main purpose of letters is the practical one of making tho ughts visible. Ruskin says that all letters are frightful things and to be endured only on occasion, that is to say, in places where the sense of the inscription is of more i mportance than external ornament. This is a sweeping statement, from which we
The main purpose of letters is the practical one of making thoughts visible. Ruskin says that all letters are frightful things and to be endured only on occasion, that is t
The main purpose of letters is the practical one of making thoughts visible. Ruskin says that all letters are frightful things and to be endured only on

7/8

TThe main purpose of letters is the practical one of making thoughts visible. Ruskin says that all letters are frightful things and to be endured only on occasion, that is t o say, in places where the sense of the inscription is of more importance than exter nal ornament. This is a sweeping statement, from which we need not suffer unduly; yet it is doubtful whether there is art in individual letters. Letters in combination m ay be satisfying and in a well composed page even beautiful as a whole, but art in l etters consists rather in the art of arranging and composing them in a pleasing and appropriate manner. The main purpose of letters is the practical one of making tho ughts visible. Ruskin says that all letters are frightful things and to be endured only on occasion, that is to say, in places where the sense of the inscription is of more i
The main purpose of letters is the practical one of making thoughts visible. Ruskin says that all letters are frightful things and to be endured only on occasion, that is t
The main purpose of letters is the practical one of making thoughts visible. Ruskin says that all letters are frightful things and to be endured only on

7/9

The main purpose of letters is the practical one of making thoughts visible. Ruskin says that all letters are frightful things and to be endured only on occasion, that is t o say, in places where the sense of the inscription is of more importance than exter nal ornament. This is a sweeping statement, from which we need not suffer unduly; yet it is doubtful whether there is art in individual letters. Letters in combination m ay be satisfying and in a well composed page even beautiful as a whole, but art in l etters consists rather in the art of arranging and composing them in a pleasing and appropriate manner. The main purpose of letters is the practical one of making tho ughts visible. Ruskin says that all letters are frightful things and to be endured only on occasion, that is to say, in places where the sense of the inscription is of more i
The main purpose of letters is the practical one of making thoughts visible. Ruskin says that all letters are frightful things and to be endured only on occasion, that is t
The main purpose of letters is the practical one of making thoughts visible. Ruskin says that all letters are frightful things and to be endured only on

7/10

The main purpose of letters is the practical one of making thoughts visible. Ruskin says that all letters are frightful things and to be endured only on occasion, that is t o say, in places where the sense of the inscription is of more importance than exter nal ornament. This is a sweeping statement, from which we need not suffer unduly; yet it is doubtful whether there is art in individual letters. Letters in combination m ay be satisfying and in a well composed page even beautiful as a whole, but art in l etters consists rather in the art of arranging and composing them in a pleasing and appropriate manner. The main purpose of letters is the practical one of making tho ughts visible. Ruskin says that all letters are frightful things and to be endured only
The main purpose of letters is the practical one of making thoughts visible. Ruskin says that all letters are frightful things and to be endured only on occasion, that is t
The main purpose of letters is the practical one of making thoughts visible. Ruskin says that all letters are frightful things and to be endured only on

ITC CHELTENHAM 8 & 9 POINT SET NORMAL

LIGHT, ITALIC, BOLD, BOLD ITALIC

ABCDEFGHIJKLMNOPQRSTUVWXYZ 1234567890 abcdefghijklmnopqrstuvwxyz

ABCDEFGHIJKLMNOPQRSTUVWXYZ 1234567890 abcdefghijklmnopqrstuvwxyz

ABCDEFGHIJKLMNOPQRSTUVWXYZ 1234567890 abcdefghijklmnopqrstuvwxyz

ABCDEFGHIJKLMNOPQRSTUVWXYZ 1234567890 abcdefghijklmnopqrstuvwxyz

8/8

The main purpose of letters is the practical one of making thoughts visib le. Ruskin says that all letters are frightful things and to be endured only on occasion, that is to say, in places where the sense of the inscription is of more importance than external ornament. This is a sweeping stateme nt, from which we need not suffer unduly; yet it is doubtful whether there is art in individual letters. Letters in combination may be satisfying and i n a well composed page even beautiful as a whole, but art in letters cons ists rather in the art of arranging and composing them in a pleasing and appropriate manner. The main purpose of letters is the practical one of *The main purpose of letters is the practical one of making thoughts visib le. Ruskin says that all letters are frightful things and to be endured only* **The main purpose of letters is the practical one of making thoug hts visible. Ruskin says that all letters are frightful things and to**

8/9

The main purpose of letters is the practical one of making thoughts visib le. Ruskin says that all letters are frightful things and to be endured only on occasion, that is to say, in places where the sense of the inscription is of more importance than external ornament. This is a sweeping stateme nt, from which we need not suffer unduly; yet it is doubtful whether there is art in individual letters. Letters in combination may be satisfying and i n a well composed page even beautiful as a whole, but art in letters cons ists rather in the art of arranging and composing them in a pleasing and *The main purpose of letters is the practical one of making thoughts visib le. Ruskin says that all letters are frightful things and to be endured only* **The main purpose of letters is the practical one of making thoug hts visible. Ruskin says that all letters are frightful things and to**

8/10

The main purpose of letters is the practical one of making thoughts visib le. Ruskin says that all letters are frightful things and to be endured only on occasion, that is to say, in places where the sense of the inscription is of more importance than external ornament. This is a sweeping stateme nt, from which we need not suffer unduly; yet it is doubtful whether there is art in individual letters. Letters in combination may be satisfying and i n a well composed page even beautiful as a whole, but art in letters cons *The main purpose of letters is the practical one of making thoughts visib le. Ruskin says that all letters are frightful things and to be endured only* **The main purpose of letters is the practical one of making thoug hts visible. Ruskin says that all letters are frightful things and to**

8/11

The main purpose of letters is the practical one of making thoughts visib le. Ruskin says that all letters are frightful things and to be endured only on occasion, that is to say, in places where the sense of the inscription is of more importance than external ornament. This is a sweeping stateme nt, from which we need not suffer unduly; yet it is doubtful whether there is art in individual letters. Letters in combination may be satisfying and i n a well composed page even beautiful as a whole, but art in letters cons *The main purpose of letters is the practical one of making thoughts visib le. Ruskin says that all letters are frightful things and to be endured only* **The main purpose of letters is the practical one of making thoug hts visible. Ruskin says that all letters are frightful things and to**

ABCDEFGHIJKLMNOPQRSTUVWXYZ 1234567890 abcdefghijklmnopqrstuvwxyz

ABCDEFGHIJKLMNOPQRSTUVWXYZ 1234567890 abcdefghijklmnopqrstuvwxyz

ABCDEFGHIJKLMNOPQRSTUVWXYZ 1234567890 abcdefghijklmnopqrstuvwxyz

ABCDEFGHIJKLMNOPQRSTUVWXYZ 1234567890 abcdefghijklmnopqrstuvwxyz

9/9

The main purpose of letters is the practical one of making thoug hts visible. Ruskin says that all letters are frightful things and to b e endured only on occasion, that is to say, in places where the se nse of the inscription is of more importance than external orna ment. This is a sweeping statement, from which we need not suff er unduly; yet it is doubtful whether there is art in individual lette rs. Letters in combination may be satisfying and in a well compo sed page even beautiful as a whole, but art in letters consists rat *The main purpose of letters is the practical one of making thoug hts visible. Ruskin says that all letters are frightful things and to* **The main purpose of letters is the practical one of making thoughts visible. Ruskin says that all letters are frightful t**

9/10

The main purpose of letters is the practical one of making thoug hts visible. Ruskin says that all letters are frightful things and to b e endured only on occasion, that is to say, in places where the se nse of the inscription is of more importance than external orna ment. This is a sweeping statement, from which we need not suff er unduly; yet it is doubtful whether there is art in individual lette rs. Letters in combination may be satisfying and in a well compo *The main purpose of letters is the practical one of making thoug hts visible. Ruskin says that all letters are frightful things and to* **The main purpose of letters is the practical one of making thoughts visible. Ruskin says that all letters are frightful t**

9/11

The main purpose of letters is the practical one of making thoug hts visible. Ruskin says that all letters are frightful things and to b e endured only on occasion, that is to say, in places where the se nse of the inscription is of more importance than external orna ment. This is a sweeping statement, from which we need not suff er unduly; yet it is doubtful whether there is art in individual lette rs. Letters in combination may be satisfying and in a well compo *The main purpose of letters is the practical one of making thoug hts visible. Ruskin says that all letters are frightful things and to* **The main purpose of letters is the practical one of making thoughts visible. Ruskin says that all letters are frightful t**

9/12

The main purpose of letters is the practical one of making thoug hts visible. Ruskin says that all letters are frightful things and to b e endured only on occasion, that is to say, in places where the se nse of the inscription is of more importance than external orna ment. This is a sweeping statement, from which we need not suff er unduly; yet it is doubtful whether there is art in individual lette rs. Letters in combination may be satisfying and in a well compo *The main purpose of letters is the practical one of making thoug hts visible. Ruskin says that all letters are frightful things and to* **The main purpose of letters is the practical one of making thoughts visible. Ruskin says that all letters are frightful t**

ITC CHELTENHAM 10 POINT SET MINUS ½ UNIT

LIGHT, ITALIC, BOLD, BOLD ITALIC

abcdefghijklmnopqrstuvwxyz — 1 UNIT
abcdefghijklmnopqrstuvwxyz — ½ UNIT
abcdefghijklmnopqrstuvwxyz NORMAL

ABCDEFGHIJKLMNOPQRSTUVWXYZ 1234567890 abcdefghijklmnopqrstuvwxyz
ABCDEFGHIJKLMNOPQRSTUVWXYZ 1234567890 abcdefghijklmnopqrstuvwxyz
ABCDEFGHIJKLMNOPQRSTUVWXYZ 1234567890 abcdefghijklmnopqrstuvwxyz
ABCDEFGHIJKLMNOPQRSTUVWXYZ 1234567890 abcdefghijklmnopqrstuvwxyz

10/10

The main purpose of letters is the practical one of making th oughts visible. Ruskin says that all letters are frightful things and to be endured only on occasion, that is to say, in places where the sense of the inscription is of more importance tha n external ornament. This is a sweeping statement, from wh ich we need not suffer unduly; yet it is doubtful whether there is art in individual letters. Letters in combination may be sati sfying and in a well composed page even beautiful as a whol e, but art in letters consists rather in the art of arranging and composing them in a pleasing and appropriate manner. The main purpose of letters is the practical one of making though ts visible. Ruskin says that all letters are frightful things and t o be endured only on occasion, that is to say, in places wher e the sense of the inscription is of more importance than ext ernal ornament. This is a sweeping statement, from which w e need not suffer unduly; yet it is doubtful whether there is art in individual letters. Letters in combination may be satisfyin g and in a well composed page even beautiful as a whole, bu t art in letters consists rather in the art of arranging and comp osing them in a pleasing and appropriate manner. The main purpose of letters is the practical one of making thoughts visi ble. Ruskin says that all letters are frightful things and to be e
The main purpose of letters is the practical one of making th oughts visible. Ruskin says that all letters are frightful things
The main purpose of letters is the practical one of ma king thoughts visible. Ruskin says that all letters are fr

10/11

The main purpose of letters is the practical one of making th oughts visible. Ruskin says that all letters are frightful things and to be endured only on occasion, that is to say, in places where the sense of the inscription is of more importance tha n external ornament. This is a sweeping statement, from wh ich we need not suffer unduly; yet it is doubtful whether there is art in individual letters. Letters in combination may be sati sfying and in a well composed page even beautiful as a whol e, but art in letters consists rather in the art of arranging and composing them in a pleasing and appropriate manner. The main purpose of letters is the practical one of making though ts visible. Ruskin says that all letters are frightful things and t o be endured only on occasion, that is to say, in places wher e the sense of the inscription is of more importance than ext ernal ornament. This is a sweeping statement, from which w e need not suffer unduly; yet it is doubtful whether there is art in individual letters. Letters in combination may be satisfyin g and in a well composed page even beautiful as a whole, bu t art in letters consists rather in the art of arranging and comp osing them in a pleasing and appropriate manner. The main
The main purpose of letters is the practical one of making th oughts visible. Ruskin says that all letters are frightful things
The main purpose of letters is the practical one of ma king thoughts visible. Ruskin says that all letters are fr

10/12

The main purpose of letters is the practical one of making th oughts visible. Ruskin says that all letters are frightful things and to be endured only on occasion, that is to say, in places where the sense of the inscription is of more importance tha n external ornament. This is a sweeping statement, from wh ich we need not suffer unduly; yet it is doubtful whether there is art in individual letters. Letters in combination may be sati sfying and in a well composed page even beautiful as a whol e, but art in letters consists rather in the art of arranging and composing them in a pleasing and appropriate manner. The main purpose of letters is the practical one of making though ts visible. Ruskin says that all letters are frightful things and t o be endured only on occasion, that is to say, in places wher e the sense of the inscription is of more importance than ext ernal ornament. This is a sweeping statement, from which w e need not suffer unduly; yet it is doubtful whether there is art in individual letters. Letters in combination may be satisfyin g and in a well composed page even beautiful as a whole, bu
The main purpose of letters is the practical one of making th oughts visible. Ruskin says that all letters are frightful things
The main purpose of letters is the practical one of ma king thoughts visible. Ruskin says that all letters are fr

10/13

The main purpose of letters is the practical one of making th oughts visible. Ruskin says that all letters are frightful things and to be endured only on occasion, that is to say, in places where the sense of the inscription is of more importance tha n external ornament. This is a sweeping statement, from wh ich we need not suffer unduly; yet it is doubtful whether there is art in individual letters. Letters in combination may be sati sfying and in a well composed page even beautiful as a whol e, but art in letters consists rather in the art of arranging and composing them in a pleasing and appropriate manner. The main purpose of letters is the practical one of making though ts visible. Ruskin says that all letters are frightful things and t o be endured only on occasion, that is to say, in places wher e the sense of the inscription is of more importance than ext ernal ornament. This is a sweeping statement, from which w e need not suffer unduly; yet it is doubtful whether there is art in individual letters. Letters in combination may be satisfyin
The main purpose of letters is the practical one of making th oughts visible. Ruskin says that all letters are frightful things
The main purpose of letters is the practical one of ma king thoughts visible. Ruskin says that all letters are fr

ITC CHELTENHAM 11 POINT SET MINUS ½ UNIT

LIGHT, ITALIC, BOLD, BOLD ITALIC

abcdefghijklmnopqrstuvwxyz – 1 UNIT
abcdefghijklmnopqrstuvwxyz – ½ UNIT
abcdefghijklmnopqrstuvwxyz NORMAL

ABCDEFGHIJKLMNOPQRSTUVWXYZ 1234567890 abcdefghijklmnopqrstuvwxyz
ABCDEFGHIJKLMNOPQRSTUVWXYZ 1234567890 abcdefghijklmnopqrstuvwxyz
ABCDEFGHIJKLMNOPQRSTUVWXYZ 1234567890 abcdefghijklmnopqrstuvwxyz
ABCDEFGHIJKLMNOPQRSTUVWXYZ 1234567890 abcdefghijklmnopqrstuvwxyz

11/11

The main purpose of letters is the practical one of maki ng thoughts visible. Ruskin says that all letters are frigh tful things and to be endured only on occasion, that is t o say, in places where the sense of the inscription is of more importance than external ornament. This is a sw eeping statement, from which we need not suffer undu ly; yet it is doubtful whether there is art in individual lett ers. Letters in combination may be satisfying and in a well composed page even beautiful as a whole, but art in letters consists rather in the art of arranging and co mposing them in a pleasing and appropriate manner. T he main purpose of letters is the practical one of makin g thoughts visible. Ruskin says that all letters are frightf ul things and to be endured only on occasion, that is to say, in places where the sense of the inscription is of m ore importance than external ornament. This is a swee ping statement, from which we need not suffer unduly; yet it is doubtful whether there is art in individual letter s. Letters in combination may be satisfying and in a wel
The main purpose of letters is the practical one of mak ing thoughts visible. Ruskin says that all letters are frig
The main purpose of letters is the practical one o f making thoughts visible. Ruskin says that all let

11/12

The main purpose of letters is the practical one of maki ng thoughts visible. Ruskin says that all letters are frigh tful things and to be endured only on occasion, that is t o say, in places where the sense of the inscription is of more importance than external ornament. This is a sw eeping statement, from which we need not suffer undu ly; yet it is doubtful whether there is art in individual lett ers. Letters in combination may be satisfying and in a well composed page even beautiful as a whole, but art in letters consists rather in the art of arranging and co mposing them in a pleasing and appropriate manner. T he main purpose of letters is the practical one of makin g thoughts visible. Ruskin says that all letters are frightf ul things and to be endured only on occasion, that is to say, in places where the sense of the inscription is of m ore importance than external ornament. This is a swee ping statement, from which we need not suffer unduly; yet it is doubtful whether there is art in individual letter
The main purpose of letters is the practical one of mak ing thoughts visible. Ruskin says that all letters are frig
The main purpose of letters is the practical one o f making thoughts visible. Ruskin says that all let

11/13

The main purpose of letters is the practical one of maki ng thoughts visible. Ruskin says that all letters are frigh tful things and to be endured only on occasion, that is t o say, in places where the sense of the inscription is of more importance than external ornament. This is a sw eeping statement, from which we need not suffer undu ly; yet it is doubtful whether there is art in individual lett ers. Letters in combination may be satisfying and in a well composed page even beautiful as a whole, but art in letters consists rather in the art of arranging and co mposing them in a pleasing and appropriate manner. T he main purpose of letters is the practical one of makin g thoughts visible. Ruskin says that all letters are frightf ul things and to be endured only on occasion, that is to say, in places where the sense of the inscription is of m ore importance than external ornament. This is a swee ping statement, from which we need not suffer unduly;
The main purpose of letters is the practical one of mak ing thoughts visible. Ruskin says that all letters are frig
The main purpose of letters is the practical one o f making thoughts visible. Ruskin says that all let

11/14

The main purpose of letters is the practical one of maki ng thoughts visible. Ruskin says that all letters are frigh tful things and to be endured only on occasion, that is t o say, in places where the sense of the inscription is of more importance than external ornament. This is a sw eeping statement, from which we need not suffer undu ly; yet it is doubtful whether there is art in individual lett ers. Letters in combination may be satisfying and in a well composed page even beautiful as a whole, but art in letters consists rather in the art of arranging and co mposing them in a pleasing and appropriate manner. T he main purpose of letters is the practical one of makin g thoughts visible. Ruskin says that all letters are frightf ul things and to be endured only on occasion, that is to say, in places where the sense of the inscription is of m ore importance than external ornament. This is a swee
The main purpose of letters is the practical one of mak ing thoughts visible. Ruskin says that all letters are frig
The main purpose of letters is the practical one o f making thoughts visible. Ruskin says that all let

ITC CHELTENHAM 12 POINT SET MINUS ½ UNIT

LIGHT, ITALIC, BOLD, BOLD ITALIC

abcdefghijklmnopqrstuvwxyz – 1 UNIT
abcdefghijklmnopqrstuvwxyz – ½ UNIT
abcdefghijklmnopqrstuvwxyz NORMAL

ABCDEFGHIJKLMNOPQRSTUVWXYZ 1234567890 abcdefghijklmnopqrstuvwxyz
ABCDEFGHIJKLMNOPQRSTUVWXYZ 1234567890 abcdefghijklmnopqrstuvwxyz
ABCDEFGHIJKLMNOPQRSTUVWXYZ 1234567890 abcdefghijklmnopqrstuvwxyz
ABCDEFGHIJKLMNOPQRSTUVWXYZ 1234567890 abcdefghijklmnopqrstuvwxyz

12/12

The main purpose of letters is the practical one of making thoughts visible. Ruskin says that all letters are frightful things and to be endured only on occa sion, that is to say, in places where the sense of the i nscription is of more importance than external orn ament. This is a sweeping statement, from which w e need not suffer unduly; yet it is doubtful whether t here is art in individual letters. Letters in combinati on may be satisfying and in a well composed page even beautiful as a whole, but art in letters consists rather in the art of arranging and composing them i n a pleasing and appropriate manner. The main pu rpose of letters is the practical one of making thoug hts visible. Ruskin says that all letters are frightful th ings and to be endured only on occasion, that is to
The main purpose of letters is the practical one of making thoughts visible. Ruskin says that all letter
The main purpose of letters is the practical o ne of making thoughts visible. Ruskin says th

12/13

The main purpose of letters is the practical one of making thoughts visible. Ruskin says that all letters are frightful things and to be endured only on occa sion, that is to say, in places where the sense of the i nscription is of more importance than external orn ament. This is a sweeping statement, from which w e need not suffer unduly; yet it is doubtful whether t here is art in individual letters. Letters in combinati on may be satisfying and in a well composed page even beautiful as a whole, but art in letters consists rather in the art of arranging and composing them i n a pleasing and appropriate manner. The main pu rpose of letters is the practical one of making thoug hts visible. Ruskin says that all letters are frightful th
The main purpose of letters is the practical one of making thoughts visible. Ruskin says that all letter
The main purpose of letters is the practical o ne of making thoughts visible. Ruskin says th

12/14

The main purpose of letters is the practical one of making thoughts visible. Ruskin says that all letters are frightful things and to be endured only on occa sion, that is to say, in places where the sense of the i nscription is of more importance than external orn ament. This is a sweeping statement, from which w e need not suffer unduly; yet it is doubtful whether t here is art in individual letters. Letters in combinati on may be satisfying and in a well composed page even beautiful as a whole, but art in letters consists rather in the art of arranging and composing them i n a pleasing and appropriate manner. The main pu rpose of letters is the practical one of making thoug hts visible. Ruskin says that all letters are frightful th ings and to be endured only on occasion, that is to
The main purpose of letters is the practical one of making thoughts visible. Ruskin says that all letter
The main purpose of letters is the practical o ne of making thoughts visible. Ruskin says th

12/15

The main purpose of letters is the practical one of making thoughts visible. Ruskin says that all letters are frightful things and to be endured only on occa sion, that is to say, in places where the sense of the i nscription is of more importance than external orn ament. This is a sweeping statement, from which w e need not suffer unduly; yet it is doubtful whether t here is art in individual letters. Letters in combinati on may be satisfying and in a well composed page even beautiful as a whole, but art in letters consists rather in the art of arranging and composing them i n a pleasing and appropriate manner. The main pu rpose of letters is the practical one of making thoug hts visible. Ruskin says that all letters are frightful th
The main purpose of letters is the practical one of making thoughts visible. Ruskin says that all letter
The main purpose of letters is the practical o ne of making thoughts visible. Ruskin says th

ITC CHELTENHAM 14 POINT SET MINUS ½ UNIT

LIGHT, ITALIC, BOLD, BOLD ITALIC

abcdefghijklmnopqrstuvwxyz – 1 UNIT
abcdefghijklmnopqrstuvwxyz ½ UNIT
abcdefghijklmnopqrstuvwxyz NORMAL

ABCDEFGHIJKLMNOPQRSTUVWXYZ abcdefghijklmnopqrstuvwxyz
ABCDEFGHIJKLMNOPQRSTUVWXYZ abcdefghijklmnopqrstuvwxyz
ABCDEFGHIJKLMNOPQRSTUVWXYZ abcdefghijklmnopqrstuvwxyz
ABCDEFGHIJKLMNOPQRSTUVWXYZ abcdefghijklmnopqrstuvwxyz

14/14

The main purpose of letters is the practical one of making thoughts visible. Ruskin say s that all letters are frightful things and to be endured only on occasion, that is to say, in places where the sense of the inscription is of more importance than external ornament. This is a sweeping statement, from which we need not suffer unduly; yet it is doubtful whether there is art in individual letters. Letters in combination may be satisfying and in a well composed page even beautiful as a whole, but art in letters consists rather in the art of arranging and composing them
The main purpose of letters is the practical one of making thoughts visible. Ruskin say
The main purpose of letters is the practical one of making thoughts visible. R

14/15

The main purpose of letters is the practical one of making thoughts visible. Ruskin say s that all letters are frightful things and to be endured only on occasion, that is to say, in places where the sense of the inscription is of more importance than external ornament. This is a sweeping statement, from which we need not suffer unduly; yet it is doubtful whether there is art in individual letters. Letters in combination may be satisfying and in a well composed page even beautiful as a whole, but art in letters consists rather i
The main purpose of letters is the practical one of making thoughts visible. Ruskin say
The main purpose of letters is the practical one of making thoughts visible. R

14/16

The main purpose of letters is the practical one of making thoughts visible. Ruskin say s that all letters are frightful things and to be endured only on occasion, that is to say, in places where the sense of the inscription is of more importance than external ornament. This is a sweeping statement, from which we need not suffer unduly; yet it is doubtful whether there is art in individual letters. Letters in combination may be satisfying and in a well composed page even beautiful as a whole, but art in letters consists rather in the art of arranging and composing them
The main purpose of letters is the practical one of making thoughts visible. Ruskin say
The main purpose of letters is the practical one of making thoughts visible. R

14/17

The main purpose of letters is the practical one of making thoughts visible. Ruskin say s that all letters are frightful things and to be endured only on occasion, that is to say, in places where the sense of the inscription is of more importance than external ornament. This is a sweeping statement, from which we need not suffer unduly; yet it is doubtful whether there is art in individual letters. Letters in combination may be satisfying and in a well composed page even beautiful as a whole, but art in letters consists rather i
The main purpose of letters is the practical one of making thoughts visible. Ruskin say
The main purpose of letters is the practical one of making thoughts visible. R

CLARENDON 6 & 7 POINT SET NORMAL

LIGHT, REGULAR, BOLD

ABCDEFGHIJKLMNOPQRSTUVWXYZ 1234567890 abcdefghijklmnopqrstuvwxyz

ABCDEFGHIJKLMNOPQRSTUVWXYZ 1234567890 abcdefghijklmnopqrstuvwxyz

ABCDEFGHIJKLMNOPQRSTUVWXYZ 1234567890 abcdefghijklmnopqrstuvwxyz

6/6

The main purpose of letters is the practical one of making thoughts visible. Ruskin s ays that all letters are frightful things and to be endured only on occasion, that is to s ay, in places where the sense of the inscription is of more importance than external o rnament. This is a sweeping statement, from which we need not suffer unduly; yet it is doubtful whether there is art in individual letters. Letters in combination may be s atisfying and in a well composed page even beautiful as a whole, but art in letters con sists rather in the art of arranging and composing them in a pleasing and appropria te manner. The main purpose of letters is the practical one of making thoughts visibl e. Ruskin says that all letters are frightful things and to be endured only on occasion, that is to say, in places where the sense of the inscription is of more importance tha n external ornament. This is a sweeping statement, from which we need not suffer u nduly; yet it is doubtful whether there is art in individual letters. Letters in combinat ion may be satisfying and in a well composed page even beautiful as a whole, but art i
The main purpose of letters is the practical one of making thoughts visible. Ruskin s ays that all letters are frightful things and to be endured only on occasion, that is to s
The main purpose of letters is the practical one of making thoughts visible. Rus kin says that all letters are frightful things and to be endured only on occasion, t

6/7

The main purpose of letters is the practical one of making thoughts visible. Ruskin s ays that all letters are frightful things and to be endured only on occasion, that is to s ay, in places where the sense of the inscription is of more importance than external o rnament. This is a sweeping statement, from which we need not suffer unduly; yet it is doubtful whether there is art in individual letters. Letters in combination may be s atisfying and in a well composed page even beautiful as a whole, but art in letters con sists rather in the art of arranging and composing them in a pleasing and appropria te manner. The main purpose of letters is the practical one of making thoughts visibl e. Ruskin says that all letters are frightful things and to be endured only on occasion, that is to say, in places where the sense of the inscription is of more importance tha n external ornament. This is a sweeping statement, from which we need not suffer u
The main purpose of letters is the practical one of making thoughts visible. Ruskin s ays that all letters are frightful things and to be endured only on occasion, that is to s
The main purpose of letters is the practical one of making thoughts visible. Rus kin says that all letters are frightful things and to be endured only on occasion, t

6/8

The main purpose of letters is the practical one of making thoughts visible. Ruskin s ays that all letters are frightful things and to be endured only on occasion, that is to s ay, in places where the sense of the inscription is of more importance than external o rnament. This is a sweeping statement, from which we need not suffer unduly; yet it is doubtful whether there is art in individual letters. Letters in combination may be s atisfying and in a well composed page even beautiful as a whole, but art in letters con sists rather in the art of arranging and composing them in a pleasing and appropria te manner. The main purpose of letters is the practical one of making thoughts visibl e. Ruskin says that all letters are frightful things and to be endured only on occasion,
The main purpose of letters is the practical one of making thoughts visible. Ruskin s ays that all letters are frightful things and to be endured only on occasion, that is to s
The main purpose of letters is the practical one of making thoughts visible. Rus kin says that all letters are frightful things and to be endured only on occasion, t

6/9

The main purpose of letters is the practical one of making thoughts visible. Ruskin s ays that all letters are frightful things and to be endured only on occasion, that is to s ay, in places where the sense of the inscription is of more importance than external o rnament. This is a sweeping statement, from which we need not suffer unduly; yet it is doubtful whether there is art in individual letters. Letters in combination may be s atisfying and in a well composed page even beautiful as a whole, but art in letters con sists rather in the art of arranging and composing them in a pleasing and appropria te manner. The main purpose of letters is the practical one of making thoughts visibl
The main purpose of letters is the practical one of making thoughts visible. Ruskin s ays that all letters are frightful things and to be endured only on occasion, that is to s
The main purpose of letters is the practical one of making thoughts visible. Rus kin says that all letters are frightful things and to be endured only on occasion, t

ABCDEFGHIJKLMNOPQRSTUVWXYZ 1234567890 abcdefghijklmnopqrstuvwxyz

ABCDEFGHIJKLMNOPQRSTUVWXYZ 1234567890 abcdefghijklmnopqrstuvwxyz

ABCDEFGHIJKLMNOPQRSTUVWXYZ 1234567890 abcdefghijklmnopqrstuvwxyz

7/7

The main purpose of letters is the practical one of making thoughts visib le. Ruskin says that all letters are frightful things and to be endured onl y on occasion, that is to say, in places where the sense of the inscription i s of more importance than external ornament. This is a sweeping statem ent, from which we need not suffer unduly; yet it is doubtful whether the re is art in individual letters. Letters in combination may be satisfying a nd in a well composed page even beautiful as a whole, but art in letters co nsists rather in the art of arranging and composing them in a pleasing a nd appropriate manner. The main purpose of letters is the practical one of making thoughts visible. Ruskin says that all letters are frightful thi ngs and to be endured only on occasion, that is to say, in places where th
The main purpose of letters is the practical one of making thoughts visib le. Ruskin says that all letters are frightful things and to be endured onl
The main purpose of letters is the practical one of making thoughts v isible. Ruskin says that all letters are frightful things and to be end

7/8

The main purpose of letters is the practical one of making thoughts visib le. Ruskin says that all letters are frightful things and to be endured onl y on occasion, that is to say, in places where the sense of the inscription i s of more importance than external ornament. This is a sweeping statem ent, from which we need not suffer unduly; yet it is doubtful whether the re is art in individual letters. Letters in combination may be satisfying a nd in a well composed page even beautiful as a whole, but art in letters co nsists rather in the art of arranging and composing them in a pleasing a nd appropriate manner. The main purpose of letters is the practical one of making thoughts visible. Ruskin says that all letters are frightful thi
The main purpose of letters is the practical one of making thoughts visib le. Ruskin says that all letters are frightful things and to be endured onl
The main purpose of letters is the practical one of making thoughts v isible. Ruskin says that all letters are frightful things and to be end

7/9

The main purpose of letters is the practical one of making thoughts visib le. Ruskin says that all letters are frightful things and to be endured onl y on occasion, that is to say, in places where the sense of the inscription i s of more importance than external ornament. This is a sweeping statem ent, from which we need not suffer unduly; yet it is doubtful whether the re is art in individual letters. Letters in combination may be satisfying a nd in a well composed page even beautiful as a whole, but art in letters co nsists rather in the art of arranging and composing them in a pleasing a nd appropriate manner. The main purpose of letters is the practical one of making thoughts visible. Ruskin says that all letters are frightful thi
The main purpose of letters is the practical one of making thoughts visib le. Ruskin says that all letters are frightful things and to be endured onl
The main purpose of letters is the practical one of making thoughts v isible. Ruskin says that all letters are frightful things and to be end

7/10

The main purpose of letters is the practical one of making thoughts visib le. Ruskin says that all letters are frightful things and to be endured onl y on occasion, that is to say, in places where the sense of the inscription i s of more importance than external ornament. This is a sweeping statem ent, from which we need not suffer unduly; yet it is doubtful whether the re is art in individual letters. Letters in combination may be satisfying a nd in a well composed page even beautiful as a whole, but art in letters co nsists rather in the art of arranging and composing them in a pleasing a nd appropriate manner. The main purpose of letters is the practical one
The main purpose of letters is the practical one of making thoughts visib le. Ruskin says that all letters are frightful things and to be endured onl
The main purpose of letters is the practical one of making thoughts v isible. Ruskin says that all letters are frightful things and to be end

CLARENDON 8 & 9 POINT SET NORMAL

LIGHT, REGULAR, BOLD

ABCDEFGHIJKLMNOPQRSTUVWXYZ 1234567890 abcdefghijklmnopqrstuvwxyz

ABCDEFGHIJKLMNOPQRSTUVWXYZ 1234567890 abcdefghijklmnopqrstuvwxyz

ABCDEFGHIJKLMNOPQRSTUVWXYZ 1234567890 abcdefghijklmnopqrstuvwxyz

8/8

The main purpose of letters is the practical one of making thou ghts visible. Ruskin says that all letters are frightful things an d to be endured only on occasion, that is to say, in places where t he sense of the inscription is of more importance than external ornament. This is a sweeping statement, from which we need n ot suffer unduly; yet it is doubtful whether there is art in indivi dual letters. Letters in combination may be satisfying and in a well composed page even beautiful as a whole, but art in letters consists rather in the art of arranging and composing them in
The main purpose of letters is the practical one of making thou ghts visible. Ruskin says that all letters are frightful things an
The main purpose of letters is the practical one of making th oughts visible. Ruskin says that all letters are frightful thi

8/9

The main purpose of letters is the practical one of making thou ghts visible. Ruskin says that all letters are frightful things an d to be endured only on occasion, that is to say, in places where t he sense of the inscription is of more importance than external ornament. This is a sweeping statement, from which we need n ot suffer unduly; yet it is doubtful whether there is art in indivi dual letters. Letters in combination may be satisfying and in a well composed page even beautiful as a whole, but art in letters
The main purpose of letters is the practical one of making thou ghts visible. Ruskin says that all letters are frightful things an
The main purpose of letters is the practical one of making th oughts visible. Ruskin says that all letters are frightful thi

8/10

The main purpose of letters is the practical one of making thou ghts visible. Ruskin says that all letters are frightful things an d to be endured only on occasion, that is to say, in places where t he sense of the inscription is of more importance than external ornament. This is a sweeping statement, from which we need n ot suffer unduly; yet it is doubtful whether there is art in indivi dual letters. Letters in combination may be satisfying and in a
The main purpose of letters is the practical one of making thou ghts visible. Ruskin says that all letters are frightful things an
The main purpose of letters is the practical one of making th oughts visible. Ruskin says that all letters are frightful thi

8/11

The main purpose of letters is the practical one of making thou ghts visible. Ruskin says that all letters are frightful things an d to be endured only on occasion, that is to say, in places where t he sense of the inscription is of more importance than external ornament. This is a sweeping statement, from which we need n ot suffer unduly; yet it is doubtful whether there is art in indivi dual letters. Letters in combination may be satisfying and in a
The main purpose of letters is the practical one of making thou ghts visible. Ruskin says that all letters are frightful things an
The main purpose of letters is the practical one of making th oughts visible. Ruskin says that all letters are frightful thi

---

ABCDEFGHIJKLMNOPQRSTUVWXYZ 1234567890 abcdefghijklmnopqrstuvwxyz

ABCDEFGHIJKLMNOPQRSTUVWXYZ 1234567890 abcdefghijklmnopqrstuvwxyz

ABCDEFGHIJKLMNOPQRSTUVWXYZ 1234567890 abcdefghijklmnopqrstuvwxyz

9/9

The main purpose of letters is the practical one of makin g thoughts visible. Ruskin says that all letters are fright ful things and to be endured only on occasion, that is to s ay, in places where the sense of the inscription is of more importance than external ornament. This is a sweeping statement, from which we need not suffer unduly; yet it is doubtful whether there is art in individual letters. Let ters in combination may be satisfying and in a well com
The main purpose of letters is the practical one of makin g thoughts visible. Ruskin says that all letters are fright
The main purpose of letters is the practical one of ma king thoughts visible. Ruskin says that all letters ar

9/10

The main purpose of letters is the practical one of makin g thoughts visible. Ruskin says that all letters are fright ful things and to be endured only on occasion, that is to s ay, in places where the sense of the inscription is of more importance than external ornament. This is a sweeping statement, from which we need not suffer unduly; yet it is doubtful whether there is art in individual letters. Let
The main purpose of letters is the practical one of makin g thoughts visible. Ruskin says that all letters are fright
The main purpose of letters is the practical one of ma king thoughts visible. Ruskin says that all letters ar

9/11

The main purpose of letters is the practical one of makin g thoughts visible. Ruskin says that all letters are fright ful things and to be endured only on occasion, that is to s ay, in places where the sense of the inscription is of more importance than external ornament. This is a sweeping statement, from which we need not suffer unduly; yet it is doubtful whether there is art in individual letters. Let
The main purpose of letters is the practical one of makin g thoughts visible. Ruskin says that all letters are fright
The main purpose of letters is the practical one of ma king thoughts visible. Ruskin says that all letters ar

9/12

The main purpose of letters is the practical one of makin g thoughts visible. Ruskin says that all letters are fright ful things and to be endured only on occasion, that is to s ay, in places where the sense of the inscription is of more importance than external ornament. This is a sweeping statement, from which we need not suffer unduly; yet it is doubtful whether there is art in individual letters. Let
The main purpose of letters is the practical one of makin g thoughts visible. Ruskin says that all letters are fright
The main purpose of letters is the practical one of ma king thoughts visible. Ruskin says that all letters ar

CLARENDON 10 POINT SET MINUS ½ UNIT

LIGHT, REGULAR, BOLD

abcdefghijklmnopqrstuvwxyz – 1 UNIT
abcdefghijklmnopqrstuvwxyz – ½ UNIT
abcdefghijklmnopqrstuvwxyz NORMAL

ABCDEFGHIJKLMNOPQRSTUVWXYZ 1234567890 abcdefghijklmnopqrstuvwxyz
ABCDEFGHIJKLMNOPQRSTUVWXYZ 1234567890 abcdefghijklmnopqrstuvwxyz
ABCDEFGHIJKLMNOPQRSTUVWXYZ 1234567890 abcdefghijklmnopqrstuvwxyz

10/10

The main purpose of letters is the practical one of ma king thoughts visible. Ruskin says that all letters ar e frightful things and to be endured only on occasion, that is to say, in places where the sense of the inscri ption is of more importance than external ornament. This is a sweeping statement, from which we need n ot suffer unduly; yet it is doubtful whether there is a rt in individual letters. Letters in combination may b e satisfying and in a well composed page even beauti ful as a whole, but art in letters consists rather in the art of arranging and composing them in a pleasing a nd appropriate manner. The main purpose of letters is the practical one of making thoughts visible. Rus kin says that all letters are frightful things and to be endured only on occasion, that is to say, in places wh ere the sense of the inscription is of more importance than external ornament. This is a sweeping stateme nt, from which we need not suffer unduly; yet it is do ubtful whether there is art in individual letters. Lett ers in combination may be satisfying and in a well co mposed page even beautiful as a whole, but art in lett ers consists rather in the art of arranging and comp

The main purpose of letters is the practical one of ma king thoughts visible. Ruskin says that all letters ar

The main purpose of letters is the practical one of making thoughts visible. Ruskin says that all let

10/11

The main purpose of letters is the practical one of ma king thoughts visible. Ruskin says that all letters ar e frightful things and to be endured only on occasion, that is to say, in places where the sense of the inscri ption is of more importance than external ornament. This is a sweeping statement, from which we need n ot suffer unduly; yet it is doubtful whether there is a rt in individual letters. Letters in combination may b e satisfying and in a well composed page even beauti ful as a whole, but art in letters consists rather in the art of arranging and composing them in a pleasing a nd appropriate manner. The main purpose of letters is the practical one of making thoughts visible. Rus kin says that all letters are frightful things and to be endured only on occasion, that is to say, in places wh ere the sense of the inscription is of more importance than external ornament. This is a sweeping stateme nt, from which we need not suffer unduly; yet it is do ubtful whether there is art in individual letters. Lett ers in combination may be satisfying and in a well co

The main purpose of letters is the practical one of ma king thoughts visible. Ruskin says that all letters ar

The main purpose of letters is the practical one of making thoughts visible. Ruskin says that all let

10/12

The main purpose of letters is the practical one of ma king thoughts visible. Ruskin says that all letters ar e frightful things and to be endured only on occasion, that is to say, in places where the sense of the inscri ption is of more importance than external ornament. This is a sweeping statement, from which we need n ot suffer unduly; yet it is doubtful whether there is a rt in individual letters. Letters in combination may b e satisfying and in a well composed page even beauti ful as a whole, but art in letters consists rather in the art of arranging and composing them in a pleasing a nd appropriate manner. The main purpose of letters is the practical one of making thoughts visible. Rus kin says that all letters are frightful things and to be endured only on occasion, that is to say, in places wh ere the sense of the inscription is of more importance than external ornament. This is a sweeping stateme nt, from which we need not suffer unduly; yet it is do

The main purpose of letters is the practical one of ma king thoughts visible. Ruskin says that all letters ar

The main purpose of letters is the practical one of making thoughts visible. Ruskin says that all let

10/13

The main purpose of letters is the practical one of ma king thoughts visible. Ruskin says that all letters ar e frightful things and to be endured only on occasion, that is to say, in places where the sense of the inscri ption is of more importance than external ornament. This is a sweeping statement, from which we need n ot suffer unduly; yet it is doubtful whether there is a rt in individual letters. Letters in combination may b e satisfying and in a well composed page even beauti ful as a whole, but art in letters consists rather in the art of arranging and composing them in a pleasing a nd appropriate manner. The main purpose of letters is the practical one of making thoughts visible. Rus kin says that all letters are frightful things and to be endured only on occasion, that is to say, in places wh ere the sense of the inscription is of more importance than external ornament. This is a sweeping stateme

The main purpose of letters is the practical one of ma king thoughts visible. Ruskin says that all letters ar

The main purpose of letters is the practical one of making thoughts visible. Ruskin says that all let

CLARENDON 11 POINT SET MINUS ½ UNIT

LIGHT, REGULAR, BOLD

abcdefghijklmnopqrstuvwxyz – 1 UNIT
abcdefghijklmnopqrstuvwxyz – ½ UNIT
abcdefghijklmnopqrstuvwxyz NORMAL

ABCDEFGHIJKLMNOPQRSTUVWXYZ 1234567890 abcdefghijklmnopqrstuvwxyz
ABCDEFGHIJKLMNOPQRSTUVWXYZ 1234567890 abcdefghijklmnopqrstuvwxyz
ABCDEFGHIJKLMNOPQRSTUVWXYZ 1234567890 abcdefghijklmnopqrstuvwxyz

11/11

The main purpose of letters is the practical one of making thoughts visible. Ruskin says that al l letters are frightful things and to be endured o nly on occasion, that is to say, in places where t he sense of the inscription is of more importanc e than external ornament. This is a sweeping st atement, from which we need not suffer unduly; yet it is doubtful whether there is art in individ ual letters. Letters in combination may be satisf ying and in a well composed page even beautifu l as a whole, but art in letters consists rather in t he art of arranging and composing them in a pl easing and appropriate manner. The main pur pose of letters is the practical one of making tho ughts visible. Ruskin says that all letters are fri ghtful things and to be endured only on occasio n, that is to say, in places where the sense of the inscription is of more importance than external ornament. This is a sweeping statement, from
The main purpose of letters is the practical one of making thoughts visible. Ruskin says that al
The main purpose of letters is the practical one of making thoughts visible. Ruskin says

11/12

The main purpose of letters is the practical one of making thoughts visible. Ruskin says that al l letters are frightful things and to be endured o nly on occasion, that is to say, in places where t he sense of the inscription is of more importanc e than external ornament. This is a sweeping st atement, from which we need not suffer unduly; yet it is doubtful whether there is art in individ ual letters. Letters in combination may be satisf ying and in a well composed page even beautifu l as a whole, but art in letters consists rather in t he art of arranging and composing them in a pl easing and appropriate manner. The main pur pose of letters is the practical one of making tho ughts visible. Ruskin says that all letters are fri ghtful things and to be endured only on occasio n, that is to say, in places where the sense of the inscription is of more importance than external
The main purpose of letters is the practical one of making thoughts visible. Ruskin says that al
The main purpose of letters is the practical one of making thoughts visible. Ruskin says

11/13

The main purpose of letters is the practical one of making thoughts visible. Ruskin says that al l letters are frightful things and to be endured o nly on occasion, that is to say, in places where t he sense of the inscription is of more importanc e than external ornament. This is a sweeping st atement, from which we need not suffer unduly; yet it is doubtful whether there is art in individ ual letters. Letters in combination may be satisf ying and in a well composed page even beautifu l as a whole, but art in letters consists rather in t he art of arranging and composing them in a pl easing and appropriate manner. The main pur pose of letters is the practical one of making tho ughts visible. Ruskin says that all letters are fri ghtful things and to be endured only on occasio n, that is to say, in places where the sense of the
The main purpose of letters is the practical one of making thoughts visible. Ruskin says that al
The main purpose of letters is the practical one of making thoughts visible. Ruskin says

11/14

The main purpose of letters is the practical one of making thoughts visible. Ruskin says that al l letters are frightful things and to be endured o nly on occasion, that is to say, in places where t he sense of the inscription is of more importanc e than external ornament. This is a sweeping st atement, from which we need not suffer unduly; yet it is doubtful whether there is art in individ ual letters. Letters in combination may be satisf ying and in a well composed page even beautifu l as a whole, but art in letters consists rather in t he art of arranging and composing them in a pl easing and appropriate manner. The main pur pose of letters is the practical one of making tho ughts visible. Ruskin says that all letters are fri ghtful things and to be endured only on occasio
The main purpose of letters is the practical one of making thoughts visible. Ruskin says that al
The main purpose of letters is the practical one of making thoughts visible. Ruskin says

CLARENDON 12 POINT SET MINUS ½ UNIT

LIGHT, REGULAR, BOLD

abcdefghijklmnopqrstuvwxyz – 1 UNIT
abcdefghijklmnopqrstuvwxyz – ½ UNIT
abcdefghijklmnopqrstuvwxyz NORMAL

ABCDEFGHIJKLMNOPQRSTUVWXYZ 1234567890 abcdefghijklmnopqrstuvwxyz
ABCDEFGHIJKLMNOPQRSTUVWXYZ 1234567890 abcdefghijklmnopqrstuvwxyz
ABCDEFGHIJKLMNOPQRSTUVWXYZ 1234567890 abcdefghijklmnopqrstuvwx

12/12

The main purpose of letters is the practical o ne of making thoughts visible. Ruskin says that all letters are frightful things and to be endured only on occasion, that is to say, in p laces where the sense of the inscription is of more importance than external ornament. T his is a sweeping statement, from which we need not suffer unduly; yet it is doubtful wh ether there is art in individual letters. Letter s in combination may be satisfying and in a well composed page even beautiful as a whol e, but art in letters consists rather in the art of arranging and composing them in a pleas ing and appropriate manner. The main pur pose of letters is the practical one of making
The main purpose of letters is the practical o ne of making thoughts visible. Ruskin says
The main purpose of letters is the practica l one of making thoughts visible. Ruskin

12/13

The main purpose of letters is the practical o ne of making thoughts visible. Ruskin says that all letters are frightful things and to be endured only on occasion, that is to say, in p laces where the sense of the inscription is of more importance than external ornament. T his is a sweeping statement, from which we need not suffer unduly; yet it is doubtful wh ether there is art in individual letters. Letter s in combination may be satisfying and in a well composed page even beautiful as a whol e, but art in letters consists rather in the art of arranging and composing them in a pleas ing and appropriate manner. The main pur
The main purpose of letters is the practical o ne of making thoughts visible. Ruskin says
The main purpose of letters is the practica l one of making thoughts visible. Ruskin

12/14

The main purpose of letters is the practical o ne of making thoughts visible. Ruskin says that all letters are frightful things and to be endured only on occasion, that is to say, in p laces where the sense of the inscription is of more importance than external ornament. T his is a sweeping statement, from which we need not suffer unduly; yet it is doubtful wh ether there is art in individual letters. Letter s in combination may be satisfying and in a well composed page even beautiful as a whol e, but art in letters consists rather in the art of arranging and composing them in a pleas ing and appropriate manner. The main pur pose of letters is the practical one of making
The main purpose of letters is the practical o ne of making thoughts visible. Ruskin says
The main purpose of letters is the practica l one of making thoughts visible. Ruskin

12/15

The main purpose of letters is the practical o ne of making thoughts visible. Ruskin says that all letters are frightful things and to be endured only on occasion, that is to say, in p laces where the sense of the inscription is of more importance than external ornament. T his is a sweeping statement, from which we need not suffer unduly; yet it is doubtful wh ether there is art in individual letters. Letter s in combination may be satisfying and in a well composed page even beautiful as a whol e, but art in letters consists rather in the art of arranging and composing them in a pleas ing and appropriate manner. The main pur
The main purpose of letters is the practical o ne of making thoughts visible. Ruskin says
The main purpose of letters is the practica l one of making thoughts visible. Ruskin

CLARENDON 14 POINT SET MINUS ½ UNIT

LIGHT, REGULAR, BOLD

abcdefghijklmnopqrstuvwxyz – 1 UNIT
abcdefghijklmnopqrstuvwxyz – ½ UNIT
abcdefghijklmnopqrstuvwxyz NORMAL

ABCDEFGHIJKLMNOPQRSTUVWXYZ abcdefghijklmnopqrstuvwxyz
ABCDEFGHIJKLMNOPQRSTUVWXYZ abcdefghijklmnopqrstuvwxyz
ABCDEFGHIJKLMNOPQRSTUVWXYZ abcdefghijklmnopqrstuvwxyz

14/14

The main purpose of letters is the pra ctical one of making thoughts visible. Ruskin says that all letters are fright ful things and to be endured only on o ccasion, that is to say, in places where the sense of the inscription is of more importance than external ornament. This is a sweeping statement, from w hich we need not suffer unduly; yet it is doubtful whether there is art in ind ividual letters. Letters in combination may be satisfying and in a well compo sed page even beautiful as a whole, bu
The main purpose of letters is the pra ctical one of making thoughts visible.
The main purpose of letters is the pr actical one of making thoughts visi

14/15

The main purpose of letters is the pra ctical one of making thoughts visible. Ruskin says that all letters are fright ful things and to be endured only on o ccasion, that is to say, in places where the sense of the inscription is of more importance than external ornament. This is a sweeping statement, from w hich we need not suffer unduly; yet it is doubtful whether there is art in ind ividual letters. Letters in combination may be satisfying and in a well compo
The main purpose of letters is the pra ctical one of making thoughts visible.
The main purpose of letters is the pr actical one of making thoughts visi

14/16

The main purpose of letters is the pra ctical one of making thoughts visible. Ruskin says that all letters are fright ful things and to be endured only on o ccasion, that is to say, in places where the sense of the inscription is of more importance than external ornament. This is a sweeping statement, from w hich we need not suffer unduly; yet it is doubtful whether there is art in ind ividual letters. Letters in combination may be satisfying and in a well compo sed page even beautiful as a whole, bu
The main purpose of letters is the pra ctical one of making thoughts visible.
The main purpose of letters is the pr actical one of making thoughts visi

14/17

The main purpose of letters is the pra ctical one of making thoughts visible. Ruskin says that all letters are fright ful things and to be endured only on o ccasion, that is to say, in places where the sense of the inscription is of more importance than external ornament. This is a sweeping statement, from w hich we need not suffer unduly; yet it is doubtful whether there is art in ind ividual letters. Letters in combination may be satisfying and in a well compo
The main purpose of letters is the pra ctical one of making thoughts visible.
The main purpose of letters is the pr actical one of making thoughts visi

ITC CLEARFACE 6 & 7 POINT SET NORMAL

ROMAN, ITALIC, HEAVY, HEAVY ITALIC

ABCDEFGHIJKLMNOPQRSTUVWXYZ 1234567890 abcdefghijklmnopqrstuvwxyz

ABCDEFGHIJKLMNOPQRSTUVWXYZ 1234567890 abcdefghijklmnopqrstuvwxyz

ABCDEFGHIJKLMNOPQRSTUVWXYZ 1234567890 abcdefghijklmnopqrstuvwxyz

ABCDEFGHIJKLMNOPQRSTUVWXYZ 1234567890 abcdefghijklmnopqrstuvwxyz

6/6

The main purpose of letters is the practical one of making thoughts visible. Ruskin says that all lette
rs are frightful things and to be endured only on occasion, that is to say, in places where the sense of t
he inscription is of more importance than external ornament. This is a sweeping statement, from w
hich we need not suffer unduly; yet it is doubtful whether there is art in individual letters. Letters in
combination may be satisfying and in a well composed page even beautiful as a whole, but art in lette
rs consists rather in the art of arranging and composing them in a pleasing and appropriate manner.
The main purpose of letters is the practical one of making thoughts visible. Ruskin says that all lette
rs are frightful things and to be endured only on occasion, that is to say, in places where the sense of t
he inscription is of more importance than external ornament. This is a sweeping statement, from w
hich we need not suffer unduly; yet it is doubtful whether there is art in individual letters. Letters in
combination may be satisfying and in a well composed page even beautiful as a whole, but art in lette
rs consists rather in the art of arranging and composing them in a pleasing and appropriate manner.
The main purpose of letters is the practical one of making thoughts visible. Ruskin says that all lette
The main purpose of letters is the practical one of making thoughts visible. Ruskin says that all lett
ers are frightful things and to be endured only on occasion, that is to say, in places where the sense
The main purpose of letters is the practical one of making thoughts visible. Ruskin says that all lett
ers are frightful things and to be endured only on occasion, that is to say, in places where the sense

6/7

The main purpose of letters is the practical one of making thoughts visible. Ruskin says that all lette
rs are frightful things and to be endured only on occasion, that is to say, in places where the sense of t
he inscription is of more importance than external ornament. This is a sweeping statement, from w
hich we need not suffer unduly; yet it is doubtful whether there is art in individual letters. Letters in
combination may be satisfying and in a well composed page even beautiful as a whole, but art in lette
rs consists rather in the art of arranging and composing them in a pleasing and appropriate manner.
The main purpose of letters is the practical one of making thoughts visible. Ruskin says that all lette
rs are frightful things and to be endured only on occasion, that is to say, in places where the sense of t
he inscription is of more importance than external ornament. This is a sweeping statement, from w
hich we need not suffer unduly; yet it is doubtful whether there is art in individual letters. Letters in
combination may be satisfying and in a well composed page even beautiful as a whole, but art in lette
The main purpose of letters is the practical one of making thoughts visible. Ruskin says that all lett
ers are frightful things and to be endured only on occasion, that is to say, in places where the sense
The main purpose of letters is the practical one of making thoughts visible. Ruskin says that all lett
ers are frightful things and to be endured only on occasion, that is to say, in places where the sense

6/8

The main purpose of letters is the practical one of making thoughts visible. Ruskin says that all lette
rs are frightful things and to be endured only on occasion, that is to say, in places where the sense of t
he inscription is of more importance than external ornament. This is a sweeping statement, from w
hich we need not suffer unduly; yet it is doubtful whether there is art in individual letters. Letters in
combination may be satisfying and in a well composed page even beautiful as a whole, but art in lette
rs consists rather in the art of arranging and composing them in a pleasing and appropriate manner.
The main purpose of letters is the practical one of making thoughts visible. Ruskin says that all lette
rs are frightful things and to be endured only on occasion, that is to say, in places where the sense of t
he inscription is of more importance than external ornament. This is a sweeping statement, from w
The main purpose of letters is the practical one of making thoughts visible. Ruskin says that all lett
ers are frightful things and to be endured only on occasion, that is to say, in places where the sense
The main purpose of letters is the practical one of making thoughts visible. Ruskin says that all lett
ers are frightful things and to be endured only on occasion, that is to say, in places where the sense

6/9

The main purpose of letters is the practical one of making thoughts visible. Ruskin says that all lette
rs are frightful things and to be endured only on occasion, that is to say, in places where the sense of t
he inscription is of more importance than external ornament. This is a sweeping statement, from w
hich we need not suffer unduly; yet it is doubtful whether there is art in individual letters. Letters in
combination may be satisfying and in a well composed page even beautiful as a whole, but art in lette
rs consists rather in the art of arranging and composing them in a pleasing and appropriate manner.
The main purpose of letters is the practical one of making thoughts visible. Ruskin says that all lette
rs are frightful things and to be endured only on occasion, that is to say, in places where the sense of t
The main purpose of letters is the practical one of making thoughts visible. Ruskin says that all lett
ers are frightful things and to be endured only on occasion, that is to say, in places where the sense
The main purpose of letters is the practical one of making thoughts visible. Ruskin says that all lett
ers are frightful things and to be endured only on occasion, that is to say, in places where the sense

---

ABCDEFGHIJKLMNOPQRSTUVWXYZ 1234567890 abcdefghijklmnopqrstuvwxyz

ABCDEFGHIJKLMNOPQRSTUVWXYZ 1234567890 abcdefghijklmnopqrstuvwxyz

ABCDEFGHIJKLMNOPQRSTUVWXYZ 1234567890 abcdefghijklmnopqrstuvwxyz

ABCDEFGHIJKLMNOPQRSTUVWXYZ 1234567890 abcdefghijklmnopqrstuvwxyz

7/7

The main purpose of letters is the practical one of making thoughts visible. Ruskin sa
ys that all letters are frightful things and to be endured only on occasion, that is to say,
in places where the sense of the inscription is of more importance than external orna
ment. This is a sweeping statement, from which we need not suffer unduly; yet it is do
ubtful whether there is art in individual letters. Letters in combination may be satisfyi
ng and in a well composed page even beautiful as a whole, but art in letters consists rat
her in the art of arranging and composing them in a pleasing and appropriate manner.
The main purpose of letters is the practical one of making thoughts visible. Ruskin sa
ys that all letters are frightful things and to be endured only on occasion, that is to say,
in places where the sense of the inscription is of more importance than external orna
ment. This is a sweeping statement, from which we need not suffer unduly; yet it is do
The main purpose of letters is the practical one of making thoughts visible. Ruskin sa
ys that all letters are frightful things and to be endured only on occasion, that is to sa
The main purpose of letters is the practical one of making thoughts visible. Ruskin
says that all letters are frightful things and to be endured only on occasion, that is to

7/8

The main purpose of letters is the practical one of making thoughts visible. Ruskin sa
ys that all letters are frightful things and to be endured only on occasion, that is to say,
in places where the sense of the inscription is of more importance than external orna
ment. This is a sweeping statement, from which we need not suffer unduly; yet it is do
ubtful whether there is art in individual letters. Letters in combination may be satisfyi
ng and in a well composed page even beautiful as a whole, but art in letters consists rat
her in the art of arranging and composing them in a pleasing and appropriate manner.
The main purpose of letters is the practical one of making thoughts visible. Ruskin sa
ys that all letters are frightful things and to be endured only on occasion, that is to say,
in places where the sense of the inscription is of more importance than external orna
The main purpose of letters is the practical one of making thoughts visible. Ruskin sa
ys that all letters are frightful things and to be endured only on occasion, that is to sa
The main purpose of letters is the practical one of making thoughts visible. Ruskin
says that all letters are frightful things and to be endured only on occasion, that is to

7/9

The main purpose of letters is the practical one of making thoughts visible. Ruskin sa
ys that all letters are frightful things and to be endured only on occasion, that is to say,
in places where the sense of the inscription is of more importance than external orna
ment. This is a sweeping statement, from which we need not suffer unduly; yet it is do
ubtful whether there is art in individual letters. Letters in combination may be satisfyi
ng and in a well composed page even beautiful as a whole, but art in letters consists rat
her in the art of arranging and composing them in a pleasing and appropriate manner.
The main purpose of letters is the practical one of making thoughts visible. Ruskin sa
ys that all letters are frightful things and to be endured only on occasion, that is to say,
in places where the sense of the inscription is of more importance than external orna
The main purpose of letters is the practical one of making thoughts visible. Ruskin sa
ys that all letters are frightful things and to be endured only on occasion, that is to sa
The main purpose of letters is the practical one of making thoughts visible. Ruskin
says that all letters are frightful things and to be endured only on occasion, that is to

7/10

The main purpose of letters is the practical one of making thoughts visible. Ruskin sa
ys that all letters are frightful things and to be endured only on occasion, that is to say,
in places where the sense of the inscription is of more importance than external orna
ment. This is a sweeping statement, from which we need not suffer unduly; yet it is do
ubtful whether there is art in individual letters. Letters in combination may be satisfyi
ng and in a well composed page even beautiful as a whole, but art in letters consists rat
her in the art of arranging and composing them in a pleasing and appropriate manner.
The main purpose of letters is the practical one of making thoughts visible. Ruskin sa
ys that all letters are frightful things and to be endured only on occasion, that is to say,
The main purpose of letters is the practical one of making thoughts visible. Ruskin sa
ys that all letters are frightful things and to be endured only on occasion, that is to sa
The main purpose of letters is the practical one of making thoughts visible. Ruskin
says that all letters are frightful things and to be endured only on occasion, that is to

ITC CLEARFACE 8 & 9 POINT SET NORMAL

ROMAN, ITALIC, HEAVY, HEAVY ITALIC

ABCDEFGHIJKLMNOPQRSTUVWXYZ 1234567890 abcdefghijklmnopqrstuvwxyz

ABCDEFGHIJKLMNOPQRSTUVWXYZ 1234567890 abcdefghijklmnopqrstuvwxyz

ABCDEFGHIJKLMNOPQRSTUVWXYZ 1234567890 abcdefghijklmnopqrstuvwxyz

ABCDEFGHIJKLMNOPQRSTUVWXYZ 1234567890 abcdefghijklmnopqrstuvwxyz

8/8

The main purpose of letters is the practical one of making thoughts visible. Ruskin says that all letters are frightful things and to be endured only on oc casion, that is to say, in places where the sense of the inscription is of more i mportance than external ornament. This is a sweeping statement, from wh ich we need not suffer unduly; yet it is doubtful whether there is art in indiv idual letters. Letters in combination may be satisfying and in a well compos ed page even beautiful as a whole, but art in letters consists rather in the art of arranging and composing them in a pleasing and appropriate manner. T he main purpose of letters is the practical one of making thoughts visible.
The main purpose of letters is the practical one of making thoughts visible. Ruskin says that all letters are frightful things and to be endured only on
The main purpose of letters is the practical one of making thoughts visible. Ruskin says that all letters are frightful things and to be endured only on

8/9

The main purpose of letters is the practical one of making thoughts visible. Ruskin says that all letters are frightful things and to be endured only on oc casion, that is to say, in places where the sense of the inscription is of more i mportance than external ornament. This is a sweeping statement, from wh ich we need not suffer unduly; yet it is doubtful whether there is art in indiv idual letters. Letters in combination may be satisfying and in a well compos ed page even beautiful as a whole, but art in letters consists rather in the art of arranging and composing them in a pleasing and appropriate manner. T
The main purpose of letters is the practical one of making thoughts visible. Ruskin says that all letters are frightful things and to be endured only on
The main purpose of letters is the practical one of making thoughts visible. Ruskin says that all letters are frightful things and to be endured only on

8/10

The main purpose of letters is the practical one of making thoughts visible. Ruskin says that all letters are frightful things and to be endured only on oc casion, that is to say, in places where the sense of the inscription is of more i mportance than external ornament. This is a sweeping statement, from wh ich we need not suffer unduly; yet it is doubtful whether there is art in indiv idual letters. Letters in combination may be satisfying and in a well compos ed page even beautiful as a whole, but art in letters consists rather in the art
The main purpose of letters is the practical one of making thoughts visible. Ruskin says that all letters are frightful things and to be endured only on
The main purpose of letters is the practical one of making thoughts visible. Ruskin says that all letters are frightful things and to be endured only on

8/11

The main purpose of letters is the practical one of making thoughts visible. Ruskin says that all letters are frightful things and to be endured only on oc casion, that is to say, in places where the sense of the inscription is of more i mportance than external ornament. This is a sweeping statement, from wh ich we need not suffer unduly; yet it is doubtful whether there is art in indiv idual letters. Letters in combination may be satisfying and in a well compos ed page even beautiful as a whole, but art in letters consists rather in the art
The main purpose of letters is the practical one of making thoughts visible. Ruskin says that all letters are frightful things and to be endured only on
The main purpose of letters is the practical one of making thoughts visible. Ruskin says that all letters are frightful things and to be endured only on

---

ABCDEFGHIJKLMNOPQRSTUVWXYZ 1234567890 abcdefghijklmnopqrstuvwxyz

ABCDEFGHIJKLMNOPQRSTUVWXYZ 1234567890 abcdefghijklmnopqrstuvwxyz

ABCDEFGHIJKLMNOPQRSTUVWXYZ 1234567890 abcdefghijklmnopqrstuvwxyz

ABCDEFGHIJKLMNOPQRSTUVWXYZ 1234567890 abcdefghijklmnopqrstuvwxyz

9/9

The main purpose of letters is the practical one of making thought s visible. Ruskin says that all letters are frightful things and to be e ndured only on occasion, that is to say, in places where the sense of the inscription is of more importance than external ornament. Thi s is a sweeping statement, from which we need not suffer unduly; y et it is doubtful whether there is art in individual letters. Letters in combination may be satisfying and in a well composed page even b eautiful as a whole, but art in letters consists rather in the art of arr
The main purpose of letters is the practical one of making thought s visible. Ruskin says that all letters are frightful things and to be e
The main purpose of letters is the practical one of making though ts visible. Ruskin says that all letters are frightful things and to be

9/10

The main purpose of letters is the practical one of making thought s visible. Ruskin says that all letters are frightful things and to be e ndured only on occasion, that is to say, in places where the sense of the inscription is of more importance than external ornament. Thi s is a sweeping statement, from which we need not suffer unduly; y et it is doubtful whether there is art in individual letters. Letters in combination may be satisfying and in a well composed page even b
The main purpose of letters is the practical one of making thought s visible. Ruskin says that all letters are frightful things and to be e
The main purpose of letters is the practical one of making though ts visible. Ruskin says that all letters are frightful things and to be

9/11

The main purpose of letters is the practical one of making thought s visible. Ruskin says that all letters are frightful things and to be e ndured only on occasion, that is to say, in places where the sense of the inscription is of more importance than external ornament. Thi s is a sweeping statement, from which we need not suffer unduly; y et it is doubtful whether there is art in individual letters. Letters in combination may be satisfying and in a well composed page even b
The main purpose of letters is the practical one of making thought s visible. Ruskin says that all letters are frightful things and to be e
The main purpose of letters is the practical one of making though ts visible. Ruskin says that all letters are frightful things and to be

9/12

The main purpose of letters is the practical one of making thought s visible. Ruskin says that all letters are frightful things and to be e ndured only on occasion, that is to say, in places where the sense of the inscription is of more importance than external ornament. Thi s is a sweeping statement, from which we need not suffer unduly; y et it is doubtful whether there is art in individual letters. Letters in combination may be satisfying and in a well composed page even b
The main purpose of letters is the practical one of making thought s visible. Ruskin says that all letters are frightful things and to be e
The main purpose of letters is the practical one of making though ts visible. Ruskin says that all letters are frightful things and to be

ITC CLEARFACE 10 POINT SET MINUS ½ UNIT

ROMAN, ITALIC, HEAVY, HEAVY ITALIC

abcdefghijklmnopqrstuvwxyz – 1 UNIT
abcdefghijklmnopqrstuvwxyz – ½ UNIT
abcdefghijklmnopqrstuvwxyz NORMAL

ABCDEFGHIJKLMNOPQRSTUVWXYZ 1234567890 abcdefghijklmnopqrstuvwxyz
ABCDEFGHIJKLMNOPQRSTUVWXYZ 1234567890 abcdefghijklmnopqrstuvwxyz
ABCDEFGHIJKLMNOPQRSTUVWXYZ 1234567890 abcdefghijklmnopqrstuvwxyz
ABCDEFGHIJKLMNOPQRSTUVWXYZ 1234567890 abcdefghijklmnopqrstuvwxyz

10/10

The main purpose of letters is the practical one of making thou ghts visible. Ruskin says that all letters are frightful things and to be endured only on occasion, that is to say, in places where t he sense of the inscription is of more importance than external ornament. This is a sweeping statement, from which we need not suffer unduly; yet it is doubtful whether there is art in indiv idual letters. Letters in combination may be satisfying and in a well composed page even beautiful as a whole, but art in letters consists rather in the art of arranging and composing them in a pleasing and appropriate manner. The main purpose of letter s is the practical one of making thoughts visible. Ruskin says th at all letters are frightful things and to be endured only on occa sion, that is to say, in places where the sense of the inscription i s of more importance than external ornament. This is a sweepi ng statement, from which we need not suffer unduly; yet it is d oubtful whether there is art in individual letters. Letters in co mbination may be satisfying and in a well composed page even beautiful as a whole, but art in letters consists rather in the art of arranging and composing them in a pleasing and appropriat e manner. The main purpose of letters is the practical one of m aking thoughts visible. Ruskin says that all letters are frightful things and to be endured only on occasion, that is to say, in pla
The main purpose of letters is the practical one of making tho ughts visible. Ruskin says that all letters are frightful things a
The main purpose of letters is the practical one of making tho ughts visible. Ruskin says that all letters are frightful things a

10/11

The main purpose of letters is the practical one of making thou ghts visible. Ruskin says that all letters are frightful things and to be endured only on occasion, that is to say, in places where t he sense of the inscription is of more importance than external ornament. This is a sweeping statement, from which we need not suffer unduly; yet it is doubtful whether there is art in indiv idual letters. Letters in combination may be satisfying and in a well composed page even beautiful as a whole, but art in letters consists rather in the art of arranging and composing them in a pleasing and appropriate manner. The main purpose of letter s is the practical one of making thoughts visible. Ruskin says th at all letters are frightful things and to be endured only on occa sion, that is to say, in places where the sense of the inscription i s of more importance than external ornament. This is a sweepi ng statement, from which we need not suffer unduly; yet it is d oubtful whether there is art in individual letters. Letters in co mbination may be satisfying and in a well composed page even beautiful as a whole, but art in letters consists rather in the art of arranging and composing them in a pleasing and appropriat e manner. The main purpose of letters is the practical one of m
The main purpose of letters is the practical one of making tho ughts visible. Ruskin says that all letters are frightful things a
The main purpose of letters is the practical one of making tho ughts visible. Ruskin says that all letters are frightful things a

10/12

The main purpose of letters is the practical one of making thou ghts visible. Ruskin says that all letters are frightful things and to be endured only on occasion, that is to say, in places where t he sense of the inscription is of more importance than external ornament. This is a sweeping statement, from which we need not suffer unduly; yet it is doubtful whether there is art in indiv idual letters. Letters in combination may be satisfying and in a well composed page even beautiful as a whole, but art in letters consists rather in the art of arranging and composing them in a pleasing and appropriate manner. The main purpose of letter s is the practical one of making thoughts visible. Ruskin says th at all letters are frightful things and to be endured only on occa sion, that is to say, in places where the sense of the inscription i s of more importance than external ornament. This is a sweepi ng statement, from which we need not suffer unduly; yet it is d oubtful whether there is art in individual letters. Letters in co mbination may be satisfying and in a well composed page even beautiful as a whole, but art in letters consists rather in the art
The main purpose of letters is the practical one of making tho ughts visible. Ruskin says that all letters are frightful things a
The main purpose of letters is the practical one of making tho ughts visible. Ruskin says that all letters are frightful things a

10/13

The main purpose of letters is the practical one of making thou ghts visible. Ruskin says that all letters are frightful things and to be endured only on occasion, that is to say, in places where t he sense of the inscription is of more importance than external ornament. This is a sweeping statement, from which we need not suffer unduly; yet it is doubtful whether there is art in indiv idual letters. Letters in combination may be satisfying and in a well composed page even beautiful as a whole, but art in letters consists rather in the art of arranging and composing them in a pleasing and appropriate manner. The main purpose of letter s is the practical one of making thoughts visible. Ruskin says th at all letters are frightful things and to be endured only on occa sion, that is to say, in places where the sense of the inscription i s of more importance than external ornament. This is a sweepi ng statement, from which we need not suffer unduly; yet it is d oubtful whether there is art in individual letters. Letters in co mbination may be satisfying and in a well composed page even
The main purpose of letters is the practical one of making tho ughts visible. Ruskin says that all letters are frightful things a
The main purpose of letters is the practical one of making tho ughts visible. Ruskin says that all letters are frightful things a

ITC CLEARFACE 11 POINT SET MINUS ½ UNIT

ROMAN, ITALIC, HEAVY, HEAVY ITALIC

abcdefghijklmnopqrstuvwxyz – 1 UNIT
abcdefghijklmnopqrstuvwxyz – ½ UNIT
abcdefghijklmnopqrstuvwxyz NORMAL

ABCDEFGHIJKLMNOPQRSTUVWXYZ 1234567890 abcdefghijklmnopqrstuvwxyz
ABCDEFGHIJKLMNOPQRSTUVWXYZ 1234567890 abcdefghijklmnopqrstuvwxyz
ABCDEFGHIJKLMNOPQRSTUVWXYZ 1234567890 abcdefghijklmnopqrstuvwxyz
ABCDEFGHIJKLMNOPQRSTUVWXYZ 1234567890 abcdefghijklmnopqrstuvwxyz

11/11

The main purpose of letters is the practical one of makin g thoughts visible. Ruskin says that all letters are frightful things and to be endured only on occasion, that is to say, in places where the sense of the inscription is of more i mportance than external ornament. This is a sweeping st atement, from which we need not suffer unduly; yet it is doubtful whether there is art in individual letters. Letter s in combination may be satisfying and in a well compose d page even beautiful as a whole, but art in letters consist s rather in the art of arranging and composing them in a pleasing and appropriate manner. The main purpose of le tters is the practical one of making thoughts visible. Rus kin says that all letters are frightful things and to be endu red only on occasion, that is to say, in places where the se nse of the inscription is of more importance than externa l ornament. This is a sweeping statement, from which we need not suffer unduly; yet it is doubtful whether there is art in individual letters. Letters in combination may be s atisfying and in a well composed page even beautiful as a
The main purpose of letters is the practical one of makin g thoughts visible. Ruskin says that all letters are frightf
The main purpose of letters is the practical one of makin g thoughts visible. Ruskin says that all letters are fright

11/12

The main purpose of letters is the practical one of makin g thoughts visible. Ruskin says that all letters are frightful things and to be endured only on occasion, that is to say, in places where the sense of the inscription is of more i mportance than external ornament. This is a sweeping st atement, from which we need not suffer unduly; yet it is doubtful whether there is art in individual letters. Letter s in combination may be satisfying and in a well compose d page even beautiful as a whole, but art in letters consist s rather in the art of arranging and composing them in a pleasing and appropriate manner. The main purpose of le tters is the practical one of making thoughts visible. Rus kin says that all letters are frightful things and to be endu red only on occasion, that is to say, in places where the se nse of the inscription is of more importance than externa l ornament. This is a sweeping statement, from which we need not suffer unduly; yet it is doubtful whether there is art in individual letters. Letters in combination may be s
The main purpose of letters is the practical one of makin g thoughts visible. Ruskin says that all letters are frightf
The main purpose of letters is the practical one of makin g thoughts visible. Ruskin says that all letters are fright

11/13

The main purpose of letters is the practical one of makin g thoughts visible. Ruskin says that all letters are frightful things and to be endured only on occasion, that is to say, in places where the sense of the inscription is of more i mportance than external ornament. This is a sweeping st atement, from which we need not suffer unduly; yet it is doubtful whether there is art in individual letters. Letter s in combination may be satisfying and in a well compose d page even beautiful as a whole, but art in letters consist s rather in the art of arranging and composing them in a pleasing and appropriate manner. The main purpose of le tters is the practical one of making thoughts visible. Rus kin says that all letters are frightful things and to be endu red only on occasion, that is to say, in places where the se nse of the inscription is of more importance than externa l ornament. This is a sweeping statement, from which we need not suffer unduly; yet it is doubtful whether there is
The main purpose of letters is the practical one of makin g thoughts visible. Ruskin says that all letters are frightf
The main purpose of letters is the practical one of makin g thoughts visible. Ruskin says that all letters are fright

11/14

The main purpose of letters is the practical one of makin g thoughts visible. Ruskin says that all letters are frightful things and to be endured only on occasion, that is to say, in places where the sense of the inscription is of more i mportance than external ornament. This is a sweeping st atement, from which we need not suffer unduly; yet it is doubtful whether there is art in individual letters. Letter s in combination may be satisfying and in a well compose d page even beautiful as a whole, but art in letters consist s rather in the art of arranging and composing them in a pleasing and appropriate manner. The main purpose of le tters is the practical one of making thoughts visible. Rus kin says that all letters are frightful things and to be endu red only on occasion, that is to say, in places where the se nse of the inscription is of more importance than externa l ornament. This is a sweeping statement, from which we
The main purpose of letters is the practical one of makin g thoughts visible. Ruskin says that all letters are frightf
The main purpose of letters is the practical one of makin g thoughts visible. Ruskin says that all letters are fright

ITC CLEARFACE 12 POINT SET MINUS ½ UNIT

ROMAN, ITALIC, HEAVY, HEAVY ITALIC

abcdefghijklmnopqrstuvwxyz – 1 UNIT
abcdefghijklmnopqrstuvwxyz – ½ UNIT
abcdefghijklmnopqrstuvwxyz NORMAL

ABCDEFGHIJKLMNOPQRSTUVWXYZ 1234567890 abcdefghijklmnopqrstuvwxyz
ABCDEFGHIJKLMNOPQRSTUVWXYZ 1234567890 abcdefghijklmnopqrstuvwxyz
ABCDEFGHIJKLMNOPQRSTUVWXYZ 1234567890 abcdefghijklmnopqrstuvwxyz
ABCDEFGHIJKLMNOPQRSTUVWXYZ 1234567890 abcdefghijklmnopqrstuvwxyz

12/12

The main purpose of letters is the practical one of ma king thoughts visible. Ruskin says that all letters are f rightful things and to be endured only on occasion, t hat is to say, in places where the sense of the inscripti on is of more importance than external ornament. T his is a sweeping statement, from which we need not suffer unduly; yet it is doubtful whether there is art i n individual letters. Letters in combination may be s atisfying and in a well composed page even beautiful as a whole, but art in letters consists rather in the art of arranging and composing them in a pleasing and a ppropriate manner. The main purpose of letters is th e practical one of making thoughts visible. Ruskin sa ys that all letters are frightful things and to be endure d only on occasion, that is to say, in places where the
The main purpose of letters is the practical one of m aking thoughts visible. Ruskin says that all letters ar
The main purpose of letters is the practical one of m aking thoughts visible. Ruskin says that all letters ar

12/13

The main purpose of letters is the practical one of ma king thoughts visible. Ruskin says that all letters are f rightful things and to be endured only on occasion, t hat is to say, in places where the sense of the inscripti on is of more importance than external ornament. T his is a sweeping statement, from which we need not suffer unduly; yet it is doubtful whether there is art i n individual letters. Letters in combination may be s atisfying and in a well composed page even beautiful as a whole, but art in letters consists rather in the art of arranging and composing them in a pleasing and a ppropriate manner. The main purpose of letters is th e practical one of making thoughts visible. Ruskin sa ys that all letters are frightful things and to be endure
The main purpose of letters is the practical one of m aking thoughts visible. Ruskin says that all letters ar
The main purpose of letters is the practical one of m aking thoughts visible. Ruskin says that all letters ar

12/14

The main purpose of letters is the practical one of ma king thoughts visible. Ruskin says that all letters are f rightful things and to be endured only on occasion, t hat is to say, in places where the sense of the inscripti on is of more importance than external ornament. T his is a sweeping statement, from which we need not suffer unduly; yet it is doubtful whether there is art i n individual letters. Letters in combination may be s atisfying and in a well composed page even beautiful as a whole, but art in letters consists rather in the art of arranging and composing them in a pleasing and a ppropriate manner. The main purpose of letters is th e practical one of making thoughts visible. Ruskin sa ys that all letters are frightful things and to be endure d only on occasion, that is to say, in places where the
The main purpose of letters is the practical one of m aking thoughts visible. Ruskin says that all letters ar
The main purpose of letters is the practical one of m aking thoughts visible. Ruskin says that all letters ar

12/15

The main purpose of letters is the practical one of ma king thoughts visible. Ruskin says that all letters are f rightful things and to be endured only on occasion, t hat is to say, in places where the sense of the inscripti on is of more importance than external ornament. T his is a sweeping statement, from which we need not suffer unduly; yet it is doubtful whether there is art i n individual letters. Letters in combination may be s atisfying and in a well composed page even beautiful as a whole, but art in letters consists rather in the art of arranging and composing them in a pleasing and a ppropriate manner. The main purpose of letters is th e practical one of making thoughts visible. Ruskin sa ys that all letters are frightful things and to be endure
The main purpose of letters is the practical one of m aking thoughts visible. Ruskin says that all letters ar
The main purpose of letters is the practical one of m aking thoughts visible. Ruskin says that all letters ar

ITC CLEARFACE 14 POINT SET MINUS ½ UNIT

ROMAN, ITALIC, HEAVY, HEAVY ITALIC

abcdefghijklmnopqrstuvwxyz – 1 UNIT
abcdefghijklmnopqrstuvwxyz – ½ UNIT
abcdefghijklmnopqrstuvwxyz NORMAL

ABCDEFGHIJKLMNOPQRSTUVWXYZ abcdefghijklmnopqrstuvwxyz
ABCDEFGHIJKLMNOPQRSTUVWXYZ abcdefghijklmnopqrstuvwxyz
ABCDEFGHIJKLMNOPQRSTUVWXYZ abcdefghijklmnopqrstuvwxyz
ABCDEFGHIJKLMNOPQRSTUVWXYZ abcdefghijklmnopqrstuvwxyz

14/14

The main purpose of letters is the practical o ne of making thoughts visible. Ruskin says t hat all letters are frightful things and to be en dured only on occasion, that is to say, in plac es where the sense of the inscription is of mo re importance than external ornament. This is a sweeping statement, from which we need not suffer unduly; yet it is doubtful whether t here is art in individual letters. Letters in co mbination may be satisfying and in a well co mposed page even beautiful as a whole, but a rt in letters consists rather in the art of arran ging and composing them in a pleasing and a
The main purpose of letters is the practical o ne of making thoughts visible. Ruskin says t
The main purpose of letters is the practical o ne of making thoughts visible. Ruskin says t

14/15

The main purpose of letters is the practical o ne of making thoughts visible. Ruskin says t hat all letters are frightful things and to be en dured only on occasion, that is to say, in plac es where the sense of the inscription is of mo re importance than external ornament. This is a sweeping statement, from which we need not suffer unduly; yet it is doubtful whether t here is art in individual letters. Letters in co mbination may be satisfying and in a well co mposed page even beautiful as a whole, but a rt in letters consists rather in the art of arran
The main purpose of letters is the practical o ne of making thoughts visible. Ruskin says t
The main purpose of letters is the practical o ne of making thoughts visible. Ruskin says t

14/16

The main purpose of letters is the practical o ne of making thoughts visible. Ruskin says t hat all letters are frightful things and to be en dured only on occasion, that is to say, in plac es where the sense of the inscription is of mo re importance than external ornament. This is a sweeping statement, from which we need not suffer unduly; yet it is doubtful whether t here is art in individual letters. Letters in co mbination may be satisfying and in a well co mposed page even beautiful as a whole, but a rt in letters consists rather in the art of arran ging and composing them in a pleasing and a
The main purpose of letters is the practical o ne of making thoughts visible. Ruskin says t
The main purpose of letters is the practical o ne of making thoughts visible. Ruskin says t

14/17

The main purpose of letters is the practical o ne of making thoughts visible. Ruskin says t hat all letters are frightful things and to be en dured only on occasion, that is to say, in plac es where the sense of the inscription is of mo re importance than external ornament. This is a sweeping statement, from which we need not suffer unduly; yet it is doubtful whether t here is art in individual letters. Letters in co mbination may be satisfying and in a well co mposed page even beautiful as a whole, but a rt in letters consists rather in the art of arran
The main purpose of letters is the practical o ne of making thoughts visible. Ruskin says t
The main purpose of letters is the practical o ne of making thoughts visible. Ruskin says t

CLOISTER 6 & 7 POINT SET NORMAL

ROMAN, ITALIC, BOLD

ABCDEFGHIJKLMNOPQRSTUVWXYZ 1234567890 abcdefghijklmnopqrstuvwxyz

ABCDEFGHIJKLMNOPQRSTUVWXYZ 1234567890 abcdefghijklmnopqrstuvwxyz

ABCDEFGHIJKLMNOPQRSTUVWXYZ 1234567890 abcdefghijklmnopqrstuvwxyz

6/6

The main purpose of letters is the practical one of making thoughts visible. Ruskin says that all letters are frightful t
hings and to be endured only on occasion, that is to say, in places where the sense of the inscription is of more impor
tance than external ornament. This is a sweeping statement, from which we need not suffer unduly; yet it is doubtful
whether there is art in individual letters. Letters in combination may be satisfying and in a well composed page even
beautiful as a whole, but art in letters consists rather in the art of arranging and composing them in a pleasing and ap
propriate manner. The main purpose of letters is the practical one of making thoughts visible. Ruskin says that all le
tters are frightful things and to be endured only on occasion, that is to say, in places where the sense of the inscripti
on is of more importance than external ornament. This is a sweeping statement, from which we need not suffer undu
ly; yet it is doubtful whether there is art in individual letters. Letters in combination may be satisfying and in a well c
omposed page even beautiful as a whole, but art in letters consists rather in the art of arranging and composing the
m in a pleasing and appropriate manner. The main purpose of letters is the practical one of making thoughts visible.
Ruskin says that all letters are frightful things and to be endured only on occasion, that is to say, in places where the
sense of the inscription is of more importance than external ornament. This is a sweeping statement, from which we
The main purpose of letters is the practical one of making thoughts visible. Ruskin says that all letters are frightful things and to b
e endured only on occasion, that is to say, in places where the sense of the inscription is of more importance than external orname
The main purpose of letters is the practical one of making thoughts visible. Ruskin says that all letters are
frightful things and to be endured only on occasion, that is to say, in places where the sense of the inscript

6/7

The main purpose of letters is the practical one of making thoughts visible. Ruskin says that all letters are frightful t
hings and to be endured only on occasion, that is to say, in places where the sense of the inscription is of more impor
tance than external ornament. This is a sweeping statement, from which we need not suffer unduly; yet it is doubtful
whether there is art in individual letters. Letters in combination may be satisfying and in a well composed page even
beautiful as a whole, but art in letters consists rather in the art of arranging and composing them in a pleasing and ap
propriate manner. The main purpose of letters is the practical one of making thoughts visible. Ruskin says that all le
tters are frightful things and to be endured only on occasion, that is to say, in places where the sense of the inscripti
on is of more importance than external ornament. This is a sweeping statement, from which we need not suffer undu
ly; yet it is doubtful whether there is art in individual letters. Letters in combination may be satisfying and in a well c
omposed page even beautiful as a whole, but art in letters consists rather in the art of arranging and composing the
m in a pleasing and appropriate manner. The main purpose of letters is the practical one of making thoughts visible.
The main purpose of letters is the practical one of making thoughts visible. Ruskin says that all letters are frightful things and to b
e endured only on occasion, that is to say, in places where the sense of the inscription is of more importance than external orname
The main purpose of letters is the practical one of making thoughts visible. Ruskin says that all letters are
frightful things and to be endured only on occasion, that is to say, in places where the sense of the inscript

6/8

The main purpose of letters is the practical one of making thoughts visible. Ruskin says that all letters are frightful t
hings and to be endured only on occasion, that is to say, in places where the sense of the inscription is of more impor
tance than external ornament. This is a sweeping statement, from which we need not suffer unduly; yet it is doubtful
whether there is art in individual letters. Letters in combination may be satisfying and in a well composed page even
beautiful as a whole, but art in letters consists rather in the art of arranging and composing them in a pleasing and ap
propriate manner. The main purpose of letters is the practical one of making thoughts visible. Ruskin says that all le
tters are frightful things and to be endured only on occasion, that is to say, in places where the sense of the inscripti
on is of more importance than external ornament. This is a sweeping statement, from which we need not suffer undu
ly; yet it is doubtful whether there is art in individual letters. Letters in combination may be satisfying and in a well c
The main purpose of letters is the practical one of making thoughts visible. Ruskin says that all letters are frightful things and to b
e endured only on occasion, that is to say, in places where the sense of the inscription is of more importance than external orname
The main purpose of letters is the practical one of making thoughts visible. Ruskin says that all letters are
frightful things and to be endured only on occasion, that is to say, in places where the sense of the inscript

6/9

The main purpose of letters is the practical one of making thoughts visible. Ruskin says that all letters are frightful t
hings and to be endured only on occasion, that is to say, in places where the sense of the inscription is of more impor
tance than external ornament. This is a sweeping statement, from which we need not suffer unduly; yet it is doubtful
whether there is art in individual letters. Letters in combination may be satisfying and in a well composed page even
beautiful as a whole, but art in letters consists rather in the art of arranging and composing them in a pleasing and ap
propriate manner. The main purpose of letters is the practical one of making thoughts visible. Ruskin says that all le
tters are frightful things and to be endured only on occasion, that is to say, in places where the sense of the inscripti
on is of more importance than external ornament. This is a sweeping statement, from which we need not suffer undu
The main purpose of letters is the practical one of making thoughts visible. Ruskin says that all letters are frightful things and to b
e endured only on occasion, that is to say, in places where the sense of the inscription is of more importance than external orname
The main purpose of letters is the practical one of making thoughts visible. Ruskin says that all letters are
frightful things and to be endured only on occasion, that is to say, in places where the sense of the inscript

---

ABCDEFGHIJKLMNOPQRSTUVWXYZ 1234567890 abcdefghijklmnopqrstuvwxyz

ABCDEFGHIJKLMNOPQRSTUVWXYZ 1234567890 abcdefghijklmnopqrstuvwxyz

ABCDEFGHIJKLMNOPQRSTUVWXYZ 1234567890 abcdefghijklmnopqrstuvwxyz

7/7

The main purpose of letters is the practical one of making thoughts visible. Ruskin says that all lett
ers are frightful things and to be endured only on occasion, that is to say, in places where the sense
of the inscription is of more importance than external ornament. This is a sweeping statement, fro
m which we need not suffer unduly; yet it is doubtful whether there is art in individual letters. Lette
rs in combination may be satisfying and in a well composed page even beautiful as a whole, but art i
n letters consists rather in the art of arranging and composing them in a pleasing and appropriate m
anner. The main purpose of letters is the practical one of making thoughts visible. Ruskin says that
all letters are frightful things and to be endured only on occasion, that is to say, in places where the
sense of the inscription is of more importance than external ornament. This is a sweeping statemen
t, from which we need not suffer unduly; yet it is doubtful whether there is art in individual letters.
Letters in combination may be satisfying and in a well composed page even beautiful as a whole, but
The main purpose of letters is the practical one of making thoughts visible. Ruskin says that all letters are frigh
tful things and to be endured only on occasion, that is to say, in places where the sense of the inscription is of mo
The main purpose of letters is the practical one of making thoughts visible. Ruskin says th
at all letters are frightful things and to be endured only on occasion, that is to say, in place

7/8

The main purpose of letters is the practical one of making thoughts visible. Ruskin says that all lett
ers are frightful things and to be endured only on occasion, that is to say, in places where the sense
of the inscription is of more importance than external ornament. This is a sweeping statement, fro
m which we need not suffer unduly; yet it is doubtful whether there is art in individual letters. Lette
rs in combination may be satisfying and in a well composed page even beautiful as a whole, but art i
n letters consists rather in the art of arranging and composing them in a pleasing and appropriate m
anner. The main purpose of letters is the practical one of making thoughts visible. Ruskin says that
all letters are frightful things and to be endured only on occasion, that is to say, in places where the
sense of the inscription is of more importance than external ornament. This is a sweeping statemen
t, from which we need not suffer unduly; yet it is doubtful whether there is art in individual letters.
The main purpose of letters is the practical one of making thoughts visible. Ruskin says that all letters are frigh
tful things and to be endured only on occasion, that is to say, in places where the sense of the inscription is of mo
The main purpose of letters is the practical one of making thoughts visible. Ruskin says th
at all letters are frightful things and to be endured only on occasion, that is to say, in place

7/9

The main purpose of letters is the practical one of making thoughts visible. Ruskin says that all lett
ers are frightful things and to be endured only on occasion, that is to say, in places where the sense
of the inscription is of more importance than external ornament. This is a sweeping statement, fro
m which we need not suffer unduly; yet it is doubtful whether there is art in individual letters. Lette
rs in combination may be satisfying and in a well composed page even beautiful as a whole, but art i
n letters consists rather in the art of arranging and composing them in a pleasing and appropriate m
anner. The main purpose of letters is the practical one of making thoughts visible. Ruskin says that
all letters are frightful things and to be endured only on occasion, that is to say, in places where the
sense of the inscription is of more importance than external ornament. This is a sweeping statemen
t, from which we need not suffer unduly; yet it is doubtful whether there is art in individual letters.
The main purpose of letters is the practical one of making thoughts visible. Ruskin says that all letters are frigh
tful things and to be endured only on occasion, that is to say, in places where the sense of the inscription is of mo
The main purpose of letters is the practical one of making thoughts visible. Ruskin says th
at all letters are frightful things and to be endured only on occasion, that is to say, in place

7/10

The main purpose of letters is the practical one of making thoughts visible. Ruskin says that all lett
ers are frightful things and to be endured only on occasion, that is to say, in places where the sense
of the inscription is of more importance than external ornament. This is a sweeping statement, fro
m which we need not suffer unduly; yet it is doubtful whether there is art in individual letters. Lette
rs in combination may be satisfying and in a well composed page even beautiful as a whole, but art i
n letters consists rather in the art of arranging and composing them in a pleasing and appropriate m
anner. The main purpose of letters is the practical one of making thoughts visible. Ruskin says that
all letters are frightful things and to be endured only on occasion, that is to say, in places where the
sense of the inscription is of more importance than external ornament. This is a sweeping statemen
The main purpose of letters is the practical one of making thoughts visible. Ruskin says that all letters are frigh
tful things and to be endured only on occasion, that is to say, in places where the sense of the inscription is of mo
The main purpose of letters is the practical one of making thoughts visible. Ruskin says th
at all letters are frightful things and to be endured only on occasion, that is to say, in place

CLOISTER 8 & 9 POINT SET NORMAL

ROMAN, ITALIC, BOLD

ABCDEFGHIJKLMNOPQRSTUVWXYZ 1234567890 abcdefghijklmnopqrstuvwxyz

ABCDEFGHIJKLMNOPQRSTUVWXYZ 1234567890 abcdefghijklmnopqrstuvwxyz

ABCDEFGHIJKLMNOPQRSTUVWXYZ 1234567890 abcdefghijklmnopqrstuvwxyz

8/8

The main purpose of letters is the practical one of making thoughts visible. Ruskin say s that all letters are frightful things and to be endured only on occasion, that is to say, i n places where the sense of the inscription is of more importance than external ornament. This is a sweeping statement, from which we need not suffer unduly; yet it is doubtf ul whether there is art in individual letters. Letters in combination may be satisfying an d in a well composed page even beautiful as a whole, but art in letters consists rather in the art of arranging and composing them in a pleasing and appropriate manner. The m ain purpose of letters is the practical one of making thoughts visible. Ruskin says that a ll letters are frightful things and to be endured only on occasion, that is to say, in places
The main purpose of letters is the practical one of making thoughts visible. Ruskin says that all le tters are frightful things and to be endured only on occasion, that is to say, in places where the sen
The main purpose of letters is the practical one of making thoughts visible. Ru skin says that all letters are frightful things and to be endured only on occasion

8/9

The main purpose of letters is the practical one of making thoughts visible. Ruskin say s that all letters are frightful things and to be endured only on occasion, that is to say, i n places where the sense of the inscription is of more importance than external ornament. This is a sweeping statement, from which we need not suffer unduly; yet it is doubtf ul whether there is art in individual letters. Letters in combination may be satisfying an d in a well composed page even beautiful as a whole, but art in letters consists rather in the art of arranging and composing them in a pleasing and appropriate manner. The m ain purpose of letters is the practical one of making thoughts visible. Ruskin says that a
The main purpose of letters is the practical one of making thoughts visible. Ruskin says that all le tters are frightful things and to be endured only on occasion, that is to say, in places where the sen
The main purpose of letters is the practical one of making thoughts visible. Ru skin says that all letters are frightful things and to be endured only on occasion

8/10

The main purpose of letters is the practical one of making thoughts visible. Ruskin say s that all letters are frightful things and to be endured only on occasion, that is to say, i n places where the sense of the inscription is of more importance than external ornament. This is a sweeping statement, from which we need not suffer unduly; yet it is doubtf ul whether there is art in individual letters. Letters in combination may be satisfying an d in a well composed page even beautiful as a whole, but art in letters consists rather in the art of arranging and composing them in a pleasing and appropriate manner. The m
The main purpose of letters is the practical one of making thoughts visible. Ruskin says that all le tters are frightful things and to be endured only on occasion, that is to say, in places where the sen
The main purpose of letters is the practical one of making thoughts visible. Ru skin says that all letters are frightful things and to be endured only on occasion

8/11

The main purpose of letters is the practical one of making thoughts visible. Ruskin say s that all letters are frightful things and to be endured only on occasion, that is to say, i n places where the sense of the inscription is of more importance than external ornament. This is a sweeping statement, from which we need not suffer unduly; yet it is doubtf ul whether there is art in individual letters. Letters in combination may be satisfying an d in a well composed page even beautiful as a whole, but art in letters consists rather in the art of arranging and composing them in a pleasing and appropriate manner. The m
The main purpose of letters is the practical one of making thoughts visible. Ruskin says that all le tters are frightful things and to be endured only on occasion, that is to say, in places where the sen
The main purpose of letters is the practical one of making thoughts visible. Ru skin says that all letters are frightful things and to be endured only on occasion

---

ABCDEFGHIJKLMNOPQRSTUVWXYZ 1234567890 abcdefghijklmnopqrstuvwxyz

ABCDEFGHIJKLMNOPQRSTUVWXYZ 1234567890 abcdefghijklmnopqrstuvwxyz

ABCDEFGHIJKLMNOPQRSTUVWXYZ 1234567890 abcdefghijklmnopqrstuvwxyz

9/9

The main purpose of letters is the practical one of making thoughts visible. R uskin says that all letters are frightful things and to be endured only on occasi on, that is to say, in places where the sense of the inscription is of more impor tance than external ornament. This is a sweeping statement, from which we n eed not suffer unduly; yet it is doubtful whether there is art in individual lette rs. Letters in combination may be satisfying and in a well composed page eve n beautiful as a whole, but art in letters consists rather in the art of arranging and composing them in a pleasing and appropriate manner. The main purpos
The main purpose of letters is the practical one of making thoughts visible. Ruskin say s that all letters are frightful things and to be endured only on occasion, that is to say, i
The main purpose of letters is the practical one of making thoughts vis ible. Ruskin says that all letters are frightful things and to be endured

9/10

The main purpose of letters is the practical one of making thoughts visible. R uskin says that all letters are frightful things and to be endured only on occasi on, that is to say, in places where the sense of the inscription is of more impor tance than external ornament. This is a sweeping statement, from which we n eed not suffer unduly; yet it is doubtful whether there is art in individual lette rs. Letters in combination may be satisfying and in a well composed page eve n beautiful as a whole, but art in letters consists rather in the art of arranging
The main purpose of letters is the practical one of making thoughts visible. Ruskin say s that all letters are frightful things and to be endured only on occasion, that is to say, i
The main purpose of letters is the practical one of making thoughts vis ible. Ruskin says that all letters are frightful things and to be endured

9/11

The main purpose of letters is the practical one of making thoughts visible. R uskin says that all letters are frightful things and to be endured only on occasi on, that is to say, in places where the sense of the inscription is of more impor tance than external ornament. This is a sweeping statement, from which we n eed not suffer unduly; yet it is doubtful whether there is art in individual lette rs. Letters in combination may be satisfying and in a well composed page eve n beautiful as a whole, but art in letters consists rather in the art of arranging
The main purpose of letters is the practical one of making thoughts visible. Ruskin say s that all letters are frightful things and to be endured only on occasion, that is to say, i
The main purpose of letters is the practical one of making thoughts vis ible. Ruskin says that all letters are frightful things and to be endured

9/12

The main purpose of letters is the practical one of making thoughts visible. R uskin says that all letters are frightful things and to be endured only on occasi on, that is to say, in places where the sense of the inscription is of more impor tance than external ornament. This is a sweeping statement, from which we n eed not suffer unduly; yet it is doubtful whether there is art in individual lette rs. Letters in combination may be satisfying and in a well composed page eve n beautiful as a whole, but art in letters consists rather in the art of arranging
The main purpose of letters is the practical one of making thoughts visible. Ruskin say s that all letters are frightful things and to be endured only on occasion, that is to say, i
The main purpose of letters is the practical one of making thoughts vis ible. Ruskin says that all letters are frightful things and to be endured

CLOISTER 10 POINT SET MINUS ½ UNIT

ROMAN, ITALIC, BOLD

abcdefghijklmnopqrstuvwxyz — 1 UNIT
abcdefghijklmnopqrstuvwxyz — ½ UNIT
abcdefghijklmnopqrstuvwxyz NORMAL

ABCDEFGHIJKLMNOPQRSTUVWXYZ 1234567890 abcdefghijklmnopqrstuvwxyz
ABCDEFGHIJKLMNOPQRSTUVWXYZ 1234567890 abcdefghijklmnopqrstuvwxyz
ABCDEFGHIJKLMNOPQRSTUVWXYZ 1234567890 abcdefghijklmnopqrstuvwxyz

10/10

The main purpose of letters is the practical one of making thoughts visibl
e. Ruskin says that all letters are frightful things and to be endured only o
n occasion, that is to say, in places where the sense of the inscription is of
more importance than external ornament. This is a sweeping statement,
from which we need not suffer unduly; yet it is doubtful whether there is
art in individual letters. Letters in combination may be satisfying and in
a well composed page even beautiful as a whole, but art in letters consists
rather in the art of arranging and composing them in a pleasing and appro
priate manner. The main purpose of letters is the practical one of making
thoughts visible. Ruskin says that all letters are frightful things and to be
endured only on occasion, that is to say, in places where the sense of the i
nscription is of more importance than external ornament. This is a sweep
ing statement, from which we need not suffer unduly; yet it is doubtful w
hether there is art in individual letters. Letters in combination may be sati
sfying and in a well composed page even beautiful as a whole, but art in le
tters consists rather in the art of arranging and composing them in a pleas
ing and appropriate manner. The main purpose of letters is the practical
one of making thoughts visible. Ruskin says that all letters are frightful th
ings and to be endured only on occasion, that is to say, in places where th
e sense of the inscription is of more importance than external ornament.
This is a sweeping statement, from which we need not suffer unduly; yet i
t is doubtful whether there is art in individual letters. Letters in combinati
The main purpose of letters is the practical one of making thoughts visible. Ruskin
says that all letters are frightful things and to be endured only on occasion, that is t
The main purpose of letters is the practical one of making though
ts visible. Ruskin says that all letters are frightful things and to be

10/11

The main purpose of letters is the practical one of making thoughts visibl
e. Ruskin says that all letters are frightful things and to be endured only o
n occasion, that is to say, in places where the sense of the inscription is of
more importance than external ornament. This is a sweeping statement,
from which we need not suffer unduly; yet it is doubtful whether there is
art in individual letters. Letters in combination may be satisfying and in
a well composed page even beautiful as a whole, but art in letters consists
rather in the art of arranging and composing them in a pleasing and appro
priate manner. The main purpose of letters is the practical one of making
thoughts visible. Ruskin says that all letters are frightful things and to be
endured only on occasion, that is to say, in places where the sense of the i
nscription is of more importance than external ornament. This is a sweep
ing statement, from which we need not suffer unduly; yet it is doubtful w
hether there is art in individual letters. Letters in combination may be sati
sfying and in a well composed page even beautiful as a whole, but art in le
tters consists rather in the art of arranging and composing them in a pleas
ing and appropriate manner. The main purpose of letters is the practical
one of making thoughts visible. Ruskin says that all letters are frightful th
ings and to be endured only on occasion, that is to say, in places where th
e sense of the inscription is of more importance than external ornament.
The main purpose of letters is the practical one of making thoughts visible. Ruskin
says that all letters are frightful things and to be endured only on occasion, that is t
The main purpose of letters is the practical one of making though
ts visible. Ruskin says that all letters are frightful things and to be

10/12

The main purpose of letters is the practical one of making thoughts visibl
e. Ruskin says that all letters are frightful things and to be endured only o
n occasion, that is to say, in places where the sense of the inscription is of
more importance than external ornament. This is a sweeping statement,
from which we need not suffer unduly; yet it is doubtful whether there is
art in individual letters. Letters in combination may be satisfying and in
a well composed page even beautiful as a whole, but art in letters consists
rather in the art of arranging and composing them in a pleasing and appro
priate manner. The main purpose of letters is the practical one of making
thoughts visible. Ruskin says that all letters are frightful things and to be
endured only on occasion, that is to say, in places where the sense of the i
nscription is of more importance than external ornament. This is a sweep
ing statement, from which we need not suffer unduly; yet it is doubtful w
hether there is art in individual letters. Letters in combination may be sati
sfying and in a well composed page even beautiful as a whole, but art in le
tters consists rather in the art of arranging and composing them in a pleas
ing and appropriate manner. The main purpose of letters is the practical
one of making thoughts visible. Ruskin says that all letters are frightful th
The main purpose of letters is the practical one of making thoughts visible. Ruskin
says that all letters are frightful things and to be endured only on occasion, that is t
The main purpose of letters is the practical one of making though
ts visible. Ruskin says that all letters are frightful things and to be

10/13

The main purpose of letters is the practical one of making thoughts visibl
e. Ruskin says that all letters are frightful things and to be endured only o
n occasion, that is to say, in places where the sense of the inscription is of
more importance than external ornament. This is a sweeping statement,
from which we need not suffer unduly; yet it is doubtful whether there is
art in individual letters. Letters in combination may be satisfying and in
a well composed page even beautiful as a whole, but art in letters consists
rather in the art of arranging and composing them in a pleasing and appro
priate manner. The main purpose of letters is the practical one of making
thoughts visible. Ruskin says that all letters are frightful things and to be
endured only on occasion, that is to say, in places where the sense of the i
nscription is of more importance than external ornament. This is a sweep
ing statement, from which we need not suffer unduly; yet it is doubtful w
hether there is art in individual letters. Letters in combination may be sati
sfying and in a well composed page even beautiful as a whole, but art in le
tters consists rather in the art of arranging and composing them in a pleas
ing and appropriate manner. The main purpose of letters is the practical
The main purpose of letters is the practical one of making thoughts visible. Ruskin
says that all letters are frightful things and to be endured only on occasion, that is t
The main purpose of letters is the practical one of making though
ts visible. Ruskin says that all letters are frightful things and to be

CLOISTER 11 POINT SET MINUS ½ UNIT

ROMAN, ITALIC, BOLD

abcdefghijklmnopqrstuvwxyz – 1 UNIT
abcdefghijklmnopqrstuvwxyz – ½ UNIT
abcdefghijklmnopqrstuvwxyz NORMAL

ABCDEFGHIJKLMNOPQRSTUVWXYZ 1234567890 abcdefghijklmnopqrstuvwxyz
ABCDEFGHIJKLMNOPQRSTUVWXYZ 1234567890 abcdefghijklmnopqrstuvwxyz
ABCDEFGHIJKLMNOPQRSTUVWXYZ 1234567890 abcdefghijklmnopqrstuvwxyz

11/11

The main purpose of letters is the practical one of making thought s visible. Ruskin says that all letters are frightful things and to be e ndured only on occasion, that is to say, in places where the sense o f the inscription is of more importance than external ornament. T his is a sweeping statement, from which we need not suffer unduly; yet it is doubtful whether there is art in individual letters. Letters in combination may be satisfying and in a well composed page eve n beautiful as a whole, but art in letters consists rather in the art of arranging and composing them in a pleasing and appropriate man ner. The main purpose of letters is the practical one of making tho ughts visible. Ruskin says that all letters are frightful things and to be endured only on occasion, that is to say, in places where the sen se of the inscription is of more importance than external ornament. This is a sweeping statement, from which we need not suffer und uly; yet it is doubtful whether there is art in individual letters. Lett ers in combination may be satisfying and in a well composed page even beautiful as a whole, but art in letters consists rather in the ar t of arranging and composing them in a pleasing and appropriate manner. The main purpose of letters is the practical one of makin
The main purpose of letters is the practical one of making thoughts visible. Ruskin says that all letters are frightful things and to be endured only on oc
The main purpose of letters is the practical one of making t houghts visible. Ruskin says that all letters are frightful thin

11/12

The main purpose of letters is the practical one of making thought s visible. Ruskin says that all letters are frightful things and to be e ndured only on occasion, that is to say, in places where the sense o f the inscription is of more importance than external ornament. T his is a sweeping statement, from which we need not suffer unduly; yet it is doubtful whether there is art in individual letters. Letters in combination may be satisfying and in a well composed page eve n beautiful as a whole, but art in letters consists rather in the art of arranging and composing them in a pleasing and appropriate man ner. The main purpose of letters is the practical one of making tho ughts visible. Ruskin says that all letters are frightful things and to be endured only on occasion, that is to say, in places where the sen se of the inscription is of more importance than external ornament. This is a sweeping statement, from which we need not suffer und uly; yet it is doubtful whether there is art in individual letters. Lett ers in combination may be satisfying and in a well composed page even beautiful as a whole, but art in letters consists rather in the ar t of arranging and composing them in a pleasing and appropriate
The main purpose of letters is the practical one of making thoughts visible. Ruskin says that all letters are frightful things and to be endured only on oc
The main purpose of letters is the practical one of making t houghts visible. Ruskin says that all letters are frightful thin

11/13

The main purpose of letters is the practical one of making thought s visible. Ruskin says that all letters are frightful things and to be e ndured only on occasion, that is to say, in places where the sense o f the inscription is of more importance than external ornament. T his is a sweeping statement, from which we need not suffer unduly; yet it is doubtful whether there is art in individual letters. Letters in combination may be satisfying and in a well composed page eve n beautiful as a whole, but art in letters consists rather in the art of arranging and composing them in a pleasing and appropriate man ner. The main purpose of letters is the practical one of making tho ughts visible. Ruskin says that all letters are frightful things and to be endured only on occasion, that is to say, in places where the sen se of the inscription is of more importance than external ornament. This is a sweeping statement, from which we need not suffer und uly; yet it is doubtful whether there is art in individual letters. Lett ers in combination may be satisfying and in a well composed page even beautiful as a whole, but art in letters consists rather in the ar
The main purpose of letters is the practical one of making thoughts visible. Ruskin says that all letters are frightful things and to be endured only on oc
The main purpose of letters is the practical one of making t houghts visible. Ruskin says that all letters are frightful thin

11/14

The main purpose of letters is the practical one of making thought s visible. Ruskin says that all letters are frightful things and to be e ndured only on occasion, that is to say, in places where the sense o f the inscription is of more importance than external ornament. T his is a sweeping statement, from which we need not suffer unduly; yet it is doubtful whether there is art in individual letters. Letters in combination may be satisfying and in a well composed page eve n beautiful as a whole, but art in letters consists rather in the art of arranging and composing them in a pleasing and appropriate man ner. The main purpose of letters is the practical one of making tho ughts visible. Ruskin says that all letters are frightful things and to be endured only on occasion, that is to say, in places where the sen se of the inscription is of more importance than external ornament. This is a sweeping statement, from which we need not suffer und uly; yet it is doubtful whether there is art in individual letters. Lett ers in combination may be satisfying and in a well composed page
The main purpose of letters is the practical one of making thoughts visible. Ruskin says that all letters are frightful things and to be endured only on oc
The main purpose of letters is the practical one of making t houghts visible. Ruskin says that all letters are frightful thin

CLOISTER 12 POINT SET MINUS ½ UNIT

ROMAN, ITALIC, BOLD

abcdefghijklmnopqrstuvwxyz — 1 UNIT
abcdefghijklmnopqrstuvwxyz — ½ UNIT
abcdefghijklmnopqrstuvwxyz NORMAL

ABCDEFGHIJKLMNOPQRSTUVWXYZ 1234567890 abcdefghijklmnopqrstuvwxyz
ABCDEFGHIJKLMNOPQRSTUVWXYZ 1234567890 abcdefghijklmnopqrstuvwxyz
ABCDEFGHIJKLMNOPQRSTUVWXYZ 1234567890 abcdefghijklmnopqrstuvwxyz

12/12

The main purpose of letters is the practical one of making tho ughts visible. Ruskin says that all letters are frightful things an d to be endured only on occasion, that is to say, in places wher e the sense of the inscription is of more importance than exter nal ornament. This is a sweeping statement, from which we ne ed not suffer unduly; yet it is doubtful whether there is art in i ndividual letters. Letters in combination may be satisfying and in a well composed page even beautiful as a whole, but art in le tters consists rather in the art of arranging and composing the m in a pleasing and appropriate manner. The main purpose of letters is the practical one of making thoughts visible. Ruskin s ays that all letters are frightful things and to be endured only on occasion, that is to say, in places where the sense of the ins cription is of more importance than external ornament. This i s a sweeping statement, from which we need not suffer unduly
The main purpose of letters is the practical one of making thoughts vi sible. Ruskin says that all letters are frightful things and to be endured
The main purpose of letters is the practical one of maki ng thoughts visible. Ruskin says that all letters are fright

12/13

The main purpose of letters is the practical one of making tho ughts visible. Ruskin says that all letters are frightful things an d to be endured only on occasion, that is to say, in places wher e the sense of the inscription is of more importance than exter nal ornament. This is a sweeping statement, from which we ne ed not suffer unduly; yet it is doubtful whether there is art in i ndividual letters. Letters in combination may be satisfying and in a well composed page even beautiful as a whole, but art in le tters consists rather in the art of arranging and composing the m in a pleasing and appropriate manner. The main purpose of letters is the practical one of making thoughts visible. Ruskin s ays that all letters are frightful things and to be endured only on occasion, that is to say, in places where the sense of the ins cription is of more importance than external ornament. This i
The main purpose of letters is the practical one of making thoughts vi sible. Ruskin says that all letters are frightful things and to be endured
The main purpose of letters is the practical one of maki ng thoughts visible. Ruskin says that all letters are fright

12/14

The main purpose of letters is the practical one of making tho ughts visible. Ruskin says that all letters are frightful things an d to be endured only on occasion, that is to say, in places wher e the sense of the inscription is of more importance than exter nal ornament. This is a sweeping statement, from which we ne ed not suffer unduly; yet it is doubtful whether there is art in i ndividual letters. Letters in combination may be satisfying and in a well composed page even beautiful as a whole, but art in le tters consists rather in the art of arranging and composing the m in a pleasing and appropriate manner. The main purpose of letters is the practical one of making thoughts visible. Ruskin s ays that all letters are frightful things and to be endured only on occasion, that is to say, in places where the sense of the ins cription is of more importance than external ornament. This i s a sweeping statement, from which we need not suffer unduly
The main purpose of letters is the practical one of making thoughts vi sible. Ruskin says that all letters are frightful things and to be endured
The main purpose of letters is the practical one of maki ng thoughts visible. Ruskin says that all letters are fright

12/15

The main purpose of letters is the practical one of making tho ughts visible. Ruskin says that all letters are frightful things an d to be endured only on occasion, that is to say, in places wher e the sense of the inscription is of more importance than exter nal ornament. This is a sweeping statement, from which we ne ed not suffer unduly; yet it is doubtful whether there is art in i ndividual letters. Letters in combination may be satisfying and in a well composed page even beautiful as a whole, but art in le tters consists rather in the art of arranging and composing the m in a pleasing and appropriate manner. The main purpose of letters is the practical one of making thoughts visible. Ruskin s ays that all letters are frightful things and to be endured only on occasion, that is to say, in places where the sense of the ins cription is of more importance than external ornament. This i
The main purpose of letters is the practical one of making thoughts vi sible. Ruskin says that all letters are frightful things and to be endured
The main purpose of letters is the practical one of maki ng thoughts visible. Ruskin says that all letters are fright

CLOISTER 14 POINT SET MINUS ½ UNIT

ROMAN, ITALIC, BOLD

abcdefghijklmnopqrstuvwxyz – 1 UNIT
abcdefghijklmnopqrstuvwxyz – ½ UNIT
abcdefghijklmnopqrstuvwxyz NORMAL

ABCDEFGHIJKLMNOPQRSTUVWXYZ abcdefghijklmnopqrstuvwxyz
ABCDEFGHIJKLMNOPQRSTUVWXYZ abcdefghijklmnopqrstuvwxyz
ABCDEFGHIJKLMNOPQRSTUVWXYZ abcdefghijklmnopqrstuvwxyz

14/14

The main purpose of letters is the practical one of m aking thoughts visible. Ruskin says that all letters ar e frightful things and to be endured only on occasion, that is to say, in places where the sense of the inscri ption is of more importance than external ornament. This is a sweeping statement, from which we need n ot suffer unduly; yet it is doubtful whether there is a rt in individual letters. Letters in combination may b e satisfying and in a well composed page even beauti ful as a whole, but art in letters consists rather in the art of arranging and composing them in a pleasing a nd appropriate manner. The main purpose of letters is the practical one of making thoughts visible. Ruski
The main purpose of letters is the practical one of making t houghts visible. Ruskin says that all letters are frightful thin
The main purpose of letters is the practical one of making thoughts visible. Ruskin says that all

14/15

The main purpose of letters is the practical one of m aking thoughts visible. Ruskin says that all letters ar e frightful things and to be endured only on occasion, that is to say, in places where the sense of the inscri ption is of more importance than external ornament. This is a sweeping statement, from which we need n ot suffer unduly; yet it is doubtful whether there is a rt in individual letters. Letters in combination may b e satisfying and in a well composed page even beauti ful as a whole, but art in letters consists rather in the art of arranging and composing them in a pleasing a nd appropriate manner. The main purpose of letters
The main purpose of letters is the practical one of making t houghts visible. Ruskin says that all letters are frightful thin
The main purpose of letters is the practical one of making thoughts visible. Ruskin says that all

14/16

The main purpose of letters is the practical one of m aking thoughts visible. Ruskin says that all letters ar e frightful things and to be endured only on occasion, that is to say, in places where the sense of the inscri ption is of more importance than external ornament. This is a sweeping statement, from which we need n ot suffer unduly; yet it is doubtful whether there is a rt in individual letters. Letters in combination may b e satisfying and in a well composed page even beauti ful as a whole, but art in letters consists rather in the art of arranging and composing them in a pleasing a nd appropriate manner. The main purpose of letters is the practical one of making thoughts visible. Ruski
The main purpose of letters is the practical one of making t houghts visible. Ruskin says that all letters are frightful thin
The main purpose of letters is the practical one of making thoughts visible. Ruskin says that all

14/17

The main purpose of letters is the practical one of m aking thoughts visible. Ruskin says that all letters ar e frightful things and to be endured only on occasion, that is to say, in places where the sense of the inscri ption is of more importance than external ornament. This is a sweeping statement, from which we need n ot suffer unduly; yet it is doubtful whether there is a rt in individual letters. Letters in combination may b e satisfying and in a well composed page even beauti ful as a whole, but art in letters consists rather in the art of arranging and composing them in a pleasing a nd appropriate manner. The main purpose of letters
The main purpose of letters is the practical one of making t houghts visible. Ruskin says that all letters are frightful thin
The main purpose of letters is the practical one of making thoughts visible. Ruskin says that all

ITC ERAS 6 & 7 POINT SET NORMAL

LIGHT, BOOK, DEMI, BOLD

ABCDEFGHIJKLMNOPQRSTUVWXYZ 1234567890 abcdefghijklmnopqrstuvwxyz

ABCDEFGHIJKLMNOPQRSTUVWXYZ 1234567890 abcdefghijklmnopqrstuvwxyz

ABCDEFGHIJKLMNOPQRSTUVWXYZ 1234567890 abcdefghijklmnopqrstuvwxyz

ABCDEFGHIJKLMNOPQRSTUVWXYZ 1234567890 abcdefghijklmnopqrstuvwxyz

6/6

The main purpose of letters is the practical one of making thoughts visible. Ruskin says that all letters a
re frightful things and to be endured only on occasion, that is to say, in places where the sense of the i
nscription is of more importance than external ornament. This is a sweeping statement, from which
we need not suffer unduly; yet it is doubtful whether there is art in individual letters. Letters in combi
nation may be satisfying and in a well composed page even beautiful as a whole, but art in letters co
nsists rather in the art of arranging and composing them in a pleasing and appropriate manner. The
main purpose of letters is the practical one of making thoughts visible. Ruskin says that all letters are fri
ghtful things and to be endured only on occasion, that is to say, in places where the sense of the inscr
iption is of more importance than external ornament. This is a sweeping statement, from which we
need not suffer unduly; yet it is doubtful whether there is art in individual letters. Letters in combinati
on may be satisfying and in a well composed page even beautiful as a whole, but art in letters consis
ts rather in the art of arranging and composing them in a pleasing and appropriate manner. The mai
n purpose of letters is the practical one of making thoughts visible. Ruskin says that all letters are fright
The main purpose of letters is the practical one of making thoughts visible. Ruskin says that all letters
are frightful things and to be endured only on occasion, that is to say, in places where the sense of th
The main purpose of letters is the practical one of making thoughts visible. Ruskin says th
at all letters are frightful things and to be endured only on occasion, that is to say, in plac

6/7

The main purpose of letters is the practical one of making thoughts visible. Ruskin says that all letters a
re frightful things and to be endured only on occasion, that is to say, in places where the sense of the i
nscription is of more importance than external ornament. This is a sweeping statement, from which
we need not suffer unduly; yet it is doubtful whether there is art in individual letters. Letters in combi
nation may be satisfying and in a well composed page even beautiful as a whole, but art in letters co
nsists rather in the art of arranging and composing them in a pleasing and appropriate manner. The
main purpose of letters is the practical one of making thoughts visible. Ruskin says that all letters are fri
ghtful things and to be endured only on occasion, that is to say, in places where the sense of the inscr
iption is of more importance than external ornament. This is a sweeping statement, from which we
need not suffer unduly; yet it is doubtful whether there is art in individual letters. Letters in combinati
on may be satisfying and in a well composed page even beautiful as a whole, but art in letters consis
The main purpose of letters is the practical one of making thoughts visible. Ruskin says that all letters
are frightful things and to be endured only on occasion, that is to say, in places where the sense of th
The main purpose of letters is the practical one of making thoughts visible. Ruskin says th
at all letters are frightful things and to be endured only on occasion, that is to say, in plac

6/8

The main purpose of letters is the practical one of making thoughts visible. Ruskin says that all letters a
re frightful things and to be endured only on occasion, that is to say, in places where the sense of the i
nscription is of more importance than external ornament. This is a sweeping statement, from which
we need not suffer unduly; yet it is doubtful whether there is art in individual letters. Letters in combi
nation may be satisfying and in a well composed page even beautiful as a whole, but art in letters co
nsists rather in the art of arranging and composing them in a pleasing and appropriate manner. The
main purpose of letters is the practical one of making thoughts visible. Ruskin says that all letters are fri
ghtful things and to be endured only on occasion, that is to say, in places where the sense of the inscr
iption is of more importance than external ornament. This is a sweeping statement, from which we
The main purpose of letters is the practical one of making thoughts visible. Ruskin says that all letters
are frightful things and to be endured only on occasion, that is to say, in places where the sense of th
The main purpose of letters is the practical one of making thoughts visible. Ruskin says th
at all letters are frightful things and to be endured only on occasion, that is to say, in plac

6/9

The main purpose of letters is the practical one of making thoughts visible. Ruskin says that all letters a
re frightful things and to be endured only on occasion, that is to say, in places where the sense of the i
nscription is of more importance than external ornament. This is a sweeping statement, from which
we need not suffer unduly; yet it is doubtful whether there is art in individual letters. Letters in combi
nation may be satisfying and in a well composed page even beautiful as a whole, but art in letters co
nsists rather in the art of arranging and composing them in a pleasing and appropriate manner. The
main purpose of letters is the practical one of making thoughts visible. Ruskin says that all letters are fri
ghtful things and to be endured only on occasion, that is to say, in places where the sense of the inscr
The main purpose of letters is the practical one of making thoughts visible. Ruskin says that all letters
are frightful things and to be endured only on occasion, that is to say, in places where the sense of th
The main purpose of letters is the practical one of making thoughts visible. Ruskin says th
at all letters are frightful things and to be endured only on occasion, that is to say, in plac

---

ABCDEFGHIJKLMNOPQRSTUVWXYZ 1234567890 abcdefghijklmnopqrstuvwxyz

ABCDEFGHIJKLMNOPQRSTUVWXYZ 1234567890 abcdefghijklmnopqrstuvwxyz

ABCDEFGHIJKLMNOPQRSTUVWXYZ 1234567890 abcdefghijklmnopqrstuvwxyz

ABCDEFGHIJKLMNOPQRSTUVWXYZ 1234567890 abcdefghijklmnopqrstuvwxyz

7/7

The main purpose of letters is the practical one of making thoughts visible. Ruskin says
that all letters are frightful things and to be endured only on occasion, that is to say, in
places where the sense of the inscription is of more importance than external orname
nt. This is a sweeping statement, from which we need not suffer unduly; yet it is doubt
ful whether there is art in individual letters. Letters in combination may be satisfying a
nd in a well composed page even beautiful as a whole, but art in letters consists rather
in the art of arranging and composing them in a pleasing and appropriate manner. Th
e main purpose of letters is the practical one of making thoughts visible. Ruskin says th
at all letters are frightful things and to be endured only on occasion, that is to say, in pla
ces where the sense of the inscription is of more importance than external ornament.
This is a sweeping statement, from which we need not suffer unduly; yet it is doubtful
The main purpose of letters is the practical one of making thoughts visible. Ruskin s
ays that all letters are frightful things and to be endured only on occasion, that is to say, i
The main purpose of letters is the practical one of making thoughts visible. R
uskin says that all letters are frightful things and to be endured only on occa

7/8

The main purpose of letters is the practical one of making thoughts visible. Ruskin says
that all letters are frightful things and to be endured only on occasion, that is to say, in
places where the sense of the inscription is of more importance than external orname
nt. This is a sweeping statement, from which we need not suffer unduly; yet it is doubt
ful whether there is art in individual letters. Letters in combination may be satisfying a
nd in a well composed page even beautiful as a whole, but art in letters consists rather
in the art of arranging and composing them in a pleasing and appropriate manner. Th
e main purpose of letters is the practical one of making thoughts visible. Ruskin says th
at all letters are frightful things and to be endured only on occasion, that is to say, in pla
ces where the sense of the inscription is of more importance than external ornament.
The main purpose of letters is the practical one of making thoughts visible. Ruskin s
ays that all letters are frightful things and to be endured only on occasion, that is to say, i
The main purpose of letters is the practical one of making thoughts visible. R
uskin says that all letters are frightful things and to be endured only on occa

7/9

The main purpose of letters is the practical one of making thoughts visible. Ruskin says
that all letters are frightful things and to be endured only on occasion, that is to say, in
places where the sense of the inscription is of more importance than external orname
nt. This is a sweeping statement, from which we need not suffer unduly; yet it is doubt
ful whether there is art in individual letters. Letters in combination may be satisfying a
nd in a well composed page even beautiful as a whole, but art in letters consists rather
in the art of arranging and composing them in a pleasing and appropriate manner. Th
e main purpose of letters is the practical one of making thoughts visible. Ruskin says th
at all letters are frightful things and to be endured only on occasion, that is to say, in pla
ces where the sense of the inscription is of more importance than external ornament.
The main purpose of letters is the practical one of making thoughts visible. Ruskin s
ays that all letters are frightful things and to be endured only on occasion, that is to say, i
The main purpose of letters is the practical one of making thoughts visible. R
uskin says that all letters are frightful things and to be endured only on occa

7/10

The main purpose of letters is the practical one of making thoughts visible. Ruskin says
that all letters are frightful things and to be endured only on occasion, that is to say, in
places where the sense of the inscription is of more importance than external orname
nt. This is a sweeping statement, from which we need not suffer unduly; yet it is doubt
ful whether there is art in individual letters. Letters in combination may be satisfying a
nd in a well composed page even beautiful as a whole, but art in letters consists rather
in the art of arranging and composing them in a pleasing and appropriate manner. Th
e main purpose of letters is the practical one of making thoughts visible. Ruskin says th
at all letters are frightful things and to be endured only on occasion, that is to say, in pla
The main purpose of letters is the practical one of making thoughts visible. Ruskin s
ays that all letters are frightful things and to be endured only on occasion, that is to say, i
The main purpose of letters is the practical one of making thoughts visible. R
uskin says that all letters are frightful things and to be endured only on occa

ITC ERAS 8 & 9 POINT SET NORMAL

LIGHT, BOOK, DEMI, BOLD

ABCDEFGHIJKLMNOPQRSTUVWXYZ 1234567890 abcdefghijklmnopqrstuvwxyz

ABCDEFGHIJKLMNOPQRSTUVWXYZ 1234567890 abcdefghijklmnopqrstuvwxyz

ABCDEFGHIJKLMNOPQRSTUVWXYZ 1234567890 abcdefghijklmnopqrstuvwxyz

ABCDEFGHIJKLMNOPQRSTUVWXYZ 1234567890 abcdefghijklmnopqrstuvwxyz

8/8

The main purpose of letters is the practical one of making thoughts visible. Ruskin says that all letters are frightful things and to be endured only on occ asion, that is to say, in places where the sense of the inscription is of more im portance than external ornament. This is a sweeping statement, from whic h we need not suffer unduly; yet it is doubtful whether there is art in individ ual letters. Letters in combination may be satisfying and in a well compose d page even beautiful as a whole, but art in letters consists rather in the art o f arranging and composing them in a pleasing and appropriate manner. Th e main purpose of letters is the practical one of making thoughts visible. Rus

The main purpose of letters is the practical one of making thoughts visible. Ruskin says that all letters are frightful things and to be endured only on oc

The main purpose of letters is the practical one of making thoughts visible. Ruskin says that all letters are frightful things and to be end

8/9

The main purpose of letters is the practical one of making thoughts visible. Ruskin says that all letters are frightful things and to be endured only on occ asion, that is to say, in places where the sense of the inscription is of more im portance than external ornament. This is a sweeping statement, from whic h we need not suffer unduly; yet it is doubtful whether there is art in individ ual letters. Letters in combination may be satisfying and in a well compose d page even beautiful as a whole, but art in letters consists rather in the art o f arranging and composing them in a pleasing and appropriate manner. Th

The main purpose of letters is the practical one of making thoughts visible. Ruskin says that all letters are frightful things and to be endured only on oc

The main purpose of letters is the practical one of making thoughts visible. Ruskin says that all letters are frightful things and to be end

8/10

The main purpose of letters is the practical one of making thoughts visible. Ruskin says that all letters are frightful things and to be endured only on occ asion, that is to say, in places where the sense of the inscription is of more im portance than external ornament. This is a sweeping statement, from whic h we need not suffer unduly; yet it is doubtful whether there is art in individ ual letters. Letters in combination may be satisfying and in a well compose d page even beautiful as a whole, but art in letters consists rather in the art o

The main purpose of letters is the practical one of making thoughts visible. Ruskin says that all letters are frightful things and to be endured only on oc

The main purpose of letters is the practical one of making thoughts visible. Ruskin says that all letters are frightful things and to be end

8/11

The main purpose of letters is the practical one of making thoughts visible. Ruskin says that all letters are frightful things and to be endured only on occ asion, that is to say, in places where the sense of the inscription is of more im portance than external ornament. This is a sweeping statement, from whic h we need not suffer unduly; yet it is doubtful whether there is art in individ ual letters. Letters in combination may be satisfying and in a well compose d page even beautiful as a whole, but art in letters consists rather in the art o

The main purpose of letters is the practical one of making thoughts visible. Ruskin says that all letters are frightful things and to be endured only on oc

The main purpose of letters is the practical one of making thoughts visible. Ruskin says that all letters are frightful things and to be end

---

ABCDEFGHIJKLMNOPQRSTUVWXYZ 1234567890 abcdefghijklmnopqrstuvwxyz

ABCDEFGHIJKLMNOPQRSTUVWXYZ 1234567890 abcdefghijklmnopqrstuvwxyz

ABCDEFGHIJKLMNOPQRSTUVWXYZ 1234567890 abcdefghijklmnopqrstuvwxyz

ABCDEFGHIJKLMNOPQRSTUVWXYZ 1234567890 abcdefghijklmnopqrstuvwxyz

9/9

The main purpose of letters is the practical one of making thoughts visible. Ruskin says that all letters are frightful things and to be endu red only on occasion, that is to say, in places where the sense of the inscription is of more importance than external ornament. This is a sweeping statement, from which we need not suffer unduly; yet it is doubtful whether there is art in individual letters. Letters in combi nation may be satisfying and in a well composed page even beaut iful as a whole, but art in letters consists rather in the art of arrangin

The main purpose of letters is the practical one of making thought s visible. Ruskin says that all letters are frightful things and to be en

The main purpose of letters is the practical one of making t houghts visible. Ruskin says that all letters are frightful thin

9/10

The main purpose of letters is the practical one of making thoughts visible. Ruskin says that all letters are frightful things and to be endu red only on occasion, that is to say, in places where the sense of the inscription is of more importance than external ornament. This is a sweeping statement, from which we need not suffer unduly; yet it is doubtful whether there is art in individual letters. Letters in combi nation may be satisfying and in a well composed page even beaut

The main purpose of letters is the practical one of making thought s visible. Ruskin says that all letters are frightful things and to be en

The main purpose of letters is the practical one of making t houghts visible. Ruskin says that all letters are frightful thin

9/11

The main purpose of letters is the practical one of making thoughts visible. Ruskin says that all letters are frightful things and to be endu red only on occasion, that is to say, in places where the sense of the inscription is of more importance than external ornament. This is a sweeping statement, from which we need not suffer unduly; yet it is doubtful whether there is art in individual letters. Letters in combi nation may be satisfying and in a well composed page even beaut

The main purpose of letters is the practical one of making thought s visible. Ruskin says that all letters are frightful things and to be en

The main purpose of letters is the practical one of making t houghts visible. Ruskin says that all letters are frightful thin

9/12

The main purpose of letters is the practical one of making thoughts visible. Ruskin says that all letters are frightful things and to be endu red only on occasion, that is to say, in places where the sense of the inscription is of more importance than external ornament. This is a sweeping statement, from which we need not suffer unduly; yet it is doubtful whether there is art in individual letters. Letters in combi nation may be satisfying and in a well composed page even beaut

The main purpose of letters is the practical one of making thought s visible. Ruskin says that all letters are frightful things and to be en

The main purpose of letters is the practical one of making t houghts visible. Ruskin says that all letters are frightful thin

10 POINT SET MINUS ½ UNIT

LIGHT, BOOK, DEMI, BOLD

abcdefghijklmnopqrstuvwxyz – 1 UNIT
abcdefghijklmnopqrstuvwxyz – ½ UNIT
abcdefghijklmnopqrstuvwxyz NORMAL

ABCDEFGHIJKLMNOPQRSTUVWXYZ 1234567890 abcdefghijklmnopqrstuvwxyz
ABCDEFGHIJKLMNOPQRSTUVWXYZ 1234567890 abcdefghijklmnopqrstuvwxyz
ABCDEFGHIJKLMNOPQRSTUVWXYZ 1234567890 abcdefghijklmnopqrstuvwxyz
ABCDEFGHIJKLMNOPQRSTUVWXYZ 1234567890 abcdefghijklmnopqrstuvwxyz

10/10

The main purpose of letters is the practical one of making thou
ghts visible. Ruskin says that all letters are frightful things and to
be endured only on occasion, that is to say, in places where the
sense of the inscription is of more importance than external orn
ament. This is a sweeping statement, from which we need not
suffer unduly; yet it is doubtful whether there is art in individual
letters. Letters in combination may be satisfying and in a well c
omposed page even beautiful as a whole, but art in letters con
sists rather in the art of arranging and composing them in a ple
asing and appropriate manner. The main purpose of letters is th
e practical one of making thoughts visible. Ruskin says that all le
tters are frightful things and to be endured only on occasion, th
at is to say, in places where the sense of the inscription is of mor
e importance than external ornament. This is a sweeping state
ment, from which we need not suffer unduly; yet it is doubtful
whether there is art in individual letters. Letters in combination
may be satisfying and in a well composed page even beautiful
as a whole, but art in letters consists rather in the art of arrangin
g and composing them in a pleasing and appropriate manner.
The main purpose of letters is the practical one of making thou
ghts visible. Ruskin says that all letters are frightful things and to
be endured only on occasion, that is to say, in places where the
The main purpose of letters is the practical one of making thou
ghts visible. Ruskin says that all letters are frightful things and to
**The main purpose of letters is the practical one of makin
g thoughts visible. Ruskin says that all letters are frightf**

10/11

The main purpose of letters is the practical one of making thou
ghts visible. Ruskin says that all letters are frightful things and to
be endured only on occasion, that is to say, in places where the
sense of the inscription is of more importance than external orn
ament. This is a sweeping statement, from which we need not
suffer unduly; yet it is doubtful whether there is art in individual
letters. Letters in combination may be satisfying and in a well c
omposed page even beautiful as a whole, but art in letters con
sists rather in the art of arranging and composing them in a ple
asing and appropriate manner. The main purpose of letters is th
e practical one of making thoughts visible. Ruskin says that all le
tters are frightful things and to be endured only on occasion, th
at is to say, in places where the sense of the inscription is of mor
e importance than external ornament. This is a sweeping state
ment, from which we need not suffer unduly; yet it is doubtful
whether there is art in individual letters. Letters in combination
may be satisfying and in a well composed page even beautiful
as a whole, but art in letters consists rather in the art of arrangin
g and composing them in a pleasing and appropriate manner.
The main purpose of letters is the practical one of making thou
The main purpose of letters is the practical one of making thou
ghts visible. Ruskin says that all letters are frightful things and to
**The main purpose of letters is the practical one of makin
g thoughts visible. Ruskin says that all letters are frightf**

10/12

The main purpose of letters is the practical one of making thou
ghts visible. Ruskin says that all letters are frightful things and to
be endured only on occasion, that is to say, in places where the
sense of the inscription is of more importance than external orn
ament. This is a sweeping statement, from which we need not
suffer unduly; yet it is doubtful whether there is art in individual
letters. Letters in combination may be satisfying and in a well c
omposed page even beautiful as a whole, but art in letters con
sists rather in the art of arranging and composing them in a ple
asing and appropriate manner. The main purpose of letters is th
e practical one of making thoughts visible. Ruskin says that all le
tters are frightful things and to be endured only on occasion, th
at is to say, in places where the sense of the inscription is of mor
e importance than external ornament. This is a sweeping state
ment, from which we need not suffer unduly; yet it is doubtful
whether there is art in individual letters. Letters in combination
may be satisfying and in a well composed page even beautiful
as a whole, but art in letters consists rather in the art of arrangin
The main purpose of letters is the practical one of making thou
ghts visible. Ruskin says that all letters are frightful things and to
**The main purpose of letters is the practical one of makin
g thoughts visible. Ruskin says that all letters are frightf**

10/13

The main purpose of letters is the practical one of making thou
ghts visible. Ruskin says that all letters are frightful things and to
be endured only on occasion, that is to say, in places where the
sense of the inscription is of more importance than external orn
ament. This is a sweeping statement, from which we need not
suffer unduly; yet it is doubtful whether there is art in individual
letters. Letters in combination may be satisfying and in a well c
omposed page even beautiful as a whole, but art in letters con
sists rather in the art of arranging and composing them in a ple
asing and appropriate manner. The main purpose of letters is th
e practical one of making thoughts visible. Ruskin says that all le
tters are frightful things and to be endured only on occasion, th
at is to say, in places where the sense of the inscription is of mor
e importance than external ornament. This is a sweeping state
ment, from which we need not suffer unduly; yet it is doubtful
whether there is art in individual letters. Letters in combination
may be satisfying and in a well composed page even beautiful
The main purpose of letters is the practical one of making thou
ghts visible. Ruskin says that all letters are frightful things and to
**The main purpose of letters is the practical one of makin
g thoughts visible. Ruskin says that all letters are frightf**

ITC ERAS 11 POINT SET MINUS ½ UNIT

LIGHT, BOOK, DEMI, BOLD

abcdefghijklmnopqrstuvwxyz – 1 UNIT
abcdefghijklmnopqrstuvwxyz – ½ UNIT
abcdefghijklmnopqrstuvwxyz NORMAL

ABCDEFGHIJKLMNOPQRSTUVWXYZ 1234567890 abcdefghijklmnopqrstuvwxyz
ABCDEFGHIJKLMNOPQRSTUVWXYZ 1234567890 abcdefghijklmnopqrstuvwxyz
ABCDEFGHIJKLMNOPQRSTUVWXYZ 1234567890 abcdefghijklmnopqrstuvwxyz
ABCDEFGHIJKLMNOPQRSTUVWXYZ 1234567890 abcdefghijklmnopqrstuvwxyz

11/11

The main purpose of letters is the practical one of making thoughts visible. Ruskin says that all letters are frightful thi ngs and to be endured only on occasion, that is to say, in places where the sense of the inscription is of more impo rtance than external ornament. This is a sweeping statem ent, from which we need not suffer unduly; yet it is doub tful whether there is art in individual letters. Letters in com bination may be satisfying and in a well composed page even beautiful as a whole, but art in letters consists rather in the art of arranging and composing them in a pleasin g and appropriate manner. The main purpose of letters is the practical one of making thoughts visible. Ruskin says t hat all letters are frightful things and to be endured only o n occasion, that is to say, in places where the sense of the inscription is of more importance than external ornamen t. This is a sweeping statement, from which we need not suffer unduly; yet it is doubtful whether there is art in indi vidual letters. Letters in combination may be satisfying an d in a well composed page even beautiful as a whole, b
The main purpose of letters is the practical one of makin g thoughts visible. Ruskin says that all letters are frightful t
The main purpose of letters is the practical one of making thoughts visible. Ruskin says that all letter

11/12

The main purpose of letters is the practical one of making thoughts visible. Ruskin says that all letters are frightful thi ngs and to be endured only on occasion, that is to say, in places where the sense of the inscription is of more impo rtance than external ornament. This is a sweeping statem ent, from which we need not suffer unduly; yet it is doub tful whether there is art in individual letters. Letters in com bination may be satisfying and in a well composed page even beautiful as a whole, but art in letters consists rather in the art of arranging and composing them in a pleasin g and appropriate manner. The main purpose of letters is the practical one of making thoughts visible. Ruskin says t hat all letters are frightful things and to be endured only o n occasion, that is to say, in places where the sense of the inscription is of more importance than external ornamen t. This is a sweeping statement, from which we need not suffer unduly; yet it is doubtful whether there is art in indi vidual letters. Letters in combination may be satisfying an
The main purpose of letters is the practical one of makin g thoughts visible. Ruskin says that all letters are frightful t
The main purpose of letters is the practical one of making thoughts visible. Ruskin says that all letter

11/13

The main purpose of letters is the practical one of making thoughts visible. Ruskin says that all letters are frightful thi ngs and to be endured only on occasion, that is to say, in places where the sense of the inscription is of more impo rtance than external ornament. This is a sweeping statem ent, from which we need not suffer unduly; yet it is doub tful whether there is art in individual letters. Letters in com bination may be satisfying and in a well composed page even beautiful as a whole, but art in letters consists rather in the art of arranging and composing them in a pleasin g and appropriate manner. The main purpose of letters is the practical one of making thoughts visible. Ruskin says t hat all letters are frightful things and to be endured only o n occasion, that is to say, in places where the sense of the inscription is of more importance than external ornamen t. This is a sweeping statement, from which we need not suffer unduly; yet it is doubtful whether there is art in indi
The main purpose of letters is the practical one of makin g thoughts visible. Ruskin says that all letters are frightful t
The main purpose of letters is the practical one of making thoughts visible. Ruskin says that all letter

11/14

The main purpose of letters is the practical one of making thoughts visible. Ruskin says that all letters are frightful thi ngs and to be endured only on occasion, that is to say, in places where the sense of the inscription is of more impo rtance than external ornament. This is a sweeping statem ent, from which we need not suffer unduly; yet it is doub tful whether there is art in individual letters. Letters in com bination may be satisfying and in a well composed page even beautiful as a whole, but art in letters consists rather in the art of arranging and composing them in a pleasin g and appropriate manner. The main purpose of letters is the practical one of making thoughts visible. Ruskin says t hat all letters are frightful things and to be endured only o n occasion, that is to say, in places where the sense of the inscription is of more importance than external ornamen t. This is a sweeping statement, from which we need not
The main purpose of letters is the practical one of makin g thoughts visible. Ruskin says that all letters are frightful t
The main purpose of letters is the practical one of making thoughts visible. Ruskin says that all letter

12 POINT SET MINUS ½ UNIT

LIGHT, BOOK, DEMI, BOLD

abcdefghijklmnopqrstuvwxyz – 1 UNIT
abcdefghijklmnopqrstuvwxyz – ½ UNIT
abcdefghijklmnopqrstuvwxyz NORMAL

ABCDEFGHIJKLMNOPQRSTUVWXYZ 1234567890 abcdefghijklmnopqrstuvwxyz
ABCDEFGHIJKLMNOPQRSTUVWXYZ 1234567890 abcdefghijklmnopqrstuvwxyz
ABCDEFGHIJKLMNOPQRSTUVWXYZ 1234567890 abcdefghijklmnopqrstuvwxyz
ABCDEFGHIJKLMNOPQRSTUVWXYZ 1234567890 abcdefghijklmnopqrstuvwxyz

12/12

The main purpose of letters is the practical one of ma king thoughts visible. Ruskin says that all letters are frig htful things and to be endured only on occasion, that is to say, in places where the sense of the inscription is of more importance than external ornament. This is a sweeping statement, from which we need not suffer unduly; yet it is doubtful whether there is art in indivi dual letters. Letters in combination may be satisfying and in a well composed page even beautiful as a w hole, but art in letters consists rather in the art of arran ging and composing them in a pleasing and approp riate manner. The main purpose of letters is the practi cal one of making thoughts visible. Ruskin says that all letters are frightful things and to be endured only on occasion, that is to say, in places where the sense of th
The main purpose of letters is the practical one of ma king thoughts visible. Ruskin says that all letters are fri
The main purpose of letters is the practical one of making thoughts visible. Ruskin says that all

12/13

The main purpose of letters is the practical one of ma king thoughts visible. Ruskin says that all letters are frig htful things and to be endured only on occasion, that is to say, in places where the sense of the inscription is of more importance than external ornament. This is a sweeping statement, from which we need not suffer unduly; yet it is doubtful whether there is art in indivi dual letters. Letters in combination may be satisfying and in a well composed page even beautiful as a w hole, but art in letters consists rather in the art of arran ging and composing them in a pleasing and approp riate manner. The main purpose of letters is the practi cal one of making thoughts visible. Ruskin says that all letters are frightful things and to be endured only on
The main purpose of letters is the practical one of ma king thoughts visible. Ruskin says that all letters are fri
The main purpose of letters is the practical one of making thoughts visible. Ruskin says that all

12/14

The main purpose of letters is the practical one of ma king thoughts visible. Ruskin says that all letters are frig htful things and to be endured only on occasion, that is to say, in places where the sense of the inscription is of more importance than external ornament. This is a sweeping statement, from which we need not suffer unduly; yet it is doubtful whether there is art in indivi dual letters. Letters in combination may be satisfying and in a well composed page even beautiful as a w hole, but art in letters consists rather in the art of arran ging and composing them in a pleasing and approp riate manner. The main purpose of letters is the practi cal one of making thoughts visible. Ruskin says that all letters are frightful things and to be endured only on occasion, that is to say, in places where the sense of th
The main purpose of letters is the practical one of ma king thoughts visible. Ruskin says that all letters are fri
The main purpose of letters is the practical one of making thoughts visible. Ruskin says that all

12/15

The main purpose of letters is the practical one of ma king thoughts visible. Ruskin says that all letters are frig htful things and to be endured only on occasion, that is to say, in places where the sense of the inscription is of more importance than external ornament. This is a sweeping statement, from which we need not suffer unduly; yet it is doubtful whether there is art in indivi dual letters. Letters in combination may be satisfying and in a well composed page even beautiful as a w hole, but art in letters consists rather in the art of arran ging and composing them in a pleasing and approp riate manner. The main purpose of letters is the practi cal one of making thoughts visible. Ruskin says that all letters are frightful things and to be endured only on
The main purpose of letters is the practical one of ma king thoughts visible. Ruskin says that all letters are fri
The main purpose of letters is the practical one of making thoughts visible. Ruskin says that all

ITC ERAS 14 POINT SET MINUS ½ UNIT

LIGHT, BOOK, DEMI, BOLD

abcdefghijklmnopqrstuvwxyz – 1 UNIT
abcdefghijklmnopqrstuvwxyz – ½ UNIT
abcdefghijklmnopqrstuvwxyz NORMAL

ABCDEFGHIJKLMNOPQRSTUVWXYZ abcdefghijklmnopqrstuvwxyz
ABCDEFGHIJKLMNOPQRSTUVWXYZ abcdefghijklmnopqrstuvwxyz
ABCDEFGHIJKLMNOPQRSTUVWXYZ abcdefghijklmnopqrstuvwxyz
ABCDEFGHIJKLMNOPQRSTUVWXYZ abcdefghijklmnopqrstuvwxyz

14/14

The main purpose of letters is the practical on
e of making thoughts visible. Ruskin says that
all letters are frightful things and to be endure
d only on occasion, that is to say, in places wh
ere the sense of the inscription is of more imp
ortance than external ornament. This is a swe
eping statement, from which we need not s
uffer unduly; yet it is doubtful whether there i
s art in individual letters. Letters in combinatio
n may be satisfying and in a well composed
page even beautiful as a whole, but art in lett
ers consists rather in the art of arranging and
composing them in a pleasing and appropri
The main purpose of letters is the practical o
ne of making thoughts visible. Ruskin says th
The main purpose of letters is the practi
cal one of making thoughts visible. Rus

14/15

The main purpose of letters is the practical on
e of making thoughts visible. Ruskin says that
all letters are frightful things and to be endure
d only on occasion, that is to say, in places wh
ere the sense of the inscription is of more imp
ortance than external ornament. This is a swe
eping statement, from which we need not s
uffer unduly; yet it is doubtful whether there i
s art in individual letters. Letters in combinatio
n may be satisfying and in a well composed
page even beautiful as a whole, but art in lett
ers consists rather in the art of arranging and
The main purpose of letters is the practical o
ne of making thoughts visible. Ruskin says th
The main purpose of letters is the practi
cal one of making thoughts visible. Rus

14/16

The main purpose of letters is the practical on
e of making thoughts visible. Ruskin says that
all letters are frightful things and to be endure
d only on occasion, that is to say, in places wh
ere the sense of the inscription is of more imp
ortance than external ornament. This is a swe
eping statement, from which we need not s
uffer unduly; yet it is doubtful whether there i
s art in individual letters. Letters in combinatio
n may be satisfying and in a well composed
page even beautiful as a whole, but art in lett
ers consists rather in the art of arranging and
composing them in a pleasing and appropri
The main purpose of letters is the practical o
ne of making thoughts visible. Ruskin says th
The main purpose of letters is the practi
cal one of making thoughts visible. Rus

14/17

The main purpose of letters is the practical on
e of making thoughts visible. Ruskin says that
all letters are frightful things and to be endure
d only on occasion, that is to say, in places wh
ere the sense of the inscription is of more imp
ortance than external ornament. This is a swe
eping statement, from which we need not s
uffer unduly; yet it is doubtful whether there i
s art in individual letters. Letters in combinatio
n may be satisfying and in a well composed
page even beautiful as a whole, but art in lett
ers consists rather in the art of arranging and
The main purpose of letters is the practical o
ne of making thoughts visible. Ruskin says th
The main purpose of letters is the practi
cal one of making thoughts visible. Rus

FRIZ QUADRATA 6 & 7 POINT SET NORMAL

ROMAN, BOLD

ABCDEFGHIJKLMNOPQRSTUVWXYZ 1234567890 abcdefghijklmnopqrstuvwxyz

ABCDEFGHIJKLMNOPQRSTUVWXYZ 1234567890 abcdefghijklmnopqrstuvwxyz

6/6

The main purpose of letters is the practical one of making thoughts visible. Ruskin says that all
letters are frightful things and to be endured only on occasion, that is to say, in places where t
he sense of the inscription is of more importance than external ornament. This is a sweeping
statement, from which we need not suffer unduly; yet it is doubtful whether there is art in indi
vidual letters. Letters in combination may be satisfying and in a well composed page even be
autiful as a whole, but art in letters consists rather in the art of arranging and composing them
in a pleasing and appropriate manner. The main purpose of letters is the practical one of maki
ng thoughts visible. Ruskin says that all letters are frightful things and to be endured only on o
ccasion, that is to say, in places where the sense of the inscription is of more importance than
external ornament. This is a sweeping statement, from which we need not suffer unduly; yet it
is doubtful whether there is art in individual letters. Letters in combination may be satisfying a
nd in a well composed page even beautiful as a whole, but art in letters consists rather in the a
rt of arranging and composing them in a pleasing and appropriate manner. The main purpos
e of letters is the practical one of making thoughts visible. Ruskin says that all letters are frightf
ul things and to be endured only on occasion, that is to say, in places where the sense of the in
**The main purpose of letters is the practical one of making thoughts visible. Ruskin says t
hat all letters are frightful things and to be endured only on occasion, that is to say, in pla**

6/7

The main purpose of letters is the practical one of making thoughts visible. Ruskin says that all
letters are frightful things and to be endured only on occasion, that is to say, in places where t
he sense of the inscription is of more importance than external ornament. This is a sweeping
statement, from which we need not suffer unduly; yet it is doubtful whether there is art in indi
vidual letters. Letters in combination may be satisfying and in a well composed page even be
autiful as a whole, but art in letters consists rather in the art of arranging and composing them
in a pleasing and appropriate manner. The main purpose of letters is the practical one of maki
ng thoughts visible. Ruskin says that all letters are frightful things and to be endured only on o
ccasion, that is to say, in places where the sense of the inscription is of more importance than
external ornament. This is a sweeping statement, from which we need not suffer unduly; yet it
is doubtful whether there is art in individual letters. Letters in combination may be satisfying a
nd in a well composed page even beautiful as a whole, but art in letters consists rather in the a
rt of arranging and composing them in a pleasing and appropriate manner. The main purpos
**The main purpose of letters is the practical one of making thoughts visible. Ruskin says t
hat all letters are frightful things and to be endured only on occasion, that is to say, in pla**

6/8

The main purpose of letters is the practical one of making thoughts visible. Ruskin says that all
letters are frightful things and to be endured only on occasion, that is to say, in places where t
he sense of the inscription is of more importance than external ornament. This is a sweeping
statement, from which we need not suffer unduly; yet it is doubtful whether there is art in indi
vidual letters. Letters in combination may be satisfying and in a well composed page even be
autiful as a whole, but art in letters consists rather in the art of arranging and composing them
in a pleasing and appropriate manner. The main purpose of letters is the practical one of maki
ng thoughts visible. Ruskin says that all letters are frightful things and to be endured only on o
ccasion, that is to say, in places where the sense of the inscription is of more importance than
external ornament. This is a sweeping statement, from which we need not suffer unduly; yet it
is doubtful whether there is art in individual letters. Letters in combination may be satisfying a
**The main purpose of letters is the practical one of making thoughts visible. Ruskin says t
hat all letters are frightful things and to be endured only on occasion, that is to say, in pla**

6/9

The main purpose of letters is the practical one of making thoughts visible. Ruskin says that all
letters are frightful things and to be endured only on occasion, that is to say, in places where t
he sense of the inscription is of more importance than external ornament. This is a sweeping
statement, from which we need not suffer unduly; yet it is doubtful whether there is art in indi
vidual letters. Letters in combination may be satisfying and in a well composed page even be
autiful as a whole, but art in letters consists rather in the art of arranging and composing them
in a pleasing and appropriate manner. The main purpose of letters is the practical one of maki
ng thoughts visible. Ruskin says that all letters are frightful things and to be endured only on o
ccasion, that is to say, in places where the sense of the inscription is of more importance than
external ornament. This is a sweeping statement, from which we need not suffer unduly; yet it
**The main purpose of letters is the practical one of making thoughts visible. Ruskin says t
hat all letters are frightful things and to be endured only on occasion, that is to say, in pla**

ABCDEFGHIJKLMNOPQRSTUVWXYZ 1234567890 abcdefghijklmnopqrstuvwxyz

ABCDEFGHIJKLMNOPQRSTUVWXYZ 1234567890 abcdefghijklmnopqrstuvwxyz

7/7

The main purpose of letters is the practical one of making thoughts visible. Ruski
n says that all letters are frightful things and to be endured only on occasion, that
is to say, in places where the sense of the inscription is of more importance than
external ornament. This is a sweeping statement, from which we need not suffer
unduly; yet it is doubtful whether there is art in individual letters. Letters in comb
ination may be satisfying and in a well composed page even beautiful as a whol
e, but art in letters consists rather in the art of arranging and composing them in
a pleasing and appropriate manner. The main purpose of letters is the practical
one of making thoughts visible. Ruskin says that all letters are frightful things an
d to be endured only on occasion, that is to say, in places where the sense of the
inscription is of more importance than external ornament. This is a sweeping sta
tement, from which we need not suffer unduly; yet it is doubtful whether there is
art in individual letters. Letters in combination may be satisfying and in a well co
**The main purpose of letters is the practical one of making thoughts visible.
Ruskin says that all letters are frightful things and to be endured only on occ**

7/8

The main purpose of letters is the practical one of making thoughts visible. Ruski
n says that all letters are frightful things and to be endured only on occasion, that
is to say, in places where the sense of the inscription is of more importance than
external ornament. This is a sweeping statement, from which we need not suffer
unduly; yet it is doubtful whether there is art in individual letters. Letters in comb
ination may be satisfying and in a well composed page even beautiful as a whol
e, but art in letters consists rather in the art of arranging and composing them in
a pleasing and appropriate manner. The main purpose of letters is the practical
one of making thoughts visible. Ruskin says that all letters are frightful things an
d to be endured only on occasion, that is to say, in places where the sense of the
inscription is of more importance than external ornament. This is a sweeping sta
tement, from which we need not suffer unduly; yet it is doubtful whether there is
**The main purpose of letters is the practical one of making thoughts visible.
Ruskin says that all letters are frightful things and to be endured only on occ**

7/9

The main purpose of letters is the practical one of making thoughts visible. Ruski
n says that all letters are frightful things and to be endured only on occasion, that
is to say, in places where the sense of the inscription is of more importance than
external ornament. This is a sweeping statement, from which we need not suffer
unduly; yet it is doubtful whether there is art in individual letters. Letters in comb
ination may be satisfying and in a well composed page even beautiful as a whol
e, but art in letters consists rather in the art of arranging and composing them in
a pleasing and appropriate manner. The main purpose of letters is the practical
one of making thoughts visible. Ruskin says that all letters are frightful things an
d to be endured only on occasion, that is to say, in places where the sense of the
inscription is of more importance than external ornament. This is a sweeping sta
tement, from which we need not suffer unduly; yet it is doubtful whether there is
**The main purpose of letters is the practical one of making thoughts visible.
Ruskin says that all letters are frightful things and to be endured only on occ**

7/10

The main purpose of letters is the practical one of making thoughts visible. Ruski
n says that all letters are frightful things and to be endured only on occasion, that
is to say, in places where the sense of the inscription is of more importance than
external ornament. This is a sweeping statement, from which we need not suffer
unduly; yet it is doubtful whether there is art in individual letters. Letters in comb
ination may be satisfying and in a well composed page even beautiful as a whol
e, but art in letters consists rather in the art of arranging and composing them in
a pleasing and appropriate manner. The main purpose of letters is the practical
one of making thoughts visible. Ruskin says that all letters are frightful things an
d to be endured only on occasion, that is to say, in places where the sense of the
inscription is of more importance than external ornament. This is a sweeping sta
**The main purpose of letters is the practical one of making thoughts visible.
Ruskin says that all letters are frightful things and to be endured only on occ**

FRIZ QUADRATA 8 & 9 POINT SET NORMAL

ROMAN, BOLD

ABCDEFGHIJKLMNOPQRSTUVWXYZ 1234567890 abcdefghijklmnopqrstuvwxyz

ABCDEFGHIJKLMNOPQRSTUVWXYZ 1234567890 abcdefghijklmnopqrstuvwxyz

8/8

The main purpose of letters is the practical one of making thoughts vis ible. Ruskin says that all letters are frightful things and to be endured o nly on occasion, that is to say, in places where the sense of the inscripti on is of more importance than external ornament. This is a sweeping s tatement, from which we need not suffer unduly; yet it is doubtful whe ther there is art in individual letters. Letters in combination may be sati sfying and in a well composed page even beautiful as a whole, but art i n letters consists rather in the art of arranging and composing them in a pleasing and appropriate manner. The main purpose of letters is the practical one of making thoughts visible. Ruskin says that all letters are frightful things and to be endured only on occasion, that is to say, in pl

The main purpose of letters is the practical one of making thought s visible. Ruskin says that all letters are frightful things and to be e

8/9

The main purpose of letters is the practical one of making thoughts vis ible. Ruskin says that all letters are frightful things and to be endured o nly on occasion, that is to say, in places where the sense of the inscripti on is of more importance than external ornament. This is a sweeping s tatement, from which we need not suffer unduly; yet it is doubtful whe ther there is art in individual letters. Letters in combination may be sati sfying and in a well composed page even beautiful as a whole, but art i n letters consists rather in the art of arranging and composing them in a pleasing and appropriate manner. The main purpose of letters is the practical one of making thoughts visible. Ruskin says that all letters are

The main purpose of letters is the practical one of making thought s visible. Ruskin says that all letters are frightful things and to be e

8/10

The main purpose of letters is the practical one of making thoughts vis ible. Ruskin says that all letters are frightful things and to be endured o nly on occasion, that is to say, in places where the sense of the inscripti on is of more importance than external ornament. This is a sweeping s tatement, from which we need not suffer unduly; yet it is doubtful whe ther there is art in individual letters. Letters in combination may be sati sfying and in a well composed page even beautiful as a whole, but art i n letters consists rather in the art of arranging and composing them in a pleasing and appropriate manner. The main purpose of letters is the

The main purpose of letters is the practical one of making thought s visible. Ruskin says that all letters are frightful things and to be e

8/11

The main purpose of letters is the practical one of making thoughts vis ible. Ruskin says that all letters are frightful things and to be endured o nly on occasion, that is to say, in places where the sense of the inscripti on is of more importance than external ornament. This is a sweeping s tatement, from which we need not suffer unduly; yet it is doubtful whe ther there is art in individual letters. Letters in combination may be sati sfying and in a well composed page even beautiful as a whole, but art i n letters consists rather in the art of arranging and composing them in a pleasing and appropriate manner. The main purpose of letters is the

The main purpose of letters is the practical one of making thought s visible. Ruskin says that all letters are frightful things and to be e

ABCDEFGHIJKLMNOPQRSTUVWXYZ 1234567890 abcdefghijklmnopqrstuvwxyz

ABCDEFGHIJKLMNOPQRSTUVWXYZ 1234567890 abcdefghijklmnopqrstuvwxyz

9/9

The main purpose of letters is the practical one of making tho ughts visible. Ruskin says that all letters are frightful things and to be endured only on occasion, that is to say, in places where the sense of the inscription is of more importance than extern al ornament. This is a sweeping statement, from which we nee d not suffer unduly; yet it is doubtful whether there is art in indi vidual letters. Letters in combination may be satisfying and in a well composed page even beautiful as a whole, but art in lette rs consists rather in the art of arranging and composing them i n a pleasing and appropriate manner. The main purpose of lett

The main purpose of letters is the practical one of making t houghts visible. Ruskin says that all letters are frightful thi

9/10

The main purpose of letters is the practical one of making tho ughts visible. Ruskin says that all letters are frightful things and to be endured only on occasion, that is to say, in places where the sense of the inscription is of more importance than extern al ornament. This is a sweeping statement, from which we nee d not suffer unduly; yet it is doubtful whether there is art in indi vidual letters. Letters in combination may be satisfying and in a well composed page even beautiful as a whole, but art in lette rs consists rather in the art of arranging and composing them i

The main purpose of letters is the practical one of making t houghts visible. Ruskin says that all letters are frightful thi

9/11

The main purpose of letters is the practical one of making tho ughts visible. Ruskin says that all letters are frightful things and to be endured only on occasion, that is to say, in places where the sense of the inscription is of more importance than extern al ornament. This is a sweeping statement, from which we nee d not suffer unduly; yet it is doubtful whether there is art in indi vidual letters. Letters in combination may be satisfying and in a well composed page even beautiful as a whole, but art in lette rs consists rather in the art of arranging and composing them i

The main purpose of letters is the practical one of making t houghts visible. Ruskin says that all letters are frightful thi

9/12

The main purpose of letters is the practical one of making tho ughts visible. Ruskin says that all letters are frightful things and to be endured only on occasion, that is to say, in places where the sense of the inscription is of more importance than extern al ornament. This is a sweeping statement, from which we nee d not suffer unduly; yet it is doubtful whether there is art in indi vidual letters. Letters in combination may be satisfying and in a well composed page even beautiful as a whole, but art in lette rs consists rather in the art of arranging and composing them i

The main purpose of letters is the practical one of making t houghts visible. Ruskin says that all letters are frightful thi

FRIZ QUADRATA 10 POINT SET MINUS ½ UNIT

ROMAN, BOLD

abcdefghijklmnopqrstuvwxyz – 1 UNIT
abcdefghijklmnopqrstuvwxyz – ½ UNIT
abcdefghijklmnopqrstuvwxyz NORMAL

ABCDEFGHIJKLMNOPQRSTUVWXYZ 1234567890 abcdefghijklmnopqrstuvwxyz
ABCDEFGHIJKLMNOPQRSTUVWXYZ 1234567890 abcdefghijklmnopqrstuvwxyz

10/10

The main purpose of letters is the practical one of making t houghts visible. Ruskin says that all letters are frightful thin gs and to be endured only on occasion, that is to say, in pla ces where the sense of the inscription is of more importan ce than external ornament. This is a sweeping statement, f rom which we need not suffer unduly; yet it is doubtful wh ether there is art in individual letters. Letters in combinatio n may be satisfying and in a well composed page even be autiful as a whole, but art in letters consists rather in the art of arranging and composing them in a pleasing and appro priate manner. The main purpose of letters is the practical one of making thoughts visible. Ruskin says that all letters are frightful things and to be endured only on occasion, th at is to say, in places where the sense of the inscription is of more importance than external ornament. This is a sweepi ng statement, from which we need not suffer unduly; yet it is doubtful whether there is art in individual letters. Letters i n combination may be satisfying and in a well composed p age even beautiful as a whole, but art in letters consists rat her in the art of arranging and composing them in a pleasi ng and appropriate manner. The main purpose of letters is the practical one of making thoughts visible. Ruskin says th at all letters are frightful things and to be endured only on occasion, that is to say, in places where the sense of the ins
The main purpose of letters is the practical one of maki ng thoughts visible. Ruskin says that all letters are frigh

10/11

The main purpose of letters is the practical one of making t houghts visible. Ruskin says that all letters are frightful thin gs and to be endured only on occasion, that is to say, in pla ces where the sense of the inscription is of more importan ce than external ornament. This is a sweeping statement, f rom which we need not suffer unduly; yet it is doubtful wh ether there is art in individual letters. Letters in combinatio n may be satisfying and in a well composed page even be autiful as a whole, but art in letters consists rather in the art of arranging and composing them in a pleasing and appro priate manner. The main purpose of letters is the practical one of making thoughts visible. Ruskin says that all letters are frightful things and to be endured only on occasion, th at is to say, in places where the sense of the inscription is of more importance than external ornament. This is a sweepi ng statement, from which we need not suffer unduly; yet it is doubtful whether there is art in individual letters. Letters i n combination may be satisfying and in a well composed p age even beautiful as a whole, but art in letters consists rat her in the art of arranging and composing them in a pleasi ng and appropriate manner. The main purpose of letters is the practical one of making thoughts visible. Ruskin says th
The main purpose of letters is the practical one of maki ng thoughts visible. Ruskin says that all letters are frigh

10/12

The main purpose of letters is the practical one of making t houghts visible. Ruskin says that all letters are frightful thin gs and to be endured only on occasion, that is to say, in pla ces where the sense of the inscription is of more importan ce than external ornament. This is a sweeping statement, f rom which we need not suffer unduly; yet it is doubtful wh ether there is art in individual letters. Letters in combinatio n may be satisfying and in a well composed page even be autiful as a whole, but art in letters consists rather in the art of arranging and composing them in a pleasing and appro priate manner. The main purpose of letters is the practical one of making thoughts visible. Ruskin says that all letters are frightful things and to be endured only on occasion, th at is to say, in places where the sense of the inscription is of more importance than external ornament. This is a sweepi ng statement, from which we need not suffer unduly; yet it is doubtful whether there is art in individual letters. Letters i n combination may be satisfying and in a well composed p age even beautiful as a whole, but art in letters consists rat her in the art of arranging and composing them in a pleasi
The main purpose of letters is the practical one of maki ng thoughts visible. Ruskin says that all letters are frigh

10/13

The main purpose of letters is the practical one of making t houghts visible. Ruskin says that all letters are frightful thin gs and to be endured only on occasion, that is to say, in pla ces where the sense of the inscription is of more importan ce than external ornament. This is a sweeping statement, f rom which we need not suffer unduly; yet it is doubtful wh ether there is art in individual letters. Letters in combinatio n may be satisfying and in a well composed page even be autiful as a whole, but art in letters consists rather in the art of arranging and composing them in a pleasing and appro priate manner. The main purpose of letters is the practical one of making thoughts visible. Ruskin says that all letters are frightful things and to be endured only on occasion, th at is to say, in places where the sense of the inscription is of more importance than external ornament. This is a sweepi ng statement, from which we need not suffer unduly; yet it is doubtful whether there is art in individual letters. Letters i n combination may be satisfying and in a well composed p age even beautiful as a whole, but art in letters consists rat
The main purpose of letters is the practical one of maki ng thoughts visible. Ruskin says that all letters are frigh

FRIZ QUADRATA 11 POINT SET MINUS ½ UNIT

ROMAN, BOLD

abcdefghijklmnopqrstuvwxyz – 1 UNIT
abcdefghijklmnopqrstuvwxyz – ½ UNIT
abcdefghijklmnopqrstuvwxyz NORMAL

ABCDEFGHIJKLMNOPQRSTUVWXYZ 1234567890 abcdefghijklmnopqrstuvwxyz
ABCDEFGHIJKLMNOPQRSTUVWXYZ 1234567890 abcdefghijklmnopqrstuvwxyz

11/11

The main purpose of letters is the practical one of ma king thoughts visible. Ruskin says that all letters are fri ghtful things and to be endured only on occasion, th at is to say, in places where the sense of the inscriptio n is of more importance than external ornament. Thi s is a sweeping statement, from which we need not s uffer unduly; yet it is doubtful whether there is art in in dividual letters. Letters in combination may be satisfy ing and in a well composed page even beautiful as a whole, but art in letters consists rather in the art of arr anging and composing them in a pleasing and appr opriate manner. The main purpose of letters is the pr actical one of making thoughts visible. Ruskin says th at all letters are frightful things and to be endured onl y on occasion, that is to say, in places where the sens e of the inscription is of more importance than exter nal ornament. This is a sweeping statement, from wh ich we need not suffer unduly; yet it is doubtful whet her there is art in individual letters. Letters in combina tion may be satisfying and in a well composed page even beautiful as a whole, but art in letters consists ra
The main purpose of letters is the practical one of making thoughts visible. Ruskin says that all letter

11/12

The main purpose of letters is the practical one of ma king thoughts visible. Ruskin says that all letters are fri ghtful things and to be endured only on occasion, th at is to say, in places where the sense of the inscriptio n is of more importance than external ornament. Thi s is a sweeping statement, from which we need not s uffer unduly; yet it is doubtful whether there is art in in dividual letters. Letters in combination may be satisfy ing and in a well composed page even beautiful as a whole, but art in letters consists rather in the art of arr anging and composing them in a pleasing and appr opriate manner. The main purpose of letters is the pr actical one of making thoughts visible. Ruskin says th at all letters are frightful things and to be endured onl y on occasion, that is to say, in places where the sens e of the inscription is of more importance than exter nal ornament. This is a sweeping statement, from wh ich we need not suffer unduly; yet it is doubtful whet her there is art in individual letters. Letters in combina tion may be satisfying and in a well composed page
The main purpose of letters is the practical one of making thoughts visible. Ruskin says that all letter

11/13

The main purpose of letters is the practical one of ma king thoughts visible. Ruskin says that all letters are fri ghtful things and to be endured only on occasion, th at is to say, in places where the sense of the inscriptio n is of more importance than external ornament. Thi s is a sweeping statement, from which we need not s uffer unduly; yet it is doubtful whether there is art in in dividual letters. Letters in combination may be satisfy ing and in a well composed page even beautiful as a whole, but art in letters consists rather in the art of arr anging and composing them in a pleasing and appr opriate manner. The main purpose of letters is the pr actical one of making thoughts visible. Ruskin says th at all letters are frightful things and to be endured onl y on occasion, that is to say, in places where the sens e of the inscription is of more importance than exter nal ornament. This is a sweeping statement, from wh ich we need not suffer unduly; yet it is doubtful whet her there is art in individual letters. Letters in combina
The main purpose of letters is the practical one of making thoughts visible. Ruskin says that all letter

11/14

The main purpose of letters is the practical one of ma king thoughts visible. Ruskin says that all letters are fri ghtful things and to be endured only on occasion, th at is to say, in places where the sense of the inscriptio n is of more importance than external ornament. Thi s is a sweeping statement, from which we need not s uffer unduly; yet it is doubtful whether there is art in in dividual letters. Letters in combination may be satisfy ing and in a well composed page even beautiful as a whole, but art in letters consists rather in the art of arr anging and composing them in a pleasing and appr opriate manner. The main purpose of letters is the pr actical one of making thoughts visible. Ruskin says th at all letters are frightful things and to be endured onl y on occasion, that is to say, in places where the sens e of the inscription is of more importance than exter nal ornament. This is a sweeping statement, from wh ich we need not suffer unduly; yet it is doubtful whet
The main purpose of letters is the practical one of making thoughts visible. Ruskin says that all letter

FRIZ QUADRATA 12 POINT SET MINUS ½ UNIT

ROMAN, BOLD

abcdefghijklmnopqrstuvwxyz – 1 UNIT
abcdefghijklmnopqrstuvwxyz – ½ UNIT
abcdefghijklmnopqrstuvwxyz NORMAL

ABCDEFGHIJKLMNOPQRSTUVWXYZ 1234567890 abcdefghijklmnopqrstuvwxyz
ABCDEFGHIJKLMNOPQRSTUVWXYZ 1234567890 abcdefghijklmnopqrstuvwxyz

12/12

The main purpose of letters is the practical one of making thoughts visible. Ruskin says that all letter s are frightful things and to be endured only on o ccasion, that is to say, in places where the sense o f the inscription is of more importance than exter nal ornament. This is a sweeping statement, from which we need not suffer unduly; yet it is doubtful whether there is art in individual letters. Letters in combination may be satisfying and in a well com posed page even beautiful as a whole, but art in l etters consists rather in the art of arranging and c omposing them in a pleasing and appropriate m anner. The main purpose of letters is the practical one of making thoughts visible. Ruskin says that a ll letters are frightful things and to be endured onl y on occasion, that is to say, in places where the s ense of the inscription is of more importance tha
The main purpose of letters is the practical on e of making thoughts visible. Ruskin says that

12/13

The main purpose of letters is the practical one of making thoughts visible. Ruskin says that all letter s are frightful things and to be endured only on o ccasion, that is to say, in places where the sense o f the inscription is of more importance than exter nal ornament. This is a sweeping statement, from which we need not suffer unduly; yet it is doubtful whether there is art in individual letters. Letters in combination may be satisfying and in a well com posed page even beautiful as a whole, but art in l etters consists rather in the art of arranging and c omposing them in a pleasing and appropriate m anner. The main purpose of letters is the practical one of making thoughts visible. Ruskin says that a ll letters are frightful things and to be endured onl y on occasion, that is to say, in places where the s
The main purpose of letters is the practical on e of making thoughts visible. Ruskin says that

12/14

The main purpose of letters is the practical one of making thoughts visible. Ruskin says that all letter s are frightful things and to be endured only on o ccasion, that is to say, in places where the sense o f the inscription is of more importance than exter nal ornament. This is a sweeping statement, from which we need not suffer unduly; yet it is doubtful whether there is art in individual letters. Letters in combination may be satisfying and in a well com posed page even beautiful as a whole, but art in l etters consists rather in the art of arranging and c omposing them in a pleasing and appropriate m anner. The main purpose of letters is the practical one of making thoughts visible. Ruskin says that a ll letters are frightful things and to be endured onl y on occasion, that is to say, in places where the s ense of the inscription is of more importance tha
The main purpose of letters is the practical on e of making thoughts visible. Ruskin says that

12/15

The main purpose of letters is the practical one of making thoughts visible. Ruskin says that all letter s are frightful things and to be endured only on o ccasion, that is to say, in places where the sense o f the inscription is of more importance than exter nal ornament. This is a sweeping statement, from which we need not suffer unduly; yet it is doubtful whether there is art in individual letters. Letters in combination may be satisfying and in a well com posed page even beautiful as a whole, but art in l etters consists rather in the art of arranging and c omposing them in a pleasing and appropriate m anner. The main purpose of letters is the practical one of making thoughts visible. Ruskin says that a ll letters are frightful things and to be endured onl y on occasion, that is to say, in places where the s
The main purpose of letters is the practical on e of making thoughts visible. Ruskin says that

FRIZ QUADRATA 14 POINT SET MINUS ½ UNIT

ROMAN, BOLD

abcdefghijklmnopqrstuvwxyz – 1 UNIT
abcdefghijklmnopqrstuvwxyz – ½ UNIT
abcdefghijklmnopqrstuvwxyz NORMAL

ABCDEFGHIJKLMNOPQRSTUVWXYZ abcdefghijklmnopqrstuvwxyz
ABCDEFGHIJKLMNOPQRSTUVWXYZ abcdefghijklmnopqrstuvwxyz

14/14

The main purpose of letters is the practica l one of making thoughts visible. Ruskin s ays that all letters are frightful things and t o be endured only on occasion, that is to say, in places where the sense of the inscri ption is of more importance than external ornament. This is a sweeping statement, f rom which we need not suffer unduly; yet it is doubtful whether there is art in individ ual letters. Letters in combination may be satisfying and in a well composed page e ven beautiful as a whole, but art in letters c onsists rather in the art of arranging and c omposing them in a pleasing and approp riate manner. The main purpose of letters i
The main purpose of letters is the practi cal one of making thoughts visible. Rus

14/15

The main purpose of letters is the practica l one of making thoughts visible. Ruskin s ays that all letters are frightful things and t o be endured only on occasion, that is to say, in places where the sense of the inscri ption is of more importance than external ornament. This is a sweeping statement, f rom which we need not suffer unduly; yet it is doubtful whether there is art in individ ual letters. Letters in combination may be satisfying and in a well composed page e ven beautiful as a whole, but art in letters c onsists rather in the art of arranging and c omposing them in a pleasing and approp
The main purpose of letters is the practi cal one of making thoughts visible. Rus

14/16

The main purpose of letters is the practica l one of making thoughts visible. Ruskin s ays that all letters are frightful things and t o be endured only on occasion, that is to say, in places where the sense of the inscri ption is of more importance than external ornament. This is a sweeping statement, f rom which we need not suffer unduly; yet it is doubtful whether there is art in individ ual letters. Letters in combination may be satisfying and in a well composed page e ven beautiful as a whole, but art in letters c onsists rather in the art of arranging and c omposing them in a pleasing and approp riate manner. The main purpose of letters i
The main purpose of letters is the practi cal one of making thoughts visible. Rus

14/17

The main purpose of letters is the practica l one of making thoughts visible. Ruskin s ays that all letters are frightful things and t o be endured only on occasion, that is to say, in places where the sense of the inscri ption is of more importance than external ornament. This is a sweeping statement, f rom which we need not suffer unduly; yet it is doubtful whether there is art in individ ual letters. Letters in combination may be satisfying and in a well composed page e ven beautiful as a whole, but art in letters c onsists rather in the art of arranging and c omposing them in a pleasing and approp
The main purpose of letters is the practi cal one of making thoughts visible. Rus

GARAMOND #3 6 & 7 POINT SET NORMAL

ROMAN, ITALIC, BOLD, BOLD ITALIC

ABCDEFGHIJKLMNOPQRSTUVWXYZ 1234567890 abcdefghijklmnopqrstuvwxyz

ABCDEFGHIJKLMNOPQRSTUVWXYZ 1234567890 abcdefghijklmnopqrstuvwxyz

ABCDEFGHIJKLMNOPQRSTUVWXYZ 1234567890 abcdefghijklmnopqrstuvwxyz

ABCDEFGHIJKLMNOPQRSTUVWXYZ 1234567890 abcdefghijklmnopqrstuvwxyz

6/6

The main purpose of letters is the practical one of making thoughts visible. Ruskin says that all letters are fr ightful things and to be endured only on occasion, that is to say, in places where the sense of the inscription is of more importance than external ornament. This is a sweeping statement, from which we need not suffer unduly; yet it is doubtful whether there is art in individual letters. Letters in combination may be satisfyin g and in a well composed page even beautiful as a whole, but art in letters consists rather in the art of arrangi ng and composing them in a pleasing and appropriate manner. The main purpose of letters is the practical o ne of making thoughts visible. Ruskin says that all letters are frightful things and to be endured only on occ asion, that is to say, in places where the sense of the inscription is of more importance than external orname nt. This is a sweeping statement, from which we need not suffer unduly; yet it is doubtful whether there is a rt in individual letters. Letters in combination may be satisfying and in a well composed page even beautifu l as a whole, but art in letters consists rather in the art of arranging and composing them in a pleasing and a ppropriate manner. The main purpose of letters is the practical one of making thoughts visible. Ruskin says that all letters are frightful things and to be endured only on occasion, that is to say, in places where the sens
The main purpose of letters is the practical one of making thoughts visible. Ruskin says that all letters are frightful thing s and to be endured only on occasion, that is to say, in places where the sense of the inscription is of more importance than e
The main purpose of letters is the practical one of making thoughts visible. Ruskin says that all lett ers are frightful things and to be endured only on occasion, that is to say, in places where the sense

6/7

The main purpose of letters is the practical one of making thoughts visible. Ruskin says that all letters are fr ightful things and to be endured only on occasion, that is to say, in places where the sense of the inscription is of more importance than external ornament. This is a sweeping statement, from which we need not suffer unduly; yet it is doubtful whether there is art in individual letters. Letters in combination may be satisfyin g and in a well composed page even beautiful as a whole, but art in letters consists rather in the art of arrangi ng and composing them in a pleasing and appropriate manner. The main purpose of letters is the practical o ne of making thoughts visible. Ruskin says that all letters are frightful things and to be endured only on occ asion, that is to say, in places where the sense of the inscription is of more importance than external orname nt. This is a sweeping statement, from which we need not suffer unduly; yet it is doubtful whether there is a rt in individual letters. Letters in combination may be satisfying and in a well composed page even beautifu l as a whole, but art in letters consists rather in the art of arranging and composing them in a pleasing and a
The main purpose of letters is the practical one of making thoughts visible. Ruskin says that all letters are frightful thing s and to be endured only on occasion, that is to say, in places where the sense of the inscription is of more importance than e
The main purpose of letters is the practical one of making thoughts visible. Ruskin says that all lett ers are frightful things and to be endured only on occasion, that is to say, in places where the sense

6/8

The main purpose of letters is the practical one of making thoughts visible. Ruskin says that all letters are fr ightful things and to be endured only on occasion, that is to say, in places where the sense of the inscription is of more importance than external ornament. This is a sweeping statement, from which we need not suffer unduly; yet it is doubtful whether there is art in individual letters. Letters in combination may be satisfyin g and in a well composed page even beautiful as a whole, but art in letters consists rather in the art of arrangi ng and composing them in a pleasing and appropriate manner. The main purpose of letters is the practical o ne of making thoughts visible. Ruskin says that all letters are frightful things and to be endured only on occ asion, that is to say, in places where the sense of the inscription is of more importance than external orname nt. This is a sweeping statement, from which we need not suffer unduly; yet it is doubtful whether there is a
The main purpose of letters is the practical one of making thoughts visible. Ruskin says that all letters are frightful thing s and to be endured only on occasion, that is to say, in places where the sense of the inscription is of more importance than e
The main purpose of letters is the practical one of making thoughts visible. Ruskin says that all lett ers are frightful things and to be endured only on occasion, that is to say, in places where the sense

6/9

The main purpose of letters is the practical one of making thoughts visible. Ruskin says that all letters are fr ightful things and to be endured only on occasion, that is to say, in places where the sense of the inscription is of more importance than external ornament. This is a sweeping statement, from which we need not suffer unduly; yet it is doubtful whether there is art in individual letters. Letters in combination may be satisfyin g and in a well composed page even beautiful as a whole, but art in letters consists rather in the art of arrangi ng and composing them in a pleasing and appropriate manner. The main purpose of letters is the practical o ne of making thoughts visible. Ruskin says that all letters are frightful things and to be endured only on occ asion, that is to say, in places where the sense of the inscription is of more importance than external orname
The main purpose of letters is the practical one of making thoughts visible. Ruskin says that all letters are frightful thing s and to be endured only on occasion, that is to say, in places where the sense of the inscription is of more importance than e
The main purpose of letters is the practical one of making thoughts visible. Ruskin says that all lett ers are frightful things and to be endured only on occasion, that is to say, in places where the sense

---

ABCDEFGHIJKLMNOPQRSTUVWXYZ 1234567890 abcdefghijklmnopqrstuvwxyz

ABCDEFGHIJKLMNOPQRSTUVWXYZ 1234567890 abcdefghijklmnopqrstuvwxyz

ABCDEFGHIJKLMNOPQRSTUVWXYZ 1234567890 abcdefghijklmnopqrstuvwxyz

ABCDEFGHIJKLMNOPQRSTUVWXYZ 1234567890 abcdefghijklmnopqrstuvwxyz

7/7

The main purpose of letters is the practical one of making thoughts visible. Ruskin says that all letters are frightful things and to be endured only on occasion, that is to say, in places wh ere the sense of the inscription is of more importance than external ornament. This is a swee ping statement, from which we need not suffer unduly; yet it is doubtful whether there is ar t in individual letters. Letters in combination may be satisfying and in a well composed pag e even beautiful as a whole, but art in letters consists rather in the art of arranging and comp osing them in a pleasing and appropriate manner. The main purpose of letters is the practica l one of making thoughts visible. Ruskin says that all letters are frightful things and to be en dured only on occasion, that is to say, in places where the sense of the inscription is of more i mportance than external ornament. This is a sweeping statement, from which we need not s uffer unduly; yet it is doubtful whether there is art in individual letters. Letters in combinat
The main purpose of letters is the practical one of making thoughts visible. Ruskin says that all letters a re frightful things and to be endured only on occasion, that is to say, in places where the sense of the inscr
The main purpose of letters is the practical one of making thoughts visible. Ruskin says that all letters are frightful things and to be endured only on occasion, that is to

7/8

The main purpose of letters is the practical one of making thoughts visible. Ruskin says that all letters are frightful things and to be endured only on occasion, that is to say, in places wh ere the sense of the inscription is of more importance than external ornament. This is a swee ping statement, from which we need not suffer unduly; yet it is doubtful whether there is ar t in individual letters. Letters in combination may be satisfying and in a well composed pag e even beautiful as a whole, but art in letters consists rather in the art of arranging and comp osing them in a pleasing and appropriate manner. The main purpose of letters is the practica l one of making thoughts visible. Ruskin says that all letters are frightful things and to be en dured only on occasion, that is to say, in places where the sense of the inscription is of more i mportance than external ornament. This is a sweeping statement, from which we need not s
The main purpose of letters is the practical one of making thoughts visible. Ruskin says that all letters a re frightful things and to be endured only on occasion, that is to say, in places where the sense of the inscr
The main purpose of letters is the practical one of making thoughts visible. Ruskin says that all letters are frightful things and to be endured only on occasion, that is to

7/9

The main purpose of letters is the practical one of making thoughts visible. Ruskin says that all letters are frightful things and to be endured only on occasion, that is to say, in places wh ere the sense of the inscription is of more importance than external ornament. This is a swee ping statement, from which we need not suffer unduly; yet it is doubtful whether there is ar t in individual letters. Letters in combination may be satisfying and in a well composed pag e even beautiful as a whole, but art in letters consists rather in the art of arranging and comp osing them in a pleasing and appropriate manner. The main purpose of letters is the practica l one of making thoughts visible. Ruskin says that all letters are frightful things and to be en dured only on occasion, that is to say, in places where the sense of the inscription is of more i mportance than external ornament. This is a sweeping statement, from which we need not s
The main purpose of letters is the practical one of making thoughts visible. Ruskin says that all letters a re frightful things and to be endured only on occasion, that is to say, in places where the sense of the inscr
The main purpose of letters is the practical one of making thoughts visible. Ruskin says that all letters are frightful things and to be endured only on occasion, that is to

7/10

The main purpose of letters is the practical one of making thoughts visible. Ruskin says that all letters are frightful things and to be endured only on occasion, that is to say, in places wh ere the sense of the inscription is of more importance than external ornament. This is a swee ping statement, from which we need not suffer unduly; yet it is doubtful whether there is ar t in individual letters. Letters in combination may be satisfying and in a well composed pag e even beautiful as a whole, but art in letters consists rather in the art of arranging and comp osing them in a pleasing and appropriate manner. The main purpose of letters is the practica l one of making thoughts visible. Ruskin says that all letters are frightful things and to be en dured only on occasion, that is to say, in places where the sense of the inscription is of more i
The main purpose of letters is the practical one of making thoughts visible. Ruskin says that all letters a re frightful things and to be endured only on occasion, that is to say, in places where the sense of the inscr
The main purpose of letters is the practical one of making thoughts visible. Ruskin says that all letters are frightful things and to be endured only on occasion, that is to

GARAMOND #3 8 & 9 POINT SET NORMAL

ROMAN, ITALIC, BOLD, BOLD ITALIC

ABCDEFGHIJKLMNOPQRSTUVWXYZ 1234567890 abcdefghijklmnopqrstuvwxyz

ABCDEFGHIJKLMNOPQRSTUVWXYZ 1234567890 abcdefghijklmnopqrstuvwxyz

ABCDEFGHIJKLMNOPQRSTUVWXYZ 1234567890 abcdefghijklmnopqrstuvwxyz

ABCDEFGHIJKLMNOPQRSTUVWXYZ 1234567890 abcdefghijklmnopqrstuvwxyz

8/8

The main purpose of letters is the practical one of making thoughts visible. Rus kin says that all letters are frightful things and to be endured only on occasion, t hat is to say, in places where the sense of the inscription is of more importance th an external ornament. This is a sweeping statement, from which we need not suf fer unduly; yet it is doubtful whether there is art in individual letters. Letters in combination may be satisfying and in a well composed page even beautiful as a w hole, but art in letters consists rather in the art of arranging and composing the m in a pleasing and appropriate manner. The main purpose of letters is the practi cal one of making thoughts visible. Ruskin says that all letters are frightful thin

The main purpose of letters is the practical one of making thoughts visible. Ruskin says tha t all letters are frightful things and to be endured only on occasion, that is to say, in places

The main purpose of letters is the practical one of making thoughts visibl e. Ruskin says that all letters are frightful things and to be endured only o

8/9

The main purpose of letters is the practical one of making thoughts visible. Rus kin says that all letters are frightful things and to be endured only on occasion, t hat is to say, in places where the sense of the inscription is of more importance th an external ornament. This is a sweeping statement, from which we need not suf fer unduly; yet it is doubtful whether there is art in individual letters. Letters in combination may be satisfying and in a well composed page even beautiful as a w hole, but art in letters consists rather in the art of arranging and composing the m in a pleasing and appropriate manner. The main purpose of letters is the practi

The main purpose of letters is the practical one of making thoughts visible. Ruskin says tha t all letters are frightful things and to be endured only on occasion, that is to say, in places

The main purpose of letters is the practical one of making thoughts visibl e. Ruskin says that all letters are frightful things and to be endured only o

8/10

The main purpose of letters is the practical one of making thoughts visible. Rus kin says that all letters are frightful things and to be endured only on occasion, t hat is to say, in places where the sense of the inscription is of more importance th an external ornament. This is a sweeping statement, from which we need not suf fer unduly; yet it is doubtful whether there is art in individual letters. Letters in combination may be satisfying and in a well composed page even beautiful as a w hole, but art in letters consists rather in the art of arranging and composing the

The main purpose of letters is the practical one of making thoughts visible. Ruskin says tha t all letters are frightful things and to be endured only on occasion, that is to say, in places

The main purpose of letters is the practical one of making thoughts visibl e. Ruskin says that all letters are frightful things and to be endured only o

8/11

The main purpose of letters is the practical one of making thoughts visible. Rus kin says that all letters are frightful things and to be endured only on occasion, t hat is to say, in places where the sense of the inscription is of more importance th an external ornament. This is a sweeping statement, from which we need not suf fer unduly; yet it is doubtful whether there is art in individual letters. Letters in combination may be satisfying and in a well composed page even beautiful as a w hole, but art in letters consists rather in the art of arranging and composing the

The main purpose of letters is the practical one of making thoughts visible. Ruskin says tha t all letters are frightful things and to be endured only on occasion, that is to say, in places

The main purpose of letters is the practical one of making thoughts visibl e. Ruskin says that all letters are frightful things and to be endured only o

ABCDEFGHIJKLMNOPQRSTUVWXYZ 1234567890 abcdefghijklmnopqrstuvwxyz

ABCDEFGHIJKLMNOPQRSTUVWXYZ 1234567890 abcdefghijklmnopqrstuvwxyz

ABCDEFGHIJKLMNOPQRSTUVWXYZ 1234567890 abcdefghijklmnopqrstuvwxyz

ABCDEFGHIJKLMNOPQRSTUVWXYZ 1234567890 abcdefghijklmnopqrstuvwxyz

9/9

The main purpose of letters is the practical one of making thoughts visi ble. Ruskin says that all letters are frightful things and to be endured o nly on occasion, that is to say, in places where the sense of the inscriptio n is of more importance than external ornament. This is a sweeping stat ement, from which we need not suffer unduly; yet it is doubtful whethe r there is art in individual letters. Letters in combination may be satisfy ing and in a well composed page even beautiful as a whole, but art in let ters consists rather in the art of arranging and composing them in a plea

The main purpose of letters is the practical one of making thoughts visible. Ruski n says that all letters are frightful things and to be endured only on occasion, tha

The main purpose of letters is the practical one of making though ts visible. Ruskin says that all letters are frightful things and to be

9/10

The main purpose of letters is the practical one of making thoughts visi ble. Ruskin says that all letters are frightful things and to be endured o nly on occasion, that is to say, in places where the sense of the inscriptio n is of more importance than external ornament. This is a sweeping stat ement, from which we need not suffer unduly; yet it is doubtful whethe r there is art in individual letters. Letters in combination may be satisfy ing and in a well composed page even beautiful as a whole, but art in let

The main purpose of letters is the practical one of making thoughts visible. Ruski n says that all letters are frightful things and to be endured only on occasion, tha

The main purpose of letters is the practical one of making though ts visible. Ruskin says that all letters are frightful things and to be

9/11

The main purpose of letters is the practical one of making thoughts visi ble. Ruskin says that all letters are frightful things and to be endured o nly on occasion, that is to say, in places where the sense of the inscriptio n is of more importance than external ornament. This is a sweeping stat ement, from which we need not suffer unduly; yet it is doubtful whethe r there is art in individual letters. Letters in combination may be satisfy ing and in a well composed page even beautiful as a whole, but art in let

The main purpose of letters is the practical one of making thoughts visible. Ruski n says that all letters are frightful things and to be endured only on occasion, tha

The main purpose of letters is the practical one of making though ts visible. Ruskin says that all letters are frightful things and to be

9/12

The main purpose of letters is the practical one of making thoughts visi ble. Ruskin says that all letters are frightful things and to be endured o nly on occasion, that is to say, in places where the sense of the inscriptio n is of more importance than external ornament. This is a sweeping stat ement, from which we need not suffer unduly; yet it is doubtful whethe r there is art in individual letters. Letters in combination may be satisfy ing and in a well composed page even beautiful as a whole, but art in let

The main purpose of letters is the practical one of making thoughts visible. Ruski n says that all letters are frightful things and to be endured only on occasion, tha

The main purpose of letters is the practical one of making though ts visible. Ruskin says that all letters are frightful things and to be

GARAMOND #3 10 POINT SET MINUS ½ UNIT

ROMAN, ITALIC, BOLD, BOLD ITALIC

abcdefghijklmnopqrstuvwxyz – 1 UNIT
abcdefghijklmnopqrstuvwxyz – ½ UNIT
abcdefghijklmnopqrstuvwxyz NORMAL

ABCDEFGHIJKLMNOPQRSTUVWXYZ 1234567890 abcdefghijklmnopqrstuvwxyz
ABCDEFGHIJKLMNOPQRSTUVWXYZ 1234567890 abcdefghijklmnopqrstuvwxyz
ABCDEFGHIJKLMNOPQRSTUVWXYZ 1234567890 abcdefghijklmnopqrstuvwxyz
ABCDEFGHIJKLMNOPQRSTUVWXYZ 1234567890 abcdefghijklmnopqrstuvwxyz

10/10

The main purpose of letters is the practical one of making thoughts visible. Ruskin says that all letters are frightful things and to be end ured only on occasion, that is to say, in places where the sense of the inscription is of more importance than external ornament. This is a sweeping statement, from which we need not suffer unduly; yet it is doubtful whether there is art in individual letters. Letters in combi nation may be satisfying and in a well composed page even beautifu l as a whole, but art in letters consists rather in the art of arranging a nd composing them in a pleasing and appropriate manner. The mai n purpose of letters is the practical one of making thoughts visible. Ruskin says that all letters are frightful things and to be endured on ly on occasion, that is to say, in places where the sense of the inscript ion is of more importance than external ornament. This is a sweepin g statement, from which we need not suffer unduly; yet it is doubtf ul whether there is art in individual letters. Letters in combination may be satisfying and in a well composed page even beautiful as a w hole, but art in letters consists rather in the art of arranging and co mposing them in a pleasing and appropriate manner. The main pur pose of letters is the practical one of making thoughts visible. Ruski n says that all letters are frightful things and to be endured only on o ccasion, that is to say, in places where the sense of the inscription is of more importance than external ornament. This is a sweeping stat
The main purpose of letters is the practical one of making thoughts visible. R uskin says that all letters are frightful things and to be endured only on occas
The main purpose of letters is the practical one of making tho ughts visible. Ruskin says that all letters are frightful things a

10/11

The main purpose of letters is the practical one of making thoughts visible. Ruskin says that all letters are frightful things and to be end ured only on occasion, that is to say, in places where the sense of the inscription is of more importance than external ornament. This is a sweeping statement, from which we need not suffer unduly; yet it is doubtful whether there is art in individual letters. Letters in combi nation may be satisfying and in a well composed page even beautifu l as a whole, but art in letters consists rather in the art of arranging a nd composing them in a pleasing and appropriate manner. The mai n purpose of letters is the practical one of making thoughts visible. Ruskin says that all letters are frightful things and to be endured on ly on occasion, that is to say, in places where the sense of the inscript ion is of more importance than external ornament. This is a sweepin g statement, from which we need not suffer unduly; yet it is doubtf ul whether there is art in individual letters. Letters in combination may be satisfying and in a well composed page even beautiful as a w hole, but art in letters consists rather in the art of arranging and co mposing them in a pleasing and appropriate manner. The main pur pose of letters is the practical one of making thoughts visible. Ruski n says that all letters are frightful things and to be endured only on o
The main purpose of letters is the practical one of making thoughts visible. R uskin says that all letters are frightful things and to be endured only on occas
The main purpose of letters is the practical one of making tho ughts visible. Ruskin says that all letters are frightful things a

10/12

The main purpose of letters is the practical one of making thoughts visible. Ruskin says that all letters are frightful things and to be end ured only on occasion, that is to say, in places where the sense of the inscription is of more importance than external ornament. This is a sweeping statement, from which we need not suffer unduly; yet it is doubtful whether there is art in individual letters. Letters in combi nation may be satisfying and in a well composed page even beautifu l as a whole, but art in letters consists rather in the art of arranging a nd composing them in a pleasing and appropriate manner. The mai n purpose of letters is the practical one of making thoughts visible. Ruskin says that all letters are frightful things and to be endured on ly on occasion, that is to say, in places where the sense of the inscript ion is of more importance than external ornament. This is a sweepin g statement, from which we need not suffer unduly; yet it is doubtf ul whether there is art in individual letters. Letters in combination may be satisfying and in a well composed page even beautiful as a w hole, but art in letters consists rather in the art of arranging and co mposing them in a pleasing and appropriate manner. The main pur
The main purpose of letters is the practical one of making thoughts visible. R uskin says that all letters are frightful things and to be endured only on occas
The main purpose of letters is the practical one of making tho ughts visible. Ruskin says that all letters are frightful things a

10/13

The main purpose of letters is the practical one of making thoughts visible. Ruskin says that all letters are frightful things and to be end ured only on occasion, that is to say, in places where the sense of the inscription is of more importance than external ornament. This is a sweeping statement, from which we need not suffer unduly; yet it is doubtful whether there is art in individual letters. Letters in combi nation may be satisfying and in a well composed page even beautifu l as a whole, but art in letters consists rather in the art of arranging a nd composing them in a pleasing and appropriate manner. The mai n purpose of letters is the practical one of making thoughts visible. Ruskin says that all letters are frightful things and to be endured on ly on occasion, that is to say, in places where the sense of the inscript ion is of more importance than external ornament. This is a sweepin g statement, from which we need not suffer unduly; yet it is doubtf ul whether there is art in individual letters. Letters in combination may be satisfying and in a well composed page even beautiful as a w hole, but art in letters consists rather in the art of arranging and co
The main purpose of letters is the practical one of making thoughts visible. R uskin says that all letters are frightful things and to be endured only on occas
The main purpose of letters is the practical one of making tho ughts visible. Ruskin says that all letters are frightful things a

GARAMOND #3 11 POINT SET MINUS ½ UNIT

ROMAN, ITALIC, BOLD, BOLD ITALIC

abcdefghijklmnopqrstuvwxyz – 1 UNIT
abcdefghijklmnopqrstuvwxyz – ½ UNIT
abcdefghijklmnopqrstuvwxyz NORMAL

ABCDEFGHIJKLMNOPQRSTUVWXYZ 1234567890 abcdefghijklmnopqrstuvwxyz
ABCDEFGHIJKLMNOPQRSTUVWXYZ 1234567890 abcdefghijklmnopqrstuvwxyz
ABCDEFGHIJKLMNOPQRSTUVWXYZ 1234567890 abcdefghijklmnopqrstuvwxyz
ABCDEFGHIJKLMNOPQRSTUVWXYZ 1234567890 abcdefghijklmnopqrstuvwxyz

11/11

The main purpose of letters is the practical one of making tho ughts visible. Ruskin says that all letters are frightful things and to be endured only on occasion, that is to say, in places w here the sense of the inscription is of more importance than ex ternal ornament. This is a sweeping statement, from which we need not suffer unduly; yet it is doubtful whether there is art in individual letters. Letters in combination may be satisf ying and in a well composed page even beautiful as a whole, b ut art in letters consists rather in the art of arranging and com posing them in a pleasing and appropriate manner. The main purpose of letters is the practical one of making thoughts visi ble. Ruskin says that all letters are frightful things and to be e ndured only on occasion, that is to say, in places where the se nse of the inscription is of more importance than external orn ament. This is a sweeping statement, from which we need no t suffer unduly; yet it is doubtful whether there is art in indivi dual letters. Letters in combination may be satisfying and in a well composed page even beautiful as a whole, but art in let ters consists rather in the art of arranging and composing the
The main purpose of letters is the practical one of making thoughts vis ible. Ruskin says that all letters are frightful things and to be endure
The main purpose of letters is the practical one of maki ng thoughts visible. Ruskin says that all letters are frigh

11/12

The main purpose of letters is the practical one of making tho ughts visible. Ruskin says that all letters are frightful things and to be endured only on occasion, that is to say, in places w here the sense of the inscription is of more importance than ex ternal ornament. This is a sweeping statement, from which we need not suffer unduly; yet it is doubtful whether there is art in individual letters. Letters in combination may be satisf ying and in a well composed page even beautiful as a whole, b ut art in letters consists rather in the art of arranging and com posing them in a pleasing and appropriate manner. The main purpose of letters is the practical one of making thoughts visi ble. Ruskin says that all letters are frightful things and to be e ndured only on occasion, that is to say, in places where the se nse of the inscription is of more importance than external orn ament. This is a sweeping statement, from which we need no t suffer unduly; yet it is doubtful whether there is art in indivi dual letters. Letters in combination may be satisfying and in a well composed page even beautiful as a whole, but art in let
The main purpose of letters is the practical one of making thoughts vis ible. Ruskin says that all letters are frightful things and to be endure
The main purpose of letters is the practical one of maki ng thoughts visible. Ruskin says that all letters are frigh

11/13

The main purpose of letters is the practical one of making tho ughts visible. Ruskin says that all letters are frightful things and to be endured only on occasion, that is to say, in places w here the sense of the inscription is of more importance than ex ternal ornament. This is a sweeping statement, from which we need not suffer unduly; yet it is doubtful whether there is art in individual letters. Letters in combination may be satisf ying and in a well composed page even beautiful as a whole, b ut art in letters consists rather in the art of arranging and com posing them in a pleasing and appropriate manner. The main purpose of letters is the practical one of making thoughts visi ble. Ruskin says that all letters are frightful things and to be e ndured only on occasion, that is to say, in places where the se nse of the inscription is of more importance than external orn ament. This is a sweeping statement, from which we need no t suffer unduly; yet it is doubtful whether there is art in indivi dual letters. Letters in combination may be satisfying and in
The main purpose of letters is the practical one of making thoughts vis ible. Ruskin says that all letters are frightful things and to be endure
The main purpose of letters is the practical one of maki ng thoughts visible. Ruskin says that all letters are frigh

11/14

The main purpose of letters is the practical one of making tho ughts visible. Ruskin says that all letters are frightful things and to be endured only on occasion, that is to say, in places w here the sense of the inscription is of more importance than ex ternal ornament. This is a sweeping statement, from which we need not suffer unduly; yet it is doubtful whether there is art in individual letters. Letters in combination may be satisf ying and in a well composed page even beautiful as a whole, b ut art in letters consists rather in the art of arranging and com posing them in a pleasing and appropriate manner. The main purpose of letters is the practical one of making thoughts visi ble. Ruskin says that all letters are frightful things and to be e ndured only on occasion, that is to say, in places where the se nse of the inscription is of more importance than external orn ament. This is a sweeping statement, from which we need no t suffer unduly; yet it is doubtful whether there is art in indivi
The main purpose of letters is the practical one of making thoughts vis ible. Ruskin says that all letters are frightful things and to be endure
The main purpose of letters is the practical one of maki ng thoughts visible. Ruskin says that all letters are frigh

GARAMOND #3 12 POINT SET MINUS ½ UNIT

ROMAN, ITALIC, BOLD, BOLD ITALIC

abcdefghijklmnopqrstuvwxyz – 1 UNIT
abcdefghijklmnopqrstuvwxyz – ½ UNIT
abcdefghijklmnopqrstuvwxyz NORMAL

ABCDEFGHIJKLMNOPQRSTUVWXYZ 1234567890 abcdefghijklmnopqrstuvwxyz
ABCDEFGHIJKLMNOPQRSTUVWXYZ 1234567890 abcdefghijklmnopqrstuvwxyz
ABCDEFGHIJKLMNOPQRSTUVWXYZ 1234567890 abcdefghijklmnopqrstuvwxyz
ABCDEFGHIJKLMNOPQRSTUVWXYZ 1234567890 abcdefghijklmnopqrstuvwxyz

12/12

The main purpose of letters is the practical one of making thoughts visible. Ruskin says that all letters are frightful things and to be endured only on occasion, that is to say, i n places where the sense of the inscription is of more imp ortance than external ornament. This is a sweeping state ment, from which we need not suffer unduly; yet it is do ubtful whether there is art in individual letters. Letters in combination may be satisfying and in a well composed p age even beautiful as a whole, but art in letters consists ra ther in the art of arranging and composing them in a plea sing and appropriate manner. The main purpose of letter s is the practical one of making thoughts visible. Ruskin says that all letters are frightful things and to be endured only on occasion, that is to say, in places where the sense o f the inscription is of more importance than external orna
The main purpose of letters is the practical one of making thought s visible. Ruskin says that all letters are frightful things and to b
The main purpose of letters is the practical one of m aking thoughts visible. Ruskin says that all letters ar

12/13

The main purpose of letters is the practical one of making thoughts visible. Ruskin says that all letters are frightful things and to be endured only on occasion, that is to say, i n places where the sense of the inscription is of more imp ortance than external ornament. This is a sweeping state ment, from which we need not suffer unduly; yet it is do ubtful whether there is art in individual letters. Letters in combination may be satisfying and in a well composed p age even beautiful as a whole, but art in letters consists ra ther in the art of arranging and composing them in a plea sing and appropriate manner. The main purpose of letter s is the practical one of making thoughts visible. Ruskin says that all letters are frightful things and to be endured only on occasion, that is to say, in places where the sense o
The main purpose of letters is the practical one of making thought s visible. Ruskin says that all letters are frightful things and to b
The main purpose of letters is the practical one of m aking thoughts visible. Ruskin says that all letters ar

12/14

The main purpose of letters is the practical one of making thoughts visible. Ruskin says that all letters are frightful things and to be endured only on occasion, that is to say, i n places where the sense of the inscription is of more imp ortance than external ornament. This is a sweeping state ment, from which we need not suffer unduly; yet it is do ubtful whether there is art in individual letters. Letters in combination may be satisfying and in a well composed p age even beautiful as a whole, but art in letters consists ra ther in the art of arranging and composing them in a plea sing and appropriate manner. The main purpose of letter s is the practical one of making thoughts visible. Ruskin says that all letters are frightful things and to be endured only on occasion, that is to say, in places where the sense o f the inscription is of more importance than external orna
The main purpose of letters is the practical one of making thought s visible. Ruskin says that all letters are frightful things and to b
The main purpose of letters is the practical one of m aking thoughts visible. Ruskin says that all letters ar

12/15

The main purpose of letters is the practical one of making thoughts visible. Ruskin says that all letters are frightful things and to be endured only on occasion, that is to say, i n places where the sense of the inscription is of more imp ortance than external ornament. This is a sweeping state ment, from which we need not suffer unduly; yet it is do ubtful whether there is art in individual letters. Letters in combination may be satisfying and in a well composed p age even beautiful as a whole, but art in letters consists ra ther in the art of arranging and composing them in a plea sing and appropriate manner. The main purpose of letter s is the practical one of making thoughts visible. Ruskin says that all letters are frightful things and to be endured only on occasion, that is to say, in places where the sense o
The main purpose of letters is the practical one of making thought s visible. Ruskin says that all letters are frightful things and to b
The main purpose of letters is the practical one of m aking thoughts visible. Ruskin says that all letters ar

GARAMOND #3 14 POINT SET MINUS ½ UNIT

ROMAN, ITALIC, BOLD, BOLD ITALIC

abcdefghijklmnopqrstuvwxyz – 1 UNIT

abcdefghijklmnopqrstuvwxyz – ½ UNIT

abcdefghijklmnopqrstuvwxyz NORMAL

ABCDEFGHIJKLMNOPQRSTUVWXYZ abcdefghijklmnopqrstuvwxyz

ABCDEFGHIJKLMNOPQRSTUVWXYZ abcdefghijklmnopqrstuvwxyz

ABCDEFGHIJKLMNOPQRSTUVWXYZ abcdefghijklmnopqrstuvwxyz

ABCDEFGHIJKLMNOPQRSTUVWXYZ abcdefghijklmnopqrstuvwxyz

14/14

The main purpose of letters is the practical one o f making thoughts visible. Ruskin says that all l etters are frightful things and to be endured only on occasion, that is to say, in places where the se nse of the inscription is of more importance than external ornament. This is a sweeping statement, from which we need not suffer unduly; yet it is doubtful whether there is art in individual letter s. Letters in combination may be satisfying and i n a well composed page even beautiful as a whol e, but art in letters consists rather in the art of arr anging and composing them in a pleasing and a ppropriate manner. The main purpose of letters i

The main purpose of letters is the practical one of maki ng thoughts visible. Ruskin says that all letters are fri

The main purpose of letters is the practical o ne of making thoughts visible. Ruskin says t

14/15

The main purpose of letters is the practical one o f making thoughts visible. Ruskin says that all l etters are frightful things and to be endured only on occasion, that is to say, in places where the se nse of the inscription is of more importance than external ornament. This is a sweeping statement, from which we need not suffer unduly; yet it is doubtful whether there is art in individual letter s. Letters in combination may be satisfying and i n a well composed page even beautiful as a whol e, but art in letters consists rather in the art of arr anging and composing them in a pleasing and a

The main purpose of letters is the practical one of maki ng thoughts visible. Ruskin says that all letters are fri

The main purpose of letters is the practical o ne of making thoughts visible. Ruskin says t

14/16

The main purpose of letters is the practical one o f making thoughts visible. Ruskin says that all l etters are frightful things and to be endured only on occasion, that is to say, in places where the se nse of the inscription is of more importance than external ornament. This is a sweeping statement, from which we need not suffer unduly; yet it is doubtful whether there is art in individual letter s. Letters in combination may be satisfying and i n a well composed page even beautiful as a whol e, but art in letters consists rather in the art of arr anging and composing them in a pleasing and a ppropriate manner. The main purpose of letters i

The main purpose of letters is the practical one of maki ng thoughts visible. Ruskin says that all letters are fri

The main purpose of letters is the practical o ne of making thoughts visible. Ruskin says t

14/17

The main purpose of letters is the practical one o f making thoughts visible. Ruskin says that all l etters are frightful things and to be endured only on occasion, that is to say, in places where the se nse of the inscription is of more importance than external ornament. This is a sweeping statement, from which we need not suffer unduly; yet it is doubtful whether there is art in individual letter s. Letters in combination may be satisfying and i n a well composed page even beautiful as a whol e, but art in letters consists rather in the art of arr anging and composing them in a pleasing and a

The main purpose of letters is the practical one of maki ng thoughts visible. Ruskin says that all letters are fri

The main purpose of letters is the practical o ne of making thoughts visible. Ruskin says t

ITC GARAMOND 6 & 7 POINT SET NORMAL

BOOK, ITALIC, BOLD, BOLD ITALIC

ABCDEFGHIJKLMNOPQRSTUVWXYZ 1234567890 abcdefghijklmnopqrstuvwxyz

ABCDEFGHIJKLMNOPQRSTUVWXYZ 1234567890 abcdefghijklmnopqrstuvwxyz

ABCDEFGHIJKLMNOPQRSTUVWXYZ 1234567890 abcdefghijklmnopqrstuvwxyz

ABCDEFGHIJKLMNOPQRSTUVWXYZ 1234567890 abcdefghijklmnopqrstuvwxyz

6/6

The main purpose of letters is the practical one of making thoughts visible. Ruskin says that all le tters are frightful things and to be endured only on occasion, that is to say, in places where the se nse of the inscription is of more importance than external ornament. This is a sweeping stateme nt, from which we need not suffer unduly; yet it is doubtful whether there is art in individual lett ers. Letters in combination may be satisfying and in a well composed page even beautiful as a wh ole, but art in letters consists rather in the art of arranging and composing them in a pleasing and appropriate manner. The main purpose of letters is the practical one of making thoughts visible. Ruskin says that all letters are frightful things and to be endured only on occasion, that is to say, in places where the sense of the inscription is of more importance than external ornament. This is a sweeping statement, from which we need not suffer unduly; yet it is doubtful whether there is art in individual letters. Letters in combination may be satisfying and in a well composed page even beautiful as a whole, but art in letters consists rather in the art of arranging and composing them in a pleasing and appropriate manner. The main purpose of letters is the practical one of m
The main purpose of letters is the practical one of making thoughts visible. Ruskin says that a ll letters are frightful things and to be endured only on occasion, that is to say, in places where
The main purpose of letters is the practical one of making thoughts visible. Ruskin say s that all letters are frightful things and to be endured only on occasion, that is to say, in

6/7

The main purpose of letters is the practical one of making thoughts visible. Ruskin says that all le tters are frightful things and to be endured only on occasion, that is to say, in places where the se nse of the inscription is of more importance than external ornament. This is a sweeping stateme nt, from which we need not suffer unduly; yet it is doubtful whether there is art in individual lett ers. Letters in combination may be satisfying and in a well composed page even beautiful as a wh ole, but art in letters consists rather in the art of arranging and composing them in a pleasing and appropriate manner. The main purpose of letters is the practical one of making thoughts visible. Ruskin says that all letters are frightful things and to be endured only on occasion, that is to say, in places where the sense of the inscription is of more importance than external ornament. This is a sweeping statement, from which we need not suffer unduly; yet it is doubtful whether there is art in individual letters. Letters in combination may be satisfying and in a well composed page
The main purpose of letters is the practical one of making thoughts visible. Ruskin says that a ll letters are frightful things and to be endured only on occasion, that is to say, in places where
The main purpose of letters is the practical one of making thoughts visible. Ruskin say s that all letters are frightful things and to be endured only on occasion, that is to say, in

6/8

The main purpose of letters is the practical one of making thoughts visible. Ruskin says that all le tters are frightful things and to be endured only on occasion, that is to say, in places where the se nse of the inscription is of more importance than external ornament. This is a sweeping stateme nt, from which we need not suffer unduly; yet it is doubtful whether there is art in individual lett ers. Letters in combination may be satisfying and in a well composed page even beautiful as a wh ole, but art in letters consists rather in the art of arranging and composing them in a pleasing and appropriate manner. The main purpose of letters is the practical one of making thoughts visible. Ruskin says that all letters are frightful things and to be endured only on occasion, that is to say, in places where the sense of the inscription is of more importance than external ornament. This
The main purpose of letters is the practical one of making thoughts visible. Ruskin says that a ll letters are frightful things and to be endured only on occasion, that is to say, in places where
The main purpose of letters is the practical one of making thoughts visible. Ruskin say s that all letters are frightful things and to be endured only on occasion, that is to say, in

6/9

The main purpose of letters is the practical one of making thoughts visible. Ruskin says that all le tters are frightful things and to be endured only on occasion, that is to say, in places where the se nse of the inscription is of more importance than external ornament. This is a sweeping stateme nt, from which we need not suffer unduly; yet it is doubtful whether there is art in individual lett ers. Letters in combination may be satisfying and in a well composed page even beautiful as a wh ole, but art in letters consists rather in the art of arranging and composing them in a pleasing and appropriate manner. The main purpose of letters is the practical one of making thoughts visible. Ruskin says that all letters are frightful things and to be endured only on occasion, that is to say,
The main purpose of letters is the practical one of making thoughts visible. Ruskin says that a ll letters are frightful things and to be endured only on occasion, that is to say, in places where
The main purpose of letters is the practical one of making thoughts visible. Ruskin say s that all letters are frightful things and to be endured only on occasion, that is to say, in

---

ABCDEFGHIJKLMNOPQRSTUVWXYZ 1234567890 abcdefghijklmnopqrstuvwxyz

ABCDEFGHIJKLMNOPQRSTUVWXYZ 1234567890 abcdefghijklmnopqrstuvwxyz

ABCDEFGHIJKLMNOPQRSTUVWXYZ 1234567890 abcdefghijklmnopqrstuvwxyz

ABCDEFGHIJKLMNOPQRSTUVWXYZ 1234567890 abcdefghijklmnopqrstuvwxyz

7/7

The main purpose of letters is the practical one of making thoughts visible. Ruskin says that all letters are frightful things and to be endured only on occasion, that is t o say, in places where the sense of the inscription is of more importance than exter nal ornament. This is a sweeping statement, from which we need not suffer unduly; yet it is doubtful whether there is art in individual letters. Letters in combination may be satisfying and in a well composed page even beautiful as a whole, but art in letters consists rather in the art of arranging and composing them in a pleasing and appropriate manner. The main purpose of letters is the practical one of making tho ughts visible. Ruskin says that all letters are frightful things and to be endured only on occasion, that is to say, in places where the sense of the inscription is of more im portance than external ornament. This is a sweeping statement, from which we ne
The main purpose of letters is the practical one of making thoughts visible. Rusk in says that all letters are frightful things and to be endured only on occasion, th
The main purpose of letters is the practical one of making thoughts visible. Ruskin says that all letters are frightful things and to be endured only on

7/8

The main purpose of letters is the practical one of making thoughts visible. Ruskin says that all letters are frightful things and to be endured only on occasion, that is t o say, in places where the sense of the inscription is of more importance than exter nal ornament. This is a sweeping statement, from which we need not suffer unduly; yet it is doubtful whether there is art in individual letters. Letters in combination may be satisfying and in a well composed page even beautiful as a whole, but art in letters consists rather in the art of arranging and composing them in a pleasing and appropriate manner. The main purpose of letters is the practical one of making tho ughts visible. Ruskin says that all letters are frightful things and to be endured only on occasion, that is to say, in places where the sense of the inscription is of more im
The main purpose of letters is the practical one of making thoughts visible. Rusk in says that all letters are frightful things and to be endured only on occasion, th
The main purpose of letters is the practical one of making thoughts visible. Ruskin says that all letters are frightful things and to be endured only on

7/9

The main purpose of letters is the practical one of making thoughts visible. Ruskin says that all letters are frightful things and to be endured only on occasion, that is t o say, in places where the sense of the inscription is of more importance than exter nal ornament. This is a sweeping statement, from which we need not suffer unduly; yet it is doubtful whether there is art in individual letters. Letters in combination may be satisfying and in a well composed page even beautiful as a whole, but art in letters consists rather in the art of arranging and composing them in a pleasing and appropriate manner. The main purpose of letters is the practical one of making tho ughts visible. Ruskin says that all letters are frightful things and to be endured only on occasion, that is to say, in places where the sense of the inscription is of more im
The main purpose of letters is the practical one of making thoughts visible. Rusk in says that all letters are frightful things and to be endured only on occasion, th
The main purpose of letters is the practical one of making thoughts visible. Ruskin says that all letters are frightful things and to be endured only on

7/10

The main purpose of letters is the practical one of making thoughts visible. Ruskin says that all letters are frightful things and to be endured only on occasion, that is t o say, in places where the sense of the inscription is of more importance than exter nal ornament. This is a sweeping statement, from which we need not suffer unduly; yet it is doubtful whether there is art in individual letters. Letters in combination may be satisfying and in a well composed page even beautiful as a whole, but art in letters consists rather in the art of arranging and composing them in a pleasing and appropriate manner. The main purpose of letters is the practical one of making tho ughts visible. Ruskin says that all letters are frightful things and to be endured only
The main purpose of letters is the practical one of making thoughts visible. Rusk in says that all letters are frightful things and to be endured only on occasion, th
The main purpose of letters is the practical one of making thoughts visible. Ruskin says that all letters are frightful things and to be endured only on

ITC GARAMOND 8 & 9 POINT SET NORMAL

BOOK, ITALIC, BOLD, BOLD ITALIC

ABCDEFGHIJKLMNOPQRSTUVWXYZ 1234567890 abcdefghijklmnopqrstuvwxyz

ABCDEFGHIJKLMNOPQRSTUVWXYZ 1234567890 abcdefghijklmnopqrstuvwxyz

ABCDEFGHIJKLMNOPQRSTUVWXYZ 1234567890 abcdefghijklmnopqrstuvwxyz

ABCDEFGHIJKLMNOPQRSTUVWXYZ 1234567890 abcdefghijklmnopqrstuvwxyz

8/8

The main purpose of letters is the practical one of making thoughts visib le. Ruskin says that all letters are frightful things and to be endured only on occasion, that is to say, in places where the sense of the inscription is of more importance than external ornament. This is a sweeping state ment, from which we need not suffer unduly; yet it is doubtful whether the re is art in individual letters. Letters in combination may be satisfying an d in a well composed page even beautiful as a whole, but art in letters co nsists rather in the art of arranging and composing them in a pleasing an d appropriate manner. The main purpose of letters is the practical one of

The main purpose of letters is the practical one of making thoughts vis ible. Ruskin says that all letters are frightful things and to be endured

The main purpose of letters is the practical one of making thoug hts visible. Ruskin says that all letters are frightful things and to b

8/9

The main purpose of letters is the practical one of making thoughts visib le. Ruskin says that all letters are frightful things and to be endured only on occasion, that is to say, in places where the sense of the inscription is of more importance than external ornament. This is a sweeping state ment, from which we need not suffer unduly; yet it is doubtful whether the re is art in individual letters. Letters in combination may be satisfying an d in a well composed page even beautiful as a whole, but art in letters co nsists rather in the art of arranging and composing them in a pleasing an

The main purpose of letters is the practical one of making thoughts vis ible. Ruskin says that all letters are frightful things and to be endured

The main purpose of letters is the practical one of making thoug hts visible. Ruskin says that all letters are frightful things and to b

8/10

The main purpose of letters is the practical one of making thoughts visib le. Ruskin says that all letters are frightful things and to be endured only on occasion, that is to say, in places where the sense of the inscription is of more importance than external ornament. This is a sweeping state ment, from which we need not suffer unduly; yet it is doubtful whether the re is art in individual letters. Letters in combination may be satisfying an d in a well composed page even beautiful as a whole, but art in letters co

The main purpose of letters is the practical one of making thoughts vis ible. Ruskin says that all letters are frightful things and to be endured

The main purpose of letters is the practical one of making thoug hts visible. Ruskin says that all letters are frightful things and to b

8/11

The main purpose of letters is the practical one of making thoughts visib le. Ruskin says that all letters are frightful things and to be endured only on occasion, that is to say, in places where the sense of the inscription is of more importance than external ornament. This is a sweeping state ment, from which we need not suffer unduly; yet it is doubtful whether the re is art in individual letters. Letters in combination may be satisfying an d in a well composed page even beautiful as a whole, but art in letters co

The main purpose of letters is the practical one of making thoughts vis ible. Ruskin says that all letters are frightful things and to be endured

The main purpose of letters is the practical one of making thoug hts visible. Ruskin says that all letters are frightful things and to b

---

ABCDEFGHIJKLMNOPQRSTUVWXYZ 1234567890 abcdefghijklmnopqrstuvwxyz

ABCDEFGHIJKLMNOPQRSTUVWXYZ 1234567890 abcdefghijklmnopqrstuvwxyz

ABCDEFGHIJKLMNOPQRSTUVWXYZ 1234567890 abcdefghijklmnopqrstuvwxyz

ABCDEFGHIJKLMNOPQRSTUVWXYZ 1234567890 abcdefghijklmnopqrstuvwxyz

9/9

The main purpose of letters is the practical one of making thoug hts visible. Ruskin says that all letters are frightful things and to b e endured only on occasion, that is to say, in places where the se nse of the inscription is of more importance than external orna ment. This is a sweeping statement, from which we need not suf fer unduly; yet it is doubtful whether there is art in individual let ters. Letters in combination may be satisfying and in a well com posed page even beautiful as a whole, but art in letters consists r

The main purpose of letters is the practical one of making tho ughts visible. Ruskin says that all letters are frightful things a

The main purpose of letters is the practical one of making thoughts visible. Ruskin says that all letters are frightful t

9/10

The main purpose of letters is the practical one of making thoug hts visible. Ruskin says that all letters are frightful things and to b e endured only on occasion, that is to say, in places where the se nse of the inscription is of more importance than external orna ment. This is a sweeping statement, from which we need not suf fer unduly; yet it is doubtful whether there is art in individual let ters. Letters in combination may be satisfying and in a well com

The main purpose of letters is the practical one of making tho ughts visible. Ruskin says that all letters are frightful things a

The main purpose of letters is the practical one of making thoughts visible. Ruskin says that all letters are frightful t

9/11

The main purpose of letters is the practical one of making thoug hts visible. Ruskin says that all letters are frightful things and to b e endured only on occasion, that is to say, in places where the se nse of the inscription is of more importance than external orna ment. This is a sweeping statement, from which we need not suf fer unduly; yet it is doubtful whether there is art in individual let ters. Letters in combination may be satisfying and in a well com

The main purpose of letters is the practical one of making tho ughts visible. Ruskin says that all letters are frightful things a

The main purpose of letters is the practical one of making thoughts visible. Ruskin says that all letters are frightful t

9/12

The main purpose of letters is the practical one of making thoug hts visible. Ruskin says that all letters are frightful things and to b e endured only on occasion, that is to say, in places where the se nse of the inscription is of more importance than external orna ment. This is a sweeping statement, from which we need not suf fer unduly; yet it is doubtful whether there is art in individual let ters. Letters in combination may be satisfying and in a well com

The main purpose of letters is the practical one of making tho ughts visible. Ruskin says that all letters are frightful things a

The main purpose of letters is the practical one of making thoughts visible. Ruskin says that all letters are frightful t

ITC GARAMOND 10 POINT SET MINUS ½ UNIT

BOOK, ITALIC, BOLD, BOLD ITALIC

abcdefghijklmnopqrstuvwxyz − 1 UNIT
abcdefghijklmnopqrstuvwxyz − ½ UNIT
abcdefghijklmnopqrstuvwxyz NORMAL

ABCDEFGHIJKLMNOPQRSTUVWXYZ 1234567890 abcdefghijklmnopqrstuvwxyz
ABCDEFGHIJKLMNOPQRSTUVWXYZ 1234567890 abcdefghijklmnopqrstuvwxyz
ABCDEFGHIJKLMNOPQRSTUVWXYZ 1234567890 abcdefghijklmnopqrstuvwxyz
ABCDEFGHIJKLMNOPQRSTUVWXYZ 1234567890 abcdefghijklmnopqrstuvwxyz

10/10

The main purpose of letters is the practical one of making th
oughts visible. Ruskin says that all letters are frightful things
and to be endured only on occasion, that is to say, in places
where the sense of the inscription is of more importance tha
n external ornament. This is a sweeping statement, from wh
ich we need not suffer unduly; yet it is doubtful whether the
re is art in individual letters. Letters in combination may be s
atisfying and in a well composed page even beautiful as a wh
ole, but art in letters consists rather in the art of arranging an
d composing them in a pleasing and appropriate manner. Th
e main purpose of letters is the practical one of making thou
ghts visible. Ruskin says that all letters are frightful things an
d to be endured only on occasion, that is to say, in places wh
ere the sense of the inscription is of more importance than e
xternal ornament. This is a sweeping statement, from which
we need not suffer unduly; yet it is doubtful whether there is
art in individual letters. Letters in combination may be satisf
ying and in a well composed page even beautiful as a whole,
but art in letters consists rather in the art of arranging and co
mposing them in a pleasing and appropriate manner. The ma
in purpose of letters is the practical one of making thoughts
visible. Ruskin says that all letters are frightful things and to b
The main purpose of letters is the practical one of making t
houghts visible. Ruskin says that all letters are frightful thi
The main purpose of letters is the practical one of ma
king thoughts visible. Ruskin says that all letters are fr

10/11

The main purpose of letters is the practical one of making th
oughts visible. Ruskin says that all letters are frightful things
and to be endured only on occasion, that is to say, in places
where the sense of the inscription is of more importance tha
n external ornament. This is a sweeping statement, from wh
ich we need not suffer unduly; yet it is doubtful whether the
re is art in individual letters. Letters in combination may be s
atisfying and in a well composed page even beautiful as a wh
ole, but art in letters consists rather in the art of arranging an
d composing them in a pleasing and appropriate manner. Th
e main purpose of letters is the practical one of making thou
ghts visible. Ruskin says that all letters are frightful things an
d to be endured only on occasion, that is to say, in places wh
ere the sense of the inscription is of more importance than e
xternal ornament. This is a sweeping statement, from which
we need not suffer unduly; yet it is doubtful whether there is
art in individual letters. Letters in combination may be satisf
ying and in a well composed page even beautiful as a whole,
but art in letters consists rather in the art of arranging and co
mposing them in a pleasing and appropriate manner. The ma
The main purpose of letters is the practical one of making t
houghts visible. Ruskin says that all letters are frightful thi
The main purpose of letters is the practical one of ma
king thoughts visible. Ruskin says that all letters are fr

10/12

The main purpose of letters is the practical one of making th
oughts visible. Ruskin says that all letters are frightful things
and to be endured only on occasion, that is to say, in places
where the sense of the inscription is of more importance tha
n external ornament. This is a sweeping statement, from wh
ich we need not suffer unduly; yet it is doubtful whether the
re is art in individual letters. Letters in combination may be s
atisfying and in a well composed page even beautiful as a wh
ole, but art in letters consists rather in the art of arranging an
d composing them in a pleasing and appropriate manner. Th
e main purpose of letters is the practical one of making thou
ghts visible. Ruskin says that all letters are frightful things an
d to be endured only on occasion, that is to say, in places wh
ere the sense of the inscription is of more importance than e
xternal ornament. This is a sweeping statement, from which
we need not suffer unduly; yet it is doubtful whether there is
art in individual letters. Letters in combination may be satisf
ying and in a well composed page even beautiful as a whole,
The main purpose of letters is the practical one of making t
houghts visible. Ruskin says that all letters are frightful thi
The main purpose of letters is the practical one of ma
king thoughts visible. Ruskin says that all letters are fr

10/13

The main purpose of letters is the practical one of making th
oughts visible. Ruskin says that all letters are frightful things
and to be endured only on occasion, that is to say, in places
where the sense of the inscription is of more importance tha
n external ornament. This is a sweeping statement, from wh
ich we need not suffer unduly; yet it is doubtful whether the
re is art in individual letters. Letters in combination may be s
atisfying and in a well composed page even beautiful as a wh
ole, but art in letters consists rather in the art of arranging an
d composing them in a pleasing and appropriate manner. Th
e main purpose of letters is the practical one of making thou
ghts visible. Ruskin says that all letters are frightful things an
d to be endured only on occasion, that is to say, in places wh
ere the sense of the inscription is of more importance than e
xternal ornament. This is a sweeping statement, from which
we need not suffer unduly; yet it is doubtful whether there is
art in individual letters. Letters in combination may be satisf
The main purpose of letters is the practical one of making t
houghts visible. Ruskin says that all letters are frightful thi
The main purpose of letters is the practical one of ma
king thoughts visible. Ruskin says that all letters are fr

ITC GARAMOND 11 POINT SET MINUS ½ UNIT

BOOK, ITALIC, BOLD, BOLD ITALIC

abcdefghijklmnopqrstuvwxyz – 1 UNIT
abcdefghijklmnopqrstuvwxyz – ½ UNIT
abcdefghijklmnopqrstuvwxyz NORMAL

ABCDEFGHIJKLMNOPQRSTUVWXYZ 1234567890 abcdefghijklmnopqrstuvwxyz
ABCDEFGHIJKLMNOPQRSTUVWXYZ 1234567890 abcdefghijklmnopqrstuvwxyz
ABCDEFGHIJKLMNOPQRSTUVWXYZ 1234567890 abcdefghijklmnopqrstuvwxyz
ABCDEFGHIJKLMNOPQRSTUVWXYZ 1234567890 abcdefghijklmnopqrstuvwxyz

11/11

The main purpose of letters is the practical one of maki
ng thoughts visible. Ruskin says that all letters are frigh
tful things and to be endured only on occasion, that is t
o say, in places where the sense of the inscription is of
more importance than external ornament. This is a sw
eeping statement, from which we need not suffer und
uly; yet it is doubtful whether there is art in individual l
etters. Letters in combination may be satisfying and in
a well composed page even beautiful as a whole, but ar
t in letters consists rather in the art of arranging and co
mposing them in a pleasing and appropriate manner. T
he main purpose of letters is the practical one of makin
g thoughts visible. Ruskin says that all letters are frightf
ul things and to be endured only on occasion, that is to
say, in places where the sense of the inscription is of m
ore importance than external ornament. This is a swee
ping statement, from which we need not suffer unduly;
yet it is doubtful whether there is art in individual lett
ers. Letters in combination may be satisfying and in a w
The main purpose of letters is the practical one of ma
king thoughts visible. Ruskin says that all letters are f
The main purpose of letters is the practical one o
f making thoughts visible. Ruskin says that all let

11/12

The main purpose of letters is the practical one of maki
ng thoughts visible. Ruskin says that all letters are frigh
tful things and to be endured only on occasion, that is t
o say, in places where the sense of the inscription is of
more importance than external ornament. This is a sw
eeping statement, from which we need not suffer und
uly; yet it is doubtful whether there is art in individual l
etters. Letters in combination may be satisfying and in
a well composed page even beautiful as a whole, but ar
t in letters consists rather in the art of arranging and co
mposing them in a pleasing and appropriate manner. T
he main purpose of letters is the practical one of makin
g thoughts visible. Ruskin says that all letters are frightf
ul things and to be endured only on occasion, that is to
say, in places where the sense of the inscription is of m
ore importance than external ornament. This is a swee
ping statement, from which we need not suffer unduly;
yet it is doubtful whether there is art in individual lett
The main purpose of letters is the practical one of ma
king thoughts visible. Ruskin says that all letters are f
The main purpose of letters is the practical one o
f making thoughts visible. Ruskin says that all let

11/13

The main purpose of letters is the practical one of maki
ng thoughts visible. Ruskin says that all letters are frigh
tful things and to be endured only on occasion, that is t
o say, in places where the sense of the inscription is of
more importance than external ornament. This is a sw
eeping statement, from which we need not suffer und
uly; yet it is doubtful whether there is art in individual l
etters. Letters in combination may be satisfying and in
a well composed page even beautiful as a whole, but ar
t in letters consists rather in the art of arranging and co
mposing them in a pleasing and appropriate manner. T
he main purpose of letters is the practical one of makin
g thoughts visible. Ruskin says that all letters are frightf
ul things and to be endured only on occasion, that is to
say, in places where the sense of the inscription is of m
ore importance than external ornament. This is a swee
ping statement, from which we need not suffer unduly;
The main purpose of letters is the practical one of ma
king thoughts visible. Ruskin says that all letters are f
The main purpose of letters is the practical one o
f making thoughts visible. Ruskin says that all let

11/14

The main purpose of letters is the practical one of maki
ng thoughts visible. Ruskin says that all letters are frigh
tful things and to be endured only on occasion, that is t
o say, in places where the sense of the inscription is of
more importance than external ornament. This is a sw
eeping statement, from which we need not suffer und
uly; yet it is doubtful whether there is art in individual l
etters. Letters in combination may be satisfying and in
a well composed page even beautiful as a whole, but ar
t in letters consists rather in the art of arranging and co
mposing them in a pleasing and appropriate manner. T
he main purpose of letters is the practical one of makin
g thoughts visible. Ruskin says that all letters are frightf
ul things and to be endured only on occasion, that is to
say, in places where the sense of the inscription is of m
ore importance than external ornament. This is a swee
The main purpose of letters is the practical one of ma
king thoughts visible. Ruskin says that all letters are f
The main purpose of letters is the practical one o
f making thoughts visible. Ruskin says that all let

ITC GARAMOND 12 POINT SET MINUS ½ UNIT

BOOK, ITALIC, BOLD, BOLD ITALIC

abcdefghijklmnopqrstuvwxyz – 1 UNIT
abcdefghijklmnopqrstuvwxyz – ½ UNIT
abcdefghijklmnopqrstuvwxyz NORMAL

ABCDEFGHIJKLMNOPQRSTUVWXYZ 1234567890 abcdefghijklmnopqrstuvwxyz
ABCDEFGHIJKLMNOPQRSTUVWXYZ 1234567890 abcdefghijklmnopqrstuvwxyz
ABCDEFGHIJKLMNOPQRSTUVWXYZ 1234567890 abcdefghijklmnopqrstuvwxyz
ABCDEFGHIJKLMNOPQRSTUVWXYZ 1234567890 abcdefghijklmnopqrstuvwxyz

12/12

The main purpose of letters is the practical one of making thoughts visible. Ruskin says that all letters are frightful things and to be endured only on occa sion, that is to say, in places where the sense of the i nscription is of more importance than external or nament. This is a sweeping statement, from which we need not suffer unduly; yet it is doubtful wheth er there is art in individual letters. Letters in combi nation may be satisfying and in a well composed pa ge even beautiful as a whole, but art in letters consi sts rather in the art of arranging and composing the m in a pleasing and appropriate manner. The main purpose of letters is the practical one of making th oughts visible. Ruskin says that all letters are frightf ul things and to be endured only on occasion, that i
The main purpose of letters is the practical one of making thoughts visible. Ruskin says that all lett
The main purpose of letters is the practical o ne of making thoughts visible. Ruskin says th

12/13

The main purpose of letters is the practical one of making thoughts visible. Ruskin says that all letters are frightful things and to be endured only on occa sion, that is to say, in places where the sense of the i nscription is of more importance than external or nament. This is a sweeping statement, from which we need not suffer unduly; yet it is doubtful wheth er there is art in individual letters. Letters in combi nation may be satisfying and in a well composed pa ge even beautiful as a whole, but art in letters consi sts rather in the art of arranging and composing the m in a pleasing and appropriate manner. The main purpose of letters is the practical one of making th oughts visible. Ruskin says that all letters are frightf
The main purpose of letters is the practical one of making thoughts visible. Ruskin says that all lett
The main purpose of letters is the practical o ne of making thoughts visible. Ruskin says th

12/14

The main purpose of letters is the practical one of making thoughts visible. Ruskin says that all letters are frightful things and to be endured only on occa sion, that is to say, in places where the sense of the i nscription is of more importance than external or nament. This is a sweeping statement, from which we need not suffer unduly; yet it is doubtful wheth er there is art in individual letters. Letters in combi nation may be satisfying and in a well composed pa ge even beautiful as a whole, but art in letters consi sts rather in the art of arranging and composing the m in a pleasing and appropriate manner. The main purpose of letters is the practical one of making th oughts visible. Ruskin says that all letters are frightf ul things and to be endured only on occasion, that i
The main purpose of letters is the practical one of making thoughts visible. Ruskin says that all lett
The main purpose of letters is the practical o ne of making thoughts visible. Ruskin says th

12/15

The main purpose of letters is the practical one of making thoughts visible. Ruskin says that all letters are frightful things and to be endured only on occa sion, that is to say, in places where the sense of the i nscription is of more importance than external or nament. This is a sweeping statement, from which we need not suffer unduly; yet it is doubtful wheth er there is art in individual letters. Letters in combi nation may be satisfying and in a well composed pa ge even beautiful as a whole, but art in letters consi sts rather in the art of arranging and composing the m in a pleasing and appropriate manner. The main purpose of letters is the practical one of making th oughts visible. Ruskin says that all letters are frightf
The main purpose of letters is the practical one of making thoughts visible. Ruskin says that all lett
The main purpose of letters is the practical o ne of making thoughts visible. Ruskin says th

ITC GARAMOND 14 POINT SET MINUS ½ UNIT

BOOK, ITALIC, BOLD, BOLD ITALIC

abcdefghijklmnopqrstuvwxyz – 1 UNIT
abcdefghijklmnopqrstuvwxyz ½ UNIT
abcdefghijklmnopqrstuvwxyz NORMAL

ABCDEFGHIJKLMNOPQRSTUVWXYZ abcdefghijklmnopqrstuvwxyz
ABCDEFGHIJKLMNOPQRSTUVWXYZ abcdefghijklmnopqrstuvwxyz
ABCDEFGHIJKLMNOPQRSTUVWXYZ abcdefghijklmnopqrstuvwxyz
ABCDEFGHIJKLMNOPQRSTUVWXYZ abcdefghijklmnopqrstuvwxyz

14/14

The main purpose of letters is the practical one of making thoughts visible. Ruskin says that all letters are frightful things and to be endured only on occasion, that is to say, in places where the sense of the inscription is of more importance than external ornament. This is a sweeping statement, from which we need not suffer unduly; yet it is doubtful whether there is art in individual letters. Letters in combination may be satisfying and in a well composed page even beautiful as a whole, but art in letters consists rather in the art of arranging and composing them
The main purpose of letters is the practical one of making thoughts visible. Ruskin s
The main purpose of letters is the practical one of making thoughts visible. R

14/15

The main purpose of letters is the practical one of making thoughts visible. Ruskin says that all letters are frightful things and to be endured only on occasion, that is to say, in places where the sense of the inscription is of more importance than external ornament. This is a sweeping statement, from which we need not suffer unduly; yet it is doubtful whether there is art in individual letters. Letters in combination may be satisfying and in a well composed page even beautiful as a whole, but art in letters consists rather i
The main purpose of letters is the practical one of making thoughts visible. Ruskin s
The main purpose of letters is the practical one of making thoughts visible. R

14/16

The main purpose of letters is the practical one of making thoughts visible. Ruskin says that all letters are frightful things and to be endured only on occasion, that is to say, in places where the sense of the inscription is of more importance than external ornament. This is a sweeping statement, from which we need not suffer unduly; yet it is doubtful whether there is art in individual letters. Letters in combination may be satisfying and in a well composed page even beautiful as a whole, but art in letters consists rather in the art of arranging and composing them
The main purpose of letters is the practical one of making thoughts visible. Ruskin s
The main purpose of letters is the practical one of making thoughts visible. R

14/17

The main purpose of letters is the practical one of making thoughts visible. Ruskin says that all letters are frightful things and to be endured only on occasion, that is to say, in places where the sense of the inscription is of more importance than external ornament. This is a sweeping statement, from which we need not suffer unduly; yet it is doubtful whether there is art in individual letters. Letters in combination may be satisfying and in a well composed page even beautiful as a whole, but art in letters consists rather i
The main purpose of letters is the practical one of making thoughts visible. Ruskin s
The main purpose of letters is the practical one of making thoughts visible. R

GOUDY OLDSTYLE 6 & 7 POINT SET NORMAL

ROMAN, ITALIC, BOLD, EXTRA BOLD

ABCDEFGHIJKLMNOPQRSTUVWXYZ 1234567890 abcdefghijklmnopqrstuvwxyz

ABCDEFGHIJKLMNOPQRSTUVWXYZ 1234567890 abcdefghijklmnopqrstuvwxyz

ABCDEFGHIJKLMNOPQRSTUVWXYZ 1234567890 abcdefghijklmnopqrstuvwxyz

ABCDEFGHIJKLMNOPQRSTUVWXYZ 1234567890 abcdefghijklmnopqrstuvwxyz

6/6

The main purpose of letters is the practical one of making thoughts visible. Ruskin says that all letters
are frightful things and to be endured only on occasion, that is to say, in places where the sense of the i
nscription is of more importance than external ornament. This is a sweeping statement, from which
we need not suffer unduly; yet it is doubtful whether there is art in individual letters. Letters in combi
nation may be satisfying and in a well composed page even beautiful as a whole, but art in letters consi
sts rather in the art of arranging and composing them in a pleasing and appropriate manner. The main
purpose of letters is the practical one of making thoughts visible. Ruskin says that all letters are frightf
ul things and to be endured only on occasion, that is to say, in places where the sense of the inscription
is of more importance than external ornament. This is a sweeping statement, from which we need not
suffer unduly; yet it is doubtful whether there is art in individual letters. Letters in combination may b
e satisfying and in a well composed page even beautiful as a whole, but art in letters consists rather in t
he art of arranging and composing them in a pleasing and appropriate manner. The main purpose of le
tters is the practical one of making thoughts visible. Ruskin says that all letters are frightful things and
The main purpose of letters is the practical one of making thoughts visible. Ruskin says that all letters are frightf
ul things and to be endured only on occasion, that is to say, in places where the sense of the inscription is of more
The main purpose of letters is the practical one of making thoughts visible. Ruskin says that all lett
ers are frightful things and to be endured only on occasion, that is to say, in places where the sense o

6/7

The main purpose of letters is the practical one of making thoughts visible. Ruskin says that all letters
are frightful things and to be endured only on occasion, that is to say, in places where the sense of the i
nscription is of more importance than external ornament. This is a sweeping statement, from which
we need not suffer unduly; yet it is doubtful whether there is art in individual letters. Letters in combi
nation may be satisfying and in a well composed page even beautiful as a whole, but art in letters consi
sts rather in the art of arranging and composing them in a pleasing and appropriate manner. The main
purpose of letters is the practical one of making thoughts visible. Ruskin says that all letters are frightf
ul things and to be endured only on occasion, that is to say, in places where the sense of the inscription
is of more importance than external ornament. This is a sweeping statement, from which we need not
suffer unduly; yet it is doubtful whether there is art in individual letters. Letters in combination may b
e satisfying and in a well composed page even beautiful as a whole, but art in letters consists rather in t
The main purpose of letters is the practical one of making thoughts visible. Ruskin says that all letters are frightf
ul things and to be endured only on occasion, that is to say, in places where the sense of the inscription is of more
The main purpose of letters is the practical one of making thoughts visible. Ruskin says that all lett
ers are frightful things and to be endured only on occasion, that is to say, in places where the sense o

6/8

The main purpose of letters is the practical one of making thoughts visible. Ruskin says that all letters
are frightful things and to be endured only on occasion, that is to say, in places where the sense of the i
nscription is of more importance than external ornament. This is a sweeping statement, from which
we need not suffer unduly; yet it is doubtful whether there is art in individual letters. Letters in combi
nation may be satisfying and in a well composed page even beautiful as a whole, but art in letters consi
sts rather in the art of arranging and composing them in a pleasing and appropriate manner. The main
purpose of letters is the practical one of making thoughts visible. Ruskin says that all letters are frightf
ul things and to be endured only on occasion, that is to say, in places where the sense of the inscription
is of more importance than external ornament. This is a sweeping statement, from which we need not
The main purpose of letters is the practical one of making thoughts visible. Ruskin says that all letters are frightf
ul things and to be endured only on occasion, that is to say, in places where the sense of the inscription is of more
The main purpose of letters is the practical one of making thoughts visible. Ruskin says that all lett
ers are frightful things and to be endured only on occasion, that is to say, in places where the sense o

6/9

The main purpose of letters is the practical one of making thoughts visible. Ruskin says that all letters
are frightful things and to be endured only on occasion, that is to say, in places where the sense of the i
nscription is of more importance than external ornament. This is a sweeping statement, from which
we need not suffer unduly; yet it is doubtful whether there is art in individual letters. Letters in combi
nation may be satisfying and in a well composed page even beautiful as a whole, but art in letters consi
sts rather in the art of arranging and composing them in a pleasing and appropriate manner. The main
purpose of letters is the practical one of making thoughts visible. Ruskin says that all letters are frightf
ul things and to be endured only on occasion, that is to say, in places where the sense of the inscription
The main purpose of letters is the practical one of making thoughts visible. Ruskin says that all letters are frightf
ul things and to be endured only on occasion, that is to say, in places where the sense of the inscription is of more
The main purpose of letters is the practical one of making thoughts visible. Ruskin says that all lett
ers are frightful things and to be endured only on occasion, that is to say, in places where the sense o

---

ABCDEFGHIJKLMNOPQRSTUVWXYZ 1234567890 abcdefghijklmnopqrstuvwxyz

ABCDEFGHIJKLMNOPQRSTUVWXYZ 1234567890 abcdefghijklmnopqrstuvwxyz

ABCDEFGHIJKLMNOPQRSTUVWXYZ 1234567890 abcdefghijklmnopqrstuvwxyz

ABCDEFGHIJKLMNOPQRSTUVWXYZ 1234567890 abcdefghijklmnopqrstuvwxyz

7/7

The main purpose of letters is the practical one of making thoughts visible. Ruskin says
that all letters are frightful things and to be endured only on occasion, that is to say, in p
laces where the sense of the inscription is of more importance than external ornament.
This is a sweeping statement, from which we need not suffer unduly; yet it is doubtful w
hether there is art in individual letters. Letters in combination may be satisfying and in
a well composed page even beautiful as a whole, but art in letters consists rather in the a
rt of arranging and composing them in a pleasing and appropriate manner. The main pu
rpose of letters is the practical one of making thoughts visible. Ruskin says that all letter
s are frightful things and to be endured only on occasion, that is to say, in places where t
he sense of the inscription is of more importance than external ornament. This is a swe
eping statement, from which we need not suffer unduly; yet it is doubtful whether there
The main purpose of letters is the practical one of making thoughts visible. Ruskin says that all l
etters are frightful things and to be endured only on occasion, that is to say, in places where the s
The main purpose of letters is the practical one of making thoughts visible. Ruskin sa
ys that all letters are frightful things and to be endured only on occasion, that is to say

7/8

The main purpose of letters is the practical one of making thoughts visible. Ruskin says
that all letters are frightful things and to be endured only on occasion, that is to say, in p
laces where the sense of the inscription is of more importance than external ornament.
This is a sweeping statement, from which we need not suffer unduly; yet it is doubtful w
hether there is art in individual letters. Letters in combination may be satisfying and in
a well composed page even beautiful as a whole, but art in letters consists rather in the a
rt of arranging and composing them in a pleasing and appropriate manner. The main pu
rpose of letters is the practical one of making thoughts visible. Ruskin says that all letter
s are frightful things and to be endured only on occasion, that is to say, in places where t
he sense of the inscription is of more importance than external ornament. This is a swe
The main purpose of letters is the practical one of making thoughts visible. Ruskin says that all l
etters are frightful things and to be endured only on occasion, that is to say, in places where the s
The main purpose of letters is the practical one of making thoughts visible. Ruskin sa
ys that all letters are frightful things and to be endured only on occasion, that is to say

7/9

The main purpose of letters is the practical one of making thoughts visible. Ruskin says
that all letters are frightful things and to be endured only on occasion, that is to say, in p
laces where the sense of the inscription is of more importance than external ornament.
This is a sweeping statement, from which we need not suffer unduly; yet it is doubtful w
hether there is art in individual letters. Letters in combination may be satisfying and in
a well composed page even beautiful as a whole, but art in letters consists rather in the a
rt of arranging and composing them in a pleasing and appropriate manner. The main pu
rpose of letters is the practical one of making thoughts visible. Ruskin says that all letter
s are frightful things and to be endured only on occasion, that is to say, in places where t
he sense of the inscription is of more importance than external ornament. This is a swe
The main purpose of letters is the practical one of making thoughts visible. Ruskin says that all l
etters are frightful things and to be endured only on occasion, that is to say, in places where the s
The main purpose of letters is the practical one of making thoughts visible. Ruskin sa
ys that all letters are frightful things and to be endured only on occasion, that is to say

7/10

The main purpose of letters is the practical one of making thoughts visible. Ruskin says
that all letters are frightful things and to be endured only on occasion, that is to say, in p
laces where the sense of the inscription is of more importance than external ornament.
This is a sweeping statement, from which we need not suffer unduly; yet it is doubtful w
hether there is art in individual letters. Letters in combination may be satisfying and in
a well composed page even beautiful as a whole, but art in letters consists rather in the a
rt of arranging and composing them in a pleasing and appropriate manner. The main pu
rpose of letters is the practical one of making thoughts visible. Ruskin says that all letter
s are frightful things and to be endured only on occasion, that is to say, in places where t
The main purpose of letters is the practical one of making thoughts visible. Ruskin says that all l
etters are frightful things and to be endured only on occasion, that is to say, in places where the s
The main purpose of letters is the practical one of making thoughts visible. Ruskin sa
ys that all letters are frightful things and to be endured only on occasion, that is to say

GOUDY OLDSTYLE 8 & 9 POINT SET NORMAL

ROMAN, ITALIC, BOLD, EXTRA BOLD

ABCDEFGHIJKLMNOPQRSTUVWXYZ 1234567890 abcdefghijklmnopqrstuvwxyz

ABCDEFGHIJKLMNOPQRSTUVWXYZ 1234567890 abcdefghijklmnopqrstuvwxyz

ABCDEFGHIJKLMNOPQRSTUVWXYZ 1234567890 abcdefghijklmnopqrstuvwxyz

ABCDEFGHIJKLMNOPQRSTUVWXYZ 1234567890 abcdefghijklmnopqrstuvwxyz

8/8

The main purpose of letters is the practical one of making thoughts visible. Ruskin says that all letters are frightful things and to be endured only on occa sion, that is to say, in places where the sense of the inscription is of more imp ortance than external ornament. This is a sweeping statement, from which we need not suffer unduly; yet it is doubtful whether there is art in individual letters. Letters in combination may be satisfying and in a well composed pag e even beautiful as a whole, but art in letters consists rather in the art of arra nging and composing them in a pleasing and appropriate manner. The main purpose of letters is the practical one of making thoughts visible. Ruskin says *The main purpose of letters is the practical one of making thoughts visible. Ruskin s ays that all letters are frightful things and to be endured only on occasion, that is to s* **The main purpose of letters is the practical one of making thoughts visible. Ruskin says that all letters are frightful things and to be endured only on o**

8/9

The main purpose of letters is the practical one of making thoughts visible. Ruskin says that all letters are frightful things and to be endured only on occa sion, that is to say, in places where the sense of the inscription is of more imp ortance than external ornament. This is a sweeping statement, from which we need not suffer unduly; yet it is doubtful whether there is art in individual letters. Letters in combination may be satisfying and in a well composed pag e even beautiful as a whole, but art in letters consists rather in the art of arra nging and composing them in a pleasing and appropriate manner. The main *The main purpose of letters is the practical one of making thoughts visible. Ruskin s ays that all letters are frightful things and to be endured only on occasion, that is to s* **The main purpose of letters is the practical one of making thoughts visible. Ruskin says that all letters are frightful things and to be endured only on o**

8/10

The main purpose of letters is the practical one of making thoughts visible. Ruskin says that all letters are frightful things and to be endured only on occa sion, that is to say, in places where the sense of the inscription is of more imp ortance than external ornament. This is a sweeping statement, from which we need not suffer unduly; yet it is doubtful whether there is art in individual letters. Letters in combination may be satisfying and in a well composed pag e even beautiful as a whole, but art in letters consists rather in the art of arra *The main purpose of letters is the practical one of making thoughts visible. Ruskin s ays that all letters are frightful things and to be endured only on occasion, that is to s* **The main purpose of letters is the practical one of making thoughts visible. Ruskin says that all letters are frightful things and to be endured only on o**

8/11

The main purpose of letters is the practical one of making thoughts visible. Ruskin says that all letters are frightful things and to be endured only on occa sion, that is to say, in places where the sense of the inscription is of more imp ortance than external ornament. This is a sweeping statement, from which we need not suffer unduly; yet it is doubtful whether there is art in individual letters. Letters in combination may be satisfying and in a well composed pag e even beautiful as a whole, but art in letters consists rather in the art of arra *The main purpose of letters is the practical one of making thoughts visible. Ruskin s ays that all letters are frightful things and to be endured only on occasion, that is to s* **The main purpose of letters is the practical one of making thoughts visible. Ruskin says that all letters are frightful things and to be endured only on o**

ABCDEFGHIJKLMNOPQRSTUVWXYZ 1234567890 abcdefghijklmnopqrstuvwxyz

ABCDEFGHIJKLMNOPQRSTUVWXYZ 1234567890 abcdefghijklmnopqrstuvwxyz

ABCDEFGHIJKLMNOPQRSTUVWXYZ 1234567890 abcdefghijklmnopqrstuvwxyz

ABCDEFGHIJKLMNOPQRSTUVWXYZ 1234567890 abcdefghijklmnopqrstuvwxyz

9/9

The main purpose of letters is the practical one of making thoughts visible. Ruskin says that all letters are frightful things and to be end ured only on occasion, that is to say, in places where the sense of the inscription is of more importance than external ornament. This is a sweeping statement, from which we need not suffer unduly; yet it is doubtful whether there is art in individual letters. Letters in combin ation may be satisfying and in a well composed page even beautiful a s a whole, but art in letters consists rather in the art of arranging and *The main purpose of letters is the practical one of making thoughts visible. Ruskin says that all letters are frightful things and to be endured only on oc* **The main purpose of letters is the practical one of making thought s visible. Ruskin says that all letters are frightful things and to be e**

9/10

The main purpose of letters is the practical one of making thoughts visible. Ruskin says that all letters are frightful things and to be end ured only on occasion, that is to say, in places where the sense of the inscription is of more importance than external ornament. This is a sweeping statement, from which we need not suffer unduly; yet it is doubtful whether there is art in individual letters. Letters in combin ation may be satisfying and in a well composed page even beautiful a *The main purpose of letters is the practical one of making thoughts visible. Ruskin says that all letters are frightful things and to be endured only on oc* **The main purpose of letters is the practical one of making thought s visible. Ruskin says that all letters are frightful things and to be e**

9/11

The main purpose of letters is the practical one of making thoughts visible. Ruskin says that all letters are frightful things and to be end ured only on occasion, that is to say, in places where the sense of the inscription is of more importance than external ornament. This is a sweeping statement, from which we need not suffer unduly; yet it is doubtful whether there is art in individual letters. Letters in combin ation may be satisfying and in a well composed page even beautiful a *The main purpose of letters is the practical one of making thoughts visible. Ruskin says that all letters are frightful things and to be endured only on oc* **The main purpose of letters is the practical one of making thought s visible. Ruskin says that all letters are frightful things and to be e**

9/12

The main purpose of letters is the practical one of making thoughts visible. Ruskin says that all letters are frightful things and to be end ured only on occasion, that is to say, in places where the sense of the inscription is of more importance than external ornament. This is a sweeping statement, from which we need not suffer unduly; yet it is doubtful whether there is art in individual letters. Letters in combin ation may be satisfying and in a well composed page even beautiful a *The main purpose of letters is the practical one of making thoughts visible. Ruskin says that all letters are frightful things and to be endured only on oc* **The main purpose of letters is the practical one of making thought s visible. Ruskin says that all letters are frightful things and to be e**

GOUDY OLDSTYLE 10 POINT SET MINUS ½ UNIT

ROMAN, ITALIC, BOLD, EXTRA BOLD

abcdefghijklmnopqrstuvwxyz – 1 UNIT
abcdefghijklmnopqrstuvwxyz – ½ UNIT
abcdefghijklmnopqrstuvwxyz NORMAL

ABCDEFGHIJKLMNOPQRSTUVWXYZ 1234567890 abcdefghijklmnopqrstuvwxyz
ABCDEFGHIJKLMNOPQRSTUVWXYZ 1234567890 abcdefghijklmnopqrstuvwxyz
ABCDEFGHIJKLMNOPQRSTUVWXYZ 1234567890 abcdefghijklmnopqrstuvwxyz
ABCDEFGHIJKLMNOPQRSTUVWXYZ 1234567890 abcdefghijklmnopqrstuvwxyz

10/10

The main purpose of letters is the practical one of making thoug hts visible. Ruskin says that all letters are frightful things and to be endured only on occasion, that is to say, in places where the s ense of the inscription is of more importance than external orna ment. This is a sweeping statement, from which we need not suf fer unduly; yet it is doubtful whether there is art in individual let ters. Letters in combination may be satisfying and in a well com posed page even beautiful as a whole, but art in letters consists ra ther in the art of arranging and composing them in a pleasing an d appropriate manner. The main purpose of letters is the practic al one of making thoughts visible. Ruskin says that all letters are frightful things and to be endured only on occasion, that is to sa y, in places where the sense of the inscription is of more importa nce than external ornament. This is a sweeping statement, fro m which we need not suffer unduly; yet it is doubtful whether th ere is art in individual letters. Letters in combination may be sat isfying and in a well composed page even beautiful as a whole, b ut art in letters consists rather in the art of arranging and compos ing them in a pleasing and appropriate manner. The main purpo se of letters is the practical one of making thoughts visible. Rus kin says that all letters are frightful things and to be endured only on occasion, that is to say, in places where the sense of the inscri
The main purpose of letters is the practical one of making thoughts visi ble. Ruskin says that all letters are frightful things and to be endured on
The main purpose of letters is the practical one of making tho ughts visible. Ruskin says that all letters are frightful things an

10/11

The main purpose of letters is the practical one of making thoug hts visible. Ruskin says that all letters are frightful things and to be endured only on occasion, that is to say, in places where the s ense of the inscription is of more importance than external orna ment. This is a sweeping statement, from which we need not suf fer unduly; yet it is doubtful whether there is art in individual let ters. Letters in combination may be satisfying and in a well com posed page even beautiful as a whole, but art in letters consists ra ther in the art of arranging and composing them in a pleasing an d appropriate manner. The main purpose of letters is the practic al one of making thoughts visible. Ruskin says that all letters are frightful things and to be endured only on occasion, that is to sa y, in places where the sense of the inscription is of more importa nce than external ornament. This is a sweeping statement, fro m which we need not suffer unduly; yet it is doubtful whether th ere is art in individual letters. Letters in combination may be sat isfying and in a well composed page even beautiful as a whole, b ut art in letters consists rather in the art of arranging and compos ing them in a pleasing and appropriate manner. The main purpo se of letters is the practical one of making thoughts visible. Rusk
The main purpose of letters is the practical one of making thoughts visi ble. Ruskin says that all letters are frightful things and to be endured on
The main purpose of letters is the practical one of making tho ughts visible. Ruskin says that all letters are frightful things an

10/12

The main purpose of letters is the practical one of making thoug hts visible. Ruskin says that all letters are frightful things and to be endured only on occasion, that is to say, in places where the s ense of the inscription is of more importance than external orna ment. This is a sweeping statement, from which we need not suf fer unduly; yet it is doubtful whether there is art in individual let ters. Letters in combination may be satisfying and in a well com posed page even beautiful as a whole, but art in letters consists ra ther in the art of arranging and composing them in a pleasing an d appropriate manner. The main purpose of letters is the practic al one of making thoughts visible. Ruskin says that all letters are frightful things and to be endured only on occasion, that is to sa y, in places where the sense of the inscription is of more importa nce than external ornament. This is a sweeping statement, fro m which we need not suffer unduly; yet it is doubtful whether th ere is art in individual letters. Letters in combination may be sat isfying and in a well composed page even beautiful as a whole, b ut art in letters consists rather in the art of arranging and compos
The main purpose of letters is the practical one of making thoughts visi ble. Ruskin says that all letters are frightful things and to be endured on
The main purpose of letters is the practical one of making tho ughts visible. Ruskin says that all letters are frightful things an

10/13

The main purpose of letters is the practical one of making thoug hts visible. Ruskin says that all letters are frightful things and to be endured only on occasion, that is to say, in places where the s ense of the inscription is of more importance than external orna ment. This is a sweeping statement, from which we need not suf fer unduly; yet it is doubtful whether there is art in individual let ters. Letters in combination may be satisfying and in a well com posed page even beautiful as a whole, but art in letters consists ra ther in the art of arranging and composing them in a pleasing an d appropriate manner. The main purpose of letters is the practic al one of making thoughts visible. Ruskin says that all letters are frightful things and to be endured only on occasion, that is to sa y, in places where the sense of the inscription is of more importa nce than external ornament. This is a sweeping statement, fro m which we need not suffer unduly; yet it is doubtful whether th ere is art in individual letters. Letters in combination may be sat isfying and in a well composed page even beautiful as a whole, b
The main purpose of letters is the practical one of making thoughts visi ble. Ruskin says that all letters are frightful things and to be endured on
The main purpose of letters is the practical one of making tho ughts visible. Ruskin says that all letters are frightful things an

GOUDY OLDSTYLE 11 POINT SET MINUS ½ UNIT

ROMAN, ITALIC, BOLD, EXTRA BOLD

abcdefghijklmnopqrstuvwxyz – 1 UNIT
abcdefghijklmnopqrstuvwxyz – ½ UNIT
abcdefghijklmnopqrstuvwxyz NORMAL

ABCDEFGHIJKLMNOPQRSTUVWXYZ 1234567890 abcdefghijklmnopqrstuvwxyz
ABCDEFGHIJKLMNOPQRSTUVWXYZ 1234567890 abcdefghijklmnopqrstuvwxyz
ABCDEFGHIJKLMNOPQRSTUVWXYZ 1234567890 abcdefghijklmnopqrstuvwxyz
ABCDEFGHIJKLMNOPQRSTUVWXYZ 1234567890 abcdefghijklmnopqrstuvwxyz

11/11

The main purpose of letters is the practical one of making thoughts visible. Ruskin says that all letters are frightful th ings and to be endured only on occasion, that is to say, in places where the sense of the inscription is of more import ance than external ornament. This is a sweeping stateme nt, from which we need not suffer unduly; yet it is doubtfu l whether there is art in individual letters. Letters in comb ination may be satisfying and in a well composed page eve n beautiful as a whole, but art in letters consists rather in t he art of arranging and composing them in a pleasing and appropriate manner. The main purpose of letters is the pra ctical one of making thoughts visible. Ruskin says that all letters are frightful things and to be endured only on occas ion, that is to say, in places where the sense of the inscripti on is of more importance than external ornament. This is a sweeping statement, from which we need not suffer und uly; yet it is doubtful whether there is art in individual lett ers. Letters in combination may be satisfying and in a well composed page even beautiful as a whole, but art in letters
The main purpose of letters is the practical one of making thoug hts visible. Ruskin says that all letters are frightful things and to
The main purpose of letters is the practical one of makin g thoughts visible. Ruskin says that all letters are frightf

11/12

The main purpose of letters is the practical one of making thoughts visible. Ruskin says that all letters are frightful th ings and to be endured only on occasion, that is to say, in places where the sense of the inscription is of more import ance than external ornament. This is a sweeping stateme nt, from which we need not suffer unduly; yet it is doubtfu l whether there is art in individual letters. Letters in comb ination may be satisfying and in a well composed page eve n beautiful as a whole, but art in letters consists rather in t he art of arranging and composing them in a pleasing and appropriate manner. The main purpose of letters is the pra ctical one of making thoughts visible. Ruskin says that all letters are frightful things and to be endured only on occas ion, that is to say, in places where the sense of the inscripti on is of more importance than external ornament. This is a sweeping statement, from which we need not suffer und uly; yet it is doubtful whether there is art in individual lett ers. Letters in combination may be satisfying and in a well
The main purpose of letters is the practical one of making thoug hts visible. Ruskin says that all letters are frightful things and to
The main purpose of letters is the practical one of makin g thoughts visible. Ruskin says that all letters are frightf

11/13

The main purpose of letters is the practical one of making thoughts visible. Ruskin says that all letters are frightful th ings and to be endured only on occasion, that is to say, in places where the sense of the inscription is of more import ance than external ornament. This is a sweeping stateme nt, from which we need not suffer unduly; yet it is doubtfu l whether there is art in individual letters. Letters in comb ination may be satisfying and in a well composed page eve n beautiful as a whole, but art in letters consists rather in t he art of arranging and composing them in a pleasing and appropriate manner. The main purpose of letters is the pra ctical one of making thoughts visible. Ruskin says that all letters are frightful things and to be endured only on occas ion, that is to say, in places where the sense of the inscripti on is of more importance than external ornament. This is a sweeping statement, from which we need not suffer und uly; yet it is doubtful whether there is art in individual lett
The main purpose of letters is the practical one of making thoug hts visible. Ruskin says that all letters are frightful things and to
The main purpose of letters is the practical one of makin g thoughts visible. Ruskin says that all letters are frightf

11/14

The main purpose of letters is the practical one of making thoughts visible. Ruskin says that all letters are frightful th ings and to be endured only on occasion, that is to say, in places where the sense of the inscription is of more import ance than external ornament. This is a sweeping stateme nt, from which we need not suffer unduly; yet it is doubtfu l whether there is art in individual letters. Letters in comb ination may be satisfying and in a well composed page eve n beautiful as a whole, but art in letters consists rather in t he art of arranging and composing them in a pleasing and appropriate manner. The main purpose of letters is the pra ctical one of making thoughts visible. Ruskin says that all letters are frightful things and to be endured only on occas ion, that is to say, in places where the sense of the inscripti on is of more importance than external ornament. This is a sweeping statement, from which we need not suffer und
The main purpose of letters is the practical one of making thoug hts visible. Ruskin says that all letters are frightful things and to
The main purpose of letters is the practical one of makin g thoughts visible. Ruskin says that all letters are frightf

GOUDY OLDSTYLE 12 POINT SET MINUS ½ UNIT

ROMAN, ITALIC, BOLD, EXTRA BOLD

abcdefghijklmnopqrstuvwxyz – 1 UNIT
abcdefghijklmnopqrstuvwxyz – ½ UNIT
abcdefghijklmnopqrstuvwxyz NORMAL

ABCDEFGHIJKLMNOPQRSTUVWXYZ 1234567890 abcdefghijklmnopqrstuvwxyz
ABCDEFGHIJKLMNOPQRSTUVWXYZ 1234567890 abcdefghijklmnopqrstuvwxyz
ABCDEFGHIJKLMNOPQRSTUVWXYZ 1234567890 abcdefghijklmnopqrstuvwxyz
ABCDEFGHIJKLMNOPQRSTUVWXYZ 1234567890 abcdefghijklmnopqrstuvwxyz

12/12

The main purpose of letters is the practical one of mak ing thoughts visible. Ruskin says that all letters are frig htful things and to be endured only on occasion, that i s to say, in places where the sense of the inscription is of more importance than external ornament. This is a sweeping statement, from which we need not suffer u nduly; yet it is doubtful whether there is art in individ ual letters. Letters in combination may be satisfying a nd in a well composed page even beautiful as a whole, but art in letters consists rather in the art of arranging and composing them in a pleasing and appropriate ma nner. The main purpose of letters is the practical one of making thoughts visible. Ruskin says that all letters are frightful things and to be endured only on occasio n, that is to say, in places where the sense of the inscri
The main purpose of letters is the practical one of making th oughts visible. Ruskin says that all letters are frightful things
The main purpose of letters is the practical one of m aking thoughts visible. Ruskin says that all letters ar

12/13

The main purpose of letters is the practical one of mak ing thoughts visible. Ruskin says that all letters are frig htful things and to be endured only on occasion, that i s to say, in places where the sense of the inscription is of more importance than external ornament. This is a sweeping statement, from which we need not suffer u nduly; yet it is doubtful whether there is art in individ ual letters. Letters in combination may be satisfying a nd in a well composed page even beautiful as a whole, but art in letters consists rather in the art of arranging and composing them in a pleasing and appropriate ma nner. The main purpose of letters is the practical one of making thoughts visible. Ruskin says that all letters are frightful things and to be endured only on occasio
The main purpose of letters is the practical one of making th oughts visible. Ruskin says that all letters are frightful things
The main purpose of letters is the practical one of m aking thoughts visible. Ruskin says that all letters ar

12/14

The main purpose of letters is the practical one of mak ing thoughts visible. Ruskin says that all letters are frig htful things and to be endured only on occasion, that i s to say, in places where the sense of the inscription is of more importance than external ornament. This is a sweeping statement, from which we need not suffer u nduly; yet it is doubtful whether there is art in individ ual letters. Letters in combination may be satisfying a nd in a well composed page even beautiful as a whole, but art in letters consists rather in the art of arranging and composing them in a pleasing and appropriate ma nner. The main purpose of letters is the practical one of making thoughts visible. Ruskin says that all letters are frightful things and to be endured only on occasio n, that is to say, in places where the sense of the inscri
The main purpose of letters is the practical one of making th oughts visible. Ruskin says that all letters are frightful things
The main purpose of letters is the practical one of m aking thoughts visible. Ruskin says that all letters ar

12/15

The main purpose of letters is the practical one of mak ing thoughts visible. Ruskin says that all letters are frig htful things and to be endured only on occasion, that i s to say, in places where the sense of the inscription is of more importance than external ornament. This is a sweeping statement, from which we need not suffer u nduly; yet it is doubtful whether there is art in individ ual letters. Letters in combination may be satisfying a nd in a well composed page even beautiful as a whole, but art in letters consists rather in the art of arranging and composing them in a pleasing and appropriate ma nner. The main purpose of letters is the practical one of making thoughts visible. Ruskin says that all letters are frightful things and to be endured only on occasio
The main purpose of letters is the practical one of making th oughts visible. Ruskin says that all letters are frightful things
The main purpose of letters is the practical one of m aking thoughts visible. Ruskin says that all letters ar

GOUDY OLDSTYLE 14 POINT SET MINUS ½ UNIT

ROMAN, ITALIC, BOLD, EXTRA BOLD

abcdefghijklmnopqrstuvwxyz – 1 UNIT
abcdefghijklmnopqrstuvwxyz – ½ UNIT
abcdefghijklmnopqrstuvwxyz NORMAL

ABCDEFGHIJKLMNOPQRSTUVWXYZ abcdefghijklmnopqrstuvwxyz
ABCDEFGHIJKLMNOPQRSTUVWXYZ abcdefghijklmnopqrstuvwxyz
ABCDEFGHIJKLMNOPQRSTUVWXYZ abcdefghijklmnopqrstuvwxyz
ABCDEFGHIJKLMNOPQRSTUVWXYZ abcdefghijklmnopqrstuvwxyz

14/14

The main purpose of letters is the practical on e of making thoughts visible. Ruskin says that all letters are frightful things and to be endure d only on occasion, that is to say, in places wh ere the sense of the inscription is of more imp ortance than external ornament. This is a swe eping statement, from which we need not suff er unduly; yet it is doubtful whether there is ar t in individual letters. Letters in combination may be satisfying and in a well composed page even beautiful as a whole, but art in letters co nsists rather in the art of arranging and compo sing them in a pleasing and appropriate mann
The main purpose of letters is the practical one of making thoughts visible. Ruskin says that all letter
The main purpose of letters is the practical o ne of making thoughts visible. Ruskin says

14/15

The main purpose of letters is the practical on e of making thoughts visible. Ruskin says that all letters are frightful things and to be endure d only on occasion, that is to say, in places wh ere the sense of the inscription is of more imp ortance than external ornament. This is a swe eping statement, from which we need not suff er unduly; yet it is doubtful whether there is ar t in individual letters. Letters in combination may be satisfying and in a well composed page even beautiful as a whole, but art in letters co nsists rather in the art of arranging and compo
The main purpose of letters is the practical one of making thoughts visible. Ruskin says that all letter
The main purpose of letters is the practical o ne of making thoughts visible. Ruskin says

14/16

The main purpose of letters is the practical on e of making thoughts visible. Ruskin says that all letters are frightful things and to be endure d only on occasion, that is to say, in places wh ere the sense of the inscription is of more imp ortance than external ornament. This is a swe eping statement, from which we need not suff er unduly; yet it is doubtful whether there is ar t in individual letters. Letters in combination may be satisfying and in a well composed page even beautiful as a whole, but art in letters co nsists rather in the art of arranging and compo sing them in a pleasing and appropriate mann
The main purpose of letters is the practical one of making thoughts visible. Ruskin says that all letter
The main purpose of letters is the practical o ne of making thoughts visible. Ruskin says

14/17

The main purpose of letters is the practical on e of making thoughts visible. Ruskin says that all letters are frightful things and to be endure d only on occasion, that is to say, in places wh ere the sense of the inscription is of more imp ortance than external ornament. This is a swe eping statement, from which we need not suff er unduly; yet it is doubtful whether there is ar t in individual letters. Letters in combination may be satisfying and in a well composed page even beautiful as a whole, but art in letters co nsists rather in the art of arranging and compo
The main purpose of letters is the practical one of making thoughts visible. Ruskin says that all letter
The main purpose of letters is the practical o ne of making thoughts visible. Ruskin says

HELVETICA 6 & 7 POINT SET NORMAL

LIGHT, ITALIC, BOLD, BOLD ITALIC

ABCDEFGHIJKLMNOPQRSTUVWXYZ 1234567890 abcdefghijklmnopqrstuvwxyz

ABCDEFGHIJKLMNOPQRSTUVWXYZ 1234567890 abcdefghijklmnopqrstuvwxyz

ABCDEFGHIJKLMNOPQRSTUVWXYZ 1234567890 abcdefghijklmnopqrstuvwxyz

ABCDEFGHIJKLMNOPQRSTUVWXYZ 1234567890 abcdefghijklmnopqrstuvwxyz

6/6

The main purpose of letters is the practical one of making thoughts visible. Ruskin says that al
l letters are frightful things and to be endured only on occasion, that is to say, in places where t
he sense of the inscription is of more importance than external ornament. This is a sweeping
statement, from which we need not suffer unduly; yet it is doubtful whether there is art in indivi
dual letters. Letters in combination may be satisfying and in a well composed page even bea
utiful as a whole, but art in letters consists rather in the art of arranging and composing them i
n a pleasing and appropriate manner. The main purpose of letters is the practical one of maki
ng thoughts visible. Ruskin says that all letters are frightful things and to be endured only on o
ccasion, that is to say, in places where the sense of the inscription is of more importance than
external ornament. This is a sweeping statement, from which we need not suffer unduly; yet it
is doubtful whether there is art in individual letters. Letters in combination may be satisfying a
nd in a well composed page even beautiful as a whole, but art in letters consists rather in the
art of arranging and composing them in a pleasing and appropriate manner. The main purpo
The main purpose of letters is the practical one of making thoughts visible. Ruskin says that al
l letters are frightful things and to be endured only on occasion, that is to say, in places where
The main purpose of letters is the practical one of making thoughts visible. Ruskin say
s that all letters are frightful things and to be endured only on occasion, that is to say, in

6/7

The main purpose of letters is the practical one of making thoughts visible. Ruskin says that al
l letters are frightful things and to be endured only on occasion, that is to say, in places where t
he sense of the inscription is of more importance than external ornament. This is a sweeping
statement, from which we need not suffer unduly; yet it is doubtful whether there is art in indivi
dual letters. Letters in combination may be satisfying and in a well composed page even bea
utiful as a whole, but art in letters consists rather in the art of arranging and composing them i
n a pleasing and appropriate manner. The main purpose of letters is the practical one of maki
ng thoughts visible. Ruskin says that all letters are frightful things and to be endured only on o
ccasion, that is to say, in places where the sense of the inscription is of more importance than
external ornament. This is a sweeping statement, from which we need not suffer unduly; yet it
is doubtful whether there is art in individual letters. Letters in combination may be satisfying a
The main purpose of letters is the practical one of making thoughts visible. Ruskin says that al
l letters are frightful things and to be endured only on occasion, that is to say, in places where
The main purpose of letters is the practical one of making thoughts visible. Ruskin say
s that all letters are frightful things and to be endured only on occasion, that is to say, in

6/8

The main purpose of letters is the practical one of making thoughts visible. Ruskin says that al
l letters are frightful things and to be endured only on occasion, that is to say, in places where t
he sense of the inscription is of more importance than external ornament. This is a sweeping
statement, from which we need not suffer unduly; yet it is doubtful whether there is art in indivi
dual letters. Letters in combination may be satisfying and in a well composed page even bea
utiful as a whole, but art in letters consists rather in the art of arranging and composing them i
n a pleasing and appropriate manner. The main purpose of letters is the practical one of maki
ng thoughts visible. Ruskin says that all letters are frightful things and to be endured only on o
ccasion, that is to say, in places where the sense of the inscription is of more importance than
The main purpose of letters is the practical one of making thoughts visible. Ruskin says that al
l letters are frightful things and to be endured only on occasion, that is to say, in places where
The main purpose of letters is the practical one of making thoughts visible. Ruskin say
s that all letters are frightful things and to be endured only on occasion, that is to say, in

6/9

The main purpose of letters is the practical one of making thoughts visible. Ruskin says that al
l letters are frightful things and to be endured only on occasion, that is to say, in places where t
he sense of the inscription is of more importance than external ornament. This is a sweeping
statement, from which we need not suffer unduly; yet it is doubtful whether there is art in indivi
dual letters. Letters in combination may be satisfying and in a well composed page even bea
utiful as a whole, but art in letters consists rather in the art of arranging and composing them i
n a pleasing and appropriate manner. The main purpose of letters is the practical one of maki
ng thoughts visible. Ruskin says that all letters are frightful things and to be endured only on o
The main purpose of letters is the practical one of making thoughts visible. Ruskin says that al
l letters are frightful things and to be endured only on occasion, that is to say, in places where
The main purpose of letters is the practical one of making thoughts visible. Ruskin say
s that all letters are frightful things and to be endured only on occasion, that is to say, in

---

ABCDEFGHIJKLMNOPQRSTUVWXYZ 1234567890 abcdefghijklmnopqrstuvwxyz

ABCDEFGHIJKLMNOPQRSTUVWXYZ 1234567890 abcdefghijklmnopqrstuvwxyz

ABCDEFGHIJKLMNOPQRSTUVWXYZ 1234567890 abcdefghijklmnopqrstuvwxyz

ABCDEFGHIJKLMNOPQRSTUVWXYZ 1234567890 abcdefghijklmnopqrstuvwxyz

7/7

The main purpose of letters is the practical one of making thoughts visible. Rusk
in says that all letters are frightful things and to be endured only on occasion, tha
t is to say, in places where the sense of the inscription is of more importance tha
n external ornament. This is a sweeping statement, from which we need not suff
er unduly; yet it is doubtful whether there is art in individual letters. Letters in co
mbination may be satisfying and in a well composed page even beautiful as a w
hole, but art in letters consists rather in the art of arranging and composing them
in a pleasing and appropriate manner. The main purpose of letters is the practic
al one of making thoughts visible. Ruskin says that all letters are frightful things
and to be endured only on occasion, that is to say, in places where the sense of t
he inscription is of more importance than external ornament. This is a sweeping
The main purpose of letters is the practical one of making thoughts visible. Rusk
in says that all letters are frightful things and to be endured only on occasion, th
The main purpose of letters is the practical one of making thoughts visible.
Ruskin says that all letters are frightful things and to be endured only o

7/8

The main purpose of letters is the practical one of making thoughts visible. Rusk
in says that all letters are frightful things and to be endured only on occasion, tha
t is to say, in places where the sense of the inscription is of more importance tha
n external ornament. This is a sweeping statement, from which we need not suff
er unduly; yet it is doubtful whether there is art in individual letters. Letters in co
mbination may be satisfying and in a well composed page even beautiful as a w
hole, but art in letters consists rather in the art of arranging and composing them
in a pleasing and appropriate manner. The main purpose of letters is the practic
al one of making thoughts visible. Ruskin says that all letters are frightful things
and to be endured only on occasion, that is to say, in places where the sense of t
The main purpose of letters is the practical one of making thoughts visible. Rusk
in says that all letters are frightful things and to be endured only on occasion, th
The main purpose of letters is the practical one of making thoughts visible.
Ruskin says that all letters are frightful things and to be endured only o

7/9

The main purpose of letters is the practical one of making thoughts visible. Rusk
in says that all letters are frightful things and to be endured only on occasion, tha
t is to say, in places where the sense of the inscription is of more importance tha
n external ornament. This is a sweeping statement, from which we need not suff
er unduly; yet it is doubtful whether there is art in individual letters. Letters in co
mbination may be satisfying and in a well composed page even beautiful as a w
hole, but art in letters consists rather in the art of arranging and composing them
in a pleasing and appropriate manner. The main purpose of letters is the practic
al one of making thoughts visible. Ruskin says that all letters are frightful things
and to be endured only on occasion, that is to say, in places where the sense of t
The main purpose of letters is the practical one of making thoughts visible. Rusk
in says that all letters are frightful things and to be endured only on occasion, th
The main purpose of letters is the practical one of making thoughts visible.
Ruskin says that all letters are frightful things and to be endured only o

7/10

The main purpose of letters is the practical one of making thoughts visible. Rusk
in says that all letters are frightful things and to be endured only on occasion, tha
t is to say, in places where the sense of the inscription is of more importance tha
n external ornament. This is a sweeping statement, from which we need not suff
er unduly; yet it is doubtful whether there is art in individual letters. Letters in co
mbination may be satisfying and in a well composed page even beautiful as a w
hole, but art in letters consists rather in the art of arranging and composing them
in a pleasing and appropriate manner. The main purpose of letters is the practic
al one of making thoughts visible. Ruskin says that all letters are frightful things
The main purpose of letters is the practical one of making thoughts visible. Rusk
in says that all letters are frightful things and to be endured only on occasion, th
The main purpose of letters is the practical one of making thoughts visible.
Ruskin says that all letters are frightful things and to be endured only o

HELVETICA 8 & 9 POINT SET NORMAL

LIGHT, ITALIC, BOLD, BOLD ITALIC

ABCDEFGHIJKLMNOPQRSTUVWXYZ 1234567890 abcdefghijklmnopqrstuvwxyz

ABCDEFGHIJKLMNOPQRSTUVWXYZ 1234567890 abcdefghijklmnopqrstuvwxyz

ABCDEFGHIJKLMNOPQRSTUVWXYZ 1234567890 abcdefghijklmnopqrstuvwxyz

ABCDEFGHIJKLMNOPQRSTUVWXYZ 1234567890 abcdefghijklmnopqrstuvwxyz

8/8

The main purpose of letters is the practical one of making thoughts vis ible. Ruskin says that all letters are frightful things and to be endured o nly on occasion, that is to say, in places where the sense of the inscript ion is of more importance than external ornament. This is a sweeping statement, from which we need not suffer unduly; yet it is doubtful whe ther there is art in individual letters. Letters in combination may be sati sfying and in a well composed page even beautiful as a whole, but art in letters consists rather in the art of arranging and composing them in a pleasing and appropriate manner. The main purpose of letters is the *The main purpose of letters is the practical one of making thoughts vis ible. Ruskin says that all letters are frightful things and to be endured o* **The main purpose of letters is the practical one of making though ts visible. Ruskin says that all letters are frightful things and to be**

8/9

The main purpose of letters is the practical one of making thoughts vis ible. Ruskin says that all letters are frightful things and to be endured o nly on occasion, that is to say, in places where the sense of the inscript ion is of more importance than external ornament. This is a sweeping statement, from which we need not suffer unduly; yet it is doubtful whe ther there is art in individual letters. Letters in combination may be sati sfying and in a well composed page even beautiful as a whole, but art in letters consists rather in the art of arranging and composing them in *The main purpose of letters is the practical one of making thoughts vis ible. Ruskin says that all letters are frightful things and to be endured o* **The main purpose of letters is the practical one of making though ts visible. Ruskin says that all letters are frightful things and to be**

8/10

The main purpose of letters is the practical one of making thoughts vis ible. Ruskin says that all letters are frightful things and to be endured o nly on occasion, that is to say, in places where the sense of the inscript ion is of more importance than external ornament. This is a sweeping statement, from which we need not suffer unduly; yet it is doubtful whe ther there is art in individual letters. Letters in combination may be sati sfying and in a well composed page even beautiful as a whole, but art *The main purpose of letters is the practical one of making thoughts vis ible. Ruskin says that all letters are frightful things and to be endured o* **The main purpose of letters is the practical one of making though ts visible. Ruskin says that all letters are frightful things and to be**

8/11

The main purpose of letters is the practical one of making thoughts vis ible. Ruskin says that all letters are frightful things and to be endured o nly on occasion, that is to say, in places where the sense of the inscript ion is of more importance than external ornament. This is a sweeping statement, from which we need not suffer unduly; yet it is doubtful whe ther there is art in individual letters. Letters in combination may be sati sfying and in a well composed page even beautiful as a whole, but art *The main purpose of letters is the practical one of making thoughts vis ible. Ruskin says that all letters are frightful things and to be endured o* **The main purpose of letters is the practical one of making though ts visible. Ruskin says that all letters are frightful things and to be**

ABCDEFGHIJKLMNOPQRSTUVWXYZ 1234567890 abcdefghijklmnopqrstuvwxyz

ABCDEFGHIJKLMNOPQRSTUVWXYZ 1234567890 abcdefghijklmnopqrstuvwxyz

ABCDEFGHIJKLMNOPQRSTUVWXYZ 1234567890 abcdefghijklmnopqrstuvwxyz

ABCDEFGHIJKLMNOPQRSTUVWXYZ 1234567890 abcdefghijklmnopqrstuvwxyz

9/9

The main purpose of letters is the practical one of making thou ghts visible. Ruskin says that all letters are frightful things and to be endured only on occasion, that is to say, in places where the sense of the inscription is of more importance than externa l ornament. This is a sweeping statement, from which we need not suffer unduly; yet it is doubtful whether there is art in indivi dual letters. Letters in combination may be satisfying and in a well composed page even beautiful as a whole, but art in lette *The main purpose of letters is the practical one of making thou ghts visible. Ruskin says that all letters are frightful things and* **The main purpose of letters is the practical one of making thoughts visible. Ruskin says that all letters are frightful t**

9/10

The main purpose of letters is the practical one of making thou ghts visible. Ruskin says that all letters are frightful things and to be endured only on occasion, that is to say, in places where the sense of the inscription is of more importance than externa l ornament. This is a sweeping statement, from which we need not suffer unduly; yet it is doubtful whether there is art in indivi dual letters. Letters in combination may be satisfying and in a *The main purpose of letters is the practical one of making thou ghts visible. Ruskin says that all letters are frightful things and* **The main purpose of letters is the practical one of making thoughts visible. Ruskin says that all letters are frightful t**

9/11

The main purpose of letters is the practical one of making thou ghts visible. Ruskin says that all letters are frightful things and to be endured only on occasion, that is to say, in places where the sense of the inscription is of more importance than externa l ornament. This is a sweeping statement, from which we need not suffer unduly; yet it is doubtful whether there is art in indivi dual letters. Letters in combination may be satisfying and in a *The main purpose of letters is the practical one of making thou ghts visible. Ruskin says that all letters are frightful things and* **The main purpose of letters is the practical one of making thoughts visible. Ruskin says that all letters are frightful t**

9/12

The main purpose of letters is the practical one of making thou ghts visible. Ruskin says that all letters are frightful things and to be endured only on occasion, that is to say, in places where the sense of the inscription is of more importance than externa l ornament. This is a sweeping statement, from which we need not suffer unduly; yet it is doubtful whether there is art in indivi dual letters. Letters in combination may be satisfying and in a *The main purpose of letters is the practical one of making thou ghts visible. Ruskin says that all letters are frightful things and* **The main purpose of letters is the practical one of making thoughts visible. Ruskin says that all letters are frightful t**

10 POINT SET MINUS ½ UNIT

LIGHT, ITALIC, BOLD, BOLD ITALIC

abcdefghijklmnopqrstuvwxyz – 1 UNIT
abcdefghijklmnopqrstuvwxyz – ½ UNIT
abcdefghijklmnopqrstuvwxyz NORMAL

ABCDEFGHIJKLMNOPQRSTUVWXYZ 1234567890 abcdefghijklmnopqrstuvwxyz
ABCDEFGHIJKLMNOPQRSTUVWXYZ 1234567890 abcdefghijklmnopqrstuvwxyz
ABCDEFGHIJKLMNOPQRSTUVWXYZ 1234567890 abcdefghijklmnopqrstuvwxyz
ABCDEFGHIJKLMNOPQRSTUVWXYZ 1234567890 abcdefghijklmnopqrstuvwxyz

10/10

The main purpose of letters is the practical one of making t
houghts visible. Ruskin says that all letters are frightful thin
gs and to be endured only on occasion, that is to say, in pl
aces where the sense of the inscription is of more importa
nce than external ornament. This is a sweeping statement,
from which we need not suffer unduly; yet it is doubtful wh
ether there is art in individual letters. Letters in combinatio
n may be satisfying and in a well composed page even be
autiful as a whole, but art in letters consists rather in the art
of arranging and composing them in a pleasing and appr
opriate manner. The main purpose of letters is the practica
l one of making thoughts visible. Ruskin says that all letters
are frightful things and to be endured only on occasion, th
at is to say, in places where the sense of the inscription is of
more importance than external ornament. This is a sweepi
ng statement, from which we need not suffer unduly; yet it i
s doubtful whether there is art in individual letters. Letters i
n combination may be satisfying and in a well composed
page even beautiful as a whole, but art in letters consists r
ather in the art of arranging and composing them in a plea
sing and appropriate manner. The main purpose of letters
is the practical one of making thoughts visible. Ruskin say
*The main purpose of letters is the practical one of making t
houghts visible. Ruskin says that all letters are frightful thin*
**The main purpose of letters is the practical one of mak
ing thoughts visible. Ruskin says that all letters are fri**

10/11

The main purpose of letters is the practical one of making t
houghts visible. Ruskin says that all letters are frightful thin
gs and to be endured only on occasion, that is to say, in pl
aces where the sense of the inscription is of more importa
nce than external ornament. This is a sweeping statement,
from which we need not suffer unduly; yet it is doubtful wh
ether there is art in individual letters. Letters in combinatio
n may be satisfying and in a well composed page even be
autiful as a whole, but art in letters consists rather in the art
of arranging and composing them in a pleasing and appr
opriate manner. The main purpose of letters is the practica
l one of making thoughts visible. Ruskin says that all letters
are frightful things and to be endured only on occasion, th
at is to say, in places where the sense of the inscription is of
more importance than external ornament. This is a sweepi
ng statement, from which we need not suffer unduly; yet it i
s doubtful whether there is art in individual letters. Letters i
n combination may be satisfying and in a well composed
page even beautiful as a whole, but art in letters consists r
ather in the art of arranging and composing them in a plea
*The main purpose of letters is the practical one of making t
houghts visible. Ruskin says that all letters are frightful thin*
**The main purpose of letters is the practical one of mak
ing thoughts visible. Ruskin says that all letters are fri**

10/12

The main purpose of letters is the practical one of making t
houghts visible. Ruskin says that all letters are frightful thin
gs and to be endured only on occasion, that is to say, in pl
aces where the sense of the inscription is of more importa
nce than external ornament. This is a sweeping statement,
from which we need not suffer unduly; yet it is doubtful wh
ether there is art in individual letters. Letters in combinatio
n may be satisfying and in a well composed page even be
autiful as a whole, but art in letters consists rather in the art
of arranging and composing them in a pleasing and appr
opriate manner. The main purpose of letters is the practica
l one of making thoughts visible. Ruskin says that all letters
are frightful things and to be endured only on occasion, th
at is to say, in places where the sense of the inscription is of
more importance than external ornament. This is a sweepi
ng statement, from which we need not suffer unduly; yet it i
s doubtful whether there is art in individual letters. Letters i
n combination may be satisfying and in a well composed
*The main purpose of letters is the practical one of making t
houghts visible. Ruskin says that all letters are frightful thin*
**The main purpose of letters is the practical one of mak
ing thoughts visible. Ruskin says that all letters are fri**

10/13

The main purpose of letters is the practical one of making t
houghts visible. Ruskin says that all letters are frightful thin
gs and to be endured only on occasion, that is to say, in pl
aces where the sense of the inscription is of more importa
nce than external ornament. This is a sweeping statement,
from which we need not suffer unduly; yet it is doubtful wh
ether there is art in individual letters. Letters in combinatio
n may be satisfying and in a well composed page even be
autiful as a whole, but art in letters consists rather in the art
of arranging and composing them in a pleasing and appr
opriate manner. The main purpose of letters is the practica
l one of making thoughts visible. Ruskin says that all letters
are frightful things and to be endured only on occasion, th
at is to say, in places where the sense of the inscription is of
more importance than external ornament. This is a sweepi
ng statement, from which we need not suffer unduly; yet it i
s doubtful whether there is art in individual letters. Letters i
*The main purpose of letters is the practical one of making t
houghts visible. Ruskin says that all letters are frightful thin*
**The main purpose of letters is the practical one of mak
ing thoughts visible. Ruskin says that all letters are fri**

HELVETICA 11 POINT SET MINUS ½ UNIT

LIGHT, ITALIC, BOLD, BOLD ITALIC

abcdefghijklmnopqrstuvwxyz – 1 UNIT
abcdefghijklmnopqrstuvwxyz – ½ UNIT
abcdefghijklmnopqrstuvwxyz NORMAL

ABCDEFGHIJKLMNOPQRSTUVWXYZ 1234567890 abcdefghijklmnopqrstuvwxyz
ABCDEFGHIJKLMNOPQRSTUVWXYZ 1234567890 abcdefghijklmnopqrstuvwxyz
ABCDEFGHIJKLMNOPQRSTUVWXYZ 1234567890 abcdefghijklmnopqrstuvwxyz
ABCDEFGHIJKLMNOPQRSTUVWXYZ 1234567890 abcdefghijklmnopqrstuvwxyz

11/11

The main purpose of letters is the practical one of ma
king thoughts visible. Ruskin says that all letters are f
rightful things and to be endured only on occasion, t
hat is to say, in places where the sense of the inscripti
on is of more importance than external ornament. Thi
s is a sweeping statement, from which we need not s
uffer unduly; yet it is doubtful whether there is art in in
dividual letters. Letters in combination may be satisf
ying and in a well composed page even beautiful as
a whole, but art in letters consists rather in the art of a
rranging and composing them in a pleasing and ap
propriate manner. The main purpose of letters is the
practical one of making thoughts visible. Ruskin say
s that all letters are frightful things and to be endured
only on occasion, that is to say, in places where the s
ense of the inscription is of more importance than ext
ernal ornament. This is a sweeping statement, from
which we need not suffer unduly; yet it is doubtful wh
ether there is art in individual letters. Letters in combi
The main purpose of letters is the practical one of ma
king thoughts visible. Ruskin says that all letters are f
The main purpose of letters is the practical one of
making thoughts visible. Ruskin says that all lett

11/12

The main purpose of letters is the practical one of ma
king thoughts visible. Ruskin says that all letters are f
rightful things and to be endured only on occasion, t
hat is to say, in places where the sense of the inscripti
on is of more importance than external ornament. Thi
s is a sweeping statement, from which we need not s
uffer unduly; yet it is doubtful whether there is art in in
dividual letters. Letters in combination may be satisf
ying and in a well composed page even beautiful as
a whole, but art in letters consists rather in the art of a
rranging and composing them in a pleasing and ap
propriate manner. The main purpose of letters is the
practical one of making thoughts visible. Ruskin say
s that all letters are frightful things and to be endured
only on occasion, that is to say, in places where the s
ense of the inscription is of more importance than ext
ernal ornament. This is a sweeping statement, from
which we need not suffer unduly; yet it is doubtful wh
The main purpose of letters is the practical one of ma
king thoughts visible. Ruskin says that all letters are f
The main purpose of letters is the practical one of
making thoughts visible. Ruskin says that all lett

11/13

The main purpose of letters is the practical one of ma
king thoughts visible. Ruskin says that all letters are f
rightful things and to be endured only on occasion, t
hat is to say, in places where the sense of the inscripti
on is of more importance than external ornament. Thi
s is a sweeping statement, from which we need not s
uffer unduly; yet it is doubtful whether there is art in in
dividual letters. Letters in combination may be satisf
ying and in a well composed page even beautiful as
a whole, but art in letters consists rather in the art of a
rranging and composing them in a pleasing and ap
propriate manner. The main purpose of letters is the
practical one of making thoughts visible. Ruskin say
s that all letters are frightful things and to be endured
only on occasion, that is to say, in places where the s
ense of the inscription is of more importance than ext
ernal ornament. This is a sweeping statement, from
The main purpose of letters is the practical one of ma
king thoughts visible. Ruskin says that all letters are f
The main purpose of letters is the practical one of
making thoughts visible. Ruskin says that all lett

11/14

The main purpose of letters is the practical one of ma
king thoughts visible. Ruskin says that all letters are f
rightful things and to be endured only on occasion, t
hat is to say, in places where the sense of the inscripti
on is of more importance than external ornament. Thi
s is a sweeping statement, from which we need not s
uffer unduly; yet it is doubtful whether there is art in in
dividual letters. Letters in combination may be satisf
ying and in a well composed page even beautiful as
a whole, but art in letters consists rather in the art of a
rranging and composing them in a pleasing and ap
propriate manner. The main purpose of letters is the
practical one of making thoughts visible. Ruskin say
s that all letters are frightful things and to be endured
only on occasion, that is to say, in places where the s
ense of the inscription is of more importance than ext
The main purpose of letters is the practical one of ma
king thoughts visible. Ruskin says that all letters are f
The main purpose of letters is the practical one of
making thoughts visible. Ruskin says that all lett

HELVETICA 12 POINT SET MINUS ½ UNIT

LIGHT, ITALIC, BOLD, BOLD ITALIC

abcdefghijklmnopqrstuvwxyz – 1 UNIT
abcdefghijklmnopqrstuvwxyz – ½ UNIT
abcdefghijklmnopqrstuvwxyz NORMAL

ABCDEFGHIJKLMNOPQRSTUVWXYZ 1234567890 abcdefghijklmnopqrstuvwxyz
ABCDEFGHIJKLMNOPQRSTUVWXYZ 1234567890 abcdefghijklmnopqrstuvwxyz
ABCDEFGHIJKLMNOPQRSTUVWXYZ 1234567890 abcdefghijklmnopqrstuvwxyz
ABCDEFGHIJKLMNOPQRSTUVWXYZ 1234567890 abcdefghijklmnopqrstuvwxyz

12/12

The main purpose of letters is the practical one of making thoughts visible. Ruskin says that all lette rs are frightful things and to be endured only on o ccasion, that is to say, in places where the sense of the inscription is of more importance than exter nal ornament. This is a sweeping statement, from which we need not suffer unduly; yet it is doubtful whether there is art in individual letters. Letters in combination may be satisfying and in a well com posed page even beautiful as a whole, but art in l etters consists rather in the art of arranging and c omposing them in a pleasing and appropriate m anner. The main purpose of letters is the practical one of making thoughts visible. Ruskin says that all letters are frightful things and to be endured o
The main purpose of letters is the practical one of making thoughts visible. Ruskin says that all lette
The main purpose of letters is the practical on e of making thoughts visible. Ruskin says tha

12/13

The main purpose of letters is the practical one of making thoughts visible. Ruskin says that all lette rs are frightful things and to be endured only on o ccasion, that is to say, in places where the sense of the inscription is of more importance than exter nal ornament. This is a sweeping statement, from which we need not suffer unduly; yet it is doubtful whether there is art in individual letters. Letters in combination may be satisfying and in a well com posed page even beautiful as a whole, but art in l etters consists rather in the art of arranging and c omposing them in a pleasing and appropriate m anner. The main purpose of letters is the practical one of making thoughts visible. Ruskin says that
The main purpose of letters is the practical one of making thoughts visible. Ruskin says that all lette
The main purpose of letters is the practical on e of making thoughts visible. Ruskin says tha

12/14

The main purpose of letters is the practical one of making thoughts visible. Ruskin says that all lette rs are frightful things and to be endured only on o ccasion, that is to say, in places where the sense of the inscription is of more importance than exter nal ornament. This is a sweeping statement, from which we need not suffer unduly; yet it is doubtful whether there is art in individual letters. Letters in combination may be satisfying and in a well com posed page even beautiful as a whole, but art in l etters consists rather in the art of arranging and c omposing them in a pleasing and appropriate m anner. The main purpose of letters is the practical one of making thoughts visible. Ruskin says that all letters are frightful things and to be endured o
The main purpose of letters is the practical one of making thoughts visible. Ruskin says that all lette
The main purpose of letters is the practical on e of making thoughts visible. Ruskin says tha

12/15

The main purpose of letters is the practical one of making thoughts visible. Ruskin says that all lette rs are frightful things and to be endured only on o ccasion, that is to say, in places where the sense of the inscription is of more importance than exter nal ornament. This is a sweeping statement, from which we need not suffer unduly; yet it is doubtful whether there is art in individual letters. Letters in combination may be satisfying and in a well com posed page even beautiful as a whole, but art in l etters consists rather in the art of arranging and c omposing them in a pleasing and appropriate m anner. The main purpose of letters is the practical one of making thoughts visible. Ruskin says that
The main purpose of letters is the practical one of making thoughts visible. Ruskin says that all lette
The main purpose of letters is the practical on e of making thoughts visible. Ruskin says tha

HELVETICA 14 POINT SET MINUS ½ UNIT

LIGHT, ITALIC, BOLD, BOLD ITALIC

abcdefghijklmnopqrstuvwxyz – 1 UNIT
abcdefghijklmnopqrstuvwxyz – ½ UNIT
abcdefghijklmnopqrstuvwxyz NORMAL

ABCDEFGHIJKLMNOPQRSTUVWXYZ abcdefghijklmnopqrstuvwxyz
ABCDEFGHIJKLMNOPQRSTUVWXYZ abcdefghijklmnopqrstuvwxyz
ABCDEFGHIJKLMNOPQRSTUVWXYZ abcdefghijklmnopqrstuvwxyz
ABCDEFGHIJKLMNOPQRSTUVWXYZ abcdefghijklmnopqrstuvwxyz

14/14

The main purpose of letters is the practic al one of making thoughts visible. Ruskin says that all letters are frightful things and to be endured only on occasion, that is to say, in places where the sense of the inscr iption is of more importance than external ornament. This is a sweeping statement, f rom which we need not suffer unduly; yet i t is doubtful whether there is art in individu al letters. Letters in combination may be s atisfying and in a well composed page ev en beautiful as a whole, but art in letters c onsists rather in the art of arranging and c
The main purpose of letters is the practic al one of making thoughts visible. Ruskin
The main purpose of letters is the pract ical one of making thoughts visible. Ru

14/16

The main purpose of letters is the practic al one of making thoughts visible. Ruskin says that all letters are frightful things and to be endured only on occasion, that is to say, in places where the sense of the inscr iption is of more importance than external ornament. This is a sweeping statement, f rom which we need not suffer unduly; yet i t is doubtful whether there is art in individu al letters. Letters in combination may be s atisfying and in a well composed page ev en beautiful as a whole, but art in letters c onsists rather in the art of arranging and c
The main purpose of letters is the practic al one of making thoughts visible. Ruskin
The main purpose of letters is the pract ical one of making thoughts visible. Ru

14/15

The main purpose of letters is the practic al one of making thoughts visible. Ruskin says that all letters are frightful things and to be endured only on occasion, that is to say, in places where the sense of the inscr iption is of more importance than external ornament. This is a sweeping statement, f rom which we need not suffer unduly; yet i t is doubtful whether there is art in individu al letters. Letters in combination may be s atisfying and in a well composed page ev en beautiful as a whole, but art in letters c
The main purpose of letters is the practic al one of making thoughts visible. Ruskin
The main purpose of letters is the pract ical one of making thoughts visible. Ru

14/17

The main purpose of letters is the practic al one of making thoughts visible. Ruskin says that all letters are frightful things and to be endured only on occasion, that is to say, in places where the sense of the inscr iption is of more importance than external ornament. This is a sweeping statement, f rom which we need not suffer unduly; yet i t is doubtful whether there is art in individu al letters. Letters in combination may be s atisfying and in a well composed page ev en beautiful as a whole, but art in letters c
The main purpose of letters is the practic al one of making thoughts visible. Ruskin
The main purpose of letters is the pract ical one of making thoughts visible. Ru

HELVETICA 6 & 7 POINT SET NORMAL

ROMAN, ITALIC, HEAVY, HEAVY ITALIC

ABCDEFGHIJKLMNOPQRSTUVWXYZ 1234567890 abcdefghijklmnopqrstuvwxyz

ABCDEFGHIJKLMNOPQRSTUVWXYZ 1234567890 abcdefghijklmnopqrstuvwxyz

ABCDEFGHIJKLMNOPQRSTUVWXYZ 1234567890 abcdefghijklmnopqrstuvwxyz

ABCDEFGHIJKLMNOPQRSTUVWXYZ 1234567890 abcdefghijklmnopqrstuvwxyz

6/6

The main purpose of letters is the practical one of making thoughts visible. Ruskin says that all
letters are frightful things and to be endured only on occasion, that is to say, in places where th
e sense of the inscription is of more importance than external ornament. This is a sweeping st
atement, from which we need not suffer unduly; yet it is doubtful whether there is art in individu
al letters. Letters in combination may be satisfying and in a well composed page even beautifu
l as a whole, but art in letters consists rather in the art of arranging and composing them in a pl
easing and appropriate manner. The main purpose of letters is the practical one of making tho
ughts visible. Ruskin says that all letters are frightful things and to be endured only on occasio
n, that is to say, in places where the sense of the inscription is of more importance than externa
l ornament. This is a sweeping statement, from which we need not suffer unduly; yet it is doubt
ful whether there is art in individual letters. Letters in combination may be satisfying and in a w
ell composed page even beautiful as a whole, but art in letters consists rather in the art of arran
ging and composing them in a pleasing and appropriate manner. The main purpose of letters i
The main purpose of letters is the practical one of making thoughts visible. Ruskin says that a
ll letters are frightful things and to be endured only on occasion, that is to say, in places where
The main purpose of letters is the practical one of making thoughts visible. Ruski
n says that all letters are frightful things and to be endured only on occasion, that

6/7

The main purpose of letters is the practical one of making thoughts visible. Ruskin says that all
letters are frightful things and to be endured only on occasion, that is to say, in places where th
e sense of the inscription is of more importance than external ornament. This is a sweeping st
atement, from which we need not suffer unduly; yet it is doubtful whether there is art in individu
al letters. Letters in combination may be satisfying and in a well composed page even beautifu
l as a whole, but art in letters consists rather in the art of arranging and composing them in a pl
easing and appropriate manner. The main purpose of letters is the practical one of making tho
ughts visible. Ruskin says that all letters are frightful things and to be endured only on occasio
n, that is to say, in places where the sense of the inscription is of more importance than externa
l ornament. This is a sweeping statement, from which we need not suffer unduly; yet it is doubt
ful whether there is art in individual letters. Letters in combination may be satisfying and in a w
The main purpose of letters is the practical one of making thoughts visible. Ruskin says that a
ll letters are frightful things and to be endured only on occasion, that is to say, in places where
The main purpose of letters is the practical one of making thoughts visible. Ruski
n says that all letters are frightful things and to be endured only on occasion, that

6/8

The main purpose of letters is the practical one of making thoughts visible. Ruskin says that all
letters are frightful things and to be endured only on occasion, that is to say, in places where th
e sense of the inscription is of more importance than external ornament. This is a sweeping st
atement, from which we need not suffer unduly; yet it is doubtful whether there is art in individu
al letters. Letters in combination may be satisfying and in a well composed page even beautifu
l as a whole, but art in letters consists rather in the art of arranging and composing them in a pl
easing and appropriate manner. The main purpose of letters is the practical one of making tho
ughts visible. Ruskin says that all letters are frightful things and to be endured only on occasio
n, that is to say, in places where the sense of the inscription is of more importance than externa
The main purpose of letters is the practical one of making thoughts visible. Ruskin says that a
ll letters are frightful things and to be endured only on occasion, that is to say, in places where
The main purpose of letters is the practical one of making thoughts visible. Ruski
n says that all letters are frightful things and to be endured only on occasion, that

6/9

The main purpose of letters is the practical one of making thoughts visible. Ruskin says that all
letters are frightful things and to be endured only on occasion, that is to say, in places where th
e sense of the inscription is of more importance than external ornament. This is a sweeping st
atement, from which we need not suffer unduly; yet it is doubtful whether there is art in individu
al letters. Letters in combination may be satisfying and in a well composed page even beautifu
l as a whole, but art in letters consists rather in the art of arranging and composing them in a pl
easing and appropriate manner. The main purpose of letters is the practical one of making tho
ughts visible. Ruskin says that all letters are frightful things and to be endured only on occasio
The main purpose of letters is the practical one of making thoughts visible. Ruskin says that a
ll letters are frightful things and to be endured only on occasion, that is to say, in places where
The main purpose of letters is the practical one of making thoughts visible. Ruski
n says that all letters are frightful things and to be endured only on occasion, that

---

ABCDEFGHIJKLMNOPQRSTUVWXYZ 1234567890 abcdefghijklmnopqrstuvwxyz

ABCDEFGHIJKLMNOPQRSTUVWXYZ 1234567890 abcdefghijklmnopqrstuvwxyz

ABCDEFGHIJKLMNOPQRSTUVWXYZ 1234567890 abcdefghijklmnopqrstuvwxyz

ABCDEFGHIJKLMNOPQRSTUVWXYZ 1234567890 abcdefghijklmnopqrstuvwxyz

7/7

The main purpose of letters is the practical one of making thoughts visible. Ruski
n says that all letters are frightful things and to be endured only on occasion, that
is to say, in places where the sense of the inscription is of more importance than
external ornament. This is a sweeping statement, from which we need not suffer
unduly; yet it is doubtful whether there is art in individual letters. Letters in combi
nation may be satisfying and in a well composed page even beautiful as a whole,
but art in letters consists rather in the art of arranging and composing them in a pl
easing and appropriate manner. The main purpose of letters is the practical one
of making thoughts visible. Ruskin says that all letters are frightful things and to b
e endured only on occasion, that is to say, in places where the sense of the inscri
ption is of more importance than external ornament. This is a sweeping stateme
The main purpose of letters is the practical one of making thoughts visible. Rusk
in says that all letters are frightful things and to be endured only on occasion, th
The main purpose of letters is the practical one of making thoughts vi
sible. Ruskin says that all letters are frightful things and to be endure

7/8

The main purpose of letters is the practical one of making thoughts visible. Ruski
n says that all letters are frightful things and to be endured only on occasion, that
is to say, in places where the sense of the inscription is of more importance than
external ornament. This is a sweeping statement, from which we need not suffer
unduly; yet it is doubtful whether there is art in individual letters. Letters in combi
nation may be satisfying and in a well composed page even beautiful as a whole,
but art in letters consists rather in the art of arranging and composing them in a pl
easing and appropriate manner. The main purpose of letters is the practical one
of making thoughts visible. Ruskin says that all letters are frightful things and to b
e endured only on occasion, that is to say, in places where the sense of the inscri
The main purpose of letters is the practical one of making thoughts visible. Rusk
in says that all letters are frightful things and to be endured only on occasion, th
The main purpose of letters is the practical one of making thoughts vi
sible. Ruskin says that all letters are frightful things and to be endure

7/9

The main purpose of letters is the practical one of making thoughts visible. Ruski
n says that all letters are frightful things and to be endured only on occasion, that
is to say, in places where the sense of the inscription is of more importance than
external ornament. This is a sweeping statement, from which we need not suffer
unduly; yet it is doubtful whether there is art in individual letters. Letters in combi
nation may be satisfying and in a well composed page even beautiful as a whole,
but art in letters consists rather in the art of arranging and composing them in a pl
easing and appropriate manner. The main purpose of letters is the practical one
of making thoughts visible. Ruskin says that all letters are frightful things and to b
e endured only on occasion, that is to say, in places where the sense of the inscri
The main purpose of letters is the practical one of making thoughts visible. Rusk
in says that all letters are frightful things and to be endured only on occasion, th
The main purpose of letters is the practical one of making thoughts vi
sible. Ruskin says that all letters are frightful things and to be endure

7/10

The main purpose of letters is the practical one of making thoughts visible. Ruski
n says that all letters are frightful things and to be endured only on occasion, that
is to say, in places where the sense of the inscription is of more importance than
external ornament. This is a sweeping statement, from which we need not suffer
unduly; yet it is doubtful whether there is art in individual letters. Letters in combi
nation may be satisfying and in a well composed page even beautiful as a whole,
but art in letters consists rather in the art of arranging and composing them in a pl
easing and appropriate manner. The main purpose of letters is the practical one
of making thoughts visible. Ruskin says that all letters are frightful things and to b
The main purpose of letters is the practical one of making thoughts visible. Rusk
in says that all letters are frightful things and to be endured only on occasion, th
The main purpose of letters is the practical one of making thoughts vi
sible. Ruskin says that all letters are frightful things and to be endure

HELVETICA 8 & 9 POINT SET NORMAL

ROMAN, ITALIC, HEAVY, HEAVY ITALIC

ABCDEFGHIJKLMNOPQRSTUVWXYZ 1234567890 abcdefghijklmnopqrstuvwxyz

ABCDEFGHIJKLMNOPQRSTUVWXYZ 1234567890 abcdefghijklmnopqrstuvwxyz

ABCDEFGHIJKLMNOPQRSTUVWXYZ 1234567890 abcdefghijklmnopqrstuvwxyz

ABCDEFGHIJKLMNOPQRSTUVWXYZ 1234567890 abcdefghijklmnopqrstuvwxyz

8/8

The main purpose of letters is the practical one of making thoughts visi ble. Ruskin says that all letters are frightful things and to be endured on ly on occasion, that is to say, in places where the sense of the inscriptio n is of more importance than external ornament. This is a sweeping sta tement, from which we need not suffer unduly; yet it is doubtful whethe r there is art in individual letters. Letters in combination may be satisfyi ng and in a well composed page even beautiful as a whole, but art in let ters consists rather in the art of arranging and composing them in a ple asing and appropriate manner. The main purpose of letters is the pract
The main purpose of letters is the practical one of making thoughts vis ible. Ruskin says that all letters are frightful things and to be endured
The main purpose of letters is the practical one of making tho ughts visible. Ruskin says that all letters are frightful things a

8/9

The main purpose of letters is the practical one of making thoughts visi ble. Ruskin says that all letters are frightful things and to be endured on ly on occasion, that is to say, in places where the sense of the inscriptio n is of more importance than external ornament. This is a sweeping sta tement, from which we need not suffer unduly; yet it is doubtful whethe r there is art in individual letters. Letters in combination may be satisfyi ng and in a well composed page even beautiful as a whole, but art in let ters consists rather in the art of arranging and composing them in a ple
The main purpose of letters is the practical one of making thoughts vis ible. Ruskin says that all letters are frightful things and to be endured
The main purpose of letters is the practical one of making tho ughts visible. Ruskin says that all letters are frightful things a

8/10

The main purpose of letters is the practical one of making thoughts visi ble. Ruskin says that all letters are frightful things and to be endured on ly on occasion, that is to say, in places where the sense of the inscriptio n is of more importance than external ornament. This is a sweeping sta tement, from which we need not suffer unduly; yet it is doubtful whethe r there is art in individual letters. Letters in combination may be satisfyi ng and in a well composed page even beautiful as a whole, but art in let
The main purpose of letters is the practical one of making thoughts vis ible. Ruskin says that all letters are frightful things and to be endured
The main purpose of letters is the practical one of making tho ughts visible. Ruskin says that all letters are frightful things a

8/11

The main purpose of letters is the practical one of making thoughts visi ble. Ruskin says that all letters are frightful things and to be endured on ly on occasion, that is to say, in places where the sense of the inscriptio n is of more importance than external ornament. This is a sweeping sta tement, from which we need not suffer unduly; yet it is doubtful whethe r there is art in individual letters. Letters in combination may be satisfyi ng and in a well composed page even beautiful as a whole, but art in let
The main purpose of letters is the practical one of making thoughts vis ible. Ruskin says that all letters are frightful things and to be endured
The main purpose of letters is the practical one of making tho ughts visible. Ruskin says that all letters are frightful things a

---

ABCDEFGHIJKLMNOPQRSTUVWXYZ 1234567890 abcdefghijklmnopqrstuvwxyz

ABCDEFGHIJKLMNOPQRSTUVWXYZ 1234567890 abcdefghijklmnopqrstuvwxyz

ABCDEFGHIJKLMNOPQRSTUVWXYZ 1234567890 abcdefghijklmnopqrstuvwxyz

ABCDEFGHIJKLMNOPQRSTUVWXYZ 1234567890 abcdefghijklmnopqrstuvwxyz

9/9

The main purpose of letters is the practical one of making thou ghts visible. Ruskin says that all letters are frightful things and t o be endured only on occasion, that is to say, in places where t he sense of the inscription is of more importance than external ornament. This is a sweeping statement, from which we need not suffer unduly; yet it is doubtful whether there is art in individ ual letters. Letters in combination may be satisfying and in a w ell composed page even beautiful as a whole, but art in letters
The main purpose of letters is the practical one of making thou ghts visible. Ruskin says that all letters are frightful things and
The main purpose of letters is the practical one of mak ing thoughts visible. Ruskin says that all letters are fri

9/10

The main purpose of letters is the practical one of making thou ghts visible. Ruskin says that all letters are frightful things and t o be endured only on occasion, that is to say, in places where t he sense of the inscription is of more importance than external ornament. This is a sweeping statement, from which we need not suffer unduly; yet it is doubtful whether there is art in individ ual letters. Letters in combination may be satisfying and in a w
The main purpose of letters is the practical one of making thou ghts visible. Ruskin says that all letters are frightful things and
The main purpose of letters is the practical one of mak ing thoughts visible. Ruskin says that all letters are fri

9/11

The main purpose of letters is the practical one of making thou ghts visible. Ruskin says that all letters are frightful things and t o be endured only on occasion, that is to say, in places where t he sense of the inscription is of more importance than external ornament. This is a sweeping statement, from which we need not suffer unduly; yet it is doubtful whether there is art in individ ual letters. Letters in combination may be satisfying and in a w
The main purpose of letters is the practical one of making thou ghts visible. Ruskin says that all letters are frightful things and
The main purpose of letters is the practical one of mak ing thoughts visible. Ruskin says that all letters are fri

9/12

The main purpose of letters is the practical one of making thou ghts visible. Ruskin says that all letters are frightful things and t o be endured only on occasion, that is to say, in places where t he sense of the inscription is of more importance than external ornament. This is a sweeping statement, from which we need not suffer unduly; yet it is doubtful whether there is art in individ ual letters. Letters in combination may be satisfying and in a w
The main purpose of letters is the practical one of making thou ghts visible. Ruskin says that all letters are frightful things and
The main purpose of letters is the practical one of mak ing thoughts visible. Ruskin says that all letters are fri

HELVETICA 10 POINT SET MINUS ½ UNIT

ROMAN, ITALIC, HEAVY, HEAVY ITALIC

abcdefghijklmnopqrstuvwxyz – 1 UNIT
abcdefghijklmnopqrstuvwxyz – ½ UNIT
abcdefghijklmnopqrstuvwxyz NORMAL

ABCDEFGHIJKLMNOPQRSTUVWXYZ 1234567890 abcdefghijklmnopqrstuvwxyz
ABCDEFGHIJKLMNOPQRSTUVWXYZ 1234567890 abcdefghijklmnopqrstuvwxyz
ABCDEFGHIJKLMNOPQRSTUVWXYZ 1234567890 abcdefghijklmnopqrstuvwxyz
ABCDEFGHIJKLMNOPQRSTUVWXYZ 1234567890 abcdefghijklmnopqrstuvwxyz

10/10

The main purpose of letters is the practical one of making t
houghts visible. Ruskin says that all letters are frightful thin
gs and to be endured only on occasion, that is to say, in pla
ces where the sense of the inscription is of more importanc
e than external ornament. This is a sweeping statement, fr
om which we need not suffer unduly; yet it is doubtful whet
her there is art in individual letters. Letters in combination
may be satisfying and in a well composed page even beaut
iful as a whole, but art in letters consists rather in the art of a
rranging and composing them in a pleasing and appropriat
e manner. The main purpose of letters is the practical one o
f making thoughts visible. Ruskin says that all letters are fri
ghtful things and to be endured only on occasion, that is to
say, in places where the sense of the inscription is of more i
mportance than external ornament. This is a sweeping stat
ement, from which we need not suffer unduly; yet it is doubt
ful whether there is art in individual letters. Letters in combi
nation may be satisfying and in a well composed page eve
n beautiful as a whole, but art in letters consists rather in th
e art of arranging and composing them in a pleasing and a
ppropriate manner. The main purpose of letters is the pract
ical one of making thoughts visible. Ruskin says that all lett
The main purpose of letters is the practical one of making t
houghts visible. Ruskin says that all letters are frightful thin
The main purpose of letters is the practical one of
making thoughts visible. Ruskin says that all letter

10/11

The main purpose of letters is the practical one of making t
houghts visible. Ruskin says that all letters are frightful thin
gs and to be endured only on occasion, that is to say, in pla
ces where the sense of the inscription is of more importanc
e than external ornament. This is a sweeping statement, fr
om which we need not suffer unduly; yet it is doubtful whet
her there is art in individual letters. Letters in combination
may be satisfying and in a well composed page even beaut
iful as a whole, but art in letters consists rather in the art of a
rranging and composing them in a pleasing and appropriat
e manner. The main purpose of letters is the practical one o
f making thoughts visible. Ruskin says that all letters are fri
ghtful things and to be endured only on occasion, that is to
say, in places where the sense of the inscription is of more i
mportance than external ornament. This is a sweeping stat
ement, from which we need not suffer unduly; yet it is doubt
ful whether there is art in individual letters. Letters in combi
nation may be satisfying and in a well composed page eve
n beautiful as a whole, but art in letters consists rather in th
e art of arranging and composing them in a pleasing and a
The main purpose of letters is the practical one of making t
houghts visible. Ruskin says that all letters are frightful thin
The main purpose of letters is the practical one of
making thoughts visible. Ruskin says that all letter

10/12

The main purpose of letters is the practical one of making t
houghts visible. Ruskin says that all letters are frightful thin
gs and to be endured only on occasion, that is to say, in pla
ces where the sense of the inscription is of more importanc
e than external ornament. This is a sweeping statement, fr
om which we need not suffer unduly; yet it is doubtful whet
her there is art in individual letters. Letters in combination
may be satisfying and in a well composed page even beaut
iful as a whole, but art in letters consists rather in the art of a
rranging and composing them in a pleasing and appropriat
e manner. The main purpose of letters is the practical one o
f making thoughts visible. Ruskin says that all letters are fri
ghtful things and to be endured only on occasion, that is to
say, in places where the sense of the inscription is of more i
mportance than external ornament. This is a sweeping stat
ement, from which we need not suffer unduly; yet it is doubt
ful whether there is art in individual letters. Letters in combi
nation may be satisfying and in a well composed page eve
The main purpose of letters is the practical one of making t
houghts visible. Ruskin says that all letters are frightful thin
The main purpose of letters is the practical one of
making thoughts visible. Ruskin says that all letter

10/13

The main purpose of letters is the practical one of making t
houghts visible. Ruskin says that all letters are frightful thin
gs and to be endured only on occasion, that is to say, in pla
ces where the sense of the inscription is of more importanc
e than external ornament. This is a sweeping statement, fr
om which we need not suffer unduly; yet it is doubtful whet
her there is art in individual letters. Letters in combination
may be satisfying and in a well composed page even beaut
iful as a whole, but art in letters consists rather in the art of a
rranging and composing them in a pleasing and appropriat
e manner. The main purpose of letters is the practical one o
f making thoughts visible. Ruskin says that all letters are fri
ghtful things and to be endured only on occasion, that is to
say, in places where the sense of the inscription is of more i
mportance than external ornament. This is a sweeping stat
ement, from which we need not suffer unduly; yet it is doubt
ful whether there is art in individual letters. Letters in combi
The main purpose of letters is the practical one of making t
houghts visible. Ruskin says that all letters are frightful thin
The main purpose of letters is the practical one of
making thoughts visible. Ruskin says that all letter

HELVETICA 11 POINT SET MINUS ½ UNIT

ROMAN, ITALIC, HEAVY, HEAVY ITALIC

abcdefghijklmnopqrstuvwxyz – 1 UNIT
abcdefghijklmnopqrstuvwxyz – ½ UNIT
abcdefghijklmnopqrstuvwxyz NORMAL

ABCDEFGHIJKLMNOPQRSTUVWXYZ 1234567890 abcdefghijklmnopqrstuvwxyz
ABCDEFGHIJKLMNOPQRSTUVWXYZ 1234567890 abcdefghijklmnopqrstuvwxyz
ABCDEFGHIJKLMNOPQRSTUVWXYZ 1234567890 abcdefghijklmnopqrstuvwxyz
ABCDEFGHIJKLMNOPQRSTUVWXYZ 1234567890 abcdefghijklmnopqrstuvwxyz

11/11

The main purpose of letters is the practical one of ma
king thoughts visible. Ruskin says that all letters are fr
ightful things and to be endured only on occasion, tha
t is to say, in places where the sense of the inscription
is of more importance than external ornament. This is
a sweeping statement, from which we need not suffer
unduly; yet it is doubtful whether there is art in individ
ual letters. Letters in combination may be satisfying a
nd in a well composed page even beautiful as a whol
e, but art in letters consists rather in the art of arrangin
g and composing them in a pleasing and appropriate
manner. The main purpose of letters is the practical o
ne of making thoughts visible. Ruskin says that all lett
ers are frightful things and to be endured only on occ
asion, that is to say, in places where the sense of the i
nscription is of more importance than external ornam
ent. This is a sweeping statement, from which we nee
d not suffer unduly; yet it is doubtful whether there is a
rt in individual letters. Letters in combination may be s
The main purpose of letters is the practical one of ma
king thoughts visible. Ruskin says that all letters are f
The main purpose of letters is the practical on
e of making thoughts visible. Ruskin says that

11/12

The main purpose of letters is the practical one of ma
king thoughts visible. Ruskin says that all letters are fr
ightful things and to be endured only on occasion, tha
t is to say, in places where the sense of the inscription
is of more importance than external ornament. This is
a sweeping statement, from which we need not suffer
unduly; yet it is doubtful whether there is art in individ
ual letters. Letters in combination may be satisfying a
nd in a well composed page even beautiful as a whol
e, but art in letters consists rather in the art of arrangin
g and composing them in a pleasing and appropriate
manner. The main purpose of letters is the practical o
ne of making thoughts visible. Ruskin says that all lett
ers are frightful things and to be endured only on occ
asion, that is to say, in places where the sense of the i
nscription is of more importance than external ornam
ent. This is a sweeping statement, from which we nee
d not suffer unduly; yet it is doubtful whether there is a
The main purpose of letters is the practical one of ma
king thoughts visible. Ruskin says that all letters are f
The main purpose of letters is the practical on
e of making thoughts visible. Ruskin says that

11/13

The main purpose of letters is the practical one of ma
king thoughts visible. Ruskin says that all letters are fr
ightful things and to be endured only on occasion, tha
t is to say, in places where the sense of the inscription
is of more importance than external ornament. This is
a sweeping statement, from which we need not suffer
unduly; yet it is doubtful whether there is art in individ
ual letters. Letters in combination may be satisfying a
nd in a well composed page even beautiful as a whol
e, but art in letters consists rather in the art of arrangin
g and composing them in a pleasing and appropriate
manner. The main purpose of letters is the practical o
ne of making thoughts visible. Ruskin says that all lett
ers are frightful things and to be endured only on occ
asion, that is to say, in places where the sense of the i
nscription is of more importance than external ornam
ent. This is a sweeping statement, from which we nee
The main purpose of letters is the practical one of ma
king thoughts visible. Ruskin says that all letters are f
The main purpose of letters is the practical on
e of making thoughts visible. Ruskin says that

11/14

The main purpose of letters is the practical one of ma
king thoughts visible. Ruskin says that all letters are fr
ightful things and to be endured only on occasion, tha
t is to say, in places where the sense of the inscription
is of more importance than external ornament. This is
a sweeping statement, from which we need not suffer
unduly; yet it is doubtful whether there is art in individ
ual letters. Letters in combination may be satisfying a
nd in a well composed page even beautiful as a whol
e, but art in letters consists rather in the art of arrangin
g and composing them in a pleasing and appropriate
manner. The main purpose of letters is the practical o
ne of making thoughts visible. Ruskin says that all lett
ers are frightful things and to be endured only on occ
asion, that is to say, in places where the sense of the i
nscription is of more importance than external ornam
The main purpose of letters is the practical one of ma
king thoughts visible. Ruskin says that all letters are f
The main purpose of letters is the practical on
e of making thoughts visible. Ruskin says that

HELVETICA 12 POINT SET MINUS ½ UNIT

ROMAN, ITALIC, HEAVY, HEAVY ITALIC

abcdefghijklmnopqrstuvwxyz – 1 UNIT
abcdefghijklmnopqrstuvwxyz – ½ UNIT
abcdefghijklmnopqrstuvwxyz NORMAL

ABCDEFGHIJKLMNOPQRSTUVWXYZ 1234567890 abcdefghijklmnopqrstuvwxyz
ABCDEFGHIJKLMNOPQRSTUVWXYZ 1234567890 abcdefghijklmnopqrstuvwxyz
ABCDEFGHIJKLMNOPQRSTUVWXYZ 1234567890 abcdefghijklmnopqrstuvwxyz
ABCDEFGHIJKLMNOPQRSTUVWXYZ 1234567890 abcdefghijklmnopqrstuvwxyz

12/12

The main purpose of letters is the practical one of making thoughts visible. Ruskin says that all letter s are frightful things and to be endured only on oc casion, that is to say, in places where the sense of the inscription is of more importance than externa l ornament. This is a sweeping statement, from w hich we need not suffer unduly; yet it is doubtful w hether there is art in individual letters. Letters in co mbination may be satisfying and in a well compos ed page even beautiful as a whole, but art in letter s consists rather in the art of arranging and comp osing them in a pleasing and appropriate manner. The main purpose of letters is the practical one of making thoughts visible. Ruskin says that all letter s are frightful things and to be endured only on oc
The main purpose of letters is the practical one of making thoughts visible. Ruskin says that all lette
The main purpose of letters is the practical one of making thoughts visible. Ruskin sa

12/13

The main purpose of letters is the practical one of making thoughts visible. Ruskin says that all letter s are frightful things and to be endured only on oc casion, that is to say, in places where the sense of the inscription is of more importance than externa l ornament. This is a sweeping statement, from w hich we need not suffer unduly; yet it is doubtful w hether there is art in individual letters. Letters in co mbination may be satisfying and in a well compos ed page even beautiful as a whole, but art in letter s consists rather in the art of arranging and comp osing them in a pleasing and appropriate manner. The main purpose of letters is the practical one of making thoughts visible. Ruskin says that all letter
The main purpose of letters is the practical one of making thoughts visible. Ruskin says that all lette
The main purpose of letters is the practical one of making thoughts visible. Ruskin sa

12/14

The main purpose of letters is the practical one of making thoughts visible. Ruskin says that all letter s are frightful things and to be endured only on oc casion, that is to say, in places where the sense of the inscription is of more importance than externa l ornament. This is a sweeping statement, from w hich we need not suffer unduly; yet it is doubtful w hether there is art in individual letters. Letters in co mbination may be satisfying and in a well compos ed page even beautiful as a whole, but art in letter s consists rather in the art of arranging and comp osing them in a pleasing and appropriate manner. The main purpose of letters is the practical one of making thoughts visible. Ruskin says that all letter s are frightful things and to be endured only on oc
The main purpose of letters is the practical one of making thoughts visible. Ruskin says that all lette
The main purpose of letters is the practical one of making thoughts visible. Ruskin sa

12/15

The main purpose of letters is the practical one of making thoughts visible. Ruskin says that all letter s are frightful things and to be endured only on oc casion, that is to say, in places where the sense of the inscription is of more importance than externa l ornament. This is a sweeping statement, from w hich we need not suffer unduly; yet it is doubtful w hether there is art in individual letters. Letters in co mbination may be satisfying and in a well compos ed page even beautiful as a whole, but art in letter s consists rather in the art of arranging and comp osing them in a pleasing and appropriate manner. The main purpose of letters is the practical one of making thoughts visible. Ruskin says that all letter
The main purpose of letters is the practical one of making thoughts visible. Ruskin says that all lette
The main purpose of letters is the practical one of making thoughts visible. Ruskin sa

HELVETICA 14 POINT SET MINUS ½ UNIT

ROMAN, ITALIC, HEAVY, HEAVY ITALIC

abcdefghijklmnopqrstuvwxyz – 1 UNIT
abcdefghijklmnopqrstuvwxyz – ½ UNIT
abcdefghijklmnopqrstuvwxyz NORMAL

ABCDEFGHIJKLMNOPQRSTUVWXYZ abcdefghijklmnopqrstuvwxyz
ABCDEFGHIJKLMNOPQRSTUVWXYZ abcdefghijklmnopqrstuvwxyz
ABCDEFGHIJKLMNOPQRSTUVWXYZ abcdefghijklmnopqrstuvwxyz
ABCDEFGHIJKLMNOPQRSTUVWXYZ abcdefghijklmnopqrstuvwxyz

14/14

The main purpose of letters is the practical one of making thoughts visible. Ruskin sa ys that all letters are frightful things and to be endured only on occasion, that is to sa y, in places where the sense of the inscripti on is of more importance than external orn ament. This is a sweeping statement, fro m which we need not suffer unduly; yet it i s doubtful whether there is art in individual letters. Letters in combination may be sati sfying and in a well composed page even beautiful as a whole, but art in letters consi sts rather in the art of arranging and comp
The main purpose of letters is the practic al one of making thoughts visible. Ruskin
The main purpose of letters is the pr actical one of making thoughts visib

14/15

The main purpose of letters is the practical one of making thoughts visible. Ruskin sa ys that all letters are frightful things and to be endured only on occasion, that is to sa y, in places where the sense of the inscripti on is of more importance than external orn ament. This is a sweeping statement, fro m which we need not suffer unduly; yet it i s doubtful whether there is art in individual letters. Letters in combination may be sati sfying and in a well composed page even beautiful as a whole, but art in letters consi
The main purpose of letters is the practic al one of making thoughts visible. Ruskin
The main purpose of letters is the pr actical one of making thoughts visib

14/16

The main purpose of letters is the practical one of making thoughts visible. Ruskin sa ys that all letters are frightful things and to be endured only on occasion, that is to sa y, in places where the sense of the inscripti on is of more importance than external orn ament. This is a sweeping statement, fro m which we need not suffer unduly; yet it i s doubtful whether there is art in individual letters. Letters in combination may be sati sfying and in a well composed page even beautiful as a whole, but art in letters consi sts rather in the art of arranging and comp
The main purpose of letters is the practic al one of making thoughts visible. Ruskin
The main purpose of letters is the pr actical one of making thoughts visib

14/17

The main purpose of letters is the practical one of making thoughts visible. Ruskin sa ys that all letters are frightful things and to be endured only on occasion, that is to sa y, in places where the sense of the inscripti on is of more importance than external orn ament. This is a sweeping statement, fro m which we need not suffer unduly; yet it i s doubtful whether there is art in individual letters. Letters in combination may be sati sfying and in a well composed page even beautiful as a whole, but art in letters consi
The main purpose of letters is the practic al one of making thoughts visible. Ruskin
The main purpose of letters is the pr actical one of making thoughts visib

JANSON 6 & 7 POINT SET NORMAL

ROMAN, ITALIC

ABCDEFGHIJKLMNOPQRSTUVWXYZ 1234567890 abcdefghijklmnopqrstuvwxyz

ABCDEFGHIJKLMNOPQRSTUVWXYZ 1234567890 abcdefghijklmnopqrstuvwxyz

6/6

The main purpose of letters is the practical one of making thoughts visible. Ruskin says that all let
ters are frightful things and to be endured only on occasion, that is to say, in places where the sens
e of the inscription is of more importance than external ornament. This is a sweeping statement, f
rom which we need not suffer unduly; yet it is doubtful whether there is art in individual letters.
Letters in combination may be satisfying and in a well composed page even beautiful as a whole, b
ut art in letters consists rather in the art of arranging and composing them in a pleasing and appro
priate manner. The main purpose of letters is the practical one of making thoughts visible. Ruskin
says that all letters are frightful things and to be endured only on occasion, that is to say, in places
where the sense of the inscription is of more importance than external ornament. This is a sweepi
ng statement, from which we need not suffer unduly; yet it is doubtful whether there is art in indi
vidual letters. Letters in combination may be satisfying and in a well composed page even beautif
ul as a whole, but art in letters consists rather in the art of arranging and composing them in a plea
sing and appropriate manner. The main purpose of letters is the practical one of making thoughts
visible. Ruskin says that all letters are frightful things and to be endured only on occasion, that is t
o say, in places where the sense of the inscription is of more importance than external ornament.
*The main purpose of letters is the practical one of making thoughts visible. Ruskin says that all letters are fright
ful things and to be endured only on occasion, that is to say, in places where the sense of the inscription is of more*

6/7

The main purpose of letters is the practical one of making thoughts visible. Ruskin says that all let
ters are frightful things and to be endured only on occasion, that is to say, in places where the sens
e of the inscription is of more importance than external ornament. This is a sweeping statement, f
rom which we need not suffer unduly; yet it is doubtful whether there is art in individual letters.
Letters in combination may be satisfying and in a well composed page even beautiful as a whole, b
ut art in letters consists rather in the art of arranging and composing them in a pleasing and appro
priate manner. The main purpose of letters is the practical one of making thoughts visible. Ruskin
says that all letters are frightful things and to be endured only on occasion, that is to say, in places
where the sense of the inscription is of more importance than external ornament. This is a sweepi
ng statement, from which we need not suffer unduly; yet it is doubtful whether there is art in indi
vidual letters. Letters in combination may be satisfying and in a well composed page even beautif
ul as a whole, but art in letters consists rather in the art of arranging and composing them in a plea
sing and appropriate manner. The main purpose of letters is the practical one of making thoughts
*The main purpose of letters is the practical one of making thoughts visible. Ruskin says that all letters are fright
ful things and to be endured only on occasion, that is to say, in places where the sense of the inscription is of more*

6/8

The main purpose of letters is the practical one of making thoughts visible. Ruskin says that all let
ters are frightful things and to be endured only on occasion, that is to say, in places where the sens
e of the inscription is of more importance than external ornament. This is a sweeping statement, f
rom which we need not suffer unduly; yet it is doubtful whether there is art in individual letters.
Letters in combination may be satisfying and in a well composed page even beautiful as a whole, b
ut art in letters consists rather in the art of arranging and composing them in a pleasing and appro
priate manner. The main purpose of letters is the practical one of making thoughts visible. Ruskin
says that all letters are frightful things and to be endured only on occasion, that is to say, in places
where the sense of the inscription is of more importance than external ornament. This is a sweepi
ng statement, from which we need not suffer unduly; yet it is doubtful whether there is art in indi
vidual letters. Letters in combination may be satisfying and in a well composed page even beautif
*The main purpose of letters is the practical one of making thoughts visible. Ruskin says that all letters are fright
ful things and to be endured only on occasion, that is to say, in places where the sense of the inscription is of more*

6/9

The main purpose of letters is the practical one of making thoughts visible. Ruskin says that all let
ters are frightful things and to be endured only on occasion, that is to say, in places where the sens
e of the inscription is of more importance than external ornament. This is a sweeping statement, f
rom which we need not suffer unduly; yet it is doubtful whether there is art in individual letters.
Letters in combination may be satisfying and in a well composed page even beautiful as a whole, b
ut art in letters consists rather in the art of arranging and composing them in a pleasing and appro
priate manner. The main purpose of letters is the practical one of making thoughts visible. Ruskin
says that all letters are frightful things and to be endured only on occasion, that is to say, in places
where the sense of the inscription is of more importance than external ornament. This is a sweepi
ng statement, from which we need not suffer unduly; yet it is doubtful whether there is art in indi
*The main purpose of letters is the practical one of making thoughts visible. Ruskin says that all letters are fright
ful things and to be endured only on occasion, that is to say, in places where the sense of the inscription is of more*

ABCDEFGHIJKLMNOPQRSTUVWXYZ 1234567890 abcdefghijklmnopqrstuvwxyz

ABCDEFGHIJKLMNOPQRSTUVWXYZ 1234567890 abcdefghijklmnopqrstuvwxyz

7/7

The main purpose of letters is the practical one of making thoughts visible. Ruskin s
ays that all letters are frightful things and to be endured only on occasion, that is to s
ay, in places where the sense of the inscription is of more importance than external o
rnament. This is a sweeping statement, from which we need not suffer unduly; yet
it is doubtful whether there is art in individual letters. Letters in combination may b
e satisfying and in a well composed page even beautiful as a whole, but art in letters
consists rather in the art of arranging and composing them in a pleasing and appropr
iate manner. The main purpose of letters is the practical one of making thoughts visi
ble. Ruskin says that all letters are frightful things and to be endured only on occasi
on, that is to say, in places where the sense of the inscription is of more importance t
han external ornament. This is a sweeping statement, from which we need not suffe
r unduly; yet it is doubtful whether there is art in individual letters. Letters in comb
ination may be satisfying and in a well composed page even beautiful as a whole, bu
*The main purpose of letters is the practical one of making thoughts visible. Ruskin says that all
letters are frightful things and to be endured only on occasion, that is to say, in places where the*

7/8

The main purpose of letters is the practical one of making thoughts visible. Ruskin s
ays that all letters are frightful things and to be endured only on occasion, that is to s
ay, in places where the sense of the inscription is of more importance than external o
rnament. This is a sweeping statement, from which we need not suffer unduly; yet
it is doubtful whether there is art in individual letters. Letters in combination may b
e satisfying and in a well composed page even beautiful as a whole, but art in letters
consists rather in the art of arranging and composing them in a pleasing and appropr
iate manner. The main purpose of letters is the practical one of making thoughts visi
ble. Ruskin says that all letters are frightful things and to be endured only on occasi
on, that is to say, in places where the sense of the inscription is of more importance t
han external ornament. This is a sweeping statement, from which we need not suffe
r unduly; yet it is doubtful whether there is art in individual letters. Letters in comb
*The main purpose of letters is the practical one of making thoughts visible. Ruskin says that all
letters are frightful things and to be endured only on occasion, that is to say, in places where the*

7/9

The main purpose of letters is the practical one of making thoughts visible. Ruskin s
ays that all letters are frightful things and to be endured only on occasion, that is to s
ay, in places where the sense of the inscription is of more importance than external o
rnament. This is a sweeping statement, from which we need not suffer unduly; yet
it is doubtful whether there is art in individual letters. Letters in combination may b
e satisfying and in a well composed page even beautiful as a whole, but art in letters
consists rather in the art of arranging and composing them in a pleasing and appropr
iate manner. The main purpose of letters is the practical one of making thoughts visi
ble. Ruskin says that all letters are frightful things and to be endured only on occasi
on, that is to say, in places where the sense of the inscription is of more importance t
han external ornament. This is a sweeping statement, from which we need not suffe
r unduly; yet it is doubtful whether there is art in individual letters. Letters in comb
*The main purpose of letters is the practical one of making thoughts visible. Ruskin says that all
letters are frightful things and to be endured only on occasion, that is to say, in places where the*

7/10

The main purpose of letters is the practical one of making thoughts visible. Ruskin s
ays that all letters are frightful things and to be endured only on occasion, that is to s
ay, in places where the sense of the inscription is of more importance than external o
rnament. This is a sweeping statement, from which we need not suffer unduly; yet
it is doubtful whether there is art in individual letters. Letters in combination may b
e satisfying and in a well composed page even beautiful as a whole, but art in letters
consists rather in the art of arranging and composing them in a pleasing and appropr
iate manner. The main purpose of letters is the practical one of making thoughts visi
ble. Ruskin says that all letters are frightful things and to be endured only on occasi
on, that is to say, in places where the sense of the inscription is of more importance t
han external ornament. This is a sweeping statement, from which we need not suffe
*The main purpose of letters is the practical one of making thoughts visible. Ruskin says that all
letters are frightful things and to be endured only on occasion, that is to say, in places where the*

JANSON 8 & 9 POINT SET NORMAL

ROMAN, ITALIC

ABCDEFGHIJKLMNOPQRSTUVWXYZ 1234567890 abcdefghijklmnopqrstuvwxyz

ABCDEFGHIJKLMNOPQRSTUVWXYZ 1234567890 abcdefghijklmnopqrstuvwxyz

8/8

The main purpose of letters is the practical one of making thoughts visibl e. Ruskin says that all letters are frightful things and to be endured only o n occasion, that is to say, in places where the sense of the inscription is of more importance than external ornament. This is a sweeping statement, from which we need not suffer unduly; yet it is doubtful whether there is art in individual letters. Letters in combination may be satisfying and in a well composed page even beautiful as a whole, but art in letters consists r ather in the art of arranging and composing them in a pleasing and appro priate manner. The main purpose of letters is the practical one of making thoughts visible. Ruskin says that all letters are frightful things and to be endured only on occasion, that is to say, in places where the sense of the i
The main purpose of letters is the practical one of making thoughts visible. Ruskin s ays that all letters are frightful things and to be endured only on occasion, that is to

8/9

The main purpose of letters is the practical one of making thoughts visibl e. Ruskin says that all letters are frightful things and to be endured only o n occasion, that is to say, in places where the sense of the inscription is of more importance than external ornament. This is a sweeping statement, from which we need not suffer unduly; yet it is doubtful whether there is art in individual letters. Letters in combination may be satisfying and in a well composed page even beautiful as a whole, but art in letters consists r ather in the art of arranging and composing them in a pleasing and appro priate manner. The main purpose of letters is the practical one of making thoughts visible. Ruskin says that all letters are frightful things and to be
The main purpose of letters is the practical one of making thoughts visible. Ruskin s ays that all letters are frightful things and to be endured only on occasion, that is to

8/10

The main purpose of letters is the practical one of making thoughts visibl e. Ruskin says that all letters are frightful things and to be endured only o n occasion, that is to say, in places where the sense of the inscription is of more importance than external ornament. This is a sweeping statement, from which we need not suffer unduly; yet it is doubtful whether there is art in individual letters. Letters in combination may be satisfying and in a well composed page even beautiful as a whole, but art in letters consists r ather in the art of arranging and composing them in a pleasing and appro priate manner. The main purpose of letters is the practical one of making
The main purpose of letters is the practical one of making thoughts visible. Ruskin s ays that all letters are frightful things and to be endured only on occasion, that is to

8/11

The main purpose of letters is the practical one of making thoughts visibl e. Ruskin says that all letters are frightful things and to be endured only o n occasion, that is to say, in places where the sense of the inscription is of more importance than external ornament. This is a sweeping statement, from which we need not suffer unduly; yet it is doubtful whether there is art in individual letters. Letters in combination may be satisfying and in a well composed page even beautiful as a whole, but art in letters consists r ather in the art of arranging and composing them in a pleasing and appro priate manner. The main purpose of letters is the practical one of making
The main purpose of letters is the practical one of making thoughts visible. Ruskin s ays that all letters are frightful things and to be endured only on occasion, that is to

ABCDEFGHIJKLMNOPQRSTUVWXYZ 1234567890 abcdefghijklmnopqrstuvwxyz

ABCDEFGHIJKLMNOPQRSTUVWXYZ 1234567890 abcdefghijklmnopqrstuvwxyz

9/9

The main purpose of letters is the practical one of making though ts visible. Ruskin says that all letters are frightful things and to be endured only on occasion, that is to say, in places where the sense of the inscription is of more importance than external ornament. This is a sweeping statement, from which we need not suffer und uly; yet it is doubtful whether there is art in individual letters. Le tters in combination may be satisfying and in a well composed pa ge even beautiful as a whole, but art in letters consists rather in th e art of arranging and composing them in a pleasing and appropri ate manner. The main purpose of letters is the practical one of ma
The main purpose of letters is the practical one of making thoughts visible. Ruskin says that all letters are frightful things and to be endured only on o

9/10

The main purpose of letters is the practical one of making though ts visible. Ruskin says that all letters are frightful things and to be endured only on occasion, that is to say, in places where the sense of the inscription is of more importance than external ornament. This is a sweeping statement, from which we need not suffer und uly; yet it is doubtful whether there is art in individual letters. Le tters in combination may be satisfying and in a well composed pa ge even beautiful as a whole, but art in letters consists rather in th e art of arranging and composing them in a pleasing and appropri
The main purpose of letters is the practical one of making thoughts visible. Ruskin says that all letters are frightful things and to be endured only on o

9/11

The main purpose of letters is the practical one of making though ts visible. Ruskin says that all letters are frightful things and to be endured only on occasion, that is to say, in places where the sense of the inscription is of more importance than external ornament. This is a sweeping statement, from which we need not suffer und uly; yet it is doubtful whether there is art in individual letters. Le tters in combination may be satisfying and in a well composed pa ge even beautiful as a whole, but art in letters consists rather in th e art of arranging and composing them in a pleasing and appropri
The main purpose of letters is the practical one of making thoughts visible. Ruskin says that all letters are frightful things and to be endured only on o

9/12

The main purpose of letters is the practical one of making though ts visible. Ruskin says that all letters are frightful things and to be endured only on occasion, that is to say, in places where the sense of the inscription is of more importance than external ornament. This is a sweeping statement, from which we need not suffer und uly; yet it is doubtful whether there is art in individual letters. Le tters in combination may be satisfying and in a well composed pa ge even beautiful as a whole, but art in letters consists rather in th e art of arranging and composing them in a pleasing and appropri
The main purpose of letters is the practical one of making thoughts visible. Ruskin says that all letters are frightful things and to be endured only on o

JANSON 10 POINT SET MINUS ½ UNIT

ROMAN, ITALIC

abcdefghijklmnopqrstuvwxyz – 1 UNIT
abcdefghijklmnopqrstuvwxyz – ½ UNIT
abcdefghijklmnopqrstuvwxyz NORMAL

ABCDEFGHIJKLMNOPQRSTUVWXYZ 1234567890 abcdefghijklmnopqrstuvwxyz
ABCDEFGHIJKLMNOPQRSTUVWXYZ 1234567890 abcdefghijklmnopqrstuvwxyz

10/10

The main purpose of letters is the practical one of making tho ughts visible. Ruskin says that all letters are frightful things a nd to be endured only on occasion, that is to say, in places wh ere the sense of the inscription is of more importance than ext ernal ornament. This is a sweeping statement, from which w e need not suffer unduly; yet it is doubtful whether there is ar t in individual letters. Letters in combination may be satisfyi ng and in a well composed page even beautiful as a whole, bu t art in letters consists rather in the art of arranging and comp osing them in a pleasing and appropriate manner. The main p urpose of letters is the practical one of making thoughts visibl e. Ruskin says that all letters are frightful things and to be end ured only on occasion, that is to say, in places where the sense of the inscription is of more importance than external orname nt. This is a sweeping statement, from which we need not suf fer unduly; yet it is doubtful whether there is art in individual letters. Letters in combination may be satisfying and in a wel l composed page even beautiful as a whole, but art in letters c onsists rather in the art of arranging and composing them in a pleasing and appropriate manner. The main purpose of letter s is the practical one of making thoughts visible. Ruskin says t hat all letters are frightful things and to be endured only on oc casion, that is to say, in places where the sense of the inscripti on is of more importance than external ornament. This is a s
The main purpose of letters is the practical one of making thoughts visi ble. Ruskin says that all letters are frightful things and to be endured o

10/11

The main purpose of letters is the practical one of making tho ughts visible. Ruskin says that all letters are frightful things a nd to be endured only on occasion, that is to say, in places wh ere the sense of the inscription is of more importance than ext ernal ornament. This is a sweeping statement, from which w e need not suffer unduly; yet it is doubtful whether there is ar t in individual letters. Letters in combination may be satisfyi ng and in a well composed page even beautiful as a whole, bu t art in letters consists rather in the art of arranging and comp osing them in a pleasing and appropriate manner. The main p urpose of letters is the practical one of making thoughts visibl e. Ruskin says that all letters are frightful things and to be end ured only on occasion, that is to say, in places where the sense of the inscription is of more importance than external orname nt. This is a sweeping statement, from which we need not suf fer unduly; yet it is doubtful whether there is art in individual letters. Letters in combination may be satisfying and in a wel l composed page even beautiful as a whole, but art in letters c onsists rather in the art of arranging and composing them in a pleasing and appropriate manner. The main purpose of letter s is the practical one of making thoughts visible. Ruskin says t hat all letters are frightful things and to be endured only on oc
The main purpose of letters is the practical one of making thoughts visi ble. Ruskin says that all letters are frightful things and to be endured o

10/12

The main purpose of letters is the practical one of making tho ughts visible. Ruskin says that all letters are frightful things a nd to be endured only on occasion, that is to say, in places wh ere the sense of the inscription is of more importance than ext ernal ornament. This is a sweeping statement, from which w e need not suffer unduly; yet it is doubtful whether there is ar t in individual letters. Letters in combination may be satisfyi ng and in a well composed page even beautiful as a whole, bu t art in letters consists rather in the art of arranging and comp osing them in a pleasing and appropriate manner. The main p urpose of letters is the practical one of making thoughts visibl e. Ruskin says that all letters are frightful things and to be end ured only on occasion, that is to say, in places where the sense of the inscription is of more importance than external orname nt. This is a sweeping statement, from which we need not suf fer unduly; yet it is doubtful whether there is art in individual letters. Letters in combination may be satisfying and in a wel l composed page even beautiful as a whole, but art in letters c onsists rather in the art of arranging and composing them in a pleasing and appropriate manner. The main purpose of letter
The main purpose of letters is the practical one of making thoughts visi ble. Ruskin says that all letters are frightful things and to be endured o

10/13

The main purpose of letters is the practical one of making tho ughts visible. Ruskin says that all letters are frightful things a nd to be endured only on occasion, that is to say, in places wh ere the sense of the inscription is of more importance than ext ernal ornament. This is a sweeping statement, from which w e need not suffer unduly; yet it is doubtful whether there is ar t in individual letters. Letters in combination may be satisfyi ng and in a well composed page even beautiful as a whole, bu t art in letters consists rather in the art of arranging and comp osing them in a pleasing and appropriate manner. The main p urpose of letters is the practical one of making thoughts visibl e. Ruskin says that all letters are frightful things and to be end ured only on occasion, that is to say, in places where the sense of the inscription is of more importance than external orname nt. This is a sweeping statement, from which we need not suf fer unduly; yet it is doubtful whether there is art in individual letters. Letters in combination may be satisfying and in a wel l composed page even beautiful as a whole, but art in letters c onsists rather in the art of arranging and composing them in a
The main purpose of letters is the practical one of making thoughts visi ble. Ruskin says that all letters are frightful things and to be endured o

JANSON 11 POINT SET MINUS ½ UNIT

ROMAN, ITALIC

abcdefghijklmnopqrstuvwxyz – 1 UNIT
abcdefghijklmnopqrstuvwxyz – ½ UNIT
abcdefghijklmnopqrstuvwxyz NORMAL

ABCDEFGHIJKLMNOPQRSTUVWXYZ 1234567890 abcdefghijklmnopqrstuvwxyz
ABCDEFGHIJKLMNOPQRSTUVWXYZ 1234567890 abcdefghijklmnopqrstuvwxyz

11/11

The main purpose of letters is the practical one of maki ng thoughts visible. Ruskin says that all letters are frigh tful things and to be endured only on occasion, that is t o say, in places where the sense of the inscription is of m ore importance than external ornament. This is a swee ping statement, from which we need not suffer unduly; yet it is doubtful whether there is art in individual letter s. Letters in combination may be satisfying and in a wel l composed page even beautiful as a whole, but art in let ters consists rather in the art of arranging and composin g them in a pleasing and appropriate manner. The main purpose of letters is the practical one of making thought s visible. Ruskin says that all letters are frightful things and to be endured only on occasion, that is to say, in pla ces where the sense of the inscription is of more import ance than external ornament. This is a sweeping statem ent, from which we need not suffer unduly; yet it is do ubtful whether there is art in individual letters. Letters in combination may be satisfying and in a well compos ed page even beautiful as a whole, but art in letters cons ists rather in the art of arranging and composing them i
The main purpose of letters is the practical one of making thoug hts visible. Ruskin says that all letters are frightful things and t

11/12

The main purpose of letters is the practical one of maki ng thoughts visible. Ruskin says that all letters are frigh tful things and to be endured only on occasion, that is t o say, in places where the sense of the inscription is of m ore importance than external ornament. This is a swee ping statement, from which we need not suffer unduly; yet it is doubtful whether there is art in individual letter s. Letters in combination may be satisfying and in a wel l composed page even beautiful as a whole, but art in let ters consists rather in the art of arranging and composin g them in a pleasing and appropriate manner. The main purpose of letters is the practical one of making thought s visible. Ruskin says that all letters are frightful things and to be endured only on occasion, that is to say, in pla ces where the sense of the inscription is of more import ance than external ornament. This is a sweeping statem ent, from which we need not suffer unduly; yet it is do ubtful whether there is art in individual letters. Letters in combination may be satisfying and in a well compos ed page even beautiful as a whole, but art in letters cons
The main purpose of letters is the practical one of making thoug hts visible. Ruskin says that all letters are frightful things and t

11/13

The main purpose of letters is the practical one of maki ng thoughts visible. Ruskin says that all letters are frigh tful things and to be endured only on occasion, that is t o say, in places where the sense of the inscription is of m ore importance than external ornament. This is a swee ping statement, from which we need not suffer unduly; yet it is doubtful whether there is art in individual letter s. Letters in combination may be satisfying and in a wel l composed page even beautiful as a whole, but art in let ters consists rather in the art of arranging and composin g them in a pleasing and appropriate manner. The main purpose of letters is the practical one of making thought s visible. Ruskin says that all letters are frightful things and to be endured only on occasion, that is to say, in pla ces where the sense of the inscription is of more import ance than external ornament. This is a sweeping statem ent, from which we need not suffer unduly; yet it is do ubtful whether there is art in individual letters. Letters in combination may be satisfying and in a well compos
The main purpose of letters is the practical one of making thoug hts visible. Ruskin says that all letters are frightful things and t

11/14

The main purpose of letters is the practical one of maki ng thoughts visible. Ruskin says that all letters are frigh tful things and to be endured only on occasion, that is t o say, in places where the sense of the inscription is of m ore importance than external ornament. This is a swee ping statement, from which we need not suffer unduly; yet it is doubtful whether there is art in individual letter s. Letters in combination may be satisfying and in a wel l composed page even beautiful as a whole, but art in let ters consists rather in the art of arranging and composin g them in a pleasing and appropriate manner. The main purpose of letters is the practical one of making thought s visible. Ruskin says that all letters are frightful things and to be endured only on occasion, that is to say, in pla ces where the sense of the inscription is of more import ance than external ornament. This is a sweeping statem ent, from which we need not suffer unduly; yet it is do ubtful whether there is art in individual letters. Letters
The main purpose of letters is the practical one of making thoug hts visible. Ruskin says that all letters are frightful things and t

JANSON 12 POINT SET MINUS ½ UNIT

ROMAN, ITALIC

abcdefghijklmnopqrstuvwxyz – 1 UNIT
abcdefghijklmnopqrstuvwxyz – ½ UNIT
abcdefghijklmnopqrstuvwxyz NORMAL

ABCDEFGHIJKLMNOPQRSTUVWXYZ 1234567890 abcdefghijklmnopqrstuvwxyz
ABCDEFGHIJKLMNOPQRSTUVWXYZ 1234567890 abcdefghijklmnopqrstuvwxyz

12/12

The main purpose of letters is the practical one of m aking thoughts visible. Ruskin says that all letters ar e frightful things and to be endured only on occasio n, that is to say, in places where the sense of the insc ription is of more importance than external orname nt. This is a sweeping statement, from which we ne ed not suffer unduly; yet it is doubtful whether ther e is art in individual letters. Letters in combination may be satisfying and in a well composed page even beautiful as a whole, but art in letters consists rather in the art of arranging and composing them in a plea sing and appropriate manner. The main purpose of letters is the practical one of making thoughts visibl e. Ruskin says that all letters are frightful things and to be endured only on occasion, that is to say, in pla ces where the sense of the inscription is of more imp ortance than external ornament. This is a sweeping
The main purpose of letters is the practical one of making th oughts visible. Ruskin says that all letters are frightful thin

12/13

The main purpose of letters is the practical one of m aking thoughts visible. Ruskin says that all letters ar e frightful things and to be endured only on occasio n, that is to say, in places where the sense of the insc ription is of more importance than external orname nt. This is a sweeping statement, from which we ne ed not suffer unduly; yet it is doubtful whether ther e is art in individual letters. Letters in combination may be satisfying and in a well composed page even beautiful as a whole, but art in letters consists rather in the art of arranging and composing them in a plea sing and appropriate manner. The main purpose of letters is the practical one of making thoughts visibl e. Ruskin says that all letters are frightful things and to be endured only on occasion, that is to say, in pla ces where the sense of the inscription is of more imp
The main purpose of letters is the practical one of making th oughts visible. Ruskin says that all letters are frightful thin

12/14

The main purpose of letters is the practical one of m aking thoughts visible. Ruskin says that all letters ar e frightful things and to be endured only on occasio n, that is to say, in places where the sense of the insc ription is of more importance than external orname nt. This is a sweeping statement, from which we ne ed not suffer unduly; yet it is doubtful whether ther e is art in individual letters. Letters in combination may be satisfying and in a well composed page even beautiful as a whole, but art in letters consists rather in the art of arranging and composing them in a plea sing and appropriate manner. The main purpose of letters is the practical one of making thoughts visibl e. Ruskin says that all letters are frightful things and to be endured only on occasion, that is to say, in pla ces where the sense of the inscription is of more imp ortance than external ornament. This is a sweeping
The main purpose of letters is the practical one of making th oughts visible. Ruskin says that all letters are frightful thin

12/15

The main purpose of letters is the practical one of m aking thoughts visible. Ruskin says that all letters ar e frightful things and to be endured only on occasio n, that is to say, in places where the sense of the insc ription is of more importance than external orname nt. This is a sweeping statement, from which we ne ed not suffer unduly; yet it is doubtful whether ther e is art in individual letters. Letters in combination may be satisfying and in a well composed page even beautiful as a whole, but art in letters consists rather in the art of arranging and composing them in a plea sing and appropriate manner. The main purpose of letters is the practical one of making thoughts visibl e. Ruskin says that all letters are frightful things and to be endured only on occasion, that is to say, in pla ces where the sense of the inscription is of more imp
The main purpose of letters is the practical one of making th oughts visible. Ruskin says that all letters are frightful thin

JANSON 14 POINT SET MINUS ½ UNIT

ROMAN, ITALIC

abcdefghijklmnopqrstuvwxyz – 1 UNIT
abcdefghijklmnopqrstuvwxyz – ½ UNIT
abcdefghijklmnopqrstuvwxyz NORMAL

ABCDEFGHIJKLMNOPQRSTUVWXYZ abcdefghijklmnopqrstuvwxyz
ABCDEFGHIJKLMNOPQRSTUVWXYZ abcdefghijklmnopqrstuvwxyz

14/14

The main purpose of letters is the practical one of making thoughts visible. Ruskin says that all letters are frightful things and to be e ndured only on occasion, that is to say, in pl aces where the sense of the inscription is of more importance than external ornament. This is a sweeping statement, from which we need not suffer unduly; yet it is doubtful whether there is art in individual letters. Le tters in combination may be satisfying and i n a well composed page even beautiful as a whole, but art in letters consists rather in th e art of arranging and composing them in a pleasing and appropriate manner. The mai n purpose of letters is the practical one of m
The main purpose of letters is the practical one of making thoughts visible. Ruskin says that all lette

14/15

The main purpose of letters is the practical one of making thoughts visible. Ruskin says that all letters are frightful things and to be e ndured only on occasion, that is to say, in pl aces where the sense of the inscription is of more importance than external ornament. This is a sweeping statement, from which we need not suffer unduly; yet it is doubtful whether there is art in individual letters. Le tters in combination may be satisfying and i n a well composed page even beautiful as a whole, but art in letters consists rather in th e art of arranging and composing them in a pleasing and appropriate manner. The mai
The main purpose of letters is the practical one of making thoughts visible. Ruskin says that all lette

14/16

The main purpose of letters is the practical one of making thoughts visible. Ruskin says that all letters are frightful things and to be e ndured only on occasion, that is to say, in pl aces where the sense of the inscription is of more importance than external ornament. This is a sweeping statement, from which we need not suffer unduly; yet it is doubtful whether there is art in individual letters. Le tters in combination may be satisfying and i n a well composed page even beautiful as a whole, but art in letters consists rather in th e art of arranging and composing them in a pleasing and appropriate manner. The mai n purpose of letters is the practical one of m
The main purpose of letters is the practical one of making thoughts visible. Ruskin says that all lette

14/17

The main purpose of letters is the practical one of making thoughts visible. Ruskin says that all letters are frightful things and to be e ndured only on occasion, that is to say, in pl aces where the sense of the inscription is of more importance than external ornament. This is a sweeping statement, from which we need not suffer unduly; yet it is doubtful whether there is art in individual letters. Le tters in combination may be satisfying and i n a well composed page even beautiful as a whole, but art in letters consists rather in th e art of arranging and composing them in a pleasing and appropriate manner. The mai
The main purpose of letters is the practical one of making thoughts visible. Ruskin says that all lette

ITC KABEL 6 & 7 POINT SET NORMAL

BOOK, MEDIUM, DEMI, BOLD

ABCDEFGHIJKLMNOPQRSTUVWXYZ 1234567890 abcdefghijklmnopqrstuvwxyz

ABCDEFGHIJKLMNOPQRSTUVWXYZ 1234567890 abcdefghijklmnopqrstuvwxyz

ABCDEFGHIJKLMNOPQRSTUVWXYZ 1234567890 abcdefghijklmnopqrstuvwxyz

ABCDEFGHIJKLMNOPQRSTUVWXYZ 1234567890 abcdefghijklmnopqrstuvwxyz

6/6

The main purpose of letters is the practical one of making thoughts visible. Ruskin says that all letters ar
e frightful things and to be endured only on occasion, that is to say, in places where the sense of the in
scription is of more importance than external ornament. This is a sweeping statement, from which we
need not suffer unduly; yet it is doubtful whether there is art in individual letters. Letters in combinatio
n may be satisfying and in a well composed page even beautiful as a whole, but art in letters consists r
ather in the art of arranging and composing them in a pleasing and appropriate manner. The main purp
ose of letters is the practical one of making thoughts visible. Ruskin says that all letters are frightful thing
s and to be endured only on occasion, that is to say, in places where the sense of the inscription is of
more importance than external ornament. This is a sweeping statement, from which we need not suff
er unduly; yet it is doubtful whether there is art in individual letters. Letters in combination may be sati
sfying and in a well composed page even beautiful as a whole, but art in letters consists rather in the ar
t of arranging and composing them in a pleasing and appropriate manner. The main purpose of letters
is the practical one of making thoughts visible. Ruskin says that all letters are frightful things and to be e
The main purpose of letters is the practical one of making thoughts visible. Ruskin says that all le
tters are frightful things and to be endured only on occasion, that is to say, in places where the s
The main purpose of letters is the practical one of making thoughts visible. Ruskin says that all
letters are frightful things and to be endured only on occasion, that is to say, in places where t

6/7

The main purpose of letters is the practical one of making thoughts visible. Ruskin says that all letters ar
e frightful things and to be endured only on occasion, that is to say, in places where the sense of the in
scription is of more importance than external ornament. This is a sweeping statement, from which we
need not suffer unduly; yet it is doubtful whether there is art in individual letters. Letters in combinatio
n may be satisfying and in a well composed page even beautiful as a whole, but art in letters consists r
ather in the art of arranging and composing them in a pleasing and appropriate manner. The main purp
ose of letters is the practical one of making thoughts visible. Ruskin says that all letters are frightful thing
s and to be endured only on occasion, that is to say, in places where the sense of the inscription is of
more importance than external ornament. This is a sweeping statement, from which we need not suff
er unduly; yet it is doubtful whether there is art in individual letters. Letters in combination may be sati
sfying and in a well composed page even beautiful as a whole, but art in letters consists rather in the ar
The main purpose of letters is the practical one of making thoughts visible. Ruskin says that all le
tters are frightful things and to be endured only on occasion, that is to say, in places where the s
The main purpose of letters is the practical one of making thoughts visible. Ruskin says that all
letters are frightful things and to be endured only on occasion, that is to say, in places where t

6/8

The main purpose of letters is the practical one of making thoughts visible. Ruskin says that all letters ar
e frightful things and to be endured only on occasion, that is to say, in places where the sense of the in
scription is of more importance than external ornament. This is a sweeping statement, from which we
need not suffer unduly; yet it is doubtful whether there is art in individual letters. Letters in combinatio
n may be satisfying and in a well composed page even beautiful as a whole, but art in letters consists r
ather in the art of arranging and composing them in a pleasing and appropriate manner. The main purp
ose of letters is the practical one of making thoughts visible. Ruskin says that all letters are frightful thing
s and to be endured only on occasion, that is to say, in places where the sense of the inscription is of
more importance than external ornament. This is a sweeping statement, from which we need not suff
The main purpose of letters is the practical one of making thoughts visible. Ruskin says that all le
tters are frightful things and to be endured only on occasion, that is to say, in places where the s
The main purpose of letters is the practical one of making thoughts visible. Ruskin says that all
letters are frightful things and to be endured only on occasion, that is to say, in places where t

6/9

The main purpose of letters is the practical one of making thoughts visible. Ruskin says that all letters ar
e frightful things and to be endured only on occasion, that is to say, in places where the sense of the in
scription is of more importance than external ornament. This is a sweeping statement, from which we
need not suffer unduly; yet it is doubtful whether there is art in individual letters. Letters in combinatio
n may be satisfying and in a well composed page even beautiful as a whole, but art in letters consists r
ather in the art of arranging and composing them in a pleasing and appropriate manner. The main purp
ose of letters is the practical one of making thoughts visible. Ruskin says that all letters are frightful thing
s and to be endured only on occasion, that is to say, in places where the sense of the inscription is of
The main purpose of letters is the practical one of making thoughts visible. Ruskin says that all le
tters are frightful things and to be endured only on occasion, that is to say, in places where the s
The main purpose of letters is the practical one of making thoughts visible. Ruskin says that all
letters are frightful things and to be endured only on occasion, that is to say, in places where t

---

ABCDEFGHIJKLMNOPQRSTUVWXYZ 1234567890 abcdefghijklmnopqrstuvwxyz

ABCDEFGHIJKLMNOPQRSTUVWXYZ 1234567890 abcdefghijklmnopqrstuvwxyz

ABCDEFGHIJKLMNOPQRSTUVWXYZ 1234567890 abcdefghijklmnopqrstuvwxyz

ABCDEFGHIJKLMNOPQRSTUVWXYZ 1234567890 abcdefghijklmnopqrstuvwxyz

7/7

The main purpose of letters is the practical one of making thoughts visible. Ruskin says t
hat all letters are frightful things and to be endured only on occasion, that is to say, in pla
ces where the sense of the inscription is of more importance than external ornament. T
his is a sweeping statement, from which we need not suffer unduly; yet it is doubtful w
hether there is art in individual letters. Letters in combination may be satisfying and in a
well composed page even beautiful as a whole, but art in letters consists rather in the ar
t of arranging and composing them in a pleasing and appropriate manner. The main pur
pose of letters is the practical one of making thoughts visible. Ruskin says that all letters a
re frightful things and to be endured only on occasion, that is to say, in places where the
sense of the inscription is of more importance than external ornament. This is a sweepi
ng statement, from which we need not suffer unduly; yet it is doubtful whether there is
The main purpose of letters is the practical one of making thoughts visible. Ruskin
says that all letters are frightful things and to be endured only on occasion, that is t
The main purpose of letters is the practical one of making thoughts visible. Ruski
n says that all letters are frightful things and to be endured only on occasion, tha

7/8

The main purpose of letters is the practical one of making thoughts visible. Ruskin says t
hat all letters are frightful things and to be endured only on occasion, that is to say, in pla
ces where the sense of the inscription is of more importance than external ornament. T
his is a sweeping statement, from which we need not suffer unduly; yet it is doubtful w
hether there is art in individual letters. Letters in combination may be satisfying and in a
well composed page even beautiful as a whole, but art in letters consists rather in the ar
t of arranging and composing them in a pleasing and appropriate manner. The main pur
pose of letters is the practical one of making thoughts visible. Ruskin says that all letters a
re frightful things and to be endured only on occasion, that is to say, in places where the
sense of the inscription is of more importance than external ornament. This is a sweepi
The main purpose of letters is the practical one of making thoughts visible. Ruskin
says that all letters are frightful things and to be endured only on occasion, that is t
The main purpose of letters is the practical one of making thoughts visible. Ruski
n says that all letters are frightful things and to be endured only on occasion, tha

7/9

The main purpose of letters is the practical one of making thoughts visible. Ruskin says t
hat all letters are frightful things and to be endured only on occasion, that is to say, in pla
ces where the sense of the inscription is of more importance than external ornament. T
his is a sweeping statement, from which we need not suffer unduly; yet it is doubtful w
hether there is art in individual letters. Letters in combination may be satisfying and in a
well composed page even beautiful as a whole, but art in letters consists rather in the ar
t of arranging and composing them in a pleasing and appropriate manner. The main pur
pose of letters is the practical one of making thoughts visible. Ruskin says that all letters a
re frightful things and to be endured only on occasion, that is to say, in places where the
sense of the inscription is of more importance than external ornament. This is a sweepi
The main purpose of letters is the practical one of making thoughts visible. Ruskin
says that all letters are frightful things and to be endured only on occasion, that is t
The main purpose of letters is the practical one of making thoughts visible. Ruski
n says that all letters are frightful things and to be endured only on occasion, tha

7/10

The main purpose of letters is the practical one of making thoughts visible. Ruskin says t
hat all letters are frightful things and to be endured only on occasion, that is to say, in pla
ces where the sense of the inscription is of more importance than external ornament. T
his is a sweeping statement, from which we need not suffer unduly; yet it is doubtful w
hether there is art in individual letters. Letters in combination may be satisfying and in a
well composed page even beautiful as a whole, but art in letters consists rather in the ar
t of arranging and composing them in a pleasing and appropriate manner. The main pur
pose of letters is the practical one of making thoughts visible. Ruskin says that all letters a
re frightful things and to be endured only on occasion, that is to say, in places where the
The main purpose of letters is the practical one of making thoughts visible. Ruskin
says that all letters are frightful things and to be endured only on occasion, that is t
The main purpose of letters is the practical one of making thoughts visible. Ruski
n says that all letters are frightful things and to be endured only on occasion, tha

ITC KABEL 8 & 9 POINT SET NORMAL

BOOK, MEDIUM, DEMI, BOLD

ABCDEFGHIJKLMNOPQRSTUVWXYZ 1234567890 abcdefghijklmnopqrstuvwxyz

ABCDEFGHIJKLMNOPQRSTUVWXYZ 1234567890 abcdefghijklmnopqrstuvwxyz

ABCDEFGHIJKLMNOPQRSTUVWXYZ 1234567890 abcdefghijklmnopqrstuvwxyz

ABCDEFGHIJKLMNOPQRSTUVWXYZ 1234567890 abcdefghijklmnopqrstuvwxyz

8/8

The main purpose of letters is the practical one of making thoughts visible. R uskin says that all letters are frightful things and to be endured only on occasi on, that is to say, in places where the sense of the inscription is of more impo rtance than external ornament. This is a sweeping statement, from which we need not suffer unduly; yet it is doubtful whether there is art in individual lett ers. Letters in combination may be satisfying and in a well composed page e ven beautiful as a whole, but art in letters consists rather in the art of arrangin g and composing them in a pleasing and appropriate manner. The main pur pose of letters is the practical one of making thoughts visible. Ruskin says that The main purpose of letters is the practical one of making thoughts visib le. Ruskin says that all letters are frightful things and to be endured only **The main purpose of letters is the practical one of making thoughts visi ble. Ruskin says that all letters are frightful things and to be endured o**

8/9

The main purpose of letters is the practical one of making thoughts visible. R uskin says that all letters are frightful things and to be endured only on occasi on, that is to say, in places where the sense of the inscription is of more impo rtance than external ornament. This is a sweeping statement, from which we need not suffer unduly; yet it is doubtful whether there is art in individual lett ers. Letters in combination may be satisfying and in a well composed page e ven beautiful as a whole, but art in letters consists rather in the art of arrangin g and composing them in a pleasing and appropriate manner. The main pur The main purpose of letters is the practical one of making thoughts visib le. Ruskin says that all letters are frightful things and to be endured only **The main purpose of letters is the practical one of making thoughts visi ble. Ruskin says that all letters are frightful things and to be endured o**

8/10

The main purpose of letters is the practical one of making thoughts visible. R uskin says that all letters are frightful things and to be endured only on occasi on, that is to say, in places where the sense of the inscription is of more impo rtance than external ornament. This is a sweeping statement, from which we need not suffer unduly; yet it is doubtful whether there is art in individual lett ers. Letters in combination may be satisfying and in a well composed page e ven beautiful as a whole, but art in letters consists rather in the art of arrangin The main purpose of letters is the practical one of making thoughts visib le. Ruskin says that all letters are frightful things and to be endured only **The main purpose of letters is the practical one of making thoughts visi ble. Ruskin says that all letters are frightful things and to be endured o**

8/11

The main purpose of letters is the practical one of making thoughts visible. R uskin says that all letters are frightful things and to be endured only on occasi on, that is to say, in places where the sense of the inscription is of more impo rtance than external ornament. This is a sweeping statement, from which we need not suffer unduly; yet it is doubtful whether there is art in individual lett ers. Letters in combination may be satisfying and in a well composed page e ven beautiful as a whole, but art in letters consists rather in the art of arrangin The main purpose of letters is the practical one of making thoughts visib le. Ruskin says that all letters are frightful things and to be endured only **The main purpose of letters is the practical one of making thoughts visi ble. Ruskin says that all letters are frightful things and to be endured o**

ABCDEFGHIJKLMNOPQRSTUVWXYZ 1234567890 abcdefghijklmnopqrstuvwxyz

ABCDEFGHIJKLMNOPQRSTUVWXYZ 1234567890 abcdefghijklmnopqrstuvwxyz

ABCDEFGHIJKLMNOPQRSTUVWXYZ 1234567890 abcdefghijklmnopqrstuvwxyz

ABCDEFGHIJKLMNOPQRSTUVWXYZ 1234567890 abcdefghijklmnopqrstuvwxyz

9/9

The main purpose of letters is the practical one of making thoughts v isible. Ruskin says that all letters are frightful things and to be endure d only on occasion, that is to say, in places where the sense of the in scription is of more importance than external ornament. This is a sw eeping statement, from which we need not suffer unduly; yet it is d oubtful whether there is art in individual letters. Letters in combinati on may be satisfying and in a well composed page even beautiful a s a whole, but art in letters consists rather in the art of arranging and The main purpose of letters is the practical one of making thoug hts visible. Ruskin says that all letters are frightful things and to b **The main purpose of letters is the practical one of making thou ghts visible. Ruskin says that all letters are frightful things and t**

9/10

The main purpose of letters is the practical one of making thoughts v isible. Ruskin says that all letters are frightful things and to be endure d only on occasion, that is to say, in places where the sense of the in scription is of more importance than external ornament. This is a sw eeping statement, from which we need not suffer unduly; yet it is d oubtful whether there is art in individual letters. Letters in combinati on may be satisfying and in a well composed page even beautiful a The main purpose of letters is the practical one of making thoug hts visible. Ruskin says that all letters are frightful things and to b **The main purpose of letters is the practical one of making thou ghts visible. Ruskin says that all letters are frightful things and t**

9/11

The main purpose of letters is the practical one of making thoughts v isible. Ruskin says that all letters are frightful things and to be endure d only on occasion, that is to say, in places where the sense of the in scription is of more importance than external ornament. This is a sw eeping statement, from which we need not suffer unduly; yet it is d oubtful whether there is art in individual letters. Letters in combinati on may be satisfying and in a well composed page even beautiful a The main purpose of letters is the practical one of making thoug hts visible. Ruskin says that all letters are frightful things and to b **The main purpose of letters is the practical one of making thou ghts visible. Ruskin says that all letters are frightful things and t**

9/12

The main purpose of letters is the practical one of making thoughts v isible. Ruskin says that all letters are frightful things and to be endure d only on occasion, that is to say, in places where the sense of the in scription is of more importance than external ornament. This is a sw eeping statement, from which we need not suffer unduly; yet it is d oubtful whether there is art in individual letters. Letters in combinati on may be satisfying and in a well composed page even beautiful a The main purpose of letters is the practical one of making thoug hts visible. Ruskin says that all letters are frightful things and to b **The main purpose of letters is the practical one of making thou ghts visible. Ruskin says that all letters are frightful things and t**

10 POINT SET MINUS ½ UNIT

BOOK, MEDIUM, DEMI, BOLD

abcdefghijklmnopqrstuvwxyz – 1 UNIT
abcdefghijklmnopqrstuvwxyz – ½ UNIT
abcdefghijklmnopqrstuvwxyz NORMAL

ABCDEFGHIJKLMNOPQRSTUVWXYZ 1234567890 abcdefghijklmnopqrstuvwxyz
ABCDEFGHIJKLMNOPQRSTUVWXYZ 1234567890 abcdefghijklmnopqrstuvwxyz
ABCDEFGHIJKLMNOPQRSTUVWXYZ 1234567890 abcdefghijklmnopqrstuvwxyz
ABCDEFGHIJKLMNOPQRSTUVWXYZ 1234567890 abcdefghijklmnopqrstuvwxyz

10/10

The main purpose of letters is the practical one of making thoug
hts visible. Ruskin says that all letters are frightful things and to be
endured only on occasion, that is to say, in places where the sen
se of the inscription is of more importance than external orname
nt. This is a sweeping statement, from which we need not suffer
unduly; yet it is doubtful whether there is art in individual letters.
Letters in combination may be satisfying and in a well compose
d page even beautiful as a whole, but art in letters consists rathe
r in the art of arranging and composing them in a pleasing and a
ppropriate manner. The main purpose of letters is the practical o
ne of making thoughts visible. Ruskin says that all letters are frightf
ul things and to be endured only on occasion, that is to say, in pl
aces where the sense of the inscription is of more importance th
an external ornament. This is a sweeping statement, from which
we need not suffer unduly; yet it is doubtful whether there is art i
n individual letters. Letters in combination may be satisfying and
in a well composed page even beautiful as a whole, but art in le
tters consists rather in the art of arranging and composing them i
n a pleasing and appropriate manner. The main purpose of lette
rs is the practical one of making thoughts visible. Ruskin says that
all letters are frightful things and to be endured only on occasion,
that is to say, in places where the sense of the inscription is of m
**The main purpose of letters is the practical one of making th
oughts visible. Ruskin says that all letters are frightful things a
The main purpose of letters is the practical one of making t
houghts visible. Ruskin says that all letters are frightful thin**

10/11

The main purpose of letters is the practical one of making thoug
hts visible. Ruskin says that all letters are frightful things and to be
endured only on occasion, that is to say, in places where the sen
se of the inscription is of more importance than external orname
nt. This is a sweeping statement, from which we need not suffer
unduly; yet it is doubtful whether there is art in individual letters.
Letters in combination may be satisfying and in a well compose
d page even beautiful as a whole, but art in letters consists rathe
r in the art of arranging and composing them in a pleasing and a
ppropriate manner. The main purpose of letters is the practical o
ne of making thoughts visible. Ruskin says that all letters are frightf
ul things and to be endured only on occasion, that is to say, in pl
aces where the sense of the inscription is of more importance th
an external ornament. This is a sweeping statement, from which
we need not suffer unduly; yet it is doubtful whether there is art i
n individual letters. Letters in combination may be satisfying and
in a well composed page even beautiful as a whole, but art in le
tters consists rather in the art of arranging and composing them i
n a pleasing and appropriate manner. The main purpose of lette
rs is the practical one of making thoughts visible. Ruskin says that
**The main purpose of letters is the practical one of making th
oughts visible. Ruskin says that all letters are frightful things a
The main purpose of letters is the practical one of making t
houghts visible. Ruskin says that all letters are frightful thin**

10/12

The main purpose of letters is the practical one of making thoug
hts visible. Ruskin says that all letters are frightful things and to be
endured only on occasion, that is to say, in places where the sen
se of the inscription is of more importance than external orname
nt. This is a sweeping statement, from which we need not suffer
unduly; yet it is doubtful whether there is art in individual letters.
Letters in combination may be satisfying and in a well compose
d page even beautiful as a whole, but art in letters consists rathe
r in the art of arranging and composing them in a pleasing and a
ppropriate manner. The main purpose of letters is the practical o
ne of making thoughts visible. Ruskin says that all letters are frightf
ul things and to be endured only on occasion, that is to say, in pl
aces where the sense of the inscription is of more importance th
an external ornament. This is a sweeping statement, from which
we need not suffer unduly; yet it is doubtful whether there is art i
n individual letters. Letters in combination may be satisfying and
in a well composed page even beautiful as a whole, but art in le
tters consists rather in the art of arranging and composing them i
**The main purpose of letters is the practical one of making th
oughts visible. Ruskin says that all letters are frightful things a
The main purpose of letters is the practical one of making t
houghts visible. Ruskin says that all letters are frightful thin**

10/13

The main purpose of letters is the practical one of making thoug
hts visible. Ruskin says that all letters are frightful things and to be
endured only on occasion, that is to say, in places where the sen
se of the inscription is of more importance than external orname
nt. This is a sweeping statement, from which we need not suffer
unduly; yet it is doubtful whether there is art in individual letters.
Letters in combination may be satisfying and in a well compose
d page even beautiful as a whole, but art in letters consists rathe
r in the art of arranging and composing them in a pleasing and a
ppropriate manner. The main purpose of letters is the practical o
ne of making thoughts visible. Ruskin says that all letters are frightf
ul things and to be endured only on occasion, that is to say, in pl
aces where the sense of the inscription is of more importance th
an external ornament. This is a sweeping statement, from which
we need not suffer unduly; yet it is doubtful whether there is art i
n individual letters. Letters in combination may be satisfying and
in a well composed page even beautiful as a whole, but art in le
**The main purpose of letters is the practical one of making th
oughts visible. Ruskin says that all letters are frightful things a
The main purpose of letters is the practical one of making t
houghts visible. Ruskin says that all letters are frightful thin**

ITC KABEL 11 POINT SET MINUS ½ UNIT

BOOK, MEDIUM, DEMI, BOLD

abcdefghijklmnopqrstuvwxyz – 1 UNIT
abcdefghijklmnopqrstuvwxyz – ½ UNIT
abcdefghijklmnopqrstuvwxyz NORMAL

ABCDEFGHIJKLMNOPQRSTUVWXYZ 1234567890 abcdefghijklmnopqrstuvwxyz
ABCDEFGHIJKLMNOPQRSTUVWXYZ 1234567890 abcdefghijklmnopqrstuvwxyz
ABCDEFGHIJKLMNOPQRSTUVWXYZ 1234567890 abcdefghijklmnopqrstuvwxyz
ABCDEFGHIJKLMNOPQRSTUVWXYZ 1234567890 abcdefghijklmnopqrstuvwxyz

11/11

The main purpose of letters is the practical one of making t
houghts visible. Ruskin says that all letters are frightful thing
s and to be endured only on occasion, that is to say, in pla
ces where the sense of the inscription is of more importan
ce than external ornament. This is a sweeping statement, fr
om which we need not suffer unduly; yet it is doubtful wh
ether there is art in individual letters. Letters in combinatio
n may be satisfying and in a well composed page even b
eautiful as a whole, but art in letters consists rather in the ar
t of arranging and composing them in a pleasing and appr
opriate manner. The main purpose of letters is the practica
l one of making thoughts visible. Ruskin says that all letters
are frightful things and to be endured only on occasion, th
at is to say, in places where the sense of the inscription is o
f more importance than external ornament. This is a swee
ping statement, from which we need not suffer unduly; ye
t it is doubtful whether there is art in individual letters. Lett
ers in combination may be satisfying and in a well compo
sed page even beautiful as a whole, but art in letters consi
The main purpose of letters is the practical one of mak
ing thoughts visible. Ruskin says that all letters are frigh
The main purpose of letters is the practical one of ma
king thoughts visible. Ruskin says that all letters are fri

11/12

The main purpose of letters is the practical one of making t
houghts visible. Ruskin says that all letters are frightful thing
s and to be endured only on occasion, that is to say, in pla
ces where the sense of the inscription is of more importan
ce than external ornament. This is a sweeping statement, fr
om which we need not suffer unduly; yet it is doubtful wh
ether there is art in individual letters. Letters in combinatio
n may be satisfying and in a well composed page even b
eautiful as a whole, but art in letters consists rather in the ar
t of arranging and composing them in a pleasing and appr
opriate manner. The main purpose of letters is the practica
l one of making thoughts visible. Ruskin says that all letters
are frightful things and to be endured only on occasion, th
at is to say, in places where the sense of the inscription is o
f more importance than external ornament. This is a swee
ping statement, from which we need not suffer unduly; ye
t it is doubtful whether there is art in individual letters. Lett
ers in combination may be satisfying and in a well compo
The main purpose of letters is the practical one of mak
ing thoughts visible. Ruskin says that all letters are frigh
The main purpose of letters is the practical one of ma
king thoughts visible. Ruskin says that all letters are fri

11/13

The main purpose of letters is the practical one of making t
houghts visible. Ruskin says that all letters are frightful thing
s and to be endured only on occasion, that is to say, in pla
ces where the sense of the inscription is of more importan
ce than external ornament. This is a sweeping statement, fr
om which we need not suffer unduly; yet it is doubtful wh
ether there is art in individual letters. Letters in combinatio
n may be satisfying and in a well composed page even b
eautiful as a whole, but art in letters consists rather in the ar
t of arranging and composing them in a pleasing and appr
opriate manner. The main purpose of letters is the practica
l one of making thoughts visible. Ruskin says that all letters
are frightful things and to be endured only on occasion, th
at is to say, in places where the sense of the inscription is o
f more importance than external ornament. This is a swee
ping statement, from which we need not suffer unduly; ye
t it is doubtful whether there is art in individual letters. Lett
The main purpose of letters is the practical one of mak
ing thoughts visible. Ruskin says that all letters are frigh
The main purpose of letters is the practical one of ma
king thoughts visible. Ruskin says that all letters are fri

11/14

The main purpose of letters is the practical one of making t
houghts visible. Ruskin says that all letters are frightful thing
s and to be endured only on occasion, that is to say, in pla
ces where the sense of the inscription is of more importan
ce than external ornament. This is a sweeping statement, fr
om which we need not suffer unduly; yet it is doubtful wh
ether there is art in individual letters. Letters in combinatio
n may be satisfying and in a well composed page even b
eautiful as a whole, but art in letters consists rather in the ar
t of arranging and composing them in a pleasing and appr
opriate manner. The main purpose of letters is the practica
l one of making thoughts visible. Ruskin says that all letters
are frightful things and to be endured only on occasion, th
at is to say, in places where the sense of the inscription is o
f more importance than external ornament. This is a swee
ping statement, from which we need not suffer unduly; ye
The main purpose of letters is the practical one of mak
ing thoughts visible. Ruskin says that all letters are frigh
The main purpose of letters is the practical one of ma
king thoughts visible. Ruskin says that all letters are fri

 12 POINT SET MINUS ½ UNIT

ITC KABEL

BOOK, MEDIUM, DEMI, BOLD

abcdefghijklmnopqrstuvwxyz – 1 UNIT
abcdefghijklmnopqrstuvwxyz – ½ UNIT
abcdefghijklmnopqrstuvwxyz NORMAL

ABCDEFGHIJKLMNOPQRSTUVWXYZ 1234567890 abcdefghijklmnopqrstuvwxyz
ABCDEFGHIJKLMNOPQRSTUVWXYZ 1234567890 abcdefghijklmnopqrstuvwxyz
ABCDEFGHIJKLMNOPQRSTUVWXYZ 1234567890 abcdefghijklmnopqrstuvwxyz
ABCDEFGHIJKLMNOPQRSTUVWXYZ 1234567890 abcdefghijklmnopqrstuvwxyz

12/12

The main purpose of letters is the practical one of mak ing thoughts visible. Ruskin says that all letters are fright ful things and to be endured only on occasion, that is t o say, in places where the sense of the inscription is of more importance than external ornament. This is a sw eeping statement, from which we need not suffer un duly; yet it is doubtful whether there is art in individual letters. Letters in combination may be satisfying and in a well composed page even beautiful as a whole, but art in letters consists rather in the art of arranging and c omposing them in a pleasing and appropriate manne r. The main purpose of letters is the practical one of m aking thoughts visible. Ruskin says that all letters are frig htful things and to be endured only on occasion, that i s to say, in places where the sense of the inscription is
The main purpose of letters is the practical one of making thoughts visible. Ruskin says that all letters
The main purpose of letters is the practical one of making thoughts visible. Ruskin says that all letter

12/13

The main purpose of letters is the practical one of mak ing thoughts visible. Ruskin says that all letters are fright ful things and to be endured only on occasion, that is t o say, in places where the sense of the inscription is of more importance than external ornament. This is a sw eeping statement, from which we need not suffer un duly; yet it is doubtful whether there is art in individual letters. Letters in combination may be satisfying and in a well composed page even beautiful as a whole, but art in letters consists rather in the art of arranging and c omposing them in a pleasing and appropriate manne r. The main purpose of letters is the practical one of m aking thoughts visible. Ruskin says that all letters are frig htful things and to be endured only on occasion, that i
The main purpose of letters is the practical one of making thoughts visible. Ruskin says that all letters
The main purpose of letters is the practical one of making thoughts visible. Ruskin says that all letter

12/14

The main purpose of letters is the practical one of mak ing thoughts visible. Ruskin says that all letters are fright ful things and to be endured only on occasion, that is t o say, in places where the sense of the inscription is of more importance than external ornament. This is a sw eeping statement, from which we need not suffer un duly; yet it is doubtful whether there is art in individual letters. Letters in combination may be satisfying and in a well composed page even beautiful as a whole, but art in letters consists rather in the art of arranging and c omposing them in a pleasing and appropriate manne r. The main purpose of letters is the practical one of m aking thoughts visible. Ruskin says that all letters are frig htful things and to be endured only on occasion, that i s to say, in places where the sense of the inscription is
The main purpose of letters is the practical one of making thoughts visible. Ruskin says that all letters
The main purpose of letters is the practical one of making thoughts visible. Ruskin says that all letter

12/15

The main purpose of letters is the practical one of mak ing thoughts visible. Ruskin says that all letters are fright ful things and to be endured only on occasion, that is t o say, in places where the sense of the inscription is of more importance than external ornament. This is a sw eeping statement, from which we need not suffer un duly; yet it is doubtful whether there is art in individual letters. Letters in combination may be satisfying and in a well composed page even beautiful as a whole, but art in letters consists rather in the art of arranging and c omposing them in a pleasing and appropriate manne r. The main purpose of letters is the practical one of m aking thoughts visible. Ruskin says that all letters are frig htful things and to be endured only on occasion, that i
The main purpose of letters is the practical one of making thoughts visible. Ruskin says that all letters
The main purpose of letters is the practical one of making thoughts visible. Ruskin says that all letter

ITC KABEL 14 POINT SET MINUS ½ UNIT

BOOK, MEDIUM, DEMI, BOLD

abcdefghijklmnopqrstuvwxyz – 1 UNIT
abcdefghijklmnopqrstuvwxyz – ½ UNIT
abcdefghijklmnopqrstuvwxyz NORMAL

ABCDEFGHIJKLMNOPQRSTUVWXYZ abcdefghijklmnopqrstuvwxyz
ABCDEFGHIJKLMNOPQRSTUVWXYZ abcdefghijklmnopqrstuvwxyz
ABCDEFGHIJKLMNOPQRSTUVWXYZ abcdefghijklmnopqrstuvwxyz
ABCDEFGHIJKLMNOPQRSTUVWXYZ abcdefghijklmnopqrstuvwxyz

14/14

The main purpose of letters is the practical on
e of making thoughts visible. Ruskin says that al
l letters are frightful things and to be endured
only on occasion, that is to say, in places wher
e the sense of the inscription is of more impor
tance than external ornament. This is a sweepi
ng statement, from which we need not suffer
unduly; yet it is doubtful whether there is art in
individual letters. Letters in combination may
be satisfying and in a well composed page e
ven beautiful as a whole, but art in letters cons
ists rather in the art of arranging and composin
g them in a pleasing and appropriate manner.
The main purpose of letters is the practical
one of making thoughts visible. Ruskin says
The main purpose of letters is the practica
l one of making thoughts visible. Ruskin sa

14/15

The main purpose of letters is the practical on
e of making thoughts visible. Ruskin says that al
l letters are frightful things and to be endured
only on occasion, that is to say, in places wher
e the sense of the inscription is of more impor
tance than external ornament. This is a sweepi
ng statement, from which we need not suffer
unduly; yet it is doubtful whether there is art in
individual letters. Letters in combination may
be satisfying and in a well composed page e
ven beautiful as a whole, but art in letters cons
ists rather in the art of arranging and composin
The main purpose of letters is the practical
one of making thoughts visible. Ruskin says
The main purpose of letters is the practica
l one of making thoughts visible. Ruskin sa

14/16

The main purpose of letters is the practical on
e of making thoughts visible. Ruskin says that al
l letters are frightful things and to be endured
only on occasion, that is to say, in places wher
e the sense of the inscription is of more impor
tance than external ornament. This is a sweepi
ng statement, from which we need not suffer
unduly; yet it is doubtful whether there is art in
individual letters. Letters in combination may
be satisfying and in a well composed page e
ven beautiful as a whole, but art in letters cons
ists rather in the art of arranging and composin
g them in a pleasing and appropriate manner.
The main purpose of letters is the practical
one of making thoughts visible. Ruskin says
The main purpose of letters is the practica
l one of making thoughts visible. Ruskin sa

14/17

The main purpose of letters is the practical on
e of making thoughts visible. Ruskin says that al
l letters are frightful things and to be endured
only on occasion, that is to say, in places wher
e the sense of the inscription is of more impor
tance than external ornament. This is a sweepi
ng statement, from which we need not suffer
unduly; yet it is doubtful whether there is art in
individual letters. Letters in combination may
be satisfying and in a well composed page e
ven beautiful as a whole, but art in letters cons
ists rather in the art of arranging and composin
The main purpose of letters is the practical
one of making thoughts visible. Ruskin says
The main purpose of letters is the practica
l one of making thoughts visible. Ruskin sa

KENNERLY 6 & 7 POINT SET NORMAL

ROMAN, ITALIC, BOLD, BOLD ITALIC

ABCDEFGHIJKLMNOPQRSTUVWXYZ 1234567890 abcdefghijklmnopqrstuvwxyz

ABCDEFGHIJKLMNOPQRSTUVWXYZ 1234567890 abcdefghijklmnopqrstuvwxyz

ABCDEFGHIJKLMNOPQRSTUVWXYZ 1234567890 abcdefghijklmnopqrstuvwxyz

ABCDEFGHIJKLMNOPQRSTUVWXYZ 1234567890 abcdefghijklmnopqrstuvwxyz

6/6

The main purpose of letters is the practical one of making thoughts visible. Ruskin says that all letters are frig
htful things and to be endured only on occasion, that is to say, in places where the sense of the inscription is o
f more importance than external ornament. This is a sweeping statement, from which we need not suffer un
duly; yet it is doubtful whether there is art in individual letters. Letters in combination may be satisfying and
in a well composed page even beautiful as a whole, but art in letters consists rather in the art of arranging and
composing them in a pleasing and appropriate manner. The main purpose of letters is the practical one of mak
ing thoughts visible. Ruskin says that all letters are frightful things and to be endured only on occasion, that i
s to say, in places where the sense of the inscription is of more importance than external ornament. This is a
sweeping statement, from which we need not suffer unduly; yet it is doubtful whether there is art in individ
ual letters. Letters in combination may be satisfying and in a well composed page even beautiful as a whole, b
ut art in letters consists rather in the art of arranging and composing them in a pleasing and appropriate mann
er. The main purpose of letters is the practical one of making thoughts visible. Ruskin says that all letters are
frightful things and to be endured only on occasion, that is to say, in places where the sense of the inscription
The main purpose of letters is the practical one of making thoughts visible. Ruskin says that all letters a
re frightful things and to be endured only on occasion, that is to say, in places where the sense of the insc
The main purpose of letters is the practical one of making thoughts visible. Ruskin says t
hat all letters are frightful things and to be endured only on occasion, that is to say, in pla

6/7

The main purpose of letters is the practical one of making thoughts visible. Ruskin says that all letters are frig
htful things and to be endured only on occasion, that is to say, in places where the sense of the inscription is o
f more importance than external ornament. This is a sweeping statement, from which we need not suffer un
duly; yet it is doubtful whether there is art in individual letters. Letters in combination may be satisfying and
in a well composed page even beautiful as a whole, but art in letters consists rather in the art of arranging and
composing them in a pleasing and appropriate manner. The main purpose of letters is the practical one of mak
ing thoughts visible. Ruskin says that all letters are frightful things and to be endured only on occasion, that i
s to say, in places where the sense of the inscription is of more importance than external ornament. This is a
sweeping statement, from which we need not suffer unduly; yet it is doubtful whether there is art in individ
ual letters. Letters in combination may be satisfying and in a well composed page even beautiful as a whole, b
ut art in letters consists rather in the art of arranging and composing them in a pleasing and appropriate mann
The main purpose of letters is the practical one of making thoughts visible. Ruskin says that all letters a
re frightful things and to be endured only on occasion, that is to say, in places where the sense of the insc
The main purpose of letters is the practical one of making thoughts visible. Ruskin says t
hat all letters are frightful things and to be endured only on occasion, that is to say, in pla

6/8

The main purpose of letters is the practical one of making thoughts visible. Ruskin says that all letters are frig
htful things and to be endured only on occasion, that is to say, in places where the sense of the inscription is o
f more importance than external ornament. This is a sweeping statement, from which we need not suffer un
duly; yet it is doubtful whether there is art in individual letters. Letters in combination may be satisfying and
in a well composed page even beautiful as a whole, but art in letters consists rather in the art of arranging and
composing them in a pleasing and appropriate manner. The main purpose of letters is the practical one of mak
ing thoughts visible. Ruskin says that all letters are frightful things and to be endured only on occasion, that i
s to say, in places where the sense of the inscription is of more importance than external ornament. This is a
sweeping statement, from which we need not suffer unduly; yet it is doubtful whether there is art in individ
The main purpose of letters is the practical one of making thoughts visible. Ruskin says that all letters a
re frightful things and to be endured only on occasion, that is to say, in places where the sense of the insc
The main purpose of letters is the practical one of making thoughts visible. Ruskin says t
hat all letters are frightful things and to be endured only on occasion, that is to say, in pla

6/9

The main purpose of letters is the practical one of making thoughts visible. Ruskin says that all letters are frig
htful things and to be endured only on occasion, that is to say, in places where the sense of the inscription is o
f more importance than external ornament. This is a sweeping statement, from which we need not suffer un
duly; yet it is doubtful whether there is art in individual letters. Letters in combination may be satisfying and
in a well composed page even beautiful as a whole, but art in letters consists rather in the art of arranging and
composing them in a pleasing and appropriate manner. The main purpose of letters is the practical one of mak
ing thoughts visible. Ruskin says that all letters are frightful things and to be endured only on occasion, that i
s to say, in places where the sense of the inscription is of more importance than external ornament. This is a
The main purpose of letters is the practical one of making thoughts visible. Ruskin says that all letters a
re frightful things and to be endured only on occasion, that is to say, in places where the sense of the insc
The main purpose of letters is the practical one of making thoughts visible. Ruskin says t
hat all letters are frightful things and to be endured only on occasion, that is to say, in pla

---

ABCDEFGHIJKLMNOPQRSTUVWXYZ 1234567890 abcdefghijklmnopqrstuvwxyz

ABCDEFGHIJKLMNOPQRSTUVWXYZ 1234567890 abcdefghijklmnopqrstuvwxyz

ABCDEFGHIJKLMNOPQRSTUVWXYZ 1234567890 abcdefghijklmnopqrstuvwxyz

ABCDEFGHIJKLMNOPQRSTUVWXYZ 1234567890 abcdefghijklmnopqrstuvwxyz

7/7

The main purpose of letters is the practical one of making thoughts visible. Ruskin says that a
ll letters are frightful things and to be endured only on occasion, that is to say, in places where
the sense of the inscription is of more importance than external ornament. This is a sweeping
statement, from which we need not suffer unduly; yet it is doubtful whether there is art in in
dividual letters. Letters in combination may be satisfying and in a well composed page even b
eautiful as a whole, but art in letters consists rather in the art of arranging and composing the
m in a pleasing and appropriate manner. The main purpose of letters is the practical one of ma
king thoughts visible. Ruskin says that all letters are frightful things and to be endured only o
n occasion, that is to say, in places where the sense of the inscription is of more importance th
an external ornament. This is a sweeping statement, from which we need not suffer unduly;
yet it is doubtful whether there is art in individual letters. Letters in combination may be sati
The main purpose of letters is the practical one of making thoughts visible. Ruskin says t
hat all letters are frightful things and to be endured only on occasion, that is to say, in pl
The main purpose of letters is the practical one of making thoughts visible.
Ruskin says that all letters are frightful things and to be endured only on oc

7/8

The main purpose of letters is the practical one of making thoughts visible. Ruskin says that a
ll letters are frightful things and to be endured only on occasion, that is to say, in places where
the sense of the inscription is of more importance than external ornament. This is a sweeping
statement, from which we need not suffer unduly; yet it is doubtful whether there is art in in
dividual letters. Letters in combination may be satisfying and in a well composed page even b
eautiful as a whole, but art in letters consists rather in the art of arranging and composing the
m in a pleasing and appropriate manner. The main purpose of letters is the practical one of ma
king thoughts visible. Ruskin says that all letters are frightful things and to be endured only o
n occasion, that is to say, in places where the sense of the inscription is of more importance th
an external ornament. This is a sweeping statement, from which we need not suffer unduly;
The main purpose of letters is the practical one of making thoughts visible. Ruskin says t
hat all letters are frightful things and to be endured only on occasion, that is to say, in pl
The main purpose of letters is the practical one of making thoughts visible.
Ruskin says that all letters are frightful things and to be endured only on oc

7/9

The main purpose of letters is the practical one of making thoughts visible. Ruskin says that a
ll letters are frightful things and to be endured only on occasion, that is to say, in places where
the sense of the inscription is of more importance than external ornament. This is a sweeping
statement, from which we need not suffer unduly; yet it is doubtful whether there is art in in
dividual letters. Letters in combination may be satisfying and in a well composed page even b
eautiful as a whole, but art in letters consists rather in the art of arranging and composing the
m in a pleasing and appropriate manner. The main purpose of letters is the practical one of ma
king thoughts visible. Ruskin says that all letters are frightful things and to be endured only o
n occasion, that is to say, in places where the sense of the inscription is of more importance th
an external ornament. This is a sweeping statement, from which we need not suffer unduly;
The main purpose of letters is the practical one of making thoughts visible. Ruskin says t
hat all letters are frightful things and to be endured only on occasion, that is to say, in pl
The main purpose of letters is the practical one of making thoughts visible.
Ruskin says that all letters are frightful things and to be endured only on oc

7/10

The main purpose of letters is the practical one of making thoughts visible. Ruskin says that a
ll letters are frightful things and to be endured only on occasion, that is to say, in places where
the sense of the inscription is of more importance than external ornament. This is a sweeping
statement, from which we need not suffer unduly; yet it is doubtful whether there is art in in
dividual letters. Letters in combination may be satisfying and in a well composed page even b
eautiful as a whole, but art in letters consists rather in the art of arranging and composing the
m in a pleasing and appropriate manner. The main purpose of letters is the practical one of ma
king thoughts visible. Ruskin says that all letters are frightful things and to be endured only o
n occasion, that is to say, in places where the sense of the inscription is of more importance th
The main purpose of letters is the practical one of making thoughts visible. Ruskin says t
hat all letters are frightful things and to be endured only on occasion, that is to say, in pl
The main purpose of letters is the practical one of making thoughts visible.
Ruskin says that all letters are frightful things and to be endured only on oc

KENNERLY 8 & 9 POINT SET NORMAL

ROMAN, ITALIC, BOLD, BOLD ITALIC

ABCDEFGHIJKLMNOPQRSTUVWXYZ 1234567890 abcdefghijklmnopqrstuvwxyz

ABCDEFGHIJKLMNOPQRSTUVWXYZ 1234567890 abcdefghijklmnopqrstuvwxyz

ABCDEFGHIJKLMNOPQRSTUVWXYZ 1234567890 abcdefghijklmnopqrstuvwxyz

ABCDEFGHIJKLMNOPQRSTUVWXYZ 1234567890 abcdefghijklmnopqrstuvwxyz

8/8

The main purpose of letters is the practical one of making thoughts visible. Ruski n says that all letters are frightful things and to be endured only on occasion, that i s to say, in places where the sense of the inscription is of more importance than ext ernal ornament. This is a sweeping statement, from which we need not suffer un duly; yet it is doubtful whether there is art in individual letters. Letters in combin ation may be satisfying and in a well composed page even beautiful as a whole, bu t art in letters consists rather in the art of arranging and composing them in a pleas ing and appropriate manner. The main purpose of letters is the practical one of ma king thoughts visible. Ruskin says that all letters are frightful things and to be end

The main purpose of letters is the practical one of making thoughts visible. R uskin says that all letters are frightful things and to be endured only on occasi

The main purpose of letters is the practical one of making thought s visible. Ruskin says that all letters are frightful things and to be e

8/9

The main purpose of letters is the practical one of making thoughts visible. Ruski n says that all letters are frightful things and to be endured only on occasion, that i s to say, in places where the sense of the inscription is of more importance than ext ernal ornament. This is a sweeping statement, from which we need not suffer un duly; yet it is doubtful whether there is art in individual letters. Letters in combin ation may be satisfying and in a well composed page even beautiful as a whole, bu t art in letters consists rather in the art of arranging and composing them in a pleas ing and appropriate manner. The main purpose of letters is the practical one of ma

The main purpose of letters is the practical one of making thoughts visible. R uskin says that all letters are frightful things and to be endured only on occasi

The main purpose of letters is the practical one of making thought s visible. Ruskin says that all letters are frightful things and to be e

8/10

The main purpose of letters is the practical one of making thoughts visible. Ruski n says that all letters are frightful things and to be endured only on occasion, that i s to say, in places where the sense of the inscription is of more importance than ext ernal ornament. This is a sweeping statement, from which we need not suffer un duly; yet it is doubtful whether there is art in individual letters. Letters in combin ation may be satisfying and in a well composed page even beautiful as a whole, bu t art in letters consists rather in the art of arranging and composing them in a pleas

The main purpose of letters is the practical one of making thoughts visible. R uskin says that all letters are frightful things and to be endured only on occasi

The main purpose of letters is the practical one of making thought s visible. Ruskin says that all letters are frightful things and to be e

8/11

The main purpose of letters is the practical one of making thoughts visible. Ruski n says that all letters are frightful things and to be endured only on occasion, that i s to say, in places where the sense of the inscription is of more importance than ext ernal ornament. This is a sweeping statement, from which we need not suffer un duly; yet it is doubtful whether there is art in individual letters. Letters in combin ation may be satisfying and in a well composed page even beautiful as a whole, bu t art in letters consists rather in the art of arranging and composing them in a pleas

The main purpose of letters is the practical one of making thoughts visible. R uskin says that all letters are frightful things and to be endured only on occasi

The main purpose of letters is the practical one of making thought s visible. Ruskin says that all letters are frightful things and to be e

---

ABCDEFGHIJKLMNOPQRSTUVWXYZ 1234567890 abcdefghijklmnopqrstuvwxyz

ABCDEFGHIJKLMNOPQRSTUVWXYZ 1234567890 abcdefghijklmnopqrstuvwxyz

ABCDEFGHIJKLMNOPQRSTUVWXYZ 1234567890 abcdefghijklmnopqrstuvwxyz

ABCDEFGHIJKLMNOPQRSTUVWXYZ 1234567890 abcdefghijklmnopqrstuvwxyz

9/9

The main purpose of letters is the practical one of making thoughts visibl e. Ruskin says that all letters are frightful things and to be endured only on occasion, that is to say, in places where the sense of the inscription is of more importance than external ornament. This is a sweeping stateme nt, from which we need not suffer unduly; yet it is doubtful whether th ere is art in individual letters. Letters in combination may be satisfying a nd in a well composed page even beautiful as a whole, but art in letters c onsists rather in the art of arranging and composing them in a pleasing an

The main purpose of letters is the practical one of making thoughts vi sible. Ruskin says that all letters are frightful things and to be endur

The main purpose of letters is the practical one of making t houghts visible. Ruskin says that all letters are frightful th

9/10

The main purpose of letters is the practical one of making thoughts visibl e. Ruskin says that all letters are frightful things and to be endured only on occasion, that is to say, in places where the sense of the inscription is of more importance than external ornament. This is a sweeping stateme nt, from which we need not suffer unduly; yet it is doubtful whether th ere is art in individual letters. Letters in combination may be satisfying a nd in a well composed page even beautiful as a whole, but art in letters c

The main purpose of letters is the practical one of making thoughts vi sible. Ruskin says that all letters are frightful things and to be endur

The main purpose of letters is the practical one of making t houghts visible. Ruskin says that all letters are frightful th

9/11

The main purpose of letters is the practical one of making thoughts visibl e. Ruskin says that all letters are frightful things and to be endured only on occasion, that is to say, in places where the sense of the inscription is of more importance than external ornament. This is a sweeping stateme nt, from which we need not suffer unduly; yet it is doubtful whether th ere is art in individual letters. Letters in combination may be satisfying a nd in a well composed page even beautiful as a whole, but art in letters c

The main purpose of letters is the practical one of making thoughts vi sible. Ruskin says that all letters are frightful things and to be endur

The main purpose of letters is the practical one of making t houghts visible. Ruskin says that all letters are frightful th

9/12

The main purpose of letters is the practical one of making thoughts visibl e. Ruskin says that all letters are frightful things and to be endured only on occasion, that is to say, in places where the sense of the inscription is of more importance than external ornament. This is a sweeping stateme nt, from which we need not suffer unduly; yet it is doubtful whether th ere is art in individual letters. Letters in combination may be satisfying a nd in a well composed page even beautiful as a whole, but art in letters c

The main purpose of letters is the practical one of making thoughts vi sible. Ruskin says that all letters are frightful things and to be endur

The main purpose of letters is the practical one of making t houghts visible. Ruskin says that all letters are frightful th

KENNERLY 10 POINT SET MINUS ½ UNIT

ROMAN, ITALIC, BOLD, BOLD ITALIC

abcdefghijklmnopqrstuvwxyz – 1 UNIT
abcdefghijklmnopqrstuvwxyz – ½ UNIT
abcdefghijklmnopqrstuvwxyz NORMAL

ABCDEFGHIJKLMNOPQRSTUVWXYZ 1234567890 abcdefghijklmnopqrstuvwxyz
ABCDEFGHIJKLMNOPQRSTUVWXYZ 1234567890 abcdefghijklmnopqrstuvwxyz
ABCDEFGHIJKLMNOPQRSTUVWXYZ 1234567890 abcdefghijklmnopqrstuvwxyz
ABCDEFGHIJKLMNOPQRSTUVWXYZ 1234567890 abcdefghijklmnopqrstuvwxyz

10/10

The main purpose of letters is the practical one of making thoughts v isible. Ruskin says that all letters are frightful things and to be endure d only on occasion, that is to say, in places where the sense of the ins cription is of more importance than external ornament. This is a swe eping statement, from which we need not suffer unduly; yet it is do ubtful whether there is art in individual letters. Letters in combinati on may be satisfying and in a well composed page even beautiful as a whole, but art in letters consists rather in the art of arranging and co mposing them in a pleasing and appropriate manner. The main purp ose of letters is the practical one of making thoughts visible. Ruskin s ays that all letters are frightful things and to be endured only on occa sion, that is to say, in places where the sense of the inscription is of m ore importance than external ornament. This is a sweeping statemen t, from which we need not suffer unduly; yet it is doubtful whether there is art in individual letters. Letters in combination may be satisf ying and in a well composed page even beautiful as a whole, but art in letters consists rather in the art of arranging and composing them in a pleasing and appropriate manner. The main purpose of letters is the practical one of making thoughts visible. Ruskin says that all lett ers are frightful things and to be endured only on occasion, that is to say, in places where the sense of the inscription is of more importanc e than external ornament. This is a sweeping statement, from whic
The main purpose of letters is the practical one of making though ts visible. Ruskin says that all letters are frightful things and to b
The main purpose of letters is the practical one of maki ng thoughts visible. Ruskin says that all letters are frig

10/11

The main purpose of letters is the practical one of making thoughts v isible. Ruskin says that all letters are frightful things and to be endure d only on occasion, that is to say, in places where the sense of the ins cription is of more importance than external ornament. This is a swe eping statement, from which we need not suffer unduly; yet it is do ubtful whether there is art in individual letters. Letters in combinati on may be satisfying and in a well composed page even beautiful as a whole, but art in letters consists rather in the art of arranging and co mposing them in a pleasing and appropriate manner. The main purp ose of letters is the practical one of making thoughts visible. Ruskin s ays that all letters are frightful things and to be endured only on occa sion, that is to say, in places where the sense of the inscription is of m ore importance than external ornament. This is a sweeping statemen t, from which we need not suffer unduly; yet it is doubtful whether there is art in individual letters. Letters in combination may be satisf ying and in a well composed page even beautiful as a whole, but art in letters consists rather in the art of arranging and composing them in a pleasing and appropriate manner. The main purpose of letters is the practical one of making thoughts visible. Ruskin says that all lett ers are frightful things and to be endured only on occasion, that is to
The main purpose of letters is the practical one of making though ts visible. Ruskin says that all letters are frightful things and to b
The main purpose of letters is the practical one of maki ng thoughts visible. Ruskin says that all letters are frig

10/12

The main purpose of letters is the practical one of making thoughts v isible. Ruskin says that all letters are frightful things and to be endure d only on occasion, that is to say, in places where the sense of the ins cription is of more importance than external ornament. This is a swe eping statement, from which we need not suffer unduly; yet it is do ubtful whether there is art in individual letters. Letters in combinati on may be satisfying and in a well composed page even beautiful as a whole, but art in letters consists rather in the art of arranging and co mposing them in a pleasing and appropriate manner. The main purp ose of letters is the practical one of making thoughts visible. Ruskin s ays that all letters are frightful things and to be endured only on occa sion, that is to say, in places where the sense of the inscription is of m ore importance than external ornament. This is a sweeping statemen t, from which we need not suffer unduly; yet it is doubtful whether there is art in individual letters. Letters in combination may be satisf ying and in a well composed page even beautiful as a whole, but art in letters consists rather in the art of arranging and composing them in a pleasing and appropriate manner. The main purpose of letters is
The main purpose of letters is the practical one of making though ts visible. Ruskin says that all letters are frightful things and to b
The main purpose of letters is the practical one of maki ng thoughts visible. Ruskin says that all letters are frig

10/13

The main purpose of letters is the practical one of making thoughts v isible. Ruskin says that all letters are frightful things and to be endure d only on occasion, that is to say, in places where the sense of the ins cription is of more importance than external ornament. This is a swe eping statement, from which we need not suffer unduly; yet it is do ubtful whether there is art in individual letters. Letters in combinati on may be satisfying and in a well composed page even beautiful as a whole, but art in letters consists rather in the art of arranging and co mposing them in a pleasing and appropriate manner. The main purp ose of letters is the practical one of making thoughts visible. Ruskin s ays that all letters are frightful things and to be endured only on occa sion, that is to say, in places where the sense of the inscription is of m ore importance than external ornament. This is a sweeping statemen t, from which we need not suffer unduly; yet it is doubtful whether there is art in individual letters. Letters in combination may be satisf ying and in a well composed page even beautiful as a whole, but art in letters consists rather in the art of arranging and composing them
The main purpose of letters is the practical one of making though ts visible. Ruskin says that all letters are frightful things and to b
The main purpose of letters is the practical one of maki ng thoughts visible. Ruskin says that all letters are frig

KENNERLY 11 POINT SET MINUS ½ UNIT

ROMAN, ITALIC, BOLD, BOLD ITALIC

abcdefghijklmnopqrstuvwxyz – 1 UNIT
abcdefghijklmnopqrstuvwxyz – ½ UNIT
abcdefghijklmnopqrstuvwxyz NORMAL

ABCDEFGHIJKLMNOPQRSTUVWXYZ 1234567890 abcdefghijklmnopqrstuvwxyz
ABCDEFGHIJKLMNOPQRSTUVWXYZ 1234567890 abcdefghijklmnopqrstuvwxyz
ABCDEFGHIJKLMNOPQRSTUVWXYZ 1234567890 abcdefghijklmnopqrstuvwxyz
ABCDEFGHIJKLMNOPQRSTUVWXYZ 1234567890 abcdefghijklmnopqrstuvwxyz

11/11

The main purpose of letters is the practical one of making tho ughts visible. Ruskin says that all letters are frightful things an d to be endured only on occasion, that is to say, in places wher e the sense of the inscription is of more importance than exter nal ornament. This is a sweeping statement, from which we n eed not suffer unduly; yet it is doubtful whether there is art in individual letters. Letters in combination may be satisfying and in a well composed page even beautiful as a whole, but art in letters consists rather in the art of arranging and composing th em in a pleasing and appropriate manner. The main purpose of letters is the practical one of making thoughts visible. Ruskin s ays that all letters are frightful things and to be endured only o n occasion, that is to say, in places where the sense of the inscr iption is of more importance than external ornament. This is a sweeping statement, from which we need not suffer unduly; yet it is doubtful whether there is art in individual letters. Lett ers in combination may be satisfying and in a well composed p age even beautiful as a whole, but art in letters consists rather i n the art of arranging and composing them in a pleasing and ap
The main purpose of letters is the practical one of making t houghts visible. Ruskin says that all letters are frightful thi
The main purpose of letters is the practical one of making thoughts visible. Ruskin says that all lett

11/12

The main purpose of letters is the practical one of making tho ughts visible. Ruskin says that all letters are frightful things an d to be endured only on occasion, that is to say, in places wher e the sense of the inscription is of more importance than exter nal ornament. This is a sweeping statement, from which we n eed not suffer unduly; yet it is doubtful whether there is art in individual letters. Letters in combination may be satisfying and in a well composed page even beautiful as a whole, but art in letters consists rather in the art of arranging and composing th em in a pleasing and appropriate manner. The main purpose of letters is the practical one of making thoughts visible. Ruskin s ays that all letters are frightful things and to be endured only o n occasion, that is to say, in places where the sense of the inscr iption is of more importance than external ornament. This is a sweeping statement, from which we need not suffer unduly; yet it is doubtful whether there is art in individual letters. Lett ers in combination may be satisfying and in a well composed p age even beautiful as a whole, but art in letters consists rather i
The main purpose of letters is the practical one of making t houghts visible. Ruskin says that all letters are frightful thi
The main purpose of letters is the practical one of making thoughts visible. Ruskin says that all lett

11/13

The main purpose of letters is the practical one of making tho ughts visible. Ruskin says that all letters are frightful things an d to be endured only on occasion, that is to say, in places wher e the sense of the inscription is of more importance than exter nal ornament. This is a sweeping statement, from which we n eed not suffer unduly; yet it is doubtful whether there is art in individual letters. Letters in combination may be satisfying and in a well composed page even beautiful as a whole, but art in letters consists rather in the art of arranging and composing th em in a pleasing and appropriate manner. The main purpose of letters is the practical one of making thoughts visible. Ruskin s ays that all letters are frightful things and to be endured only o n occasion, that is to say, in places where the sense of the inscr iption is of more importance than external ornament. This is a sweeping statement, from which we need not suffer unduly; yet it is doubtful whether there is art in individual letters. Lett ers in combination may be satisfying and in a well composed p
The main purpose of letters is the practical one of making t houghts visible. Ruskin says that all letters are frightful thi
The main purpose of letters is the practical one of making thoughts visible. Ruskin says that all lett

11/14

The main purpose of letters is the practical one of making tho ughts visible. Ruskin says that all letters are frightful things an d to be endured only on occasion, that is to say, in places wher e the sense of the inscription is of more importance than exter nal ornament. This is a sweeping statement, from which we n eed not suffer unduly; yet it is doubtful whether there is art in individual letters. Letters in combination may be satisfying and in a well composed page even beautiful as a whole, but art in letters consists rather in the art of arranging and composing th em in a pleasing and appropriate manner. The main purpose of letters is the practical one of making thoughts visible. Ruskin s ays that all letters are frightful things and to be endured only o n occasion, that is to say, in places where the sense of the inscr iption is of more importance than external ornament. This is a sweeping statement, from which we need not suffer unduly; yet it is doubtful whether there is art in individual letters. Lett
The main purpose of letters is the practical one of making t houghts visible. Ruskin says that all letters are frightful thi
The main purpose of letters is the practical one of making thoughts visible. Ruskin says that all lett

12 POINT SET MINUS ½ UNIT

ROMAN, ITALIC, BOLD, BOLD ITALIC

abcdefghijklmnopqrstuvwxyz – 1 UNIT
abcdefghijklmnopqrstuvwxyz – ½ UNIT
abcdefghijklmnopqrstuvwxyz NORMAL

ABCDEFGHIJKLMNOPQRSTUVWXYZ 1234567890 abcdefghijklmnopqrstuvwxyz
ABCDEFGHIJKLMNOPQRSTUVWXYZ 1234567890 abcdefghijklmnopqrstuvwxyz
ABCDEFGHIJKLMNOPQRSTUVWXYZ 1234567890 abcdefghijklmnopqrstuvwxyz
ABCDEFGHIJKLMNOPQRSTUVWXYZ 1234567890 abcdefghijklmnopqrstuvwxyz

12/12

The main purpose of letters is the practical one of making thoughts visible. Ruskin says that all letters are frightful t hings and to be endured only on occasion, that is to say, in places where the sense of the inscription is of more import ance than external ornament. This is a sweeping statemen t, from which we need not suffer unduly; yet it is doubtf ul whether there is art in individual letters. Letters in com bination may be satisfying and in a well composed page ev en beautiful as a whole, but art in letters consists rather in the art of arranging and composing them in a pleasing and appropriate manner. The main purpose of letters is the pra ctical one of making thoughts visible. Ruskin says that all l etters are frightful things and to be endured only on occasi on, that is to say, in places where the sense of the inscripti on is of more importance than external ornament. This is
The main purpose of letters is the practical one of maki ng thoughts visible. Ruskin says that all letters are frig
The main purpose of letters is the practical one of making thoughts visible. Ruskin says that a

12/13

The main purpose of letters is the practical one of making thoughts visible. Ruskin says that all letters are frightful t hings and to be endured only on occasion, that is to say, in places where the sense of the inscription is of more import ance than external ornament. This is a sweeping statemen t, from which we need not suffer unduly; yet it is doubtf ul whether there is art in individual letters. Letters in com bination may be satisfying and in a well composed page ev en beautiful as a whole, but art in letters consists rather in the art of arranging and composing them in a pleasing and appropriate manner. The main purpose of letters is the pra ctical one of making thoughts visible. Ruskin says that all l etters are frightful things and to be endured only on occasi on, that is to say, in places where the sense of the inscripti
The main purpose of letters is the practical one of maki ng thoughts visible. Ruskin says that all letters are frig
The main purpose of letters is the practical one of making thoughts visible. Ruskin says that a

12/14

The main purpose of letters is the practical one of making thoughts visible. Ruskin says that all letters are frightful t hings and to be endured only on occasion, that is to say, in places where the sense of the inscription is of more import ance than external ornament. This is a sweeping statemen t, from which we need not suffer unduly; yet it is doubtf ul whether there is art in individual letters. Letters in com bination may be satisfying and in a well composed page ev en beautiful as a whole, but art in letters consists rather in the art of arranging and composing them in a pleasing and appropriate manner. The main purpose of letters is the pra ctical one of making thoughts visible. Ruskin says that all l etters are frightful things and to be endured only on occasi on, that is to say, in places where the sense of the inscripti on is of more importance than external ornament. This is
The main purpose of letters is the practical one of maki ng thoughts visible. Ruskin says that all letters are frig
The main purpose of letters is the practical one of making thoughts visible. Ruskin says that a

12/15

The main purpose of letters is the practical one of making thoughts visible. Ruskin says that all letters are frightful t hings and to be endured only on occasion, that is to say, in places where the sense of the inscription is of more import ance than external ornament. This is a sweeping statemen t, from which we need not suffer unduly; yet it is doubtf ul whether there is art in individual letters. Letters in com bination may be satisfying and in a well composed page ev en beautiful as a whole, but art in letters consists rather in the art of arranging and composing them in a pleasing and appropriate manner. The main purpose of letters is the pra ctical one of making thoughts visible. Ruskin says that all l etters are frightful things and to be endured only on occasi on, that is to say, in places where the sense of the inscripti
The main purpose of letters is the practical one of maki ng thoughts visible. Ruskin says that all letters are frig
The main purpose of letters is the practical one of making thoughts visible. Ruskin says that a

KENNERLY 14 POINT SET MINUS ½ UNIT

ROMAN, ITALIC, BOLD, BOLD ITALIC

abcdefghijklmnopqrstuvwxyz – 1 UNIT
abcdefghijklmnopqrstuvwxyz ½ UNIT
abcdefghijklmnopqrstuvwxyz NORMAL

ABCDEFGHIJKLMNOPQRSTUVWXYZ abcdefghijklmnopqrstuvwxyz
ABCDEFGHIJKLMNOPQRSTUVWXYZ abcdefghijklmnopqrstuvwxyz
ABCDEFGHIJKLMNOPQRSTUVWXYZ abcdefghijklmnopqrstuvwxyz
ABCDEFGHIJKLMNOPQRSTUVWXYZ abcdefghijklmnopqrstuvwxyz

14/14

The main purpose of letters is the practical one of making thoughts visible. Ruskin says that all lette rs are frightful things and to be endured only on o ccasion, that is to say, in places where the sense of the inscription is of more importance than exte rnal ornament. This is a sweeping statement, fr om which we need not suffer unduly; yet it is do ubtful whether there is art in individual letters. L etters in combination may be satisfying and in a well composed page even beautiful as a whole, bu t art in letters consists rather in the art of arrangin g and composing them in a pleasing and appropri ate manner. The main purpose of letters is the pr
The main purpose of letters is the practical one of making thoughts visible. Ruskin says that al
The main purpose of letters is the practi cal one of making thoughts visible. Rus

14/15

The main purpose of letters is the practical one of making thoughts visible. Ruskin says that all lette rs are frightful things and to be endured only on o ccasion, that is to say, in places where the sense of the inscription is of more importance than exte rnal ornament. This is a sweeping statement, fr om which we need not suffer unduly; yet it is do ubtful whether there is art in individual letters. L etters in combination may be satisfying and in a well composed page even beautiful as a whole, bu t art in letters consists rather in the art of arrangin g and composing them in a pleasing and appropri
The main purpose of letters is the practical one of making thoughts visible. Ruskin says that al
The main purpose of letters is the practi cal one of making thoughts visible. Rus

14/16

The main purpose of letters is the practical one of making thoughts visible. Ruskin says that all lette rs are frightful things and to be endured only on o ccasion, that is to say, in places where the sense of the inscription is of more importance than exte rnal ornament. This is a sweeping statement, fr om which we need not suffer unduly; yet it is do ubtful whether there is art in individual letters. L etters in combination may be satisfying and in a well composed page even beautiful as a whole, bu t art in letters consists rather in the art of arrangin g and composing them in a pleasing and appropri ate manner. The main purpose of letters is the pr
The main purpose of letters is the practical one of making thoughts visible. Ruskin says that al
The main purpose of letters is the practi cal one of making thoughts visible. Rus

14/17

The main purpose of letters is the practical one of making thoughts visible. Ruskin says that all lette rs are frightful things and to be endured only on o ccasion, that is to say, in places where the sense of the inscription is of more importance than exte rnal ornament. This is a sweeping statement, fr om which we need not suffer unduly; yet it is do ubtful whether there is art in individual letters. L etters in combination may be satisfying and in a well composed page even beautiful as a whole, bu t art in letters consists rather in the art of arrangin g and composing them in a pleasing and appropri
The main purpose of letters is the practical one of making thoughts visible. Ruskin says that al
The main purpose of letters is the practi cal one of making thoughts visible. Rus

ITC KORINNA 6 & 7 POINT SET NORMAL

ROMAN, ITALIC, EXTRA BOLD, EXTRA BOLD ITALIC

ABCDEFGHIJKLMNOPQRSTUVWXYZ 1234567890 abcdefghijklmnopqrstuvwxyz

ABCDEFGHIJKLMNOPQRSTUVWXYZ 1234567890 abcdefghijklmnopqrstuvwxyz

ABCDEFGHIJKLMNOPQRSTUVWXYZ 1234567890 abcdefghijklmnopqrstuvwxyz

ABCDEFGHIJKLMNOPQRSTUVWXYZ 1234567890 abcdefghijklmnopqrstuvwxyz

6/6

The main purpose of letters is the practical one of making thoughts visible. Ruskin says that all lett ers are frightful things and to be endured only on occasion, that is to say, in places where the sense of the inscription is of more importance than external ornament. This is a sweeping statement, fro m which we need not suffer unduly; yet it is doubtful whether there is art in individual letters. Letter s in combination may be satisfying and in a well composed page even beautiful as a whole, but art in letters consists rather in the art of arranging and composing them in a pleasing and appropriat e manner. The main purpose of letters is the practical one of making thoughts visible. Ruskin says that all letters are frightful things and to be endured only on occasion, that is to say, in places wher e the sense of the inscription is of more importance than external ornament. This is a sweeping st atement, from which we need not suffer unduly; yet it is doubtful whether there is art in individual l etters. Letters in combination may be satisfying and in a well composed page even beautiful as a whole, but art in letters consists rather in the art of arranging and composing them in a pleasing a nd appropriate manner. The main purpose of letters is the practical one of making thoughts visibl
The main purpose of letters is the practical one of making thoughts visible. Ruskin says that a ll letters are frightful things and to be endured only on occasion, that is to say, in places where
The main purpose of letters is the practical one of making thoughts visible. Ruskin says that all letters are frightful things and to be endured only on occasion, that is to say, in p

6/7

The main purpose of letters is the practical one of making thoughts visible. Ruskin says that all lett ers are frightful things and to be endured only on occasion, that is to say, in places where the sense of the inscription is of more importance than external ornament. This is a sweeping statement, fro m which we need not suffer unduly; yet it is doubtful whether there is art in individual letters. Letter s in combination may be satisfying and in a well composed page even beautiful as a whole, but art in letters consists rather in the art of arranging and composing them in a pleasing and appropriat e manner. The main purpose of letters is the practical one of making thoughts visible. Ruskin says that all letters are frightful things and to be endured only on occasion, that is to say, in places wher e the sense of the inscription is of more importance than external ornament. This is a sweeping st atement, from which we need not suffer unduly; yet it is doubtful whether there is art in individual l etters. Letters in combination may be satisfying and in a well composed page even beautiful as a
The main purpose of letters is the practical one of making thoughts visible. Ruskin says that a ll letters are frightful things and to be endured only on occasion, that is to say, in places where
The main purpose of letters is the practical one of making thoughts visible. Ruskin says that all letters are frightful things and to be endured only on occasion, that is to say, in p

6/8

The main purpose of letters is the practical one of making thoughts visible. Ruskin says that all lett ers are frightful things and to be endured only on occasion, that is to say, in places where the sense of the inscription is of more importance than external ornament. This is a sweeping statement, fro m which we need not suffer unduly; yet it is doubtful whether there is art in individual letters. Letter s in combination may be satisfying and in a well composed page even beautiful as a whole, but art in letters consists rather in the art of arranging and composing them in a pleasing and appropriat e manner. The main purpose of letters is the practical one of making thoughts visible. Ruskin says that all letters are frightful things and to be endured only on occasion, that is to say, in places wher e the sense of the inscription is of more importance than external ornament. This is a sweeping st
The main purpose of letters is the practical one of making thoughts visible. Ruskin says that a ll letters are frightful things and to be endured only on occasion, that is to say, in places where
The main purpose of letters is the practical one of making thoughts visible. Ruskin says that all letters are frightful things and to be endured only on occasion, that is to say, in p

6/9

The main purpose of letters is the practical one of making thoughts visible. Ruskin says that all lett ers are frightful things and to be endured only on occasion, that is to say, in places where the sense of the inscription is of more importance than external ornament. This is a sweeping statement, fro m which we need not suffer unduly; yet it is doubtful whether there is art in individual letters. Letter s in combination may be satisfying and in a well composed page even beautiful as a whole, but art in letters consists rather in the art of arranging and composing them in a pleasing and appropriat e manner. The main purpose of letters is the practical one of making thoughts visible. Ruskin says that all letters are frightful things and to be endured only on occasion, that is to say, in places wher
The main purpose of letters is the practical one of making thoughts visible. Ruskin says that a ll letters are frightful things and to be endured only on occasion, that is to say, in places where
The main purpose of letters is the practical one of making thoughts visible. Ruskin says that all letters are frightful things and to be endured only on occasion, that is to say, in p

---

ABCDEFGHIJKLMNOPQRSTUVWXYZ 1234567890 abcdefghijklmnopqrstuvwxyz

ABCDEFGHIJKLMNOPQRSTUVWXYZ 1234567890 abcdefghijklmnopqrstuvwxyz

ABCDEFGHIJKLMNOPQRSTUVWXYZ 1234567890 abcdefghijklmnopqrstuvwxyz

ABCDEFGHIJKLMNOPQRSTUVWXYZ 1234567890 abcdefghijklmnopqrstuvwxyz

7/7

The main purpose of letters is the practical one of making thoughts visible. Ruskin s ays that all letters are frightful things and to be endured only on occasion, that is to s ay, in places where the sense of the inscription is of more importance than external ornament. This is a sweeping statement, from which we need not suffer unduly; yet i t is doubtful whether there is art in individual letters. Letters in combination may be s atisfying and in a well composed page even beautiful as a whole, but art in letters co nsists rather in the art of arranging and composing them in a pleasing and appropri ate manner. The main purpose of letters is the practical one of making thoughts visi ble. Ruskin says that all letters are frightful things and to be endured only on occasio n, that is to say, in places where the sense of the inscription is of more importance th an external ornament. This is a sweeping statement, from which we need not suffer
The main purpose of letters is the practical one of making thoughts visible. Rusk in says that all letters are frightful things and to be endured only on occasion, th
The main purpose of letters is the practical one of making thoughts visible. Ruskin says that all letters are frightful things and to be endured only on oc

7/8

The main purpose of letters is the practical one of making thoughts visible. Ruskin s ays that all letters are frightful things and to be endured only on occasion, that is to s ay, in places where the sense of the inscription is of more importance than external ornament. This is a sweeping statement, from which we need not suffer unduly; yet i t is doubtful whether there is art in individual letters. Letters in combination may be s atisfying and in a well composed page even beautiful as a whole, but art in letters co nsists rather in the art of arranging and composing them in a pleasing and appropri ate manner. The main purpose of letters is the practical one of making thoughts visi ble. Ruskin says that all letters are frightful things and to be endured only on occasio n, that is to say, in places where the sense of the inscription is of more importance th
The main purpose of letters is the practical one of making thoughts visible. Rusk in says that all letters are frightful things and to be endured only on occasion, th
The main purpose of letters is the practical one of making thoughts visible. Ruskin says that all letters are frightful things and to be endured only on oc

7/9

The main purpose of letters is the practical one of making thoughts visible. Ruskin s ays that all letters are frightful things and to be endured only on occasion, that is to s ay, in places where the sense of the inscription is of more importance than external ornament. This is a sweeping statement, from which we need not suffer unduly; yet i t is doubtful whether there is art in individual letters. Letters in combination may be s atisfying and in a well composed page even beautiful as a whole, but art in letters co nsists rather in the art of arranging and composing them in a pleasing and appropri ate manner. The main purpose of letters is the practical one of making thoughts visi ble. Ruskin says that all letters are frightful things and to be endured only on occasio n, that is to say, in places where the sense of the inscription is of more importance th
The main purpose of letters is the practical one of making thoughts visible. Rusk in says that all letters are frightful things and to be endured only on occasion, th
The main purpose of letters is the practical one of making thoughts visible. Ruskin says that all letters are frightful things and to be endured only on oc

7/10

The main purpose of letters is the practical one of making thoughts visible. Ruskin s ays that all letters are frightful things and to be endured only on occasion, that is to s ay, in places where the sense of the inscription is of more importance than external ornament. This is a sweeping statement, from which we need not suffer unduly; yet i t is doubtful whether there is art in individual letters. Letters in combination may be s atisfying and in a well composed page even beautiful as a whole, but art in letters co nsists rather in the art of arranging and composing them in a pleasing and appropri ate manner. The main purpose of letters is the practical one of making thoughts visi ble. Ruskin says that all letters are frightful things and to be endured only on occasio
The main purpose of letters is the practical one of making thoughts visible. Rusk in says that all letters are frightful things and to be endured only on occasion, th
The main purpose of letters is the practical one of making thoughts visible. Ruskin says that all letters are frightful things and to be endured only on oc

ITC KORINNA 8 & 9 POINT SET NORMAL

ROMAN, ITALIC, EXTRA BOLD, EXTRA BOLD ITALIC

ABCDEFGHIJKLMNOPQRSTUVWXYZ 1234567890 abcdefghijklmnopqrstuvwxyz

ABCDEFGHIJKLMNOPQRSTUVWXYZ 1234567890 abcdefghijklmnopqrstuvwxyz

ABCDEFGHIJKLMNOPQRSTUVWXYZ 1234567890 abcdefghijklmnopqrstuvwxyz

ABCDEFGHIJKLMNOPQRSTUVWXYZ 1234567890 abcdefghijklmnopqrstuvwxyz

8/8

The main purpose of letters is the practical one of making thoughts visibl e. Ruskin says that all letters are frightful things and to be endured only on occasion, that is to say, in places where the sense of the inscription is of m ore importance than external ornament. This is a sweeping statement, fr om which we need not suffer unduly; yet it is doubtful whether there is art in individual letters. Letters in combination may be satisfying and in a well composed page even beautiful as a whole, but art in letters consists rathe r in the art of arranging and composing them in a pleasing and appropria te manner. The main purpose of letters is the practical one of making tho *The main purpose of letters is the practical one of making thoughts vis ible. Ruskin says that all letters are frightful things and to be endured* **The main purpose of letters is the practical one of making though ts visible. Ruskin says that all letters are frightful things and to be**

8/9

The main purpose of letters is the practical one of making thoughts visibl e. Ruskin says that all letters are frightful things and to be endured only on occasion, that is to say, in places where the sense of the inscription is of m ore importance than external ornament. This is a sweeping statement, fr om which we need not suffer unduly; yet it is doubtful whether there is art in individual letters. Letters in combination may be satisfying and in a well composed page even beautiful as a whole, but art in letters consists rathe r in the art of arranging and composing them in a pleasing and appropria *The main purpose of letters is the practical one of making thoughts vis ible. Ruskin says that all letters are frightful things and to be endured* **The main purpose of letters is the practical one of making though ts visible. Ruskin says that all letters are frightful things and to be**

8/10

The main purpose of letters is the practical one of making thoughts visibl e. Ruskin says that all letters are frightful things and to be endured only on occasion, that is to say, in places where the sense of the inscription is of m ore importance than external ornament. This is a sweeping statement, fr om which we need not suffer unduly; yet it is doubtful whether there is art in individual letters. Letters in combination may be satisfying and in a well composed page even beautiful as a whole, but art in letters consists rathe *The main purpose of letters is the practical one of making thoughts vis ible. Ruskin says that all letters are frightful things and to be endured* **The main purpose of letters is the practical one of making though ts visible. Ruskin says that all letters are frightful things and to be**

8/11

The main purpose of letters is the practical one of making thoughts visibl e. Ruskin says that all letters are frightful things and to be endured only on occasion, that is to say, in places where the sense of the inscription is of m ore importance than external ornament. This is a sweeping statement, fr om which we need not suffer unduly; yet it is doubtful whether there is art in individual letters. Letters in combination may be satisfying and in a well composed page even beautiful as a whole, but art in letters consists rathe *The main purpose of letters is the practical one of making thoughts vis ible. Ruskin says that all letters are frightful things and to be endured* **The main purpose of letters is the practical one of making though ts visible. Ruskin says that all letters are frightful things and to be**

ABCDEFGHIJKLMNOPQRSTUVWXYZ 1234567890 abcdefghijklmnopqrstuvwxyz

ABCDEFGHIJKLMNOPQRSTUVWXYZ 1234567890 abcdefghijklmnopqrstuvwxyz

ABCDEFGHIJKLMNOPQRSTUVWXYZ 1234567890 abcdefghijklmnopqrstuvwxyz

ABCDEFGHIJKLMNOPQRSTUVWXYZ 1234567890 abcdefghijklmnopqrstuvwxyz

9/9

The main purpose of letters is the practical one of making thoug hts visible. Ruskin says that all letters are frightful things and to be endured only on occasion, that is to say, in places where the sens e of the inscription is of more importance than external ornamen t. This is a sweeping statement, from which we need not suffer un duly; yet it is doubtful whether there is art in individual letters. Lett ers in combination may be satisfying and in a well composed pa ge even beautiful as a whole, but art in letters consists rather in th *The main purpose of letters is the practical one of making tho ughts visible. Ruskin says that all letters are frightful things an* **The main purpose of letters is the practical one of making thoughts visible. Ruskin says that all letters are frightful t**

9/10

The main purpose of letters is the practical one of making thoug hts visible. Ruskin says that all letters are frightful things and to be endured only on occasion, that is to say, in places where the sens e of the inscription is of more importance than external ornamen t. This is a sweeping statement, from which we need not suffer un duly; yet it is doubtful whether there is art in individual letters. Lett ers in combination may be satisfying and in a well composed pa *The main purpose of letters is the practical one of making tho ughts visible. Ruskin says that all letters are frightful things an* **The main purpose of letters is the practical one of making thoughts visible. Ruskin says that all letters are frightful t**

9/11

The main purpose of letters is the practical one of making thoug hts visible. Ruskin says that all letters are frightful things and to be endured only on occasion, that is to say, in places where the sens e of the inscription is of more importance than external ornamen t. This is a sweeping statement, from which we need not suffer un duly; yet it is doubtful whether there is art in individual letters. Lett ers in combination may be satisfying and in a well composed pa *The main purpose of letters is the practical one of making tho ughts visible. Ruskin says that all letters are frightful things an* **The main purpose of letters is the practical one of making thoughts visible. Ruskin says that all letters are frightful t**

9/12

The main purpose of letters is the practical one of making thoug hts visible. Ruskin says that all letters are frightful things and to be endured only on occasion, that is to say, in places where the sens e of the inscription is of more importance than external ornamen t. This is a sweeping statement, from which we need not suffer un duly; yet it is doubtful whether there is art in individual letters. Lett ers in combination may be satisfying and in a well composed pa *The main purpose of letters is the practical one of making tho ughts visible. Ruskin says that all letters are frightful things an* **The main purpose of letters is the practical one of making thoughts visible. Ruskin says that all letters are frightful t**

ITC KORINNA 10 POINT SET MINUS ½ UNIT

ROMAN, ITALIC, EXTRA BOLD, EXTRA BOLD ITALIC

abcdefghijklmnopqrstuvwxyz — 1 UNIT
abcdefghijklmnopqrstuvwxyz — ½ UNIT
abcdefghijklmnopqrstuvwxyz NORMAL

ABCDEFGHIJKLMNOPQRSTUVWXYZ 1234567890 abcdefghijklmnopqrstuvwxyz
ABCDEFGHIJKLMNOPQRSTUVWXYZ 1234567890 abcdefghijklmnopqrstuvwxyz
ABCDEFGHIJKLMNOPQRSTUVWXYZ 1234567890 abcdefghijklmnopqrstuvwxyz
ABCDEFGHIJKLMNOPQRSTUVWXYZ 1234567890 abcdefghijklmnopqrstuvwxyz

10/10

The main purpose of letters is the practical one of making th
oughts visible. Ruskin says that all letters are frightful things a
nd to be endured only on occasion, that is to say, in places wh
ere the sense of the inscription is of more importance than ex
ternal ornament. This is a sweeping statement, from which w
e need not suffer unduly; yet it is doubtful whether there is art i
n individual letters. Letters in combination may be satisfying
and in a well composed page even beautiful as a whole, but a
rt in letters consists rather in the art of arranging and composi
ng them in a pleasing and appropriate manner. The main pur
pose of letters is the practical one of making thoughts visible.
Ruskin says that all letters are frightful things and to be endur
ed only on occasion, that is to say, in places where the sense o
f the inscription is of more importance than external orname
nt. This is a sweeping statement, from which we need not suff
er unduly; yet it is doubtful whether there is art in individual let
ters. Letters in combination may be satisfying and in a well co
mposed page even beautiful as a whole, but art in letters cons
ists rather in the art of arranging and composing them in a pl
easing and appropriate manner. The main purpose of letters i
s the practical one of making thoughts visible. Ruskin says th
at all letters are frightful things and to be endured only on occ
*The main purpose of letters is the practical one of making t
houghts visible. Ruskin says that all letters are frightful thi*
**The main purpose of letters is the practical one of mak
ing thoughts visible. Ruskin says that all letters are fri**

10/11

The main purpose of letters is the practical one of making th
oughts visible. Ruskin says that all letters are frightful things a
nd to be endured only on occasion, that is to say, in places wh
ere the sense of the inscription is of more importance than ex
ternal ornament. This is a sweeping statement, from which w
e need not suffer unduly; yet it is doubtful whether there is art i
n individual letters. Letters in combination may be satisfying
and in a well composed page even beautiful as a whole, but a
rt in letters consists rather in the art of arranging and composi
ng them in a pleasing and appropriate manner. The main pur
pose of letters is the practical one of making thoughts visible.
Ruskin says that all letters are frightful things and to be endur
ed only on occasion, that is to say, in places where the sense o
f the inscription is of more importance than external orname
nt. This is a sweeping statement, from which we need not suff
er unduly; yet it is doubtful whether there is art in individual let
ters. Letters in combination may be satisfying and in a well co
mposed page even beautiful as a whole, but art in letters cons
ists rather in the art of arranging and composing them in a pl
easing and appropriate manner. The main purpose of letters i
*The main purpose of letters is the practical one of making t
houghts visible. Ruskin says that all letters are frightful thi*
**The main purpose of letters is the practical one of mak
ing thoughts visible. Ruskin says that all letters are fri**

10/12

The main purpose of letters is the practical one of making th
oughts visible. Ruskin says that all letters are frightful things a
nd to be endured only on occasion, that is to say, in places wh
ere the sense of the inscription is of more importance than ex
ternal ornament. This is a sweeping statement, from which w
e need not suffer unduly; yet it is doubtful whether there is art i
n individual letters. Letters in combination may be satisfying
and in a well composed page even beautiful as a whole, but a
rt in letters consists rather in the art of arranging and composi
ng them in a pleasing and appropriate manner. The main pur
pose of letters is the practical one of making thoughts visible.
Ruskin says that all letters are frightful things and to be endur
ed only on occasion, that is to say, in places where the sense o
f the inscription is of more importance than external orname
nt. This is a sweeping statement, from which we need not suff
er unduly; yet it is doubtful whether there is art in individual let
ters. Letters in combination may be satisfying and in a well co
mposed page even beautiful as a whole, but art in letters cons
*The main purpose of letters is the practical one of making t
houghts visible. Ruskin says that all letters are frightful thi*
**The main purpose of letters is the practical one of mak
ing thoughts visible. Ruskin says that all letters are fri**

10/13

The main purpose of letters is the practical one of making th
oughts visible. Ruskin says that all letters are frightful things a
nd to be endured only on occasion, that is to say, in places wh
ere the sense of the inscription is of more importance than ex
ternal ornament. This is a sweeping statement, from which w
e need not suffer unduly; yet it is doubtful whether there is art i
n individual letters. Letters in combination may be satisfying
and in a well composed page even beautiful as a whole, but a
rt in letters consists rather in the art of arranging and composi
ng them in a pleasing and appropriate manner. The main pur
pose of letters is the practical one of making thoughts visible.
Ruskin says that all letters are frightful things and to be endur
ed only on occasion, that is to say, in places where the sense o
f the inscription is of more importance than external orname
nt. This is a sweeping statement, from which we need not suff
er unduly; yet it is doubtful whether there is art in individual let
ters. Letters in combination may be satisfying and in a well co
*The main purpose of letters is the practical one of making t
houghts visible. Ruskin says that all letters are frightful thi*
**The main purpose of letters is the practical one of mak
ing thoughts visible. Ruskin says that all letters are fri**

ITC KORINNA 11 POINT SET MINUS ½ UNIT

ROMAN, ITALIC, EXTRA BOLD, EXTRA BOLD ITALIC

abcdefghijklmnopqrstuvwxyz – 1 UNIT
abcdefghijklmnopqrstuvwxyz – 1½ UNIT
abcdefghijklmnopqrstuvwxyz NORMAL

ABCDEFGHIJKLMNOPQRSTUVWXYZ 1234567890 abcdefghijklmnopqrstuvwxyz
ABCDEFGHIJKLMNOPQRSTUVWXYZ 1234567890 abcdefghijklmnopqrstuvwxyz
ABCDEFGHIJKLMNOPQRSTUVWXYZ 1234567890 abcdefghijklmnopqrstuvwxyz
ABCDEFGHIJKLMNOPQRSTUVWXYZ 1234567890 abcdefghijklmnopqrstuvwxyz

11/11

The main purpose of letters is the practical one of maki ng thoughts visible. Ruskin says that all letters are frightf ul things and to be endured only on occasion, that is to say, in places where the sense of the inscription is of mo re importance than external ornament. This is a sweepi ng statement, from which we need not suffer unduly; ye t it is doubtful whether there is art in individual letters. Le tters in combination may be satisfying and in a well co mposed page even beautiful as a whole, but art in letter s consists rather in the art of arranging and composing them in a pleasing and appropriate manner. The main purpose of letters is the practical one of making though ts visible. Ruskin says that all letters are frightful things a nd to be endured only on occasion, that is to say, in plac es where the sense of the inscription is of more importa nce than external ornament. This is a sweeping statem ent, from which we need not suffer unduly; yet it is doub tful whether there is art in individual letters. Letters in co mbination may be satisfying and in a well composed p
The main purpose of letters is the practical one of ma king thoughts visible. Ruskin says that all letters are f
The main purpose of letters is the practical one of making thoughts visible. Ruskin says that all lett

11/12

The main purpose of letters is the practical one of maki ng thoughts visible. Ruskin says that all letters are frightf ul things and to be endured only on occasion, that is to say, in places where the sense of the inscription is of mo re importance than external ornament. This is a sweepi ng statement, from which we need not suffer unduly; ye t it is doubtful whether there is art in individual letters. Le tters in combination may be satisfying and in a well co mposed page even beautiful as a whole, but art in letter s consists rather in the art of arranging and composing them in a pleasing and appropriate manner. The main purpose of letters is the practical one of making though ts visible. Ruskin says that all letters are frightful things a nd to be endured only on occasion, that is to say, in plac es where the sense of the inscription is of more importa nce than external ornament. This is a sweeping statem ent, from which we need not suffer unduly; yet it is doub tful whether there is art in individual letters. Letters in co
The main purpose of letters is the practical one of ma king thoughts visible. Ruskin says that all letters are f
The main purpose of letters is the practical one of making thoughts visible. Ruskin says that all lett

11/13

The main purpose of letters is the practical one of maki ng thoughts visible. Ruskin says that all letters are frightf ul things and to be endured only on occasion, that is to say, in places where the sense of the inscription is of mo re importance than external ornament. This is a sweepi ng statement, from which we need not suffer unduly; ye t it is doubtful whether there is art in individual letters. Le tters in combination may be satisfying and in a well co mposed page even beautiful as a whole, but art in letter s consists rather in the art of arranging and composing them in a pleasing and appropriate manner. The main purpose of letters is the practical one of making though ts visible. Ruskin says that all letters are frightful things a nd to be endured only on occasion, that is to say, in plac es where the sense of the inscription is of more importa nce than external ornament. This is a sweeping statem ent, from which we need not suffer unduly; yet it is doub
The main purpose of letters is the practical one of ma king thoughts visible. Ruskin says that all letters are f
The main purpose of letters is the practical one of making thoughts visible. Ruskin says that all lett

11/14

The main purpose of letters is the practical one of maki ng thoughts visible. Ruskin says that all letters are frightf ul things and to be endured only on occasion, that is to say, in places where the sense of the inscription is of mo re importance than external ornament. This is a sweepi ng statement, from which we need not suffer unduly; ye t it is doubtful whether there is art in individual letters. Le tters in combination may be satisfying and in a well co mposed page even beautiful as a whole, but art in letter s consists rather in the art of arranging and composing them in a pleasing and appropriate manner. The main purpose of letters is the practical one of making though ts visible. Ruskin says that all letters are frightful things a nd to be endured only on occasion, that is to say, in plac es where the sense of the inscription is of more importa nce than external ornament. This is a sweeping statem
The main purpose of letters is the practical one of ma king thoughts visible. Ruskin says that all letters are f
The main purpose of letters is the practical one of making thoughts visible. Ruskin says that all lett

ITC KORINNA 12 POINT SET MINUS ½ UNIT

ROMAN, ITALIC, EXTRA BOLD, EXTRA BOLD ITALIC

abcdefghijklmnopqrstuvwxyz – 1 UNIT
abcdefghijklmnopqrstuvwxyz – ½ UNIT
abcdefghijklmnopqrstuvwxyz NORMAL

ABCDEFGHIJKLMNOPQRSTUVWXYZ 1234567890 abcdefghijklmnopqrstuvwxyz
ABCDEFGHIJKLMNOPQRSTUVWXYZ 1234567890 abcdefghijklmnopqrstuvwxyz
ABCDEFGHIJKLMNOPQRSTUVWXYZ 1234567890 abcdefghijklmnopqrstuvwxyz
ABCDEFGHIJKLMNOPQRSTUVWXYZ 1234567890 abcdefghijklmnopqrstuvwxyz

12/12

The main purpose of letters is the practical one of making thoughts visible. Ruskin says that all letters are frightful things and to be endured only on occas ion, that is to say, in places where the sense of the in scription is of more importance than external orna ment. This is a sweeping statement, from which we need not suffer unduly; yet it is doubtful whether the re is art in individual letters. Letters in combination may be satisfying and in a well composed page eve n beautiful as a whole, but art in letters consists rath er in the art of arranging and composing them in a pleasing and appropriate manner. The main purpo se of letters is the practical one of making thoughts visible. Ruskin says that all letters are frightful things and to be endured only on occasion, that is to say, in
The main purpose of letters is the practical one of making thoughts visible. Ruskin says that all lett
The main purpose of letters is the practical on e of making thoughts visible. Ruskin says tha

12/13

The main purpose of letters is the practical one of making thoughts visible. Ruskin says that all letters are frightful things and to be endured only on occas ion, that is to say, in places where the sense of the in scription is of more importance than external orna ment. This is a sweeping statement, from which we need not suffer unduly; yet it is doubtful whether the re is art in individual letters. Letters in combination may be satisfying and in a well composed page eve n beautiful as a whole, but art in letters consists rath er in the art of arranging and composing them in a pleasing and appropriate manner. The main purpo se of letters is the practical one of making thoughts visible. Ruskin says that all letters are frightful things
The main purpose of letters is the practical one of making thoughts visible. Ruskin says that all lett
The main purpose of letters is the practical on e of making thoughts visible. Ruskin says tha

12/14

The main purpose of letters is the practical one of making thoughts visible. Ruskin says that all letters are frightful things and to be endured only on occas ion, that is to say, in places where the sense of the in scription is of more importance than external orna ment. This is a sweeping statement, from which we need not suffer unduly; yet it is doubtful whether the re is art in individual letters. Letters in combination may be satisfying and in a well composed page eve n beautiful as a whole, but art in letters consists rath er in the art of arranging and composing them in a pleasing and appropriate manner. The main purpo se of letters is the practical one of making thoughts visible. Ruskin says that all letters are frightful things and to be endured only on occasion, that is to say, in
The main purpose of letters is the practical one of making thoughts visible. Ruskin says that all lett
The main purpose of letters is the practical on e of making thoughts visible. Ruskin says tha

12/15

The main purpose of letters is the practical one of making thoughts visible. Ruskin says that all letters are frightful things and to be endured only on occas ion, that is to say, in places where the sense of the in scription is of more importance than external orna ment. This is a sweeping statement, from which we need not suffer unduly; yet it is doubtful whether the re is art in individual letters. Letters in combination may be satisfying and in a well composed page eve n beautiful as a whole, but art in letters consists rath er in the art of arranging and composing them in a pleasing and appropriate manner. The main purpo se of letters is the practical one of making thoughts visible. Ruskin says that all letters are frightful things
The main purpose of letters is the practical one of making thoughts visible. Ruskin says that all lett
The main purpose of letters is the practical on e of making thoughts visible. Ruskin says tha

ITC KORINNA 14 POINT SET MINUS ½ UNIT

ROMAN, ITALIC, EXTRA BOLD, EXTRA BOLD ITALIC

abcdefghijklmnopqrstuvwxyz – 1 UNIT
abcdefghijklmnopqrstuvwxyz – ½ UNIT
abcdefghijklmnopqrstuvwxyz NORMAL

ABCDEFGHIJKLMNOPQRSTUVWXYZ abcdefghijklmnopqrstuvwxyz
ABCDEFGHIJKLMNOPQRSTUVWXYZ abcdefghijklmnopqrstuvwxyz
ABCDEFGHIJKLMNOPQRSTUVWXYZ abcdefghijklmnopqrstuvwxyz
ABCDEFGHIJKLMNOPQRSTUVWXYZ abcdefghijklmnopqrstuvwxyz

14/14

The main purpose of letters is the practical one of making thoughts visible. Ruskin says that all letters are frightful things and to be e ndured only on occasion, that is to say, in pl aces where the sense of the inscription is of more importance than external ornament. This is a sweeping statement, from which w e need not suffer unduly; yet it is doubtful w hether there is art in individual letters. Letter s in combination may be satisfying and in a well composed page even beautiful as a wh ole, but art in letters consists rather in the art of arranging and composing them in a plea
The main purpose of letters is the practica l one of making thoughts visible. Ruskin s
The main purpose of letters is the pract ical one of making thoughts visible. Ru

14/15

The main purpose of letters is the practical one of making thoughts visible. Ruskin says that all letters are frightful things and to be e ndured only on occasion, that is to say, in pl aces where the sense of the inscription is of more importance than external ornament. This is a sweeping statement, from which w e need not suffer unduly; yet it is doubtful w hether there is art in individual letters. Letter s in combination may be satisfying and in a well composed page even beautiful as a wh ole, but art in letters consists rather in the art
The main purpose of letters is the practica l one of making thoughts visible. Ruskin s
The main purpose of letters is the pract ical one of making thoughts visible. Ru

14/16

The main purpose of letters is the practical one of making thoughts visible. Ruskin says that all letters are frightful things and to be e ndured only on occasion, that is to say, in pl aces where the sense of the inscription is of more importance than external ornament. This is a sweeping statement, from which w e need not suffer unduly; yet it is doubtful w hether there is art in individual letters. Letter s in combination may be satisfying and in a well composed page even beautiful as a wh ole, but art in letters consists rather in the art of arranging and composing them in a plea
The main purpose of letters is the practica l one of making thoughts visible. Ruskin s
The main purpose of letters is the pract ical one of making thoughts visible. Ru

14/17

The main purpose of letters is the practical one of making thoughts visible. Ruskin says that all letters are frightful things and to be e ndured only on occasion, that is to say, in pl aces where the sense of the inscription is of more importance than external ornament. This is a sweeping statement, from which w e need not suffer unduly; yet it is doubtful w hether there is art in individual letters. Letter s in combination may be satisfying and in a well composed page even beautiful as a wh ole, but art in letters consists rather in the art
The main purpose of letters is the practica l one of making thoughts visible. Ruskin s
The main purpose of letters is the pract ical one of making thoughts visible. Ru

MELIOR 6 & 7 POINT SET NORMAL

ROMAN, ITALIC, BOLD, BOLD ITALIC

ABCDEFGHIJKLMNOPQRSTUVWXYZ 1234567890 abcdefghijklmnopqrstuvwxyz

ABCDEFGHIJKLMNOPQRSTUVWXYZ 1234567890 abcdefghijklmnopqrstuvwxyz

ABCDEFGHIJKLMNOPQRSTUVWXYZ 1234567890 abcdefghijklmnopqrstuvwxyz

ABCDEFGHIJKLMNOPQRSTUVWXYZ 1234567890 abcdefghijklmnopqrstuvwxyz

6/6

The main purpose of letters is the practical one of making thoughts visible. Ruskin says th at all letters are frightful things and to be endured only on occasion, that is to say, in places where the sense of the inscription is of more importance than external ornament. This is a sweeping statement, from which we need not suffer unduly; yet it is doubtful whether the re is art in individual letters. Letters in combination may be satisfying and in a well compo sed page even beautiful as a whole, but art in letters consists rather in the art of arranging a nd composing them in a pleasing and appropriate manner. The main purpose of letters is t he practical one of making thoughts visible. Ruskin says that all letters are frightful things and to be endured only on occasion, that is to say, in places where the sense of the inscripti on is of more importance than external ornament. This is a sweeping statement, from whic h we need not suffer unduly; yet it is doubtful whether there is art in individual letters. Let ters in combination may be satisfying and in a well composed page even beautiful as a wh ole, but art in letters consists rather in the art of arranging and composing them in a pleasi
The main purpose of letters is the practical one of making thoughts visible. Ruskin says th at all letters are frightful things and to be endured only on occasion, that is to say, in place
The main purpose of letters is the practical one of making thoughts visible. Ruskin says t hat all letters are frightful things and to be endured only on occasion, that is to say, in pla

6/7

The main purpose of letters is the practical one of making thoughts visible. Ruskin says th at all letters are frightful things and to be endured only on occasion, that is to say, in places where the sense of the inscription is of more importance than external ornament. This is a sweeping statement, from which we need not suffer unduly; yet it is doubtful whether the re is art in individual letters. Letters in combination may be satisfying and in a well compo sed page even beautiful as a whole, but art in letters consists rather in the art of arranging a nd composing them in a pleasing and appropriate manner. The main purpose of letters is t he practical one of making thoughts visible. Ruskin says that all letters are frightful things and to be endured only on occasion, that is to say, in places where the sense of the inscripti on is of more importance than external ornament. This is a sweeping statement, from whic h we need not suffer unduly; yet it is doubtful whether there is art in individual letters. Let
The main purpose of letters is the practical one of making thoughts visible. Ruskin says th at all letters are frightful things and to be endured only on occasion, that is to say, in place
The main purpose of letters is the practical one of making thoughts visible. Ruskin says t hat all letters are frightful things and to be endured only on occasion, that is to say, in pla

6/8

The main purpose of letters is the practical one of making thoughts visible. Ruskin says th at all letters are frightful things and to be endured only on occasion, that is to say, in places where the sense of the inscription is of more importance than external ornament. This is a sweeping statement, from which we need not suffer unduly; yet it is doubtful whether the re is art in individual letters. Letters in combination may be satisfying and in a well compo sed page even beautiful as a whole, but art in letters consists rather in the art of arranging a nd composing them in a pleasing and appropriate manner. The main purpose of letters is t he practical one of making thoughts visible. Ruskin says that all letters are frightful things and to be endured only on occasion, that is to say, in places where the sense of the inscripti
The main purpose of letters is the practical one of making thoughts visible. Ruskin says th at all letters are frightful things and to be endured only on occasion, that is to say, in place
The main purpose of letters is the practical one of making thoughts visible. Ruskin says t hat all letters are frightful things and to be endured only on occasion, that is to say, in pla

6/9

The main purpose of letters is the practical one of making thoughts visible. Ruskin says th at all letters are frightful things and to be endured only on occasion, that is to say, in places where the sense of the inscription is of more importance than external ornament. This is a sweeping statement, from which we need not suffer unduly; yet it is doubtful whether the re is art in individual letters. Letters in combination may be satisfying and in a well compo sed page even beautiful as a whole, but art in letters consists rather in the art of arranging a nd composing them in a pleasing and appropriate manner. The main purpose of letters is t he practical one of making thoughts visible. Ruskin says that all letters are frightful things
The main purpose of letters is the practical one of making thoughts visible. Ruskin says th at all letters are frightful things and to be endured only on occasion, that is to say, in place
The main purpose of letters is the practical one of making thoughts visible. Ruskin says t hat all letters are frightful things and to be endured only on occasion, that is to say, in pla

---

ABCDEFGHIJKLMNOPQRSTUVWXYZ 1234567890 abcdefghijklmnopqrstuvwxyz

ABCDEFGHIJKLMNOPQRSTUVWXYZ 1234567890 abcdefghijklmnopqrstuvwxyz

ABCDEFGHIJKLMNOPQRSTUVWXYZ 1234567890 abcdefghijklmnopqrstuvwxyz

ABCDEFGHIJKLMNOPQRSTUVWXYZ 1234567890 abcdefghijklmnopqrstuvwxyz

7/7

The main purpose of letters is the practical one of making thoughts visible. R uskin says that all letters are frightful things and to be endured only on occasi on, that is to say, in places where the sense of the inscription is of more import ance than external ornament. This is a sweeping statement, from which we n eed not suffer unduly; yet it is doubtful whether there is art in individual lette rs. Letters in combination may be satisfying and in a well composed page eve n beautiful as a whole, but art in letters consists rather in the art of arranging a nd composing them in a pleasing and appropriate manner. The main purpos e of letters is the practical one of making thoughts visible. Ruskin says that all letters are frightful things and to be endured only on occasion, that is to say, i n places where the sense of the inscription is of more importance than extern
The main purpose of letters is the practical one of making thoughts visible. R uskin says that all letters are frightful things and to be endured only on occas
The main purpose of letters is the practical one of making thoughts visible. Ruskin says that all letters are frightful things and to be endured only on occ

7/8

The main purpose of letters is the practical one of making thoughts visible. R uskin says that all letters are frightful things and to be endured only on occasi on, that is to say, in places where the sense of the inscription is of more import ance than external ornament. This is a sweeping statement, from which we n eed not suffer unduly; yet it is doubtful whether there is art in individual lette rs. Letters in combination may be satisfying and in a well composed page eve n beautiful as a whole, but art in letters consists rather in the art of arranging a nd composing them in a pleasing and appropriate manner. The main purpos e of letters is the practical one of making thoughts visible. Ruskin says that all letters are frightful things and to be endured only on occasion, that is to say, i
The main purpose of letters is the practical one of making thoughts visible. R uskin says that all letters are frightful things and to be endured only on occas
The main purpose of letters is the practical one of making thoughts visible. Ruskin says that all letters are frightful things and to be endured only on occ

7/9

The main purpose of letters is the practical one of making thoughts visible. R uskin says that all letters are frightful things and to be endured only on occasi on, that is to say, in places where the sense of the inscription is of more import ance than external ornament. This is a sweeping statement, from which we n eed not suffer unduly; yet it is doubtful whether there is art in individual lette rs. Letters in combination may be satisfying and in a well composed page eve n beautiful as a whole, but art in letters consists rather in the art of arranging a nd composing them in a pleasing and appropriate manner. The main purpos e of letters is the practical one of making thoughts visible. Ruskin says that all letters are frightful things and to be endured only on occasion, that is to say, i
The main purpose of letters is the practical one of making thoughts visible. R uskin says that all letters are frightful things and to be endured only on occas
The main purpose of letters is the practical one of making thoughts visible. Ruskin says that all letters are frightful things and to be endured only on occ

7/10

The main purpose of letters is the practical one of making thoughts visible. R uskin says that all letters are frightful things and to be endured only on occasi on, that is to say, in places where the sense of the inscription is of more import ance than external ornament. This is a sweeping statement, from which we n eed not suffer unduly; yet it is doubtful whether there is art in individual lette rs. Letters in combination may be satisfying and in a well composed page eve n beautiful as a whole, but art in letters consists rather in the art of arranging a nd composing them in a pleasing and appropriate manner. The main purpos e of letters is the practical one of making thoughts visible. Ruskin says that all
The main purpose of letters is the practical one of making thoughts visible. R uskin says that all letters are frightful things and to be endured only on occas
The main purpose of letters is the practical one of making thoughts visible. Ruskin says that all letters are frightful things and to be endured only on occ

MELIOR 8 & 9 POINT SET NORMAL

ROMAN, ITALIC, BOLD, BOLD ITALIC

ABCDEFGHIJKLMNOPQRSTUVWXYZ 1234567890 abcdefghijklmnopqrstuvwxyz

ABCDEFGHIJKLMNOPQRSTUVWXYZ 1234567890 abcdefghijklmnopqrstuvwxyz

ABCDEFGHIJKLMNOPQRSTUVWXYZ 1234567890 abcdefghijklmnopqrstuvwxyz

ABCDEFGHIJKLMNOPQRSTUVWXYZ 1234567890 abcdefghijklmnopqrstuvwxyz

8/8

The main purpose of letters is the practical one of making thoughts visible. Ruskin says that all letters are frightful things and to be end ured only on occasion, that is to say, in places where the sense of the inscription is of more importance than external ornament. This is a sweeping statement, from which we need not suffer unduly; yet it i s doubtful whether there is art in individual letters. Letters in comb ination may be satisfying and in a well composed page even beautif ul as a whole, but art in letters consists rather in the art of arranging and composing them in a pleasing and appropriate manner. The ma
The main purpose of letters is the practical one of making thoughts visible. Ruskin says that all letters are frightful things and to be end
The main purpose of letters is the practical one of making though ts visible. Ruskin says that all letters are frightful things and to be

8/9

The main purpose of letters is the practical one of making thoughts visible. Ruskin says that all letters are frightful things and to be end ured only on occasion, that is to say, in places where the sense of the inscription is of more importance than external ornament. This is a sweeping statement, from which we need not suffer unduly; yet it i s doubtful whether there is art in individual letters. Letters in comb ination may be satisfying and in a well composed page even beautif ul as a whole, but art in letters consists rather in the art of arranging
The main purpose of letters is the practical one of making thoughts visible. Ruskin says that all letters are frightful things and to be end
The main purpose of letters is the practical one of making though ts visible. Ruskin says that all letters are frightful things and to be

8/10

The main purpose of letters is the practical one of making thoughts visible. Ruskin says that all letters are frightful things and to be end ured only on occasion, that is to say, in places where the sense of the inscription is of more importance than external ornament. This is a sweeping statement, from which we need not suffer unduly; yet it i s doubtful whether there is art in individual letters. Letters in comb ination may be satisfying and in a well composed page even beautif
The main purpose of letters is the practical one of making thoughts visible. Ruskin says that all letters are frightful things and to be end
The main purpose of letters is the practical one of making though ts visible. Ruskin says that all letters are frightful things and to be

8/11

The main purpose of letters is the practical one of making thoughts visible. Ruskin says that all letters are frightful things and to be end ured only on occasion, that is to say, in places where the sense of the inscription is of more importance than external ornament. This is a sweeping statement, from which we need not suffer unduly; yet it i s doubtful whether there is art in individual letters. Letters in comb ination may be satisfying and in a well composed page even beautif
The main purpose of letters is the practical one of making thoughts visible. Ruskin says that all letters are frightful things and to be end
The main purpose of letters is the practical one of making though ts visible. Ruskin says that all letters are frightful things and to be

---

ABCDEFGHIJKLMNOPQRSTUVWXYZ 1234567890 abcdefghijklmnopqrstuvwxyz

ABCDEFGHIJKLMNOPQRSTUVWXYZ 1234567890 abcdefghijklmnopqrstuvwxyz

ABCDEFGHIJKLMNOPQRSTUVWXYZ 1234567890 abcdefghijklmnopqrstuvwxyz

ABCDEFGHIJKLMNOPQRSTUVWXYZ 1234567890 abcdefghijklmnopqrstuvwxyz

9/9

The main purpose of letters is the practical one of making th oughts visible. Ruskin says that all letters are frightful thing s and to be endured only on occasion, that is to say, in places where the sense of the inscription is of more importance tha n external ornament. This is a sweeping statement, from wh ich we need not suffer unduly; yet it is doubtful whether the re is art in individual letters. Letters in combination may be satisfying and in a well composed page even beautiful as a
The main purpose of letters is the practical one of making th oughts visible. Ruskin says that all letters are frightful thing
The main purpose of letters is the practical one of making t houghts visible. Ruskin says that all letters are frightful thi

9/10

The main purpose of letters is the practical one of making th oughts visible. Ruskin says that all letters are frightful thing s and to be endured only on occasion, that is to say, in places where the sense of the inscription is of more importance tha n external ornament. This is a sweeping statement, from wh ich we need not suffer unduly; yet it is doubtful whether the re is art in individual letters. Letters in combination may be
The main purpose of letters is the practical one of making th oughts visible. Ruskin says that all letters are frightful thing
The main purpose of letters is the practical one of making t houghts visible. Ruskin says that all letters are frightful thi

9/11

The main purpose of letters is the practical one of making th oughts visible. Ruskin says that all letters are frightful thing s and to be endured only on occasion, that is to say, in places where the sense of the inscription is of more importance tha n external ornament. This is a sweeping statement, from wh ich we need not suffer unduly; yet it is doubtful whether the re is art in individual letters. Letters in combination may be
The main purpose of letters is the practical one of making th oughts visible. Ruskin says that all letters are frightful thing
The main purpose of letters is the practical one of making t houghts visible. Ruskin says that all letters are frightful thi

9/12

The main purpose of letters is the practical one of making th oughts visible. Ruskin says that all letters are frightful thing s and to be endured only on occasion, that is to say, in places where the sense of the inscription is of more importance tha n external ornament. This is a sweeping statement, from wh ich we need not suffer unduly; yet it is doubtful whether the re is art in individual letters. Letters in combination may be
The main purpose of letters is the practical one of making th oughts visible. Ruskin says that all letters are frightful thing
The main purpose of letters is the practical one of making t houghts visible. Ruskin says that all letters are frightful thi

MELIOR 10 POINT SET MINUS ½ UNIT

ROMAN, ITALIC, BOLD, BOLD ITALIC

abcdefghijklmnopqrstuvwxyz – 1 UNIT
abcdefghijklmnopqrstuvwxyz – ½ UNIT
abcdefghijklmnopqrstuvwxyz NORMAL

ABCDEFGHIJKLMNOPQRSTUVWXYZ 1234567890 abcdefghijklmnopqrstuvwxyz
ABCDEFGHIJKLMNOPQRSTUVWXYZ 1234567890 abcdefghijklmnopqrstuvwxyz
ABCDEFGHIJKLMNOPQRSTUVWXYZ 1234567890 abcdefghijklmnopqrstuvwxyz
ABCDEFGHIJKLMNOPQRSTUVWXYZ 1234567890 abcdefghijklmnopqrstuvwxyz

10/10

The main purpose of letters is the practical one of makin g thoughts visible. Ruskin says that all letters are frightf ul things and to be endured only on occasion, that is to s ay, in places where the sense of the inscription is of more importance than external ornament. This is a sweeping statement, from which we need not suffer unduly; yet it is doubtful whether there is art in individual letters. Lett ers in combination may be satisfying and in a well comp osed page even beautiful as a whole, but art in letters co nsists rather in the art of arranging and composing them in a pleasing and appropriate manner. The main purpo se of letters is the practical one of making thoughts visib le. Ruskin says that all letters are frightful things and to be endured only on occasion, that is to say, in places whe re the sense of the inscription is of more importance th an external ornament. This is a sweeping statement, fro m which we need not suffer unduly; yet it is doubtful wh ether there is art in individual letters. Letters in combina tion may be satisfying and in a well composed page eve n beautiful as a whole, but art in letters consists rather in the art of arranging and composing them in a pleasing and appropriate manner. The main purpose of letters is

The main purpose of letters is the practical one of maki ng thoughts visible. Ruskin says that all letters are fright

The main purpose of letters is the practical one of maki ng thoughts visible. Ruskin says that all letters are frigh

10/11

The main purpose of letters is the practical one of makin g thoughts visible. Ruskin says that all letters are frightf ul things and to be endured only on occasion, that is to s ay, in places where the sense of the inscription is of more importance than external ornament. This is a sweeping statement, from which we need not suffer unduly; yet it is doubtful whether there is art in individual letters. Lett ers in combination may be satisfying and in a well comp osed page even beautiful as a whole, but art in letters co nsists rather in the art of arranging and composing them in a pleasing and appropriate manner. The main purpo se of letters is the practical one of making thoughts visib le. Ruskin says that all letters are frightful things and to be endured only on occasion, that is to say, in places whe re the sense of the inscription is of more importance th an external ornament. This is a sweeping statement, fro m which we need not suffer unduly; yet it is doubtful wh ether there is art in individual letters. Letters in combina tion may be satisfying and in a well composed page eve n beautiful as a whole, but art in letters consists rather in

The main purpose of letters is the practical one of maki ng thoughts visible. Ruskin says that all letters are fright

The main purpose of letters is the practical one of maki ng thoughts visible. Ruskin says that all letters are frigh

10/12

The main purpose of letters is the practical one of makin g thoughts visible. Ruskin says that all letters are frightf ul things and to be endured only on occasion, that is to s ay, in places where the sense of the inscription is of more importance than external ornament. This is a sweeping statement, from which we need not suffer unduly; yet it is doubtful whether there is art in individual letters. Lett ers in combination may be satisfying and in a well comp osed page even beautiful as a whole, but art in letters co nsists rather in the art of arranging and composing them in a pleasing and appropriate manner. The main purpo se of letters is the practical one of making thoughts visib le. Ruskin says that all letters are frightful things and to be endured only on occasion, that is to say, in places whe re the sense of the inscription is of more importance th an external ornament. This is a sweeping statement, fro m which we need not suffer unduly; yet it is doubtful wh ether there is art in individual letters. Letters in combina

The main purpose of letters is the practical one of maki ng thoughts visible. Ruskin says that all letters are fright

The main purpose of letters is the practical one of maki ng thoughts visible. Ruskin says that all letters are frigh

10/13

The main purpose of letters is the practical one of makin g thoughts visible. Ruskin says that all letters are frightf ul things and to be endured only on occasion, that is to s ay, in places where the sense of the inscription is of more importance than external ornament. This is a sweeping statement, from which we need not suffer unduly; yet it is doubtful whether there is art in individual letters. Lett ers in combination may be satisfying and in a well comp osed page even beautiful as a whole, but art in letters co nsists rather in the art of arranging and composing them in a pleasing and appropriate manner. The main purpo se of letters is the practical one of making thoughts visib le. Ruskin says that all letters are frightful things and to be endured only on occasion, that is to say, in places whe re the sense of the inscription is of more importance th an external ornament. This is a sweeping statement, fro m which we need not suffer unduly; yet it is doubtful wh

The main purpose of letters is the practical one of maki ng thoughts visible. Ruskin says that all letters are fright

The main purpose of letters is the practical one of maki ng thoughts visible. Ruskin says that all letters are frigh

MELIOR 11 POINT SET MINUS ½ UNIT

ROMAN, ITALIC, BOLD, BOLD ITALIC

abcdefghijklmnopqrstuvwxyz – 1 UNIT
abcdefghijklmnopqrstuvwxyz – ½ UNIT
abcdefghijklmnopqrstuvwxyz NORMAL

ABCDEFGHIJKLMNOPQRSTUVWXYZ 1234567890 abcdefghijklmnopqrstuvwxyz
ABCDEFGHIJKLMNOPQRSTUVWXYZ 1234567890 abcdefghijklmnopqrstuvwxyz
ABCDEFGHIJKLMNOPQRSTUVWXYZ 1234567890 abcdefghijklmnopqrstuvwxyz
ABCDEFGHIJKLMNOPQRSTUVWXYZ 1234567890 abcdefghijklmnopqrstuvwxyz

11/11

The main purpose of letters is the practical one of making thoughts visible. Ruskin says that all letter s are frightful things and to be endured only on occ asion, that is to say, in places where the sense of the inscription is of more importance than external or nament. This is a sweeping statement, from which we need not suffer unduly; yet it is doubtful wheth er there is art in individual letters. Letters in combi nation may be satisfying and in a well composed p age even beautiful as a whole, but art in letters cons ists rather in the art of arranging and composing th em in a pleasing and appropriate manner. The mai n purpose of letters is the practical one of making t houghts visible. Ruskin says that all letters are frig htful things and to be endured only on occasion, th at is to say, in places where the sense of the inscript ion is of more importance than external ornament. This is a sweeping statement, from which we need not suffer unduly; yet it is doubtful whether there i
The main purpose of letters is the practical one of making thoughts visible. Ruskin says that all letter
The main purpose of letters is the practical one of making thoughts visible. Ruskin says that all lette

11/12

The main purpose of letters is the practical one of making thoughts visible. Ruskin says that all letter s are frightful things and to be endured only on occ asion, that is to say, in places where the sense of the inscription is of more importance than external or nament. This is a sweeping statement, from which we need not suffer unduly; yet it is doubtful wheth er there is art in individual letters. Letters in combi nation may be satisfying and in a well composed p age even beautiful as a whole, but art in letters cons ists rather in the art of arranging and composing th em in a pleasing and appropriate manner. The mai n purpose of letters is the practical one of making t houghts visible. Ruskin says that all letters are frig htful things and to be endured only on occasion, th at is to say, in places where the sense of the inscript ion is of more importance than external ornament. This is a sweeping statement, from which we need
The main purpose of letters is the practical one of making thoughts visible. Ruskin says that all letter
The main purpose of letters is the practical one of making thoughts visible. Ruskin says that all lette

11/13

The main purpose of letters is the practical one of making thoughts visible. Ruskin says that all letter s are frightful things and to be endured only on occ asion, that is to say, in places where the sense of the inscription is of more importance than external or nament. This is a sweeping statement, from which we need not suffer unduly; yet it is doubtful wheth er there is art in individual letters. Letters in combi nation may be satisfying and in a well composed p age even beautiful as a whole, but art in letters cons ists rather in the art of arranging and composing th em in a pleasing and appropriate manner. The mai n purpose of letters is the practical one of making t houghts visible. Ruskin says that all letters are frig htful things and to be endured only on occasion, th at is to say, in places where the sense of the inscript ion is of more importance than external ornament.
The main purpose of letters is the practical one of making thoughts visible. Ruskin says that all letter
The main purpose of letters is the practical one of making thoughts visible. Ruskin says that all lette

11/14

The main purpose of letters is the practical one of making thoughts visible. Ruskin says that all letter s are frightful things and to be endured only on occ asion, that is to say, in places where the sense of the inscription is of more importance than external or nament. This is a sweeping statement, from which we need not suffer unduly; yet it is doubtful wheth er there is art in individual letters. Letters in combi nation may be satisfying and in a well composed p age even beautiful as a whole, but art in letters cons ists rather in the art of arranging and composing th em in a pleasing and appropriate manner. The mai n purpose of letters is the practical one of making t houghts visible. Ruskin says that all letters are frig htful things and to be endured only on occasion, th at is to say, in places where the sense of the inscript
The main purpose of letters is the practical one of making thoughts visible. Ruskin says that all letter
The main purpose of letters is the practical one of making thoughts visible. Ruskin says that all lette

MELIOR 12 POINT SET MINUS ½ UNIT

ROMAN, ITALIC, BOLD, BOLD ITALIC

abcdefghijklmnopqrstuvwxyz – 1 UNIT
abcdefghijklmnopqrstuvwxyz – ½ UNIT
abcdefghijklmnopqrstuvwxyz NORMAL

ABCDEFGHIJKLMNOPQRSTUVWXYZ 1234567890 abcdefghijklmnopqrstuvwxyz
ABCDEFGHIJKLMNOPQRSTUVWXYZ 1234567890 abcdefghijklmnopqrstuvwxyz
ABCDEFGHIJKLMNOPQRSTUVWXYZ 1234567890 abcdefghijklmnopqrstuvwxyz
ABCDEFGHIJKLMNOPQRSTUVWXYZ 1234567890 abcdefghijklmnopqrstuvwxyz

12/12

The main purpose of letters is the practical one of making thoughts visible. Ruskin says that all letters are frightful things and to be endured on ly on occasion, that is to say, in places where th e sense of the inscription is of more importance than external ornament. This is a sweeping stat ement, from which we need not suffer unduly; yet it is doubtful whether there is art in individ ual letters. Letters in combination may be satisf ying and in a well composed page even beautif ul as a whole, but art in letters consists rather in the art of arranging and composing them in a pl easing and appropriate manner. The main purp ose of letters is the practical one of making thou ghts visible. Ruskin says that all letters are frigh
The main purpose of letters is the practical one of making thoughts visible. Ruskin says that all
The main purpose of letters is the practical one of making thoughts visible. Ruskin says that al

12/13

The main purpose of letters is the practical one of making thoughts visible. Ruskin says that all letters are frightful things and to be endured on ly on occasion, that is to say, in places where th e sense of the inscription is of more importance than external ornament. This is a sweeping stat ement, from which we need not suffer unduly; yet it is doubtful whether there is art in individ ual letters. Letters in combination may be satisf ying and in a well composed page even beautif ul as a whole, but art in letters consists rather in the art of arranging and composing them in a pl easing and appropriate manner. The main purp ose of letters is the practical one of making thou
The main purpose of letters is the practical one of making thoughts visible. Ruskin says that all
The main purpose of letters is the practical one of making thoughts visible. Ruskin says that al

12/14

The main purpose of letters is the practical one of making thoughts visible. Ruskin says that all letters are frightful things and to be endured on ly on occasion, that is to say, in places where th e sense of the inscription is of more importance than external ornament. This is a sweeping stat ement, from which we need not suffer unduly; yet it is doubtful whether there is art in individ ual letters. Letters in combination may be satisf ying and in a well composed page even beautif ul as a whole, but art in letters consists rather in the art of arranging and composing them in a pl easing and appropriate manner. The main purp ose of letters is the practical one of making thou ghts visible. Ruskin says that all letters are frigh
The main purpose of letters is the practical one of making thoughts visible. Ruskin says that all
The main purpose of letters is the practical one of making thoughts visible. Ruskin says that al

12/15

The main purpose of letters is the practical one of making thoughts visible. Ruskin says that all letters are frightful things and to be endured on ly on occasion, that is to say, in places where th e sense of the inscription is of more importance than external ornament. This is a sweeping stat ement, from which we need not suffer unduly; yet it is doubtful whether there is art in individ ual letters. Letters in combination may be satisf ying and in a well composed page even beautif ul as a whole, but art in letters consists rather in the art of arranging and composing them in a pl easing and appropriate manner. The main purp ose of letters is the practical one of making thou
The main purpose of letters is the practical one of making thoughts visible. Ruskin says that all
The main purpose of letters is the practical one of making thoughts visible. Ruskin says that al

MELIOR 14 POINT SET MINUS ½ UNIT

ROMAN, ITALIC, BOLD, BOLD ITALIC

abcdefghijklmnopqrstuvwxyz – 1 UNIT
abcdefghijklmnopqrstuvwxyz – ½ UNIT
abcdefghijklmnopqrstuvwxyz NORMAL

ABCDEFGHIJKLMNOPQRSTUVWXYZ abcdefghijklmnopqrstuvwxyz
ABCDEFGHIJKLMNOPQRSTUVWXYZ abcdefghijklmnopqrstuvwxyz
ABCDEFGHIJKLMNOPQRSTUVWXYZ abcdefghijklmnopqrstuvwxyz
ABCDEFGHIJKLMNOPQRSTUVWXYZ abcdefghijklmnopqrstuvwxyz

14/14

The main purpose of letters is the practi cal one of making thoughts visible. Rus kin says that all letters are frightful thing s and to be endured only on occasion, th at is to say, in places where the sense of t he inscription is of more importance tha n external ornament. This is a sweeping statement, from which we need not suff er unduly; yet it is doubtful whether the re is art in individual letters. Letters in c ombination may be satisfying and in a well composed page even beautiful as a whole, but art in letters consists rather in
The main purpose of letters is the practi cal one of making thoughts visible. Rus
The main purpose of letters is the practi cal one of making thoughts visible. Rus

14/15

The main purpose of letters is the practi cal one of making thoughts visible. Rus kin says that all letters are frightful thing s and to be endured only on occasion, th at is to say, in places where the sense of t he inscription is of more importance tha n external ornament. This is a sweeping statement, from which we need not suff er unduly; yet it is doubtful whether the re is art in individual letters. Letters in c ombination may be satisfying and in a well composed page even beautiful as a
The main purpose of letters is the practi cal one of making thoughts visible. Rus
The main purpose of letters is the practi cal one of making thoughts visible. Rus

14/16

The main purpose of letters is the practi cal one of making thoughts visible. Rus kin says that all letters are frightful thing s and to be endured only on occasion, th at is to say, in places where the sense of t he inscription is of more importance tha n external ornament. This is a sweeping statement, from which we need not suff er unduly; yet it is doubtful whether the re is art in individual letters. Letters in c ombination may be satisfying and in a well composed page even beautiful as a whole, but art in letters consists rather in
The main purpose of letters is the practi cal one of making thoughts visible. Rus
The main purpose of letters is the practi cal one of making thoughts visible. Rus

14/17

The main purpose of letters is the practi cal one of making thoughts visible. Rus kin says that all letters are frightful thing s and to be endured only on occasion, th at is to say, in places where the sense of t he inscription is of more importance tha n external ornament. This is a sweeping statement, from which we need not suff er unduly; yet it is doubtful whether the re is art in individual letters. Letters in c ombination may be satisfying and in a well composed page even beautiful as a
The main purpose of letters is the practi cal one of making thoughts visible. Rus
The main purpose of letters is the practi cal one of making thoughts visible. Rus

MEMPHIS 6 & 7 POINT SET NORMAL

LIGHT, ITALIC, BOLD, BOLD ITALIC

ABCDEFGHIJKLMNOPQRSTUVWXYZ 1234567890 abcdefghijklmnopqrstuvwxyz
ABCDEFGHIJKLMNOPQRSTUVWXYZ 1234567890 abcdefghijklmnopqrstuvwxyz
ABCDEFGHIJKLMNOPQRSTUVWXYZ 1234567890 abcdefghijklmnopqrstuvwxyz
ABCDEFGHIJKLMNOPQRSTUVWXYZ 1234567890 abcdefghijklmnopqrstuvwxyz

6/6

The main purpose of letters is the practical one of making thoughts visible. Ruskin says th
at all letters are frightful things and to be endured only on occasion, that is to say, in place
s where the sense of the inscription is of more importance than external ornament. This is
a sweeping statement, from which we need not suffer unduly; yet it is doubtful whether th
ere is art in individual letters. Letters in combination may be satisfying and in a well comp
osed page even beautiful as a whole, but art in letters consists rather in the art of arrangin
g and composing them in a pleasing and appropriate manner. The main purpose of letter
s is the practical one of making thoughts visible. Ruskin says that all letters are frightful thi
ngs and to be endured only on occasion, that is to say, in places where the sense of the ins
cription is of more importance than external ornament. This is a sweeping statement, fro
m which we need not suffer unduly; yet it is doubtful whether there is art in individual lett
ers. Letters in combination may be satisfying and in a well composed page even beautifu
l as a whole, but art in letters consists rather in the art of arranging and composing them i
The main purpose of letters is the practical one of making thoughts visible. Ruskin says th
at all letters are frightful things and to be endured only on occasion, that is to say, in place
The main purpose of letters is the practical one of making thoughts visible. Ruskin say
s that all letters are frightful things and to be endured only on occasion, that is to say, i

6/7

The main purpose of letters is the practical one of making thoughts visible. Ruskin says th
at all letters are frightful things and to be endured only on occasion, that is to say, in place
s where the sense of the inscription is of more importance than external ornament. This is
a sweeping statement, from which we need not suffer unduly; yet it is doubtful whether th
ere is art in individual letters. Letters in combination may be satisfying and in a well comp
osed page even beautiful as a whole, but art in letters consists rather in the art of arrangin
g and composing them in a pleasing and appropriate manner. The main purpose of letter
s is the practical one of making thoughts visible. Ruskin says that all letters are frightful thi
ngs and to be endured only on occasion, that is to say, in places where the sense of the ins
cription is of more importance than external ornament. This is a sweeping statement, fro
m which we need not suffer unduly; yet it is doubtful whether there is art in individual lett
The main purpose of letters is the practical one of making thoughts visible. Ruskin says th
at all letters are frightful things and to be endured only on occasion, that is to say, in place
The main purpose of letters is the practical one of making thoughts visible. Ruskin say
s that all letters are frightful things and to be endured only on occasion, that is to say, i

6/8

The main purpose of letters is the practical one of making thoughts visible. Ruskin says th
at all letters are frightful things and to be endured only on occasion, that is to say, in place
s where the sense of the inscription is of more importance than external ornament. This is
a sweeping statement, from which we need not suffer unduly; yet it is doubtful whether th
ere is art in individual letters. Letters in combination may be satisfying and in a well comp
osed page even beautiful as a whole, but art in letters consists rather in the art of arrangin
g and composing them in a pleasing and appropriate manner. The main purpose of letter
s is the practical one of making thoughts visible. Ruskin says that all letters are frightful thi
ngs and to be endured only on occasion, that is to say, in places where the sense of the ins
The main purpose of letters is the practical one of making thoughts visible. Ruskin says th
at all letters are frightful things and to be endured only on occasion, that is to say, in place
The main purpose of letters is the practical one of making thoughts visible. Ruskin say
s that all letters are frightful things and to be endured only on occasion, that is to say, i

6/9

The main purpose of letters is the practical one of making thoughts visible. Ruskin says th
at all letters are frightful things and to be endured only on occasion, that is to say, in place
s where the sense of the inscription is of more importance than external ornament. This is
a sweeping statement, from which we need not suffer unduly; yet it is doubtful whether th
ere is art in individual letters. Letters in combination may be satisfying and in a well comp
osed page even beautiful as a whole, but art in letters consists rather in the art of arrangin
g and composing them in a pleasing and appropriate manner. The main purpose of letter
s is the practical one of making thoughts visible. Ruskin says that all letters are frightful thi
The main purpose of letters is the practical one of making thoughts visible. Ruskin says th
at all letters are frightful things and to be endured only on occasion, that is to say, in place
The main purpose of letters is the practical one of making thoughts visible. Ruskin say
s that all letters are frightful things and to be endured only on occasion, that is to say, i

---

ABCDEFGHIJKLMNOPQRSTUVWXYZ 1234567890 abcdefghijklmnopqrstuvwxyz
ABCDEFGHIJKLMNOPQRSTUVWXYZ 1234567890 abcdefghijklmnopqrstuvwxyz
ABCDEFGHIJKLMNOPQRSTUVWXYZ 1234567890 abcdefghijklmnopqrstuvwxyz
ABCDEFGHIJKLMNOPQRSTUVWXYZ 1234567890 abcdefghijklmnopqrstuvwxyz

7/7

The main purpose of letters is the practical one of making thoughts visible. R
uskin says that all letters are frightful things and to be endured only on occas
ion, that is to say, in places where the sense of the inscription is of more impor
tance than external ornament. This is a sweeping statement, from which we
need not suffer unduly; yet it is doubtful whether there is art in individual lett
ers. Letters in combination may be satisfying and in a well composed page e
ven beautiful as a whole, but art in letters consists rather in the art of arrangi
ng and composing them in a pleasing and appropriate manner. The main p
urpose of letters is the practical one of making thoughts visible. Ruskin says t
hat all letters are frightful things and to be endured only on occasion, that is t
o say, in places where the sense of the inscription is of more importance than
The main purpose of letters is the practical one of making thoughts visible. R
uskin says that all letters are frightful things and to be endured only on occas
The main purpose of letters is the practical one of making thoughts visible.
Ruskin says that all letters are frightful things and to be endured only on

7/8

The main purpose of letters is the practical one of making thoughts visible. R
uskin says that all letters are frightful things and to be endured only on occas
ion, that is to say, in places where the sense of the inscription is of more impor
tance than external ornament. This is a sweeping statement, from which we
need not suffer unduly; yet it is doubtful whether there is art in individual lett
ers. Letters in combination may be satisfying and in a well composed page e
ven beautiful as a whole, but art in letters consists rather in the art of arrangi
ng and composing them in a pleasing and appropriate manner. The main p
urpose of letters is the practical one of making thoughts visible. Ruskin says t
hat all letters are frightful things and to be endured only on occasion, that is t
The main purpose of letters is the practical one of making thoughts visible. R
uskin says that all letters are frightful things and to be endured only on occas
The main purpose of letters is the practical one of making thoughts visible.
Ruskin says that all letters are frightful things and to be endured only on

7/9

The main purpose of letters is the practical one of making thoughts visible. R
uskin says that all letters are frightful things and to be endured only on occas
ion, that is to say, in places where the sense of the inscription is of more impor
tance than external ornament. This is a sweeping statement, from which we
need not suffer unduly; yet it is doubtful whether there is art in individual lett
ers. Letters in combination may be satisfying and in a well composed page e
ven beautiful as a whole, but art in letters consists rather in the art of arrangi
ng and composing them in a pleasing and appropriate manner. The main p
urpose of letters is the practical one of making thoughts visible. Ruskin says t
hat all letters are frightful things and to be endured only on occasion, that is t
The main purpose of letters is the practical one of making thoughts visible. R
uskin says that all letters are frightful things and to be endured only on occas
The main purpose of letters is the practical one of making thoughts visible.
Ruskin says that all letters are frightful things and to be endured only on

7/10

The main purpose of letters is the practical one of making thoughts visible. R
uskin says that all letters are frightful things and to be endured only on occas
ion, that is to say, in places where the sense of the inscription is of more impor
tance than external ornament. This is a sweeping statement, from which we
need not suffer unduly; yet it is doubtful whether there is art in individual lett
ers. Letters in combination may be satisfying and in a well composed page e
ven beautiful as a whole, but art in letters consists rather in the art of arrangi
ng and composing them in a pleasing and appropriate manner. The main p
urpose of letters is the practical one of making thoughts visible. Ruskin says t
The main purpose of letters is the practical one of making thoughts visible. R
uskin says that all letters are frightful things and to be endured only on occas
The main purpose of letters is the practical one of making thoughts visible.
Ruskin says that all letters are frightful things and to be endured only on

MEMPHIS 8 & 9 POINT SET NORMAL

LIGHT, ITALIC, BOLD, BOLD ITALIC

ABCDEFGHIJKLMNOPQRSTUVWXYZ 1234567890 abcdefghijklmnopqrstuvwxyz

ABCDEFGHIJKLMNOPQRSTUVWXYZ 1234567890 abcdefghijklmnopqrstuvwxyz

ABCDEFGHIJKLMNOPQRSTUVWXYZ 1234567890 abcdefghijklmnopqrstuvwxyz

ABCDEFGHIJKLMNOPQRSTUVWXYZ 1234567890 abcdefghijklmnopqrstuvwxyz

8/8

The main purpose of letters is the practical one of making thoughts visible. Ruskin says that all letters are frightful things and to be end ured only on occasion, that is to say, in places where the sense of th e inscription is of more importance than external ornament. This is a sweeping statement, from which we need not suffer unduly; yet it is doubtful whether there is art in individual letters. Letters in comb ination may be satisfying and in a well composed page even beaut iful as a whole, but art in letters consists rather in the art of arrangin g and composing them in a pleasing and appropriate manner. The

The main purpose of letters is the practical one of making thoughts visible. Ruskin says that all letters are frightful things and to be end

The main purpose of letters is the practical one of making though ts visible. Ruskin says that all letters are frightful things and to b

8/9

The main purpose of letters is the practical one of making thoughts visible. Ruskin says that all letters are frightful things and to be end ured only on occasion, that is to say, in places where the sense of th e inscription is of more importance than external ornament. This is a sweeping statement, from which we need not suffer unduly; yet it is doubtful whether there is art in individual letters. Letters in comb ination may be satisfying and in a well composed page even beaut iful as a whole, but art in letters consists rather in the art of arrangin

The main purpose of letters is the practical one of making thoughts visible. Ruskin says that all letters are frightful things and to be end

The main purpose of letters is the practical one of making though ts visible. Ruskin says that all letters are frightful things and to b

8/10

The main purpose of letters is the practical one of making thoughts visible. Ruskin says that all letters are frightful things and to be end ured only on occasion, that is to say, in places where the sense of th e inscription is of more importance than external ornament. This is a sweeping statement, from which we need not suffer unduly; yet it is doubtful whether there is art in individual letters. Letters in comb ination may be satisfying and in a well composed page even beaut

The main purpose of letters is the practical one of making thoughts visible. Ruskin says that all letters are frightful things and to be end

The main purpose of letters is the practical one of making though ts visible. Ruskin says that all letters are frightful things and to b

8/11

The main purpose of letters is the practical one of making thoughts visible. Ruskin says that all letters are frightful things and to be end ured only on occasion, that is to say, in places where the sense of th e inscription is of more importance than external ornament. This is a sweeping statement, from which we need not suffer unduly; yet it is doubtful whether there is art in individual letters. Letters in comb ination may be satisfying and in a well composed page even beaut

The main purpose of letters is the practical one of making thoughts visible. Ruskin says that all letters are frightful things and to be end

The main purpose of letters is the practical one of making though ts visible. Ruskin says that all letters are frightful things and to b

---

ABCDEFGHIJKLMNOPQRSTUVWXYZ 1234567890 abcdefghijklmnopqrstuvwxyz

ABCDEFGHIJKLMNOPQRSTUVWXYZ 1234567890 abcdefghijklmnopqrstuvwxyz

ABCDEFGHIJKLMNOPQRSTUVWXYZ 1234567890 abcdefghijklmnopqrstuvwxyz

ABCDEFGHIJKLMNOPQRSTUVWXYZ 1234567890 abcdefghijklmnopqrstuvwxyz

9/9

The main purpose of letters is the practical one of making th oughts visible. Ruskin says that all letters are frightful thing s and to be endured only on occasion, that is to say, in place s where the sense of the inscription is of more importance th an external ornament. This is a sweeping statement, from which we need not suffer unduly; yet it is doubtful whether t here is art in individual letters. Letters in combination may be satisfying and in a well composed page even beautiful a

The main purpose of letters is the practical one of making th oughts visible. Ruskin says that all letters are frightful thing

The main purpose of letters is the practical one of making thoughts visible. Ruskin says that all letters are frightful t

9/10

The main purpose of letters is the practical one of making th oughts visible. Ruskin says that all letters are frightful thing s and to be endured only on occasion, that is to say, in place s where the sense of the inscription is of more importance th an external ornament. This is a sweeping statement, from which we need not suffer unduly; yet it is doubtful whether t here is art in individual letters. Letters in combination may

The main purpose of letters is the practical one of making th oughts visible. Ruskin says that all letters are frightful thing

The main purpose of letters is the practical one of making thoughts visible. Ruskin says that all letters are frightful t

9/11

The main purpose of letters is the practical one of making th oughts visible. Ruskin says that all letters are frightful thing s and to be endured only on occasion, that is to say, in place s where the sense of the inscription is of more importance th an external ornament. This is a sweeping statement, from which we need not suffer unduly; yet it is doubtful whether t here is art in individual letters. Letters in combination may

The main purpose of letters is the practical one of making th oughts visible. Ruskin says that all letters are frightful thing

The main purpose of letters is the practical one of making thoughts visible. Ruskin says that all letters are frightful t

9/12

The main purpose of letters is the practical one of making th oughts visible. Ruskin says that all letters are frightful thing s and to be endured only on occasion, that is to say, in place s where the sense of the inscription is of more importance th an external ornament. This is a sweeping statement, from which we need not suffer unduly; yet it is doubtful whether t here is art in individual letters. Letters in combination may

The main purpose of letters is the practical one of making th oughts visible. Ruskin says that all letters are frightful thing

The main purpose of letters is the practical one of making thoughts visible. Ruskin says that all letters are frightful t

MEMPHIS 10 POINT SET MINUS ½ UNIT

LIGHT, ITALIC, BOLD, BOLD ITALIC

abcdefghijklmnopqrstuvwxyz – 1 UNIT
abcdefghijklmnopqrstuvwxyz – ½ UNIT
abcdefghijklmnopqrstuvwxyz NORMAL

ABCDEFGHIJKLMNOPQRSTUVWXYZ 1234567890 abcdefghijklmnopqrstuvwxyz
ABCDEFGHIJKLMNOPQRSTUVWXYZ 1234567890 abcdefghijklmnopqrstuvwxyz
ABCDEFGHIJKLMNOPQRSTUVWXYZ 1234567890 abcdefghijklmnopqrstuvwxyz
ABCDEFGHIJKLMNOPQRSTUVWXYZ 1234567890 abcdefghijklmnopqrstuvwxyz

10/10

The main purpose of letters is the practical one of makin g thoughts visible. Ruskin says that all letters are frightf ul things and to be endured only on occasion, that is to s ay, in places where the sense of the inscription is of mor e importance than external ornament. This is a sweepin g statement, from which we need not suffer unduly; yet i t is doubtful whether there is art in individual letters. Lett ers in combination may be satisfying and in a well com posed page even beautiful as a whole, but art in letters consists rather in the art of arranging and composing th em in a pleasing and appropriate manner. The main p urpose of letters is the practical one of making thoughts visible. Ruskin says that all letters are frightful things an d to be endured only on occasion, that is to say, in place s where the sense of the inscription is of more importanc e than external ornament. This is a sweeping statement, from which we need not suffer unduly; yet it is doubtful whether there is art in individual letters. Letters in comb ination may be satisfying and in a well composed page even beautiful as a whole, but art in letters consists rath er in the art of arranging and composing them in a plea sing and appropriate manner. The main purpose of lett

The main purpose of letters is the practical one of makin g thoughts visible. Ruskin says that all letters are frightf

The main purpose of letters is the practical one of mak ing thoughts visible. Ruskin says that all letters are fri

10/11

The main purpose of letters is the practical one of makin g thoughts visible. Ruskin says that all letters are frightf ul things and to be endured only on occasion, that is to s ay, in places where the sense of the inscription is of mor e importance than external ornament. This is a sweepin g statement, from which we need not suffer unduly; yet i t is doubtful whether there is art in individual letters. Lett ers in combination may be satisfying and in a well com posed page even beautiful as a whole, but art in letters consists rather in the art of arranging and composing th em in a pleasing and appropriate manner. The main p urpose of letters is the practical one of making thoughts visible. Ruskin says that all letters are frightful things an d to be endured only on occasion, that is to say, in place s where the sense of the inscription is of more importanc e than external ornament. This is a sweeping statement, from which we need not suffer unduly; yet it is doubtful whether there is art in individual letters. Letters in comb ination may be satisfying and in a well composed page even beautiful as a whole, but art in letters consists rath

The main purpose of letters is the practical one of makin g thoughts visible. Ruskin says that all letters are frightf

The main purpose of letters is the practical one of mak ing thoughts visible. Ruskin says that all letters are fri

10/12

The main purpose of letters is the practical one of makin g thoughts visible. Ruskin says that all letters are frightf ul things and to be endured only on occasion, that is to s ay, in places where the sense of the inscription is of mor e importance than external ornament. This is a sweepin g statement, from which we need not suffer unduly; yet i t is doubtful whether there is art in individual letters. Lett ers in combination may be satisfying and in a well com posed page even beautiful as a whole, but art in letters consists rather in the art of arranging and composing th em in a pleasing and appropriate manner. The main p urpose of letters is the practical one of making thoughts visible. Ruskin says that all letters are frightful things an d to be endured only on occasion, that is to say, in place s where the sense of the inscription is of more importanc e than external ornament. This is a sweeping statement, from which we need not suffer unduly; yet it is doubtful whether there is art in individual letters. Letters in comb

The main purpose of letters is the practical one of makin g thoughts visible. Ruskin says that all letters are frightf

The main purpose of letters is the practical one of mak ing thoughts visible. Ruskin says that all letters are fri

10/13

The main purpose of letters is the practical one of makin g thoughts visible. Ruskin says that all letters are frightf ul things and to be endured only on occasion, that is to s ay, in places where the sense of the inscription is of mor e importance than external ornament. This is a sweepin g statement, from which we need not suffer unduly; yet i t is doubtful whether there is art in individual letters. Lett ers in combination may be satisfying and in a well com posed page even beautiful as a whole, but art in letters consists rather in the art of arranging and composing th em in a pleasing and appropriate manner. The main p urpose of letters is the practical one of making thoughts visible. Ruskin says that all letters are frightful things an d to be endured only on occasion, that is to say, in place s where the sense of the inscription is of more importanc e than external ornament. This is a sweeping statement, from which we need not suffer unduly; yet it is doubtful

The main purpose of letters is the practical one of makin g thoughts visible. Ruskin says that all letters are frightf

The main purpose of letters is the practical one of mak ing thoughts visible. Ruskin says that all letters are fri

MEMPHIS 11 POINT SET MINUS ½ UNIT

LIGHT, ITALIC, BOLD, BOLD ITALIC

abcdefghijklmnopqrstuvwxyz – 1 UNIT
abcdefghijklmnopqrstuvwxyz – ½ UNIT
abcdefghijklmnopqrstuvwxyz NORMAL

ABCDEFGHIJKLMNOPQRSTUVWXYZ 1234567890 abcdefghijklmnopqrstuvwxyz
ABCDEFGHIJKLMNOPQRSTUVWXYZ 1234567890 abcdefghijklmnopqrstuvwxyz
ABCDEFGHIJKLMNOPQRSTUVWXYZ 1234567890 abcdefghijklmnopqrstuvwxyz
ABCDEFGHIJKLMNOPQRSTUVWXYZ 1234567890 abcdefghijklmnopqrstuvwxyz

11/11

The main purpose of letters is the practical one of making thoughts visible. Ruskin says that all letter s are frightful things and to be endured only on occ asion, that is to say, in places where the sense of th e inscription is of more importance than external o rnament. This is a sweeping statement, from whic h we need not suffer unduly; yet it is doubtful whet her there is art in individual letters. Letters in comb ination may be satisfying and in a well composed page even beautiful as a whole, but art in letters c onsists rather in the art of arranging and composin g them in a pleasing and appropriate manner. Th e main purpose of letters is the practical one of ma king thoughts visible. Ruskin says that all letters ar e frightful things and to be endured only on occasi on, that is to say, in places where the sense of the in scription is of more importance than external orna ment. This is a sweeping statement, from which w e need not suffer unduly; yet it is doubtful whether t
The main purpose of letters is the practical one of making thoughts visible. Ruskin says that all letter
The main purpose of letters is the practical one of making thoughts visible. Ruskin says that all lett

11/12

The main purpose of letters is the practical one of making thoughts visible. Ruskin says that all letter s are frightful things and to be endured only on occ asion, that is to say, in places where the sense of th e inscription is of more importance than external o rnament. This is a sweeping statement, from whic h we need not suffer unduly; yet it is doubtful whet her there is art in individual letters. Letters in comb ination may be satisfying and in a well composed page even beautiful as a whole, but art in letters c onsists rather in the art of arranging and composin g them in a pleasing and appropriate manner. Th e main purpose of letters is the practical one of ma king thoughts visible. Ruskin says that all letters ar e frightful things and to be endured only on occasi on, that is to say, in places where the sense of the in scription is of more importance than external orna ment. This is a sweeping statement, from which w
The main purpose of letters is the practical one of making thoughts visible. Ruskin says that all letter
The main purpose of letters is the practical one of making thoughts visible. Ruskin says that all lett

11/13

The main purpose of letters is the practical one of making thoughts visible. Ruskin says that all letter s are frightful things and to be endured only on occ asion, that is to say, in places where the sense of th e inscription is of more importance than external o rnament. This is a sweeping statement, from whic h we need not suffer unduly; yet it is doubtful whet her there is art in individual letters. Letters in comb ination may be satisfying and in a well composed page even beautiful as a whole, but art in letters c onsists rather in the art of arranging and composin g them in a pleasing and appropriate manner. Th e main purpose of letters is the practical one of ma king thoughts visible. Ruskin says that all letters ar e frightful things and to be endured only on occasi on, that is to say, in places where the sense of the in scription is of more importance than external orna
The main purpose of letters is the practical one of making thoughts visible. Ruskin says that all letter
The main purpose of letters is the practical one of making thoughts visible. Ruskin says that all lett

11/14

The main purpose of letters is the practical one of making thoughts visible. Ruskin says that all letter s are frightful things and to be endured only on occ asion, that is to say, in places where the sense of th e inscription is of more importance than external o rnament. This is a sweeping statement, from whic h we need not suffer unduly; yet it is doubtful whet her there is art in individual letters. Letters in comb ination may be satisfying and in a well composed page even beautiful as a whole, but art in letters c onsists rather in the art of arranging and composin g them in a pleasing and appropriate manner. Th e main purpose of letters is the practical one of ma king thoughts visible. Ruskin says that all letters ar e frightful things and to be endured only on occasi on, that is to say, in places where the sense of the in
The main purpose of letters is the practical one of making thoughts visible. Ruskin says that all letter
The main purpose of letters is the practical one of making thoughts visible. Ruskin says that all lett

MEMPHIS 12 POINT SET MINUS ½ UNIT

LIGHT, ITALIC, BOLD, BOLD ITALIC

abcdefghijklmnopqrstuvwxyz – 1 UNIT
abcdefghijklmnopqrstuvwxyz – ½ UNIT
abcdefghijklmnopqrstuvwxyz NORMAL

ABCDEFGHIJKLMNOPQRSTUVWXYZ 1234567890 abcdefghijklmnopqrstuvwxyz
ABCDEFGHIJKLMNOPQRSTUVWXYZ 1234567890 abcdefghijklmnopqrstuvwxyz
ABCDEFGHIJKLMNOPQRSTUVWXYZ 1234567890 abcdefghijklmnopqrstuvwxyz
ABCDEFGHIJKLMNOPQRSTUVWXYZ 1234567890 abcdefghijklmnopqrstuvwxyz

12/12

The main purpose of letters is the practical one of making thoughts visible. Ruskin says that all letters are frightful things and to be endured on ly on occasion, that is to say, in places where th e sense of the inscription is of more importance than external ornament. This is a sweeping sta tement, from which we need not suffer unduly; yet it is doubtful whether there is art in individu al letters. Letters in combination may be satisfy ing and in a well composed page even beautif ul as a whole, but art in letters consists rather in the art of arranging and composing them in a pleasing and appropriate manner. The main p urpose of letters is the practical one of making thoughts visible. Ruskin says that all letters are *The main purpose of letters is the practical one of making thoughts visible. Ruskin says that all* **The main purpose of letters is the practical on e of making thoughts visible. Ruskin says tha**

12/13

The main purpose of letters is the practical one of making thoughts visible. Ruskin says that all letters are frightful things and to be endured on ly on occasion, that is to say, in places where th e sense of the inscription is of more importance than external ornament. This is a sweeping sta tement, from which we need not suffer unduly; yet it is doubtful whether there is art in individu al letters. Letters in combination may be satisfy ing and in a well composed page even beautif ul as a whole, but art in letters consists rather in the art of arranging and composing them in a pleasing and appropriate manner. The main p urpose of letters is the practical one of making *The main purpose of letters is the practical one of making thoughts visible. Ruskin says that all* **The main purpose of letters is the practical on e of making thoughts visible. Ruskin says tha**

12/14

The main purpose of letters is the practical one of making thoughts visible. Ruskin says that all letters are frightful things and to be endured on ly on occasion, that is to say, in places where th e sense of the inscription is of more importance than external ornament. This is a sweeping sta tement, from which we need not suffer unduly; yet it is doubtful whether there is art in individu al letters. Letters in combination may be satisfy ing and in a well composed page even beautif ul as a whole, but art in letters consists rather in the art of arranging and composing them in a pleasing and appropriate manner. The main p urpose of letters is the practical one of making thoughts visible. Ruskin says that all letters are *The main purpose of letters is the practical one of making thoughts visible. Ruskin says that all* **The main purpose of letters is the practical on e of making thoughts visible. Ruskin says tha**

12/15

The main purpose of letters is the practical one of making thoughts visible. Ruskin says that all letters are frightful things and to be endured on ly on occasion, that is to say, in places where th e sense of the inscription is of more importance than external ornament. This is a sweeping sta tement, from which we need not suffer unduly; yet it is doubtful whether there is art in individu al letters. Letters in combination may be satisfy ing and in a well composed page even beautif ul as a whole, but art in letters consists rather in the art of arranging and composing them in a pleasing and appropriate manner. The main p urpose of letters is the practical one of making *The main purpose of letters is the practical one of making thoughts visible. Ruskin says that all* **The main purpose of letters is the practical on e of making thoughts visible. Ruskin says tha**

MEMPHIS 14 POINT SET MINUS ½ UNIT

LIGHT, ITALIC, BOLD, BOLD ITALIC

abcdefghijklmnopqrstuvwxyz – 1 UNIT
abcdefghijklmnopqrstuvwxyz – ½ UNIT
abcdefghijklmnopqrstuvwxyz NORMAL

ABCDEFGHIJKLMNOPQRSTUVWXYZ abcdefghijklmnopqrstuvwxyz
ABCDEFGHIJKLMNOPQRSTUVWXYZ abcdefghijklmnopqrstuvwxyz
ABCDEFGHIJKLMNOPQRSTUVWXYZ abcdefghijklmnopqrstuvwxyz
ABCDEFGHIJKLMNOPQRSTUVWXYZ abcdefghijklmnopqrstuvwxyz

14/14

The main purpose of letters is the practic al one of making thoughts visible. Ruski n says that all letters are frightful things and to be endured only on occasion, th at is to say, in places where the sense of t he inscription is of more importance tha n external ornament. This is a sweeping statement, from which we need not suff er unduly; yet it is doubtful whether ther e is art in individual letters. Letters in co mbination may be satisfying and in a w ell composed page even beautiful as a whole, but art in letters consists rather in
The main purpose of letters is the practi cal one of making thoughts visible. Rus
The main purpose of letters is the pract ical one of making thoughts visible. R

14/15

The main purpose of letters is the practic al one of making thoughts visible. Ruski n says that all letters are frightful things and to be endured only on occasion, th at is to say, in places where the sense of t he inscription is of more importance tha n external ornament. This is a sweeping statement, from which we need not suff er unduly; yet it is doubtful whether ther e is art in individual letters. Letters in co mbination may be satisfying and in a w ell composed page even beautiful as a
The main purpose of letters is the practi cal one of making thoughts visible. Rus
The main purpose of letters is the pract ical one of making thoughts visible. R

14/16

The main purpose of letters is the practic al one of making thoughts visible. Ruski n says that all letters are frightful things and to be endured only on occasion, th at is to say, in places where the sense of t he inscription is of more importance tha n external ornament. This is a sweeping statement, from which we need not suff er unduly; yet it is doubtful whether ther e is art in individual letters. Letters in co mbination may be satisfying and in a w ell composed page even beautiful as a whole, but art in letters consists rather in
The main purpose of letters is the practi cal one of making thoughts visible. Rus
The main purpose of letters is the pract ical one of making thoughts visible. R

14/17

The main purpose of letters is the practic al one of making thoughts visible. Ruski n says that all letters are frightful things and to be endured only on occasion, th at is to say, in places where the sense of t he inscription is of more importance tha n external ornament. This is a sweeping statement, from which we need not suff er unduly; yet it is doubtful whether ther e is art in individual letters. Letters in co mbination may be satisfying and in a w ell composed page even beautiful as a
The main purpose of letters is the practi cal one of making thoughts visible. Rus
The main purpose of letters is the pract ical one of making thoughts visible. R

MEMPHIS 6 & 7 POINT SET NORMAL

MEDIUM, ITALIC, EXTRA BOLD, EXTRA BOLD ITALIC

ABCDEFGHIJKLMNOPQRSTUVWXYZ 1234567890 abcdefghijklmnopqrstuvwxyz

ABCDEFGHIJKLMNOPQRSTUVWXYZ 1234567890 abcdefghijklmnopqrstuvwxyz

ABCDEFGHIJKLMNOPQRSTUVWXYZ 1234567890 abcdefghijklmnopqrstuvwxyz

ABCDEFGHIJKLMNOPQRSTUVWXYZ 1234567890 abcdefghijklmnopqrstuvwxyz

6/6

The main purpose of letters is the practical one of making thoughts visible. Ruskin say s that all letters are frightful things and to be endured only on occasion, that is to say, in places where the sense of the inscription is of more importance than external ornament. This is a sweeping statement, from which we need not suffer unduly; yet it is doubtful whether there is art in individual letters. Letters in combination may be satisfying and in a well composed page even beautiful as a whole, but art in letters consists rather in t he art of arranging and composing them in a pleasing and appropriate manner. The m ain purpose of letters is the practical one of making thoughts visible. Ruskin says that all letters are frightful things and to be endured only on occasion, that is to say, in plac es where the sense of the inscription is of more importance than external ornament. Thi s is a sweeping statement, from which we need not suffer unduly; yet it is doubtful whe ther there is art in individual letters. Letters in combination may be satisfying and in a well composed page even beautiful as a whole, but art in letters consists rather in the a
The main purpose of letters is the practical one of making thoughts visible. Ruskin says that all letters are frightful things and to be endured only on occasion, that is to say, in p
The main purpose of letters is the practical one of making thoughts visible. Ruskin says that all letters are frightful things and to be endured only on

6/7

The main purpose of letters is the practical one of making thoughts visible. Ruskin say s that all letters are frightful things and to be endured only on occasion, that is to say, in places where the sense of the inscription is of more importance than external ornament. This is a sweeping statement, from which we need not suffer unduly; yet it is doubtful whether there is art in individual letters. Letters in combination may be satisfying and in a well composed page even beautiful as a whole, but art in letters consists rather in t he art of arranging and composing them in a pleasing and appropriate manner. The m ain purpose of letters is the practical one of making thoughts visible. Ruskin says that all letters are frightful things and to be endured only on occasion, that is to say, in plac es where the sense of the inscription is of more importance than external ornament. Thi s is a sweeping statement, from which we need not suffer unduly; yet it is doubtful whe
The main purpose of letters is the practical one of making thoughts visible. Ruskin says that all letters are frightful things and to be endured only on occasion, that is to say, in p
The main purpose of letters is the practical one of making thoughts visible. Ruskin says that all letters are frightful things and to be endured only on

6/8

The main purpose of letters is the practical one of making thoughts visible. Ruskin say s that all letters are frightful things and to be endured only on occasion, that is to say, in places where the sense of the inscription is of more importance than external ornament. This is a sweeping statement, from which we need not suffer unduly; yet it is doubtful whether there is art in individual letters. Letters in combination may be satisfying and in a well composed page even beautiful as a whole, but art in letters consists rather in t he art of arranging and composing them in a pleasing and appropriate manner. The m ain purpose of letters is the practical one of making thoughts visible. Ruskin says that all letters are frightful things and to be endured only on occasion, that is to say, in plac
The main purpose of letters is the practical one of making thoughts visible. Ruskin says that all letters are frightful things and to be endured only on occasion, that is to say, in p
The main purpose of letters is the practical one of making thoughts visible. Ruskin says that all letters are frightful things and to be endured only on

6/9

The main purpose of letters is the practical one of making thoughts visible. Ruskin say s that all letters are frightful things and to be endured only on occasion, that is to say, in places where the sense of the inscription is of more importance than external ornament. This is a sweeping statement, from which we need not suffer unduly; yet it is doubtful whether there is art in individual letters. Letters in combination may be satisfying and in a well composed page even beautiful as a whole, but art in letters consists rather in t he art of arranging and composing them in a pleasing and appropriate manner. The m ain purpose of letters is the practical one of making thoughts visible. Ruskin says that
The main purpose of letters is the practical one of making thoughts visible. Ruskin says that all letters are frightful things and to be endured only on occasion, that is to say, in p
The main purpose of letters is the practical one of making thoughts visible. Ruskin says that all letters are frightful things and to be endured only on

---

ABCDEFGHIJKLMNOPQRSTUVWXYZ 1234567890 abcdefghijklmnopqrstuvwxyz

ABCDEFGHIJKLMNOPQRSTUVWXYZ 1234567890 abcdefghijklmnopqrstuvwxyz

ABCDEFGHIJKLMNOPQRSTUVWXYZ 1234567890 abcdefghijklmnopqrstuvwxyz

ABCDEFGHIJKLMNOPQRSTUVWXYZ 1234567890 abcdefghijklmnopqrstuvwxyz

7/7

The main purpose of letters is the practical one of making thoughts visible. Ruskin says that all letters are frightful things and to be endured only on occasion, that is to say, in places where the sense of the inscription is of mo re importance than external ornament. This is a sweeping statement, from which we need not suffer unduly; yet it is doubtful whether there is art in in dividual letters. Letters in combination may be satisfying and in a well co mposed page even beautiful as a whole, but art in letters consists rather in the art of arranging and composing them in a pleasing and appropriate m anner. The main purpose of letters is the practical one of making thoughts visible. Ruskin says that all letters are frightful things and to be endured o nly on occasion, that is to say, in places where the sense of the inscription i
The main purpose of letters is the practical one of making thoughts visible. Ruskin says that all letters are frightful things and to be endured only on oc
The main purpose of letters is the practical one of making thou ghts visible. Ruskin says that all letters are frightful things and

7/8

The main purpose of letters is the practical one of making thoughts visible. Ruskin says that all letters are frightful things and to be endured only on occasion, that is to say, in places where the sense of the inscription is of mo re importance than external ornament. This is a sweeping statement, from which we need not suffer unduly; yet it is doubtful whether there is art in in dividual letters. Letters in combination may be satisfying and in a well co mposed page even beautiful as a whole, but art in letters consists rather in the art of arranging and composing them in a pleasing and appropriate m anner. The main purpose of letters is the practical one of making thoughts visible. Ruskin says that all letters are frightful things and to be endured o
The main purpose of letters is the practical one of making thoughts visible. Ruskin says that all letters are frightful things and to be endured only on oc
The main purpose of letters is the practical one of making thou ghts visible. Ruskin says that all letters are frightful things and

7/9

The main purpose of letters is the practical one of making thoughts visible. Ruskin says that all letters are frightful things and to be endured only on occasion, that is to say, in places where the sense of the inscription is of mo re importance than external ornament. This is a sweeping statement, from which we need not suffer unduly; yet it is doubtful whether there is art in in dividual letters. Letters in combination may be satisfying and in a well co mposed page even beautiful as a whole, but art in letters consists rather in the art of arranging and composing them in a pleasing and appropriate m anner. The main purpose of letters is the practical one of making thoughts visible. Ruskin says that all letters are frightful things and to be endured o
The main purpose of letters is the practical one of making thoughts visible. Ruskin says that all letters are frightful things and to be endured only on oc
The main purpose of letters is the practical one of making thou ghts visible. Ruskin says that all letters are frightful things and

7/10

The main purpose of letters is the practical one of making thoughts visible. Ruskin says that all letters are frightful things and to be endured only on occasion, that is to say, in places where the sense of the inscription is of mo re importance than external ornament. This is a sweeping statement, from which we need not suffer unduly; yet it is doubtful whether there is art in in dividual letters. Letters in combination may be satisfying and in a well co mposed page even beautiful as a whole, but art in letters consists rather in the art of arranging and composing them in a pleasing and appropriate m anner. The main purpose of letters is the practical one of making thoughts
The main purpose of letters is the practical one of making thoughts visible. Ruskin says that all letters are frightful things and to be endured only on oc
The main purpose of letters is the practical one of making thou ghts visible. Ruskin says that all letters are frightful things and

MEMPHIS 8 & 9 POINT SET NORMAL

MEDIUM, ITALIC, EXTRA BOLD, EXTRA BOLD ITALIC

ABCDEFGHIJKLMNOPQRSTUVWXYZ 1234567890 abcdefghijklmnopqrstuvwxyz

ABCDEFGHIJKLMNOPQRSTUVWXYZ 1234567890 abcdefghijklmnopqrstuvwxyz

ABCDEFGHIJKLMNOPQRSTUVWXYZ 1234567890 abcdefghijklmnopqrstuvwxyz

ABCDEFGHIJKLMNOPQRSTUVWXYZ 1234567890 abcdefghijklmnopqrstuvwxyz

8/8

The main purpose of letters is the practical one of making though ts visible. Ruskin says that all letters are frightful things and to b e endured only on occasion, that is to say, in places where the sen se of the inscription is of more importance than external ornamen t. This is a sweeping statement, from which we need not suffer un duly; yet it is doubtful whether there is art in individual letters. L etters in combination may be satisfying and in a well composed page even beautiful as a whole, but art in letters consists rather i n the art of arranging and composing them in a pleasing and app
The main purpose of letters is the practical one of making thought s visible. Ruskin says that all letters are frightful things and to be
The main purpose of letters is the practical one of maki ng thoughts visible. Ruskin says that all letters are frig

8/9

The main purpose of letters is the practical one of making though ts visible. Ruskin says that all letters are frightful things and to b e endured only on occasion, that is to say, in places where the sen se of the inscription is of more importance than external ornamen t. This is a sweeping statement, from which we need not suffer un duly; yet it is doubtful whether there is art in individual letters. L etters in combination may be satisfying and in a well composed page even beautiful as a whole, but art in letters consists rather i
The main purpose of letters is the practical one of making thought s visible. Ruskin says that all letters are frightful things and to be
The main purpose of letters is the practical one of maki ng thoughts visible. Ruskin says that all letters are frig

8/10

The main purpose of letters is the practical one of making though ts visible. Ruskin says that all letters are frightful things and to b e endured only on occasion, that is to say, in places where the sen se of the inscription is of more importance than external ornamen t. This is a sweeping statement, from which we need not suffer un duly; yet it is doubtful whether there is art in individual letters. L etters in combination may be satisfying and in a well composed
The main purpose of letters is the practical one of making thought s visible. Ruskin says that all letters are frightful things and to be
The main purpose of letters is the practical one of maki ng thoughts visible. Ruskin says that all letters are frig

8/11

The main purpose of letters is the practical one of making though ts visible. Ruskin says that all letters are frightful things and to b e endured only on occasion, that is to say, in places where the sen se of the inscription is of more importance than external ornamen t. This is a sweeping statement, from which we need not suffer un duly; yet it is doubtful whether there is art in individual letters. L etters in combination may be satisfying and in a well composed
The main purpose of letters is the practical one of making thought s visible. Ruskin says that all letters are frightful things and to be
The main purpose of letters is the practical one of maki ng thoughts visible. Ruskin says that all letters are frig

---

ABCDEFGHIJKLMNOPQRSTUVWXYZ 1234567890 abcdefghijklmnopqrstuvwxyz

ABCDEFGHIJKLMNOPQRSTUVWXYZ 1234567890 abcdefghijklmnopqrstuvwxyz

ABCDEFGHIJKLMNOPQRSTUVWXYZ 1234567890 abcdefghijklmnopqrstuvwxyz

ABCDEFGHIJKLMNOPQRSTUVWXYZ 1234567890 abcdefghijklmnopqrstuvwxyz

9/9

The main purpose of letters is the practical one of making thoughts visible. Ruskin says that all letters are frightful t hings and to be endured only on occasion, that is to say, in places where the sense of the inscription is of more import ance than external ornament. This is a sweeping stateme nt, from which we need not suffer unduly; yet it is doubtful whether there is art in individual letters. Letters in combi nation may be satisfying and in a well composed page ev
The main purpose of letters is the practical one of making t houghts visible. Ruskin says that all letters are frightful th
The main purpose of letters is the practical one of making thoughts visible. Ruskin says that all lett

9/10

The main purpose of letters is the practical one of making thoughts visible. Ruskin says that all letters are frightful t hings and to be endured only on occasion, that is to say, in places where the sense of the inscription is of more import ance than external ornament. This is a sweeping stateme nt, from which we need not suffer unduly; yet it is doubtful whether there is art in individual letters. Letters in combi
The main purpose of letters is the practical one of making t houghts visible. Ruskin says that all letters are frightful th
The main purpose of letters is the practical one of making thoughts visible. Ruskin says that all lett

9/11

The main purpose of letters is the practical one of making thoughts visible. Ruskin says that all letters are frightful t hings and to be endured only on occasion, that is to say, in places where the sense of the inscription is of more import ance than external ornament. This is a sweeping stateme nt, from which we need not suffer unduly; yet it is doubtful whether there is art in individual letters. Letters in combi
The main purpose of letters is the practical one of making t houghts visible. Ruskin says that all letters are frightful th
The main purpose of letters is the practical one of making thoughts visible. Ruskin says that all lett

9/12

The main purpose of letters is the practical one of making thoughts visible. Ruskin says that all letters are frightful t hings and to be endured only on occasion, that is to say, in places where the sense of the inscription is of more import ance than external ornament. This is a sweeping stateme nt, from which we need not suffer unduly; yet it is doubtful whether there is art in individual letters. Letters in combi
The main purpose of letters is the practical one of making t houghts visible. Ruskin says that all letters are frightful th
The main purpose of letters is the practical one of making thoughts visible. Ruskin says that all lett

MEMPHIS 10 POINT SET MINUS ½ UNIT

MEDIUM, ITALIC, EXTRA BOLD, EXTRA BOLD ITALIC

abcdefghijklmnopqrstuvwxyz – 1 UNIT
abcdefghijklmnopqrstuvwxyz – ½ UNIT
abcdefghijklmnopqrstuvwxyz NORMAL

ABCDEFGHIJKLMNOPQRSTUVWXYZ 1234567890 abcdefghijklmnopqrstuvwxyz
ABCDEFGHIJKLMNOPQRSTUVWXYZ 1234567890 abcdefghijklmnopqrstuvwxyz
ABCDEFGHIJKLMNOPQRSTUVWXYZ 1234567890 abcdefghijklmnopqrstuvwxyz
ABCDEFGHIJKLMNOPQRSTUVWXYZ 1234567890 abcdefghijklmnopqrstuvwxyz

10/10

The main purpose of letters is the practical one of mak ing thoughts visible. Ruskin says that all letters are fri ghtful things and to be endured only on occasion, that is to say, in places where the sense of the inscription is of more importance than external ornament. This is a sweeping statement, from which we need not suffer u nduly; yet it is doubtful whether there is art in individu al letters. Letters in combination may be satisfying an d in a well composed page even beautiful as a whole, but art in letters consists rather in the art of arranging and composing them in a pleasing and appropriate m anner. The main purpose of letters is the practical one of making thoughts visible. Ruskin says that all letter s are frightful things and to be endured only on occasi on, that is to say, in places where the sense of the inscr iption is of more importance than external ornament. This is a sweeping statement, from which we need not suffer unduly; yet it is doubtful whether there is art in i ndividual letters. Letters in combination may be satisf ying and in a well composed page even beautiful as a whole, but art in letters consists rather in the art of arr anging and composing them in a pleasing and appro
The main purpose of letters is the practical one of maki ng thoughts visible. Ruskin says that all letters are frig
The main purpose of letters is the practical on e of making thoughts visible. Ruskin says that

10/11

The main purpose of letters is the practical one of mak ing thoughts visible. Ruskin says that all letters are fri ghtful things and to be endured only on occasion, that is to say, in places where the sense of the inscription is of more importance than external ornament. This is a sweeping statement, from which we need not suffer u nduly; yet it is doubtful whether there is art in individu al letters. Letters in combination may be satisfying an d in a well composed page even beautiful as a whole, but art in letters consists rather in the art of arranging and composing them in a pleasing and appropriate m anner. The main purpose of letters is the practical one of making thoughts visible. Ruskin says that all letter s are frightful things and to be endured only on occasi on, that is to say, in places where the sense of the inscr iption is of more importance than external ornament. This is a sweeping statement, from which we need not suffer unduly; yet it is doubtful whether there is art in i ndividual letters. Letters in combination may be satisf ying and in a well composed page even beautiful as a
The main purpose of letters is the practical one of maki ng thoughts visible. Ruskin says that all letters are frig
The main purpose of letters is the practical on e of making thoughts visible. Ruskin says that

10/12

The main purpose of letters is the practical one of mak ing thoughts visible. Ruskin says that all letters are fri ghtful things and to be endured only on occasion, that is to say, in places where the sense of the inscription is of more importance than external ornament. This is a sweeping statement, from which we need not suffer u nduly; yet it is doubtful whether there is art in individu al letters. Letters in combination may be satisfying an d in a well composed page even beautiful as a whole, but art in letters consists rather in the art of arranging and composing them in a pleasing and appropriate m anner. The main purpose of letters is the practical one of making thoughts visible. Ruskin says that all letter s are frightful things and to be endured only on occasi on, that is to say, in places where the sense of the inscr iption is of more importance than external ornament. This is a sweeping statement, from which we need not suffer unduly; yet it is doubtful whether there is art in i
The main purpose of letters is the practical one of maki ng thoughts visible. Ruskin says that all letters are frig
The main purpose of letters is the practical on e of making thoughts visible. Ruskin says that

10/13

The main purpose of letters is the practical one of mak ing thoughts visible. Ruskin says that all letters are fri ghtful things and to be endured only on occasion, that is to say, in places where the sense of the inscription is of more importance than external ornament. This is a sweeping statement, from which we need not suffer u nduly; yet it is doubtful whether there is art in individu al letters. Letters in combination may be satisfying an d in a well composed page even beautiful as a whole, but art in letters consists rather in the art of arranging and composing them in a pleasing and appropriate m anner. The main purpose of letters is the practical one of making thoughts visible. Ruskin says that all letter s are frightful things and to be endured only on occasi on, that is to say, in places where the sense of the inscr iption is of more importance than external ornament. This is a sweeping statement, from which we need not
The main purpose of letters is the practical one of maki ng thoughts visible. Ruskin says that all letters are frig
The main purpose of letters is the practical on e of making thoughts visible. Ruskin says that

MEMPHIS 11 POINT SET MINUS ½ UNIT

MEDIUM, ITALIC, EXTRA BOLD, EXTRA BOLD ITALIC

abcdefghijklmnopqrstuvwxyz – 1 UNIT
abcdefghijklmnopqrstuvwxyz – ½ UNIT
abcdefghijklmnopqrstuvwxyz NORMAL

ABCDEFGHIJKLMNOPQRSTUVWXYZ 1234567890 abcdefghijklmnopqrstuvwxyz
ABCDEFGHIJKLMNOPQRSTUVWXYZ 1234567890 abcdefghijklmnopqrstuvwxyz
ABCDEFGHIJKLMNOPQRSTUVWXYZ 1234567890 abcdefghijklmnopqrstuvwx
ABCDEFGHIJKLMNOPQRSTUVWXYZ 1234567890 abcdefghijklmnopqrstuvwx

11/11

The main purpose of letters is the practical one of making thoughts visible. Ruskin says that all lett ers are frightful things and to be endured only on occasion, that is to say, in places where the sense of the inscription is of more importance than exte rnal ornament. This is a sweeping statement, fro m which we need not suffer unduly; yet it is doub tful whether there is art in individual letters. Lett ers in combination may be satisfying and in a we ll composed page even beautiful as a whole, but art in letters consists rather in the art of arrangin g and composing them in a pleasing and approp riate manner. The main purpose of letters is the p ractical one of making thoughts visible. Ruskin s ays that all letters are frightful things and to be e ndured only on occasion, that is to say, in places where the sense of the inscription is of more impo rtance than external ornament. This is a sweepin g statement, from which we need not suffer undu
The main purpose of letters is the practical one of making thoughts visible. Ruskin says that all lett
The main purpose of letters is the practic al one of making thoughts visible. Ruskin

11/12

The main purpose of letters is the practical one of making thoughts visible. Ruskin says that all lett ers are frightful things and to be endured only on occasion, that is to say, in places where the sense of the inscription is of more importance than exte rnal ornament. This is a sweeping statement, fro m which we need not suffer unduly; yet it is doub tful whether there is art in individual letters. Lett ers in combination may be satisfying and in a we ll composed page even beautiful as a whole, but art in letters consists rather in the art of arrangin g and composing them in a pleasing and approp riate manner. The main purpose of letters is the p ractical one of making thoughts visible. Ruskin s ays that all letters are frightful things and to be e ndured only on occasion, that is to say, in places where the sense of the inscription is of more impo rtance than external ornament. This is a sweepin
The main purpose of letters is the practical one of making thoughts visible. Ruskin says that all lett
The main purpose of letters is the practic al one of making thoughts visible. Ruskin

11/13

The main purpose of letters is the practical one of making thoughts visible. Ruskin says that all lett ers are frightful things and to be endured only on occasion, that is to say, in places where the sense of the inscription is of more importance than exte rnal ornament. This is a sweeping statement, fro m which we need not suffer unduly; yet it is doub tful whether there is art in individual letters. Lett ers in combination may be satisfying and in a we ll composed page even beautiful as a whole, but art in letters consists rather in the art of arrangin g and composing them in a pleasing and approp riate manner. The main purpose of letters is the p ractical one of making thoughts visible. Ruskin s ays that all letters are frightful things and to be e ndured only on occasion, that is to say, in places where the sense of the inscription is of more impo
The main purpose of letters is the practical one of making thoughts visible. Ruskin says that all lett
The main purpose of letters is the practic al one of making thoughts visible. Ruskin

11/14

The main purpose of letters is the practical one of making thoughts visible. Ruskin says that all lett ers are frightful things and to be endured only on occasion, that is to say, in places where the sense of the inscription is of more importance than exte rnal ornament. This is a sweeping statement, fro m which we need not suffer unduly; yet it is doub tful whether there is art in individual letters. Lett ers in combination may be satisfying and in a we ll composed page even beautiful as a whole, but art in letters consists rather in the art of arrangin g and composing them in a pleasing and approp riate manner. The main purpose of letters is the p ractical one of making thoughts visible. Ruskin s ays that all letters are frightful things and to be e ndured only on occasion, that is to say, in places
The main purpose of letters is the practical one of making thoughts visible. Ruskin says that all lett
The main purpose of letters is the practic al one of making thoughts visible. Ruskin

MEMPHIS 12 POINT SET MINUS ½ UNIT

MEDIUM, ITALIC, EXTRA BOLD, EXTRA BOLD ITALIC

abcdefghijklmnopqrstuvwxyz – 1 UNIT
abcdefghijklmnopqrstuvwxyz – ½ UNIT
abcdefghijklmnopqrstuvwxyz NORMAL

ABCDEFGHIJKLMNOPQRSTUVWXYZ 1234567890 abcdefghijklmnopqrstuvwxyz
ABCDEFGHIJKLMNOPQRSTUVWXYZ 1234567890 abcdefghijklmnopqrstuvwxyz
ABCDEFGHIJKLMNOPQRSTUVWXYZ 1234567890 abcdefghijklmnopqrs
ABCDEFGHIJKLMNOPQRSTUVWXYZ 1234567890 abcdefghijklmnopqrs

12/12

The main purpose of letters is the practical on e of making thoughts visible. Ruskin says tha t all letters are frightful things and to be endu red only on occasion, that is to say, in places where the sense of the inscription is of more i mportance than external ornament. This is a sweeping statement, from which we need not suffer unduly; yet it is doubtful whether there is art in individual letters. Letters in combinat ion may be satisfying and in a well composed page even beautiful as a whole, but art in lett ers consists rather in the art of arranging and composing them in a pleasing and appropria te manner. The main purpose of letters is the practical one of making thoughts visible. Rus
The main purpose of letters is the practical on e of making thoughts visible. Ruskin says that
The main purpose of letters is the prac tical one of making thoughts visible. R

12/13

The main purpose of letters is the practical on e of making thoughts visible. Ruskin says tha t all letters are frightful things and to be endu red only on occasion, that is to say, in places where the sense of the inscription is of more i mportance than external ornament. This is a sweeping statement, from which we need not suffer unduly; yet it is doubtful whether there is art in individual letters. Letters in combinat ion may be satisfying and in a well composed page even beautiful as a whole, but art in lett ers consists rather in the art of arranging and composing them in a pleasing and appropria te manner. The main purpose of letters is the
The main purpose of letters is the practical on e of making thoughts visible. Ruskin says that
The main purpose of letters is the prac tical one of making thoughts visible. R

12/14

The main purpose of letters is the practical on e of making thoughts visible. Ruskin says tha t all letters are frightful things and to be endu red only on occasion, that is to say, in places where the sense of the inscription is of more i mportance than external ornament. This is a sweeping statement, from which we need not suffer unduly; yet it is doubtful whether there is art in individual letters. Letters in combinat ion may be satisfying and in a well composed page even beautiful as a whole, but art in lett ers consists rather in the art of arranging and composing them in a pleasing and appropria te manner. The main purpose of letters is the practical one of making thoughts visible. Rus
The main purpose of letters is the practical on e of making thoughts visible. Ruskin says that
The main purpose of letters is the prac tical one of making thoughts visible. R

12/15

The main purpose of letters is the practical on e of making thoughts visible. Ruskin says tha t all letters are frightful things and to be endu red only on occasion, that is to say, in places where the sense of the inscription is of more i mportance than external ornament. This is a sweeping statement, from which we need not suffer unduly; yet it is doubtful whether there is art in individual letters. Letters in combinat ion may be satisfying and in a well composed page even beautiful as a whole, but art in lett ers consists rather in the art of arranging and composing them in a pleasing and appropria te manner. The main purpose of letters is the
The main purpose of letters is the practical on e of making thoughts visible. Ruskin says that
The main purpose of letters is the prac tical one of making thoughts visible. R

MEMPHIS 14 POINT SET MINUS ½ UNIT

MEDIUM, ITALIC, EXTRA BOLD, EXTRA BOLD ITALIC

abcdefghijklmnopqrstuvwxyz – 1 UNIT
abcdefghijklmnopqrstuvwxyz – ½ UNIT
abcdefghijklmnopqrstuvwxyz NORMAL

ABCDEFGHIJKLMNOPQRSTUVWXYZ abcdefghijklmnopqrstuvwxyz
ABCDEFGHIJKLMNOPQRSTUVWXYZ abcdefghijklmnopqrstuvwxyz
ABCDEFGHIJKLMNOPQRSTUVWXYZ abcdefghijklmnopqrstuv
ABCDEFGHIJKLMNOPQRSTUVWXYZ abcdefghijklmnopqrstuv

14/14

The main purpose of letters is the pract ical one of making thoughts visible. R uskin says that all letters are frightful t hings and to be endured only on occasi on, that is to say, in places where the s ense of the inscription is of more impor tance than external ornament. This is a sweeping statement, from which we need not suffer unduly; yet it is doubtfu l whether there is art in individual lette rs. Letters in combination may be satis fying and in a well composed page eve n beautiful as a whole, but art in letter
The main purpose of letters is the pract ical one of making thoughts visible. R
The main purpose of letters is th e practical one of making thoug

14/15

The main purpose of letters is the pract ical one of making thoughts visible. R uskin says that all letters are frightful t hings and to be endured only on occasi on, that is to say, in places where the s ense of the inscription is of more impor tance than external ornament. This is a sweeping statement, from which we need not suffer unduly; yet it is doubtfu l whether there is art in individual lette rs. Letters in combination may be satis fying and in a well composed page eve
The main purpose of letters is the pract ical one of making thoughts visible. R
The main purpose of letters is th e practical one of making thoug

14/16

The main purpose of letters is the pract ical one of making thoughts visible. R uskin says that all letters are frightful t hings and to be endured only on occasi on, that is to say, in places where the s ense of the inscription is of more impor tance than external ornament. This is a sweeping statement, from which we need not suffer unduly; yet it is doubtfu l whether there is art in individual lette rs. Letters in combination may be satis fying and in a well composed page eve n beautiful as a whole, but art in letter
The main purpose of letters is the pract ical one of making thoughts visible. R
The main purpose of letters is th e practical one of making thoug

14/17

The main purpose of letters is the pract ical one of making thoughts visible. R uskin says that all letters are frightful t hings and to be endured only on occasi on, that is to say, in places where the s ense of the inscription is of more impor tance than external ornament. This is a sweeping statement, from which we need not suffer unduly; yet it is doubtfu l whether there is art in individual lette rs. Letters in combination may be satis fying and in a well composed page eve
The main purpose of letters is the pract ical one of making thoughts visible. R
The main purpose of letters is th e practical one of making thoug

OPTIMA 6 & 7 POINT SET NORMAL

ROMAN, ITALIC, BOLD, BOLD ITALIC

ABCDEFGHIJKLMNOPQRSTUVWXYZ 1234567890 abcdefghijklmnopqrstuvwxyz

ABCDEFGHIJKLMNOPQRSTUVWXYZ 1234567890 abcdefghijklmnopqrstuvwxyz

ABCDEFGHIJKLMNOPQRSTUVWXYZ 1234567890 abcdefghijklmnopqrstuvwxyz

ABCDEFGHIJKLMNOPQRSTUVWXYZ 1234567890 abcdefghijklmnopqrstuvwxyz

6/6

The main purpose of letters is the practical one of making thoughts visible. Ruskin says that all let
ters are frightful things and to be endured only on occasion, that is to say, in places where the sen
se of the inscription is of more importance than external ornament. This is a sweeping statement,
from which we need not suffer unduly; yet it is doubtful whether there is art in individual letters.
Letters in combination may be satisfying and in a well composed page even beautiful as a whole,
but art in letters consists rather in the art of arranging and composing them in a pleasing and appr
opriate manner. The main purpose of letters is the practical one of making thoughts visible. Ruski
n says that all letters are frightful things and to be endured only on occasion, that is to say, in plac
es where the sense of the inscription is of more importance than external ornament. This is a swe
eping statement, from which we need not suffer unduly; yet it is doubtful whether there is art in i
ndividual letters. Letters in combination may be satisfying and in a well composed page even be
autiful as a whole, but art in letters consists rather in the art of arranging and composing them in a
pleasing and appropriate manner. The main purpose of letters is the practical one of making thou
The main purpose of letters is the practical one of making thoughts visible. Ruskin says that all let
ters are frightful things and to be endured only on occasion, that is to say, in places where the sen
The main purpose of letters is the practical one of making thoughts visible. Ruskin says that all l
etters are frightful things and to be endured only on occasion, that is to say, in places where the

6/7

The main purpose of letters is the practical one of making thoughts visible. Ruskin says that all let
ters are frightful things and to be endured only on occasion, that is to say, in places where the sen
se of the inscription is of more importance than external ornament. This is a sweeping statement,
from which we need not suffer unduly; yet it is doubtful whether there is art in individual letters.
Letters in combination may be satisfying and in a well composed page even beautiful as a whole,
but art in letters consists rather in the art of arranging and composing them in a pleasing and appr
opriate manner. The main purpose of letters is the practical one of making thoughts visible. Ruski
n says that all letters are frightful things and to be endured only on occasion, that is to say, in plac
es where the sense of the inscription is of more importance than external ornament. This is a swe
eping statement, from which we need not suffer unduly; yet it is doubtful whether there is art in i
ndividual letters. Letters in combination may be satisfying and in a well composed page even be
The main purpose of letters is the practical one of making thoughts visible. Ruskin says that all let
ters are frightful things and to be endured only on occasion, that is to say, in places where the sen
The main purpose of letters is the practical one of making thoughts visible. Ruskin says that all l
etters are frightful things and to be endured only on occasion, that is to say, in places where the

6/8

The main purpose of letters is the practical one of making thoughts visible. Ruskin says that all let
ters are frightful things and to be endured only on occasion, that is to say, in places where the sen
se of the inscription is of more importance than external ornament. This is a sweeping statement,
from which we need not suffer unduly; yet it is doubtful whether there is art in individual letters.
Letters in combination may be satisfying and in a well composed page even beautiful as a whole,
but art in letters consists rather in the art of arranging and composing them in a pleasing and appr
opriate manner. The main purpose of letters is the practical one of making thoughts visible. Ruski
n says that all letters are frightful things and to be endured only on occasion, that is to say, in plac
es where the sense of the inscription is of more importance than external ornament. This is a swe
The main purpose of letters is the practical one of making thoughts visible. Ruskin says that all let
ters are frightful things and to be endured only on occasion, that is to say, in places where the sen
The main purpose of letters is the practical one of making thoughts visible. Ruskin says that all l
etters are frightful things and to be endured only on occasion, that is to say, in places where the

6/9

The main purpose of letters is the practical one of making thoughts visible. Ruskin says that all let
ters are frightful things and to be endured only on occasion, that is to say, in places where the sen
se of the inscription is of more importance than external ornament. This is a sweeping statement,
from which we need not suffer unduly; yet it is doubtful whether there is art in individual letters.
Letters in combination may be satisfying and in a well composed page even beautiful as a whole,
but art in letters consists rather in the art of arranging and composing them in a pleasing and appr
opriate manner. The main purpose of letters is the practical one of making thoughts visible. Ruski
n says that all letters are frightful things and to be endured only on occasion, that is to say, in plac
The main purpose of letters is the practical one of making thoughts visible. Ruskin says that all let
ters are frightful things and to be endured only on occasion, that is to say, in places where the sen
The main purpose of letters is the practical one of making thoughts visible. Ruskin says that all l
etters are frightful things and to be endured only on occasion, that is to say, in places where the

---

ABCDEFGHIJKLMNOPQRSTUVWXYZ 1234567890 abcdefghijklmnopqrstuvwxyz

ABCDEFGHIJKLMNOPQRSTUVWXYZ 1234567890 abcdefghijklmnopqrstuvwxyz

ABCDEFGHIJKLMNOPQRSTUVWXYZ 1234567890 abcdefghijklmnopqrstuvwxyz

ABCDEFGHIJKLMNOPQRSTUVWXYZ 1234567890 abcdefghijklmnopqrstuvwxyz

7/7

The main purpose of letters is the practical one of making thoughts visible. Ruskin s
ays that all letters are frightful things and to be endured only on occasion, that is to s
ay, in places where the sense of the inscription is of more importance than external
ornament. This is a sweeping statement, from which we need not suffer unduly; yet
it is doubtful whether there is art in individual letters. Letters in combination may b
e satisfying and in a well composed page even beautiful as a whole, but art in letter
s consists rather in the art of arranging and composing them in a pleasing and appr
opriate manner. The main purpose of letters is the practical one of making thoughts
visible. Ruskin says that all letters are frightful things and to be endured only on occ
asion, that is to say, in places where the sense of the inscription is of more importan
ce than external ornament. This is a sweeping statement, from which we need not s
The main purpose of letters is the practical one of making thoughts visible. Ruskin
says that all letters are frightful things and to be endured only on occasion, that is to
The main purpose of letters is the practical one of making thoughts visible. Ruskin
says that all letters are frightful things and to be endured only on occasion, that is

7/8

The main purpose of letters is the practical one of making thoughts visible. Ruskin s
ays that all letters are frightful things and to be endured only on occasion, that is to s
ay, in places where the sense of the inscription is of more importance than external
ornament. This is a sweeping statement, from which we need not suffer unduly; yet
it is doubtful whether there is art in individual letters. Letters in combination may b
e satisfying and in a well composed page even beautiful as a whole, but art in letter
s consists rather in the art of arranging and composing them in a pleasing and appr
opriate manner. The main purpose of letters is the practical one of making thoughts
visible. Ruskin says that all letters are frightful things and to be endured only on occ
asion, that is to say, in places where the sense of the inscription is of more importan
The main purpose of letters is the practical one of making thoughts visible. Ruskin
says that all letters are frightful things and to be endured only on occasion, that is to
The main purpose of letters is the practical one of making thoughts visible. Ruskin
says that all letters are frightful things and to be endured only on occasion, that is

7/9

The main purpose of letters is the practical one of making thoughts visible. Ruskin s
ays that all letters are frightful things and to be endured only on occasion, that is to s
ay, in places where the sense of the inscription is of more importance than external
ornament. This is a sweeping statement, from which we need not suffer unduly; yet
it is doubtful whether there is art in individual letters. Letters in combination may b
e satisfying and in a well composed page even beautiful as a whole, but art in letter
s consists rather in the art of arranging and composing them in a pleasing and appr
opriate manner. The main purpose of letters is the practical one of making thoughts
visible. Ruskin says that all letters are frightful things and to be endured only on occ
asion, that is to say, in places where the sense of the inscription is of more importan
The main purpose of letters is the practical one of making thoughts visible. Ruskin
says that all letters are frightful things and to be endured only on occasion, that is to
The main purpose of letters is the practical one of making thoughts visible. Ruskin
says that all letters are frightful things and to be endured only on occasion, that is

7/10

The main purpose of letters is the practical one of making thoughts visible. Ruskin s
ays that all letters are frightful things and to be endured only on occasion, that is to s
ay, in places where the sense of the inscription is of more importance than external
ornament. This is a sweeping statement, from which we need not suffer unduly; yet
it is doubtful whether there is art in individual letters. Letters in combination may b
e satisfying and in a well composed page even beautiful as a whole, but art in letter
s consists rather in the art of arranging and composing them in a pleasing and appr
opriate manner. The main purpose of letters is the practical one of making thoughts
visible. Ruskin says that all letters are frightful things and to be endured only on occ
The main purpose of letters is the practical one of making thoughts visible. Ruskin
says that all letters are frightful things and to be endured only on occasion, that is to
The main purpose of letters is the practical one of making thoughts visible. Ruskin
says that all letters are frightful things and to be endured only on occasion, that is

OPTIMA 8 & 9 POINT SET NORMAL

ROMAN, ITALIC, BOLD, BOLD ITALIC

ABCDEFGHIJKLMNOPQRSTUVWXYZ 1234567890 abcdefghijklmnopqrstuvwxyz

ABCDEFGHIJKLMNOPQRSTUVWXYZ 1234567890 abcdefghijklmnopqrstuvwxyz

ABCDEFGHIJKLMNOPQRSTUVWXYZ 1234567890 abcdefghijklmnopqrstuvwxyz

ABCDEFGHIJKLMNOPQRSTUVWXYZ 1234567890 abcdefghijklmnopqrstuvwxyz

8/8

The main purpose of letters is the practical one of making thoughts visibl e. Ruskin says that all letters are frightful things and to be endured only o n occasion, that is to say, in places where the sense of the inscription is of more importance than external ornament. This is a sweeping statement, from which we need not suffer unduly; yet it is doubtful whether there is art in individual letters. Letters in combination may be satisfying and in a well composed page even beautiful as a whole, but art in letters consists rather in the art of arranging and composing them in a pleasing and appr opriate manner. The main purpose of letters is the practical one of makin
The main purpose of letters is the practical one of making thoughts visibl e. Ruskin says that all letters are frightful things and to be endured only o
The main purpose of letters is the practical one of making thoughts visi ble. Ruskin says that all letters are frightful things and to be endured onl

8/9

The main purpose of letters is the practical one of making thoughts visibl e. Ruskin says that all letters are frightful things and to be endured only o n occasion, that is to say, in places where the sense of the inscription is of more importance than external ornament. This is a sweeping statement, from which we need not suffer unduly; yet it is doubtful whether there is art in individual letters. Letters in combination may be satisfying and in a well composed page even beautiful as a whole, but art in letters consists rather in the art of arranging and composing them in a pleasing and appr
The main purpose of letters is the practical one of making thoughts visibl e. Ruskin says that all letters are frightful things and to be endured only o
The main purpose of letters is the practical one of making thoughts visi ble. Ruskin says that all letters are frightful things and to be endured onl

8/10

The main purpose of letters is the practical one of making thoughts visibl e. Ruskin says that all letters are frightful things and to be endured only o n occasion, that is to say, in places where the sense of the inscription is of more importance than external ornament. This is a sweeping statement, from which we need not suffer unduly; yet it is doubtful whether there is art in individual letters. Letters in combination may be satisfying and in a well composed page even beautiful as a whole, but art in letters consists
The main purpose of letters is the practical one of making thoughts visibl e. Ruskin says that all letters are frightful things and to be endured only o
The main purpose of letters is the practical one of making thoughts visi ble. Ruskin says that all letters are frightful things and to be endured onl

8/11

The main purpose of letters is the practical one of making thoughts visibl e. Ruskin says that all letters are frightful things and to be endured only o n occasion, that is to say, in places where the sense of the inscription is of more importance than external ornament. This is a sweeping statement, from which we need not suffer unduly; yet it is doubtful whether there is art in individual letters. Letters in combination may be satisfying and in a well composed page even beautiful as a whole, but art in letters consists
The main purpose of letters is the practical one of making thoughts visibl e. Ruskin says that all letters are frightful things and to be endured only o
The main purpose of letters is the practical one of making thoughts visi ble. Ruskin says that all letters are frightful things and to be endured onl

---

ABCDEFGHIJKLMNOPQRSTUVWXYZ 1234567890 abcdefghijklmnopqrstuvwxyz

ABCDEFGHIJKLMNOPQRSTUVWXYZ 1234567890 abcdefghijklmnopqrstuvwxyz

ABCDEFGHIJKLMNOPQRSTUVWXYZ 1234567890 abcdefghijklmnopqrstuvwxyz

ABCDEFGHIJKLMNOPQRSTUVWXYZ 1234567890 abcdefghijklmnopqrstuvwxyz

9/9

The main purpose of letters is the practical one of making thoug hts visible. Ruskin says that all letters are frightful things and to b e endured only on occasion, that is to say, in places where the se nse of the inscription is of more importance than external ornam ent. This is a sweeping statement, from which we need not suffer unduly; yet it is doubtful whether there is art in individual letters. Letters in combination may be satisfying and in a well compose d page even beautiful as a whole, but art in letters consists rather
The main purpose of letters is the practical one of making thoug hts visible. Ruskin says that all letters are frightful things and to b
The main purpose of letters is the practical one of making thou ghts visible. Ruskin says that all letters are frightful things and t

9/10

The main purpose of letters is the practical one of making thoug hts visible. Ruskin says that all letters are frightful things and to b e endured only on occasion, that is to say, in places where the se nse of the inscription is of more importance than external ornam ent. This is a sweeping statement, from which we need not suffer unduly; yet it is doubtful whether there is art in individual letters. Letters in combination may be satisfying and in a well compose
The main purpose of letters is the practical one of making thoug hts visible. Ruskin says that all letters are frightful things and to b
The main purpose of letters is the practical one of making thou ghts visible. Ruskin says that all letters are frightful things and t

9/11

The main purpose of letters is the practical one of making thoug hts visible. Ruskin says that all letters are frightful things and to b e endured only on occasion, that is to say, in places where the se nse of the inscription is of more importance than external ornam ent. This is a sweeping statement, from which we need not suffer unduly; yet it is doubtful whether there is art in individual letters. Letters in combination may be satisfying and in a well compose
The main purpose of letters is the practical one of making thoug hts visible. Ruskin says that all letters are frightful things and to b
The main purpose of letters is the practical one of making thou ghts visible. Ruskin says that all letters are frightful things and t

9/12

The main purpose of letters is the practical one of making thoug hts visible. Ruskin says that all letters are frightful things and to b e endured only on occasion, that is to say, in places where the se nse of the inscription is of more importance than external ornam ent. This is a sweeping statement, from which we need not suffer unduly; yet it is doubtful whether there is art in individual letters. Letters in combination may be satisfying and in a well compose
The main purpose of letters is the practical one of making thoug hts visible. Ruskin says that all letters are frightful things and to b
The main purpose of letters is the practical one of making thou ghts visible. Ruskin says that all letters are frightful things and t

OPTIMA 10 POINT SET MINUS ½ UNIT

ROMAN, ITALIC, BOLD, BOLD ITALIC

abcdefghijklmnopqrstuvwxyz – 1 UNIT
abcdefghijklmnopqrstuvwxyz – ½ UNIT
abcdefghijklmnopqrstuvwxyz NORMAL

ABCDEFGHIJKLMNOPQRSTUVWXYZ 1234567890 abcdefghijklmnopqrstuvwxyz
ABCDEFGHIJKLMNOPQRSTUVWXYZ 1234567890 abcdefghijklmnopqrstuvwxyz
ABCDEFGHIJKLMNOPQRSTUVWXYZ 1234567890 abcdefghijklmnopqrstuvwxyz
ABCDEFGHIJKLMNOPQRSTUVWXYZ 1234567890 abcdefghijklmnopqrstuvwxyz

10/10

The main purpose of letters is the practical one of making tho
ughts visible. Ruskin says that all letters are frightful things an
d to be endured only on occasion, that is to say, in places wh
ere the sense of the inscription is of more importance than ex
ternal ornament. This is a sweeping statement, from which
we need not suffer unduly; yet it is doubtful whether there is
art in individual letters. Letters in combination may be satisfy
ing and in a well composed page even beautiful as a whole,
but art in letters consists rather in the art of arranging and co
mposing them in a pleasing and appropriate manner. The m
ain purpose of letters is the practical one of making thoughts
visible. Ruskin says that all letters are frightful things and to b
e endured only on occasion, that is to say, in places where th
e sense of the inscription is of more importance than external
ornament. This is a sweeping statement, from which we nee
d not suffer unduly; yet it is doubtful whether there is art in in
dividual letters. Letters in combination may be satisfying and
in a well composed page even beautiful as a whole, but art i
n letters consists rather in the art of arranging and composing
them in a pleasing and appropriate manner. The main purpo
se of letters is the practical one of making thoughts visible. R
uskin says that all letters are frightful things and to be endure
The main purpose of letters is the practical one of making tho
ughts visible. Ruskin says that all letters are frightful things an
The main purpose of letters is the practical one of making t
houghts visible. Ruskin says that all letters are frightful thin

10/11

The main purpose of letters is the practical one of making tho
ughts visible. Ruskin says that all letters are frightful things an
d to be endured only on occasion, that is to say, in places wh
ere the sense of the inscription is of more importance than ex
ternal ornament. This is a sweeping statement, from which
we need not suffer unduly; yet it is doubtful whether there is
art in individual letters. Letters in combination may be satisfy
ing and in a well composed page even beautiful as a whole,
but art in letters consists rather in the art of arranging and co
mposing them in a pleasing and appropriate manner. The m
ain purpose of letters is the practical one of making thoughts
visible. Ruskin says that all letters are frightful things and to b
e endured only on occasion, that is to say, in places where th
e sense of the inscription is of more importance than external
ornament. This is a sweeping statement, from which we nee
d not suffer unduly; yet it is doubtful whether there is art in in
dividual letters. Letters in combination may be satisfying and
in a well composed page even beautiful as a whole, but art i
n letters consists rather in the art of arranging and composing
them in a pleasing and appropriate manner. The main purpo
The main purpose of letters is the practical one of making tho
ughts visible. Ruskin says that all letters are frightful things an
The main purpose of letters is the practical one of making t
houghts visible. Ruskin says that all letters are frightful thin

10/12

The main purpose of letters is the practical one of making tho
ughts visible. Ruskin says that all letters are frightful things an
d to be endured only on occasion, that is to say, in places wh
ere the sense of the inscription is of more importance than ex
ternal ornament. This is a sweeping statement, from which
we need not suffer unduly; yet it is doubtful whether there is
art in individual letters. Letters in combination may be satisfy
ing and in a well composed page even beautiful as a whole,
but art in letters consists rather in the art of arranging and co
mposing them in a pleasing and appropriate manner. The m
ain purpose of letters is the practical one of making thoughts
visible. Ruskin says that all letters are frightful things and to b
e endured only on occasion, that is to say, in places where th
e sense of the inscription is of more importance than external
ornament. This is a sweeping statement, from which we nee
d not suffer unduly; yet it is doubtful whether there is art in in
dividual letters. Letters in combination may be satisfying and
in a well composed page even beautiful as a whole, but art i
The main purpose of letters is the practical one of making tho
ughts visible. Ruskin says that all letters are frightful things an
The main purpose of letters is the practical one of making t
houghts visible. Ruskin says that all letters are frightful thin

10/13

The main purpose of letters is the practical one of making tho
ughts visible. Ruskin says that all letters are frightful things an
d to be endured only on occasion, that is to say, in places wh
ere the sense of the inscription is of more importance than ex
ternal ornament. This is a sweeping statement, from which
we need not suffer unduly; yet it is doubtful whether there is
art in individual letters. Letters in combination may be satisfy
ing and in a well composed page even beautiful as a whole,
but art in letters consists rather in the art of arranging and co
mposing them in a pleasing and appropriate manner. The m
ain purpose of letters is the practical one of making thoughts
visible. Ruskin says that all letters are frightful things and to b
e endured only on occasion, that is to say, in places where th
e sense of the inscription is of more importance than external
ornament. This is a sweeping statement, from which we nee
d not suffer unduly; yet it is doubtful whether there is art in in
dividual letters. Letters in combination may be satisfying and
The main purpose of letters is the practical one of making tho
ughts visible. Ruskin says that all letters are frightful things an
The main purpose of letters is the practical one of making t
houghts visible. Ruskin says that all letters are frightful thin

OPTIMA 11 POINT SET MINUS ½ UNIT

ROMAN, ITALIC, BOLD, BOLD ITALIC

abcdefghijklmnopqrstuvwxyz – 1 UNIT
abcdefghijklmnopqrstuvwxyz – ½ UNIT
abcdefghijklmnopqrstuvwxyz NORMAL

ABCDEFGHIJKLMNOPQRSTUVWXYZ 1234567890 abcdefghijklmnopqrstuvwxyz
ABCDEFGHIJKLMNOPQRSTUVWXYZ 1234567890 abcdefghijklmnopqrstuvwxyz
ABCDEFGHIJKLMNOPQRSTUVWXYZ 1234567890 abcdefghijklmnopqrstuvwxyz
ABCDEFGHIJKLMNOPQRSTUVWXYZ 1234567890 abcdefghijklmnopqrstuvwxyz

11/11

The main purpose of letters is the practical one of maki ng thoughts visible. Ruskin says that all letters are fright ful things and to be endured only on occasion, that is to say, in places where the sense of the inscription is of m ore importance than external ornament. This is a swee ping statement, from which we need not suffer unduly; yet it is doubtful whether there is art in individual letter s. Letters in combination may be satisfying and in a wel l composed page even beautiful as a whole, but art in l etters consists rather in the art of arranging and compos ing them in a pleasing and appropriate manner. The m ain purpose of letters is the practical one of making tho ughts visible. Ruskin says that all letters are frightful thi ngs and to be endured only on occasion, that is to say, in places where the sense of the inscription is of more importance than external ornament. This is a sweepin g statement, from which we need not suffer unduly; yet it is doubtful whether there is art in individual letters. Le tters in combination may be satisfying and in a well co
The main purpose of letters is the practical one of maki ng thoughts visible. Ruskin says that all letters are fright
The main purpose of letters is the practical one of ma king thoughts visible. Ruskin says that all letters are fri

11/12

The main purpose of letters is the practical one of maki ng thoughts visible. Ruskin says that all letters are fright ful things and to be endured only on occasion, that is to say, in places where the sense of the inscription is of m ore importance than external ornament. This is a swee ping statement, from which we need not suffer unduly; yet it is doubtful whether there is art in individual letter s. Letters in combination may be satisfying and in a wel l composed page even beautiful as a whole, but art in l etters consists rather in the art of arranging and compos ing them in a pleasing and appropriate manner. The m ain purpose of letters is the practical one of making tho ughts visible. Ruskin says that all letters are frightful thi ngs and to be endured only on occasion, that is to say, in places where the sense of the inscription is of more importance than external ornament. This is a sweepin g statement, from which we need not suffer unduly; yet it is doubtful whether there is art in individual letters. Le
The main purpose of letters is the practical one of maki ng thoughts visible. Ruskin says that all letters are fright
The main purpose of letters is the practical one of ma king thoughts visible. Ruskin says that all letters are fri

11/13

The main purpose of letters is the practical one of maki ng thoughts visible. Ruskin says that all letters are fright ful things and to be endured only on occasion, that is to say, in places where the sense of the inscription is of m ore importance than external ornament. This is a swee ping statement, from which we need not suffer unduly; yet it is doubtful whether there is art in individual letter s. Letters in combination may be satisfying and in a wel l composed page even beautiful as a whole, but art in l etters consists rather in the art of arranging and compos ing them in a pleasing and appropriate manner. The m ain purpose of letters is the practical one of making tho ughts visible. Ruskin says that all letters are frightful thi ngs and to be endured only on occasion, that is to say, in places where the sense of the inscription is of more importance than external ornament. This is a sweepin g statement, from which we need not suffer unduly; yet
The main purpose of letters is the practical one of maki ng thoughts visible. Ruskin says that all letters are fright
The main purpose of letters is the practical one of ma king thoughts visible. Ruskin says that all letters are fri

11/14

The main purpose of letters is the practical one of maki ng thoughts visible. Ruskin says that all letters are fright ful things and to be endured only on occasion, that is to say, in places where the sense of the inscription is of m ore importance than external ornament. This is a swee ping statement, from which we need not suffer unduly; yet it is doubtful whether there is art in individual letter s. Letters in combination may be satisfying and in a wel l composed page even beautiful as a whole, but art in l etters consists rather in the art of arranging and compos ing them in a pleasing and appropriate manner. The m ain purpose of letters is the practical one of making tho ughts visible. Ruskin says that all letters are frightful thi ngs and to be endured only on occasion, that is to say, in places where the sense of the inscription is of more importance than external ornament. This is a sweepin
The main purpose of letters is the practical one of maki ng thoughts visible. Ruskin says that all letters are fright
The main purpose of letters is the practical one of ma king thoughts visible. Ruskin says that all letters are fri

OPTIMA 12 POINT SET MINUS ½ UNIT

ROMAN, ITALIC, BOLD, BOLD ITALIC

abcdefghijklmnopqrstuvwxyz – 1 UNIT
abcdefghijklmnopqrstuvwxyz – ½ UNIT
abcdefghijklmnopqrstuvwxyz NORMAL

ABCDEFGHIJKLMNOPQRSTUVWXYZ 1234567890 abcdefghijklmnopqrstuvwxyz
ABCDEFGHIJKLMNOPQRSTUVWXYZ 1234567890 abcdefghijklmnopqrstuvwxyz
ABCDEFGHIJKLMNOPQRSTUVWXYZ 1234567890 abcdefghijklmnopqrstuvwxyz
ABCDEFGHIJKLMNOPQRSTUVWXYZ 1234567890 abcdefghijklmnopqrstuvwxyz

12/12

The main purpose of letters is the practical one of making thoughts visible. Ruskin says that all letters are frightful things and to be endured only on occas ion, that is to say, in places where the sense of the in scription is of more importance than external orna ment. This is a sweeping statement, from which we need not suffer unduly; yet it is doubtful whether th ere is art in individual letters. Letters in combinatio n may be satisfying and in a well composed page e ven beautiful as a whole, but art in letters consists r ather in the art of arranging and composing them in a pleasing and appropriate manner. The main purp ose of letters is the practical one of making thought s visible. Ruskin says that all letters are frightful thin gs and to be endured only on occasion, that is to sa
The main purpose of letters is the practical one of making thoughts visible. Ruskin says that all letters
The main purpose of letters is the practical one of making thoughts visible. Ruskin says that all letter

12/13

The main purpose of letters is the practical one of making thoughts visible. Ruskin says that all letters are frightful things and to be endured only on occas ion, that is to say, in places where the sense of the in scription is of more importance than external orna ment. This is a sweeping statement, from which we need not suffer unduly; yet it is doubtful whether th ere is art in individual letters. Letters in combinatio n may be satisfying and in a well composed page e ven beautiful as a whole, but art in letters consists r ather in the art of arranging and composing them in a pleasing and appropriate manner. The main purp ose of letters is the practical one of making thought s visible. Ruskin says that all letters are frightful thin
The main purpose of letters is the practical one of making thoughts visible. Ruskin says that all letters
The main purpose of letters is the practical one of making thoughts visible. Ruskin says that all letter

12/14

The main purpose of letters is the practical one of making thoughts visible. Ruskin says that all letters are frightful things and to be endured only on occas ion, that is to say, in places where the sense of the in scription is of more importance than external orna ment. This is a sweeping statement, from which we need not suffer unduly; yet it is doubtful whether th ere is art in individual letters. Letters in combinatio n may be satisfying and in a well composed page e ven beautiful as a whole, but art in letters consists r ather in the art of arranging and composing them in a pleasing and appropriate manner. The main purp ose of letters is the practical one of making thought s visible. Ruskin says that all letters are frightful thin gs and to be endured only on occasion, that is to sa
The main purpose of letters is the practical one of making thoughts visible. Ruskin says that all letters
The main purpose of letters is the practical one of making thoughts visible. Ruskin says that all letter

12/15

The main purpose of letters is the practical one of making thoughts visible. Ruskin says that all letters are frightful things and to be endured only on occas ion, that is to say, in places where the sense of the in scription is of more importance than external orna ment. This is a sweeping statement, from which we need not suffer unduly; yet it is doubtful whether th ere is art in individual letters. Letters in combinatio n may be satisfying and in a well composed page e ven beautiful as a whole, but art in letters consists r ather in the art of arranging and composing them in a pleasing and appropriate manner. The main purp ose of letters is the practical one of making thought s visible. Ruskin says that all letters are frightful thin
The main purpose of letters is the practical one of making thoughts visible. Ruskin says that all letters
The main purpose of letters is the practical one of making thoughts visible. Ruskin says that all letter

OPTIMA 14 POINT SET MINUS ½ UNIT

ROMAN, ITALIC, BOLD, BOLD ITALIC

abcdefghijklmnopqrstuvwxyz – 1 UNIT
abcdefghijklmnopqrstuvwxyz – ½ UNIT
abcdefghijklmnopqrstuvwxyz NORMAL

ABCDEFGHIJKLMNOPQRSTUVWXYZ abcdefghijklmnopqrstuvwxyz
ABCDEFGHIJKLMNOPQRSTUVWXYZ abcdefghijklmnopqrstuvwxyz
ABCDEFGHIJKLMNOPQRSTUVWXYZ abcdefghijklmnopqrstuvwxyz
ABCDEFGHIJKLMNOPQRSTUVWXYZ abcdefghijklmnopqrstuvwxyz

14/14

The main purpose of letters is the practical one of making thoughts visible. Ruskin says that all letters are frightful things and to be e ndured only on occasion, that is to say, in pl aces where the sense of the inscription is of more importance than external ornament. This is a sweeping statement, from which w e need not suffer unduly; yet it is doubtful whether there is art in individual letters. Let ters in combination may be satisfying and in a well composed page even beautiful as a whole, but art in letters consists rather in the art of arranging and composing them in
The main purpose of letters is the practical one of making thoughts visible. Ruskin says
The main purpose of letters is the practical one of making thoughts visible. Ruskin say

14/15

The main purpose of letters is the practical one of making thoughts visible. Ruskin says that all letters are frightful things and to be e ndured only on occasion, that is to say, in pl aces where the sense of the inscription is of more importance than external ornament. This is a sweeping statement, from which w e need not suffer unduly; yet it is doubtful whether there is art in individual letters. Let ters in combination may be satisfying and in a well composed page even beautiful as a whole, but art in letters consists rather in
The main purpose of letters is the practical one of making thoughts visible. Ruskin says
The main purpose of letters is the practical one of making thoughts visible. Ruskin say

14/16

The main purpose of letters is the practical one of making thoughts visible. Ruskin says that all letters are frightful things and to be e ndured only on occasion, that is to say, in pl aces where the sense of the inscription is of more importance than external ornament. This is a sweeping statement, from which w e need not suffer unduly; yet it is doubtful whether there is art in individual letters. Let ters in combination may be satisfying and in a well composed page even beautiful as a whole, but art in letters consists rather in the art of arranging and composing them in
The main purpose of letters is the practical one of making thoughts visible. Ruskin says
The main purpose of letters is the practical one of making thoughts visible. Ruskin say

14/17

The main purpose of letters is the practical one of making thoughts visible. Ruskin says that all letters are frightful things and to be e ndured only on occasion, that is to say, in pl aces where the sense of the inscription is of more importance than external ornament. This is a sweeping statement, from which w e need not suffer unduly; yet it is doubtful whether there is art in individual letters. Let ters in combination may be satisfying and in a well composed page even beautiful as a whole, but art in letters consists rather in
The main purpose of letters is the practical one of making thoughts visible. Ruskin says
The main purpose of letters is the practical one of making thoughts visible. Ruskin say

PALATINO 6 & 7 POINT SET NORMAL

ROMAN, ITALIC, BOLD, BOLD ITALIC

ABCDEFGHIJKLMNOPQRSTUVWXYZ 1234567890 abcdefghijklmnopqrstuvwxyz

ABCDEFGHIJKLMNOPQRSTUVWXYZ 1234567890 abcdefghijklmnopqrstuvwxyz

ABCDEFGHIJKLMNOPQRSTUVWXYZ 1234567890 abcdefghijklmnopqrstuvwxyz

ABCDEFGHIJKLMNOPQRSTUVWXYZ 1234567890 abcdefghijklmnopqrstuvwxyz

6/6

The main purpose of letters is the practical one of making thoughts visible. Ruskin says that all letters are frightful things and to be endured only on occasion, that is to say, in places wh ere the sense of the inscription is of more importance than external ornament. This is a swee ping statement, from which we need not suffer unduly; yet it is doubtful whether there is ar t in individual letters. Letters in combination may be satisfying and in a well composed pag e even beautiful as a whole, but art in letters consists rather in the art of arranging and comp osing them in a pleasing and appropriate manner. The main purpose of letters is the practic al one of making thoughts visible. Ruskin says that all letters are frightful things and to be e ndured only on occasion, that is to say, in places where the sense of the inscription is of mor e importance than external ornament. This is a sweeping statement, from which we need n ot suffer unduly; yet it is doubtful whether there is art in individual letters. Letters in combi nation may be satisfying and in a well composed page even beautiful as a whole, but art in l etters consists rather in the art of arranging and composing them in a pleasing and appropri
The main purpose of letters is the practical one of making thoughts visible. Ruskin says that all letters are frightful things and to be endured only on occasion, that is to say, in places where the sense of the i
The main purpose of letters is the practical one of making thoughts visible. Ruskin says th at all letters are frightful things and to be endured only on occasion, that is to say, in places

6/7

The main purpose of letters is the practical one of making thoughts visible. Ruskin says that all letters are frightful things and to be endured only on occasion, that is to say, in places wh ere the sense of the inscription is of more importance than external ornament. This is a swee ping statement, from which we need not suffer unduly; yet it is doubtful whether there is ar t in individual letters. Letters in combination may be satisfying and in a well composed pag e even beautiful as a whole, but art in letters consists rather in the art of arranging and comp osing them in a pleasing and appropriate manner. The main purpose of letters is the practic al one of making thoughts visible. Ruskin says that all letters are frightful things and to be e ndured only on occasion, that is to say, in places where the sense of the inscription is of mor e importance than external ornament. This is a sweeping statement, from which we need n ot suffer unduly; yet it is doubtful whether there is art in individual letters. Letters in combi
The main purpose of letters is the practical one of making thoughts visible. Ruskin says that all letters are frightful things and to be endured only on occasion, that is to say, in places where the sense of the i
The main purpose of letters is the practical one of making thoughts visible. Ruskin says th at all letters are frightful things and to be endured only on occasion, that is to say, in places

6/8

The main purpose of letters is the practical one of making thoughts visible. Ruskin says that all letters are frightful things and to be endured only on occasion, that is to say, in places wh ere the sense of the inscription is of more importance than external ornament. This is a swee ping statement, from which we need not suffer unduly; yet it is doubtful whether there is ar t in individual letters. Letters in combination may be satisfying and in a well composed pag e even beautiful as a whole, but art in letters consists rather in the art of arranging and comp osing them in a pleasing and appropriate manner. The main purpose of letters is the practic al one of making thoughts visible. Ruskin says that all letters are frightful things and to be e ndured only on occasion, that is to say, in places where the sense of the inscription is of mor
The main purpose of letters is the practical one of making thoughts visible. Ruskin says that all letters are frightful things and to be endured only on occasion, that is to say, in places where the sense of the i
The main purpose of letters is the practical one of making thoughts visible. Ruskin says th at all letters are frightful things and to be endured only on occasion, that is to say, in places

6/9

The main purpose of letters is the practical one of making thoughts visible. Ruskin says that all letters are frightful things and to be endured only on occasion, that is to say, in places wh ere the sense of the inscription is of more importance than external ornament. This is a swee ping statement, from which we need not suffer unduly; yet it is doubtful whether there is ar t in individual letters. Letters in combination may be satisfying and in a well composed pag e even beautiful as a whole, but art in letters consists rather in the art of arranging and comp osing them in a pleasing and appropriate manner. The main purpose of letters is the practic al one of making thoughts visible. Ruskin says that all letters are frightful things and to be e
The main purpose of letters is the practical one of making thoughts visible. Ruskin says that all letters are frightful things and to be endured only on occasion, that is to say, in places where the sense of the i
The main purpose of letters is the practical one of making thoughts visible. Ruskin says th at all letters are frightful things and to be endured only on occasion, that is to say, in places

---

ABCDEFGHIJKLMNOPQRSTUVWXYZ 1234567890 abcdefghijklmnopqrstuvwxyz

ABCDEFGHIJKLMNOPQRSTUVWXYZ 1234567890 abcdefghijklmnopqrstuvwxyz

ABCDEFGHIJKLMNOPQRSTUVWXYZ 1234567890 abcdefghijklmnopqrstuvwxyz

ABCDEFGHIJKLMNOPQRSTUVWXYZ 1234567890 abcdefghijklmnopqrstuvwxyz

7/7

The main purpose of letters is the practical one of making thoughts visible. Ru skin says that all letters are frightful things and to be endured only on occasion, that is to say, in places where the sense of the inscription is of more importanc e than external ornament. This is a sweeping statement, from which we need not suffer unduly; yet it is doubtful whether there is art in individual letters. Le tters in combination may be satisfying and in a well composed page even beau tiful as a whole, but art in letters consists rather in the art of arranging and com posing them in a pleasing and appropriate manner. The main purpose of letter s is the practical one of making thoughts visible. Ruskin says that all letters are frightful things and to be endured only on occasion, that is to say, in places wh ere the sense of the inscription is of more importance than external ornament.
The main purpose of letters is the practical one of making thoughts visible. Ruskin says that all letters are frightful things and to be endured only on occasion, that is to say, in p
The main purpose of letters is the practical one of making thoughts visible. R uskin says that all letters are frightful things and to be endured only on occas

7/8

The main purpose of letters is the practical one of making thoughts visible. Ru skin says that all letters are frightful things and to be endured only on occasion, that is to say, in places where the sense of the inscription is of more importanc e than external ornament. This is a sweeping statement, from which we need not suffer unduly; yet it is doubtful whether there is art in individual letters. Le tters in combination may be satisfying and in a well composed page even beau tiful as a whole, but art in letters consists rather in the art of arranging and com posing them in a pleasing and appropriate manner. The main purpose of letter s is the practical one of making thoughts visible. Ruskin says that all letters are frightful things and to be endured only on occasion, that is to say, in places wh
The main purpose of letters is the practical one of making thoughts visible. Ruskin says that all letters are frightful things and to be endured only on occasion, that is to say, in p
The main purpose of letters is the practical one of making thoughts visible. R uskin says that all letters are frightful things and to be endured only on occas

7/9

The main purpose of letters is the practical one of making thoughts visible. Ru skin says that all letters are frightful things and to be endured only on occasion, that is to say, in places where the sense of the inscription is of more importanc e than external ornament. This is a sweeping statement, from which we need not suffer unduly; yet it is doubtful whether there is art in individual letters. Le tters in combination may be satisfying and in a well composed page even beau tiful as a whole, but art in letters consists rather in the art of arranging and com posing them in a pleasing and appropriate manner. The main purpose of letter s is the practical one of making thoughts visible. Ruskin says that all letters are frightful things and to be endured only on occasion, that is to say, in places wh
The main purpose of letters is the practical one of making thoughts visible. Ruskin says that all letters are frightful things and to be endured only on occasion, that is to say, in p
The main purpose of letters is the practical one of making thoughts visible. R uskin says that all letters are frightful things and to be endured only on occas

7/10

The main purpose of letters is the practical one of making thoughts visible. Ru skin says that all letters are frightful things and to be endured only on occasion, that is to say, in places where the sense of the inscription is of more importanc e than external ornament. This is a sweeping statement, from which we need not suffer unduly; yet it is doubtful whether there is art in individual letters. Le tters in combination may be satisfying and in a well composed page even beau tiful as a whole, but art in letters consists rather in the art of arranging and com posing them in a pleasing and appropriate manner. The main purpose of letter s is the practical one of making thoughts visible. Ruskin says that all letters are
The main purpose of letters is the practical one of making thoughts visible. Ruskin says that all letters are frightful things and to be endured only on occasion, that is to say, in p
The main purpose of letters is the practical one of making thoughts visible. R uskin says that all letters are frightful things and to be endured only on occas

PALATINO 8 & 9 POINT SET NORMAL

ROMAN, ITALIC, BOLD, BOLD ITALIC

ABCDEFGHIJKLMNOPQRSTUVWXYZ 1234567890 abcdefghijklmnopqrstuvwxyz
ABCDEFGHIJKLMNOPQRSTUVWXYZ 1234567890 abcdefghijklmnopqrstuvwxyz
ABCDEFGHIJKLMNOPQRSTUVWXYZ 1234567890 abcdefghijklmnopqrstuvwxyz
ABCDEFGHIJKLMNOPQRSTUVWXYZ 1234567890 abcdefghijklmnopqrstuvwxyz

8/8

The main purpose of letters is the practical one of making thoughts v isible. Ruskin says that all letters are frightful things and to be endur ed only on occasion, that is to say, in places where the sense of the in scription is of more importance than external ornament. This is a sw eeping statement, from which we need not suffer unduly; yet it is do ubtful whether there is art in individual letters. Letters in combinatio n may be satisfying and in a well composed page even beautiful as a whole, but art in letters consists rather in the art of arranging and co mposing them in a pleasing and appropriate manner. The main purp
The main purpose of letters is the practical one of making thoughts visible. R uskin says that all letters are frightful things and to be endured only on occas
The main purpose of letters is the practical one of making thoughts visible. Ruskin says that all letters are frightful things and to be en

8/9

The main purpose of letters is the practical one of making thoughts v isible. Ruskin says that all letters are frightful things and to be endur ed only on occasion, that is to say, in places where the sense of the in scription is of more importance than external ornament. This is a sw eeping statement, from which we need not suffer unduly; yet it is do ubtful whether there is art in individual letters. Letters in combinatio n may be satisfying and in a well composed page even beautiful as a whole, but art in letters consists rather in the art of arranging and co
The main purpose of letters is the practical one of making thoughts visible. R uskin says that all letters are frightful things and to be endured only on occas
The main purpose of letters is the practical one of making thoughts visible. Ruskin says that all letters are frightful things and to be en

8/10

The main purpose of letters is the practical one of making thoughts v isible. Ruskin says that all letters are frightful things and to be endur ed only on occasion, that is to say, in places where the sense of the in scription is of more importance than external ornament. This is a sw eeping statement, from which we need not suffer unduly; yet it is do ubtful whether there is art in individual letters. Letters in combinatio n may be satisfying and in a well composed page even beautiful as a
The main purpose of letters is the practical one of making thoughts visible. R uskin says that all letters are frightful things and to be endured only on occas
The main purpose of letters is the practical one of making thoughts visible. Ruskin says that all letters are frightful things and to be en

8/11

The main purpose of letters is the practical one of making thoughts v isible. Ruskin says that all letters are frightful things and to be endur ed only on occasion, that is to say, in places where the sense of the in scription is of more importance than external ornament. This is a sw eeping statement, from which we need not suffer unduly; yet it is do ubtful whether there is art in individual letters. Letters in combinatio n may be satisfying and in a well composed page even beautiful as a
The main purpose of letters is the practical one of making thoughts visible. R uskin says that all letters are frightful things and to be endured only on occas
The main purpose of letters is the practical one of making thoughts visible. Ruskin says that all letters are frightful things and to be en

---

ABCDEFGHIJKLMNOPQRSTUVWXYZ 1234567890 abcdefghijklmnopqrstuvwxyz
ABCDEFGHIJKLMNOPQRSTUVWXYZ 1234567890 abcdefghijklmnopqrstuvwxyz
ABCDEFGHIJKLMNOPQRSTUVWXYZ 1234567890 abcdefghijklmnopqrstuvwxyz
ABCDEFGHIJKLMNOPQRSTUVWXYZ 1234567890 abcdefghijklmnopqrstuvwxyz

9/9

The main purpose of letters is the practical one of making tho ughts visible. Ruskin says that all letters are frightful things a nd to be endured only on occasion, that is to say, in places wh ere the sense of the inscription is of more importance than ext ernal ornament. This is a sweeping statement, from which w e need not suffer unduly; yet it is doubtful whether there is ar t in individual letters. Letters in combination may be satisfyi ng and in a well composed page even beautiful as a whole, b
The main purpose of letters is the practical one of making thoughts v isible. Ruskin says that all letters are frightful things and to be endu
The main purpose of letters is the practical one of making th oughts visible. Ruskin says that all letters are frightful thin

9/10

The main purpose of letters is the practical one of making tho ughts visible. Ruskin says that all letters are frightful things a nd to be endured only on occasion, that is to say, in places wh ere the sense of the inscription is of more importance than ext ernal ornament. This is a sweeping statement, from which w e need not suffer unduly; yet it is doubtful whether there is ar t in individual letters. Letters in combination may be satisfyi
The main purpose of letters is the practical one of making thoughts v isible. Ruskin says that all letters are frightful things and to be endu
The main purpose of letters is the practical one of making th oughts visible. Ruskin says that all letters are frightful thin

9/11

The main purpose of letters is the practical one of making tho ughts visible. Ruskin says that all letters are frightful things a nd to be endured only on occasion, that is to say, in places wh ere the sense of the inscription is of more importance than ext ernal ornament. This is a sweeping statement, from which w e need not suffer unduly; yet it is doubtful whether there is ar t in individual letters. Letters in combination may be satisfyi
The main purpose of letters is the practical one of making thoughts v isible. Ruskin says that all letters are frightful things and to be endu
The main purpose of letters is the practical one of making th oughts visible. Ruskin says that all letters are frightful thin

9/12

The main purpose of letters is the practical one of making tho ughts visible. Ruskin says that all letters are frightful things a nd to be endured only on occasion, that is to say, in places wh ere the sense of the inscription is of more importance than ext ernal ornament. This is a sweeping statement, from which w e need not suffer unduly; yet it is doubtful whether there is ar t in individual letters. Letters in combination may be satisfyi
The main purpose of letters is the practical one of making thoughts v isible. Ruskin says that all letters are frightful things and to be endu
The main purpose of letters is the practical one of making th oughts visible. Ruskin says that all letters are frightful thin

PALATINO 10 POINT SET MINUS ½ UNIT

ROMAN, ITALIC, BOLD, BOLD ITALIC

abcdefghijklmnopqrstuvwxyz – 1 UNIT
abcdefghijklmnopqrstuvwxyz – ½ UNIT
abcdefghijklmnopqrstuvwxyz NORMAL

ABCDEFGHIJKLMNOPQRSTUVWXYZ 1234567890 abcdefghijklmnopqrstuvwxyz
ABCDEFGHIJKLMNOPQRSTUVWXYZ 1234567890 abcdefghijklmnopqrstuvwxyz
ABCDEFGHIJKLMNOPQRSTUVWXYZ 1234567890 abcdefghijklmnopqrstuvwxyz
ABCDEFGHIJKLMNOPQRSTUVWXYZ 1234567890 abcdefghijklmnopqrstuvwxyz

10/10

The main purpose of letters is the practical one of making thoughts visible. Ruskin says that all letters are frightful t hings and to be endured only on occasion, that is to say, i n places where the sense of the inscription is of more imp ortance than external ornament. This is a sweeping state ment, from which we need not suffer unduly; yet it is do ubtful whether there is art in individual letters. Letters in combination may be satisfying and in a well composed p age even beautiful as a whole, but art in letters consists ra ther in the art of arranging and composing them in a plea sing and appropriate manner. The main purpose of letter s is the practical one of making thoughts visible. Ruskin s ays that all letters are frightful things and to be endured only on occasion, that is to say, in places where the sense of the inscription is of more importance than external orn ament. This is a sweeping statement, from which we nee d not suffer unduly; yet it is doubtful whether there is art in individual letters. Letters in combination may be satis fying and in a well composed page even beautiful as a w hole, but art in letters consists rather in the art of arrangin g and composing them in a pleasing and appropriate ma nner. The main purpose of letters is the practical one of m

The main purpose of letters is the practical one of making thoug hts visible. Ruskin says that all letters are frightful things and to

The main purpose of letters is the practical one of makin g thoughts visible. Ruskin says that all letters are frightf

10/11

The main purpose of letters is the practical one of making thoughts visible. Ruskin says that all letters are frightful t hings and to be endured only on occasion, that is to say, i n places where the sense of the inscription is of more imp ortance than external ornament. This is a sweeping state ment, from which we need not suffer unduly; yet it is do ubtful whether there is art in individual letters. Letters in combination may be satisfying and in a well composed p age even beautiful as a whole, but art in letters consists ra ther in the art of arranging and composing them in a plea sing and appropriate manner. The main purpose of letter s is the practical one of making thoughts visible. Ruskin s ays that all letters are frightful things and to be endured only on occasion, that is to say, in places where the sense of the inscription is of more importance than external orn ament. This is a sweeping statement, from which we nee d not suffer unduly; yet it is doubtful whether there is art in individual letters. Letters in combination may be satis fying and in a well composed page even beautiful as a w hole, but art in letters consists rather in the art of arrangin

The main purpose of letters is the practical one of making thoug hts visible. Ruskin says that all letters are frightful things and to

The main purpose of letters is the practical one of makin g thoughts visible. Ruskin says that all letters are frightf

10/12

The main purpose of letters is the practical one of making thoughts visible. Ruskin says that all letters are frightful t hings and to be endured only on occasion, that is to say, i n places where the sense of the inscription is of more imp ortance than external ornament. This is a sweeping state ment, from which we need not suffer unduly; yet it is do ubtful whether there is art in individual letters. Letters in combination may be satisfying and in a well composed p age even beautiful as a whole, but art in letters consists ra ther in the art of arranging and composing them in a plea sing and appropriate manner. The main purpose of letter s is the practical one of making thoughts visible. Ruskin s ays that all letters are frightful things and to be endured only on occasion, that is to say, in places where the sense of the inscription is of more importance than external orn ament. This is a sweeping statement, from which we nee d not suffer unduly; yet it is doubtful whether there is art in individual letters. Letters in combination may be satis

The main purpose of letters is the practical one of making thoug hts visible. Ruskin says that all letters are frightful things and to

The main purpose of letters is the practical one of makin g thoughts visible. Ruskin says that all letters are frightf

10/13

The main purpose of letters is the practical one of making thoughts visible. Ruskin says that all letters are frightful t hings and to be endured only on occasion, that is to say, i n places where the sense of the inscription is of more imp ortance than external ornament. This is a sweeping state ment, from which we need not suffer unduly; yet it is do ubtful whether there is art in individual letters. Letters in combination may be satisfying and in a well composed p age even beautiful as a whole, but art in letters consists ra ther in the art of arranging and composing them in a plea sing and appropriate manner. The main purpose of letter s is the practical one of making thoughts visible. Ruskin s ays that all letters are frightful things and to be endured only on occasion, that is to say, in places where the sense of the inscription is of more importance than external orn ament. This is a sweeping statement, from which we nee d not suffer unduly; yet it is doubtful whether there is art

The main purpose of letters is the practical one of making thoug hts visible. Ruskin says that all letters are frightful things and to

The main purpose of letters is the practical one of makin g thoughts visible. Ruskin says that all letters are frightf

PALATINO 11 POINT SET MINUS ½ UNIT

ROMAN, ITALIC, BOLD BOLD ITALIC

abcdefghijklmnopqrstuvwxyz – 1 UNIT
abcdefghijklmnopqrstuvwxyz – ½ UNIT
abcdefghijklmnopqrstuvwxyz NORMAL

ABCDEFGHIJKLMNOPQRSTUVWXYZ 1234567890 abcdefghijklmnopqrstuvwxyz
ABCDEFGHIJKLMNOPQRSTUVWXYZ 1234567890 abcdefghijklmnopqrstuvwxyz
ABCDEFGHIJKLMNOPQRSTUVWXYZ 1234567890 abcdefghijklmnopqrstuvwxyz
ABCDEFGHIJKLMNOPQRSTUVWXYZ 1234567890 abcdefghijklmnopqrstuvwxyz

11/11

The main purpose of letters is the practical one of m aking thoughts visible. Ruskin says that all letters ar e frightful things and to be endured only on occasio n, that is to say, in places where the sense of the insc ription is of more importance than external orname nt. This is a sweeping statement, from which we ne ed not suffer unduly; yet it is doubtful whether ther e is art in individual letters. Letters in combination may be satisfying and in a well composed page eve n beautiful as a whole, but art in letters consists rath er in the art of arranging and composing them in a p leasing and appropriate manner. The main purpose of letters is the practical one of making thoughts visi ble. Ruskin says that all letters are frightful things a nd to be endured only on occasion, that is to say, in places where the sense of the inscription is of more i mportance than external ornament. This is a sweepi ng statement, from which we need not suffer undul y; yet it is doubtful whether there is art in individual

The main purpose of letters is the practical one of making thoughts visible. Ruskin says that all letters are frightful

The main purpose of letters is the practical one of making thoughts visible. Ruskin says that all lette

11/12

The main purpose of letters is the practical one of m aking thoughts visible. Ruskin says that all letters ar e frightful things and to be endured only on occasio n, that is to say, in places where the sense of the insc ription is of more importance than external orname nt. This is a sweeping statement, from which we ne ed not suffer unduly; yet it is doubtful whether ther e is art in individual letters. Letters in combination may be satisfying and in a well composed page eve n beautiful as a whole, but art in letters consists rath er in the art of arranging and composing them in a p leasing and appropriate manner. The main purpose of letters is the practical one of making thoughts visi ble. Ruskin says that all letters are frightful things a nd to be endured only on occasion, that is to say, in places where the sense of the inscription is of more i mportance than external ornament. This is a sweepi ng statement, from which we need not suffer undul

The main purpose of letters is the practical one of making thoughts visible. Ruskin says that all letters are frightful

The main purpose of letters is the practical one of making thoughts visible. Ruskin says that all lette

11/13

The main purpose of letters is the practical one of m aking thoughts visible. Ruskin says that all letters ar e frightful things and to be endured only on occasio n, that is to say, in places where the sense of the insc ription is of more importance than external orname nt. This is a sweeping statement, from which we ne ed not suffer unduly; yet it is doubtful whether ther e is art in individual letters. Letters in combination may be satisfying and in a well composed page eve n beautiful as a whole, but art in letters consists rath er in the art of arranging and composing them in a p leasing and appropriate manner. The main purpose of letters is the practical one of making thoughts visi ble. Ruskin says that all letters are frightful things a nd to be endured only on occasion, that is to say, in places where the sense of the inscription is of more i mportance than external ornament. This is a sweepi

The main purpose of letters is the practical one of making thoughts visible. Ruskin says that all letters are frightful

The main purpose of letters is the practical one of making thoughts visible. Ruskin says that all lette

11/14

The main purpose of letters is the practical one of m aking thoughts visible. Ruskin says that all letters ar e frightful things and to be endured only on occasio n, that is to say, in places where the sense of the insc ription is of more importance than external orname nt. This is a sweeping statement, from which we ne ed not suffer unduly; yet it is doubtful whether ther e is art in individual letters. Letters in combination may be satisfying and in a well composed page eve n beautiful as a whole, but art in letters consists rath er in the art of arranging and composing them in a p leasing and appropriate manner. The main purpose of letters is the practical one of making thoughts visi ble. Ruskin says that all letters are frightful things a nd to be endured only on occasion, that is to say, in places where the sense of the inscription is of more i

The main purpose of letters is the practical one of making thoughts visible. Ruskin says that all letters are frightful

The main purpose of letters is the practical one of making thoughts visible. Ruskin says that all lette

PALATINO 12 POINT SET MINUS ½ UNIT

ROMAN, ITALIC, BOLD, BOLD ITALIC

abcdefghijklmnopqrstuvwxyz – 1 UNIT
abcdefghijklmnopqrstuvwxyz – ½ UNIT
abcdefghijklmnopqrstuvwxyz NORMAL

ABCDEFGHIJKLMNOPQRSTUVWXYZ 1234567890 abcdefghijklmnopqrstuvwxyz
ABCDEFGHIJKLMNOPQRSTUVWXYZ 1234567890 abcdefghijklmnopqrstuvwxyz
ABCDEFGHIJKLMNOPQRSTUVWXYZ 1234567890 abcdefghijklmnopqrstuvwxyz
ABCDEFGHIJKLMNOPQRSTUVWXYZ 1234567890 abcdefghijklmnopqrstuvwxyz

12/12

The main purpose of letters is the practical one o f making thoughts visible. Ruskin says that all le tters are frightful things and to be endured only on occasion, that is to say, in places where the se nse of the inscription is of more importance than external ornament. This is a sweeping statemen t, from which we need not suffer unduly; yet it i s doubtful whether there is art in individual lette rs. Letters in combination may be satisfying and in a well composed page even beautiful as a wh ole, but art in letters consists rather in the art of a rranging and composing them in a pleasing and appropriate manner. The main purpose of letter s is the practical one of making thoughts visible. Ruskin says that all letters are frightful things an
The main purpose of letters is the practical one of maki ng thoughts visible. Ruskin says that all letters are fri
The main purpose of letters is the practical one of making thoughts visible. Ruskin says that al

12/13

The main purpose of letters is the practical one o f making thoughts visible. Ruskin says that all le tters are frightful things and to be endured only on occasion, that is to say, in places where the se nse of the inscription is of more importance than external ornament. This is a sweeping statemen t, from which we need not suffer unduly; yet it i s doubtful whether there is art in individual lette rs. Letters in combination may be satisfying and in a well composed page even beautiful as a wh ole, but art in letters consists rather in the art of a rranging and composing them in a pleasing and appropriate manner. The main purpose of letter s is the practical one of making thoughts visible.
The main purpose of letters is the practical one of maki ng thoughts visible. Ruskin says that all letters are fri
The main purpose of letters is the practical one of making thoughts visible. Ruskin says that al

12/14

The main purpose of letters is the practical one o f making thoughts visible. Ruskin says that all le tters are frightful things and to be endured only on occasion, that is to say, in places where the se nse of the inscription is of more importance than external ornament. This is a sweeping statemen t, from which we need not suffer unduly; yet it i s doubtful whether there is art in individual lette rs. Letters in combination may be satisfying and in a well composed page even beautiful as a wh ole, but art in letters consists rather in the art of a rranging and composing them in a pleasing and appropriate manner. The main purpose of letter s is the practical one of making thoughts visible. Ruskin says that all letters are frightful things an
The main purpose of letters is the practical one of maki ng thoughts visible. Ruskin says that all letters are fri
The main purpose of letters is the practical one of making thoughts visible. Ruskin says that al

12/15

The main purpose of letters is the practical one o f making thoughts visible. Ruskin says that all le tters are frightful things and to be endured only on occasion, that is to say, in places where the se nse of the inscription is of more importance than external ornament. This is a sweeping statemen t, from which we need not suffer unduly; yet it i s doubtful whether there is art in individual lette rs. Letters in combination may be satisfying and in a well composed page even beautiful as a wh ole, but art in letters consists rather in the art of a rranging and composing them in a pleasing and appropriate manner. The main purpose of letter s is the practical one of making thoughts visible.
The main purpose of letters is the practical one of maki ng thoughts visible. Ruskin says that all letters are fri
The main purpose of letters is the practical one of making thoughts visible. Ruskin says that al

PALATINO 14 POINT SET MINUS ½ UNIT

ROMAN, ITALIC, BOLD, BOLD ITALIC

abcdefghijklmnopqrstuvwxyz – 1 UNIT
abcdefghijklmnopqrstuvwxyz – ½ UNIT
abcdefghijklmnopqrstuvwxyz NORMAL

ABCDEFGHIJKLMNOPQRSTUVWXYZ abcdefghijklmnopqrstuvwxyz
ABCDEFGHIJKLMNOPQRSTUVWXYZ abcdefghijklmnopqrstuvwxyz
ABCDEFGHIJKLMNOPQRSTUVWXYZ abcdefghijklmnopqrstuvwxyz
ABCDEFGHIJKLMNOPQRSTUVWXYZ abcdefghijklmnopqrstuvwxyz

14/14

The main purpose of letters is the practic al one of making thoughts visible. Ruski n says that all letters are frightful things and to be endured only on occasion, that is to say, in places where the sense of the inscription is of more importance than ex ternal ornament. This is a sweeping state ment, from which we need not suffer un duly; yet it is doubtful whether there is ar t in individual letters. Letters in combina tion may be satisfying and in a well comp osed page even beautiful as a whole, but art in letters consists rather in the art of ar
The main purpose of letters is the practical one of making thoughts visible. Ruskin says that
The main purpose of letters is the practi cal one of making thoughts visible. Rus

14/15

The main purpose of letters is the practic al one of making thoughts visible. Ruski n says that all letters are frightful things and to be endured only on occasion, that is to say, in places where the sense of the inscription is of more importance than ex ternal ornament. This is a sweeping state ment, from which we need not suffer un duly; yet it is doubtful whether there is ar t in individual letters. Letters in combina tion may be satisfying and in a well comp osed page even beautiful as a whole, but
The main purpose of letters is the practical one of making thoughts visible. Ruskin says that
The main purpose of letters is the practi cal one of making thoughts visible. Rus

14/16

The main purpose of letters is the practic al one of making thoughts visible. Ruski n says that all letters are frightful things and to be endured only on occasion, that is to say, in places where the sense of the inscription is of more importance than ex ternal ornament. This is a sweeping state ment, from which we need not suffer un duly; yet it is doubtful whether there is ar t in individual letters. Letters in combina tion may be satisfying and in a well comp osed page even beautiful as a whole, but art in letters consists rather in the art of ar
The main purpose of letters is the practical one of making thoughts visible. Ruskin says that
The main purpose of letters is the practi cal one of making thoughts visible. Rus

14/17

The main purpose of letters is the practic al one of making thoughts visible. Ruski n says that all letters are frightful things and to be endured only on occasion, that is to say, in places where the sense of the inscription is of more importance than ex ternal ornament. This is a sweeping state ment, from which we need not suffer un duly; yet it is doubtful whether there is ar t in individual letters. Letters in combina tion may be satisfying and in a well comp osed page even beautiful as a whole, but
The main purpose of letters is the practical one of making thoughts visible. Ruskin says that
The main purpose of letters is the practi cal one of making thoughts visible. Rus

PERPETUA 6 & 7 POINT SET NORMAL

ROMAN, ITALIC, BOLD, BOLD ITALIC

ABCDEFGHIJKLMNOPQRSTUVWXYZ 1234567890 abcdefghijklmnopqrstuvwxyz

ABCDEFGHIJKLMNOPQRSTUVWXYZ 1234567890 abcdefghijklmnopqrstuvwxyz

ABCDEFGHIJKLMNOPQRSTUVWXYZ 1234567890 abcdefghijklmnopqrstuvwxyz

ABCDEFGHIJKLMNOPQRSTUVWXYZ 1234567890 abcdefghijklmnopqrstuvwxyz

6/6

The main purpose of letters is the practical one of making thoughts visible. Ruskin says that all letters are frightful t
hings and to be endured only on occasion, that is to say, in places where the sense of the inscription is of more impo
rtance than external ornament. This is a sweeping statement, from which we need not suffer unduly; yet it is doubt
ful whether there is art in individual letters. Letters in combination may be satisfying and in a well composed page e
ven beautiful as a whole, but art in letters consists rather in the art of arranging and composing them in a pleasing a
nd appropriate manner. The main purpose of letters is the practical one of making thoughts visible. Ruskin says tha
t all letters are frightful things and to be endured only on occasion, that is to say, in places where the sense of the ins
cription is of more importance than external ornament. This is a sweeping statement, from which we need not suff
er unduly; yet it is doubtful whether there is art in individual letters. Letters in combination may be satisfying and i
n a well composed page even beautiful as a whole, but art in letters consists rather in the art of arranging and comp
osing them in a pleasing and appropriate manner. The main purpose of letters is the practical one of making though
ts visible. Ruskin says that all letters are frightful things and to be endured only on occasion, that is to say, in places
where the sense of the inscription is of more importance than external ornament. This is a sweeping statement, fro
The main purpose of letters is the practical one of making thoughts visible. Ruskin says that all letters are frightful things and to be e
ndured only on occasion, that is to say, in places where the sense of the inscription is of more importance than external ornament. Thi
The main purpose of letters is the practical one of making thoughts visible. Ruskin says that all lett
ers are frightful things and to be endured only on occasion, that is to say, in places where the sense

6/7

The main purpose of letters is the practical one of making thoughts visible. Ruskin says that all letters are frightful t
hings and to be endured only on occasion, that is to say, in places where the sense of the inscription is of more impo
rtance than external ornament. This is a sweeping statement, from which we need not suffer unduly; yet it is doubt
ful whether there is art in individual letters. Letters in combination may be satisfying and in a well composed page e
ven beautiful as a whole, but art in letters consists rather in the art of arranging and composing them in a pleasing a
nd appropriate manner. The main purpose of letters is the practical one of making thoughts visible. Ruskin says tha
t all letters are frightful things and to be endured only on occasion, that is to say, in places where the sense of the ins
cription is of more importance than external ornament. This is a sweeping statement, from which we need not suff
er unduly; yet it is doubtful whether there is art in individual letters. Letters in combination may be satisfying and i
n a well composed page even beautiful as a whole, but art in letters consists rather in the art of arranging and comp
osing them in a pleasing and appropriate manner. The main purpose of letters is the practical one of making though
The main purpose of letters is the practical one of making thoughts visible. Ruskin says that all letters are frightful things and to be e
ndured only on occasion, that is to say, in places where the sense of the inscription is of more importance than external ornament. Thi
The main purpose of letters is the practical one of making thoughts visible. Ruskin says that all lett
ers are frightful things and to be endured only on occasion, that is to say, in places where the sense

6/8

The main purpose of letters is the practical one of making thoughts visible. Ruskin says that all letters are frightful t
hings and to be endured only on occasion, that is to say, in places where the sense of the inscription is of more impo
rtance than external ornament. This is a sweeping statement, from which we need not suffer unduly; yet it is doubt
ful whether there is art in individual letters. Letters in combination may be satisfying and in a well composed page e
ven beautiful as a whole, but art in letters consists rather in the art of arranging and composing them in a pleasing a
nd appropriate manner. The main purpose of letters is the practical one of making thoughts visible. Ruskin says tha
t all letters are frightful things and to be endured only on occasion, that is to say, in places where the sense of the ins
cription is of more importance than external ornament. This is a sweeping statement, from which we need not suff
er unduly; yet it is doubtful whether there is art in individual letters. Letters in combination may be satisfying and i
The main purpose of letters is the practical one of making thoughts visible. Ruskin says that all letters are frightful things and to be e
ndured only on occasion, that is to say, in places where the sense of the inscription is of more importance than external ornament. Thi
The main purpose of letters is the practical one of making thoughts visible. Ruskin says that all lett
ers are frightful things and to be endured only on occasion, that is to say, in places where the sense

6/9

The main purpose of letters is the practical one of making thoughts visible. Ruskin says that all letters are frightful t
hings and to be endured only on occasion, that is to say, in places where the sense of the inscription is of more impo
rtance than external ornament. This is a sweeping statement, from which we need not suffer unduly; yet it is doubt
ful whether there is art in individual letters. Letters in combination may be satisfying and in a well composed page e
ven beautiful as a whole, but art in letters consists rather in the art of arranging and composing them in a pleasing a
nd appropriate manner. The main purpose of letters is the practical one of making thoughts visible. Ruskin says tha
t all letters are frightful things and to be endured only on occasion, that is to say, in places where the sense of the ins
cription is of more importance than external ornament. This is a sweeping statement, from which we need not suff
The main purpose of letters is the practical one of making thoughts visible. Ruskin says that all letters are frightful things and to be e
ndured only on occasion, that is to say, in places where the sense of the inscription is of more importance than external ornament. Thi
The main purpose of letters is the practical one of making thoughts visible. Ruskin says that all lett
ers are frightful things and to be endured only on occasion, that is to say, in places where the sense

---

ABCDEFGHIJKLMNOPQRSTUVWXYZ 1234567890 abcdefghijklmnopqrstuvwxyz

ABCDEFGHIJKLMNOPQRSTUVWXYZ 1234567890 abcdefghijklmnopqrstuvwxyz

ABCDEFGHIJKLMNOPQRSTUVWXYZ 1234567890 abcdefghijklmnopqrstuvwxyz

ABCDEFGHIJKLMNOPQRSTUVWXYZ 1234567890 abcdefghijklmnopqrstuvwxyz

7/7

The main purpose of letters is the practical one of making thoughts visible. Ruskin says that all lett
ers are frightful things and to be endured only on occasion, that is to say, in places where the sense
of the inscription is of more importance than external ornament. This is a sweeping statement, fro
m which we need not suffer unduly; yet it is doubtful whether there is art in individual letters. Lett
ers in combination may be satisfying and in a well composed page even beautiful as a whole, but art
in letters consists rather in the art of arranging and composing them in a pleasing and appropriate
manner. The main purpose of letters is the practical one of making thoughts visible. Ruskin says th
at all letters are frightful things and to be endured only on occasion, that is to say, in places where t
he sense of the inscription is of more importance than external ornament. This is a sweeping state
ment, from which we need not suffer unduly; yet it is doubtful whether there is art in individual let
ters. Letters in combination may be satisfying and in a well composed page even beautiful as a whol
The main purpose of letters is the practical one of making thoughts visible. Ruskin says that all letters are frightfu
l things and to be endured only on occasion, that is to say, in places where the sense of the inscription is of more im
The main purpose of letters is the practical one of making thoughts visible. Ruskin sa
ys that all letters are frightful things and to be endured only on occasion, that is to sa

7/8

The main purpose of letters is the practical one of making thoughts visible. Ruskin says that all lett
ers are frightful things and to be endured only on occasion, that is to say, in places where the sense
of the inscription is of more importance than external ornament. This is a sweeping statement, fro
m which we need not suffer unduly; yet it is doubtful whether there is art in individual letters. Lett
ers in combination may be satisfying and in a well composed page even beautiful as a whole, but art
in letters consists rather in the art of arranging and composing them in a pleasing and appropriate
manner. The main purpose of letters is the practical one of making thoughts visible. Ruskin says th
at all letters are frightful things and to be endured only on occasion, that is to say, in places where t
he sense of the inscription is of more importance than external ornament. This is a sweeping state
ment, from which we need not suffer unduly; yet it is doubtful whether there is art in individual let
The main purpose of letters is the practical one of making thoughts visible. Ruskin says that all letters are frightfu
l things and to be endured only on occasion, that is to say, in places where the sense of the inscription is of more im
The main purpose of letters is the practical one of making thoughts visible. Ruskin sa
ys that all letters are frightful things and to be endured only on occasion, that is to sa

7/9

The main purpose of letters is the practical one of making thoughts visible. Ruskin says that all lett
ers are frightful things and to be endured only on occasion, that is to say, in places where the sense
of the inscription is of more importance than external ornament. This is a sweeping statement, fro
m which we need not suffer unduly; yet it is doubtful whether there is art in individual letters. Lett
ers in combination may be satisfying and in a well composed page even beautiful as a whole, but art
in letters consists rather in the art of arranging and composing them in a pleasing and appropriate
manner. The main purpose of letters is the practical one of making thoughts visible. Ruskin says th
at all letters are frightful things and to be endured only on occasion, that is to say, in places where t
he sense of the inscription is of more importance than external ornament. This is a sweeping state
ment, from which we need not suffer unduly; yet it is doubtful whether there is art in individual let
The main purpose of letters is the practical one of making thoughts visible. Ruskin says that all letters are frightfu
l things and to be endured only on occasion, that is to say, in places where the sense of the inscription is of more im
The main purpose of letters is the practical one of making thoughts visible. Ruskin sa
ys that all letters are frightful things and to be endured only on occasion, that is to sa

7/10

The main purpose of letters is the practical one of making thoughts visible. Ruskin says that all lett
ers are frightful things and to be endured only on occasion, that is to say, in places where the sense
of the inscription is of more importance than external ornament. This is a sweeping statement, fro
m which we need not suffer unduly; yet it is doubtful whether there is art in individual letters. Lett
ers in combination may be satisfying and in a well composed page even beautiful as a whole, but art
in letters consists rather in the art of arranging and composing them in a pleasing and appropriate
manner. The main purpose of letters is the practical one of making thoughts visible. Ruskin says th
at all letters are frightful things and to be endured only on occasion, that is to say, in places where t
he sense of the inscription is of more importance than external ornament. This is a sweeping state
The main purpose of letters is the practical one of making thoughts visible. Ruskin says that all letters are frightfu
l things and to be endured only on occasion, that is to say, in places where the sense of the inscription is of more im
The main purpose of letters is the practical one of making thoughts visible. Ruskin sa
ys that all letters are frightful things and to be endured only on occasion, that is to sa

PERPETUA 8 & 9 POINT SET NORMAL

ROMAN, ITALIC, BOLD, BOLD ITALIC

ABCDEFGHIJKLMNOPQRSTUVWXYZ 1234567890 abcdefghijklmnopqrstuvwxyz

ABCDEFGHIJKLMNOPQRSTUVWXYZ 1234567890 abcdefghijklmnopqrstuvwxyz

ABCDEFGHIJKLMNOPQRSTUVWXYZ 1234567890 abcdefghijklmnopqrstuvwxyz

ABCDEFGHIJKLMNOPQRSTUVWXYZ 1234567890 abcdefghijklmnopqrstuvwxyz

8/8

The main purpose of letters is the practical one of making thoughts visible. Ruskin say s that all letters are frightful things and to be endured only on occasion, that is to say, i n places where the sense of the inscription is of more importance than external ornam ent. This is a sweeping statement, from which we need not suffer unduly; yet it is doub tful whether there is art in individual letters. Letters in combination may be satisfying and in a well composed page even beautiful as a whole, but art in letters consists rather in the art of arranging and composing them in a pleasing and appropriate manner. The main purpose of letters is the practical one of making thoughts visible. Ruskin says tha t all letters are frightful things and to be endured only on occasion, that is to say, in pla

The main purpose of letters is the practical one of making thoughts visible. Ruskin says that all lette rs are frightful things and to be endured only on occasion, that is to say, in places where the sense of

The main purpose of letters is the practical one of making thoughts visible. Ruskin says that all letters are frightful things and to be endured only on

8/9

The main purpose of letters is the practical one of making thoughts visible. Ruskin say s that all letters are frightful things and to be endured only on occasion, that is to say, i n places where the sense of the inscription is of more importance than external ornam ent. This is a sweeping statement, from which we need not suffer unduly; yet it is doub tful whether there is art in individual letters. Letters in combination may be satisfying and in a well composed page even beautiful as a whole, but art in letters consists rather in the art of arranging and composing them in a pleasing and appropriate manner. The main purpose of letters is the practical one of making thoughts visible. Ruskin says tha

The main purpose of letters is the practical one of making thoughts visible. Ruskin says that all lette rs are frightful things and to be endured only on occasion, that is to say, in places where the sense of

The main purpose of letters is the practical one of making thoughts visible. Ruskin says that all letters are frightful things and to be endured only on

8/10

The main purpose of letters is the practical one of making thoughts visible. Ruskin say s that all letters are frightful things and to be endured only on occasion, that is to say, i n places where the sense of the inscription is of more importance than external ornam ent. This is a sweeping statement, from which we need not suffer unduly; yet it is doub tful whether there is art in individual letters. Letters in combination may be satisfying and in a well composed page even beautiful as a whole, but art in letters consists rather in the art of arranging and composing them in a pleasing and appropriate manner. The

The main purpose of letters is the practical one of making thoughts visible. Ruskin says that all lette rs are frightful things and to be endured only on occasion, that is to say, in places where the sense of

The main purpose of letters is the practical one of making thoughts visible. Ruskin says that all letters are frightful things and to be endured only on

8/11

The main purpose of letters is the practical one of making thoughts visible. Ruskin say s that all letters are frightful things and to be endured only on occasion, that is to say, i n places where the sense of the inscription is of more importance than external ornam ent. This is a sweeping statement, from which we need not suffer unduly; yet it is doub tful whether there is art in individual letters. Letters in combination may be satisfying and in a well composed page even beautiful as a whole, but art in letters consists rather in the art of arranging and composing them in a pleasing and appropriate manner. The

The main purpose of letters is the practical one of making thoughts visible. Ruskin says that all lette rs are frightful things and to be endured only on occasion, that is to say, in places where the sense of

The main purpose of letters is the practical one of making thoughts visible. Ruskin says that all letters are frightful things and to be endured only on

---

ABCDEFGHIJKLMNOPQRSTUVWXYZ 1234567890 abcdefghijklmnopqrstuvwxyz

ABCDEFGHIJKLMNOPQRSTUVWXYZ 1234567890 abcdefghijklmnopqrstuvwxyz

ABCDEFGHIJKLMNOPQRSTUVWXYZ 1234567890 abcdefghijklmnopqrstuvwxyz

ABCDEFGHIJKLMNOPQRSTUVWXYZ 1234567890 abcdefghijklmnopqrstuvwxyz

9/9

The main purpose of letters is the practical one of making thoughts visible. R uskin says that all letters are frightful things and to be endured only on occasi on, that is to say, in places where the sense of the inscription is of more impor tance than external ornament. This is a sweeping statement, from which we need not suffer unduly; yet it is doubtful whether there is art in individual let ters. Letters in combination may be satisfying and in a well composed page e ven beautiful as a whole, but art in letters consists rather in the art of arrangi ng and composing them in a pleasing and appropriate manner. The main pur

The main purpose of letters is the practical one of making thoughts visible. Ruskin says t hat all letters are frightful things and to be endured only on occasion, that is to say, in pl

The main purpose of letters is the practical one of making thought s visible. Ruskin says that all letters are frightful things and to be e

9/10

The main purpose of letters is the practical one of making thoughts visible. R uskin says that all letters are frightful things and to be endured only on occasi on, that is to say, in places where the sense of the inscription is of more impor tance than external ornament. This is a sweeping statement, from which we need not suffer unduly; yet it is doubtful whether there is art in individual let ters. Letters in combination may be satisfying and in a well composed page e ven beautiful as a whole, but art in letters consists rather in the art of arrangi

The main purpose of letters is the practical one of making thoughts visible. Ruskin says t hat all letters are frightful things and to be endured only on occasion, that is to say, in pl

The main purpose of letters is the practical one of making thought s visible. Ruskin says that all letters are frightful things and to be e

9/11

The main purpose of letters is the practical one of making thoughts visible. R uskin says that all letters are frightful things and to be endured only on occasi on, that is to say, in places where the sense of the inscription is of more impor tance than external ornament. This is a sweeping statement, from which we need not suffer unduly; yet it is doubtful whether there is art in individual let ters. Letters in combination may be satisfying and in a well composed page e ven beautiful as a whole, but art in letters consists rather in the art of arrangi

The main purpose of letters is the practical one of making thoughts visible. Ruskin says t hat all letters are frightful things and to be endured only on occasion, that is to say, in pl

The main purpose of letters is the practical one of making thought s visible. Ruskin says that all letters are frightful things and to be e

9/12

The main purpose of letters is the practical one of making thoughts visible. R uskin says that all letters are frightful things and to be endured only on occasi on, that is to say, in places where the sense of the inscription is of more impor tance than external ornament. This is a sweeping statement, from which we need not suffer unduly; yet it is doubtful whether there is art in individual let ters. Letters in combination may be satisfying and in a well composed page e ven beautiful as a whole, but art in letters consists rather in the art of arrangi

The main purpose of letters is the practical one of making thoughts visible. Ruskin says t hat all letters are frightful things and to be endured only on occasion, that is to say, in pl

The main purpose of letters is the practical one of making thought s visible. Ruskin says that all letters are frightful things and to be e

PERPETUA 10 POINT SET MINUS ½ UNIT

ROMAN, ITALIC, BOLD, BOLD ITALIC

abcdefghijklmnopqrstuvwxyz – 1 UNIT
abcdefghijklmnopqrstuvwxyz – ½ UNIT
abcdefghijklmnopqrstuvwxyz NORMAL

ABCDEFGHIJKLMNOPQRSTUVWXYZ 1234567890 abcdefghijklmnopqrstuvwxyz
ABCDEFGHIJKLMNOPQRSTUVWXYZ 1234567890 abcdefghijklmnopqrstuvwxyz
ABCDEFGHIJKLMNOPQRSTUVWXYZ 1234567890 abcdefghijklmnopqrstuvwxyz
ABCDEFGHIJKLMNOPQRSTUVWXYZ 1234567890 abcdefghijklmnopqrstuvwxyz

10/10

The main purpose of letters is the practical one of making thoughts visibl e. Ruskin says that all letters are frightful things and to be endured only o n occasion, that is to say, in places where the sense of the inscription is of more importance than external ornament. This is a sweeping statement, from which we need not suffer unduly; yet it is doubtful whether there is art in individual letters. Letters in combination may be satisfying and in a well composed page even beautiful as a whole, but art in letters consists r ather in the art of arranging and composing them in a pleasing and appro priate manner. The main purpose of letters is the practical one of making thoughts visible. Ruskin says that all letters are frightful things and to be endured only on occasion, that is to say, in places where the sense of the i nscription is of more importance than external ornament. This is a swee ping statement, from which we need not suffer unduly; yet it is doubtful whether there is art in individual letters. Letters in combination may be s atisfying and in a well composed page even beautiful as a whole, but art i n letters consists rather in the art of arranging and composing them in a p leasing and appropriate manner. The main purpose of letters is the practi cal one of making thoughts visible. Ruskin says that all letters are frightfu l things and to be endured only on occasion, that is to say, in places where the sense of the inscription is of more importance than external orname nt. This is a sweeping statement, from which we need not suffer unduly; yet it is doubtful whether there is art in individual letters. Letters in com

The main purpose of letters is the practical one of making thoughts visible. Ruskin sa ys that all letters are frightful things and to be endured only on occasion, that is to s

The main purpose of letters is the practical one of making tho ughts visible. Ruskin says that all letters are frightful things an

10/11

The main purpose of letters is the practical one of making thoughts visibl e. Ruskin says that all letters are frightful things and to be endured only o n occasion, that is to say, in places where the sense of the inscription is of more importance than external ornament. This is a sweeping statement, from which we need not suffer unduly; yet it is doubtful whether there is art in individual letters. Letters in combination may be satisfying and in a well composed page even beautiful as a whole, but art in letters consists r ather in the art of arranging and composing them in a pleasing and appro priate manner. The main purpose of letters is the practical one of making thoughts visible. Ruskin says that all letters are frightful things and to be endured only on occasion, that is to say, in places where the sense of the i nscription is of more importance than external ornament. This is a swee ping statement, from which we need not suffer unduly; yet it is doubtful whether there is art in individual letters. Letters in combination may be s atisfying and in a well composed page even beautiful as a whole, but art i n letters consists rather in the art of arranging and composing them in a p leasing and appropriate manner. The main purpose of letters is the practi cal one of making thoughts visible. Ruskin says that all letters are frightfu l things and to be endured only on occasion, that is to say, in places where the sense of the inscription is of more importance than external orname

The main purpose of letters is the practical one of making thoughts visible. Ruskin sa ys that all letters are frightful things and to be endured only on occasion, that is to s

The main purpose of letters is the practical one of making tho ughts visible. Ruskin says that all letters are frightful things an

10/12

The main purpose of letters is the practical one of making thoughts visibl e. Ruskin says that all letters are frightful things and to be endured only o n occasion, that is to say, in places where the sense of the inscription is of more importance than external ornament. This is a sweeping statement, from which we need not suffer unduly; yet it is doubtful whether there is art in individual letters. Letters in combination may be satisfying and in a well composed page even beautiful as a whole, but art in letters consists r ather in the art of arranging and composing them in a pleasing and appro priate manner. The main purpose of letters is the practical one of making thoughts visible. Ruskin says that all letters are frightful things and to be endured only on occasion, that is to say, in places where the sense of the i nscription is of more importance than external ornament. This is a swee ping statement, from which we need not suffer unduly; yet it is doubtful whether there is art in individual letters. Letters in combination may be s atisfying and in a well composed page even beautiful as a whole, but art i n letters consists rather in the art of arranging and composing them in a p leasing and appropriate manner. The main purpose of letters is the practi cal one of making thoughts visible. Ruskin says that all letters are frightfu

The main purpose of letters is the practical one of making thoughts visible. Ruskin sa ys that all letters are frightful things and to be endured only on occasion, that is to s

The main purpose of letters is the practical one of making tho ughts visible. Ruskin says that all letters are frightful things an

10/13

The main purpose of letters is the practical one of making thoughts visibl e. Ruskin says that all letters are frightful things and to be endured only o n occasion, that is to say, in places where the sense of the inscription is of more importance than external ornament. This is a sweeping statement, from which we need not suffer unduly; yet it is doubtful whether there is art in individual letters. Letters in combination may be satisfying and in a well composed page even beautiful as a whole, but art in letters consists r ather in the art of arranging and composing them in a pleasing and appro priate manner. The main purpose of letters is the practical one of making thoughts visible. Ruskin says that all letters are frightful things and to be endured only on occasion, that is to say, in places where the sense of the i nscription is of more importance than external ornament. This is a swee ping statement, from which we need not suffer unduly; yet it is doubtful whether there is art in individual letters. Letters in combination may be s atisfying and in a well composed page even beautiful as a whole, but art i n letters consists rather in the art of arranging and composing them in a p leasing and appropriate manner. The main purpose of letters is the practi

The main purpose of letters is the practical one of making thoughts visible. Ruskin sa ys that all letters are frightful things and to be endured only on occasion, that is to s

The main purpose of letters is the practical one of making tho ughts visible. Ruskin says that all letters are frightful things an

PERPETUA 11 POINT SET MINUS ½ UNIT

ROMAN, ITALIC, BOLD, BOLD ITALIC

abcdefghijklmnopqrstuvwxyz – 1 UNIT
abcdefghijklmnopqrstuvwxyz – ½ UNIT
abcdefghijklmnopqrstuvwxyz NORMAL

ABCDEFGHIJKLMNOPQRSTUVWXYZ 1234567890 abcdefghijklmnopqrstuvwxyz
ABCDEFGHIJKLMNOPQRSTUVWXYZ 1234567890 abcdefghijklmnopqrstuvwxyz
ABCDEFGHIJKLMNOPQRSTUVWXYZ 1234567890 abcdefghijklmnopqrstuvwxyz
ABCDEFGHIJKLMNOPQRSTUVWXYZ 1234567890 abcdefghijklmnopqrstuvwxyz

11/11

The main purpose of letters is the practical one of making though ts visible. Ruskin says that all letters are frightful things and to be e ndured only on occasion, that is to say, in places where the sense o f the inscription is of more importance than external ornament. T his is a sweeping statement, from which we need not suffer undul y; yet it is doubtful whether there is art in individual letters. Lette rs in combination may be satisfying and in a well composed page e ven beautiful as a whole, but art in letters consists rather in the art of arranging and composing them in a pleasing and appropriate m anner. The main purpose of letters is the practical one of making t houghts visible. Ruskin says that all letters are frightful things and to be endured only on occasion, that is to say, in places where the s ense of the inscription is of more importance than external ornam ent. This is a sweeping statement, from which we need not suffer unduly; yet it is doubtful whether there is art in individual letters. Letters in combination may be satisfying and in a well composed page even beautiful as a whole, but art in letters consists rather in the art of arranging and composing them in a pleasing and approp riate manner. The main purpose of letters is the practical one of m

The main purpose of letters is the practical one of making thoughts visible. R uskin says that all letters are frightful things and to be endured only on occas

The main purpose of letters is the practical one of makin g thoughts visible. Ruskin says that all letters are frightf

11/12

The main purpose of letters is the practical one of making though ts visible. Ruskin says that all letters are frightful things and to be e ndured only on occasion, that is to say, in places where the sense o f the inscription is of more importance than external ornament. T his is a sweeping statement, from which we need not suffer undul y; yet it is doubtful whether there is art in individual letters. Lette rs in combination may be satisfying and in a well composed page e ven beautiful as a whole, but art in letters consists rather in the art of arranging and composing them in a pleasing and appropriate m anner. The main purpose of letters is the practical one of making t houghts visible. Ruskin says that all letters are frightful things and to be endured only on occasion, that is to say, in places where the s ense of the inscription is of more importance than external ornam ent. This is a sweeping statement, from which we need not suffer unduly; yet it is doubtful whether there is art in individual letters. Letters in combination may be satisfying and in a well composed page even beautiful as a whole, but art in letters consists rather in the art of arranging and composing them in a pleasing and approp

The main purpose of letters is the practical one of making thoughts visible. R uskin says that all letters are frightful things and to be endured only on occas

The main purpose of letters is the practical one of makin g thoughts visible. Ruskin says that all letters are frightf

11/13

The main purpose of letters is the practical one of making though ts visible. Ruskin says that all letters are frightful things and to be e ndured only on occasion, that is to say, in places where the sense o f the inscription is of more importance than external ornament. T his is a sweeping statement, from which we need not suffer undul y; yet it is doubtful whether there is art in individual letters. Lette rs in combination may be satisfying and in a well composed page e ven beautiful as a whole, but art in letters consists rather in the art of arranging and composing them in a pleasing and appropriate m anner. The main purpose of letters is the practical one of making t houghts visible. Ruskin says that all letters are frightful things and to be endured only on occasion, that is to say, in places where the s ense of the inscription is of more importance than external ornam ent. This is a sweeping statement, from which we need not suffer unduly; yet it is doubtful whether there is art in individual letters. Letters in combination may be satisfying and in a well composed page even beautiful as a whole, but art in letters consists rather in

The main purpose of letters is the practical one of making thoughts visible. R uskin says that all letters are frightful things and to be endured only on occas

The main purpose of letters is the practical one of makin g thoughts visible. Ruskin says that all letters are frightf

11/14

The main purpose of letters is the practical one of making though ts visible. Ruskin says that all letters are frightful things and to be e ndured only on occasion, that is to say, in places where the sense o f the inscription is of more importance than external ornament. T his is a sweeping statement, from which we need not suffer undul y; yet it is doubtful whether there is art in individual letters. Lette rs in combination may be satisfying and in a well composed page e ven beautiful as a whole, but art in letters consists rather in the art of arranging and composing them in a pleasing and appropriate m anner. The main purpose of letters is the practical one of making t houghts visible. Ruskin says that all letters are frightful things and to be endured only on occasion, that is to say, in places where the s ense of the inscription is of more importance than external ornam ent. This is a sweeping statement, from which we need not suffer unduly; yet it is doubtful whether there is art in individual letters. Letters in combination may be satisfying and in a well composed

The main purpose of letters is the practical one of making thoughts visible. R uskin says that all letters are frightful things and to be endured only on occas

The main purpose of letters is the practical one of makin g thoughts visible. Ruskin says that all letters are frightf

PERPETUA 12 POINT SET MINUS ½ UNIT

ROMAN, ITALIC, BOLD, BOLD ITALIC

abcdefghijklmnopqrstuvwxyz – 1 UNIT
abcdefghijklmnopqrstuvwxyz – ½ UNIT
abcdefghijklmnopqrstuvwxyz NORMAL

ABCDEFGHIJKLMNOPQRSTUVWXYZ 1234567890 abcdefghijklmnopqrstuvwxyz
ABCDEFGHIJKLMNOPQRSTUVWXYZ 1234567890 abcdefghijklmnopqrstuvwxyz
ABCDEFGHIJKLMNOPQRSTUVWXYZ 1234567890 abcdefghijklmnopqrstuvwxyz
ABCDEFGHIJKLMNOPQRSTUVWXYZ 1234567890 abcdefghijklmnopqrstuvwxyz

12/12

The main purpose of letters is the practical one of making tho ughts visible. Ruskin says that all letters are frightful things an d to be endured only on occasion, that is to say, in places wher e the sense of the inscription is of more importance than exte rnal ornament. This is a sweeping statement, from which we need not suffer unduly; yet it is doubtful whether there is art i n individual letters. Letters in combination may be satisfying and in a well composed page even beautiful as a whole, but ar t in letters consists rather in the art of arranging and composi ng them in a pleasing and appropriate manner. The main pur pose of letters is the practical one of making thoughts visible. Ruskin says that all letters are frightful things and to be endur ed only on occasion, that is to say, in places where the sense of the inscription is of more importance than external ornamen t. This is a sweeping statement, from which we need not suffe
The main purpose of letters is the practical one of making thoughts visib le. Ruskin says that all letters are frightful things and to be endured onl
The main purpose of letters is the practical one of m aking thoughts visible. Ruskin says that all letters ar

12/13

The main purpose of letters is the practical one of making tho ughts visible. Ruskin says that all letters are frightful things an d to be endured only on occasion, that is to say, in places wher e the sense of the inscription is of more importance than exte rnal ornament. This is a sweeping statement, from which we need not suffer unduly; yet it is doubtful whether there is art i n individual letters. Letters in combination may be satisfying and in a well composed page even beautiful as a whole, but ar t in letters consists rather in the art of arranging and composi ng them in a pleasing and appropriate manner. The main pur pose of letters is the practical one of making thoughts visible. Ruskin says that all letters are frightful things and to be endur ed only on occasion, that is to say, in places where the sense of the inscription is of more importance than external ornamen
The main purpose of letters is the practical one of making thoughts visib le. Ruskin says that all letters are frightful things and to be endured onl
The main purpose of letters is the practical one of m aking thoughts visible. Ruskin says that all letters ar

12/14

The main purpose of letters is the practical one of making tho ughts visible. Ruskin says that all letters are frightful things an d to be endured only on occasion, that is to say, in places wher e the sense of the inscription is of more importance than exte rnal ornament. This is a sweeping statement, from which we need not suffer unduly; yet it is doubtful whether there is art i n individual letters. Letters in combination may be satisfying and in a well composed page even beautiful as a whole, but ar t in letters consists rather in the art of arranging and composi ng them in a pleasing and appropriate manner. The main pur pose of letters is the practical one of making thoughts visible. Ruskin says that all letters are frightful things and to be endur ed only on occasion, that is to say, in places where the sense of the inscription is of more importance than external ornamen t. This is a sweeping statement, from which we need not suffe
The main purpose of letters is the practical one of making thoughts visib le. Ruskin says that all letters are frightful things and to be endured onl
The main purpose of letters is the practical one of m aking thoughts visible. Ruskin says that all letters ar

12/15

The main purpose of letters is the practical one of making tho ughts visible. Ruskin says that all letters are frightful things an d to be endured only on occasion, that is to say, in places wher e the sense of the inscription is of more importance than exte rnal ornament. This is a sweeping statement, from which we need not suffer unduly; yet it is doubtful whether there is art i n individual letters. Letters in combination may be satisfying and in a well composed page even beautiful as a whole, but ar t in letters consists rather in the art of arranging and composi ng them in a pleasing and appropriate manner. The main pur pose of letters is the practical one of making thoughts visible. Ruskin says that all letters are frightful things and to be endur ed only on occasion, that is to say, in places where the sense of the inscription is of more importance than external ornamen
The main purpose of letters is the practical one of making thoughts visib le. Ruskin says that all letters are frightful things and to be endured onl
The main purpose of letters is the practical one of m aking thoughts visible. Ruskin says that all letters ar

PERPETUA 14 POINT SET MINUS ½ UNIT

ROMAN, ITALIC, BOLD, BOLD ITALIC

abcdefghijklmnopqrstuvwxyz – 1 UNIT

abcdefghijklmnopqrstuvwxyz – ½ UNIT

abcdefghijklmnopqrstuvwxyz NORMAL

ABCDEFGHIJKLMNOPQRSTUVWXYZ abcdefghijklmnopqrstuvwxyz

ABCDEFGHIJKLMNOPQRSTUVWXYZ abcdefghijklmnopqrstuvwxyz

ABCDEFGHIJKLMNOPQRSTUVWXYZ abcdefghijklmnopqrstuvwxyz

ABCDEFGHIJKLMNOPQRSTUVWXYZ abcdefghijklmnopqrstuvwxyz

14/14

The main purpose of letters is the practical one of m aking thoughts visible. Ruskin says that all letters are frightful things and to be endured only on occasion, that is to say, in places where the sense of the inscrip tion is of more importance than external ornament. This is a sweeping statement, from which we need n ot suffer unduly; yet it is doubtful whether there is a rt in individual letters. Letters in combination may b e satisfying and in a well composed page even beauti ful as a whole, but art in letters consists rather in the art of arranging and composing them in a pleasing a nd appropriate manner. The main purpose of letters is the practical one of making thoughts visible. Rusk

The main purpose of letters is the practical one of making th oughts visible. Ruskin says that all letters are frightful things

The main purpose of letters is the practical o ne of making thoughts visible. Ruskin says t

14/15

The main purpose of letters is the practical one of m aking thoughts visible. Ruskin says that all letters are frightful things and to be endured only on occasion, that is to say, in places where the sense of the inscrip tion is of more importance than external ornament. This is a sweeping statement, from which we need n ot suffer unduly; yet it is doubtful whether there is a rt in individual letters. Letters in combination may b e satisfying and in a well composed page even beauti ful as a whole, but art in letters consists rather in the art of arranging and composing them in a pleasing a nd appropriate manner. The main purpose of letters

The main purpose of letters is the practical one of making th oughts visible. Ruskin says that all letters are frightful things

The main purpose of letters is the practical o ne of making thoughts visible. Ruskin says t

14/16

The main purpose of letters is the practical one of m aking thoughts visible. Ruskin says that all letters are frightful things and to be endured only on occasion, that is to say, in places where the sense of the inscrip tion is of more importance than external ornament. This is a sweeping statement, from which we need n ot suffer unduly; yet it is doubtful whether there is a rt in individual letters. Letters in combination may b e satisfying and in a well composed page even beauti ful as a whole, but art in letters consists rather in the art of arranging and composing them in a pleasing a nd appropriate manner. The main purpose of letters is the practical one of making thoughts visible. Rusk

The main purpose of letters is the practical one of making th oughts visible. Ruskin says that all letters are frightful things

The main purpose of letters is the practical o ne of making thoughts visible. Ruskin says t

14/17

The main purpose of letters is the practical one of m aking thoughts visible. Ruskin says that all letters are frightful things and to be endured only on occasion, that is to say, in places where the sense of the inscrip tion is of more importance than external ornament. This is a sweeping statement, from which we need n ot suffer unduly; yet it is doubtful whether there is a rt in individual letters. Letters in combination may b e satisfying and in a well composed page even beauti ful as a whole, but art in letters consists rather in the art of arranging and composing them in a pleasing a nd appropriate manner. The main purpose of letters

The main purpose of letters is the practical one of making th oughts visible. Ruskin says that all letters are frightful things

The main purpose of letters is the practical o ne of making thoughts visible. Ruskin says t

PLANTIN 6 & 7 POINT SET NORMAL

ROMAN, ITALIC, BOLD, BOLD ITALIC

ABCDEFGHIJKLMNOPQRSTUVWXYZ 1234567890 abcdefghijklmnopqrstuvwxyz

ABCDEFGHIJKLMNOPQRSTUVWXYZ 1234567890 abcdefghijklmnopqrstuvwxyz

ABCDEFGHIJKLMNOPQRSTUVWXYZ 1234567890 abcdefghijklmnopqrstuvwxyz

ABCDEFGHIJKLMNOPQRSTUVWXYZ 1234567890 abcdefghijklmnopqrstuvwxyz

6/6

The main purpose of letters is the practical one of making thoughts visible. Ruskin says th at all letters are frightful things and to be endured only on occasion, that is to say, in places where the sense of the inscription is of more importance than external ornament. This is a sweeping statement, from which we need not suffer unduly; yet it is doubtful whether ther e is art in individual letters. Letters in combination may be satisfying and in a well compos ed page even beautiful as a whole, but art in letters consists rather in the art of arranging an d composing them in a pleasing and appropriate manner. The main purpose of letters is the practical one of making thoughts visible. Ruskin says that all letters are frightful things an d to be endured only on occasion, that is to say, in places where the sense of the inscription is of more importance than external ornament. This is a sweeping statement, from which we need not suffer unduly; yet it is doubtful whether there is art in individual letters. Lette rs in combination may be satisfying and in a well composed page even beautiful as a whol e, but art in letters consists rather in the art of arranging and composing them in a pleasing

The main purpose of letters is the practical one of making thoughts visible. Ruskin says that all letters are frightful things and to be endured only on occasion, that is to say, in places where

The main purpose of letters is the practical one of making thoughts visible. Ruskin says t hat all letters are frightful things and to be endured only on occasion, that is to say, in plac

6/7

The main purpose of letters is the practical one of making thoughts visible. Ruskin says th at all letters are frightful things and to be endured only on occasion, that is to say, in places where the sense of the inscription is of more importance than external ornament. This is a sweeping statement, from which we need not suffer unduly; yet it is doubtful whether ther e is art in individual letters. Letters in combination may be satisfying and in a well compos ed page even beautiful as a whole, but art in letters consists rather in the art of arranging an d composing them in a pleasing and appropriate manner. The main purpose of letters is the practical one of making thoughts visible. Ruskin says that all letters are frightful things an d to be endured only on occasion, that is to say, in places where the sense of the inscription is of more importance than external ornament. This is a sweeping statement, from which we need not suffer unduly; yet it is doubtful whether there is art in individual letters. Lette

The main purpose of letters is the practical one of making thoughts visible. Ruskin says that all letters are frightful things and to be endured only on occasion, that is to say, in places where

The main purpose of letters is the practical one of making thoughts visible. Ruskin says t hat all letters are frightful things and to be endured only on occasion, that is to say, in plac

6/8

The main purpose of letters is the practical one of making thoughts visible. Ruskin says th at all letters are frightful things and to be endured only on occasion, that is to say, in places where the sense of the inscription is of more importance than external ornament. This is a sweeping statement, from which we need not suffer unduly; yet it is doubtful whether ther e is art in individual letters. Letters in combination may be satisfying and in a well compos ed page even beautiful as a whole, but art in letters consists rather in the art of arranging an d composing them in a pleasing and appropriate manner. The main purpose of letters is the practical one of making thoughts visible. Ruskin says that all letters are frightful things an d to be endured only on occasion, that is to say, in places where the sense of the inscription

The main purpose of letters is the practical one of making thoughts visible. Ruskin says that all letters are frightful things and to be endured only on occasion, that is to say, in places where

The main purpose of letters is the practical one of making thoughts visible. Ruskin says t hat all letters are frightful things and to be endured only on occasion, that is to say, in plac

6/9

The main purpose of letters is the practical one of making thoughts visible. Ruskin says th at all letters are frightful things and to be endured only on occasion, that is to say, in places where the sense of the inscription is of more importance than external ornament. This is a sweeping statement, from which we need not suffer unduly; yet it is doubtful whether ther e is art in individual letters. Letters in combination may be satisfying and in a well compos ed page even beautiful as a whole, but art in letters consists rather in the art of arranging an d composing them in a pleasing and appropriate manner. The main purpose of letters is the practical one of making thoughts visible. Ruskin says that all letters are frightful things an

The main purpose of letters is the practical one of making thoughts visible. Ruskin says that all letters are frightful things and to be endured only on occasion, that is to say, in places where

The main purpose of letters is the practical one of making thoughts visible. Ruskin says t hat all letters are frightful things and to be endured only on occasion, that is to say, in plac

---

ABCDEFGHIJKLMNOPQRSTUVWXYZ 1234567890 abcdefghijklmnopqrstuvwxyz

ABCDEFGHIJKLMNOPQRSTUVWXYZ 1234567890 abcdefghijklmnopqrstuvwxyz

ABCDEFGHIJKLMNOPQRSTUVWXYZ 1234567890 abcdefghijklmnopqrstuvwxyz

ABCDEFGHIJKLMNOPQRSTUVWXYZ 1234567890 abcdefghijklmnopqrstuvwxyz

7/7

The main purpose of letters is the practical one of making thoughts visible. R uskin says that all letters are frightful things and to be endured only on occasi on, that is to say, in places where the sense of the inscription is of more import ance than external ornament. This is a sweeping statement, from which we n eed not suffer unduly; yet it is doubtful whether there is art in individual letter s. Letters in combination may be satisfying and in a well composed page even beautiful as a whole, but art in letters consists rather in the art of arranging an d composing them in a pleasing and appropriate manner. The main purpose o f letters is the practical one of making thoughts visible. Ruskin says that all let ters are frightful things and to be endured only on occasion, that is to say, in pl aces where the sense of the inscription is of more importance than external or

The main purpose of letters is the practical one of making thoughts visible. Rusk in says that all letters are frightful things and to be endured only on occasion, tha

The main purpose of letters is the practical one of making thoughts visible. Ruskin says that all letters are frightful things and to be endured only on occ

7/8

The main purpose of letters is the practical one of making thoughts visible. R uskin says that all letters are frightful things and to be endured only on occasi on, that is to say, in places where the sense of the inscription is of more import ance than external ornament. This is a sweeping statement, from which we n eed not suffer unduly; yet it is doubtful whether there is art in individual letter s. Letters in combination may be satisfying and in a well composed page even beautiful as a whole, but art in letters consists rather in the art of arranging an d composing them in a pleasing and appropriate manner. The main purpose o f letters is the practical one of making thoughts visible. Ruskin says that all let ters are frightful things and to be endured only on occasion, that is to say, in pl

The main purpose of letters is the practical one of making thoughts visible. Rusk in says that all letters are frightful things and to be endured only on occasion, tha

The main purpose of letters is the practical one of making thoughts visible. Ruskin says that all letters are frightful things and to be endured only on occ

7/9

The main purpose of letters is the practical one of making thoughts visible. R uskin says that all letters are frightful things and to be endured only on occasi on, that is to say, in places where the sense of the inscription is of more import ance than external ornament. This is a sweeping statement, from which we n eed not suffer unduly; yet it is doubtful whether there is art in individual letter s. Letters in combination may be satisfying and in a well composed page even beautiful as a whole, but art in letters consists rather in the art of arranging an d composing them in a pleasing and appropriate manner. The main purpose o f letters is the practical one of making thoughts visible. Ruskin says that all let ters are frightful things and to be endured only on occasion, that is to say, in pl

The main purpose of letters is the practical one of making thoughts visible. Rusk in says that all letters are frightful things and to be endured only on occasion, tha

The main purpose of letters is the practical one of making thoughts visible. Ruskin says that all letters are frightful things and to be endured only on occ

7/10

The main purpose of letters is the practical one of making thoughts visible. R uskin says that all letters are frightful things and to be endured only on occasi on, that is to say, in places where the sense of the inscription is of more import ance than external ornament. This is a sweeping statement, from which we n eed not suffer unduly; yet it is doubtful whether there is art in individual letter s. Letters in combination may be satisfying and in a well composed page even beautiful as a whole, but art in letters consists rather in the art of arranging an d composing them in a pleasing and appropriate manner. The main purpose o f letters is the practical one of making thoughts visible. Ruskin says that all let

The main purpose of letters is the practical one of making thoughts visible. Rusk in says that all letters are frightful things and to be endured only on occasion, tha

The main purpose of letters is the practical one of making thoughts visible. Ruskin says that all letters are frightful things and to be endured only on occ

PLANTIN 8 & 9 POINT SET NORMAL

ROMAN, ITALIC, BOLD, BOLD ITALIC

ABCDEFGHIJKLMNOPQRSTUVWXYZ 1234567890 abcdefghijklmnopqrstuvwxyz

ABCDEFGHIJKLMNOPQRSTUVWXYZ 1234567890 abcdefghijklmnopqrstuvwxyz

ABCDEFGHIJKLMNOPQRSTUVWXYZ 1234567890 abcdefghijklmnopqrstuvwxyz

ABCDEFGHIJKLMNOPQRSTUVWXYZ 1234567890 abcdefghijklmnopqrstuvwxyz

8/8

The main purpose of letters is the practical one of making thoughts visible. Ruskin says that all letters are frightful things and to be end ured only on occasion, that is to say, in places where the sense of the inscription is of more importance than external ornament. This is a sweeping statement, from which we need not suffer unduly; yet it is doubtful whether there is art in individual letters. Letters in combin ation may be satisfying and in a well composed page even beautiful as a whole, but art in letters consists rather in the art of arranging an d composing them in a pleasing and appropriate manner. The main
The main purpose of letters is the practical one of making thoughts vis ible. Ruskin says that all letters are frightful things and to be endured
The main purpose of letters is the practical one of making thoughts visible. Ruskin says that all letters are frightful things and to be en

8/9

The main purpose of letters is the practical one of making thoughts visible. Ruskin says that all letters are frightful things and to be end ured only on occasion, that is to say, in places where the sense of the inscription is of more importance than external ornament. This is a sweeping statement, from which we need not suffer unduly; yet it is doubtful whether there is art in individual letters. Letters in combin ation may be satisfying and in a well composed page even beautiful as a whole, but art in letters consists rather in the art of arranging an
The main purpose of letters is the practical one of making thoughts vis ible. Ruskin says that all letters are frightful things and to be endured
The main purpose of letters is the practical one of making thoughts visible. Ruskin says that all letters are frightful things and to be en

8/10

The main purpose of letters is the practical one of making thoughts visible. Ruskin says that all letters are frightful things and to be end ured only on occasion, that is to say, in places where the sense of the inscription is of more importance than external ornament. This is a sweeping statement, from which we need not suffer unduly; yet it is doubtful whether there is art in individual letters. Letters in combin ation may be satisfying and in a well composed page even beautiful
The main purpose of letters is the practical one of making thoughts vis ible. Ruskin says that all letters are frightful things and to be endured
The main purpose of letters is the practical one of making thoughts visible. Ruskin says that all letters are frightful things and to be en

8/11

The main purpose of letters is the practical one of making thoughts visible. Ruskin says that all letters are frightful things and to be end ured only on occasion, that is to say, in places where the sense of the inscription is of more importance than external ornament. This is a sweeping statement, from which we need not suffer unduly; yet it is doubtful whether there is art in individual letters. Letters in combin ation may be satisfying and in a well composed page even beautiful
The main purpose of letters is the practical one of making thoughts vis ible. Ruskin says that all letters are frightful things and to be endured
The main purpose of letters is the practical one of making thoughts visible. Ruskin says that all letters are frightful things and to be en

---

ABCDEFGHIJKLMNOPQRSTUVWXYZ 1234567890 abcdefghijklmnopqrstuvwxyz

ABCDEFGHIJKLMNOPQRSTUVWXYZ 1234567890 abcdefghijklmnopqrstuvwxyz

ABCDEFGHIJKLMNOPQRSTUVWXYZ 1234567890 abcdefghijklmnopqrstuvwxyz

ABCDEFGHIJKLMNOPQRSTUVWXYZ 1234567890 abcdefghijklmnopqrstuvwxyz

9/9

The main purpose of letters is the practical one of making th oughts visible. Ruskin says that all letters are frightful thing s and to be endured only on occasion, that is to say, in places where the sense of the inscription is of more importance tha n external ornament. This is a sweeping statement, from wh ich we need not suffer unduly; yet it is doubtful whether ther e is art in individual letters. Letters in combination may be s atisfying and in a well composed page even beautiful as a wh
The main purpose of letters is the practical one of making thou ghts vsible. Ruskin says that all letters are frightful things an
The main purpose of letters is the practical one of making t houghts visible. Ruskin says that all letters are frightful thi

9/10

The main purpose of letters is the practical one of making th oughts visible. Ruskin says that all letters are frightful thing s and to be endured only on occasion, that is to say, in places where the sense of the inscription is of more importance tha n external ornament. This is a sweeping statement, from wh ich we need not suffer unduly; yet it is doubtful whether ther e is art in individual letters. Letters in combination may be s
The main purpose of letters is the practical one of making thou ghts vsible. Ruskin says that all letters are frightful things an
The main purpose of letters is the practical one of making t houghts visible. Ruskin says that all letters are frightful thi

9/11

The main purpose of letters is the practical one of making th oughts visible. Ruskin says that all letters are frightful thing s and to be endured only on occasion, that is to say, in places where the sense of the inscription is of more importance tha n external ornament. This is a sweeping statement, from wh ich we need not suffer unduly; yet it is doubtful whether ther e is art in individual letters. Letters in combination may be s
The main purpose of letters is the practical one of making thou ghts vsible. Ruskin says that all letters are frightful things an
The main purpose of letters is the practical one of making t houghts visible. Ruskin says that all letters are frightful thi

9/12

The main purpose of letters is the practical one of making th oughts visible. Ruskin says that all letters are frightful thing s and to be endured only on occasion, that is to say, in places where the sense of the inscription is of more importance tha n external ornament. This is a sweeping statement, from wh ich we need not suffer unduly; yet it is doubtful whether ther e is art in individual letters. Letters in combination may be s
The main purpose of letters is the practical one of making thou ghts vsible. Ruskin says that all letters are frightful things an
The main purpose of letters is the practical one of making t houghts visible. Ruskin says that all letters are frightful thi

PLANTIN 10 POINT SET MINUS ½ UNIT

ROMAN, ITALIC, BOLD, BOLD ITALIC

abcdefghijklmnopqrstuvwxyz – 1 UNIT
abcdefghijklmnopqrstuvwxyz – ½ UNIT
abcdefghijklmnopqrstuvwxyz NORMAL

ABCDEFGHIJKLMNOPQRSTUVWXYZ 1234567890 abcdefghijklmnopqrstuvwxyz
ABCDEFGHIJKLMNOPQRSTUVWXYZ 1234567890 abcdefghijklmnopqrstuvwxyz
ABCDEFGHIJKLMNOPQRSTUVWXYZ 1234567890 abcdefghijklmnopqrstuvwxyz
ABCDEFGHIJKLMNOPQRSTUVWXYZ 1234567890 abcdefghijklmnopqrstuvwxyz

10/10

The main purpose of letters is the practical one of mak
ing thoughts visible. Ruskin says that all letters are fri
ghtful things and to be endured only on occasion, that
is to say, in places where the sense of the inscription is
of more importance than external ornament. This is a
sweeping statement, from which we need not suffer u
nduly; yet it is doubtful whether there is art in individ
ual letters. Letters in combination may be satisfying a
nd in a well composed page even beautiful as a whole,
but art in letters consists rather in the art of arranging
and composing them in a pleasing and appropriate ma
nner. The main purpose of letters is the practical one o
f making thoughts visible. Ruskin says that all letters
are frightful things and to be endured only on occasi
on, that is to say, in places where the sense of the inscri
ption is of more importance than external ornament.
This is a sweeping statement, from which we need no
t suffer unduly; yet it is doubtful whether there is art
in individual letters. Letters in combination may be sa
tisfying and in a well composed page even beautiful as
a whole, but art in letters consists rather in the art of ar
ranging and composing them in a pleasing and approp
The main purpose of letters is the practical one of making t
houghts visible. Ruskin says that all letters are frightful th
The main purpose of letters is the practical one of maki
ng thoughts visible. Ruskin says that all letters are frigh

10/11

The main purpose of letters is the practical one of mak
ing thoughts visible. Ruskin says that all letters are fri
ghtful things and to be endured only on occasion, that
is to say, in places where the sense of the inscription is
of more importance than external ornament. This is a
sweeping statement, from which we need not suffer u
nduly; yet it is doubtful whether there is art in individ
ual letters. Letters in combination may be satisfying a
nd in a well composed page even beautiful as a whole,
but art in letters consists rather in the art of arranging
and composing them in a pleasing and appropriate ma
nner. The main purpose of letters is the practical one o
f making thoughts visible. Ruskin says that all letters
are frightful things and to be endured only on occasi
on, that is to say, in places where the sense of the inscri
ption is of more importance than external ornament.
This is a sweeping statement, from which we need no
t suffer unduly; yet it is doubtful whether there is art
in individual letters. Letters in combination may be sa
tisfying and in a well composed page even beautiful as
The main purpose of letters is the practical one of making t
houghts visible. Ruskin says that all letters are frightful th
The main purpose of letters is the practical one of maki
ng thoughts visible. Ruskin says that all letters are frigh

10/12

The main purpose of letters is the practical one of mak
ing thoughts visible. Ruskin says that all letters are fri
ghtful things and to be endured only on occasion, that
is to say, in places where the sense of the inscription is
of more importance than external ornament. This is a
sweeping statement, from which we need not suffer u
nduly; yet it is doubtful whether there is art in individ
ual letters. Letters in combination may be satisfying a
nd in a well composed page even beautiful as a whole,
but art in letters consists rather in the art of arranging
and composing them in a pleasing and appropriate ma
nner. The main purpose of letters is the practical one o
f making thoughts visible. Ruskin says that all letters
are frightful things and to be endured only on occasi
on, that is to say, in places where the sense of the inscri
ption is of more importance than external ornament.
This is a sweeping statement, from which we need no
t suffer unduly; yet it is doubtful whether there is art
The main purpose of letters is the practical one of making t
houghts visible. Ruskin says that all letters are frightful th
The main purpose of letters is the practical one of maki
ng thoughts visible. Ruskin says that all letters are frigh

10/13

The main purpose of letters is the practical one of mak
ing thoughts visible. Ruskin says that all letters are fri
ghtful things and to be endured only on occasion, that
is to say, in places where the sense of the inscription is
of more importance than external ornament. This is a
sweeping statement, from which we need not suffer u
nduly; yet it is doubtful whether there is art in individ
ual letters. Letters in combination may be satisfying a
nd in a well composed page even beautiful as a whole,
but art in letters consists rather in the art of arranging
and composing them in a pleasing and appropriate ma
nner. The main purpose of letters is the practical one o
f making thoughts visible. Ruskin says that all letters
are frightful things and to be endured only on occasi
on, that is to say, in places where the sense of the inscri
ption is of more importance than external ornament.
This is a sweeping statement, from which we need no
The main purpose of letters is the practical one of making t
houghts visible. Ruskin says that all letters are frightful th
The main purpose of letters is the practical one of maki
ng thoughts visible. Ruskin says that all letters are frigh

PLANTIN 11 POINT SET MINUS ½ UNIT

ROMAN, ITALIC, BOLD, BOLD ITALIC

abcdefghijklmnopqrstuvwxyz – 1 UNIT
abcdefghijklmnopqrstuvwxyz – ½ UNIT
abcdefghijklmnopqrstuvwxyz NORMAL

ABCDEFGHIJKLMNOPQRSTUVWXYZ 1234567890 abcdefghijklmnopqrstuvwxyz
ABCDEFGHIJKLMNOPQRSTUVWXYZ 1234567890 abcdefghijklmnopqrstuvwxyz
ABCDEFGHIJKLMNOPQRSTUVWXYZ 1234567890 abcdefghijklmnopqrstuvwxyz
ABCDEFGHIJKLMNOPQRSTUVWXYZ 1234567890 abcdefghijklmnopqrstuvwxyz

11/11

The main purpose of letters is the practical one of making thoughts visible. Ruskin says that all lett ers are frightful things and to be endured only on occasion, that is to say, in places where the sense of the inscription is of more importance than exte rnal ornament. This is a sweeping statement, fro m which we need not suffer unduly; yet it is doub tful whether there is art in individual letters. Lett ers in combination may be satisfying and in a wel l composed page even beautiful as a whole, but ar t in letters consists rather in the art of arranging a nd composing them in a pleasing and appropriate manner. The main purpose of letters is the practi cal one of making thoughts visible. Ruskin says t hat all letters are frightful things and to be endure d only on occasion, that is to say, in places where the sense of the inscription is of more importance than external ornament. This is a sweeping state ment, from which we need not suffer unduly; yet
The main purpose of letters is the practical one of ma king thoughts visible. Ruskin says that all letters are
The main purpose of letters is the practical one of making thoughts visible. Ruskin says that all letter

11/12

The main purpose of letters is the practical one of making thoughts visible. Ruskin says that all lett ers are frightful things and to be endured only on occasion, that is to say, in places where the sense of the inscription is of more importance than exte rnal ornament. This is a sweeping statement, fro m which we need not suffer unduly; yet it is doub tful whether there is art in individual letters. Lett ers in combination may be satisfying and in a wel l composed page even beautiful as a whole, but ar t in letters consists rather in the art of arranging a nd composing them in a pleasing and appropriate manner. The main purpose of letters is the practi cal one of making thoughts visible. Ruskin says t hat all letters are frightful things and to be endure d only on occasion, that is to say, in places where the sense of the inscription is of more importance than external ornament. This is a sweeping state
The main purpose of letters is the practical one of ma king thoughts visible. Ruskin says that all letters are
The main purpose of letters is the practical one of making thoughts visible. Ruskin says that all letter

11/13

The main purpose of letters is the practical one of making thoughts visible. Ruskin says that all lett ers are frightful things and to be endured only on occasion, that is to say, in places where the sense of the inscription is of more importance than exte rnal ornament. This is a sweeping statement, fro m which we need not suffer unduly; yet it is doub tful whether there is art in individual letters. Lett ers in combination may be satisfying and in a wel l composed page even beautiful as a whole, but ar t in letters consists rather in the art of arranging a nd composing them in a pleasing and appropriate manner. The main purpose of letters is the practi cal one of making thoughts visible. Ruskin says t hat all letters are frightful things and to be endure d only on occasion, that is to say, in places where the sense of the inscription is of more importance
The main purpose of letters is the practical one of ma king thoughts visible. Ruskin says that all letters are
The main purpose of letters is the practical one of making thoughts visible. Ruskin says that all letter

11/14

The main purpose of letters is the practical one of making thoughts visible. Ruskin says that all lett ers are frightful things and to be endured only on occasion, that is to say, in places where the sense of the inscription is of more importance than exte rnal ornament. This is a sweeping statement, fro m which we need not suffer unduly; yet it is doub tful whether there is art in individual letters. Lett ers in combination may be satisfying and in a wel l composed page even beautiful as a whole, but ar t in letters consists rather in the art of arranging a nd composing them in a pleasing and appropriate manner. The main purpose of letters is the practi cal one of making thoughts visible. Ruskin says t hat all letters are frightful things and to be endure d only on occasion, that is to say, in places where
The main purpose of letters is the practical one of ma king thoughts visible. Ruskin says that all letters are
The main purpose of letters is the practical one of making thoughts visible. Ruskin says that all letter

PLANTIN 12 POINT SET MINUS ½ UNIT

ROMAN, ITALIC, BOLD, BOLD ITALIC

abcdefghijklmnopqrstuvwxyz – 1 UNIT
abcdefghijklmnopqrstuvwxyz – ½ UNIT
abcdefghijklmnopqrstuvwxyz NORMAL

ABCDEFGHIJKLMNOPQRSTUVWXYZ 1234567890 abcdefghijklmnopqrstuvwxyz
ABCDEFGHIJKLMNOPQRSTUVWXYZ 1234567890 abcdefghijklmnopqrstuvwxyz
ABCDEFGHIJKLMNOPQRSTUVWXYZ 1234567890 abcdefghijklmnopqrstuvwxyz
ABCDEFGHIJKLMNOPQRSTUVWXYZ 1234567890 abcdefghijklmnopqrstuvwxyz

12/12

The main purpose of letters is the practical on e of making thoughts visible. Ruskin says th at all letters are frightful things and to be end ured only on occasion, that is to say, in places where the sense of the inscription is of more importance than external ornament. This is a sweeping statement, from which we need n ot suffer unduly; yet it is doubtful whether th ere is art in individual letters. Letters in com bination may be satisfying and in a well comp osed page even beautiful as a whole, but art in letters consists rather in the art of arranging a nd composing them in a pleasing and approp riate manner. The main purpose of letters is t he practical one of making thoughts visible.
The main purpose of letters is the practical one of making thoughts visible. Ruskin says that all lett
The main purpose of letters is the practical one of making thoughts visible. Ruskin says that all

12/13

The main purpose of letters is the practical on e of making thoughts visible. Ruskin says th at all letters are frightful things and to be end ured only on occasion, that is to say, in places where the sense of the inscription is of more importance than external ornament. This is a sweeping statement, from which we need n ot suffer unduly; yet it is doubtful whether th ere is art in individual letters. Letters in com bination may be satisfying and in a well comp osed page even beautiful as a whole, but art in letters consists rather in the art of arranging a nd composing them in a pleasing and approp riate manner. The main purpose of letters is t
The main purpose of letters is the practical one of making thoughts visible. Ruskin says that all lett
The main purpose of letters is the practical one of making thoughts visible. Ruskin says that all

12/14

The main purpose of letters is the practical on e of making thoughts visible. Ruskin says th at all letters are frightful things and to be end ured only on occasion, that is to say, in places where the sense of the inscription is of more importance than external ornament. This is a sweeping statement, from which we need n ot suffer unduly; yet it is doubtful whether th ere is art in individual letters. Letters in com bination may be satisfying and in a well comp osed page even beautiful as a whole, but art in letters consists rather in the art of arranging a nd composing them in a pleasing and approp riate manner. The main purpose of letters is t he practical one of making thoughts visible.
The main purpose of letters is the practical one of making thoughts visible. Ruskin says that all lett
The main purpose of letters is the practical one of making thoughts visible. Ruskin says that all

12/15

The main purpose of letters is the practical on e of making thoughts visible. Ruskin says th at all letters are frightful things and to be end ured only on occasion, that is to say, in places where the sense of the inscription is of more importance than external ornament. This is a sweeping statement, from which we need n ot suffer unduly; yet it is doubtful whether th ere is art in individual letters. Letters in com bination may be satisfying and in a well comp osed page even beautiful as a whole, but art in letters consists rather in the art of arranging a nd composing them in a pleasing and approp riate manner. The main purpose of letters is t
The main purpose of letters is the practical one of making thoughts visible. Ruskin says that all lett
The main purpose of letters is the practical one of making thoughts visible. Ruskin says that all

PLANTIN 14 POINT SET MINUS ½ UNIT

ROMAN, ITALIC, BOLD, BOLD ITALIC

abcdefghijklmnopqrstuvwxyz – 1 UNIT
abcdefghijklmnopqrstuvwxyz – ½ UNIT
abcdefghijklmnopqrstuvwxyz NORMAL

ABCDEFGHIJKLMNOPQRSTUVWXYZ abcdefghijklmnopqrstuvwxyz
ABCDEFGHIJKLMNOPQRSTUVWXYZ abcdefghijklmnopqrstuvwxyz
ABCDEFGHIJKLMNOPQRSTUVWXYZ abcdefghijklmnopqrstuvwxyz
ABCDEFGHIJKLMNOPQRSTUVWXYZ abcdefghijklmnopqrstuvwxyz

14/14

The main purpose of letters is the prac tical one of making thoughts visible. R uskin says that all letters are frightful t hings and to be endured only on occasi on, that is to say, in places where the se nse of the inscription is of more import ance than external ornament. This is a sweeping statement, from which we n eed not suffer unduly; yet it is doubtful whether there is art in individual letter s. Letters in combination may be satisf ying and in a well composed page even beautiful as a whole, but art in letters c
The main purpose of letters is the practica l one of making thoughts visible. Ruskin s
The main purpose of letters is the practi cal one of making thoughts visible. Rus

14/15

The main purpose of letters is the prac tical one of making thoughts visible. R uskin says that all letters are frightful t hings and to be endured only on occasi on, that is to say, in places where the se nse of the inscription is of more import ance than external ornament. This is a sweeping statement, from which we n eed not suffer unduly; yet it is doubtful whether there is art in individual letter s. Letters in combination may be satisf ying and in a well composed page even
The main purpose of letters is the practica l one of making thoughts visible. Ruskin s
The main purpose of letters is the practi cal one of making thoughts visible. Rus

14/16

The main purpose of letters is the prac tical one of making thoughts visible. R uskin says that all letters are frightful t hings and to be endured only on occasi on, that is to say, in places where the se nse of the inscription is of more import ance than external ornament. This is a sweeping statement, from which we n eed not suffer unduly; yet it is doubtful whether there is art in individual letter s. Letters in combination may be satisf ying and in a well composed page even beautiful as a whole, but art in letters c
The main purpose of letters is the practica l one of making thoughts visible. Ruskin s
The main purpose of letters is the practi cal one of making thoughts visible. Rus

14/17

The main purpose of letters is the prac tical one of making thoughts visible. R uskin says that all letters are frightful t hings and to be endured only on occasi on, that is to say, in places where the se nse of the inscription is of more import ance than external ornament. This is a sweeping statement, from which we n eed not suffer unduly; yet it is doubtful whether there is art in individual letter s. Letters in combination may be satisf ying and in a well composed page even
The main purpose of letters is the practica l one of making thoughts visible. Ruskin s
The main purpose of letters is the practi cal one of making thoughts visible. Rus

PRIMER 6 & 7 POINT SET NORMAL

ROMAN, ITALIC

ABCDEFGHIJKLMNOPQRSTUVWXYZ 1234567890 abcdefghijklmnopqrstuvwxyz

ABCDEFGHIJKLMNOPQRSTUVWXYZ 1234567890 abcdefghijklmnopqrstuvwxyz

6/6

The main purpose of letters is the practical one of making thoughts visible. Ruskin says that all letters are frightful things and to be endured only on occasion, that is to say, in places whe re the sense of the inscription is of more importance than external ornament. This is a sweepi ng statement, from which we need not suffer unduly; yet it is doubtful whether there is art in individual letters. Letters in combination may be satisfying and in a well composed page eve n beautiful as a whole, but art in letters consists rather in the art of arranging and composing them in a pleasing and appropriate manner. The main purpose of letters is the practical one o f making thoughts visible. Ruskin says that all letters are frightful things and to be endured o nly on occasion, that is to say, in places where the sense of the inscription is of more importan ce than external ornament. This is a sweeping statement, from which we need not suffer un duly; yet it is doubtful whether there is art in individual letters. Letters in combination may b e satisfying and in a well composed page even beautiful as a whole, but art in letters consists r ather in the art of arranging and composing them in a pleasing and appropriate manner. The main purpose of letters is the practical one of making thoughts visible. Ruskin says that all le tters are frightful things and to be endured only on occasion, that is to say, in places where th *The main purpose of letters is the practical one of making thoughts visible. Ruskin says that all letters are frightful things and to be endured only on occasion, that is to say, in places wh*

6/7

The main purpose of letters is the practical one of making thoughts visible. Ruskin says that all letters are frightful things and to be endured only on occasion, that is to say, in places whe re the sense of the inscription is of more importance than external ornament. This is a sweepi ng statement, from which we need not suffer unduly; yet it is doubtful whether there is art in individual letters. Letters in combination may be satisfying and in a well composed page eve n beautiful as a whole, but art in letters consists rather in the art of arranging and composing them in a pleasing and appropriate manner. The main purpose of letters is the practical one o f making thoughts visible. Ruskin says that all letters are frightful things and to be endured o nly on occasion, that is to say, in places where the sense of the inscription is of more importan ce than external ornament. This is a sweeping statement, from which we need not suffer un duly; yet it is doubtful whether there is art in individual letters. Letters in combination may b e satisfying and in a well composed page even beautiful as a whole, but art in letters consists r ather in the art of arranging and composing them in a pleasing and appropriate manner. The *The main purpose of letters is the practical one of making thoughts visible. Ruskin says that all letters are frightful things and to be endured only on occasion, that is to say, in places wh*

6/8

The main purpose of letters is the practical one of making thoughts visible. Ruskin says that all letters are frightful things and to be endured only on occasion, that is to say, in places whe re the sense of the inscription is of more importance than external ornament. This is a sweepi ng statement, from which we need not suffer unduly; yet it is doubtful whether there is art in individual letters. Letters in combination may be satisfying and in a well composed page eve n beautiful as a whole, but art in letters consists rather in the art of arranging and composing them in a pleasing and appropriate manner. The main purpose of letters is the practical one o f making thoughts visible. Ruskin says that all letters are frightful things and to be endured o nly on occasion, that is to say, in places where the sense of the inscription is of more importan ce than external ornament. This is a sweeping statement, from which we need not suffer un duly; yet it is doubtful whether there is art in individual letters. Letters in combination may b *The main purpose of letters is the practical one of making thoughts visible. Ruskin says that all letters are frightful things and to be endured only on occasion, that is to say, in places wh*

6/9

The main purpose of letters is the practical one of making thoughts visible. Ruskin says that all letters are frightful things and to be endured only on occasion, that is to say, in places whe re the sense of the inscription is of more importance than external ornament. This is a sweepi ng statement, from which we need not suffer unduly; yet it is doubtful whether there is art in individual letters. Letters in combination may be satisfying and in a well composed page eve n beautiful as a whole, but art in letters consists rather in the art of arranging and composing them in a pleasing and appropriate manner. The main purpose of letters is the practical one o f making thoughts visible. Ruskin says that all letters are frightful things and to be endured o nly on occasion, that is to say, in places where the sense of the inscription is of more importan ce than external ornament. This is a sweeping statement, from which we need not suffer un *The main purpose of letters is the practical one of making thoughts visible. Ruskin says that all letters are frightful things and to be endured only on occasion, that is to say, in places wh*

ABCDEFGHIJKLMNOPQRSTUVWXYZ 1234567890 abcdefghijklmnopqrstuvwxyz

ABCDEFGHIJKLMNOPQRSTUVWXYZ 1234567890 abcdefghijklmnopqrstuvwxyz

7/7

The main purpose of letters is the practical one of making thoughts visible. Rus kin says that all letters are frightful things and to be endured only on occasion, t hat is to say, in places where the sense of the inscription is of more importance t han external ornament. This is a sweeping statement, from which we need not suffer unduly; yet it is doubtful whether there is art in individual letters. Letters in combination may be satisfying and in a well composed page even beautiful as a whole, but art in letters consists rather in the art of arranging and composing t hem in a pleasing and appropriate manner. The main purpose of letters is the pr actical one of making thoughts visible. Ruskin says that all letters are frightful t hings and to be endured only on occasion, that is to say, in places where the sen se of the inscription is of more importance than external ornament. This is a sw eeping statement, from which we need not suffer unduly; yet it is doubtful whe ther there is art in individual letters. Letters in combination may be satisfying a *The main purpose of letters is the practical one of making thoughts visible. Rus kin says that all letters are frightful things and to be endured only on occasion,*

7/8

The main purpose of letters is the practical one of making thoughts visible. Rus kin says that all letters are frightful things and to be endured only on occasion, t hat is to say, in places where the sense of the inscription is of more importance t han external ornament. This is a sweeping statement, from which we need not suffer unduly; yet it is doubtful whether there is art in individual letters. Letters in combination may be satisfying and in a well composed page even beautiful as a whole, but art in letters consists rather in the art of arranging and composing t hem in a pleasing and appropriate manner. The main purpose of letters is the pr actical one of making thoughts visible. Ruskin says that all letters are frightful t hings and to be endured only on occasion, that is to say, in places where the sen se of the inscription is of more importance than external ornament. This is a sw eeping statement, from which we need not suffer unduly; yet it is doubtful whe *The main purpose of letters is the practical one of making thoughts visible. Rus kin says that all letters are frightful things and to be endured only on occasion,*

7/9

The main purpose of letters is the practical one of making thoughts visible. Rus kin says that all letters are frightful things and to be endured only on occasion, t hat is to say, in places where the sense of the inscription is of more importance t han external ornament. This is a sweeping statement, from which we need not suffer unduly; yet it is doubtful whether there is art in individual letters. Letters in combination may be satisfying and in a well composed page even beautiful as a whole, but art in letters consists rather in the art of arranging and composing t hem in a pleasing and appropriate manner. The main purpose of letters is the pr actical one of making thoughts visible. Ruskin says that all letters are frightful t hings and to be endured only on occasion, that is to say, in places where the sen se of the inscription is of more importance than external ornament. This is a sw eeping statement, from which we need not suffer unduly; yet it is doubtful whe *The main purpose of letters is the practical one of making thoughts visible. Rus kin says that all letters are frightful things and to be endured only on occasion,*

7/10

The main purpose of letters is the practical one of making thoughts visible. Rus kin says that all letters are frightful things and to be endured only on occasion, t hat is to say, in places where the sense of the inscription is of more importance t han external ornament. This is a sweeping statement, from which we need not suffer unduly; yet it is doubtful whether there is art in individual letters. Letters in combination may be satisfying and in a well composed page even beautiful as a whole, but art in letters consists rather in the art of arranging and composing t hem in a pleasing and appropriate manner. The main purpose of letters is the pr actical one of making thoughts visible. Ruskin says that all letters are frightful t hings and to be endured only on occasion, that is to say, in places where the sen se of the inscription is of more importance than external ornament. This is a sw *The main purpose of letters is the practical one of making thoughts visible. Rus kin says that all letters are frightful things and to be endured only on occasion,*

PRIMER 8 & 9 POINT SET NORMAL

ROMAN, ITALIC

ABCDEFGHIJKLMNOPQRSTUVWXYZ 1234567890 abcdefghijklmnopqrstuvwxyz

ABCDEFGHIJKLMNOPQRSTUVWXYZ 1234567890 abcdefghijklmnopqrstuvwxyz

8/8

The main purpose of letters is the practical one of making thoughts vi sible. Ruskin says that all letters are frightful things and to be endure d only on occasion, that is to say, in places where the sense of the insc ription is of more importance than external ornament. This is a sweep ing statement, from which we need not suffer unduly; yet it is doubtf ul whether there is art in individual letters. Letters in combination m ay be satisfying and in a well composed page even beautiful as a whol e, but art in letters consists rather in the art of arranging and composi ng them in a pleasing and appropriate manner. The main purpose of l etters is the practical one of making thoughts visible. Ruskin says tha t all letters are frightful things and to be endured only on occasion, th
The main purpose of letters is the practical one of making thoughts vi sible. Ruskin says that all letters are frightful things and to be endur

8/9

The main purpose of letters is the practical one of making thoughts vi sible. Ruskin says that all letters are frightful things and to be endure d only on occasion, that is to say, in places where the sense of the insc ription is of more importance than external ornament. This is a sweep ing statement, from which we need not suffer unduly; yet it is doubtf ul whether there is art in individual letters. Letters in combination m ay be satisfying and in a well composed page even beautiful as a whol e, but art in letters consists rather in the art of arranging and composi ng them in a pleasing and appropriate manner. The main purpose of l etters is the practical one of making thoughts visible. Ruskin says tha
The main purpose of letters is the practical one of making thoughts vi sible. Ruskin says that all letters are frightful things and to be endur

8/10

The main purpose of letters is the practical one of making thoughts vi sible. Ruskin says that all letters are frightful things and to be endure d only on occasion, that is to say, in places where the sense of the insc ription is of more importance than external ornament. This is a sweep ing statement, from which we need not suffer unduly; yet it is doubtf ul whether there is art in individual letters. Letters in combination m ay be satisfying and in a well composed page even beautiful as a whol e, but art in letters consists rather in the art of arranging and composi ng them in a pleasing and appropriate manner. The main purpose of l
The main purpose of letters is the practical one of making thoughts vi sible. Ruskin says that all letters are frightful things and to be endur

8/11

The main purpose of letters is the practical one of making thoughts vi sible. Ruskin says that all letters are frightful things and to be endure d only on occasion, that is to say, in places where the sense of the insc ription is of more importance than external ornament. This is a sweep ing statement, from which we need not suffer unduly; yet it is doubtf ul whether there is art in individual letters. Letters in combination m ay be satisfying and in a well composed page even beautiful as a whol e, but art in letters consists rather in the art of arranging and composi ng them in a pleasing and appropriate manner. The main purpose of l
The main purpose of letters is the practical one of making thoughts vi sible. Ruskin says that all letters are frightful things and to be endur

ABCDEFGHIJKLMNOPQRSTUVWXYZ 1234567890 abcdefghijklmnopqrstuvwxyz

ABCDEFGHIJKLMNOPQRSTUVWXYZ 1234567890 abcdefghijklmnopqrstuvwxyz

9/9

The main purpose of letters is the practical one of making tho ughts visible. Ruskin says that all letters are frightful things a nd to be endured only on occasion, that is to say, in places whe re the sense of the inscription is of more importance than exte rnal ornament. This is a sweeping statement, from which we need not suffer unduly; yet it is doubtful whether there is art i n individual letters. Letters in combination may be satisfying and in a well composed page even beautiful as a whole, but art in letters consists rather in the art of arranging and composin g them in a pleasing and appropriate manner. The main purp
The main purpose of letters is the practical one of making tho ughts visible. Ruskin says that all letters are frightful things

9/10

The main purpose of letters is the practical one of making tho ughts visible. Ruskin says that all letters are frightful things a nd to be endured only on occasion, that is to say, in places whe re the sense of the inscription is of more importance than exte rnal ornament. This is a sweeping statement, from which we need not suffer unduly; yet it is doubtful whether there is art i n individual letters. Letters in combination may be satisfying and in a well composed page even beautiful as a whole, but art in letters consists rather in the art of arranging and composin
The main purpose of letters is the practical one of making tho ughts visible. Ruskin says that all letters are frightful things

9/11

The main purpose of letters is the practical one of making tho ughts visible. Ruskin says that all letters are frightful things a nd to be endured only on occasion, that is to say, in places whe re the sense of the inscription is of more importance than exte rnal ornament. This is a sweeping statement, from which we need not suffer unduly; yet it is doubtful whether there is art i n individual letters. Letters in combination may be satisfying and in a well composed page even beautiful as a whole, but art in letters consists rather in the art of arranging and composin
The main purpose of letters is the practical one of making tho ughts visible. Ruskin says that all letters are frightful things

9/12

The main purpose of letters is the practical one of making tho ughts visible. Ruskin says that all letters are frightful things a nd to be endured only on occasion, that is to say, in places whe re the sense of the inscription is of more importance than exte rnal ornament. This is a sweeping statement, from which we need not suffer unduly; yet it is doubtful whether there is art i n individual letters. Letters in combination may be satisfying and in a well composed page even beautiful as a whole, but art in letters consists rather in the art of arranging and composin
The main purpose of letters is the practical one of making tho ughts visible. Ruskin says that all letters are frightful things

PRIMER 10 POINT SET MINUS ½ UNIT

ROMAN, ITALIC

abcdefghijklmnopqrstuvwxyz – 1 UNIT
abcdefghijklmnopqrstuvwxyz – ½ UNIT
abcdefghijklmnopqrstuvwxyz NORMAL

ABCDEFGHIJKLMNOPQRSTUVWXYZ 1234567890 abcdefghijklmnopqrstuvwxyz
ABCDEFGHIJKLMNOPQRSTUVWXYZ 1234567890 abcdefghijklmnopqrstuvwxyz

10/10

The main purpose of letters is the practical one of making
thoughts visible. Ruskin says that all letters are frightful t
hings and to be endured only on occasion, that is to say, in
places where the sense of the inscription is of more import
ance than external ornament. This is a sweeping stateme
nt, from which we need not suffer unduly; yet it is doubtf
ul whether there is art in individual letters. Letters in com
bination may be satisfying and in a well composed page ev
en beautiful as a whole, but art in letters consists rather in
the art of arranging and composing them in a pleasing an
d appropriate manner. The main purpose of letters is the p
ractical one of making thoughts visible. Ruskin says that a
ll letters are frightful things and to be endured only on occ
asion, that is to say, in places where the sense of the inscri
ption is of more importance than external ornament. This
is a sweeping statement, from which we need not suffer u
nduly; yet it is doubtful whether there is art in individual l
etters. Letters in combination may be satisfying and in a w
ell composed page even beautiful as a whole, but art in lett
ers consists rather in the art of arranging and composing t
hem in a pleasing and appropriate manner. The main pur
pose of letters is the practical one of making thoughts visib
le. Ruskin says that all letters are frightful things and to be
endured only on occasion, that is to say, in places where th
The main purpose of letters is the practical one of making
thoughts visible. Ruskin says that all letters are frightful

10/11

The main purpose of letters is the practical one of making
thoughts visible. Ruskin says that all letters are frightful t
hings and to be endured only on occasion, that is to say, in
places where the sense of the inscription is of more import
ance than external ornament. This is a sweeping stateme
nt, from which we need not suffer unduly; yet it is doubtf
ul whether there is art in individual letters. Letters in com
bination may be satisfying and in a well composed page ev
en beautiful as a whole, but art in letters consists rather in
the art of arranging and composing them in a pleasing an
d appropriate manner. The main purpose of letters is the p
ractical one of making thoughts visible. Ruskin says that a
ll letters are frightful things and to be endured only on occ
asion, that is to say, in places where the sense of the inscri
ption is of more importance than external ornament. This
is a sweeping statement, from which we need not suffer u
nduly; yet it is doubtful whether there is art in individual l
etters. Letters in combination may be satisfying and in a w
ell composed page even beautiful as a whole, but art in lett
ers consists rather in the art of arranging and composing t
hem in a pleasing and appropriate manner. The main pur
pose of letters is the practical one of making thoughts visib
The main purpose of letters is the practical one of making
thoughts visible. Ruskin says that all letters are frightful

10/12

The main purpose of letters is the practical one of making
thoughts visible. Ruskin says that all letters are frightful t
hings and to be endured only on occasion, that is to say, in
places where the sense of the inscription is of more import
ance than external ornament. This is a sweeping stateme
nt, from which we need not suffer unduly; yet it is doubtf
ul whether there is art in individual letters. Letters in com
bination may be satisfying and in a well composed page ev
en beautiful as a whole, but art in letters consists rather in
the art of arranging and composing them in a pleasing an
d appropriate manner. The main purpose of letters is the p
ractical one of making thoughts visible. Ruskin says that a
ll letters are frightful things and to be endured only on occ
asion, that is to say, in places where the sense of the inscri
ption is of more importance than external ornament. This
is a sweeping statement, from which we need not suffer u
nduly; yet it is doubtful whether there is art in individual l
etters. Letters in combination may be satisfying and in a w
ell composed page even beautiful as a whole, but art in lett
ers consists rather in the art of arranging and composing t
The main purpose of letters is the practical one of making
thoughts visible. Ruskin says that all letters are frightful

10/13

The main purpose of letters is the practical one of making
thoughts visible. Ruskin says that all letters are frightful t
hings and to be endured only on occasion, that is to say, in
places where the sense of the inscription is of more import
ance than external ornament. This is a sweeping stateme
nt, from which we need not suffer unduly; yet it is doubtf
ul whether there is art in individual letters. Letters in com
bination may be satisfying and in a well composed page ev
en beautiful as a whole, but art in letters consists rather in
the art of arranging and composing them in a pleasing an
d appropriate manner. The main purpose of letters is the p
ractical one of making thoughts visible. Ruskin says that a
ll letters are frightful things and to be endured only on occ
asion, that is to say, in places where the sense of the inscri
ption is of more importance than external ornament. This
is a sweeping statement, from which we need not suffer u
nduly; yet it is doubtful whether there is art in individual l
etters. Letters in combination may be satisfying and in a w
ell composed page even beautiful as a whole, but art in lett
The main purpose of letters is the practical one of making
thoughts visible. Ruskin says that all letters are frightful

PRIMER 11 POINT SET MINUS ½ UNIT

ROMAN, ITALIC

abcdefghijklmnopqrstuvwxyz – 1 UNIT
abcdefghijklmnopqrstuvwxyz – ½ UNIT
abcdefghijklmnopqrstuvwxyz NORMAL

ABCDEFGHIJKLMNOPQRSTUVWXYZ 1234567890 abcdefghijklmnopqrstuvwxyz
ABCDEFGHIJKLMNOPQRSTUVWXYZ 1234567890 abcdefghijklmnopqrstuvwxyz

11/11

The main purpose of letters is the practical one of ma king thoughts visible. Ruskin says that all letters are frightful things and to be endured only on occasion, that is to say, in places where the sense of the inscrip tion is of more importance than external ornament. This is a sweeping statement, from which we need n ot suffer unduly; yet it is doubtful whether there is ar t in individual letters. Letters in combination may be satisfying and in a well composed page even beautif ul as a whole, but art in letters consists rather in the a rt of arranging and composing them in a pleasing an d appropriate manner. The main purpose of letters is the practical one of making thoughts visible. Ruskin says that all letters are frightful things and to be end ured only on occasion, that is to say, in places where the sense of the inscription is of more importance th an external ornament. This is a sweeping statement, from which we need not suffer unduly; yet it is doub tful whether there is art in individual letters. Letters in combination may be satisfying and in a well comp osed page even beautiful as a whole, but art in letters
The main purpose of letters is the practical one of m aking thoughts visible. Ruskin says that all letters a

11/12

The main purpose of letters is the practical one of ma king thoughts visible. Ruskin says that all letters are frightful things and to be endured only on occasion, that is to say, in places where the sense of the inscrip tion is of more importance than external ornament. This is a sweeping statement, from which we need n ot suffer unduly; yet it is doubtful whether there is ar t in individual letters. Letters in combination may be satisfying and in a well composed page even beautif ul as a whole, but art in letters consists rather in the a rt of arranging and composing them in a pleasing an d appropriate manner. The main purpose of letters is the practical one of making thoughts visible. Ruskin says that all letters are frightful things and to be end ured only on occasion, that is to say, in places where the sense of the inscription is of more importance th an external ornament. This is a sweeping statement, from which we need not suffer unduly; yet it is doub tful whether there is art in individual letters. Letters in combination may be satisfying and in a well comp
The main purpose of letters is the practical one of m aking thoughts visible. Ruskin says that all letters a

11/13

The main purpose of letters is the practical one of ma king thoughts visible. Ruskin says that all letters are frightful things and to be endured only on occasion, that is to say, in places where the sense of the inscrip tion is of more importance than external ornament. This is a sweeping statement, from which we need n ot suffer unduly; yet it is doubtful whether there is ar t in individual letters. Letters in combination may be satisfying and in a well composed page even beautif ul as a whole, but art in letters consists rather in the a rt of arranging and composing them in a pleasing an d appropriate manner. The main purpose of letters is the practical one of making thoughts visible. Ruskin says that all letters are frightful things and to be end ured only on occasion, that is to say, in places where the sense of the inscription is of more importance th an external ornament. This is a sweeping statement, from which we need not suffer unduly; yet it is doub tful whether there is art in individual letters. Letters
The main purpose of letters is the practical one of m aking thoughts visible. Ruskin says that all letters a

11/14

The main purpose of letters is the practical one of ma king thoughts visible. Ruskin says that all letters are frightful things and to be endured only on occasion, that is to say, in places where the sense of the inscrip tion is of more importance than external ornament. This is a sweeping statement, from which we need n ot suffer unduly; yet it is doubtful whether there is ar t in individual letters. Letters in combination may be satisfying and in a well composed page even beautif ul as a whole, but art in letters consists rather in the a rt of arranging and composing them in a pleasing an d appropriate manner. The main purpose of letters is the practical one of making thoughts visible. Ruskin says that all letters are frightful things and to be end ured only on occasion, that is to say, in places where the sense of the inscription is of more importance th an external ornament. This is a sweeping statement, from which we need not suffer unduly; yet it is doub
The main purpose of letters is the practical one of m aking thoughts visible. Ruskin says that all letters a

PRIMER 12 POINT SET MINUS ½ UNIT

ROMAN, ITALIC

abcdefghijklmnopqrstuvwxyz – 1 UNIT
abcdefghijklmnopqrstuvwxyz – ½ UNIT
abcdefghijklmnopqrstuvwxyz NORMAL

ABCDEFGHIJKLMNOPQRSTUVWXYZ 1234567890 abcdefghijklmnopqrstuvwxyz
ABCDEFGHIJKLMNOPQRSTUVWXYZ 1234567890 abcdefghijklmnopqrstuvwxyz

12/12

The main purpose of letters is the practical one of making thoughts visible. Ruskin says that all lett ers are frightful things and to be endured only on occasion, that is to say, in places where the sense of the inscription is of more importance than ext ernal ornament. This is a sweeping statement, fr om which we need not suffer unduly; yet it is do ubtful whether there is art in individual letters. L etters in combination may be satisfying and in a well composed page even beautiful as a whole, b ut art in letters consists rather in the art of arrang ing and composing them in a pleasing and appro priate manner. The main purpose of letters is the practical one of making thoughts visible. Ruskin says that all letters are frightful things and to be e ndured only on occasion, that is to say, in places where the sense of the inscription is of more imp *The main purpose of letters is the practical one o f making thoughts visible. Ruskin says that all le*

12/13

The main purpose of letters is the practical one of making thoughts visible. Ruskin says that all lett ers are frightful things and to be endured only on occasion, that is to say, in places where the sense of the inscription is of more importance than ext ernal ornament. This is a sweeping statement, fr om which we need not suffer unduly; yet it is do ubtful whether there is art in individual letters. L etters in combination may be satisfying and in a well composed page even beautiful as a whole, b ut art in letters consists rather in the art of arrang ing and composing them in a pleasing and appro priate manner. The main purpose of letters is the practical one of making thoughts visible. Ruskin says that all letters are frightful things and to be e ndured only on occasion, that is to say, in places *The main purpose of letters is the practical one o f making thoughts visible. Ruskin says that all le*

12/14

The main purpose of letters is the practical one of making thoughts visible. Ruskin says that all lett ers are frightful things and to be endured only on occasion, that is to say, in places where the sense of the inscription is of more importance than ext ernal ornament. This is a sweeping statement, fr om which we need not suffer unduly; yet it is do ubtful whether there is art in individual letters. L etters in combination may be satisfying and in a well composed page even beautiful as a whole, b ut art in letters consists rather in the art of arrang ing and composing them in a pleasing and appro priate manner. The main purpose of letters is the practical one of making thoughts visible. Ruskin says that all letters are frightful things and to be e ndured only on occasion, that is to say, in places where the sense of the inscription is of more imp *The main purpose of letters is the practical one o f making thoughts visible. Ruskin says that all le*

12/15

The main purpose of letters is the practical one of making thoughts visible. Ruskin says that all lett ers are frightful things and to be endured only on occasion, that is to say, in places where the sense of the inscription is of more importance than ext ernal ornament. This is a sweeping statement, fr om which we need not suffer unduly; yet it is do ubtful whether there is art in individual letters. L etters in combination may be satisfying and in a well composed page even beautiful as a whole, b ut art in letters consists rather in the art of arrang ing and composing them in a pleasing and appro priate manner. The main purpose of letters is the practical one of making thoughts visible. Ruskin says that all letters are frightful things and to be e ndured only on occasion, that is to say, in places *The main purpose of letters is the practical one o f making thoughts visible. Ruskin says that all le*

PRIMER 14 POINT SET MINUS ½ UNIT

ROMAN, ITALIC

abcdefghijklmnopqrstuvwxyz – 1 UNIT
abcdefghijklmnopqrstuvwxyz – ½ UNIT
abcdefghijklmnopqrstuvwxyz NORMAL

ABCDEFGHIJKLMNOPQRSTUVWXYZ abcdefghijklmnopqrstuvwxyz
ABCDEFGHIJKLMNOPQRSTUVWXYZ abcdefghijklmnopqrstuvwxyz

14/14

The main purpose of letters is the practic al one of making thoughts visible. Ruskin says that all letters are frightful things an d to be endured only on occasion, that is t o say, in places where the sense of the ins cription is of more importance than exter nal ornament. This is a sweeping stateme nt, from which we need not suffer unduly; yet it is doubtful whether there is art in i ndividual letters. Letters in combination may be satisfying and in a well composed page even beautiful as a whole, but art in l etters consists rather in the art of arrangi ng and composing them in a pleasing an d appropriate manner. The main purpose
The main purpose of letters is the practic al one of making thoughts visible. Ruskin

14/15

The main purpose of letters is the practic al one of making thoughts visible. Ruskin says that all letters are frightful things an d to be endured only on occasion, that is t o say, in places where the sense of the ins cription is of more importance than exter nal ornament. This is a sweeping stateme nt, from which we need not suffer unduly; yet it is doubtful whether there is art in i ndividual letters. Letters in combination may be satisfying and in a well composed page even beautiful as a whole, but art in l etters consists rather in the art of arrangi ng and composing them in a pleasing an
The main purpose of letters is the practic al one of making thoughts visible. Ruskin

14/16

The main purpose of letters is the practic al one of making thoughts visible. Ruskin says that all letters are frightful things an d to be endured only on occasion, that is t o say, in places where the sense of the ins cription is of more importance than exter nal ornament. This is a sweeping stateme nt, from which we need not suffer unduly; yet it is doubtful whether there is art in i ndividual letters. Letters in combination may be satisfying and in a well composed page even beautiful as a whole, but art in l etters consists rather in the art of arrangi ng and composing them in a pleasing an d appropriate manner. The main purpose
The main purpose of letters is the practic al one of making thoughts visible. Ruskin

14/17

The main purpose of letters is the practic al one of making thoughts visible. Ruskin says that all letters are frightful things an d to be endured only on occasion, that is t o say, in places where the sense of the ins cription is of more importance than exter nal ornament. This is a sweeping stateme nt, from which we need not suffer unduly; yet it is doubtful whether there is art in i ndividual letters. Letters in combination may be satisfying and in a well composed page even beautiful as a whole, but art in l etters consists rather in the art of arrangi ng and composing them in a pleasing an
The main purpose of letters is the practic al one of making thoughts visible. Ruskin

SABON 6 & 7 POINT SET NORMAL

ROMAN, ITALIC, BOLD

ABCDEFGHIJKLMNOPQRSTUVWXYZ 1234567890 abcdefghijklmnopqrstuvwxyz

ABCDEFGHIJKLMNOPQRSTUVWXYZ 1234567890 abcdefghijklmnopqrstuvwxyz

ABCDEFGHIJKLMNOPQRSTUVWXYZ 1234567890 abcdefghijklmnopqrstuvwxyz

6/6

The main purpose of letters is the practical one of making thoughts visible. Ruskin says that all le
tters are frightful things and to be endured only on occasion, that is to say, in places where the se
nse of the inscription is of more importance than external ornament. This is a sweeping statemen
t, from which we need not suffer unduly; yet it is doubtful whether there is art in individual letter
s. Letters in combination may be satisfying and in a well composed page even beautiful as a whol
e, but art in letters consists rather in the art of arranging and composing them in a pleasing and a
ppropriate manner. The main purpose of letters is the practical one of making thoughts visible.
Ruskin says that all letters are frightful things and to be endured only on occasion, that is to say, i
n places where the sense of the inscription is of more importance than external ornament. This is
a sweeping statement, from which we need not suffer unduly; yet it is doubtful whether there is a
rt in individual letters. Letters in combination may be satisfying and in a well composed page eve
n beautiful as a whole, but art in letters consists rather in the art of arranging and composing the
m in a pleasing and appropriate manner. The main purpose of letters is the practical one of maki

*The main purpose of letters is the practical one of making thoughts visible. Ruskin says that all le
tters are frightful things and to be endured only on occasion, that is to say, in places where the se*

**The main purpose of letters is the practical one of making thoughts visible. Ruskin says that all l
etters are frightful things and to be endured only on occasion, that is to say, in places where the se**

6/7

The main purpose of letters is the practical one of making thoughts visible. Ruskin says that all le
tters are frightful things and to be endured only on occasion, that is to say, in places where the se
nse of the inscription is of more importance than external ornament. This is a sweeping statemen
t, from which we need not suffer unduly; yet it is doubtful whether there is art in individual letter
s. Letters in combination may be satisfying and in a well composed page even beautiful as a whol
e, but art in letters consists rather in the art of arranging and composing them in a pleasing and a
ppropriate manner. The main purpose of letters is the practical one of making thoughts visible.
Ruskin says that all letters are frightful things and to be endured only on occasion, that is to say, i
n places where the sense of the inscription is of more importance than external ornament. This is
a sweeping statement, from which we need not suffer unduly; yet it is doubtful whether there is a
rt in individual letters. Letters in combination may be satisfying and in a well composed page eve

*The main purpose of letters is the practical one of making thoughts visible. Ruskin says that all le
tters are frightful things and to be endured only on occasion, that is to say, in places where the se*

**The main purpose of letters is the practical one of making thoughts visible. Ruskin says that all l
etters are frightful things and to be endured only on occasion, that is to say, in places where the se**

6/8

The main purpose of letters is the practical one of making thoughts visible. Ruskin says that all le
tters are frightful things and to be endured only on occasion, that is to say, in places where the se
nse of the inscription is of more importance than external ornament. This is a sweeping statemen
t, from which we need not suffer unduly; yet it is doubtful whether there is art in individual letter
s. Letters in combination may be satisfying and in a well composed page even beautiful as a whol
e, but art in letters consists rather in the art of arranging and composing them in a pleasing and a
ppropriate manner. The main purpose of letters is the practical one of making thoughts visible.
Ruskin says that all letters are frightful things and to be endured only on occasion, that is to say, i
n places where the sense of the inscription is of more importance than external ornament. This is

*The main purpose of letters is the practical one of making thoughts visible. Ruskin says that all le
tters are frightful things and to be endured only on occasion, that is to say, in places where the se*

**The main purpose of letters is the practical one of making thoughts visible. Ruskin says that all l
etters are frightful things and to be endured only on occasion, that is to say, in places where the se**

6/9

The main purpose of letters is the practical one of making thoughts visible. Ruskin says that all le
tters are frightful things and to be endured only on occasion, that is to say, in places where the se
nse of the inscription is of more importance than external ornament. This is a sweeping statemen
t, from which we need not suffer unduly; yet it is doubtful whether there is art in individual letter
s. Letters in combination may be satisfying and in a well composed page even beautiful as a whol
e, but art in letters consists rather in the art of arranging and composing them in a pleasing and a
ppropriate manner. The main purpose of letters is the practical one of making thoughts visible.
Ruskin says that all letters are frightful things and to be endured only on occasion, that is to say, i

*The main purpose of letters is the practical one of making thoughts visible. Ruskin says that all le
tters are frightful things and to be endured only on occasion, that is to say, in places where the se*

**The main purpose of letters is the practical one of making thoughts visible. Ruskin says that all l
etters are frightful things and to be endured only on occasion, that is to say, in places where the se**

ABCDEFGHIJKLMNOPQRSTUVWXYZ 1234567890 abcdefghijklmnopqrstuvwxyz

ABCDEFGHIJKLMNOPQRSTUVWXYZ 1234567890 abcdefghijklmnopqrstuvwxyz

ABCDEFGHIJKLMNOPQRSTUVWXYZ 1234567890 abcdefghijklmnopqrstuvwxyz

7/7

The main purpose of letters is the practical one of making thoughts visible. Ruskin
says that all letters are frightful things and to be endured only on occasion, that is t
o say, in places where the sense of the inscription is of more importance than exter
nal ornament. This is a sweeping statement, from which we need not suffer unduly;
yet it is doubtful whether there is art in individual letters. Letters in combination
may be satisfying and in a well composed page even beautiful as a whole, but art in
letters consists rather in the art of arranging and composing them in a pleasing and
appropriate manner. The main purpose of letters is the practical one of making tho
ughts visible. Ruskin says that all letters are frightful things and to be endured only
on occasion, that is to say, in places where the sense of the inscription is of more im
portance than external ornament. This is a sweeping statement, from which we ne

*The main purpose of letters is the practical one of making thoughts visible. Ruskin
says that all letters are frightful things and to be endured only on occasion, that is t*

**The main purpose of letters is the practical one of making thoughts visible. Ruskin
says that all letters are frightful things and to be endured only on occasion, that is t**

7/8

The main purpose of letters is the practical one of making thoughts visible. Ruskin
says that all letters are frightful things and to be endured only on occasion, that is t
o say, in places where the sense of the inscription is of more importance than exter
nal ornament. This is a sweeping statement, from which we need not suffer unduly;
yet it is doubtful whether there is art in individual letters. Letters in combination
may be satisfying and in a well composed page even beautiful as a whole, but art in
letters consists rather in the art of arranging and composing them in a pleasing and
appropriate manner. The main purpose of letters is the practical one of making tho
ughts visible. Ruskin says that all letters are frightful things and to be endured only
on occasion, that is to say, in places where the sense of the inscription is of more im

*The main purpose of letters is the practical one of making thoughts visible. Ruskin
says that all letters are frightful things and to be endured only on occasion, that is t*

**The main purpose of letters is the practical one of making thoughts visible. Ruskin
says that all letters are frightful things and to be endured only on occasion, that is t**

7/9

The main purpose of letters is the practical one of making thoughts visible. Ruskin
says that all letters are frightful things and to be endured only on occasion, that is t
o say, in places where the sense of the inscription is of more importance than exter
nal ornament. This is a sweeping statement, from which we need not suffer unduly;
yet it is doubtful whether there is art in individual letters. Letters in combination
may be satisfying and in a well composed page even beautiful as a whole, but art in
letters consists rather in the art of arranging and composing them in a pleasing and
appropriate manner. The main purpose of letters is the practical one of making tho
ughts visible. Ruskin says that all letters are frightful things and to be endured only
on occasion, that is to say, in places where the sense of the inscription is of more im

*The main purpose of letters is the practical one of making thoughts visible. Ruskin
says that all letters are frightful things and to be endured only on occasion, that is t*

**The main purpose of letters is the practical one of making thoughts visible. Ruskin
says that all letters are frightful things and to be endured only on occasion, that is t**

7/10

The main purpose of letters is the practical one of making thoughts visible. Ruskin
says that all letters are frightful things and to be endured only on occasion, that is t
o say, in places where the sense of the inscription is of more importance than exter
nal ornament. This is a sweeping statement, from which we need not suffer unduly;
yet it is doubtful whether there is art in individual letters. Letters in combination
may be satisfying and in a well composed page even beautiful as a whole, but art in
letters consists rather in the art of arranging and composing them in a pleasing and
appropriate manner. The main purpose of letters is the practical one of making tho
ughts visible. Ruskin says that all letters are frightful things and to be endured only

*The main purpose of letters is the practical one of making thoughts visible. Ruskin
says that all letters are frightful things and to be endured only on occasion, that is t*

**The main purpose of letters is the practical one of making thoughts visible. Ruskin
says that all letters are frightful things and to be endured only on occasion, that is t**

SABON 8 & 9 POINT SET NORMAL

ROMAN, ITALIC, BOLD

ABCDEFGHIJKLMNOPQRSTUVWXYZ 1234567890 abcdefghijklmnopqrstuvwxyz
ABCDEFGHIJKLMNOPQRSTUVWXYZ 1234567890 abcdefghijklmnopqrstuvwxyz
ABCDEFGHIJKLMNOPQRSTUVWXYZ 1234567890 abcdefghijklmnopqrstuvwxyz

8/8

The main purpose of letters is the practical one of making thoughts visib
le. Ruskin says that all letters are frightful things and to be endured only
on occasion, that is to say, in places where the sense of the inscription is
of more importance than external ornament. This is a sweeping stateme
nt, from which we need not suffer unduly; yet it is doubtful whether ther
e is art in individual letters. Letters in combination may be satisfying an
d in a well composed page even beautiful as a whole, but art in letters co
nsists rather in the art of arranging and composing them in a pleasing an
d appropriate manner. The main purpose of letters is the practical one of
The main purpose of letters is the practical one of making thoughts visib
le. Ruskin says that all letters are frightful things and to be endured only
The main purpose of letters is the practical one of making thoughts visib
le. Ruskin says that all letters are frightful things and to be endured only

8/9

The main purpose of letters is the practical one of making thoughts visib
le. Ruskin says that all letters are frightful things and to be endured only
on occasion, that is to say, in places where the sense of the inscription is
of more importance than external ornament. This is a sweeping stateme
nt, from which we need not suffer unduly; yet it is doubtful whether ther
e is art in individual letters. Letters in combination may be satisfying an
d in a well composed page even beautiful as a whole, but art in letters co
nsists rather in the art of arranging and composing them in a pleasing an
The main purpose of letters is the practical one of making thoughts visib
le. Ruskin says that all letters are frightful things and to be endured only
The main purpose of letters is the practical one of making thoughts visib
le. Ruskin says that all letters are frightful things and to be endured only

8/10

The main purpose of letters is the practical one of making thoughts visib
le. Ruskin says that all letters are frightful things and to be endured only
on occasion, that is to say, in places where the sense of the inscription is
of more importance than external ornament. This is a sweeping stateme
nt, from which we need not suffer unduly; yet it is doubtful whether ther
e is art in individual letters. Letters in combination may be satisfying an
d in a well composed page even beautiful as a whole, but art in letters co
The main purpose of letters is the practical one of making thoughts visib
le. Ruskin says that all letters are frightful things and to be endured only
The main purpose of letters is the practical one of making thoughts visib
le. Ruskin says that all letters are frightful things and to be endured only

8/11

The main purpose of letters is the practical one of making thoughts visib
le. Ruskin says that all letters are frightful things and to be endured only
on occasion, that is to say, in places where the sense of the inscription is
of more importance than external ornament. This is a sweeping stateme
nt, from which we need not suffer unduly; yet it is doubtful whether ther
e is art in individual letters. Letters in combination may be satisfying an
d in a well composed page even beautiful as a whole, but art in letters co
The main purpose of letters is the practical one of making thoughts visib
le. Ruskin says that all letters are frightful things and to be endured only
The main purpose of letters is the practical one of making thoughts visib
le. Ruskin says that all letters are frightful things and to be endured only

ABCDEFGHIJKLMNOPQRSTUVWXYZ 1234567890 abcdefghijklmnopqrstuvwxyz
ABCDEFGHIJKLMNOPQRSTUVWXYZ 1234567890 abcdefghijklmnopqrstuvwxyz
ABCDEFGHIJKLMNOPQRSTUVWXYZ 1234567890 abcdefghijklmnopqrstuvwxyz

9/9

The main purpose of letters is the practical one of making thoug
hts visible. Ruskin says that all letters are frightful things and to
be endured only on occasion, that is to say, in places where the se
nse of the inscription is of more importance than external orna
ment. This is a sweeping statement, from which we need not suff
er unduly; yet it is doubtful whether there is art in individual lett
ers. Letters in combination may be satisfying and in a well comp
osed page even beautiful as a whole, but art in letters consists rat
The main purpose of letters is the practical one of making thoug
hts visible. Ruskin says that all letters are frightful things and to
The main purpose of letters is the practical one of making thoug
hts visible. Ruskin says that all letters are frightful things and to

9/10

The main purpose of letters is the practical one of making thoug
hts visible. Ruskin says that all letters are frightful things and to
be endured only on occasion, that is to say, in places where the se
nse of the inscription is of more importance than external orna
ment. This is a sweeping statement, from which we need not suff
er unduly; yet it is doubtful whether there is art in individual lett
ers. Letters in combination may be satisfying and in a well comp
The main purpose of letters is the practical one of making thoug
hts visible. Ruskin says that all letters are frightful things and to
The main purpose of letters is the practical one of making thoug
hts visible. Ruskin says that all letters are frightful things and to

9/11

The main purpose of letters is the practical one of making thoug
hts visible. Ruskin says that all letters are frightful things and to
be endured only on occasion, that is to say, in places where the se
nse of the inscription is of more importance than external orna
ment. This is a sweeping statement, from which we need not suff
er unduly; yet it is doubtful whether there is art in individual lett
ers. Letters in combination may be satisfying and in a well comp
The main purpose of letters is the practical one of making thoug
hts visible. Ruskin says that all letters are frightful things and to
The main purpose of letters is the practical one of making thoug
hts visible. Ruskin says that all letters are frightful things and to

9/12

The main purpose of letters is the practical one of making thoug
hts visible. Ruskin says that all letters are frightful things and to
be endured only on occasion, that is to say, in places where the se
nse of the inscription is of more importance than external orna
ment. This is a sweeping statement, from which we need not suff
er unduly; yet it is doubtful whether there is art in individual lett
ers. Letters in combination may be satisfying and in a well comp
The main purpose of letters is the practical one of making thoug
hts visible. Ruskin says that all letters are frightful things and to
The main purpose of letters is the practical one of making thoug
hts visible. Ruskin says that all letters are frightful things and to

10 POINT SET MINUS ½ UNIT

ROMAN, ITALIC, BOLD

abcdefghijklmnopqrstuvwxyz – 1 UNIT
abcdefghijklmnopqrstuvwxyz – ½ UNIT
abcdefghijklmnopqrstuvwxyz NORMAL

ABCDEFGHIJKLMNOPQRSTUVWXYZ 1234567890 abcdefghijklmnopqrstuvwxyz
ABCDEFGHIJKLMNOPQRSTUVWXYZ 1234567890 abcdefghijklmnopqrstuvwxyz
ABCDEFGHIJKLMNOPQRSTUVWXYZ 1234567890 abcdefghijklmnopqrstuvwxyz

10/10

The main purpose of letters is the practical one of making th oughts visible. Ruskin says that all letters are frightful things and to be endured only on occasion, that is to say, in places where the sense of the inscription is of more importance tha n external ornament. This is a sweeping statement, from whi ch we need not suffer unduly; yet it is doubtful whether there is art in individual letters. Letters in combination may be sati sfying and in a well composed page even beautiful as a whole, but art in letters consists rather in the art of arranging and c omposing them in a pleasing and appropriate manner. The main purpose of letters is the practical one of making thoug hts visible. Ruskin says that all letters are frightful things and to be endured only on occasion, that is to say, in places wher e the sense of the inscription is of more importance than exte rnal ornament. This is a sweeping statement, from which we need not suffer unduly; yet it is doubtful whether there is art in individual letters. Letters in combination may be satisfyin g and in a well composed page even beautiful as a whole, but art in letters consists rather in the art of arranging and comp osing them in a pleasing and appropriate manner. The main purpose of letters is the practical one of making thoughts vis ible. Ruskin says that all letters are frightful things and to be

The main purpose of letters is the practical one of making th oughts visible. Ruskin says that all letters are frightful things

The main purpose of letters is the practical one of making th oughts visible. Ruskin says that all letters are frightful things

10/11

The main purpose of letters is the practical one of making th oughts visible. Ruskin says that all letters are frightful things and to be endured only on occasion, that is to say, in places where the sense of the inscription is of more importance tha n external ornament. This is a sweeping statement, from whi ch we need not suffer unduly; yet it is doubtful whether there is art in individual letters. Letters in combination may be sati sfying and in a well composed page even beautiful as a whole, but art in letters consists rather in the art of arranging and c omposing them in a pleasing and appropriate manner. The main purpose of letters is the practical one of making thoug hts visible. Ruskin says that all letters are frightful things and to be endured only on occasion, that is to say, in places wher e the sense of the inscription is of more importance than exte rnal ornament. This is a sweeping statement, from which we need not suffer unduly; yet it is doubtful whether there is art in individual letters. Letters in combination may be satisfyin g and in a well composed page even beautiful as a whole, but art in letters consists rather in the art of arranging and comp osing them in a pleasing and appropriate manner. The main

The main purpose of letters is the practical one of making th oughts visible. Ruskin says that all letters are frightful things

The main purpose of letters is the practical one of making th oughts visible. Ruskin says that all letters are frightful things

10/12

The main purpose of letters is the practical one of making th oughts visible. Ruskin says that all letters are frightful things and to be endured only on occasion, that is to say, in places where the sense of the inscription is of more importance tha n external ornament. This is a sweeping statement, from whi ch we need not suffer unduly; yet it is doubtful whether there is art in individual letters. Letters in combination may be sati sfying and in a well composed page even beautiful as a whole, but art in letters consists rather in the art of arranging and c omposing them in a pleasing and appropriate manner. The main purpose of letters is the practical one of making thoug hts visible. Ruskin says that all letters are frightful things and to be endured only on occasion, that is to say, in places wher e the sense of the inscription is of more importance than exte rnal ornament. This is a sweeping statement, from which we need not suffer unduly; yet it is doubtful whether there is art in individual letters. Letters in combination may be satisfyin g and in a well composed page even beautiful as a whole, but

The main purpose of letters is the practical one of making th oughts visible. Ruskin says that all letters are frightful things

The main purpose of letters is the practical one of making th oughts visible. Ruskin says that all letters are frightful things

10/13

The main purpose of letters is the practical one of making th oughts visible. Ruskin says that all letters are frightful things and to be endured only on occasion, that is to say, in places where the sense of the inscription is of more importance tha n external ornament. This is a sweeping statement, from whi ch we need not suffer unduly; yet it is doubtful whether there is art in individual letters. Letters in combination may be sati sfying and in a well composed page even beautiful as a whole, but art in letters consists rather in the art of arranging and c omposing them in a pleasing and appropriate manner. The main purpose of letters is the practical one of making thoug hts visible. Ruskin says that all letters are frightful things and to be endured only on occasion, that is to say, in places wher e the sense of the inscription is of more importance than exte rnal ornament. This is a sweeping statement, from which we need not suffer unduly; yet it is doubtful whether there is art in individual letters. Letters in combination may be satisfyin

The main purpose of letters is the practical one of making th oughts visible. Ruskin says that all letters are frightful things

The main purpose of letters is the practical one of making th oughts visible. Ruskin says that all letters are frightful things

SABON 11 POINT SET MINUS ½ UNIT

ROMAN, ITALIC, BOLD

abcdefghijklmnopqrstuvwxyz – 1 UNIT
abcdefghijklmnopqrstuvwxyz – ½ UNIT
abcdefghijklmnopqrstuvwxyz NORMAL

ABCDEFGHIJKLMNOPQRSTUVWXYZ 1234567890 abcdefghijklmnopqrstuvwxyz
ABCDEFGHIJKLMNOPQRSTUVWXYZ 1234567890 abcdefghijklmnopqrstuvwxyz
ABCDEFGHIJKLMNOPQRSTUVWXYZ 1234567890 abcdefghijklmnopqrstuvwxyz

11/11

The main purpose of letters is the practical one of maki ng thoughts visible. Ruskin says that all letters are frig htful things and to be endured only on occasion, that is to say, in places where the sense of the inscription is of more importance than external ornament. This is a sw eeping statement, from which we need not suffer undu ly; yet it is doubtful whether there is art in individual le tters. Letters in combination may be satisfying and in a well composed page even beautiful as a whole, but art i n letters consists rather in the art of arranging and com posing them in a pleasing and appropriate manner. Th e main purpose of letters is the practical one of making thoughts visible. Ruskin says that all letters are frightf ul things and to be endured only on occasion, that is to say, in places where the sense of the inscription is of mo re importance than external ornament. This is a sweep ing statement, from which we need not suffer unduly; yet it is doubtful whether there is art in individual letter s. Letters in combination may be satisfying and in a we
The main purpose of letters is the practical one of maki ng thoughts visible. Ruskin says that all letters are frig
The main purpose of letters is the practical one of mak ing thoughts visible. Ruskin says that all letters are frig

11/12

The main purpose of letters is the practical one of maki ng thoughts visible. Ruskin says that all letters are frig htful things and to be endured only on occasion, that is to say, in places where the sense of the inscription is of more importance than external ornament. This is a sw eeping statement, from which we need not suffer undu ly; yet it is doubtful whether there is art in individual le tters. Letters in combination may be satisfying and in a well composed page even beautiful as a whole, but art i n letters consists rather in the art of arranging and com posing them in a pleasing and appropriate manner. Th e main purpose of letters is the practical one of making thoughts visible. Ruskin says that all letters are frightf ul things and to be endured only on occasion, that is to say, in places where the sense of the inscription is of mo re importance than external ornament. This is a sweep ing statement, from which we need not suffer unduly; yet it is doubtful whether there is art in individual letter
The main purpose of letters is the practical one of maki ng thoughts visible. Ruskin says that all letters are frig
The main purpose of letters is the practical one of mak ing thoughts visible. Ruskin says that all letters are frig

11/13

The main purpose of letters is the practical one of maki ng thoughts visible. Ruskin says that all letters are frig htful things and to be endured only on occasion, that is to say, in places where the sense of the inscription is of more importance than external ornament. This is a sw eeping statement, from which we need not suffer undu ly; yet it is doubtful whether there is art in individual le tters. Letters in combination may be satisfying and in a well composed page even beautiful as a whole, but art i n letters consists rather in the art of arranging and com posing them in a pleasing and appropriate manner. Th e main purpose of letters is the practical one of making thoughts visible. Ruskin says that all letters are frightf ul things and to be endured only on occasion, that is to say, in places where the sense of the inscription is of mo re importance than external ornament. This is a sweep ing statement, from which we need not suffer unduly;
The main purpose of letters is the practical one of maki ng thoughts visible. Ruskin says that all letters are frig
The main purpose of letters is the practical one of mak ing thoughts visible. Ruskin says that all letters are frig

11/14

The main purpose of letters is the practical one of maki ng thoughts visible. Ruskin says that all letters are frig htful things and to be endured only on occasion, that is to say, in places where the sense of the inscription is of more importance than external ornament. This is a sw eeping statement, from which we need not suffer undu ly; yet it is doubtful whether there is art in individual le tters. Letters in combination may be satisfying and in a well composed page even beautiful as a whole, but art i n letters consists rather in the art of arranging and com posing them in a pleasing and appropriate manner. Th e main purpose of letters is the practical one of making thoughts visible. Ruskin says that all letters are frightf ul things and to be endured only on occasion, that is to say, in places where the sense of the inscription is of mo re importance than external ornament. This is a sweep
The main purpose of letters is the practical one of maki ng thoughts visible. Ruskin says that all letters are frig
The main purpose of letters is the practical one of mak ing thoughts visible. Ruskin says that all letters are frig

12 POINT SET MINUS ½ UNIT

ROMAN, ITALIC, BOLD

abcdefghijklmnopqrstuvwxyz – 1 UNIT
abcdefghijklmnopqrstuvwxyz – ½ UNIT
abcdefghijklmnopqrstuvwxyz NORMAL

ABCDEFGHIJKLMNOPQRSTUVWXYZ 1234567890 abcdefghijklmnopqrstuvwxyz
ABCDEFGHIJKLMNOPQRSTUVWXYZ 1234567890 abcdefghijklmnopqrstuvwxyz
ABCDEFGHIJKLMNOPQRSTUVWXYZ 1234567890 abcdefghijklmnopqrstuvwxyz

12/12

The main purpose of letters is the practical one of
making thoughts visible. Ruskin says that all letter
s are frightful things and to be endured only on occ
asion, that is to say, in places where the sense of the
inscription is of more importance than external or
nament. This is a sweeping statement, from which
we need not suffer unduly; yet it is doubtful whethe
r there is art in individual letters. Letters in combin
ation may be satisfying and in a well composed pag
e even beautiful as a whole, but art in letters consist
s rather in the art of arranging and composing the
m in a pleasing and appropriate manner. The main
purpose of letters is the practical one of making th
oughts visible. Ruskin says that all letters are fright
ful things and to be endured only on occasion, that
The main purpose of letters is the practical one of
making thoughts visible. Ruskin says that all letter
The main purpose of letters is the practical one of
making thoughts visible. Ruskin says that all letter

12/13

The main purpose of letters is the practical one of
making thoughts visible. Ruskin says that all letter
s are frightful things and to be endured only on occ
asion, that is to say, in places where the sense of the
inscription is of more importance than external or
nament. This is a sweeping statement, from which
we need not suffer unduly; yet it is doubtful whethe
r there is art in individual letters. Letters in combin
ation may be satisfying and in a well composed pag
e even beautiful as a whole, but art in letters consist
s rather in the art of arranging and composing the
m in a pleasing and appropriate manner. The main
purpose of letters is the practical one of making th
oughts visible. Ruskin says that all letters are fright
The main purpose of letters is the practical one of
making thoughts visible. Ruskin says that all letter
The main purpose of letters is the practical one of
making thoughts visible. Ruskin says that all letter

12/14

The main purpose of letters is the practical one of
making thoughts visible. Ruskin says that all letter
s are frightful things and to be endured only on occ
asion, that is to say, in places where the sense of the
inscription is of more importance than external or
nament. This is a sweeping statement, from which
we need not suffer unduly; yet it is doubtful whethe
r there is art in individual letters. Letters in combin
ation may be satisfying and in a well composed pag
e even beautiful as a whole, but art in letters consist
s rather in the art of arranging and composing the
m in a pleasing and appropriate manner. The main
purpose of letters is the practical one of making th
oughts visible. Ruskin says that all letters are fright
ful things and to be endured only on occasion, that
The main purpose of letters is the practical one of
making thoughts visible. Ruskin says that all letter
The main purpose of letters is the practical one of
making thoughts visible. Ruskin says that all letter

12/15

The main purpose of letters is the practical one of
making thoughts visible. Ruskin says that all letter
s are frightful things and to be endured only on occ
asion, that is to say, in places where the sense of the
inscription is of more importance than external or
nament. This is a sweeping statement, from which
we need not suffer unduly; yet it is doubtful whethe
r there is art in individual letters. Letters in combin
ation may be satisfying and in a well composed pag
e even beautiful as a whole, but art in letters consist
s rather in the art of arranging and composing the
m in a pleasing and appropriate manner. The main
purpose of letters is the practical one of making th
oughts visible. Ruskin says that all letters are fright
The main purpose of letters is the practical one of
making thoughts visible. Ruskin says that all letter
The main purpose of letters is the practical one of
making thoughts visible. Ruskin says that all letter

SABON 14 POINT SET MINUS ½ UNIT

ROMAN, ITALIC, BOLD

abcdefghijklmnopqrstuvwxyz – 1 UNIT
abcdefghijklmnopqrstuvwxyz – ½ UNIT
abcdefghijklmnopqrstuvwxyz NORMAL

ABCDEFGHIJKLMNOPQRSTUVWXYZ abcdefghijklmnopqrstuvwxyz
ABCDEFGHIJKLMNOPQRSTUVWXYZ abcdefghijklmnopqrstuvwxyz
ABCDEFGHIJKLMNOPQRSTUVWXYZ abcdefghijklmnopqrstuvwxyz

14/14

The main purpose of letters is the practical one of making thoughts visible. Ruskin say s that all letters are frightful things and to b e endured only on occasion, that is to say, i n places where the sense of the inscription i s of more importance than external ornam ent. This is a sweeping statement, from whi ch we need not suffer unduly; yet it is doubt ful whether there is art in individual letters. Letters in combination may be satisfying a nd in a well composed page even beautiful as a whole, but art in letters consists rather in the art of arranging and composing the
The main purpose of letters is the practical one of making thoughts visible. Ruskin say
The main purpose of letters is the practical one of making thoughts visible. Ruskin say

14/15

The main purpose of letters is the practical one of making thoughts visible. Ruskin say s that all letters are frightful things and to b e endured only on occasion, that is to say, i n places where the sense of the inscription i s of more importance than external ornam ent. This is a sweeping statement, from whi ch we need not suffer unduly; yet it is doubt ful whether there is art in individual letters. Letters in combination may be satisfying a nd in a well composed page even beautiful as a whole, but art in letters consists rather
The main purpose of letters is the practical one of making thoughts visible. Ruskin say
The main purpose of letters is the practical one of making thoughts visible. Ruskin say

14/16

The main purpose of letters is the practical one of making thoughts visible. Ruskin say s that all letters are frightful things and to b e endured only on occasion, that is to say, i n places where the sense of the inscription i s of more importance than external ornam ent. This is a sweeping statement, from whi ch we need not suffer unduly; yet it is doubt ful whether there is art in individual letters. Letters in combination may be satisfying a nd in a well composed page even beautiful as a whole, but art in letters consists rather in the art of arranging and composing the
The main purpose of letters is the practical one of making thoughts visible. Ruskin say
The main purpose of letters is the practical one of making thoughts visible. Ruskin say

14/17

The main purpose of letters is the practical one of making thoughts visible. Ruskin say s that all letters are frightful things and to b e endured only on occasion, that is to say, i n places where the sense of the inscription i s of more importance than external ornam ent. This is a sweeping statement, from whi ch we need not suffer unduly; yet it is doubt ful whether there is art in individual letters. Letters in combination may be satisfying a nd in a well composed page even beautiful as a whole, but art in letters consists rather
The main purpose of letters is the practical one of making thoughts visible. Ruskin say
The main purpose of letters is the practical one of making thoughts visible. Ruskin say

ITC SOUVENIR 6 & 7 POINT SET NORMAL

LIGHT, ITALIC, DEMI, DEMI ITALIC

ABCDEFGHIJKLMNOPQRSTUVWXYZ 1234567890 abcdefghijklmnopqrstuvwxyz

ABCDEFGHIJKLMNOPQRSTUVWXYZ 1234567890 abcdefghijklmnopqrstuvwxyz

ABCDEFGHIJKLMNOPQRSTUVWXYZ 1234567890 abcdefghijklmnopqrstuvwxyz

ABCDEFGHIJKLMNOPQRSTUVWXYZ 1234567890 abcdefghijklmnopqrstuvwxyz

6/6

The main purpose of letters is the practical one of making thoughts visible. Ruskin says that all lette
rs are frightful things and to be endured only on occasion, that is to say, in places where the sense o
f the inscription is of more importance than external ornament. This is a sweeping statement, from
which we need not suffer unduly; yet it is doubtful whether there is art in individual letters. Letters i
n combination may be satisfying and in a well composed page even beautiful as a whole, but art in
letters consists rather in the art of arranging and composing them in a pleasing and appropriate ma
nner. The main purpose of letters is the practical one of making thoughts visible. Ruskin says that a
ll letters are frightful things and to be endured only on occasion, that is to say, in places where the se
nse of the inscription is of more importance than external ornament. This is a sweeping statement,
from which we need not suffer unduly; yet it is doubtful whether there is art in individual letters. Let
ters in combination may be satisfying and in a well composed page even beautiful as a whole, but
art in letters consists rather in the art of arranging and composing them in a pleasing and appropria
te manner. The main purpose of letters is the practical one of making thoughts visible. Ruskin says
The main purpose of letters is the practical one of making thoughts visible. Ruskin says that all lette
rs are frightful things and to be endured only on occasion, that is to say, in places where the sense o
The main purpose of letters is the practical one of making thoughts visible. Ruskin sa
ys that all letters are frightful things and to be endured only on occasion, that is to say,

6/7

The main purpose of letters is the practical one of making thoughts visible. Ruskin says that all lette
rs are frightful things and to be endured only on occasion, that is to say, in places where the sense o
f the inscription is of more importance than external ornament. This is a sweeping statement, from
which we need not suffer unduly; yet it is doubtful whether there is art in individual letters. Letters i
n combination may be satisfying and in a well composed page even beautiful as a whole, but art in
letters consists rather in the art of arranging and composing them in a pleasing and appropriate ma
nner. The main purpose of letters is the practical one of making thoughts visible. Ruskin says that a
ll letters are frightful things and to be endured only on occasion, that is to say, in places where the se
nse of the inscription is of more importance than external ornament. This is a sweeping statement,
from which we need not suffer unduly; yet it is doubtful whether there is art in individual letters. Let
ters in combination may be satisfying and in a well composed page even beautiful as a whole, but
The main purpose of letters is the practical one of making thoughts visible. Ruskin says that all lette
rs are frightful things and to be endured only on occasion, that is to say, in places where the sense o
The main purpose of letters is the practical one of making thoughts visible. Ruskin sa
ys that all letters are frightful things and to be endured only on occasion, that is to say,

6/8

The main purpose of letters is the practical one of making thoughts visible. Ruskin says that all lette
rs are frightful things and to be endured only on occasion, that is to say, in places where the sense o
f the inscription is of more importance than external ornament. This is a sweeping statement, from
which we need not suffer unduly; yet it is doubtful whether there is art in individual letters. Letters i
n combination may be satisfying and in a well composed page even beautiful as a whole, but art in
letters consists rather in the art of arranging and composing them in a pleasing and appropriate ma
nner. The main purpose of letters is the practical one of making thoughts visible. Ruskin says that a
ll letters are frightful things and to be endured only on occasion, that is to say, in places where the se
nse of the inscription is of more importance than external ornament. This is a sweeping statement,
The main purpose of letters is the practical one of making thoughts visible. Ruskin says that all lette
rs are frightful things and to be endured only on occasion, that is to say, in places where the sense o
The main purpose of letters is the practical one of making thoughts visible. Ruskin sa
ys that all letters are frightful things and to be endured only on occasion, that is to say,

6/9

The main purpose of letters is the practical one of making thoughts visible. Ruskin says that all lette
rs are frightful things and to be endured only on occasion, that is to say, in places where the sense o
f the inscription is of more importance than external ornament. This is a sweeping statement, from
which we need not suffer unduly; yet it is doubtful whether there is art in individual letters. Letters i
n combination may be satisfying and in a well composed page even beautiful as a whole, but art in
letters consists rather in the art of arranging and composing them in a pleasing and appropriate ma
nner. The main purpose of letters is the practical one of making thoughts visible. Ruskin says that a
ll letters are frightful things and to be endured only on occasion, that is to say, in places where the se
The main purpose of letters is the practical one of making thoughts visible. Ruskin says that all lette
rs are frightful things and to be endured only on occasion, that is to say, in places where the sense o
The main purpose of letters is the practical one of making thoughts visible. Ruskin sa
ys that all letters are frightful things and to be endured only on occasion, that is to say,

---

ABCDEFGHIJKLMNOPQRSTUVWXYZ 1234567890 abcdefghijklmnopqrstuvwxyz

ABCDEFGHIJKLMNOPQRSTUVWXYZ 1234567890 abcdefghijklmnopqrstuvwxyz

ABCDEFGHIJKLMNOPQRSTUVWXYZ 1234567890 abcdefghijklmnopqrstuvwxyz

ABCDEFGHIJKLMNOPQRSTUVWXYZ 1234567890 abcdefghijklmnopqrstuvwxyz

7/7

The main purpose of letters is the practical one of making thoughts visible. Ruskin sa
ys that all letters are frightful things and to be endured only on occasion, that is to say,
in places where the sense of the inscription is of more importance than external orn
ament. This is a sweeping statement, from which we need not suffer unduly; yet it is
doubtful whether there is art in individual letters. Letters in combination may be satis
fying and in a well composed page even beautiful as a whole, but art in letters consist
s rather in the art of arranging and composing them in a pleasing and appropriate m
anner. The main purpose of letters is the practical one of making thoughts visible. Ru
skin says that all letters are frightful things and to be endured only on occasion, that is
to say, in places where the sense of the inscription is of more importance than extern
al ornament. This is a sweeping statement, from which we need not suffer unduly; y
The main purpose of letters is the practical one of making thoughts visible. Ruskin sa
ys that all letters are frightful things and to be endured only on occasion, that is to say,
The main purpose of letters is the practical one of making thoughts visibl
e. Ruskin says that all letters are frightful things and to be endured only o

7/8

The main purpose of letters is the practical one of making thoughts visible. Ruskin sa
ys that all letters are frightful things and to be endured only on occasion, that is to say,
in places where the sense of the inscription is of more importance than external orn
ament. This is a sweeping statement, from which we need not suffer unduly; yet it is
doubtful whether there is art in individual letters. Letters in combination may be satis
fying and in a well composed page even beautiful as a whole, but art in letters consist
s rather in the art of arranging and composing them in a pleasing and appropriate m
anner. The main purpose of letters is the practical one of making thoughts visible. Ru
skin says that all letters are frightful things and to be endured only on occasion, that is
to say, in places where the sense of the inscription is of more importance than extern
The main purpose of letters is the practical one of making thoughts visible. Ruskin sa
ys that all letters are frightful things and to be endured only on occasion, that is to say,
The main purpose of letters is the practical one of making thoughts visibl
e. Ruskin says that all letters are frightful things and to be endured only o

7/9

The main purpose of letters is the practical one of making thoughts visible. Ruskin sa
ys that all letters are frightful things and to be endured only on occasion, that is to say,
in places where the sense of the inscription is of more importance than external orn
ament. This is a sweeping statement, from which we need not suffer unduly; yet it is
doubtful whether there is art in individual letters. Letters in combination may be satis
fying and in a well composed page even beautiful as a whole, but art in letters consist
s rather in the art of arranging and composing them in a pleasing and appropriate m
anner. The main purpose of letters is the practical one of making thoughts visible. Ru
skin says that all letters are frightful things and to be endured only on occasion, that is
to say, in places where the sense of the inscription is of more importance than extern
The main purpose of letters is the practical one of making thoughts visible. Ruskin sa
ys that all letters are frightful things and to be endured only on occasion, that is to say,
The main purpose of letters is the practical one of making thoughts visibl
e. Ruskin says that all letters are frightful things and to be endured only o

7/10

The main purpose of letters is the practical one of making thoughts visible. Ruskin sa
ys that all letters are frightful things and to be endured only on occasion, that is to say,
in places where the sense of the inscription is of more importance than external orn
ament. This is a sweeping statement, from which we need not suffer unduly; yet it is
doubtful whether there is art in individual letters. Letters in combination may be satis
fying and in a well composed page even beautiful as a whole, but art in letters consist
s rather in the art of arranging and composing them in a pleasing and appropriate m
anner. The main purpose of letters is the practical one of making thoughts visible. Ru
skin says that all letters are frightful things and to be endured only on occasion, that is
The main purpose of letters is the practical one of making thoughts visible. Ruskin sa
ys that all letters are frightful things and to be endured only on occasion, that is to say,
The main purpose of letters is the practical one of making thoughts visibl
e. Ruskin says that all letters are frightful things and to be endured only o

ITC SOUVENIR 8 & 9 POINT SET NORMAL

LIGHT, ITALIC, DEMI, DEMI ITALIC

ABCDEFGHIJKLMNOPQRSTUVWXYZ 1234567890 abcdefghijklmnopqrstuvwxyz

ABCDEFGHIJKLMNOPQRSTUVWXYZ 1234567890 abcdefghijklmnopqrstuvwxyz

ABCDEFGHIJKLMNOPQRSTUVWXYZ 1234567890 abcdefghijklmnopqrstuvwxyz

ABCDEFGHIJKLMNOPQRSTUVWXYZ 1234567890 abcdefghijklmnopqrstuvwxyz

8/8

The main purpose of letters is the practical one of making thoughts visible. Ruskin says that all letters are frightful things and to be endured only on o ccasion, that is to say, in places where the sense of the inscription is of mor e importance than external ornament. This is a sweeping statement, from which we need not suffer unduly; yet it is doubtful whether there is art in in dividual letters. Letters in combination may be satisfying and in a well co mposed page even beautiful as a whole, but art in letters consists rather in the art of arranging and composing them in a pleasing and appropriate m anner. The main purpose of letters is the practical one of making thoughts
The main purpose of letters is the practical one of making thoughts visible. Ruskin says that all letters are frightful things and to be endured only on
The main purpose of letters is the practical one of making thoug hts visible. Ruskin says that all letters are frightful things and to

8/9

The main purpose of letters is the practical one of making thoughts visible. Ruskin says that all letters are frightful things and to be endured only on o ccasion, that is to say, in places where the sense of the inscription is of mor e importance than external ornament. This is a sweeping statement, from which we need not suffer unduly; yet it is doubtful whether there is art in in dividual letters. Letters in combination may be satisfying and in a well co mposed page even beautiful as a whole, but art in letters consists rather in the art of arranging and composing them in a pleasing and appropriate m
The main purpose of letters is the practical one of making thoughts visible. Ruskin says that all letters are frightful things and to be endured only on
The main purpose of letters is the practical one of making thoug hts visible. Ruskin says that all letters are frightful things and to

8/10

The main purpose of letters is the practical one of making thoughts visible. Ruskin says that all letters are frightful things and to be endured only on o ccasion, that is to say, in places where the sense of the inscription is of mor e importance than external ornament. This is a sweeping statement, from which we need not suffer unduly; yet it is doubtful whether there is art in in dividual letters. Letters in combination may be satisfying and in a well co mposed page even beautiful as a whole, but art in letters consists rather in
The main purpose of letters is the practical one of making thoughts visible. Ruskin says that all letters are frightful things and to be endured only on
The main purpose of letters is the practical one of making thoug hts visible. Ruskin says that all letters are frightful things and to

8/11

The main purpose of letters is the practical one of making thoughts visible. Ruskin says that all letters are frightful things and to be endured only on o ccasion, that is to say, in places where the sense of the inscription is of mor e importance than external ornament. This is a sweeping statement, from which we need not suffer unduly; yet it is doubtful whether there is art in in dividual letters. Letters in combination may be satisfying and in a well co mposed page even beautiful as a whole, but art in letters consists rather in
The main purpose of letters is the practical one of making thoughts visible. Ruskin says that all letters are frightful things and to be endured only on
The main purpose of letters is the practical one of making thoug hts visible. Ruskin says that all letters are frightful things and to

---

ABCDEFGHIJKLMNOPQRSTUVWXYZ 1234567890 abcdefghijklmnopqrstuvwxyz

ABCDEFGHIJKLMNOPQRSTUVWXYZ 1234567890 abcdefghijklmnopqrstuvwxyz

ABCDEFGHIJKLMNOPQRSTUVWXYZ 1234567890 abcdefghijklmnopqrstuvwxyz

ABCDEFGHIJKLMNOPQRSTUVWXYZ 1234567890 abcdefghijklmnopqrstuvwxyz

9/9

The main purpose of letters is the practical one of making thought s visible. Ruskin says that all letters are frightful things and to be e ndured only on occasion, that is to say, in places where the sense of the inscription is of more importance than external ornament. This is a sweeping statement, from which we need not suffer und uly; yet it is doubtful whether there is art in individual letters. Lette rs in combination may be satisfying and in a well composed page even beautiful as a whole, but art in letters consists rather in the ar
The main purpose of letters is the practical one of making thought s visible. Ruskin says that all letters are frightful things and to be e
The main purpose of letters is the practical one of makin g thoughts visible. Ruskin says that all letters are frightfu

9/10

The main purpose of letters is the practical one of making thought s visible. Ruskin says that all letters are frightful things and to be e ndured only on occasion, that is to say, in places where the sense of the inscription is of more importance than external ornament. This is a sweeping statement, from which we need not suffer und uly; yet it is doubtful whether there is art in individual letters. Lette rs in combination may be satisfying and in a well composed page
The main purpose of letters is the practical one of making thought s visible. Ruskin says that all letters are frightful things and to be e
The main purpose of letters is the practical one of makin g thoughts visible. Ruskin says that all letters are frightfu

9/11

The main purpose of letters is the practical one of making thought s visible. Ruskin says that all letters are frightful things and to be e ndured only on occasion, that is to say, in places where the sense of the inscription is of more importance than external ornament. This is a sweeping statement, from which we need not suffer und uly; yet it is doubtful whether there is art in individual letters. Lette rs in combination may be satisfying and in a well composed page
The main purpose of letters is the practical one of making thought s visible. Ruskin says that all letters are frightful things and to be e
The main purpose of letters is the practical one of makin g thoughts visible. Ruskin says that all letters are frightfu

9/12

The main purpose of letters is the practical one of making thought s visible. Ruskin says that all letters are frightful things and to be e ndured only on occasion, that is to say, in places where the sense of the inscription is of more importance than external ornament. This is a sweeping statement, from which we need not suffer und uly; yet it is doubtful whether there is art in individual letters. Lette rs in combination may be satisfying and in a well composed page
The main purpose of letters is the practical one of making thought s visible. Ruskin says that all letters are frightful things and to be e
The main purpose of letters is the practical one of makin g thoughts visible. Ruskin says that all letters are frightfu

ITC SOUVENIR 10 POINT SET MINUS ½ UNIT

LIGHT, ITALIC, DEMI, DEMI ITALIC

abcdefghijklmnopqrstuvwxyz – 1 UNIT
abcdefghijklmnopqrstuvwxyz – ½ UNIT
abcdefghijklmnopqrstuvwxyz NORMAL

ABCDEFGHIJKLMNOPQRSTUVWXYZ 1234567890 abcdefghijklmnopqrstuvwxyz
ABCDEFGHIJKLMNOPQRSTUVWXYZ 1234567890 abcdefghijklmnopqrstuvwxyz
ABCDEFGHIJKLMNOPQRSTUVWXYZ 1234567890 abcdefghijklmnopqrstuvwxyz
ABCDEFGHIJKLMNOPQRSTUVWXYZ 1234567890 abcdefghijklmnopqrstuvwxyz

10/10

The main purpose of letters is the practical one of making tho ughts visible. Ruskin says that all letters are frightful things and to be endured only on occasion, that is to say, in places where the sense of the inscription is of more importance than extern al ornament. This is a sweeping statement, from which we ne ed not suffer unduly; yet it is doubtful whether there is art in in dividual letters. Letters in combination may be satisfying and i n a well composed page even beautiful as a whole, but art in l etters consists rather in the art of arranging and composing th em in a pleasing and appropriate manner. The main purpose of letters is the practical one of making thoughts visible. Ruski n says that all letters are frightful things and to be endured onl y on occasion, that is to say, in places where the sense of the in scription is of more importance than external ornament. This i s a sweeping statement, from which we need not suffer undul y; yet it is doubtful whether there is art in individual letters. Let ters in combination may be satisfying and in a well composed page even beautiful as a whole, but art in letters consists rathe r in the art of arranging and composing them in a pleasing and appropriate manner. The main purpose of letters is the practic al one of making thoughts visible. Ruskin says that all letters ar e frightful things and to be endured only on occasion, that is to
The main purpose of letters is the practical one of making tho ughts visible. Ruskin says that all letters are frightful things and
The main purpose of letters is the practical one of ma king thoughts visible. Ruskin says that all letters are f

10/11

The main purpose of letters is the practical one of making tho ughts visible. Ruskin says that all letters are frightful things and to be endured only on occasion, that is to say, in places where the sense of the inscription is of more importance than extern al ornament. This is a sweeping statement, from which we ne ed not suffer unduly; yet it is doubtful whether there is art in in dividual letters. Letters in combination may be satisfying and i n a well composed page even beautiful as a whole, but art in l etters consists rather in the art of arranging and composing th em in a pleasing and appropriate manner. The main purpose of letters is the practical one of making thoughts visible. Ruski n says that all letters are frightful things and to be endured onl y on occasion, that is to say, in places where the sense of the in scription is of more importance than external ornament. This i s a sweeping statement, from which we need not suffer undul y; yet it is doubtful whether there is art in individual letters. Let ters in combination may be satisfying and in a well composed page even beautiful as a whole, but art in letters consists rathe r in the art of arranging and composing them in a pleasing and appropriate manner. The main purpose of letters is the practic
The main purpose of letters is the practical one of making tho ughts visible. Ruskin says that all letters are frightful things and
The main purpose of letters is the practical one of ma king thoughts visible. Ruskin says that all letters are f

10/12

The main purpose of letters is the practical one of making tho ughts visible. Ruskin says that all letters are frightful things and to be endured only on occasion, that is to say, in places where the sense of the inscription is of more importance than extern al ornament. This is a sweeping statement, from which we ne ed not suffer unduly; yet it is doubtful whether there is art in in dividual letters. Letters in combination may be satisfying and i n a well composed page even beautiful as a whole, but art in l etters consists rather in the art of arranging and composing th em in a pleasing and appropriate manner. The main purpose of letters is the practical one of making thoughts visible. Ruski n says that all letters are frightful things and to be endured onl y on occasion, that is to say, in places where the sense of the in scription is of more importance than external ornament. This i s a sweeping statement, from which we need not suffer undul y; yet it is doubtful whether there is art in individual letters. Let ters in combination may be satisfying and in a well composed page even beautiful as a whole, but art in letters consists rathe
The main purpose of letters is the practical one of making tho ughts visible. Ruskin says that all letters are frightful things and
The main purpose of letters is the practical one of ma king thoughts visible. Ruskin says that all letters are f

10/13

The main purpose of letters is the practical one of making tho ughts visible. Ruskin says that all letters are frightful things and to be endured only on occasion, that is to say, in places where the sense of the inscription is of more importance than extern al ornament. This is a sweeping statement, from which we ne ed not suffer unduly; yet it is doubtful whether there is art in in dividual letters. Letters in combination may be satisfying and i n a well composed page even beautiful as a whole, but art in l etters consists rather in the art of arranging and composing th em in a pleasing and appropriate manner. The main purpose of letters is the practical one of making thoughts visible. Ruski n says that all letters are frightful things and to be endured onl y on occasion, that is to say, in places where the sense of the in scription is of more importance than external ornament. This i s a sweeping statement, from which we need not suffer undul y; yet it is doubtful whether there is art in individual letters. Let ters in combination may be satisfying and in a well composed
The main purpose of letters is the practical one of making tho ughts visible. Ruskin says that all letters are frightful things and
The main purpose of letters is the practical one of ma king thoughts visible. Ruskin says that all letters are f

ITC SOUVENIR 11 POINT SET MINUS ½ UNIT

LIGHT, ITALIC, DEMI, DEMI ITALIC

abcdefghijklmnopqrstuvwxyz – 1 UNIT
abcdefghijklmnopqrstuvwxyz – ½ UNIT
abcdefghijklmnopqrstuvwxyz NORMAL

ABCDEFGHIJKLMNOPQRSTUVWXYZ 1234567890 abcdefghijklmnopqrstuvwxyz
ABCDEFGHIJKLMNOPQRSTUVWXYZ 1234567890 abcdefghijklmnopqrstuvwxyz
ABCDEFGHIJKLMNOPQRSTUVWXYZ 1234567890 abcdefghijklmnopqrstuvwxyz
ABCDEFGHIJKLMNOPQRSTUVWXYZ 1234567890 abcdefghijklmnopqrstuvwxyz

11/11

The main purpose of letters is the practical one of makin g thoughts visible. Ruskin says that all letters are frightful things and to be endured only on occasion, that is to say, in places where the sense of the inscription is of more i mportance than external ornament. This is a sweeping s tatement, from which we need not suffer unduly; yet it is doubtful whether there is art in individual letters. Letters in combination may be satisfying and in a well compose d page even beautiful as a whole, but art in letters consis ts rather in the art of arranging and composing them in a pleasing and appropriate manner. The main purpose of letters is the practical one of making thoughts visible. Ru skin says that all letters are frightful things and to be end ured only on occasion, that is to say, in places where the sense of the inscription is of more importance than exter nal ornament. This is a sweeping statement, from which we need not suffer unduly; yet it is doubtful whether the re is art in individual letters. Letters in combination may be satisfying and in a well composed page even beautif
The main purpose of letters is the practical one of makin g thoughts visible. Ruskin says that all letters are frightful
The main purpose of letters is the practical one of making thoughts visible. Ruskin says that all l

11/12

The main purpose of letters is the practical one of makin g thoughts visible. Ruskin says that all letters are frightful things and to be endured only on occasion, that is to say, in places where the sense of the inscription is of more i mportance than external ornament. This is a sweeping s tatement, from which we need not suffer unduly; yet it is doubtful whether there is art in individual letters. Letters in combination may be satisfying and in a well compose d page even beautiful as a whole, but art in letters consis ts rather in the art of arranging and composing them in a pleasing and appropriate manner. The main purpose of letters is the practical one of making thoughts visible. Ru skin says that all letters are frightful things and to be end ured only on occasion, that is to say, in places where the sense of the inscription is of more importance than exter nal ornament. This is a sweeping statement, from which we need not suffer unduly; yet it is doubtful whether the re is art in individual letters. Letters in combination may
The main purpose of letters is the practical one of makin g thoughts visible. Ruskin says that all letters are frightful
The main purpose of letters is the practical one of making thoughts visible. Ruskin says that all l

11/13

The main purpose of letters is the practical one of makin g thoughts visible. Ruskin says that all letters are frightful things and to be endured only on occasion, that is to say, in places where the sense of the inscription is of more i mportance than external ornament. This is a sweeping s tatement, from which we need not suffer unduly; yet it is doubtful whether there is art in individual letters. Letters in combination may be satisfying and in a well compose d page even beautiful as a whole, but art in letters consis ts rather in the art of arranging and composing them in a pleasing and appropriate manner. The main purpose of letters is the practical one of making thoughts visible. Ru skin says that all letters are frightful things and to be end ured only on occasion, that is to say, in places where the sense of the inscription is of more importance than exter nal ornament. This is a sweeping statement, from which we need not suffer unduly; yet it is doubtful whether the
The main purpose of letters is the practical one of makin g thoughts visible. Ruskin says that all letters are frightful
The main purpose of letters is the practical one of making thoughts visible. Ruskin says that all l

11/14

The main purpose of letters is the practical one of makin g thoughts visible. Ruskin says that all letters are frightful things and to be endured only on occasion, that is to say, in places where the sense of the inscription is of more i mportance than external ornament. This is a sweeping s tatement, from which we need not suffer unduly; yet it is doubtful whether there is art in individual letters. Letters in combination may be satisfying and in a well compose d page even beautiful as a whole, but art in letters consis ts rather in the art of arranging and composing them in a pleasing and appropriate manner. The main purpose of letters is the practical one of making thoughts visible. Ru skin says that all letters are frightful things and to be end ured only on occasion, that is to say, in places where the sense of the inscription is of more importance than exter nal ornament. This is a sweeping statement, from which
The main purpose of letters is the practical one of makin g thoughts visible. Ruskin says that all letters are frightful
The main purpose of letters is the practical one of making thoughts visible. Ruskin says that all l

ITC SOUVENIR 12 POINT SET MINUS ½ UNIT

LIGHT, ITALIC, DEMI, DEMI ITALIC

abcdefghijklmnopqrstuvwxyz – 1 UNIT
abcdefghijklmnopqrstuvwxyz – ½ UNIT
abcdefghijklmnopqrstuvwxyz NORMAL

ABCDEFGHIJKLMNOPQRSTUVWXYZ 1234567890 abcdefghijklmnopqrstuvwxyz
ABCDEFGHIJKLMNOPQRSTUVWXYZ 1234567890 abcdefghijklmnopqrstuvwxyz
ABCDEFGHIJKLMNOPQRSTUVWXYZ 1234567890 abcdefghijklmnopqrstuvwxyz
ABCDEFGHIJKLMNOPQRSTUVWXYZ 1234567890 abcdefghijklmnopqrstuvwxyz

12/12

The main purpose of letters is the practical one of m aking thoughts visible. Ruskin says that all letters are frightful things and to be endured only on occasion, that is to say, in places where the sense of the inscript ion is of more importance than external ornament. This is a sweeping statement, from which we need n ot suffer unduly; yet it is doubtful whether there is art in individual letters. Letters in combination may be s atisfying and in a well composed page even beautif ul as a whole, but art in letters consists rather in the a rt of arranging and composing them in a pleasing an d appropriate manner. The main purpose of letters i s the practical one of making thoughts visible. Ruski n says that all letters are frightful things and to be en dured only on occasion, that is to say, in places wher
The main purpose of letters is the practical one of m aking thoughts visible. Ruskin says that all letters are
The main purpose of letters is the practical o ne of making thoughts visible. Ruskin says t

12/13

The main purpose of letters is the practical one of m aking thoughts visible. Ruskin says that all letters are frightful things and to be endured only on occasion, that is to say, in places where the sense of the inscript ion is of more importance than external ornament. This is a sweeping statement, from which we need n ot suffer unduly; yet it is doubtful whether there is art in individual letters. Letters in combination may be s atisfying and in a well composed page even beautif ul as a whole, but art in letters consists rather in the a rt of arranging and composing them in a pleasing an d appropriate manner. The main purpose of letters i s the practical one of making thoughts visible. Ruski n says that all letters are frightful things and to be en
The main purpose of letters is the practical one of m aking thoughts visible. Ruskin says that all letters are
The main purpose of letters is the practical o ne of making thoughts visible. Ruskin says t

12/14

The main purpose of letters is the practical one of m aking thoughts visible. Ruskin says that all letters are frightful things and to be endured only on occasion, that is to say, in places where the sense of the inscript ion is of more importance than external ornament. This is a sweeping statement, from which we need n ot suffer unduly; yet it is doubtful whether there is art in individual letters. Letters in combination may be s atisfying and in a well composed page even beautif ul as a whole, but art in letters consists rather in the a rt of arranging and composing them in a pleasing an d appropriate manner. The main purpose of letters i s the practical one of making thoughts visible. Ruski n says that all letters are frightful things and to be en dured only on occasion, that is to say, in places wher
The main purpose of letters is the practical one of m aking thoughts visible. Ruskin says that all letters are
The main purpose of letters is the practical o ne of making thoughts visible. Ruskin says t

12/15

The main purpose of letters is the practical one of m aking thoughts visible. Ruskin says that all letters are frightful things and to be endured only on occasion, that is to say, in places where the sense of the inscript ion is of more importance than external ornament. This is a sweeping statement, from which we need n ot suffer unduly; yet it is doubtful whether there is art in individual letters. Letters in combination may be s atisfying and in a well composed page even beautif ul as a whole, but art in letters consists rather in the a rt of arranging and composing them in a pleasing an d appropriate manner. The main purpose of letters i s the practical one of making thoughts visible. Ruski n says that all letters are frightful things and to be en
The main purpose of letters is the practical one of m aking thoughts visible. Ruskin says that all letters are
The main purpose of letters is the practical o ne of making thoughts visible. Ruskin says t

ITC SOUVENIR 14 POINT SET MINUS ½ UNIT

LIGHT, ITALIC, DEMI, DEMI ITALIC

abcdefghijklmnopqrstuvwxyz – 1 UNIT
abcdefghijklmnopqrstuvwxyz – ½ UNIT
abcdefghijklmnopqrstuvwxyz NORMAL

ABCDEFGHIJKLMNOPQRSTUVWXYZ abcdefghijklmnopqrstuvwxyz
ABCDEFGHIJKLMNOPQRSTUVWXYZ abcdefghijklmnopqrstuvwxyz
ABCDEFGHIJKLMNOPQRSTUVWXYZ abcdefghijklmnopqrstuvwxyz
ABCDEFGHIJKLMNOPQRSTUVWXYZ abcdefghijklmnopqrstuvwxyz

14/14

The main purpose of letters is the practical o ne of making thoughts visible. Ruskin says t hat all letters are frightful things and to be en dured only on occasion, that is to say, in plac es where the sense of the inscription is of mo re importance than external ornament. This is a sweeping statement, from which we nee d not suffer unduly; yet it is doubtful whethe r there is art in individual letters. Letters in co mbination may be satisfying and in a well co mposed page even beautiful as a whole, but art in letters consists rather in the art of arran ging and composing them in a pleasing and
The main purpose of letters is the practical o ne of making thoughts visible. Ruskin says t
The main purpose of letters is the prac tical one of making thoughts visible.

14/15

The main purpose of letters is the practical o ne of making thoughts visible. Ruskin says t hat all letters are frightful things and to be en dured only on occasion, that is to say, in plac es where the sense of the inscription is of mo re importance than external ornament. This is a sweeping statement, from which we nee d not suffer unduly; yet it is doubtful whethe r there is art in individual letters. Letters in co mbination may be satisfying and in a well co mposed page even beautiful as a whole, but art in letters consists rather in the art of arran
The main purpose of letters is the practical o ne of making thoughts visible. Ruskin says t
The main purpose of letters is the prac tical one of making thoughts visible.

14/16

The main purpose of letters is the practical o ne of making thoughts visible. Ruskin says t hat all letters are frightful things and to be en dured only on occasion, that is to say, in plac es where the sense of the inscription is of mo re importance than external ornament. This is a sweeping statement, from which we nee d not suffer unduly; yet it is doubtful whethe r there is art in individual letters. Letters in co mbination may be satisfying and in a well co mposed page even beautiful as a whole, but art in letters consists rather in the art of arran ging and composing them in a pleasing and
The main purpose of letters is the practical o ne of making thoughts visible. Ruskin says t
The main purpose of letters is the prac tical one of making thoughts visible.

14/17

The main purpose of letters is the practical o ne of making thoughts visible. Ruskin says t hat all letters are frightful things and to be en dured only on occasion, that is to say, in plac es where the sense of the inscription is of mo re importance than external ornament. This is a sweeping statement, from which we nee d not suffer unduly; yet it is doubtful whethe r there is art in individual letters. Letters in co mbination may be satisfying and in a well co mposed page even beautiful as a whole, but art in letters consists rather in the art of arran
The main purpose of letters is the practical o ne of making thoughts visible. Ruskin says t
The main purpose of letters is the prac tical one of making thoughts visible.

ITC SOUVENIR 6 & 7 POINT SET NORMAL

MEDIUM, ITALIC, BOLD, BOLD ITALIC

ABCDEFGHIJKLMNOPQRSTUVWXYZ 1234567890 abcdefghijklmnopqrstuvwxyz

ABCDEFGHIJKLMNOPQRSTUVWXYZ 1234567890 abcdefghijklmnopqrstuvwxyz

ABCDEFGHIJKLMNOPQRSTUVWXYZ 1234567890 abcdefghijklmnopqrstuvwxyz

ABCDEFGHIJKLMNOPQRSTUVWXYZ 1234567890 abcdefghijklmnopqrstuvwxyz

6/6

The main purpose of letters is the practical one of making thoughts visible. Ruskin says that all letters are frightful things and to be endured only on occasion, that is to say, in places whe re the sense of the inscription is of more importance than external ornament. This is a sweepi ng statement, from which we need not suffer unduly; yet it is doubtful whether there is art in i ndividual letters. Letters in combination may be satisfying and in a well composed page even beautiful as a whole, but art in letters consists rather in the art of arranging and composing t hem in a pleasing and appropriate manner. The main purpose of letters is the practical one of making thoughts visible. Ruskin says that all letters are frightful things and to be endured on ly on occasion, that is to say, in places where the sense of the inscription is of more importanc e than external ornament. This is a sweeping statement, from which we need not suffer undul y; yet it is doubtful whether there is art in individual letters. Letters in combination may be sat isfying and in a well composed page even beautiful as a whole, but art in letters consists rathe r in the art of arranging and composing them in a pleasing and appropriate manner. The mai

The main purpose of letters is the practical one of making thoughts visible. Ruskin says that all letters are frightful things and to be endured only on occasion, that is to say, in places whe

The main purpose of letters is the practical one of making thoughts visible. Rus kin says that all letters are frightful things and to be endured only on occasion, t

6/7

The main purpose of letters is the practical one of making thoughts visible. Ruskin says that all letters are frightful things and to be endured only on occasion, that is to say, in places whe re the sense of the inscription is of more importance than external ornament. This is a sweepi ng statement, from which we need not suffer unduly; yet it is doubtful whether there is art in i ndividual letters. Letters in combination may be satisfying and in a well composed page even beautiful as a whole, but art in letters consists rather in the art of arranging and composing t hem in a pleasing and appropriate manner. The main purpose of letters is the practical one of making thoughts visible. Ruskin says that all letters are frightful things and to be endured on ly on occasion, that is to say, in places where the sense of the inscription is of more importanc e than external ornament. This is a sweeping statement, from which we need not suffer undul y; yet it is doubtful whether there is art in individual letters. Letters in combination may be sat

The main purpose of letters is the practical one of making thoughts visible. Ruskin says that all letters are frightful things and to be endured only on occasion, that is to say, in places whe

The main purpose of letters is the practical one of making thoughts visible. Rus kin says that all letters are frightful things and to be endured only on occasion, t

6/8

The main purpose of letters is the practical one of making thoughts visible. Ruskin says that all letters are frightful things and to be endured only on occasion, that is to say, in places whe re the sense of the inscription is of more importance than external ornament. This is a sweepi ng statement, from which we need not suffer unduly; yet it is doubtful whether there is art in i ndividual letters. Letters in combination may be satisfying and in a well composed page even beautiful as a whole, but art in letters consists rather in the art of arranging and composing t hem in a pleasing and appropriate manner. The main purpose of letters is the practical one of making thoughts visible. Ruskin says that all letters are frightful things and to be endured on ly on occasion, that is to say, in places where the sense of the inscription is of more importanc

The main purpose of letters is the practical one of making thoughts visible. Ruskin says that all letters are frightful things and to be endured only on occasion, that is to say, in places whe

The main purpose of letters is the practical one of making thoughts visible. Rus kin says that all letters are frightful things and to be endured only on occasion, t

6/9

The main purpose of letters is the practical one of making thoughts visible. Ruskin says that all letters are frightful things and to be endured only on occasion, that is to say, in places whe re the sense of the inscription is of more importance than external ornament. This is a sweepi ng statement, from which we need not suffer unduly; yet it is doubtful whether there is art in i ndividual letters. Letters in combination may be satisfying and in a well composed page even beautiful as a whole, but art in letters consists rather in the art of arranging and composing t hem in a pleasing and appropriate manner. The main purpose of letters is the practical one of making thoughts visible. Ruskin says that all letters are frightful things and to be endured on

The main purpose of letters is the practical one of making thoughts visible. Ruskin says that all letters are frightful things and to be endured only on occasion, that is to say, in places whe

The main purpose of letters is the practical one of making thoughts visible. Rus kin says that all letters are frightful things and to be endured only on occasion, t

---

ABCDEFGHIJKLMNOPQRSTUVWXYZ 1234567890 abcdefghijklmnopqrstuvwxyz

ABCDEFGHIJKLMNOPQRSTUVWXYZ 1234567890 abcdefghijklmnopqrstuvwxyz

ABCDEFGHIJKLMNOPQRSTUVWXYZ 1234567890 abcdefghijklmnopqrstuvwxyz

ABCDEFGHIJKLMNOPQRSTUVWXYZ 1234567890 abcdefghijklmnopqrstuvwxyz

7/7

The main purpose of letters is the practical one of making thoughts visible. Rus kin says that all letters are frightful things and to be endured only on occasion, t hat is to say, in places where the sense of the inscription is of more importance t han external ornament. This is a sweeping statement, from which we need not s uffer unduly; yet it is doubtful whether there is art in individual letters. Letters in combination may be satisfying and in a well composed page even beautiful as a whole, but art in letters consists rather in the art of arranging and composing th em in a pleasing and appropriate manner. The main purpose of letters is the pra ctical one of making thoughts visible. Ruskin says that all letters are frightful th ings and to be endured only on occasion, that is to say, in places where the sens e of the inscription is of more importance than external ornament. This is a swe

The main purpose of letters is the practical one of making thoughts visible. Rus kin says that all letters are frightful things and to be endured only on occasion, t

The main purpose of letters is the practical one of making thoughts v isible. Ruskin says that all letters are frightful things and to be endur

7/8

The main purpose of letters is the practical one of making thoughts visible. Rus kin says that all letters are frightful things and to be endured only on occasion, t hat is to say, in places where the sense of the inscription is of more importance t han external ornament. This is a sweeping statement, from which we need not s uffer unduly; yet it is doubtful whether there is art in individual letters. Letters in combination may be satisfying and in a well composed page even beautiful as a whole, but art in letters consists rather in the art of arranging and composing th em in a pleasing and appropriate manner. The main purpose of letters is the pra ctical one of making thoughts visible. Ruskin says that all letters are frightful th ings and to be endured only on occasion, that is to say, in places where the sens

The main purpose of letters is the practical one of making thoughts visible. Rus kin says that all letters are frightful things and to be endured only on occasion, t

The main purpose of letters is the practical one of making thoughts v isible. Ruskin says that all letters are frightful things and to be endur

7/9

The main purpose of letters is the practical one of making thoughts visible. Rus kin says that all letters are frightful things and to be endured only on occasion, t hat is to say, in places where the sense of the inscription is of more importance t han external ornament. This is a sweeping statement, from which we need not s uffer unduly; yet it is doubtful whether there is art in individual letters. Letters in combination may be satisfying and in a well composed page even beautiful as a whole, but art in letters consists rather in the art of arranging and composing th em in a pleasing and appropriate manner. The main purpose of letters is the pra ctical one of making thoughts visible. Ruskin says that all letters are frightful th ings and to be endured only on occasion, that is to say, in places where the sens

The main purpose of letters is the practical one of making thoughts visible. Rus kin says that all letters are frightful things and to be endured only on occasion, t

The main purpose of letters is the practical one of making thoughts v isible. Ruskin says that all letters are frightful things and to be endur

7/10

The main purpose of letters is the practical one of making thoughts visible. Rus kin says that all letters are frightful things and to be endured only on occasion, t hat is to say, in places where the sense of the inscription is of more importance t han external ornament. This is a sweeping statement, from which we need not s uffer unduly; yet it is doubtful whether there is art in individual letters. Letters in combination may be satisfying and in a well composed page even beautiful as a whole, but art in letters consists rather in the art of arranging and composing th em in a pleasing and appropriate manner. The main purpose of letters is the pra ctical one of making thoughts visible. Ruskin says that all letters are frightful th

The main purpose of letters is the practical one of making thoughts visible. Rus kin says that all letters are frightful things and to be endured only on occasion, t

The main purpose of letters is the practical one of making thoughts v isible. Ruskin says that all letters are frightful things and to be endur

ITC SOUVENIR 8 & 9 POINT SET NORMAL

MEDIUM, ITALIC, BOLD, BOLD ITALIC

ABCDEFGHIJKLMNOPQRSTUVWXYZ 1234567890 abcdefghijklmnopqrstuvwxyz
ABCDEFGHIJKLMNOPQRSTUVWXYZ 1234567890 abcdefghijklmnopqrstuvwxyz
ABCDEFGHIJKLMNOPQRSTUVWXYZ 1234567890 abcdefghijklmnopqrstuvwxyz
ABCDEFGHIJKLMNOPQRSTUVWXYZ 1234567890 abcdefghijklmnopqrstuvwxyz

8/8

The main purpose of letters is the practical one of making thoughts vi sible. Ruskin says that all letters are frightful things and to be endure d only on occasion, that is to say, in places where the sense of the insc ription is of more importance than external ornament. This is a sweep ing statement, from which we need not suffer unduly; yet it is doubtful whether there is art in individual letters. Letters in combination may be satisfying and in a well composed page even beautiful as a whole, b ut art in letters consists rather in the art of arranging and composing t hem in a pleasing and appropriate manner. The main purpose of lette
The main purpose of letters is the practical one of making thoughts vi sible. Ruskin says that all letters are frightful things and to be endure
The main purpose of letters is the practical one of making th oughts visible. Ruskin says that all letters are frightful thing

8/10

The main purpose of letters is the practical one of making thoughts vi sible. Ruskin says that all letters are frightful things and to be endure d only on occasion, that is to say, in places where the sense of the insc ription is of more importance than external ornament. This is a sweep ing statement, from which we need not suffer unduly; yet it is doubtful whether there is art in individual letters. Letters in combination may be satisfying and in a well composed page even beautiful as a whole, b
The main purpose of letters is the practical one of making thoughts vi sible. Ruskin says that all letters are frightful things and to be endure
The main purpose of letters is the practical one of making th oughts visible. Ruskin says that all letters are frightful thing

8/9

The main purpose of letters is the practical one of making thoughts vi sible. Ruskin says that all letters are frightful things and to be endure d only on occasion, that is to say, in places where the sense of the insc ription is of more importance than external ornament. This is a sweep ing statement, from which we need not suffer unduly; yet it is doubtful whether there is art in individual letters. Letters in combination may be satisfying and in a well composed page even beautiful as a whole, b ut art in letters consists rather in the art of arranging and composing t
The main purpose of letters is the practical one of making thoughts vi sible. Ruskin says that all letters are frightful things and to be endure
The main purpose of letters is the practical one of making th oughts visible. Ruskin says that all letters are frightful thing

8/11

The main purpose of letters is the practical one of making thoughts vi sible. Ruskin says that all letters are frightful things and to be endure d only on occasion, that is to say, in places where the sense of the insc ription is of more importance than external ornament. This is a sweep ing statement, from which we need not suffer unduly; yet it is doubtful whether there is art in individual letters. Letters in combination may be satisfying and in a well composed page even beautiful as a whole, b
The main purpose of letters is the practical one of making thoughts vi sible. Ruskin says that all letters are frightful things and to be endure
The main purpose of letters is the practical one of making th oughts visible. Ruskin says that all letters are frightful thing

---

ABCDEFGHIJKLMNOPQRSTUVWXYZ 1234567890 abcdefghijklmnopqrstuvwxyz
ABCDEFGHIJKLMNOPQRSTUVWXYZ 1234567890 abcdefghijklmnopqrstuvwxyz
ABCDEFGHIJKLMNOPQRSTUVWXYZ 1234567890 abcdefghijklmnopqrstuvwxyz
ABCDEFGHIJKLMNOPQRSTUVWXYZ 1234567890 abcdefghijklmnopqrstuvwxyz

9/9

The main purpose of letters is the practical one of making tho ughts visible. Ruskin says that all letters are frightful things a nd to be endured only on occasion, that is to say, in places whe re the sense of the inscription is of more importance than exte rnal ornament. This is a sweeping statement, from which we n eed not suffer unduly; yet it is doubtful whether there is art i n individual letters. Letters in combination may be satisfying an d in a well composed page even beautiful as a whole, but art in
The main purpose of letters is the practical one of making tho ughts visible. Ruskin says that all letters are frightful things a
The main purpose of letters is the practical one of ma king thoughts visible. Ruskin says that all letters are f

9/11

The main purpose of letters is the practical one of making tho ughts visible. Ruskin says that all letters are frightful things a nd to be endured only on occasion, that is to say, in places whe re the sense of the inscription is of more importance than exte rnal ornament. This is a sweeping statement, from which we n eed not suffer unduly; yet it is doubtful whether there is art i n individual letters. Letters in combination may be satisfying an
The main purpose of letters is the practical one of making tho ughts visible. Ruskin says that all letters are frightful things a
The main purpose of letters is the practical one of ma king thoughts visible. Ruskin says that all letters are f

9/10

The main purpose of letters is the practical one of making tho ughts visible. Ruskin says that all letters are frightful things a nd to be endured only on occasion, that is to say, in places whe re the sense of the inscription is of more importance than exte rnal ornament. This is a sweeping statement, from which we n eed not suffer unduly; yet it is doubtful whether there is art i n individual letters. Letters in combination may be satisfying an
The main purpose of letters is the practical one of making tho ughts visible. Ruskin says that all letters are frightful things a
The main purpose of letters is the practical one of ma king thoughts visible. Ruskin says that all letters are f

9/12

The main purpose of letters is the practical one of making tho ughts visible. Ruskin says that all letters are frightful things a nd to be endured only on occasion, that is to say, in places whe re the sense of the inscription is of more importance than exte rnal ornament. This is a sweeping statement, from which we n eed not suffer unduly; yet it is doubtful whether there is art i n individual letters. Letters in combination may be satisfying an
The main purpose of letters is the practical one of making tho ughts visible. Ruskin says that all letters are frightful things a
The main purpose of letters is the practical one of ma king thoughts visible. Ruskin says that all letters are f

ITC SOUVENIR 10 POINT SET MINUS ½ UNIT

MEDIUM, ITALIC, BOLD, BOLD ITALIC

abcdefghijklmnopqrstuvwxyz – 1 UNIT
abcdefghijklmnopqrstuvwxyz – ½ UNIT
abcdefghijklmnopqrstuvwxyz NORMAL

ABCDEFGHIJKLMNOPQRSTUVWXYZ 1234567890 abcdefghijklmnopqrstuvwxyz
ABCDEFGHIJKLMNOPQRSTUVWXYZ 1234567890 abcdefghijklmnopqrstuvwxyz
ABCDEFGHIJKLMNOPQRSTUVWXYZ 1234567890 abcdefghijklmnopqrstuvwxyz
ABCDEFGHIJKLMNOPQRSTUVWXYZ 1234567890 abcdefghijklmnopqrstuvwxyz

10/10

The main purpose of letters is the practical one of making thoughts visible. Ruskin says that all letters are frightful t hings and to be endured only on occasion, that is to say, in places where the sense of the inscription is of more import ance than external ornament. This is a sweeping stateme nt, from which we need not suffer unduly; yet it is doubtful whether there is art in individual letters. Letters in combin ation may be satisfying and in a well composed page even beautiful as a whole, but art in letters consists rather in the art of arranging and composing them in a pleasing and ap propriate manner. The main purpose of letters is the pract ical one of making thoughts visible. Ruskin says that all le tters are frightful things and to be endured only on occasio n, that is to say, in places where the sense of the inscriptio n is of more importance than external ornament. This is a sweeping statement, from which we need not suffer undul y; yet it is doubtful whether there is art in individual letters. Letters in combination may be satisfying and in a well co mposed page even beautiful as a whole, but art in letters c onsists rather in the art of arranging and composing them in a pleasing and appropriate manner. The main purpose of letters is the practical one of making thoughts visible. R
The main purpose of letters is the practical one of making thoughts visible. Ruskin says that all letters are frightful t
The main purpose of letters is the practical one of making thoughts visible. Ruskin says that all lette

10/11

The main purpose of letters is the practical one of making thoughts visible. Ruskin says that all letters are frightful t hings and to be endured only on occasion, that is to say, in places where the sense of the inscription is of more import ance than external ornament. This is a sweeping stateme nt, from which we need not suffer unduly; yet it is doubtful whether there is art in individual letters. Letters in combin ation may be satisfying and in a well composed page even beautiful as a whole, but art in letters consists rather in the art of arranging and composing them in a pleasing and ap propriate manner. The main purpose of letters is the pract ical one of making thoughts visible. Ruskin says that all le tters are frightful things and to be endured only on occasio n, that is to say, in places where the sense of the inscriptio n is of more importance than external ornament. This is a sweeping statement, from which we need not suffer undul y; yet it is doubtful whether there is art in individual letters. Letters in combination may be satisfying and in a well co mposed page even beautiful as a whole, but art in letters c onsists rather in the art of arranging and composing them
The main purpose of letters is the practical one of making thoughts visible. Ruskin says that all letters are frightful t
The main purpose of letters is the practical one of making thoughts visible. Ruskin says that all lette

10/12

The main purpose of letters is the practical one of making thoughts visible. Ruskin says that all letters are frightful t hings and to be endured only on occasion, that is to say, in places where the sense of the inscription is of more import ance than external ornament. This is a sweeping stateme nt, from which we need not suffer unduly; yet it is doubtful whether there is art in individual letters. Letters in combin ation may be satisfying and in a well composed page even beautiful as a whole, but art in letters consists rather in the art of arranging and composing them in a pleasing and ap propriate manner. The main purpose of letters is the pract ical one of making thoughts visible. Ruskin says that all le tters are frightful things and to be endured only on occasio n, that is to say, in places where the sense of the inscriptio n is of more importance than external ornament. This is a sweeping statement, from which we need not suffer undul y; yet it is doubtful whether there is art in individual letters. Letters in combination may be satisfying and in a well co
The main purpose of letters is the practical one of making thoughts visible. Ruskin says that all letters are frightful t
The main purpose of letters is the practical one of making thoughts visible. Ruskin says that all lette

10/13

The main purpose of letters is the practical one of making thoughts visible. Ruskin says that all letters are frightful t hings and to be endured only on occasion, that is to say, in places where the sense of the inscription is of more import ance than external ornament. This is a sweeping stateme nt, from which we need not suffer unduly; yet it is doubtful whether there is art in individual letters. Letters in combin ation may be satisfying and in a well composed page even beautiful as a whole, but art in letters consists rather in the art of arranging and composing them in a pleasing and ap propriate manner. The main purpose of letters is the pract ical one of making thoughts visible. Ruskin says that all le tters are frightful things and to be endured only on occasio n, that is to say, in places where the sense of the inscriptio n is of more importance than external ornament. This is a sweeping statement, from which we need not suffer undul y; yet it is doubtful whether there is art in individual letters.
The main purpose of letters is the practical one of making thoughts visible. Ruskin says that all letters are frightful t
The main purpose of letters is the practical one of making thoughts visible. Ruskin says that all lette

ITC SOUVENIR 11 POINT SET MINUS ½ UNIT

MEDIUM, ITALIC, BOLD, BOLD ITALIC

abcdefghijklmnopqrstuvwxyz – 1 UNIT
abcdefghijklmnopqrstuvwxyz – ½ UNIT
abcdefghijklmnopqrstuvwxyz NORMAL

ABCDEFGHIJKLMNOPQRSTUVWXYZ 1234567890 abcdefghijklmnopqrstuvwxyz
ABCDEFGHIJKLMNOPQRSTUVWXYZ 1234567890 abcdefghijklmnopqrstuvwxyz
ABCDEFGHIJKLMNOPQRSTUVWXYZ 1234567890 abcdefghijklmnopqrstuvwxyz
ABCDEFGHIJKLMNOPQRSTUVWXYZ 1234567890 abcdefghijklmnopqrstuvwxyz

11/11

The main purpose of letters is the practical one of m aking thoughts visible. Ruskin says that all letters ar e frightful things and to be endured only on occasion, that is to say, in places where the sense of the inscri ption is of more importance than external ornament. This is a sweeping statement, from which we need n ot suffer unduly; yet it is doubtful whether there is art in individual letters. Letters in combination may be s atisfying and in a well composed page even beautiful as a whole, but art in letters consists rather in the art of arranging and composing them in a pleasing and appropriate manner. The main purpose of letters is t he practical one of making thoughts visible. Ruskin says that all letters are frightful things and to be end ured only on occasion, that is to say, in places where the sense of the inscription is of more importance th an external ornament. This is a sweeping statement, from which we need not suffer unduly; yet it is doubtf ul whether there is art in individual letters. Letters in
The main purpose of letters is the practical one of m aking thoughts visible. Ruskin says that all letters ar
The main purpose of letters is the practical o ne of making thoughts visible. Ruskin says th

11/12

The main purpose of letters is the practical one of m aking thoughts visible. Ruskin says that all letters ar e frightful things and to be endured only on occasion, that is to say, in places where the sense of the inscri ption is of more importance than external ornament. This is a sweeping statement, from which we need n ot suffer unduly; yet it is doubtful whether there is art in individual letters. Letters in combination may be s atisfying and in a well composed page even beautiful as a whole, but art in letters consists rather in the art of arranging and composing them in a pleasing and appropriate manner. The main purpose of letters is t he practical one of making thoughts visible. Ruskin says that all letters are frightful things and to be end ured only on occasion, that is to say, in places where the sense of the inscription is of more importance th an external ornament. This is a sweeping statement, from which we need not suffer unduly; yet it is doubtf
The main purpose of letters is the practical one of m aking thoughts visible. Ruskin says that all letters ar
The main purpose of letters is the practical o ne of making thoughts visible. Ruskin says th

11/13

The main purpose of letters is the practical one of m aking thoughts visible. Ruskin says that all letters ar e frightful things and to be endured only on occasion, that is to say, in places where the sense of the inscri ption is of more importance than external ornament. This is a sweeping statement, from which we need n ot suffer unduly; yet it is doubtful whether there is art in individual letters. Letters in combination may be s atisfying and in a well composed page even beautiful as a whole, but art in letters consists rather in the art of arranging and composing them in a pleasing and appropriate manner. The main purpose of letters is t he practical one of making thoughts visible. Ruskin says that all letters are frightful things and to be end ured only on occasion, that is to say, in places where the sense of the inscription is of more importance th an external ornament. This is a sweeping statement,
The main purpose of letters is the practical one of m aking thoughts visible. Ruskin says that all letters ar
The main purpose of letters is the practical o ne of making thoughts visible. Ruskin says th

11/14

The main purpose of letters is the practical one of m aking thoughts visible. Ruskin says that all letters ar e frightful things and to be endured only on occasion, that is to say, in places where the sense of the inscri ption is of more importance than external ornament. This is a sweeping statement, from which we need n ot suffer unduly; yet it is doubtful whether there is art in individual letters. Letters in combination may be s atisfying and in a well composed page even beautiful as a whole, but art in letters consists rather in the art of arranging and composing them in a pleasing and appropriate manner. The main purpose of letters is t he practical one of making thoughts visible. Ruskin says that all letters are frightful things and to be end ured only on occasion, that is to say, in places where the sense of the inscription is of more importance th
The main purpose of letters is the practical one of m aking thoughts visible. Ruskin says that all letters ar
The main purpose of letters is the practical o ne of making thoughts visible. Ruskin says th

ITC SOUVENIR 12 POINT SET MINUS ½ UNIT

MEDIUM, ITALIC, BOLD, BOLD ITALIC

abcdefghijklmnopqrstuvwxyz – 1 UNIT
abcdefghijklmnopqrstuvwxyz – ½ UNIT
abcdefghijklmnopqrstuvwxyz NORMAL

ABCDEFGHIJKLMNOPQRSTUVWXYZ 1234567890 abcdefghijklmnopqrstuvwxyz
ABCDEFGHIJKLMNOPQRSTUVWXYZ 1234567890 abcdefghijklmnopqrstuvwxyz
ABCDEFGHIJKLMNOPQRSTUVWXYZ 1234567890 abcdefghijklmnopqrstuvw
ABCDEFGHIJKLMNOPQRSTUVWXYZ 1234567890 abcdefghijklmnopqrstuvw

12/12

The main purpose of letters is the practical one o f making thoughts visible. Ruskin says that all let ters are frightful things and to be endured only on occasion, that is to say, in places where the sense of the inscription is of more importance than ext ernal ornament. This is a sweeping statement, fr om which we need not suffer unduly; yet it is dou btful whether there is art in individual letters. Let ters in combination may be satisfying and in a we ll composed page even beautiful as a whole, but art in letters consists rather in the art of arrangin g and composing them in a pleasing and approp riate manner. The main purpose of letters is the p ractical one of making thoughts visible. Ruskin s ays that all letters are frightful things and to be e
The main purpose of letters is the practical one o f making thoughts visible. Ruskin says that all le
The main purpose of letters is the practic al one of making thoughts visible. Ruskin

12/13

The main purpose of letters is the practical one o f making thoughts visible. Ruskin says that all let ters are frightful things and to be endured only on occasion, that is to say, in places where the sense of the inscription is of more importance than ext ernal ornament. This is a sweeping statement, fr om which we need not suffer unduly; yet it is dou btful whether there is art in individual letters. Let ters in combination may be satisfying and in a we ll composed page even beautiful as a whole, but art in letters consists rather in the art of arrangin g and composing them in a pleasing and approp riate manner. The main purpose of letters is the p ractical one of making thoughts visible. Ruskin s
The main purpose of letters is the practical one o f making thoughts visible. Ruskin says that all le
The main purpose of letters is the practic al one of making thoughts visible. Ruskin

12/14

The main purpose of letters is the practical one o f making thoughts visible. Ruskin says that all let ters are frightful things and to be endured only on occasion, that is to say, in places where the sense of the inscription is of more importance than ext ernal ornament. This is a sweeping statement, fr om which we need not suffer unduly; yet it is dou btful whether there is art in individual letters. Let ters in combination may be satisfying and in a we ll composed page even beautiful as a whole, but art in letters consists rather in the art of arrangin g and composing them in a pleasing and approp riate manner. The main purpose of letters is the p ractical one of making thoughts visible. Ruskin s ays that all letters are frightful things and to be e
The main purpose of letters is the practical one o f making thoughts visible. Ruskin says that all le
The main purpose of letters is the practic al one of making thoughts visible. Ruskin

12/15

The main purpose of letters is the practical one o f making thoughts visible. Ruskin says that all let ters are frightful things and to be endured only on occasion, that is to say, in places where the sense of the inscription is of more importance than ext ernal ornament. This is a sweeping statement, fr om which we need not suffer unduly; yet it is dou btful whether there is art in individual letters. Let ters in combination may be satisfying and in a we ll composed page even beautiful as a whole, but art in letters consists rather in the art of arrangin g and composing them in a pleasing and approp riate manner. The main purpose of letters is the p ractical one of making thoughts visible. Ruskin s
The main purpose of letters is the practical one o f making thoughts visible. Ruskin says that all le
The main purpose of letters is the practic al one of making thoughts visible. Ruskin

ITC SOUVENIR 14 POINT SET MINUS ½ UNIT

MEDIUM, ITALIC, BOLD, BOLD ITALIC

abcdefghijklmnopqrstuvwxyz – 1 UNIT
abcdefghijklmnopqrstuvwxyz – ½ UNIT
abcdefghijklmnopqrstuvwxyz NORMAL

ABCDEFGHIJKLMNOPQRSTUVWXYZ abcdefghijklmnopqrstuvwxyz
ABCDEFGHIJKLMNOPQRSTUVWXYZ abcdefghijklmnopqrstuvwxyz
ABCDEFGHIJKLMNOPQRSTUVWXYZ abcdefghijklmnopqrstuvwxyz
ABCDEFGHIJKLMNOPQRSTUVWXYZ abcdefghijklmnopqrstuvwxyz

14/14

The main purpose of letters is the practic al one of making thoughts visible. Ruskin says that all letters are frightful things an d to be endured only on occasion, that is t o say, in places where the sense of the ins cription is of more importance than exter nal ornament. This is a sweeping stateme nt, from which we need not suffer unduly; yet it is doubtful whether there is art in ind ividual letters. Letters in combination ma y be satisfying and in a well composed pa ge even beautiful as a whole, but art in lett ers consists rather in the art of arranging
The main purpose of letters is the practic al one of making thoughts visible. Ruskin
The main purpose of letters is the p ractical one of making thoughts visi

14/15

The main purpose of letters is the practic al one of making thoughts visible. Ruskin says that all letters are frightful things an d to be endured only on occasion, that is t o say, in places where the sense of the ins cription is of more importance than exter nal ornament. This is a sweeping stateme nt, from which we need not suffer unduly; yet it is doubtful whether there is art in ind ividual letters. Letters in combination ma y be satisfying and in a well composed pa ge even beautiful as a whole, but art in lett
The main purpose of letters is the practic al one of making thoughts visible. Ruskin
The main purpose of letters is the p ractical one of making thoughts visi

14/16

The main purpose of letters is the practic al one of making thoughts visible. Ruskin says that all letters are frightful things an d to be endured only on occasion, that is t o say, in places where the sense of the ins cription is of more importance than exter nal ornament. This is a sweeping stateme nt, from which we need not suffer unduly; yet it is doubtful whether there is art in ind ividual letters. Letters in combination ma y be satisfying and in a well composed pa ge even beautiful as a whole, but art in lett ers consists rather in the art of arranging
The main purpose of letters is the practic al one of making thoughts visible. Ruskin
The main purpose of letters is the p ractical one of making thoughts visi

14/17

The main purpose of letters is the practic al one of making thoughts visible. Ruskin says that all letters are frightful things an d to be endured only on occasion, that is t o say, in places where the sense of the ins cription is of more importance than exter nal ornament. This is a sweeping stateme nt, from which we need not suffer unduly; yet it is doubtful whether there is art in ind ividual letters. Letters in combination ma y be satisfying and in a well composed pa ge even beautiful as a whole, but art in lett
The main purpose of letters is the practic al one of making thoughts visible. Ruskin
The main purpose of letters is the p ractical one of making thoughts visi

SPARTAN 6 & 7 POINT SET NORMAL

LIGHT, ITALIC, HEAVY, HEAVY ITALIC

ABCDEFGHIJKLMNOPQRSTUVWXYZ 1234567890 abcdefghijklmnopqrstuvwxyz

ABCDEFGHIJKLMNOPQRSTUVWXYZ 1234567890 abcdefghijklmnopqrstuvwxyz

ABCDEFGHIJKLMNOPQRSTUVWXYZ 1234567890 abcdefghijklmnopqrstuvwxyz

ABCDEFGHIJKLMNOPQRSTUVWXYZ 1234567890 abcdefghijklmnopqrstuvwxyz

6/6

The main purpose of letters is the practical one of making thoughts visible. Ruskin says that all letters are frightf
ul things and to be endured only on occasion, that is to say, in places where the sense of the inscription is of mo
re importance than external ornament. This is a sweeping statement, from which we need not suffer unduly; ye
t it is doubtful whether there is art in individual letters. Letters in combination may be satisfying and in a well co
mposed page even beautiful as a whole, but art in letters consists rather in the art of arranging and composing
them in a pleasing and appropriate manner. The main purpose of letters is the practical one of making thought
s visible. Ruskin says that all letters are frightful things and to be endured only on occasion, that is to say, in pla
ces where the sense of the inscription is of more importance than external ornament. This is a sweeping statem
ent, from which we need not suffer unduly; yet it is doubtful whether there is art in individual letters. Letters in c
ombination may be satisfying and in a well composed page even beautiful as a whole, but art in letters consist
s rather in the art of arranging and composing them in a pleasing and appropriate manner. The main purpose
of letters is the practical one of making thoughts visible. Ruskin says that all letters are frightful things and to be
endured only on occasion, that is to say, in places where the sense of the inscription is of more importance than
*The main purpose of letters is the practical one of making thoughts visible. Ruskin says that all letters are frightf
ul things and to be endured only on occasion, that is to say, in places where the sense of the inscription is of mo*
**The main purpose of letters is the practical one of making thoughts visible. Ruskin says that all le
tters are frightful things and to be endured only on occasion, that is to say, in places where the se**

6/7

The main purpose of letters is the practical one of making thoughts visible. Ruskin says that all letters are frightf
ul things and to be endured only on occasion, that is to say, in places where the sense of the inscription is of mo
re importance than external ornament. This is a sweeping statement, from which we need not suffer unduly; ye
t it is doubtful whether there is art in individual letters. Letters in combination may be satisfying and in a well co
mposed page even beautiful as a whole, but art in letters consists rather in the art of arranging and composing
them in a pleasing and appropriate manner. The main purpose of letters is the practical one of making thought
s visible. Ruskin says that all letters are frightful things and to be endured only on occasion, that is to say, in pla
ces where the sense of the inscription is of more importance than external ornament. This is a sweeping statem
ent, from which we need not suffer unduly; yet it is doubtful whether there is art in individual letters. Letters in c
ombination may be satisfying and in a well composed page even beautiful as a whole, but art in letters consist
s rather in the art of arranging and composing them in a pleasing and appropriate manner. The main purpose
*The main purpose of letters is the practical one of making thoughts visible. Ruskin says that all letters are frightf
ul things and to be endured only on occasion, that is to say, in places where the sense of the inscription is of mo*
**The main purpose of letters is the practical one of making thoughts visible. Ruskin says that all le
tters are frightful things and to be endured only on occasion, that is to say, in places where the se**

6/8

The main purpose of letters is the practical one of making thoughts visible. Ruskin says that all letters are frightf
ul things and to be endured only on occasion, that is to say, in places where the sense of the inscription is of mo
re importance than external ornament. This is a sweeping statement, from which we need not suffer unduly; ye
t it is doubtful whether there is art in individual letters. Letters in combination may be satisfying and in a well co
mposed page even beautiful as a whole, but art in letters consists rather in the art of arranging and composing
them in a pleasing and appropriate manner. The main purpose of letters is the practical one of making thought
s visible. Ruskin says that all letters are frightful things and to be endured only on occasion, that is to say, in pla
ces where the sense of the inscription is of more importance than external ornament. This is a sweeping statem
ent, from which we need not suffer unduly; yet it is doubtful whether there is art in individual letters. Letters in c
*The main purpose of letters is the practical one of making thoughts visible. Ruskin says that all letters are frightf
ul things and to be endured only on occasion, that is to say, in places where the sense of the inscription is of mo*
**The main purpose of letters is the practical one of making thoughts visible. Ruskin says that all le
tters are frightful things and to be endured only on occasion, that is to say, in places where the se**

6/9

The main purpose of letters is the practical one of making thoughts visible. Ruskin says that all letters are frightf
ul things and to be endured only on occasion, that is to say, in places where the sense of the inscription is of mo
re importance than external ornament. This is a sweeping statement, from which we need not suffer unduly; ye
t it is doubtful whether there is art in individual letters. Letters in combination may be satisfying and in a well co
mposed page even beautiful as a whole, but art in letters consists rather in the art of arranging and composing
them in a pleasing and appropriate manner. The main purpose of letters is the practical one of making thought
s visible. Ruskin says that all letters are frightful things and to be endured only on occasion, that is to say, in pla
ces where the sense of the inscription is of more importance than external ornament. This is a sweeping statem
*The main purpose of letters is the practical one of making thoughts visible. Ruskin says that all letters are frightf
ul things and to be endured only on occasion, that is to say, in places where the sense of the inscription is of mo*
**The main purpose of letters is the practical one of making thoughts visible. Ruskin says that all le
tters are frightful things and to be endured only on occasion, that is to say, in places where the se**

ABCDEFGHIJKLMNOPQRSTUVWXYZ 1234567890 abcdefghijklmnopqrstuvwxyz

ABCDEFGHIJKLMNOPQRSTUVWXYZ 1234567890 abcdefghijklmnopqrstuvwxyz

ABCDEFGHIJKLMNOPQRSTUVWXYZ 1234567890 abcdefghijklmnopqrstuvwxyz

ABCDEFGHIJKLMNOPQRSTUVWXYZ 1234567890 abcdefghijklmnopqrstuvwxyz

7/7

The main purpose of letters is the practical one of making thoughts visible. Ruskin says that all l
etters are frightful things and to be endured only on occasion, that is to say, in places where th
e sense of the inscription is of more importance than external ornament. This is a sweeping stat
ement, from which we need not suffer unduly; yet it is doubtful whether there is art in individual
letters. Letters in combination may be satisfying and in a well composed page even beautiful a
s a whole, but art in letters consists rather in the art of arranging and composing them in a plea
sing and appropriate manner. The main purpose of letters is the practical one of making thoug
hts visible. Ruskin says that all letters are frightful things and to be endured only on occasion, th
at is to say, in places where the sense of the inscription is of more importance than external orn
ament. This is a sweeping statement, from which we need not suffer unduly; yet it is doubtful w
hether there is art in individual letters. Letters in combination may be satisfying and in a well co
*The main purpose of letters is the practical one of making thoughts visible. Ruskin says that all l
etters are frightful things and to be endured only on occasion, that is to say, in places where th*
**The main purpose of letters is the practical one of making thoughts visible. Ruskin
says that all letters are frightful things and to be endured only on occasion, that is t**

7/8

The main purpose of letters is the practical one of making thoughts visible. Ruskin says that all l
etters are frightful things and to be endured only on occasion, that is to say, in places where th
e sense of the inscription is of more importance than external ornament. This is a sweeping stat
ement, from which we need not suffer unduly; yet it is doubtful whether there is art in individual
letters. Letters in combination may be satisfying and in a well composed page even beautiful a
s a whole, but art in letters consists rather in the art of arranging and composing them in a plea
sing and appropriate manner. The main purpose of letters is the practical one of making thoug
hts visible. Ruskin says that all letters are frightful things and to be endured only on occasion, th
at is to say, in places where the sense of the inscription is of more importance than external orn
ament. This is a sweeping statement, from which we need not suffer unduly; yet it is doubtful w
*The main purpose of letters is the practical one of making thoughts visible. Ruskin says that all l
etters are frightful things and to be endured only on occasion, that is to say, in places where th*
**The main purpose of letters is the practical one of making thoughts visible. Ruskin
says that all letters are frightful things and to be endured only on occasion, that is t**

7/9

The main purpose of letters is the practical one of making thoughts visible. Ruskin says that all l
etters are frightful things and to be endured only on occasion, that is to say, in places where th
e sense of the inscription is of more importance than external ornament. This is a sweeping stat
ement, from which we need not suffer unduly; yet it is doubtful whether there is art in individual
letters. Letters in combination may be satisfying and in a well composed page even beautiful a
s a whole, but art in letters consists rather in the art of arranging and composing them in a plea
sing and appropriate manner. The main purpose of letters is the practical one of making thoug
hts visible. Ruskin says that all letters are frightful things and to be endured only on occasion, th
at is to say, in places where the sense of the inscription is of more importance than external orn
ament. This is a sweeping statement, from which we need not suffer unduly; yet it is doubtful w
*The main purpose of letters is the practical one of making thoughts visible. Ruskin says that all l
etters are frightful things and to be endured only on occasion, that is to say, in places where th*
**The main purpose of letters is the practical one of making thoughts visible. Ruskin
says that all letters are frightful things and to be endured only on occasion, that is t**

7/10

The main purpose of letters is the practical one of making thoughts visible. Ruskin says that all l
etters are frightful things and to be endured only on occasion, that is to say, in places where th
e sense of the inscription is of more importance than external ornament. This is a sweeping stat
ement, from which we need not suffer unduly; yet it is doubtful whether there is art in individual
letters. Letters in combination may be satisfying and in a well composed page even beautiful a
s a whole, but art in letters consists rather in the art of arranging and composing them in a plea
sing and appropriate manner. The main purpose of letters is the practical one of making thoug
hts visible. Ruskin says that all letters are frightful things and to be endured only on occasion, th
at is to say, in places where the sense of the inscription is of more importance than external orn
*The main purpose of letters is the practical one of making thoughts visible. Ruskin says that all l
etters are frightful things and to be endured only on occasion, that is to say, in places where th*
**The main purpose of letters is the practical one of making thoughts visible. Ruskin
says that all letters are frightful things and to be endured only on occasion, that is t**

SPARTAN 8 & 9 POINT SET NORMAL

LIGHT, ITALIC, HEAVY, HEAVY ITALIC

ABCDEFGHIJKLMNOPQRSTUVWXYZ 1234567890 abcdefghijklmnopqrstuvwxyz

ABCDEFGHIJKLMNOPQRSTUVWXYZ 1234567890 abcdefghijklmnopqrstuvwxyz

ABCDEFGHIJKLMNOPQRSTUVWXYZ 1234567890 abcdefghijklmnopqrstuvwxyz

ABCDEFGHIJKLMNOPQRSTUVWXYZ 1234567890 abcdefghijklmnopqrstuvwxyz

8/8

The main purpose of letters is the practical one of making thoughts visible. Ruskin s ays that all letters are frightful things and to be endured only on occasion, that is to say, in places where the sense of the inscription is of more importance than externa l ornament. This is a sweeping statement, from which we need not suffer unduly; ye t it is doubtful whether there is art in individual letters. Letters in combination may b e satisfying and in a well composed page even beautiful as a whole, but art in lette rs consists rather in the art of arranging and composing them in a pleasing and ap propriate manner. The main purpose of letters is the practical one of making thoug hts visible. Ruskin says that all letters are frightful things and to be endured only on *The main purpose of letters is the practical one of making thoughts visible. Ruskin s ays that all letters are frightful things and to be endured only on occasion, that is to* **The main purpose of letters is the practical one of making thoughts visibl e. Ruskin says that all letters are frightful things and to be endured only**

8/9

The main purpose of letters is the practical one of making thoughts visible. Ruskin s ays that all letters are frightful things and to be endured only on occasion, that is to say, in places where the sense of the inscription is of more importance than externa l ornament. This is a sweeping statement, from which we need not suffer unduly; ye t it is doubtful whether there is art in individual letters. Letters in combination may b e satisfying and in a well composed page even beautiful as a whole, but art in lette rs consists rather in the art of arranging and composing them in a pleasing and ap propriate manner. The main purpose of letters is the practical one of making thoug *The main purpose of letters is the practical one of making thoughts visible. Ruskin s ays that all letters are frightful things and to be endured only on occasion, that is to* **The main purpose of letters is the practical one of making thoughts visibl e. Ruskin says that all letters are frightful things and to be endured only**

8/10

The main purpose of letters is the practical one of making thoughts visible. Ruskin s ays that all letters are frightful things and to be endured only on occasion, that is to say, in places where the sense of the inscription is of more importance than externa l ornament. This is a sweeping statement, from which we need not suffer unduly; ye t it is doubtful whether there is art in individual letters. Letters in combination may b e satisfying and in a well composed page even beautiful as a whole, but art in lette rs consists rather in the art of arranging and composing them in a pleasing and ap *The main purpose of letters is the practical one of making thoughts visible. Ruskin s ays that all letters are frightful things and to be endured only on occasion, that is to* **The main purpose of letters is the practical one of making thoughts visibl e. Ruskin says that all letters are frightful things and to be endured only**

8/11

The main purpose of letters is the practical one of making thoughts visible. Ruskin s ays that all letters are frightful things and to be endured only on occasion, that is to say, in places where the sense of the inscription is of more importance than externa l ornament. This is a sweeping statement, from which we need not suffer unduly; ye t it is doubtful whether there is art in individual letters. Letters in combination may b e satisfying and in a well composed page even beautiful as a whole, but art in lette rs consists rather in the art of arranging and composing them in a pleasing and ap *The main purpose of letters is the practical one of making thoughts visible. Ruskin s ays that all letters are frightful things and to be endured only on occasion, that is to* **The main purpose of letters is the practical one of making thoughts visibl e. Ruskin says that all letters are frightful things and to be endured only**

ABCDEFGHIJKLMNOPQRSTUVWXYZ 1234567890 abcdefghijklmnopqrstuvwxyz

ABCDEFGHIJKLMNOPQRSTUVWXYZ 1234567890 abcdefghijklmnopqrstuvwxyz

ABCDEFGHIJKLMNOPQRSTUVWXYZ 1234567890 abcdefghijklmnopqrstuvwxyz

ABCDEFGHIJKLMNOPQRSTUVWXYZ 1234567890 abcdefghijklmnopqrstuvwxyz

9/9

The main purpose of letters is the practical one of making thoughts visible. Ruskin says that all letters are frightful things and to be endured only on occasion, that is to say, in places where the sense of the inscription is of m ore importance than external ornament. This is a sweeping statement, fro m which we need not suffer unduly; yet it is doubtful whether there is art in individual letters. Letters in combination may be satisfying and in a well c omposed page even beautiful as a whole, but art in letters consists rather in the art of arranging and composing them in a pleasing and appropriat *The main purpose of letters is the practical one of making thoughts visible. Ruskin says that all letters are frightful things and to be endured only on* **The main purpose of letters is the practical one of making thoug hts visible. Ruskin says that all letters are frightful things and to**

9/10

The main purpose of letters is the practical one of making thoughts visible. Ruskin says that all letters are frightful things and to be endured only on occasion, that is to say, in places where the sense of the inscription is of m ore importance then external ornament. This is a sweeping statement, fro m which we need not suffer unduly; yet it is doubtful whether there is art in individual letters. Letters in combination may be satisfying and in a well c omposed page even beautiful as a whole, but art in letters consists rather *The main purpose of letters is the practical one of making thoughts visible. Ruskin says tla$ all letters are frightful things and to be endured only on* **The main purpose of letters is the practical one of making thoug hts visible. Rskin says that all letters are frightful things and to**

9/11

The main purpose of letters is the practical one . . on making thoughts visible. Ruskin says that all letters ave frightful things and to be endured only on occasion, that is to say, in places where the sense of the inscription is . . on m ore importance than external ornament. This is a sweeping statement, fro m which we nmed not suffer unduly; yet it is doubtful whether there is art in individual letters. Letters in combination may be satisfying and in a well c ompowed page even beautiful as a whole, but art in letters consists rather *The main prpose of letters is the practical one of making thoughts visible. Ruskin says that all lmtters are frightful things end to be endured only on* **The main purpose of lettgrs is the practical one of maoing thoug hts visible. Ruskin says that all letters are frightful things and to**

9/12

The main purpose of letters is the . . pzactical one of making thoughts visible. Ruskin says that all letters are frightful things and to be endured only on occasion, that is to say, in places where the sense of the inscription is of m ore importance than external ornament. This is a sweeping statement, fro m which we need not suffer unduly; yet it is doubtful whether there is art in individual letters. Letters in combination may be satisfying and in a well c omposed page even beautiful as a whole, but art in letters consists rather *The main purpose of letters is the practical one of making thoughts visible. Ruskin says that all letters are frightful things and to be endured only on* **The main purpose of letters is the practical one of making thoug hts visible. Ruskin says that all letters are frightful things and . . to**

SPARTAN 10 POINT SET MINUS ½ UNIT

LIGHT, ITALIC, HEAVY, HEAVY ITALIC

abcdefghijklmnopqrstuvwxyz – 1 UNIT
abcdefghijklmnopqrstuvwxyz – ½ UNIT
abcdefghijklmnopqrstuvwxyz NORMAL

ABCDEFGHIJKLMNOPQRSTUVWXYZ 1234567890 abcdefghijklmnopqrstuvwxyz
ABCDEFGHIJKLMNOPQRSTUVWXYZ 1234567890 abcdefghijklmnopqrstuvwxyz
ABCDEFGHIJKLMNOPQRSTUVWXYZ 1234567890 abcdefghijklmnopqrstuvwxyz
ABCDEFGHIJKLMNOPQRSTUVWXYZ 1234567890 abcdefghijklmnopqrstuvwxyz

10/10

The main purpose of letters is the practical one of making thoughts visi ble. Ruskin says that all letters are frightful things and to be endured o nly on occasion, that is to say, in places where the sense of the inscript ion is of more importance than external ornament. This is a sweeping statement, from which we need not suffer unduly; yet it is doubtful wh ether there is art in individual letters. Letters in combination may be sa tisfying and in a well composed page even beautiful as a whole, but art in letters consists rather in the art of arranging and composing the m in a pleasing and appropriate manner. The main purpose of letters is the practical one of making thoughts visible. Ruskin says that all lette rs are frightful things and to be endured only on occasion, that is to sa y, in places where the sense of the inscription is of more importance th an external ornament. This is a sweeping statement, from which we n eed not suffer unduly; yet it is doubtful whether there is art in individua l letters. Letters in combination may be satisfying and in a well compo sed page even beautiful as a whole, but art in letters consists rather in the art of arranging and composing them in a pleasing and appropri ate manner. The main purpose of letters is the practical one of making thoughts visible. Ruskin says that all letters are frightful things and to b e endured only on occasion, that is to say, in places where the sense o f the inscription is of more importance than external ornament. This is a sweeping statement, from which we need not suffer unduly; yet it is
The main purpose of letters is the practical one of making thoughts visi ble. Ruskin says that all letters are frightful things and to be endured o
The main purpose of letters is the practical one of making th oughts visible. Ruskin says that all letters are frightful thing

10/11

The main purpose of letters is the practical one of making thoughts visi ble. Ruskin says that all letters are frightful things and to be endured o nly on occasion, that is to say, in places where the sense of the inscript ion is of more importance than external ornament. This is a sweeping statement, from which we need not suffer unduly; yet it is doubtful wh ether there is art in individual letters. Letters in combination may be sa tisfying and in a well composed page even beautiful as a whole, but art in letters consists rather in the art of arranging and composing the m in a pleasing and appropriate manner. The main purpose of letters is the practical one of making thoughts visible. Ruskin says that all lette rs are frightful things and to be endured only on occasion, that is to sa y, in places where the sense of the inscription is of more importance th an external ornament. This is a sweeping statement, from which we n eed not suffer unduly; yet it is doubtful whether there is art in individua l letters. Letters in combination may be satisfying and in a well compo sed page even beautiful as a whole, but art in letters consists rather in the art of arranging and composing them in a pleasing and appropri ate manner. The main purpose of letters is the practical one of making thoughts visible. Ruskin says that all letters are frightful things and to b e endured only on occasion, that is to say, in places where the sense o
The main purpose of letters is the practical one of making thoughts visi ble. Ruskin says that all letters are frightful things and to be endured o
The main purpose of letters is the practical one of making th oughts visible. Ruskin says that all letters are frightful thing

10/12

The main purpose of letters is the practical one of making thoughts visi ble. Ruskin says that all letters are frightful things and to be endured o nly on occasion, that is to say, in places where the sense of the inscript ion is of more importance than external ornament. This is a sweeping statement, from which we need not suffer unduly; yet it is doubtful wh ether there is art in individual letters. Letters in combination may be sa tisfying and in a well composed page even beautiful as a whole, but art in letters consists rather in the art of arranging and composing the m in a pleasing and appropriate manner. The main purpose of letters is the practical one of making thoughts visible. Ruskin says that all lette rs are frightful things and to be endured only on occasion, that is to sa y, in places where the sense of the inscription is of more importance th an external ornament. This is a sweeping statement, from which we n eed not suffer unduly; yet it is doubtful whether there is art in individua l letters. Letters in combination may be satisfying and in a well compo sed page even beautiful as a whole, but art in letters consists rather in the art of arranging and composing them in a pleasing and appropri ate manner. The main purpose of letters is the practical one of making
The main purpose of letters is the practical one of making thoughts visi ble. Ruskin says that all letters are frightful things and to be endured o
The main purpose of letters is the practical one of making th oughts visible. Ruskin says that all letters are frightful thing

10/13

The main purpose of letters is the practical one of making thoughts visi ble. Ruskin says that all letters are frightful things and to be endured o nly on occasion, that is to say, in places where the sense of the inscript ion is of more importance than external ornament. This is a sweeping statement, from which we need not suffer unduly; yet it is doubtful wh ether there is art in individual letters. Letters in combination may be sa tisfying and in a well composed page even beautiful as a whole, but art in letters consists rather in the art of arranging and composing the m in a pleasing and appropriate manner. The main purpose of letters is the practical one of making thoughts visible. Ruskin says that all lette rs are frightful things and to be endured only on occasion, that is to sa y, in places where the sense of the inscription is of more importance th an external ornament. This is a sweeping statement, from which we n eed not suffer unduly; yet it is doubtful whether there is art in individua l letters. Letters in combination may be satisfying and in a well compo sed page even beautiful as a whole, but art in letters consists rather in the art of arranging and composing them in a pleasing and appropri
The main purpose of letters is the practical one of making thoughts visi ble. Ruskin says that all letters are frightful things and to be endured o
The main purpose of letters is the practical one of making th oughts visible. Ruskin says that all letters are frightful thing

SPARTAN 11 POINT SET MINUS ½ UNIT

LIGHT, ITALIC, HEAVY, HEAVY ITALIC

abcdefghijklmnopqrstuvwxyz – 1 UNIT
abcdefghijklmnopqrstuvwxyz – ½ UNIT
abcdefghijklmnopqrstuvwxyz NORMAL

ABCDEFGHIJKLMNOPQRSTUVWXYZ 1234567890 abcdefghijklmnopqrstuvwxyz
ABCDEFGHIJKLMNOPQRSTUVWXYZ 1234567890 abcdefghijklmnopqrstuvwxyz
ABCDEFGHIJKLMNOPQRSTUVWXYZ 1234567890 abcdefghijklmnopqrstuvwxyz
ABCDEFGHIJKLMNOPQRSTUVWXYZ 1234567890 abcdefghijklmnopqrstuvwxyz

11/11

The main purpose of letters is the practical one of making thou ghts visible. Ruskin says that all letters are frightful things and to be endured only on occasion, that is to say, in places where the sense of the inscription is of more importance than external orn ament. This is a sweeping statement, from which we need not s uffer unduly; yet it is doubtful whether there is art in individual l etters. Letters in combination may be satisfying and in a well co mposed page even beautiful as a whole, but art in letters consi sts rather in the art of arranging and composing them in a plea sing and appropriate manner. The main purpose of letters is th e practical one of making thoughts visible. Ruskin says that all l etters are frightful things and to be endured only on occasion, t hat is to say, in places where the sense of the inscription is of m ore importance than external ornament. This is a sweeping stat ement, from which we need not suffer unduly; yet it is doubtful whether there is art in individual letters. Letters in combination may be satisfying and in a well composed page even beautiful as a whole, but art in letters consists rather in the art of arrangi ng and composing them in a pleasing and appropriate manne
The main purpose of letters is the practical one of making thou ghts visible. Ruskin says that all letters are frightful things and to
The main purpose of letters is the practical one of maki ng thoughts visible. Ruskin says that all letters are frig

11/12

The main purpose of letters is the practical one of making thou ghts visible. Ruskin says that all letters are frightful things and to be endured only on occasion, that is to say, in places where the sense of the inscription is of more importance than external orn ament. This is a sweeping statement, from which we need not s uffer unduly; yet it is doubtful whether there is art in individual l etters. Letters in combination may be satisfying and in a well co mposed page even beautiful as a whole, but art in letters consi sts rather in the art of arranging and composing them in a plea sing and appropriate manner. The main purpose of letters is th e practical one of making thoughts visible. Ruskin says that all l etters are frightful things and to be endured only on occasion, t hat is to say, in places where the sense of the inscription is of m ore importance than external ornament. This is a sweeping stat ement, from which we need not suffer unduly; yet it is doubtful whether there is art in individual letters. Letters in combination may be satisfying and in a well composed page even beautiful as a whole, but art in letters consists rather in the art of arrangi
The main purpose of letters is the practical one of making thou ghts visible. Ruskin says that all letters are frightful things and to
The main purpose of letters is the practical one of maki ng thoughts visible. Ruskin says that all letters are frig

11/13

The main purpose of letters is the practical one of making thou ghts visible. Ruskin says that all letters are frightful things and to be endured only on occasion, that is to say, in places where the sense of the inscription is of more importance than external orn ament. This is a sweeping statement, from which we need not s uffer unduly; yet it is doubtful whether there is art in individual l etters. Letters in combination may be satisfying and in a well co mposed page even beautiful as a whole, but art in letters consi sts rather in the art of arranging and composing them in a plea sing and appropriate manner. The main purpose of letters is th e practical one of making thoughts visible. Ruskin says that all l etters are frightful things and to be endured only on occasion, t hat is to say, in places where the sense of the inscription is of m ore importance than external ornament. This is a sweeping stat ement, from which we need not suffer unduly; yet it is doubtful whether there is art in individual letters. Letters in combination may be satisfying and in a well composed page even beautiful
The main purpose of letters is the practical one of making thou ghts visible. Ruskin says that all letters are frightful things and to
The main purpose of letters is the practical one of maki ng thoughts visible. Ruskin says that all letters are frig

11/14

The main purpose of letters is the practical one of making thou ghts visible. Ruskin says that all letters are frightful things and to be endured only on occasion, that is to say, in places where the sense of the inscription is of more importance than external orn ament. This is a sweeping statement, from which we need not s uffer unduly; yet it is doubtful whether there is art in individual l etters. Letters in combination may be satisfying and in a well co mposed page even beautiful as a whole, but art in letters consi sts rather in the art of arranging and composing them in a plea sing and appropriate manner. The main purpose of letters is th e practical one of making thoughts visible. Ruskin says that all l etters are frightful things and to be endured only on occasion, t hat is to say, in places where the sense of the inscription is of m ore importance than external ornament. This is a sweeping stat ement, from which we need not suffer unduly; yet it is doubtful whether there is art in individual letters. Letters in combination
The main purpose of letters is the practical one of making thou ghts visible. Ruskin says that all letters are frightful things and to
The main purpose of letters is the practical one of maki ng thoughts visible. Ruskin says that all letters are frig

SPARTAN 12 POINT SET MINUS ½ UNIT

LIGHT, ITALIC, HEAVY, HEAVY ITALIC

abcdefghijklmnopqrstuvwxyz – 1 UNIT
abcdefghijklmnopqrstuvwxyz – ½ UNIT
abcdefghijklmnopqrstuvwxyz NORMAL

ABCDEFGHIJKLMNOPQRSTUVWXYZ 1234567890 abcdefghijklmnopqrstuvwxyz
ABCDEFGHIJKLMNOPQRSTUVWXYZ 1234567890 abcdefghijklmnopqrstuvwxyz
ABCDEFGHIJKLMNOPQRSTUVWXYZ 1234567890 abcdefghijklmnopqrstuvwxyz
ABCDEFGHIJKLMNOPQRSTUVWXYZ 1234567890 abcdefghijklmnopqrstuvwxyz

12/12

The main purpose of letters is the practical one of making t houghts visible. Ruskin says that all letters are frightful thing s and to be endured only on occasion, that is to say, in plac es where the sense of the inscription is of more importance than external ornament. This is a sweeping statement, fro m which we need not suffer unduly; yet it is doubtful wheth er there is art in individual letters. Letters in combination m ay be satisfying and in a well composed page even beautif ul as a whole, but art in letters consists rather in the art of a rranging and composing them in a pleasing and appropri ate manner. The main purpose of letters is the practical one of making thoughts visible. Ruskin says that all letters are fri ghtful things and to be endured only on occasion, that is to say, in places where the sense of the inscription is of more i mportance than external ornament. This is a sweeping stat
The main purpose of letters is the practical one of making t houghts visible. Ruskin says that all letters are frightful thing
The main purpose of letters is the practical one of m aking thoughts visible. Ruskin says that all letters

12/13

The main purpose of letters is the practical one of making t houghts visible. Ruskin says that all letters are frightful thing s and to be endured only on occasion, that is to say, in plac es where the sense of the inscription is of more importance than external ornament. This is a sweeping statement, fro m which we need not suffer unduly; yet it is doubtful wheth er there is art in individual letters. Letters in combination m ay be satisfying and in a well composed page even beautif ul as a whole, but art in letters consists rather in the art of a rranging and composing them in a pleasing and appropri ate manner. The main purpose of letters is the practical one of making thoughts visible. Ruskin says that all letters are fri ghtful things and to be endured only on occasion, that is to say, in places where the sense of the inscription is of more i
The main purpose of letters is the practical one of making t houghts visible. Ruskin says that all letters are frightful thing
The main purpose of letters is the practical one of m aking thoughts visible. Ruskin says that all letters

12/14

The main purpose of letters is the practical one of making t houghts visible. Ruskin says that all letters are frightful thing s and to be endured only on occasion, that is to say, in plac es where the sense of the inscription is of more importance than external ornament. This is a sweeping statement, fro m which we need not suffer unduly; yet it is doubtful wheth er there is art in individual letters. Letters in combination m ay be satisfying and in a well composed page even beautif ul as a whole, but art in letters consists rather in the art of a rranging and composing them in a pleasing and appropri ate manner. The main purpose of letters is the practical one of making thoughts visible. Ruskin says that all letters are fri ghtful things and to be endured only on occasion, that is to say, in places where the sense of the inscription is of more i mportance than external ornament. This is a sweeping stat
The main purpose of letters is the practical one of making t houghts visible. Ruskin says that all letters are frightful thing
The main purpose of letters is the practical one of m aking thoughts visible. Ruskin says that all letters

12/15

The main purpose of letters is the practical one of making t houghts visible. Ruskin says that all letters are frightful thing s and to be endured only on occasion, that is to say, in plac es where the sense of the inscription is of more importance than external ornament. This is a sweeping statement, fro m which we need not suffer unduly; yet it is doubtful wheth er there is art in individual letters. Letters in combination m ay be satisfying and in a well composed page even beautif ul as a whole, but art in letters consists rather in the art of a rranging and composing them in a pleasing and appropri ate manner. The main purpose of letters is the practical one of making thoughts visible. Ruskin says that all letters are fri ghtful things and to be endured only on occasion, that is to say, in places where the sense of the inscription is of more i
The main purpose of letters is the practical one of making t houghts visible. Ruskin says that all letters are frightful thing
The main purpose of letters is the practical one of m aking thoughts visible. Ruskin says that all letters

SPARTAN 14 POINT SET MINUS ½ UNIT

LIGHT, ITALIC, HEAVY, HEAVY ITALIC

abcdefghijklmnopqrstuvwxyz – 1 UNIT

abcdefghijklmnopqrstuvwxyz – ½ UNIT

abcdefghijklmnopqrstuvwxyz NORMAL

ABCDEFGHIJKLMNOPQRSTUVWXYZ abcdefghijklmnopqrstuvwxyz

ABCDEFGHIJKLMNOPQRSTUVWXYZ abcdefghijklmnopqrstuvwxyz

ABCDEFGHIJKLMNOPQRSTUVWXYZ abcdefghijklmnopqrstuvwxyz

ABCDEFGHIJKLMNOPQRSTUVWXYZ abcdefghijklmnopqrstuvwxyz

14/14

The main purpose of letters is the practical one of making thoughts visible. Ruskin says that all letters are frightful things and to be endured only on occ asion, that is to say, in places where the sense of t he inscription is of more importance than external ornament. This is a sweeping statement, from whi ch we need not suffer unduly; yet it is doubtful whe ther there is art in individual letters. Letters in com bination may be satisfying and in a well compose d page even beautiful as a whole, but art in letters consists rather in the art of arranging and compos ing them in a pleasing and appropriate manner. T he main purpose of letters is the practical one of

The main purpose of letters is the practical one of making thoughts visible. Ruskin says that all letters

The main purpose of letters is the practical one of making thoughts visible. Ruskin say

14/15

The main purpose of letters is the practical one of making thoughts visible. Ruskin says that all letters are frightful things and to be endured only on occ asion, that is to say, in places where the sense of t he inscription is of more importance than external ornament. This is a sweeping statement, from whi ch we need not suffer unduly; yet it is doubtful whe ther there is art in individual letters. Letters in com bination may be satisfying and in a well compose d page even beautiful as a whole, but art in letters consists rather in the art of arranging and compos ing them in a pleasing and appropriate manner. T

The main purpose of letters is the practical one of making thoughts visible. Ruskin says that all letters

The main purpose of letters is the practical one of making thoughts visible. Ruskin say

14/16

The main purpose of letters is the practical one of making thoughts visible. Ruskin says that all letters are frightful things and to be endured only on occ asion, that is to say, in places where the sense of t he inscription is of more importance than external ornament. This is a sweeping statement, from whi ch we need not suffer unduly; yet it is doubtful whe ther there is art in individual letters. Letters in com bination may be satisfying and in a well compose d page even beautiful as a whole, but art in letters consists rather in the art of arranging and compos ing them in a pleasing and appropriate manner. T he main purpose of letters is the practical one of

The main purpose of letters is the practical one of making thoughts visible. Ruskin says that all letters

The main purpose of letters is the practical one of making thoughts visible. Ruskin say

14/17

The main purpose of letters is the practical one of making thoughts visible. Ruskin says that all letters are frightful things and to be endured only on occ asion, that is to say, in places where the sense of t he inscription is of more importance than external ornament. This is a sweeping statement, from whi ch we need not suffer unduly; yet it is doubtful whe ther there is art in individual letters. Letters in com bination may be satisfying and in a well compose d page even beautiful as a whole, but art in letters consists rather in the art of arranging and compos ing them in a pleasing and appropriate manner. T

The main purpose of letters is the practical one of making thoughts visible. Ruskin says that all letters

The main purpose of letters is the practical one of making thoughts visible. Ruskin say

SPARTAN 6 & 7 POINT SET NORMAL

MEDIUM, ITALIC, BLACK, BLACK ITALIC

ABCDEFGHIJKLMNOPQRSTUVWXYZ 1234567890 abcdefghijklmnopqrstuvwxyz

ABCDEFGHIJKLMNOPQRSTUVWXYZ 1234567890 abcdefghijklmnopqrstuvwxyz

ABCDEFGHIJKLMNOPQRSTUVWXYZ 1234567890 abcdefghijklmnopqrstuvwxyz

ABCDEFGHIJKLMNOPQRSTUVWXYZ 1234567890 abcdefghijklmnopqrstuvwxyz

6/6

The main purpose of letters is the practical one of making thoughts visible. Ruskin says that all letters are frig
htful things and to be endured only on occasion, that is to say, in places where the sense of the inscription is of
more importance than external ornament. This is a sweeping statement, from which we need not suffer undul
y; yet it is doubtful whether there is art in individual letters. Letters in combination may be satisfying and in a
well composed page even beautiful as a whole, but art in letters consists rather in the art of arranging and co
mposing them in a pleasing and appropriate manner. The main purpose of letters is the practical one of maki
ng thoughts visible. Ruskin says that all letters are frightful things and to be endured only on occasion, that is
to say, in places where the sense of the inscription is of more importance than external ornament. This is a swe
eping statement, from which we need not suffer unduly; yet it is doubtful whether there is art in individual lett
ers. Letters in combination may be satisfying and in a well composed page even beautiful as a whole, but art
in letters consists rather in the art of arranging and composing them in a pleasing and appropriate manner. T
he main purpose of letters is the practical one of making thoughts visible. Ruskin says that all letters are fright
ful things and to be endured only on occasion, that is to say, in places where the sense of the inscription is of m
The main purpose of letters is the practical one of making thoughts visible. Ruskin says that all letters are fright
ful things and to be endured only on occasion, that is to say, in places where the sense of the inscription is of m
The main purpose of letters is the practical one of making thoughts visible. Ruskin say
s that all letters are frightful things and to be endured only on occasion, that is to say, i

6/7

The main purpose of letters is the practical one of making thoughts visible. Ruskin says that all letters are frig
htful things and to be endured only on occasion, that is to say, in places where the sense of the inscription is of
more importance than external ornament. This is a sweeping statement, from which we need not suffer undul
y; yet it is doubtful whether there is art in individual letters. Letters in combination may be satisfying and in a
well composed page even beautiful as a whole, but art in letters consists rather in the art of arranging and co
mposing them in a pleasing and appropriate manner. The main purpose of letters is the practical one of maki
ng thoughts visible. Ruskin says that all letters are frightful things and to be endured only on occasion, that is
to say, in places where the sense of the inscription is of more importance than external ornament. This is a swe
eping statement, from which we need not suffer unduly; yet it is doubtful whether there is art in individual lett
ers. Letters in combination may be satisfying and in a well composed page even beautiful as a whole, but art
in letters consists rather in the art of arranging and composing them in a pleasing and appropriate manner. T
The main purpose of letters is the practical one of making thoughts visible. Ruskin says that all letters are fright
ful things and to be endured only on occasion, that is to say, in places where the sense of the inscription is of m
The main purpose of letters is the practical one of making thoughts visible. Ruskin say
s that all letters are frightful things and to be endured only on occasion, that is to say, i

6/8

The main purpose of letters is the practical one of making thoughts visible. Ruskin says that all letters are frig
htful things and to be endured only on occasion, that is to say, in places where the sense of the inscription is of
more importance than external ornament. This is a sweeping statement, from which we need not suffer undul
y; yet it is doubtful whether there is art in individual letters. Letters in combination may be satisfying and in a
well composed page even beautiful as a whole, but art in letters consists rather in the art of arranging and co
mposing them in a pleasing and appropriate manner. The main purpose of letters is the practical one of maki
ng thoughts visible. Ruskin says that all letters are frightful things and to be endured only on occasion, that is
to say, in places where the sense of the inscription is of more importance than external ornament. This is a swe
eping statement, from which we need not suffer unduly; yet it is doubtful whether there is art in individual lett
The main purpose of letters is the practical one of making thoughts visible. Ruskin says that all letters are fright
ful things and to be endured only on occasion, that is to say, in places where the sense of the inscription is of m
The main purpose of letters is the practical one of making thoughts visible. Ruskin say
s that all letters are frightful things and to be endured only on occasion, that is to say, i

6/9

The main purpose of letters is the practical one of making thoughts visible. Ruskin says that all letters are frig
htful things and to be endured only on occasion, that is to say, in places where the sense of the inscription is of
more importance than external ornament. This is a sweeping statement, from which we need not suffer undul
y; yet it is doubtful whether there is art in individual letters. Letters in combination may be satisfying and in a
well composed page even beautiful as a whole, but art in letters consists rather in the art of arranging and co
mposing them in a pleasing and appropriate manner. The main purpose of letters is the practical one of maki
ng thoughts visible. Ruskin says that all letters are frightful things and to be endured only on occasion, that is
to say, in places where the sense of the inscription is of more importance than external ornament. This is a swe
The main purpose of letters is the practical one of making thoughts visible. Ruskin says that all letters are fright
ful things and to be endured only on occasion, that is to say, in places where the sense of the inscription is of m
The main purpose of letters is the practical one of making thoughts visible. Ruskin say
s that all letters are frightful things and to be endured only on occasion, that is to say, i

ABCDEFGHIJKLMNOPQRSTUVWXYZ 1234567890 abcdefghijklmnopqrstuvwxyz

ABCDEFGHIJKLMNOPQRSTUVWXYZ 1234567890 abcdefghijklmnopqrstuvwxyz

ABCDEFGHIJKLMNOPQRSTUVWXYZ 1234567890 abcdefghijklmnopqrstuvwxyz

ABCDEFGHIJKLMNOPQRSTUVWXYZ 1234567890 abcdefghijklmnopqrstuvwxyz

7/7

The main purpose of letters is the practical one of making thoughts visible. Ruskin says that all
letters are frightful things and to be endured only on occasion, that is to say, in places where t
he sense of the inscription is of more importance than external ornament. This is a sweeping st
atement, from which we need not suffer unduly; yet it is doubtful whether there is art in individ
ual letters. Letters in combination may be satisfying and in a well composed page even beauti
ful as a whole, but art in letters consists rather in the art of arranging and composing them in
a pleasing and appropriate manner. The main purpose of letters is the practical one of makin
g thoughts visible. Ruskin says that all letters are frightful things and to be endured only on oc
casion, that is to say, in places where the sense of the inscription is of more importance than e
xternal ornament. This is a sweeping statement, from which we need not suffer unduly; yet it is
doubtful whether there is art in individual letters. Letters in combination may be satisfying an
The main purpose of letters is the practical one of making thoughts visible. Ruskin says that all
letters are frightful things and to be endured only on occasion, that is to say, in places where t
The main purpose of letters is the practical one of making thoughts visible.
Ruskin says that all letters are frightful things and to be endured only on

7/8

The main purpose of letters is the practical one of making thoughts visible. Ruskin says that all
letters are frightful things and to be endured only on occasion, that is to say, in places where t
he sense of the inscription is of more importance than external ornament. This is a sweeping st
atement, from which we need not suffer unduly; yet it is doubtful whether there is art in individ
ual letters. Letters in combination may be satisfying and in a well composed page even beauti
ful as a whole, but art in letters consists rather in the art of arranging and composing them in
a pleasing and appropriate manner. The main purpose of letters is the practical one of makin
g thoughts visible. Ruskin says that all letters are frightful things and to be endured only on oc
casion, that is to say, in places where the sense of the inscription is of more importance than e
xternal ornament. This is a sweeping statement, from which we need not suffer unduly; yet it is
The main purpose of letters is the practical one of making thoughts visible. Ruskin says that all
letters are frightful things and to be endured only on occasion, that is to say, in places where t
The main purpose of letters is the practical one of making thoughts visible.
Ruskin says that all letters are frightful things and to be endured only on

7/9

The main purpose of letters is the practical one of making thoughts visible. Ruskin says that all
letters are frightful things and to be endured only on occasion, that is to say, in places where t
he sense of the inscription is of more importance than external ornament. This is a sweeping st
atement, from which we need not suffer unduly; yet it is doubtful whether there is art in individ
ual letters. Letters in combination may be satisfying and in a well composed page even beauti
ful as a whole, but art in letters consists rather in the art of arranging and composing them in
a pleasing and appropriate manner. The main purpose of letters is the practical one of makin
g thoughts visible. Ruskin says that all letters are frightful things and to be endured only on oc
casion, that is to say, in places where the sense of the inscription is of more importance than e
xternal ornament. This is a sweeping statement, from which we need not suffer unduly; yet it is
The main purpose of letters is the practical one of making thoughts visible. Ruskin says that all
letters are frightful things and to be endured only on occasion, that is to say, in places where t
The main purpose of letters is the practical one of making thoughts visible.
Ruskin says that all letters are frightful things and to be endured only on

7/10

The main purpose of letters is the practical one of making thoughts visible. Ruskin says that all
letters are frightful things and to be endured only on occasion, that is to say, in places where t
he sense of the inscription is of more importance than external ornament. This is a sweeping st
atement, from which we need not suffer unduly; yet it is doubtful whether there is art in individ
ual letters. Letters in combination may be satisfying and in a well composed page even beauti
ful as a whole, but art in letters consists rather in the art of arranging and composing them in
a pleasing and appropriate manner. The main purpose of letters is the practical one of makin
g thoughts visible. Ruskin says that all letters are frightful things and to be endured only on oc
casion, that is to say, in places where the sense of the inscription is of more importance than e
The main purpose of letters is the practical one of making thoughts visible. Ruskin says that all
letters are frightful things and to be endured only on occasion, that is to say, in places where t
The main purpose of letters is the practical one of making thoughts visible.
Ruskin says that all letters are frightful things and to be endured only on

SPARTAN 8 & 9 POINT SET NORMAL

MEDIUM, ITALIC, BLACK, BLACK ITALIC

ABCDEFGHIJKLMNOPQRSTUVWXYZ 1234567890 abcdefghijklmnopqrstuvwxyz

ABCDEFGHIJKLMNOPQRSTUVWXYZ 1234567890 abcdefghijklmnopqrstuvwxyz

ABCDEFGHIJKLMNOPQRSTUVWXYZ 1234567890 abcdefghijklmnopqrstuvwxyz

ABCDEFGHIJKLMNOPQRSTUVWXYZ 1234567890 abcdefghijklmnopqrstuvwxyz

8/8

The main purpose of letters is the practical one of making thoughts visible. Ruskin says that all letters are frightful things and to be endured only on occasion, that is to say, in places where the sense of the inscription is of more importance than exte rnal ornament. This is a sweeping statement, from which we need not suffer undul y; yet it is doubtful whether there is art in individual letters. Letters in combination may be satisfying and in a well composed page even beautiful as a whole, but art in letters consists rather in the art of arranging and composing them in a pleasing and appropriate manner. The main purpose of letters is the practical one of makin g thoughts visible. Ruskin says that all letters are frightful things and to be endure

The main purpose of letters is the practical one of making thoughts visible. Ruskin s ays that all letters are frightful things and to be endured only on occasion, that is t

The main purpose of letters is the practical one of making thoug hts visible. Ruskin says that all letters are frightful things and to

8/9

The main purpose of letters is the practical one of making thoughts visible. Ruskin says that all letters are frightful things and to be endured only on occasion, that is to say, in places where the sense of the inscription is of more importance than exte rnal ornament. This is a sweeping statement, from which we need not suffer undul y; yet it is doubtful whether there is art in individual letters. Letters in combination may be satisfying and in a well composed page even beautiful as a whole, but art in letters consists rather in the art of arranging and composing them in a pleasing and appropriate manner. The main purpose of letters is the practical one of makin

The main purpose of letters is the practical one of making thoughts visible. Ruskin s ays that all letters are frightful things and to be endured only on occasion, that is t

The main purpose of letters is the practical one of making thoug hts visible. Ruskin says that all letters are frightful things and to

8/10

The main purpose of letters is the practical one of making thoughts visible. Ruskin says that all letters are frightful things and to be endured only on occasion, that is to say, in places where the sense of the inscription is of more importance than exte rnal ornament. This is a sweeping statement, from which we need not suffer undul y; yet it is doubtful whether there is art in individual letters. Letters in combination may be satisfying and in a well composed page even beautiful as a whole, but art in letters consists rather in the art of arranging and composing them in a pleasing

The main purpose of letters is the practical one of making thoughts visible. Ruskin s ays that all letters are frightful things and to be endured only on occasion, that is t

The main purpose of letters is the practical one of making thoug hts visible. Ruskin says that all letters are frightful things and to

8/11

The main purpose of letters is the practical one of making thoughts visible. Ruskin says that all letters are frightful things and to be endured only on occasion, that is to say, in places where the sense of the inscription is of more importance than exte rnal ornament. This is a sweeping statement, from which we need not suffer undul y; yet it is doubtful whether there is art in individual letters. Letters in combination may be satisfying and in a well composed page even beautiful as a whole, but art in letters consists rather in the art of arranging and composing them in a pleasing

The main purpose of letters is the practical one of making thoughts visible. Ruskin s ays that all letters are frightful things and to be endured only on occasion, that is t

The main purpose of letters is the practical one of making thoug hts visible. Ruskin says that all letters are frightful things and to

---

ABCDEFGHIJKLMNOPQRSTUVWXYZ 1234567890 abcdefghijklmnopqrstuvwxyz

ABCDEFGHIJKLMNOPQRSTUVWXYZ 1234567890 abcdefghijklmnopqrstuvwxyz

ABCDEFGHIJKLMNOPQRSTUVWXYZ 1234567890 abcdefghijklmnopqrstuvwxyz

ABCDEFGHIJKLMNOPQRSTUVWXYZ 1234567890 abcdefghijklmnopqrstuvwxyz

9/9

The main purpose of letters is the practical one of making thoughts visibl e. Ruskin says that all letters are frightful things and to be endured only o n occasion, that is to say, in places where the sense of the inscription is of more importance than external ornament. This is a sweeping statement, from which we need not suffer unduly; yet it is doubtful whether there is a rt in individual letters. Letters in combination may be satisfying and in a well composed page even beautiful as a whole, but art in letters consists rather in the art of arranging and composing them in a pleasing and app

The main purpose of letters is the practical one of making thoughts visible. Ruskin says that all letters are frightful things and to be endured only on

The main purpose of letters is the practical one of making thoughts visible. Ruskin says that all letters are frightful

9/10

The main purpose of letters is the practical one of making thoughts visibl e. Ruskin says that all letters are frightful things and to be endured only o n occasion, that is to say, in places where the sense of the inscription is of more importance than external ornament. This is a sweeping statement, from which we need not suffer unduly; yet it is doubtful whether there is a rt in individual letters. Letters in combination may be satisfying and in a well composed page even beautiful as a whole, but art in letters consists

The main purpose of letters is the practical one of making thoughts visible. Ruskin says that all letters are frightful things and to be endured only on

The main purpose of letters is the practical one of making thoughts visible. Ruskin says that all letters are frightful

9/11

The main purpose of letters is the practical one of making thoughts visibl e. Ruskin says that all letters are frightful things and to be endured only o n occasion, that is to say, in places where the sense of the inscription is of more importance than external ornament. This is a sweeping statement, from which we need not suffer unduly; yet it is doubtful whether there is a rt in individual letters. Letters in combination may be satisfying and in a well composed page even beautiful as a whole, but art in letters consists

The main purpose of letters is the practical one of making thoughts visible. Ruskin says that all letters are frightful things and to be endured only on

The main purpose of letters is the practical one of making thoughts visible. Ruskin says that all letters are frightful

9/12

The main purpose of letters is the practical one of making thoughts visibl e. Ruskin says that all letters are frightful things and to be endured only o n occasion, that is to say, in places where the sense of the inscription is of more importance than external ornament. This is a sweeping statement, from which we need not suffer unduly; yet it is doubtful whether there is a rt in individual letters. Letters in combination may be satisfying and in a well composed page even beautiful as a whole, but art in letters consists

The main purpose of letters is the practical one of making thoughts visible. Ruskin says that all letters are frightful things and to be endured only on

The main purpose of letters is the practical one of making thoughts visible. Ruskin says that all letters are frightful

SPARTAN 10 POINT SET MINUS ½ UNIT

MEDIUM, ITALIC, BLACK, BLACK ITALIC

abcdefghijklmnopqrstuvwxyz – 1 UNIT
abcdefghijklmnopqrstuvwxyz – ½ UNIT
abcdefghijklmnopqrstuvwxyz NORMAL

ABCDEFGHIJKLMNOPQRSTUVWXYZ 1234567890 abcdefghijklmnopqrstuvwxyz
ABCDEFGHIJKLMNOPQRSTUVWXYZ 1234567890 abcdefghijklmnopqrstuvwxyz
ABCDEFGHIJKLMNOPQRSTUVWXYZ 1234567890 abcdefghijklmnopqrstuvwxyz
ABCDEFGHIJKLMNOPQRSTUVWXYZ 1234567890 abcdefghijklmnopqrstuvwxyz

10/10

The main purpose of letters is the practical one of making thoughts vi sible. Ruskin says that all letters are frightful things and to be endure d only on occasion, that is to say, in places where the sense of the insc ription is of more importance than external ornament. This is a swee ping statement, from which we need not suffer unduly; yet it is doubtf ul whether there is art in individual letters. Letters in combination ma y be satisfying and in a well composed page even beautiful as a whol e, but art in letters consists rather in the art of arranging and compos ing them in a pleasing and appropriate manner. The main purpose of letters is the practical one of making thoughts visible. Ruskin says tha t all letters are frightful things and to be endured only on occasion, th at is to say, in places where the sense of the inscription is of more imp ortance than external ornament. This is a sweeping statement, from which we need not suffer unduly; yet it is doubtful whether there is art in individual letters. Letters in combination may be satisfying and in a well composed page even beautiful as a whole, but art in letters cons ists rather in the art of arranging and composing them in a pleasing and appropriate manner. The main purpose of letters is the practical one of making thoughts visible. Ruskin says that all letters are frightf ul things and to be endured only on occasion, that is to say, in places where the sense of the inscription is of more importance than extern al ornament. This is a sweeping statement, from which we need not suf
The main purpose of letters is the practical one of making thoughts vis ible. Ruskin says that all letters are frightful things and to be endured
The main purpose of letters is the practical one of mak ing thoughts visible. Ruskin says that all letters are fr

10/11

The main purpose of letters is the practical one of making thoughts vi sible. Ruskin says that all letters are frightful things and to be endure d only on occasion, that is to say, in places where the sense of the insc ription is of more importance than external ornament. This is a swee ping statement, from which we need not suffer unduly; yet it is doubtf ul whether there is art in individual letters. Letters in combination ma y be satisfying and in a well composed page even beautiful as a whol e, but art in letters consists rather in the art of arranging and compos ing them in a pleasing and appropriate manner. The main purpose of letters is the practical one of making thoughts visible. Ruskin says tha t all letters are frightful things and to be endured only on occasion, th at is to say, in places where the sense of the inscription is of more imp ortance than external ornament. This is a sweeping statement, from which we need not suffer unduly; yet it is doubtful whether there is art in individual letters. Letters in combination may be satisfying and in a well composed page even beautiful as a whole, but art in letters cons ists rather in the art of arranging and composing them in a pleasing and appropriate manner. The main purpose of letters is the practical one of making thoughts visible. Ruskin says that all letters are frightf ul things and to be endured only on occasion, that is to say, in places
The main purpose of letters is the practical one of making thoughts vis ible. Ruskin says that all letters are frightful things and to be endured
The main purpose of letters is the practical one of mak ing thoughts visible. Ruskin says that all letters are fr

10/12

The main purpose of letters is the practical one of making thoughts vi sible. Ruskin says that all letters are frightful things and to be endure d only on occasion, that is to say, in places where the sense of the insc ription is of more importance than external ornament. This is a swee ping statement, from which we need not suffer unduly; yet it is doubtf ul whether there is art in individual letters. Letters in combination ma y be satisfying and in a well composed page even beautiful as a whol e, but art in letters consists rather in the art of arranging and compos ing them in a pleasing and appropriate manner. The main purpose of letters is the practical one of making thoughts visible. Ruskin says tha t all letters are frightful things and to be endured only on occasion, th at is to say, in places where the sense of the inscription is of more imp ortance than external ornament. This is a sweeping statement, from which we need not suffer unduly; yet it is doubtful whether there is art in individual letters. Letters in combination may be satisfying and in a well composed page even beautiful as a whole, but art in letters cons ists rather in the art of arranging and composing them in a pleasing and appropriate manner. The main purpose of letters is the practical
The main purpose of letters is the practical one of making thoughts vis ible. Ruskin says that all letters are frightful things and to be endured
The main purpose of letters is the practical one of mak ing thoughts visible. Ruskin says that all letters are fr

10/13

The main purpose of letters is the practical one of making thoughts vi sible. Ruskin says that all letters are frightful things and to be endure d only on occasion, that is to say, in places where the sense of the insc ription is of more importance than external ornament. This is a swee ping statement, from which we need not suffer unduly; yet it is doubtf ul whether there is art in individual letters. Letters in combination ma y be satisfying and in a well composed page even beautiful as a whol e, but art in letters consists rather in the art of arranging and compos ing them in a pleasing and appropriate manner. The main purpose of letters is the practical one of making thoughts visible. Ruskin says tha t all letters are frightful things and to be endured only on occasion, th at is to say, in places where the sense of the inscription is of more imp ortance than external ornament. This is a sweeping statement, from which we need not suffer unduly; yet it is doubtful whether there is art in individual letters. Letters in combination may be satisfying and in a well composed page even beautiful as a whole, but art in letters cons ists rather in the art of arranging and composing them in a pleasing
The main purpose of letters is the practical one of making thoughts vis ible. Ruskin says that all letters are frightful things and to be endured
The main purpose of letters is the practical one of mak ing thoughts visible. Ruskin says that all letters are fr

SPARTAN 11 POINT SET MINUS ½ UNIT

MEDIUM, ITALIC, BLACK, BLACK ITALIC

abcdefghijklmnopqrstuvwxyz – 1 UNIT
abcdefghijklmnopqrstuvwxyz – ½ UNIT
abcdefghijklmnopqrstuvwxyz NORMAL

ABCDEFGHIJKLMNOPQRSTUVWXYZ 1234567890 abcdefghijklmnopqrstuvwxyz
ABCDEFGHIJKLMNOPQRSTUVWXYZ 1234567890 abcdefghijklmnopqrstuvwxyz
ABCDEFGHIJKLMNOPQRSTUVWXYZ 1234567890 abcdefghijklmnopqrstuvwxyz
ABCDEFGHIJKLMNOPQRSTUVWXYZ 1234567890 abcdefghijklmnopqrstuvwxyz

11/11

The main purpose of letters is the practical one of making thou ghts visible. Ruskin says that all letters are frightful things and t o be endured only on occasion, that is to say, in places where t he sense of the inscription is of more importance than external ornament. This is a sweeping statement, from which we need n ot suffer unduly; yet it is doubtful whether there is art in individ ual letters. Letters in combination may be satisfying and in a w ell composed page even beautiful as a whole, but art in letters consists rather in the art of arranging and composing them in a pleasing and appropriate manner. The main purpose of lette rs is the practical one of making thoughts visible. Ruskin says t hat all letters are frightful things and to be endured only on oc casion, that is to say, in places where the sense of the inscriptio n is of more importance than external ornament. This is a swee ping statement, from which we need not suffer unduly; yet it is doubtful whether there is art in individual letters. Letters in co mbination may be satisfying and in a well composed page eve n beautiful as a whole, but art in letters consists rather in the a rt of arranging and composing them in a pleasing and app
The main purpose of letters is the practical one of making thou ghts visible. Ruskin says that all letters are frightful things and t
The main purpose of letters is the practical one o f making thoughts visible. Ruskin says that all le

11/12

The main purpose of letters is the practical one of making thou ghts visible. Ruskin says that all letters are frightful things and t o be endured only on occasion, that is to say, in places where t he sense of the inscription is of more importance than external ornament. This is a sweeping statement, from which we need n ot suffer unduly; yet it is doubtful whether there is art in individ ual letters. Letters in combination may be satisfying and in a w ell composed page even beautiful as a whole, but art in letters consists rather in the art of arranging and composing them in a pleasing and appropriate manner. The main purpose of lette rs is the practical one of making thoughts visible. Ruskin says t hat all letters are frightful things and to be endured only on oc casion, that is to say, in places where the sense of the inscriptio n is of more importance than external ornament. This is a swee ping statement, from which we need not suffer unduly; yet it is doubtful whether there is art in individual letters. Letters in co mbination may be satisfying and in a well composed page eve n beautiful as a whole, but art in letters consists rather in the a
The main purpose of letters is the practical one of making thou ghts visible. Ruskin says that all letters are frightful things and t
The main purpose of letters is the practical one o f making thoughts visible. Ruskin says that all le

11/13

The main purpose of letters is the practical one of making thou ghts visible. Ruskin says that all letters are frightful things and t o be endured only on occasion, that is to say, in places where t he sense of the inscription is of more importance than external ornament. This is a sweeping statement, from which we need n ot suffer unduly; yet it is doubtful whether there is art in individ ual letters. Letters in combination may be satisfying and in a w ell composed page even beautiful as a whole, but art in letters consists rather in the art of arranging and composing them in a pleasing and appropriate manner. The main purpose of lette rs is the practical one of making thoughts visible. Ruskin says t hat all letters are frightful things and to be endured only on oc casion, that is to say, in places where the sense of the inscriptio n is of more importance than external ornament. This is a swee ping statement, from which we need not suffer unduly; yet it is doubtful whether there is art in individual letters. Letters in co mbination may be satisfying and in a well composed page eve
The main purpose of letters is the practical one of making thou ghts visible. Ruskin says that all letters are frightful things and t
The main purpose of letters is the practical one o f making thoughts visible. Ruskin says that all le

11/14

The main purpose of letters is the practical one of making thou ghts visible. Ruskin says that all letters are frightful things and t o be endured only on occasion, that is to say, in places where t he sense of the inscription is of more importance than external ornament. This is a sweeping statement, from which we need n ot suffer unduly; yet it is doubtful whether there is art in individ ual letters. Letters in combination may be satisfying and in a w ell composed page even beautiful as a whole, but art in letters consists rather in the art of arranging and composing them in a pleasing and appropriate manner. The main purpose of lette rs is the practical one of making thoughts visible. Ruskin says t hat all letters are frightful things and to be endured only on oc casion, that is to say, in places where the sense of the inscriptio n is of more importance than external ornament. This is a swee ping statement, from which we need not suffer unduly; yet it is doubtful whether there is art in individual letters. Letters in co
The main purpose of letters is the practical one of making thou ghts visible. Ruskin says that all letters are frightful things and t
The main purpose of letters is the practical one o f making thoughts visible. Ruskin says that all le

SPARTAN 12 POINT SET MINUS ½ UNIT

MEDIUM, ITALIC, BLACK, BLACK ITALIC

abcdefghijklmnopqrstuvwxyz – 1 UNIT
abcdefghijklmnopqrstuvwxyz – ½ UNIT
abcdefghijklmnopqrstuvwxyz NORMAL

ABCDEFGHIJKLMNOPQRSTUVWXYZ 1234567890 abcdefghijklmnopqrstuvwxyz
ABCDEFGHIJKLMNOPQRSTUVWXYZ 1234567890 abcdefghijklmnopqrstuvwxyz
ABCDEFGHIJKLMNOPQRSTUVWXYZ 1234567890 abcdefghijklmnopqrstuvwxyz
ABCDEFGHIJKLMNOPQRSTUVWXYZ 1234567890 abcdefghijklmnopqrstuvwxyz

12/12

The main purpose of letters is the practical one of making thoughts visible. Ruskin says that all letters are frightful thi ngs and to be endured only on occasion, that is to say, in p laces where the sense of the inscription is of more importa nce than external ornament. This is a sweeping statement, from which we need not suffer unduly; yet it is doubtful wh ether there is art in individual letters. Letters in combinatio n may be satisfying and in a well composed page even be autiful as a whole, but art in letters consists rather in the ar t of arranging and composing them in a pleasing and app ropriate manner. The main purpose of letters is the practic al one of making thoughts visible. Ruskin says that all lette rs are frightful things and to be endured only on occasion, that is to say, in places where the sense of the inscription is of more importance than external ornament. This is a swe
The main purpose of letters is the practical one of making t houghts visible. Ruskin says that all letters are frightful thin
The main purpose of letters is the practical on e of making thoughts visible. Ruskin says tha

12/13

The main purpose of letters is the practical one of making thoughts visible. Ruskin says that all letters are frightful thi ngs and to be endured only on occasion, that is to say, in p laces where the sense of the inscription is of more importa nce than external ornament. This is a sweeping statement, from which we need not suffer unduly; yet it is doubtful wh ether there is art in individual letters. Letters in combinatio n may be satisfying and in a well composed page even be autiful as a whole, but art in letters consists rather in the ar t of arranging and composing them in a pleasing and app ropriate manner. The main purpose of letters is the practic al one of making thoughts visible. Ruskin says that all lette rs are frightful things and to be endured only on occasion, that is to say, in places where the sense of the inscription is
The main purpose of letters is the practical one of making t houghts visible. Ruskin says that all letters are frightful thin
The main purpose of letters is the practical on e of making thoughts visible. Ruskin says tha

12/14

The main purpose of letters is the practical one of making thoughts visible. Ruskin says that all letters are frightful thi ngs and to be endured only on occasion, that is to say, in p laces where the sense of the inscription is of more importa nce than external ornament. This is a sweeping statement, from which we need not suffer unduly; yet it is doubtful wh ether there is art in individual letters. Letters in combinatio n may be satisfying and in a well composed page even be autiful as a whole, but art in letters consists rather in the ar t of arranging and composing them in a pleasing and app ropriate manner. The main purpose of letters is the practic al one of making thoughts visible. Ruskin says that all lette rs are frightful things and to be endured only on occasion, that is to say, in places where the sense of the inscription is of more importance than external ornament. This is a swe
The main purpose of letters is the practical one of making t houghts visible. Ruskin says that all letters are frightful thin
The main purpose of letters is the practical on e of making thoughts visible. Ruskin says tha

12/15

The main purpose of letters is the practical one of making thoughts visible. Ruskin says that all letters are frightful thi ngs and to be endured only on occasion, that is to say, in p laces where the sense of the inscription is of more importa nce than external ornament. This is a sweeping statement, from which we need not suffer unduly; yet it is doubtful wh ether there is art in individual letters. Letters in combinatio n may be satisfying and in a well composed page even be autiful as a whole, but art in letters consists rather in the ar t of arranging and composing them in a pleasing and app ropriate manner. The main purpose of letters is the practic al one of making thoughts visible. Ruskin says that all lette rs are frightful things and to be endured only on occasion, that is to say, in places where the sense of the inscription is
The main purpose of letters is the practical one of making t houghts visible. Ruskin says that all letters are frightful thin
The main purpose of letters is the practical on e of making thoughts visible. Ruskin says tha

SPARTAN 14 POINT SET MINUS ½ UNIT

MEDIUM, ITALIC, BLACK, BLACK ITALIC

abcdefghijklmnopqrstuvwxyz – 1 UNIT

abcdefghijklmnopqrstuvwxyz – ½ UNIT

abcdefghijklmnopqrstuvwxyz NORMAL

ABCDEFGHIJKLMNOPQRSTUVWXYZ abcdefghijklmnopqrstuvwxyz

ABCDEFGHIJKLMNOPQRSTUVWXYZ abcdefghijklmnopqrstuvwxyz

ABCDEFGHIJKLMNOPQRSTUVWXYZ abcdefghijklmnopqrstuvwxyz

ABCDEFGHIJKLMNOPQRSTUVWXYZ abcdefghijklmnopqrstuvwxyz

14/14

The main purpose of letters is the practical one of making thoughts visible. Ruskin says that all lette rs are frightful things and to be endured only on o ccasion, that is to say, in places where the sense o f the inscription is of more importance than exter nal ornament. This is a sweeping statement, from which we need not suffer unduly; yet it is doubtful whether there is art in individual letters. Letters in combination may be satisfying and in a well com posed page even beautiful as a whole, but art in l etters consists rather in the art of arranging and c omposing them in a pleasing and appropriate m anner. The main purpose of letters is the practical

The main purpose of letters is the practical one of making thoughts visible. Ruskin says that all letter

The main purpose of letters is the prac tical one of making thoughts visible. R

14/15

The main purpose of letters is the practical one of making thoughts visible. Ruskin says that all lette rs are frightful things and to be endured only on o ccasion, that is to say, in places where the sense o f the inscription is of more importance than exter nal ornament. This is a sweeping statement, from which we need not suffer unduly; yet it is doubtful whether there is art in individual letters. Letters in combination may be satisfying and in a well com posed page even beautiful as a whole, but art in l etters consists rather in the art of arranging and c omposing them in a pleasing and appropriate m

The main purpose of letters is the practical one of making thoughts visible. Ruskin says that all letter

The main purpose of letters is the prac tical one of making thoughts visible. R

14/16

The main purpose of letters is the practical one of making thoughts visible. Ruskin says that all lette rs are frightful things and to be endured only on o ccasion, that is to say, in places where the sense o f the inscription is of more importance than exter nal ornament. This is a sweeping statement, from which we need not suffer unduly; yet it is doubtful whether there is art in individual letters. Letters in combination may be satisfying and in a well com posed page even beautiful as a whole, but art in l etters consists rather in the art of arranging and c omposing them in a pleasing and appropriate m anner. The main purpose of letters is the practical

The main purpose of letters is the practical one of making thoughts visible. Ruskin says that all letter

The main purpose of letters is the prac tical one of making thoughts visible. R

14/17

The main purpose of letters is the practical one of making thoughts visible. Ruskin says that all lette rs are frightful things and to be endured only on o ccasion, that is to say, in places where the sense o f the inscription is of more importance than exter nal ornament. This is a sweeping statement, from which we need not suffer unduly; yet it is doubtful whether there is art in individual letters. Letters in combination may be satisfying and in a well com posed page even beautiful as a whole, but art in l etters consists rather in the art of arranging and c omposing them in a pleasing and appropriate m

The main purpose of letters is the practical one of making thoughts visible. Ruskin says that all letter

The main purpose of letters is the prac tical one of making thoughts visible. R

TIMES ROMAN 6 & 7 POINT SET NORMAL

ROMAN, ITALIC, BOLD, BOLD ITALIC

ABCDEFGHIJKLMNOPQRSTUVWXYZ 1234567890 abcdefghijklmnopqrstuvwxyz

ABCDEFGHIJKLMNOPQRSTUVWXYZ 1234567890 abcdefghijklmnopqrstuvwxyz

ABCDEFGHIJKLMNOPQRSTUVWXYZ 1234567890 abcdefghijklmnopqrstuvwxyz

ABCDEFGHIJKLMNOPQRSTUVWXYZ 1234567890 abcdefghijklmnopqrstuvwxyz

6/6

The main purpose of letters is the practical one of making thoughts visible. Ruskin says that all letters a
re frightful things and to be endured only on occasion, that is to say, in places where the sense of the ins
cription is of more importance than external ornament. This is a sweeping statement, from which we n
eed not suffer unduly; yet it is doubtful whether there is art in individual letters. Letters in combination
may be satisfying and in a well composed page even beautiful as a whole, but art in letters consists rath
er in the art of arranging and composing them in a pleasing and appropriate manner. The main purpose
of letters is the practical one of making thoughts visible. Ruskin says that all letters are frightful things
and to be endured only on occasion, that is to say, in places where the sense of the inscription is of more
importance than external ornament. This is a sweeping statement, from which we need not suffer undu
ly; yet it is doubtful whether there is art in individual letters. Letters in combination may be satisfying a
nd in a well composed page even beautiful as a whole, but art in letters consists rather in the art of arran
ging and composing them in a pleasing and appropriate manner. The main purpose of letters is the prac
tical one of making thoughts visible. Ruskin says that all letters are frightful things and to be endured o
The main purpose of letters is the practical one of making thoughts visible. Ruskin says that all letters
are frightful things and to be endured only on occasion, that is to say, in places where the sense of the in
The main purpose of letters is the practical one of making thoughts visible. Ruskin says that all le
tters are frightful things and to be endured only on occasion, that is to say, in places where the sen

6/7

The main purpose of letters is the practical one of making thoughts visible. Ruskin says that all letters a
re frightful things and to be endured only on occasion, that is to say, in places where the sense of the ins
cription is of more importance than external ornament. This is a sweeping statement, from which we n
eed not suffer unduly; yet it is doubtful whether there is art in individual letters. Letters in combination
may be satisfying and in a well composed page even beautiful as a whole, but art in letters consists rath
er in the art of arranging and composing them in a pleasing and appropriate manner. The main purpose
of letters is the practical one of making thoughts visible. Ruskin says that all letters are frightful things
and to be endured only on occasion, that is to say, in places where the sense of the inscription is of more
importance than external ornament. This is a sweeping statement, from which we need not suffer undu
ly; yet it is doubtful whether there is art in individual letters. Letters in combination may be satisfying a
nd in a well composed page even beautiful as a whole, but art in letters consists rather in the art of arran
The main purpose of letters is the practical one of making thoughts visible. Ruskin says that all letters
are frightful things and to be endured only on occasion, that is to say, in places where the sense of the in
The main purpose of letters is the practical one of making thoughts visible. Ruskin says that all le
tters are frightful things and to be endured only on occasion, that is to say, in places where the sen

6/8

The main purpose of letters is the practical one of making thoughts visible. Ruskin says that all letters a
re frightful things and to be endured only on occasion, that is to say, in places where the sense of the ins
cription is of more importance than external ornament. This is a sweeping statement, from which we n
eed not suffer unduly; yet it is doubtful whether there is art in individual letters. Letters in combination
may be satisfying and in a well composed page even beautiful as a whole, but art in letters consists rath
er in the art of arranging and composing them in a pleasing and appropriate manner. The main purpose
of letters is the practical one of making thoughts visible. Ruskin says that all letters are frightful things
and to be endured only on occasion, that is to say, in places where the sense of the inscription is of more
importance than external ornament. This is a sweeping statement, from which we need not suffer undu
The main purpose of letters is the practical one of making thoughts visible. Ruskin says that all letters
are frightful things and to be endured only on occasion, that is to say, in places where the sense of the in
The main purpose of letters is the practical one of making thoughts visible. Ruskin says that all le
tters are frightful things and to be endured only on occasion, that is to say, in places where the sen

6/9

The main purpose of letters is the practical one of making thoughts visible. Ruskin says that all letters a
re frightful things and to be endured only on occasion, that is to say, in places where the sense of the ins
cription is of more importance than external ornament. This is a sweeping statement, from which we n
eed not suffer unduly; yet it is doubtful whether there is art in individual letters. Letters in combination
may be satisfying and in a well composed page even beautiful as a whole, but art in letters consists rath
er in the art of arranging and composing them in a pleasing and appropriate manner. The main purpose
of letters is the practical one of making thoughts visible. Ruskin says that all letters are frightful things
and to be endured only on occasion, that is to say, in places where the sense of the inscription is of more
The main purpose of letters is the practical one of making thoughts visible. Ruskin says that all letters
are frightful things and to be endured only on occasion, that is to say, in places where the sense of the in
The main purpose of letters is the practical one of making thoughts visible. Ruskin says that all le
tters are frightful things and to be endured only on occasion, that is to say, in places where the sen

ABCDEFGHIJKLMNOPQRSTUVWXYZ 1234567890 abcdefghijklmnopqrstuvwxyz

ABCDEFGHIJKLMNOPQRSTUVWXYZ 1234567890 abcdefghijklmnopqrstuvwxyz

ABCDEFGHIJKLMNOPQRSTUVWXYZ 1234567890 abcdefghijklmnopqrstuvwxyz

ABCDEFGHIJKLMNOPQRSTUVWXYZ 1234567890 abcdefghijklmnopqrstuvwxyz

7/7

The main purpose of letters is the practical one of making thoughts visible. Ruskin says
that all letters are frightful things and to be endured only on occasion, that is to say, in pl
aces where the sense of the inscription is of more importance than external ornament. T
his is a sweeping statement, from which we need not suffer unduly; yet it is doubtful wh
ether there is art in individual letters. Letters in combination may be satisfying and in a
well composed page even beautiful as a whole, but art in letters consists rather in the art
of arranging and composing them in a pleasing and appropriate manner. The main purp
ose of letters is the practical one of making thoughts visible. Ruskin says that all letters a
re frightful things and to be endured only on occasion, that is to say, in places where the
sense of the inscription is of more importance than external ornament. This is a sweepin
g statement, from which we need not suffer unduly; yet it is doubtful whether there is art
The main purpose of letters is the practical one of making thoughts visible. Ruskin says t
hat all letters are frightful things and to be endured only on occasion, that is to say, in pl
The main purpose of letters is the practical one of making thoughts visible. Ruskin
says that all letters are frightful things and to be endured only on occasion, that is t

7/8

The main purpose of letters is the practical one of making thoughts visible. Ruskin says
that all letters are frightful things and to be endured only on occasion, that is to say, in pl
aces where the sense of the inscription is of more importance than external ornament. T
his is a sweeping statement, from which we need not suffer unduly; yet it is doubtful wh
ether there is art in individual letters. Letters in combination may be satisfying and in a
well composed page even beautiful as a whole, but art in letters consists rather in the art
of arranging and composing them in a pleasing and appropriate manner. The main purp
ose of letters is the practical one of making thoughts visible. Ruskin says that all letters a
re frightful things and to be endured only on occasion, that is to say, in places where the
sense of the inscription is of more importance than external ornament. This is a sweepin
The main purpose of letters is the practical one of making thoughts visible. Ruskin says t
hat all letters are frightful things and to be endured only on occasion, that is to say, in pl
The main purpose of letters is the practical one of making thoughts visible. Ruskin
says that all letters are frightful things and to be endured only on occasion, that is t

7/9

The main purpose of letters is the practical one of making thoughts visible. Ruskin says
that all letters are frightful things and to be endured only on occasion, that is to say, in pl
aces where the sense of the inscription is of more importance than external ornament. T
his is a sweeping statement, from which we need not suffer unduly; yet it is doubtful wh
ether there is art in individual letters. Letters in combination may be satisfying and in a
well composed page even beautiful as a whole, but art in letters consists rather in the art
of arranging and composing them in a pleasing and appropriate manner. The main purp
ose of letters is the practical one of making thoughts visible. Ruskin says that all letters a
re frightful things and to be endured only on occasion, that is to say, in places where the
sense of the inscription is of more importance than external ornament. This is a sweepin
The main purpose of letters is the practical one of making thoughts visible. Ruskin says t
hat all letters are frightful things and to be endured only on occasion, that is to say, in pl
The main purpose of letters is the practical one of making thoughts visible. Ruskin
says that all letters are frightful things and to be endured only on occasion, that is t

7/10

The main purpose of letters is the practical one of making thoughts visible. Ruskin says
that all letters are frightful things and to be endured only on occasion, that is to say, in pl
aces where the sense of the inscription is of more importance than external ornament. T
his is a sweeping statement, from which we need not suffer unduly; yet it is doubtful wh
ether there is art in individual letters. Letters in combination may be satisfying and in a
well composed page even beautiful as a whole, but art in letters consists rather in the art
of arranging and composing them in a pleasing and appropriate manner. The main purp
ose of letters is the practical one of making thoughts visible. Ruskin says that all letters a
re frightful things and to be endured only on occasion, that is to say, in places where the
sense of the inscription is of more importance than external ornament. This is a sweepin
The main purpose of letters is the practical one of making thoughts visible. Ruskin says t
hat all letters are frightful things and to be endured only on occasion, that is to say, in pl
The main purpose of letters is the practical one of making thoughts visible. Ruskin
says that all letters are frightful things and to be endured only on occasion, that is t

TIMES ROMAN 8 & 9 POINT SET NORMAL

ROMAN, ITALIC, BOLD, BOLD ITALIC

ABCDEFGHIJKLMNOPQRSTUVWXYZ 1234567890 abcdefghijklmnopqrstuvwxyz

ABCDEFGHIJKLMNOPQRSTUVWXYZ 1234567890 abcdefghijklmnopqrstuvwxyz

ABCDEFGHIJKLMNOPQRSTUVWXYZ 1234567890 abcdefghijklmnopqrstuvwxyz

ABCDEFGHIJKLMNOPQRSTUVWXYZ 1234567890 abcdefghijklmnopqrstuvwxyz

8/8

The main purpose of letters is the practical one of making thoughts visible. R uskin says that all letters are frightful things and to be endured only on occasi on, that is to say, in places where the sense of the inscription is of more impor tance than external ornament. This is a sweeping statement, from which we n eed not suffer unduly; yet it is doubtful whether there is art in individual letter s. Letters in combination may be satisfying and in a well composed page eve n beautiful as a whole, but art in letters consists rather in the art of arranging a nd composing them in a pleasing and appropriate manner. The main purpose of letters is the practical one of making thoughts visible. Ruskin says that all l

The main purpose of letters is the practical one of making thoughts visible. R uskin says that all letters are frightful things and to be endured only on occasi

The main purpose of letters is the practical one of making thoughts visib le. Ruskin says that all letters are frightful things and to be endured only

8/10

The main purpose of letters is the practical one of making thoughts visible. R uskin says that all letters are frightful things and to be endured only on occasi on, that is to say, in places where the sense of the inscription is of more impor tance than external ornament. This is a sweeping statement, from which we n eed not suffer unduly; yet it is doubtful whether there is art in individual letter s. Letters in combination may be satisfying and in a well composed page eve n beautiful as a whole, but art in letters consists rather in the art of arranging a

The main purpose of letters is the practical one of making thoughts visible. R uskin says that all letters are frightful things and to be endured only on occasi

The main purpose of letters is the practical one of making thoughts visib le. Ruskin says that all letters are frightful things and to be endured only

8/9

The main purpose of letters is the practical one of making thoughts visible. R uskin says that all letters are frightful things and to be endured only on occasi on, that is to say, in places where the sense of the inscription is of more impor tance than external ornament. This is a sweeping statement, from which we n eed not suffer unduly; yet it is doubtful whether there is art in individual letter s. Letters in combination may be satisfying and in a well composed page eve n beautiful as a whole, but art in letters consists rather in the art of arranging a nd composing them in a pleasing and appropriate manner. The main purpose

The main purpose of letters is the practical one of making thoughts visible. R uskin says that all letters are frightful things and to be endured only on occasi

The main purpose of letters is the practical one of making thoughts visib le. Ruskin says that all letters are frightful things and to be endured only

8/11

The main purpose of letters is the practical one of making thoughts visible. R uskin says that all letters are frightful things and to be endured only on occasi on, that is to say, in places where the sense of the inscription is of more impor tance than external ornament. This is a sweeping statement, from which we n eed not suffer unduly; yet it is doubtful whether there is art in individual letter s. Letters in combination may be satisfying and in a well composed page eve n beautiful as a whole, but art in letters consists rather in the art of arranging a

The main purpose of letters is the practical one of making thoughts visible. R uskin says that all letters are frightful things and to be endured only on occasi

The main purpose of letters is the practical one of making thoughts visib le. Ruskin says that all letters are frightful things and to be endured only

---

ABCDEFGHIJKLMNOPQRSTUVWXYZ 1234567890 abcdefghijklmnopqrstuvwxyz

ABCDEFGHIJKLMNOPQRSTUVWXYZ 1234567890 abcdefghijklmnopqrstuvwxyz

ABCDEFGHIJKLMNOPQRSTUVWXYZ 1234567890 abcdefghijklmnopqrstuvwxyz

ABCDEFGHIJKLMNOPQRSTUVWXYZ 1234567890 abcdefghijklmnopqrstuvwxyz

9/9

The main purpose of letters is the practical one of making thoughts v isible. Ruskin says that all letters are frightful things and to be endur ed only on occasion, that is to say, in places where the sense of the in scription is of more importance than external ornament. This is a sw eeping statement, from which we need not suffer unduly; yet it is do ubtful whether there is art in individual letters. Letters in combinatio n may be satisfying and in a well composed page even beautiful as a whole, but art in letters consists rather in the art of arranging and co

The main purpose of letters is the practical one of making thoughts v isible. Ruskin says that all letters are frightful things and to be endur

The main purpose of letters is the practical one of making thoug hts visible. Ruskin says that all letters are frightful things and to

9/11

The main purpose of letters is the practical one of making thoughts v isible. Ruskin says that all letters are frightful things and to be endur ed only on occasion, that is to say, in places where the sense of the in scription is of more importance than external ornament. This is a sw eeping statement, from which we need not suffer unduly; yet it is do ubtful whether there is art in individual letters. Letters in combinatio n may be satisfying and in a well composed page even beautiful as a

The main purpose of letters is the practical one of making thoughts v isible. Ruskin says that all letters are frightful things and to be endur

The main purpose of letters is the practical one of making thoug hts visible. Ruskin says that all letters are frightful things and to

9/10

The main purpose of letters is the practical one of making thoughts v isible. Ruskin says that all letters are frightful things and to be endur ed only on occasion, that is to say, in places where the sense of the in scription is of more importance than external ornament. This is a sw eeping statement, from which we need not suffer unduly; yet it is do ubtful whether there is art in individual letters. Letters in combinatio n may be satisfying and in a well composed page even beautiful as a

The main purpose of letters is the practical one of making thoughts v isible. Ruskin says that all letters are frightful things and to be endur

The main purpose of letters is the practical one of making thoug hts visible. Ruskin says that all letters are frightful things and to

9/12

The main purpose of letters is the practical one of making thoughts v isible. Ruskin says that all letters are frightful things and to be endur ed only on occasion, that is to say, in places where the sense of the in scription is of more importance than external ornament. This is a sw eeping statement, from which we need not suffer unduly; yet it is do ubtful whether there is art in individual letters. Letters in combinatio n may be satisfying and in a well composed page even beautiful as a

The main purpose of letters is the practical one of making thoughts v isible. Ruskin says that all letters are frightful things and to be endur

The main purpose of letters is the practical one of making thoug hts visible. Ruskin says that all letters are frightful things and to

TIMES ROMAN 10 POINT SET MINUS ½ UNIT

ROMAN, ITALIC, BOLD, BOLD ITALIC

abcdefghijklmnopqrstuvwxyz – 1 UNIT
abcdefghijklmnopqrstuvwxyz – ½ UNIT
abcdefghijklmnopqrstuvwxyz NORMAL

ABCDEFGHIJKLMNOPQRSTUVWXYZ 1234567890 abcdefghijklmnopqrstuvwxyz
ABCDEFGHIJKLMNOPQRSTUVWXYZ 1234567890 abcdefghijklmnopqrstuvwxyz
ABCDEFGHIJKLMNOPQRSTUVWXYZ 1234567890 abcdefghijklmnopqrstuvwxyz
ABCDEFGHIJKLMNOPQRSTUVWXYZ 1234567890 abcdefghijklmnopqrstuvwxyz

10/10

The main purpose of letters is the practical one of making though ts visible. Ruskin says that all letters are frightful things and to be endured only on occasion, that is to say, in places where the sens e of the inscription is of more importance than external ornamen t. This is a sweeping statement, from which we need not suffer u nduly; yet it is doubtful whether there is art in individual letters. Letters in combination may be satisfying and in a well compose d page even beautiful as a whole, but art in letters consists rather in the art of arranging and composing them in a pleasing and app ropriate manner. The main purpose of letters is the practical one of making thoughts visible. Ruskin says that all letters are frightf ul things and to be endured only on occasion, that is to say, in pla ces where the sense of the inscription is of more importance than external ornament. This is a sweeping statement, from which w e need not suffer unduly; yet it is doubtful whether there is art in i ndividual letters. Letters in combination may be satisfying and i n a well composed page even beautiful as a whole, but art in lette rs consists rather in the art of arranging and composing them in a pleasing and appropriate manner. The main purpose of letters is t he practical one of making thoughts visible. Ruskin says that all l etters are frightful things and to be endured only on occasion, tha t is to say, in places where the sense of the inscription is of more i

The main purpose of letters is the practical one of making thoug hts visible. Ruskin says that all letters are frightful things and to

The main purpose of letters is the practical one of making th oughts visible. Ruskin says that all letters are frightful things

10/11

The main purpose of letters is the practical one of making though ts visible. Ruskin says that all letters are frightful things and to be endured only on occasion, that is to say, in places where the sens e of the inscription is of more importance than external ornamen t. This is a sweeping statement, from which we need not suffer u nduly; yet it is doubtful whether there is art in individual letters. Letters in combination may be satisfying and in a well compose d page even beautiful as a whole, but art in letters consists rather in the art of arranging and composing them in a pleasing and app ropriate manner. The main purpose of letters is the practical one of making thoughts visible. Ruskin says that all letters are frightf ul things and to be endured only on occasion, that is to say, in pla ces where the sense of the inscription is of more importance than external ornament. This is a sweeping statement, from which w e need not suffer unduly; yet it is doubtful whether there is art in i ndividual letters. Letters in combination may be satisfying and i n a well composed page even beautiful as a whole, but art in lette rs consists rather in the art of arranging and composing them in a pleasing and appropriate manner. The main purpose of letters is t he practical one of making thoughts visible. Ruskin says that all l

The main purpose of letters is the practical one of making thoug hts visible. Ruskin says that all letters are frightful things and to

The main purpose of letters is the practical one of making th oughts visible. Ruskin says that all letters are frightful things

10/12

The main purpose of letters is the practical one of making though ts visible. Ruskin says that all letters are frightful things and to be endured only on occasion, that is to say, in places where the sens e of the inscription is of more importance than external ornamen t. This is a sweeping statement, from which we need not suffer u nduly; yet it is doubtful whether there is art in individual letters. Letters in combination may be satisfying and in a well compose d page even beautiful as a whole, but art in letters consists rather in the art of arranging and composing them in a pleasing and app ropriate manner. The main purpose of letters is the practical one of making thoughts visible. Ruskin says that all letters are frightf ul things and to be endured only on occasion, that is to say, in pla ces where the sense of the inscription is of more importance than external ornament. This is a sweeping statement, from which w e need not suffer unduly; yet it is doubtful whether there is art in i ndividual letters. Letters in combination may be satisfying and i n a well composed page even beautiful as a whole, but art in lette rs consists rather in the art of arranging and composing them in a

The main purpose of letters is the practical one of making thoug hts visible. Ruskin says that all letters are frightful things and to

The main purpose of letters is the practical one of making th oughts visible. Ruskin says that all letters are frightful things

10/13

The main purpose of letters is the practical one of making though ts visible. Ruskin says that all letters are frightful things and to be endured only on occasion, that is to say, in places where the sens e of the inscription is of more importance than external ornamen t. This is a sweeping statement, from which we need not suffer u nduly; yet it is doubtful whether there is art in individual letters. Letters in combination may be satisfying and in a well compose d page even beautiful as a whole, but art in letters consists rather in the art of arranging and composing them in a pleasing and app ropriate manner. The main purpose of letters is the practical one of making thoughts visible. Ruskin says that all letters are frightf ul things and to be endured only on occasion, that is to say, in pla ces where the sense of the inscription is of more importance than external ornament. This is a sweeping statement, from which w e need not suffer unduly; yet it is doubtful whether there is art in i ndividual letters. Letters in combination may be satisfying and i n a well composed page even beautiful as a whole, but art in lette

The main purpose of letters is the practical one of making thoug hts visible. Ruskin says that all letters are frightful things and to

The main purpose of letters is the practical one of making th oughts visible. Ruskin says that all letters are frightful things

TIMES ROMAN 11 POINT SET MINUS ½ UNIT

ROMAN, ITALIC, BOLD, BOLD ITALIC

abcdefghijklmnopqrstuvwxyz – 1 UNIT
abcdefghijklmnopqrstuvwxyz – ½ UNIT
abcdefghijklmnopqrstuvwxyz NORMAL

ABCDEFGHIJKLMNOPQRSTUVWXYZ 1234567890 abcdefghijklmnopqrstuvwxyz
ABCDEFGHIJKLMNOPQRSTUVWXYZ 1234567890 abcdefghijklmnopqrstuvwxyz
ABCDEFGHIJKLMNOPQRSTUVWXYZ 1234567890 abcdefghijklmnopqrstuvwxyz
ABCDEFGHIJKLMNOPQRSTUVWXYZ 1234567890 abcdefghijklmnopqrstuvwxyz

11/11

The main purpose of letters is the practical one of making t houghts visible. Ruskin says that all letters are frightful thi ngs and to be endured only on occasion, that is to say, in pl aces where the sense of the inscription is of more importan ce than external ornament. This is a sweeping statement, f rom which we need not suffer unduly; yet it is doubtful wh ether there is art in individual letters. Letters in combinatio n may be satisfying and in a well composed page even bea utiful as a whole, but art in letters consists rather in the art of arranging and composing them in a pleasing and approp riate manner. The main purpose of letters is the practical o ne of making thoughts visible. Ruskin says that all letters a re frightful things and to be endured only on occasion, that is to say, in places where the sense of the inscription is of m ore importance than external ornament. This is a sweeping statement, from which we need not suffer unduly; yet it is doubtful whether there is art in individual letters. Letters i n combination may be satisfying and in a well composed p age even beautiful as a whole, but art in letters consists rat
The main purpose of letters is the practical one of making t houghts visible. Ruskin says that all letters are frightful thi
The main purpose of letters is the practical one of maki ng thoughts visible. Ruskin says that all letters are frig

11/12

The main purpose of letters is the practical one of making t houghts visible. Ruskin says that all letters are frightful thi ngs and to be endured only on occasion, that is to say, in pl aces where the sense of the inscription is of more importan ce than external ornament. This is a sweeping statement, f rom which we need not suffer unduly; yet it is doubtful wh ether there is art in individual letters. Letters in combinatio n may be satisfying and in a well composed page even bea utiful as a whole, but art in letters consists rather in the art of arranging and composing them in a pleasing and approp riate manner. The main purpose of letters is the practical o ne of making thoughts visible. Ruskin says that all letters a re frightful things and to be endured only on occasion, that is to say, in places where the sense of the inscription is of m ore importance than external ornament. This is a sweeping statement, from which we need not suffer unduly; yet it is doubtful whether there is art in individual letters. Letters i n combination may be satisfying and in a well composed p
The main purpose of letters is the practical one of making t houghts visible. Ruskin says that all letters are frightful thi
The main purpose of letters is the practical one of maki ng thoughts visible. Ruskin says that all letters are frig

11/13

The main purpose of letters is the practical one of making t houghts visible. Ruskin says that all letters are frightful thi ngs and to be endured only on occasion, that is to say, in pl aces where the sense of the inscription is of more importan ce than external ornament. This is a sweeping statement, f rom which we need not suffer unduly; yet it is doubtful wh ether there is art in individual letters. Letters in combinatio n may be satisfying and in a well composed page even bea utiful as a whole, but art in letters consists rather in the art of arranging and composing them in a pleasing and approp riate manner. The main purpose of letters is the practical o ne of making thoughts visible. Ruskin says that all letters a re frightful things and to be endured only on occasion, that is to say, in places where the sense of the inscription is of m ore importance than external ornament. This is a sweeping statement, from which we need not suffer unduly; yet it is doubtful whether there is art in individual letters. Letters i
The main purpose of letters is the practical one of making t houghts visible. Ruskin says that all letters are frightful thi
The main purpose of letters is the practical one of maki ng thoughts visible. Ruskin says that all letters are frig

11/14

The main purpose of letters is the practical one of making t houghts visible. Ruskin says that all letters are frightful thi ngs and to be endured only on occasion, that is to say, in pl aces where the sense of the inscription is of more importan ce than external ornament. This is a sweeping statement, f rom which we need not suffer unduly; yet it is doubtful wh ether there is art in individual letters. Letters in combinatio n may be satisfying and in a well composed page even bea utiful as a whole, but art in letters consists rather in the art of arranging and composing them in a pleasing and approp riate manner. The main purpose of letters is the practical o ne of making thoughts visible. Ruskin says that all letters a re frightful things and to be endured only on occasion, that is to say, in places where the sense of the inscription is of m ore importance than external ornament. This is a sweeping statement, from which we need not suffer unduly; yet it is
The main purpose of letters is the practical one of making t houghts visible. Ruskin says that all letters are frightful thi
The main purpose of letters is the practical one of maki ng thoughts visible. Ruskin says that all letters are frig

TIMES ROMAN 12 POINT SET MINUS ½ UNIT

ROMAN, ITALIC, BOLD, BOLD ITALIC

abcdefghijklmnopqrstuvwxyz – 1 UNIT
abcdefghijklmnopqrstuvwxyz – ½ UNIT
abcdefghijklmnopqrstuvwxyz NORMAL

ABCDEFGHIJKLMNOPQRSTUVWXYZ 1234567890 abcdefghijklmnopqrstuvwxyz
ABCDEFGHIJKLMNOPQRSTUVWXYZ 1234567890 abcdefghijklmnopqrstuvwxyz
ABCDEFGHIJKLMNOPQRSTUVWXYZ 1234567890 abcdefghijklmnopqrstuvwxyz
ABCDEFGHIJKLMNOPQRSTUVWXYZ 1234567890 abcdefghijklmnopqrstuvwxyz

12/12

The main purpose of letters is the practical one of maki ng thoughts visible. Ruskin says that all letters are frig htful things and to be endured only on occasion, that is to say, in places where the sense of the inscription is of more importance than external ornament. This is a sw eeping statement, from which we need not suffer undu ly; yet it is doubtful whether there is art in individual le tters. Letters in combination may be satisfying and in a well composed page even beautiful as a whole, but art in letters consists rather in the art of arranging and com posing them in a pleasing and appropriate manner. Th e main purpose of letters is the practical one of making thoughts visible. Ruskin says that all letters are frightf ul things and to be endured only on occasion, that is to say, in places where the sense of the inscription is of m
The main purpose of letters is the practical one of mak ing thoughts visible. Ruskin says that all letters are fri
The main purpose of letters is the practical one of making thoughts visible. Ruskin says that all letter

12/13

The main purpose of letters is the practical one of maki ng thoughts visible. Ruskin says that all letters are frig htful things and to be endured only on occasion, that is to say, in places where the sense of the inscription is of more importance than external ornament. This is a sw eeping statement, from which we need not suffer undu ly; yet it is doubtful whether there is art in individual le tters. Letters in combination may be satisfying and in a well composed page even beautiful as a whole, but art in letters consists rather in the art of arranging and com posing them in a pleasing and appropriate manner. Th e main purpose of letters is the practical one of making thoughts visible. Ruskin says that all letters are frightf ul things and to be endured only on occasion, that is to
The main purpose of letters is the practical one of mak ing thoughts visible. Ruskin says that all letters are fri
The main purpose of letters is the practical one of making thoughts visible. Ruskin says that all letter

12/14

The main purpose of letters is the practical one of maki ng thoughts visible. Ruskin says that all letters are frig htful things and to be endured only on occasion, that is to say, in places where the sense of the inscription is of more importance than external ornament. This is a sw eeping statement, from which we need not suffer undu ly; yet it is doubtful whether there is art in individual le tters. Letters in combination may be satisfying and in a well composed page even beautiful as a whole, but art in letters consists rather in the art of arranging and com posing them in a pleasing and appropriate manner. Th e main purpose of letters is the practical one of making thoughts visible. Ruskin says that all letters are frightf ul things and to be endured only on occasion, that is to say, in places where the sense of the inscription is of m
The main purpose of letters is the practical one of mak ing thoughts visible. Ruskin says that all letters are fri
The main purpose of letters is the practical one of making thoughts visible. Ruskin says that all letter

12/15

The main purpose of letters is the practical one of maki ng thoughts visible. Ruskin says that all letters are frig htful things and to be endured only on occasion, that is to say, in places where the sense of the inscription is of more importance than external ornament. This is a sw eeping statement, from which we need not suffer undu ly; yet it is doubtful whether there is art in individual le tters. Letters in combination may be satisfying and in a well composed page even beautiful as a whole, but art in letters consists rather in the art of arranging and com posing them in a pleasing and appropriate manner. Th e main purpose of letters is the practical one of making thoughts visible. Ruskin says that all letters are frightf ul things and to be endured only on occasion, that is to
The main purpose of letters is the practical one of mak ing thoughts visible. Ruskin says that all letters are fri
The main purpose of letters is the practical one of making thoughts visible. Ruskin says that all letter

TIMES ROMAN 14 POINT SET MINUS ½ UNIT

ROMAN, ITALIC, BOLD, BOLD ITALIC

abcdefghijklmnopqrstuvwxyz – 1 UNIT
abcdefghijklmnopqrstuvwxyz – ½ UNIT
abcdefghijklmnopqrstuvwxyz NORMAL

ABCDEFGHIJKLMNOPQRSTUVWXYZ abcdefghijklmnopqrstuvwxyz
ABCDEFGHIJKLMNOPQRSTUVWXYZ abcdefghijklmnopqrstuvwxyz
ABCDEFGHIJKLMNOPQRSTUVWXYZ abcdefghijklmnopqrstuvwxyz
ABCDEFGHIJKLMNOPQRSTUVWXYZ abcdefghijklmnopqrstuvwxyz

14/14

The main purpose of letters is the practical one of making thoughts visible. Ruskin says that a ll letters are frightful things and to be endured only on occasion, that is to say, in places wher e the sense of the inscription is of more import ance than external ornament. This is a sweepi ng statement, from which we need not suffer u nduly; yet it is doubtful whether there is art in i ndividual letters. Letters in combination may be satisfying and in a well composed page eve n beautiful as a whole, but art in letters consist s rather in the art of arranging and composing t hem in a pleasing and appropriate manner. Th
The main purpose of letters is the practical on e of making thoughts visible. Ruskin says that
The main purpose of letters is the practical one of making thoughts visible. Ruskin say

14/15

The main purpose of letters is the practical one of making thoughts visible. Ruskin says that a ll letters are frightful things and to be endured only on occasion, that is to say, in places wher e the sense of the inscription is of more import ance than external ornament. This is a sweepi ng statement, from which we need not suffer u nduly; yet it is doubtful whether there is art in i ndividual letters. Letters in combination may be satisfying and in a well composed page eve n beautiful as a whole, but art in letters consist s rather in the art of arranging and composing t
The main purpose of letters is the practical on e of making thoughts visible. Ruskin says that
The main purpose of letters is the practical one of making thoughts visible. Ruskin say

14/16

The main purpose of letters is the practical one of making thoughts visible. Ruskin says that a ll letters are frightful things and to be endured only on occasion, that is to say, in places wher e the sense of the inscription is of more import ance than external ornament. This is a sweepi ng statement, from which we need not suffer u nduly; yet it is doubtful whether there is art in i ndividual letters. Letters in combination may be satisfying and in a well composed page eve n beautiful as a whole, but art in letters consist s rather in the art of arranging and composing t hem in a pleasing and appropriate manner. Th
The main purpose of letters is the practical on e of making thoughts visible. Ruskin says that
The main purpose of letters is the practical one of making thoughts visible. Ruskin say

14/17

The main purpose of letters is the practical one of making thoughts visible. Ruskin says that a ll letters are frightful things and to be endured only on occasion, that is to say, in places wher e the sense of the inscription is of more import ance than external ornament. This is a sweepi ng statement, from which we need not suffer u nduly; yet it is doubtful whether there is art in i ndividual letters. Letters in combination may be satisfying and in a well composed page eve n beautiful as a whole, but art in letters consist s rather in the art of arranging and composing t
The main purpose of letters is the practical on e of making thoughts visible. Ruskin says that
The main purpose of letters is the practical one of making thoughts visible. Ruskin say

TRADE GOTHIC 6 & 7 POINT SET NORMAL

LIGHT, ITALIC, BOLD, BOLD ITALIC

ABCDEFGHIJKLMNOPQRSTUVWXYZ 1234567890 abcdefghijklmnopqrstuvwxyz

ABCDEFGHIJKLMNOPQRSTUVWXYZ 1234567890 abcdefghijklmnopqrstuvwxyz

ABCDEFGHIJKLMNOPQRSTUVWXYZ 1234567890 abcdefghijklmnopqrstuvwxyz

ABCDEFGHIJKLMNOPQRSTUVWXYZ 1234567890 abcdefghijklmnopqrstuvwxyz

6/6

The main purpose of letters is the practical one of making thoughts visible. Ruskin says that all lette
rs are frightful things and to be endured only on occasion, that is to say, in places where the sense o
f the inscription is of more importance than external ornament. This is a sweeping statement, from
which we need not suffer unduly; yet it is doubtful whether there is art in individual letters. Letters i
n combination may be satisfying and in a well composed page even beautiful as a whole, but art in l
etters consists rather in the art of arranging and composing them in a pleasing and appropriate ma
nner. The main purpose of letters is the practical one of making thoughts visible. Ruskin says that a
ll letters are frightful things and to be endured only on occasion, that is to say, in places where the s
ense of the inscription is of more importance than external ornament. This is a sweeping statement,
from which we need not suffer unduly; yet it is doubtful whether there is art in individual letters. Le
tters in combination may be satisfying and in a well composed page even beautiful as a whole, but
art in letters consists rather in the art of arranging and composing them in a pleasing and appropria
te manner. The main purpose of letters is the practical one of making thoughts visible. Ruskin says
The main purpose of letters is the practical one of making thoughts visible. Ruskin says that all lette
rs are frightful things and to be endured only on occasion, that is to say, in places where the sense o
The main purpose of letters is the practical one of making thoughts visible. Ruskin says that all l
etters are frightful things and to be endured only on occasion, that is to say, in places where the s

6/7

The main purpose of letters is the practical one of making thoughts visible. Ruskin says that all lette
rs are frightful things and to be endured only on occasion, that is to say, in places where the sense o
f the inscription is of more importance than external ornament. This is a sweeping statement, from
which we need not suffer unduly; yet it is doubtful whether there is art in individual letters. Letters i
n combination may be satisfying and in a well composed page even beautiful as a whole, but art in l
etters consists rather in the art of arranging and composing them in a pleasing and appropriate ma
nner. The main purpose of letters is the practical one of making thoughts visible. Ruskin says that a
ll letters are frightful things and to be endured only on occasion, that is to say, in places where the s
ense of the inscription is of more importance than external ornament. This is a sweeping statement,
from which we need not suffer unduly; yet it is doubtful whether there is art in individual letters. Le
tters in combination may be satisfying and in a well composed page even beautiful as a whole, but
The main purpose of letters is the practical one of making thoughts visible. Ruskin says that all lette
rs are frightful things and to be endured only on occasion, that is to say, in places where the sense o
The main purpose of letters is the practical one of making thoughts visible. Ruskin says that all l
etters are frightful things and to be endured only on occasion, that is to say, in places where the s

6/8

The main purpose of letters is the practical one of making thoughts visible. Ruskin says that all lette
rs are frightful things and to be endured only on occasion, that is to say, in places where the sense o
f the inscription is of more importance than external ornament. This is a sweeping statement, from
which we need not suffer unduly; yet it is doubtful whether there is art in individual letters. Letters i
n combination may be satisfying and in a well composed page even beautiful as a whole, but art in l
etters consists rather in the art of arranging and composing them in a pleasing and appropriate ma
nner. The main purpose of letters is the practical one of making thoughts visible. Ruskin says that a
ll letters are frightful things and to be endured only on occasion, that is to say, in places where the s
ense of the inscription is of more importance than external ornament. This is a sweeping statement,
The main purpose of letters is the practical one of making thoughts visible. Ruskin says that all lette
rs are frightful things and to be endured only on occasion, that is to say, in places where the sense o
The main purpose of letters is the practical one of making thoughts visible. Ruskin says that all l
etters are frightful things and to be endured only on occasion, that is to say, in places where the s

6/9

The main purpose of letters is the practical one of making thoughts visible. Ruskin says that all lette
rs are frightful things and to be endured only on occasion, that is to say, in places where the sense o
f the inscription is of more importance than external ornament. This is a sweeping statement, from
which we need not suffer unduly; yet it is doubtful whether there is art in individual letters. Letters i
n combination may be satisfying and in a well composed page even beautiful as a whole, but art in l
etters consists rather in the art of arranging and composing them in a pleasing and appropriate ma
nner. The main purpose of letters is the practical one of making thoughts visible. Ruskin says that a
ll letters are frightful things and to be endured only on occasion, that is to say, in places where the s
The main purpose of letters is the practical one of making thoughts visible. Ruskin says that all lette
rs are frightful things and to be endured only on occasion, that is to say, in places where the sense o
The main purpose of letters is the practical one of making thoughts visible. Ruskin says that all l
etters are frightful things and to be endured only on occasion, that is to say, in places where the s

---

ABCDEFGHIJKLMNOPQRSTUVWXYZ 1234567890 abcdefghijklmnopqrstuvwxyz

ABCDEFGHIJKLMNOPQRSTUVWXYZ 1234567890 abcdefghijklmnopqrstuvwxyz

ABCDEFGHIJKLMNOPQRSTUVWXYZ 1234567890 abcdefghijklmnopqrstuvwxyz

ABCDEFGHIJKLMNOPQRSTUVWXYZ 1234567890 abcdefghijklmnopqrstuvwxyz

7/7

The main purpose of letters is the practical one of making thoughts visible. Ruskin sa
ys that all letters are frightful things and to be endured only on occasion, that is to say,
in places where the sense of the inscription is of more importance than external orn
ament. This is a sweeping statement, from which we need not suffer unduly; yet it is
doubtful whether there is art in individual letters. Letters in combination may be satis
fying and in a well composed page even beautiful as a whole, but art in letters consist
s rather in the art of arranging and composing them in a pleasing and appropriate m
anner. The main purpose of letters is the practical one of making thoughts visible. Ru
skin says that all letters are frightful things and to be endured only on occasion, that i
s to say, in places where the sense of the inscription is of more importance than exter
nal ornament. This is a sweeping statement, from which we need not suffer unduly; y
The main purpose of letters is the practical one of making thoughts visible. Ruskin sa
ys that all letters are frightful things and to be endured only on occasion, that is to say,
The main purpose of letters is the practical one of making thoughts visible. Ruskin
says that all letters are frightful things and to be endured only on occasion, that is t

7/8

The main purpose of letters is the practical one of making thoughts visible. Ruskin sa
ys that all letters are frightful things and to be endured only on occasion, that is to say,
in places where the sense of the inscription is of more importance than external orn
ament. This is a sweeping statement, from which we need not suffer unduly; yet it is
doubtful whether there is art in individual letters. Letters in combination may be satis
fying and in a well composed page even beautiful as a whole, but art in letters consist
s rather in the art of arranging and composing them in a pleasing and appropriate m
anner. The main purpose of letters is the practical one of making thoughts visible. Ru
skin says that all letters are frightful things and to be endured only on occasion, that i
s to say, in places where the sense of the inscription is of more importance than exter
The main purpose of letters is the practical one of making thoughts visible. Ruskin sa
ys that all letters are frightful things and to be endured only on occasion, that is to say,
The main purpose of letters is the practical one of making thoughts visible. Ruskin
says that all letters are frightful things and to be endured only on occasion, that is t

7/9

The main purpose of letters is the practical one of making thoughts visible. Ruskin sa
ys that all letters are frightful things and to be endured only on occasion, that is to say,
in places where the sense of the inscription is of more importance than external orn
ament. This is a sweeping statement, from which we need not suffer unduly; yet it is
doubtful whether there is art in individual letters. Letters in combination may be satis
fying and in a well composed page even beautiful as a whole, but art in letters consist
s rather in the art of arranging and composing them in a pleasing and appropriate m
anner. The main purpose of letters is the practical one of making thoughts visible. Ru
skin says that all letters are frightful things and to be endured only on occasion, that i
s to say, in places where the sense of the inscription is of more importance than exter
The main purpose of letters is the practical one of making thoughts visible. Ruskin sa
ys that all letters are frightful things and to be endured only on occasion, that is to say,
The main purpose of letters is the practical one of making thoughts visible. Ruskin
says that all letters are frightful things and to be endured only on occasion, that is t

7/10

The main purpose of letters is the practical one of making thoughts visible. Ruskin sa
ys that all letters are frightful things and to be endured only on occasion, that is to say,
in places where the sense of the inscription is of more importance than external orn
ament. This is a sweeping statement, from which we need not suffer unduly; yet it is
doubtful whether there is art in individual letters. Letters in combination may be satis
fying and in a well composed page even beautiful as a whole, but art in letters consist
s rather in the art of arranging and composing them in a pleasing and appropriate m
anner. The main purpose of letters is the practical one of making thoughts visible. Ru
skin says that all letters are frightful things and to be endured only on occasion, that i
The main purpose of letters is the practical one of making thoughts visible. Ruskin sa
ys that all letters are frightful things and to be endured only on occasion, that is to say,
The main purpose of letters is the practical one of making thoughts visible. Ruskin
says that all letters are frightful things and to be endured only on occasion, that is t

TRADE GOTHIC 8 & 9 POINT SET NORMAL

LIGHT, ITALIC, BOLD, BOLD ITALIC

ABCDEFGHIJKLMNOPQRSTUVWXYZ 1234567890 abcdefghijklmnopqrstuvwxyz

ABCDEFGHIJKLMNOPQRSTUVWXYZ 1234567890 abcdefghijklmnopqrstuvwxyz

ABCDEFGHIJKLMNOPQRSTUVWXYZ 1234567890 abcdefghijklmnopqrstuvwxyz

ABCDEFGHIJKLMNOPQRSTUVWXYZ 1234567890 abcdefghijklmnopqrstuvwxyz

8/8

The main purpose of letters is the practical one of making thoughts visible. Ruskin says that all letters are frightful things and to be endured only on o ccasion, that is to say, in places where the sense of the inscription is of mo re importance than external ornament. This is a sweeping statement, fro m which we need not suffer unduly; yet it is doubtful whether there is art in individual letters. Letters in combination may be satisfying and in a well co mposed page even beautiful as a whole, but art in letters consists rather in the art of arranging and composing them in a pleasing and appropriate m anner. The main purpose of letters is the practical one of making thoughts

The main purpose of letters is the practical one of making thoughts visible. Ruskin says that all letters are frightful things and to be endured only on o

The main purpose of letters is the practical one of making thoughts visib le. Ruskin says that all letters are frightful things and to be endured only

8/9

The main purpose of letters is the practical one of making thoughts visible. Ruskin says that all letters are frightful things and to be endured only on o ccasion, that is to say, in places where the sense of the inscription is of mo re importance than external ornament. This is a sweeping statement, fro m which we need not suffer unduly; yet it is doubtful whether there is art in individual letters. Letters in combination may be satisfying and in a well co mposed page even beautiful as a whole, but art in letters consists rather in the art of arranging and composing them in a pleasing and appropriate m

The main purpose of letters is the practical one of making thoughts visible. Ruskin says that all letters are frightful things and to be endured only on o

The main purpose of letters is the practical one of making thoughts visib le. Ruskin says that all letters are frightful things and to be endured only

8/10

The main purpose of letters is the practical one of making thoughts visible. Ruskin says that all letters are frightful things and to be endured only on o ccasion, that is to say, in places where the sense of the inscription is of mo re importance than external ornament. This is a sweeping statement, fro m which we need not suffer unduly; yet it is doubtful whether there is art in individual letters. Letters in combination may be satisfying and in a well co mposed page even beautiful as a whole, but art in letters consists rather in

The main purpose of letters is the practical one of making thoughts visible. Ruskin says that all letters are frightful things and to be endured only on o

The main purpose of letters is the practical one of making thoughts visib le. Ruskin says that all letters are frightful things and to be endured only

8/11

The main purpose of letters is the practical one of making thoughts visible. Ruskin says that all letters are frightful things and to be endured only on o ccasion, that is to say, in places where the sense of the inscription is of mo re importance than external ornament. This is a sweeping statement, fro m which we need not suffer unduly; yet it is doubtful whether there is art in individual letters. Letters in combination may be satisfying and in a well co mposed page even beautiful as a whole, but art in letters consists rather in

The main purpose of letters is the practical one of making thoughts visible. Ruskin says that all letters are frightful things and to be endured only on o

The main purpose of letters is the practical one of making thoughts visib le. Ruskin says that all letters are frightful things and to be endured only

---

ABCDEFGHIJKLMNOPQRSTUVWXYZ 1234567890 abcdefghijklmnopqrstuvwxyz

ABCDEFGHIJKLMNOPQRSTUVWXYZ 1234567890 abcdefghijklmnopqrstuvwxyz

ABCDEFGHIJKLMNOPQRSTUVWXYZ 1234567890 abcdefghijklmnopqrstuvwxyz

ABCDEFGHIJKLMNOPQRSTUVWXYZ 1234567890 abcdefghijklmnopqrstuvwxyz

9/9

The main purpose of letters is the practical one of making thought s visible. Ruskin says that all letters are frightful things and to be e ndured only on occasion, that is to say, in places where the sense of the inscription is of more importance than external ornament. T his is a sweeping statement, from which we need not suffer undul y; yet it is doubtful whether there is art in individual letters. Letters in combination may be satisfying and in a well composed page ev en beautiful as a whole, but art in letters consists rather in the art o

The main purpose of letters is the practical one of making thought s visible. Ruskin says that all letters are frightful things and to be e

The main purpose of letters is the practical one of making thoug hts visible. Ruskin says that all letters are frightful things and to

9/10

The main purpose of letters is the practical one of making thought s visible. Ruskin says that all letters are frightful things and to be e ndured only on occasion, that is to say, in places where the sense of the inscription is of more importance than external ornament. T his is a sweeping statement, from which we need not suffer undul y; yet it is doubtful whether there is art in individual letters. Letters in combination may be satisfying and in a well composed page ev

The main purpose of letters is the practical one of making thought s visible. Ruskin says that all letters are frightful things and to be e

The main purpose of letters is the practical one of making thoug hts visible. Ruskin says that all letters are frightful things and to

9/11

The main purpose of letters is the practical one of making thought s visible. Ruskin says that all letters are frightful things and to be e ndured only on occasion, that is to say, in places where the sense of the inscription is of more importance than external ornament. T his is a sweeping statement, from which we need not suffer undul y; yet it is doubtful whether there is art in individual letters. Letters in combination may be satisfying and in a well composed page ev

The main purpose of letters is the practical one of making thought s visible. Ruskin says that all letters are frightful things and to be e

The main purpose of letters is the practical one of making thoug hts visible. Ruskin says that all letters are frightful things and to

9/12

The main purpose of letters is the practical one of making thought s visible. Ruskin says that all letters are frightful things and to be e ndured only on occasion, that is to say, in places where the sense of the inscription is of more importance than external ornament. T his is a sweeping statement, from which we need not suffer undul y; yet it is doubtful whether there is art in individual letters. Letters in combination may be satisfying and in a well composed page ev

The main purpose of letters is the practical one of making thought s visible. Ruskin says that all letters are frightful things and to be e

The main purpose of letters is the practical one of making thoug hts visible. Ruskin says that all letters are frightful things and to

TRADE GOTHIC 10 POINT SET MINUS ½ UNIT

LIGHT, ITALIC, BOLD, BOLD ITALIC

abcdefghijklmnopqrstuvwxyz – 1 UNIT
abcdefghijklmnopqrstuvwxyz – ½ UNIT
abcdefghijklmnopqrstuvwxyz NORMAL

ABCDEFGHIJKLMNOPQRSTUVWXYZ 1234567890 abcdefghijklmnopqrstuvwxyz
ABCDEFGHIJKLMNOPQRSTUVWXYZ 1234567890 abcdefghijklmnopqrstuvwxyz
ABCDEFGHIJKLMNOPQRSTUVWXYZ 1234567890 abcdefghijklmnopqrstuvwxyz
ABCDEFGHIJKLMNOPQRSTUVWXYZ 1234567890 abcdefghijklmnopqrstuvwxyz

10/10

The main purpose of letters is the practical one of making tho ughts visible. Ruskin says that all letters are frightful things an d to be endured only on occasion, that is to say, in places wher e the sense of the inscription is of more importance than exter nal ornament. This is a sweeping statement, from which we n eed not suffer unduly; yet it is doubtful whether there is art in i ndividual letters. Letters in combination may be satisfying and in a well composed page even beautiful as a whole, but art in l etters consists rather in the art of arranging and composing th em in a pleasing and appropriate manner. The main purpose of letters is the practical one of making thoughts visible. Ruski n says that all letters are frightful things and to be endured onl y on occasion, that is to say, in places where the sense of the i nscription is of more importance than external ornament. Thi s is a sweeping statement, from which we need not suffer und uly; yet it is doubtful whether there is art in individual letters. L etters in combination may be satisfying and in a well compose d page even beautiful as a whole, but art in letters consists rat her in the art of arranging and composing them in a pleasing a nd appropriate manner. The main purpose of letters is the pra ctical one of making thoughts visible. Ruskin says that all lette rs are frightful things and to be endured only on occasion, that

The main purpose of letters is the practical one of making tho ughts visible. Ruskin says that all letters are frightful things an

The main purpose of letters is the practical one of making th oughts visible. Ruskin says that all letters are frightful thing

10/11

The main purpose of letters is the practical one of making tho ughts visible. Ruskin says that all letters are frightful things an d to be endured only on occasion, that is to say, in places wher e the sense of the inscription is of more importance than exter nal ornament. This is a sweeping statement, from which we n eed not suffer unduly; yet it is doubtful whether there is art in i ndividual letters. Letters in combination may be satisfying and in a well composed page even beautiful as a whole, but art in l etters consists rather in the art of arranging and composing th em in a pleasing and appropriate manner. The main purpose of letters is the practical one of making thoughts visible. Ruski n says that all letters are frightful things and to be endured onl y on occasion, that is to say, in places where the sense of the i nscription is of more importance than external ornament. Thi s is a sweeping statement, from which we need not suffer und uly; yet it is doubtful whether there is art in individual letters. L etters in combination may be satisfying and in a well compose d page even beautiful as a whole, but art in letters consists rat her in the art of arranging and composing them in a pleasing a nd appropriate manner. The main purpose of letters is the pra

The main purpose of letters is the practical one of making tho ughts visible. Ruskin says that all letters are frightful things an

The main purpose of letters is the practical one of making th oughts visible. Ruskin says that all letters are frightful thing

10/12

The main purpose of letters is the practical one of making tho ughts visible. Ruskin says that all letters are frightful things an d to be endured only on occasion, that is to say, in places wher e the sense of the inscription is of more importance than exter nal ornament. This is a sweeping statement, from which we n eed not suffer unduly; yet it is doubtful whether there is art in i ndividual letters. Letters in combination may be satisfying and in a well composed page even beautiful as a whole, but art in l etters consists rather in the art of arranging and composing th em in a pleasing and appropriate manner. The main purpose of letters is the practical one of making thoughts visible. Ruski n says that all letters are frightful things and to be endured onl y on occasion, that is to say, in places where the sense of the i nscription is of more importance than external ornament. Thi s is a sweeping statement, from which we need not suffer und uly; yet it is doubtful whether there is art in individual letters. L etters in combination may be satisfying and in a well compose d page even beautiful as a whole, but art in letters consists rat

The main purpose of letters is the practical one of making tho ughts visible. Ruskin says that all letters are frightful things an

The main purpose of letters is the practical one of making th oughts visible. Ruskin says that all letters are frightful thing

10/13

The main purpose of letters is the practical one of making tho ughts visible. Ruskin says that all letters are frightful things an d to be endured only on occasion, that is to say, in places wher e the sense of the inscription is of more importance than exter nal ornament. This is a sweeping statement, from which we n eed not suffer unduly; yet it is doubtful whether there is art in i ndividual letters. Letters in combination may be satisfying and in a well composed page even beautiful as a whole, but art in l etters consists rather in the art of arranging and composing th em in a pleasing and appropriate manner. The main purpose of letters is the practical one of making thoughts visible. Ruski n says that all letters are frightful things and to be endured onl y on occasion, that is to say, in places where the sense of the i nscription is of more importance than external ornament. Thi s is a sweeping statement, from which we need not suffer und uly; yet it is doubtful whether there is art in individual letters. L etters in combination may be satisfying and in a well compose

The main purpose of letters is the practical one of making tho ughts visible. Ruskin says that all letters are frightful things an

The main purpose of letters is the practical one of making th oughts visible. Ruskin says that all letters are frightful thing

TRADE GOTHIC 11 POINT SET MINUS ½ UNIT

LIGHT, ITALIC, BOLD, BOLD ITALIC

abcdefghijklmnopqrstuvwxyz – 1 UNIT
abcdefghijklmnopqrstuvwxyz – ½ UNIT
abcdefghijklmnopqrstuvwxyz NORMAL

ABCDEFGHIJKLMNOPQRSTUVWXYZ 1234567890 abcdefghijklmnopqrstuvwxyz
ABCDEFGHIJKLMNOPQRSTUVWXYZ 1234567890 abcdefghijklmnopqrstuvwxyz
ABCDEFGHIJKLMNOPQRSTUVWXYZ 1234567890 abcdefghijklmnopqrstuvwxyz
ABCDEFGHIJKLMNOPQRSTUVWXYZ 1234567890 abcdefghijklmnopqrstuvwxyz

11/11

The main purpose of letters is the practical one of makin g thoughts visible. Ruskin says that all letters are frightfu l things and to be endured only on occasion, that is to sa y, in places where the sense of the inscription is of more importance than external ornament. This is a sweeping statement, from which we need not suffer unduly; yet it i s doubtful whether there is art in individual letters. Letter s in combination may be satisfying and in a well compos ed page even beautiful as a whole, but art in letters cons ists rather in the art of arranging and composing them in a pleasing and appropriate manner. The main purpose of letters is the practical one of making thoughts visible. Ruskin says that all letters are frightful things and to be e ndured only on occasion, that is to say, in places where t he sense of the inscription is of more importance than e xternal ornament. This is a sweeping statement, from w hich we need not suffer unduly; yet it is doubtful whethe r there is art in individual letters. Letters in combination may be satisfying and in a well composed page even be
The main purpose of letters is the practical one of makin g thoughts visible. Ruskin says that all letters are frightfu
The main purpose of letters is the practical one of mak ing thoughts visible. Ruskin says that all letters are frig

11/12

The main purpose of letters is the practical one of makin g thoughts visible. Ruskin says that all letters are frightfu l things and to be endured only on occasion, that is to sa y, in places where the sense of the inscription is of more importance than external ornament. This is a sweeping statement, from which we need not suffer unduly; yet it i s doubtful whether there is art in individual letters. Letter s in combination may be satisfying and in a well compos ed page even beautiful as a whole, but art in letters cons ists rather in the art of arranging and composing them in a pleasing and appropriate manner. The main purpose of letters is the practical one of making thoughts visible. Ruskin says that all letters are frightful things and to be e ndured only on occasion, that is to say, in places where t he sense of the inscription is of more importance than e xternal ornament. This is a sweeping statement, from w hich we need not suffer unduly; yet it is doubtful whethe r there is art in individual letters. Letters In combination
The main purpose of letters is the practical one of makin g thoughts visible. Ruskin says that all letters are frightfu
The main purpose of letters is the practical one of mak ing thoughts visible. Ruskin says that all letters are frig

11/13

The main purpose of letters is the practical one of makin g thoughts visible. Ruskin says that all letters are frightfu l things and to be endured only on occasion, that is to sa y, in places where the sense of the inscription is of more importance than external ornament. This is a sweeping statement, from which we need not suffer unduly; yet it i s doubtful whether there is art in individual letters. Letter s in combination may be satisfying and in a well compos ed page even beautiful as a whole, but art in letters cons ists rather in the art of arranging and composing them in a pleasing and appropriate manner. The main purpose of letters is the practical one of making thoughts visible. Ruskin says that all letters are frightful things and to be e ndured only on occasion, that is to say, in places where t he sense of the inscription is of more importance than e xternal ornament. This is a sweeping statement, from w hich we need not suffer unduly; yet it is doubtful whethe
The main purpose of letters is the practical one of makin g thoughts visible. Ruskin says that all letters are frightfu
The main purpose of letters is the practical one of mak ing thoughts visible. Ruskin says that all letters are frig

11/14

The main purpose of letters is the practical one of makin g thoughts visible. Ruskin says that all letters are frightfu l things and to be endured only on occasion, that is to sa y, in places where the sense of the inscription is of more importance than external ornament. This is a sweeping statement, from which we need not suffer unduly; yet it i s doubtful whether there is art in individual letters. Letter s in combination may be satisfying and in a well compos ed page even beautiful as a whole, but art in letters cons ists rather in the art of arranging and composing them in a pleasing and appropriate manner. The main purpose of letters is the practical one of making thoughts visible. Ruskin says that all letters are frightful things and to be e ndured only on occasion, that is to say, in places where t he sense of the inscription is of more importance than e xternal ornament. This is a sweeping statement, from w
The main purpose of letters is the practical one of makin g thoughts visible. Ruskin says that all letters are frightfu
The main purpose of letters is the practical one of mak ing thoughts visible. Ruskin says that all letters are frig

TRADE GOTHIC 12 POINT SET MINUS ½ UNIT

LIGHT, ITALIC, BOLD, BOLD ITALIC

abcdefghijklmnopqrstuvwxyz – 1 UNIT
abcdefghijklmnopqrstuvwxyz – ½ UNIT
abcdefghijklmnopqrstuvwxyz NORMAL

ABCDEFGHIJKLMNOPQRSTUVWXYZ 1234567890 abcdefghijklmnopqrstuvwxyz
ABCDEFGHIJKLMNOPQRSTUVWXYZ 1234567890 abcdefghijklmnopqrstuvwxyz
ABCDEFGHIJKLMNOPQRSTUVWXYZ 1234567890 abcdefghijklmnopqrstuvwxyz
ABCDEFGHIJKLMNOPQRSTUVWXYZ 1234567890 abcdefghijklmnopqrstuvwxyz

12/12

The main purpose of letters is the practical one of m aking thoughts visible. Ruskin says that all letters ar e frightful things and to be endured only on occasio n, that is to say, in places where the sense of the insc ription is of more importance than external ornamen t. This is a sweeping statement, from which we need not suffer unduly; yet it is doubtful whether there is a rt in individual letters. Letters in combination may be satisfying and in a well composed page even beautif ul as a whole, but art in letters consists rather in the a rt of arranging and composing them in a pleasing an d appropriate manner. The main purpose of letters i s the practical one of making thoughts visible. Ruski n says that all letters are frightful things and to be en dured only on occasion, that is to say, in places wher
The main purpose of letters is the practical one of m aking thoughts visible. Ruskin says that all letters ar
The main purpose of letters is the practical one of making thoughts visible. Ruskin says that all letter

12/13

The main purpose of letters is the practical one of m aking thoughts visible. Ruskin says that all letters ar e frightful things and to be endured only on occasio n, that is to say, in places where the sense of the insc ription is of more importance than external ornamen t. This is a sweeping statement, from which we need not suffer unduly; yet it is doubtful whether there is a rt in individual letters. Letters in combination may be satisfying and in a well composed page even beautif ul as a whole, but art in letters consists rather in the a rt of arranging and composing them in a pleasing an d appropriate manner. The main purpose of letters i s the practical one of making thoughts visible. Ruski n says that all letters are frightful things and to be en
The main purpose of letters is the practical one of m aking thoughts visible. Ruskin says that all letters ar
The main purpose of letters is the practical one of making thoughts visible. Ruskin says that all letter

12/14

The main purpose of letters is the practical one of m aking thoughts visible. Ruskin says that all letters ar e frightful things and to be endured only on occasio n, that is to say, in places where the sense of the insc ription is of more importance than external ornamen t. This is a sweeping statement, from which we need not suffer unduly; yet it is doubtful whether there is a rt in individual letters. Letters in combination may be satisfying and in a well composed page even beautif ul as a whole, but art in letters consists rather in the a rt of arranging and composing them in a pleasing an d appropriate manner. The main purpose of letters i s the practical one of making thoughts visible. Ruski n says that all letters are frightful things and to be en dured only on occasion, that is to say, in places wher
The main purpose of letters is the practical one of m aking thoughts visible. Ruskin says that all letters ar
The main purpose of letters is the practical one of making thoughts visible. Ruskin says that all letter

12/15

The main purpose of letters is the practical one of m aking thoughts visible. Ruskin says that all letters ar e frightful things and to be endured only on occasio n, that is to say, in places where the sense of the insc ription is of more importance than external ornamen t. This is a sweeping statement, from which we need not suffer unduly; yet it is doubtful whether there is a rt in individual letters. Letters in combination may be satisfying and in a well composed page even beautif ul as a whole, but art in letters consists rather in the a rt of arranging and composing them in a pleasing an d appropriate manner. The main purpose of letters i s the practical one of making thoughts visible. Ruski n says that all letters are frightful things and to be en
The main purpose of letters is the practical one of m aking thoughts visible. Ruskin says that all letters ar
The main purpose of letters is the practical one of making thoughts visible. Ruskin says that all letter

TRADE GOTHIC 14 POINT SET MINUS ½ UNIT

LIGHT, ITALIC, BOLD, BOLD ITALIC

abcdefghijklmnopqrstuvwxyz – 1 UNIT
abcdefghijklmnopqrstuvwxyz – ½ UNIT
abcdefghijklmnopqrstuvwxyz NORMAL

ABCDEFGHIJKLMNOPQRSTUVWXYZ abcdefghijklmnopqrstuvwxyz
ABCDEFGHIJKLMNOPQRSTUVWXYZ abcdefghijklmnopqrstuvwxyz
ABCDEFGHIJKLMNOPQRSTUVWXYZ abcdefghijklmnopqrstuvwxyz
ABCDEFGHIJKLMNOPQRSTUVWXYZ abcdefghijklmnopqrstuvwxyz

14/14

The main purpose of letters is the practical o ne of making thoughts visible. Ruskin says t hat all letters are frightful things and to be en dured only on occasion, that is to say, in plac es where the sense of the inscription is of mo re importance than external ornament. This is a sweeping statement, from which we nee d not suffer unduly; yet it is doubtful whether there is art in individual letters. Letters in co mbination may be satisfying and in a well co mposed page even beautiful as a whole, but art in letters consists rather in the art of arran ging and composing them in a pleasing and
The main purpose of letters is the practical o ne of making thoughts visible. Ruskin says t
The main purpose of letters is the practical one of making thoughts visible. Ruskin say

14/15

The main purpose of letters is the practical o ne of making thoughts visible. Ruskin says t hat all letters are frightful things and to be en dured only on occasion, that is to say, in plac es where the sense of the inscription is of mo re importance than external ornament. This is a sweeping statement, from which we nee d not suffer unduly; yet it is doubtful whether there is art in individual letters. Letters in co mbination may be satisfying and in a well co mposed page even beautiful as a whole, but art in letters consists rather in the art of arran
The main purpose of letters is the practical o ne of making thoughts visible. Ruskin says t
The main purpose of letters is the practical one of making thoughts visible. Ruskin say

14/16

The main purpose of letters is the practical o ne of making thoughts visible. Ruskin says t hat all letters are frightful things and to be en dured only on occasion, that is to say, in plac es where the sense of the inscription is of mo re importance than external ornament. This is a sweeping statement, from which we nee d not suffer unduly; yet it is doubtful whether there is art in individual letters. Letters in co mbination may be satisfying and in a well co mposed page even beautiful as a whole, but art in letters consists rather in the art of arran ging and composing them in a pleasing and
The main purpose of letters is the practical o ne of making thoughts visible. Ruskin says t
The main purpose of letters is the practical one of making thoughts visible. Ruskin say

14/17

The main purpose of letters is the practical o ne of making thoughts visible. Ruskin says t hat all letters are frightful things and to be en dured only on occasion, that is to say, in plac es where the sense of the inscription is of mo re importance than external ornament. This is a sweeping statement, from which we nee d not suffer unduly; yet it is doubtful whether there is art in individual letters. Letters in co mbination may be satisfying and in a well co mposed page even beautiful as a whole, but art in letters consists rather in the art of arran
The main purpose of letters is the practical o ne of making thoughts visible. Ruskin says t
The main purpose of letters is the practical one of making thoughts visible. Ruskin say

TRUMP 6 & 7 POINT SET NORMAL

ROMAN, ITALIC, BOLD, BOLD ITALIC

ABCDEFGHIJKLMNOPQRSTUVWXYZ 1234567890 abcdefghijklmnopqrstuvwxyz

ABCDEFGHIJKLMNOPQRSTUVWXYZ 1234567890 abcdefghijklmnopqrstuvwxyz

ABCDEFGHIJKLMNOPQRSTUVWXYZ 1234567890 abcdefghijklmnopqrstuvwxyz

ABCDEFGHIJKLMNOPQRSTUVWXYZ 1234567890 abcdefghijklmnopqrstuvwxyz

6/6

The main purpose of letters is the practical one of making thoughts visible. Ruskin says t hat all letters are frightful things and to be endured only on occasion, that is to say, in plac es where the sense of the inscription is of more importance than external ornament. This is a sweeping statement, from which we need not suffer unduly; yet it is doubtful whether there is art in individual letters. Letters in combination may be satisfying and in a well co mposed page even beautiful as a whole, but art in letters consists rather in the art of arrang ing and composing them in a pleasing and appropriate manner. The main purpose of letter s is the practical one of making thoughts visible. Ruskin says that all letters are frightful t hings and to be endured only on occasion, that is to say, in places where the sense of the in scription is of more importance than external ornament. This is a sweeping statement, fr om which we need not suffer unduly; yet it is doubtful whether there is art in individual l etters. Letters in combination may be satisfying and in a well composed page even beautif ul as a whole, but art in letters consists rather in the art of arranging and composing them
The main purpose of letters is the practical one of making thoughts visible. Ruskin says t hat all letters are frightful things and to be endured only on occasion, that is to say, in pla
The main purpose of letters is the practical one of making thoughts visible. Ruskin says t hat all letters are frightful things and to be endured only on occasion, that is to say, in plac

6/7

The main purpose of letters is the practical one of making thoughts visible. Ruskin says t hat all letters are frightful things and to be endured only on occasion, that is to say, in plac es where the sense of the inscription is of more importance than external ornament. This is a sweeping statement, from which we need not suffer unduly; yet it is doubtful whether there is art in individual letters. Letters in combination may be satisfying and in a well co mposed page even beautiful as a whole, but art in letters consists rather in the art of arrang ing and composing them in a pleasing and appropriate manner. The main purpose of letter s is the practical one of making thoughts visible. Ruskin says that all letters are frightful t hings and to be endured only on occasion, that is to say, in places where the sense of the in scription is of more importance than external ornament. This is a sweeping statement, fr om which we need not suffer unduly; yet it is doubtful whether there is art in individual l
The main purpose of letters is the practical one of making thoughts visible. Ruskin says t hat all letters are frightful things and to be endured only on occasion, that is to say, in pla
The main purpose of letters is the practical one of making thoughts visible. Ruskin says t hat all letters are frightful things and to be endured only on occasion, that is to say, in plac

6/8

The main purpose of letters is the practical one of making thoughts visible. Ruskin says t hat all letters are frightful things and to be endured only on occasion, that is to say, in plac es where the sense of the inscription is of more importance than external ornament. This is a sweeping statement, from which we need not suffer unduly; yet it is doubtful whether there is art in individual letters. Letters in combination may be satisfying and in a well co mposed page even beautiful as a whole, but art in letters consists rather in the art of arrang ing and composing them in a pleasing and appropriate manner. The main purpose of letter s is the practical one of making thoughts visible. Ruskin says that all letters are frightful t hings and to be endured only on occasion, that is to say, in places where the sense of the in
The main purpose of letters is the practical one of making thoughts visible. Ruskin says t hat all letters are frightful things and to be endured only on occasion, that is to say, in pla
The main purpose of letters is the practical one of making thoughts visible. Ruskin says t hat all letters are frightful things and to be endured only on occasion, that is to say, in plac

6/9

The main purpose of letters is the practical one of making thoughts visible. Ruskin says t hat all letters are frightful things and to be endured only on occasion, that is to say, in plac es where the sense of the inscription is of more importance than external ornament. This is a sweeping statement, from which we need not suffer unduly; yet it is doubtful whether there is art in individual letters. Letters in combination may be satisfying and in a well co mposed page even beautiful as a whole, but art in letters consists rather in the art of arrang ing and composing them in a pleasing and appropriate manner. The main purpose of letter s is the practical one of making thoughts visible. Ruskin says that all letters are frightful t
The main purpose of letters is the practical one of making thoughts visible. Ruskin says t hat all letters are frightful things and to be endured only on occasion, that is to say, in pla
The main purpose of letters is the practical one of making thoughts visible. Ruskin says t hat all letters are frightful things and to be endured only on occasion, that is to say, in plac

---

ABCDEFGHIJKLMNOPQRSTUVWXYZ 1234567890 abcdefghijklmnopqrstuvwxyz

ABCDEFGHIJKLMNOPQRSTUVWXYZ 1234567890 abcdefghijklmnopqrstuvwxyz

ABCDEFGHIJKLMNOPQRSTUVWXYZ 1234567890 abcdefghijklmnopqrstuvwxyz

ABCDEFGHIJKLMNOPQRSTUVWXYZ 1234567890 abcdefghijklmnopqrstuvwxyz

7/7

The main purpose of letters is the practical one of making thoughts visible. R uskin says that all letters are frightful things and to be endured only on occas ion, that is to say, in places where the sense of the inscription is of more impo rtance than external ornament. This is a sweeping statement, from which we need not suffer unduly; yet it is doubtful whether there is art in individual let ters. Letters in combination may be satisfying and in a well composed page e ven beautiful as a whole, but art in letters consists rather in the art of arrangi ng and composing them in a pleasing and appropriate manner. The main pur pose of letters is the practical one of making thoughts visible. Ruskin says th at all letters are frightful things and to be endured only on occasion, that is to say, in places where the sense of the inscription is of more importance than e
The main purpose of letters is the practical one of making thoughts visible. Ruskin says that all letters are frightful things and to be endured only on occ
The main purpose of letters is the practical one of making thoughts visible. R uskin says that all letters are frightful things and to be endured only on occas

7/8

The main purpose of letters is the practical one of making thoughts visible. R uskin says that all letters are frightful things and to be endured only on occas ion, that is to say, in places where the sense of the inscription is of more impo rtance than external ornament. This is a sweeping statement, from which we need not suffer unduly; yet it is doubtful whether there is art in individual let ters. Letters in combination may be satisfying and in a well composed page e ven beautiful as a whole, but art in letters consists rather in the art of arrangi ng and composing them in a pleasing and appropriate manner. The main pur pose of letters is the practical one of making thoughts visible. Ruskin says th at all letters are frightful things and to be endured only on occasion, that is to
The main purpose of letters is the practical one of making thoughts visible. Ruskin says that all letters are frightful things and to be endured only on occ
The main purpose of letters is the practical one of making thoughts visible. R uskin says that all letters are frightful things and to be endured only on occas

7/9

The main purpose of letters is the practical one of making thoughts visible. R uskin says that all letters are frightful things and to be endured only on occas ion, that is to say, in places where the sense of the inscription is of more impo rtance than external ornament. This is a sweeping statement, from which we need not suffer unduly; yet it is doubtful whether there is art in individual let ters. Letters in combination may be satisfying and in a well composed page e ven beautiful as a whole, but art in letters consists rather in the art of arrangi ng and composing them in a pleasing and appropriate manner. The main pur pose of letters is the practical one of making thoughts visible. Ruskin says th at all letters are frightful things and to be endured only on occasion, that is to
The main purpose of letters is the practical one of making thoughts visible. Ruskin says that all letters are frightful things and to be endured only on occ
The main purpose of letters is the practical one of making thoughts visible. R uskin says that all letters are frightful things and to be endured only on occas

7/10

The main purpose of letters is the practical one of making thoughts visible. R uskin says that all letters are frightful things and to be endured only on occas ion, that is to say, in places where the sense of the inscription is of more impo rtance than external ornament. This is a sweeping statement, from which we need not suffer unduly; yet it is doubtful whether there is art in individual let ters. Letters in combination may be satisfying and in a well composed page e ven beautiful as a whole, but art in letters consists rather in the art of arrangi ng and composing them in a pleasing and appropriate manner. The main pur pose of letters is the practical one of making thoughts visible. Ruskin says th
The main purpose of letters is the practical one of making thoughts visible. Ruskin says that all letters are frightful things and to be endured only on occ
The main purpose of letters is the practical one of making thoughts visible. R uskin says that all letters are frightful things and to be endured only on occas

TRUMP 8 & 9 POINT SET NORMAL

ROMAN, ITALIC, BOLD, BOLD ITALIC

ABCDEFGHIJKLMNOPQRSTUVWXYZ 1234567890 abcdefghijklmnopqrstuvwxyz
ABCDEFGHIJKLMNOPQRSTUVWXYZ 1234567890 abcdefghijklmnopqrstuvwxyz
ABCDEFGHIJKLMNOPQRSTUVWXYZ 1234567890 abcdefghijklmnopqrstuvwxyz
ABCDEFGHIJKLMNOPQRSTUVWXYZ 1234567890 abcdefghijklmnopqrstuvwxyz

8/8

The main purpose of letters is the practical one of making thoughts visible. Ruskin says that all letters are frightful things and to be end ured only on occasion, that is to say, in places where the sense of th e inscription is of more importance than external ornament. This i s a sweeping statement, from which we need not suffer unduly; yet it is doubtful whether there is art in individual letters. Letters in co mbination may be satisfying and in a well composed page even bea utiful as a whole, but art in letters consists rather in the art of arran ging and composing them in a pleasing and appropriate manner. Th
The main purpose of letters is the practical one of making thought s visible. Ruskin says that all letters are frightful things and to be e
The main purpose of letters is the practical one of making thoughts visible. Ruskin says that all letters are frightful things and to be end

8/9

The main purpose of letters is the practical one of making thoughts visible. Ruskin says that all letters are frightful things and to be end ured only on occasion, that is to say, in places where the sense of th e inscription is of more importance than external ornament. This i s a sweeping statement, from which we need not suffer unduly; yet it is doubtful whether there is art in individual letters. Letters in co mbination may be satisfying and in a well composed page even bea utiful as a whole, but art in letters consists rather in the art of arran
The main purpose of letters is the practical one of making thought s visible. Ruskin says that all letters are frightful things and to be e
The main purpose of letters is the practical one of making thoughts visible. Ruskin says that all letters are frightful things and to be end

8/10

The main purpose of letters is the practical one of making thoughts visible. Ruskin says that all letters are frightful things and to be end ured only on occasion, that is to say, in places where the sense of th e inscription is of more importance than external ornament. This i s a sweeping statement, from which we need not suffer unduly; yet it is doubtful whether there is art in individual letters. Letters in co mbination may be satisfying and in a well composed page even bea
The main purpose of letters is the practical one of making thought s visible. Ruskin says that all letters are frightful things and to be e
The main purpose of letters is the practical one of making thoughts visible. Ruskin says that all letters are frightful things and to be end

8/11

The main purpose of letters is the practical one of making thoughts visible. Ruskin says that all letters are frightful things and to be end ured only on occasion, that is to say, in places where the sense of th e inscription is of more importance than external ornament. This i s a sweeping statement, from which we need not suffer unduly; yet it is doubtful whether there is art in individual letters. Letters in co mbination may be satisfying and in a well composed page even bea
The main purpose of letters is the practical one of making thought s visible. Ruskin says that all letters are frightful things and to be e
The main purpose of letters is the practical one of making thoughts visible. Ruskin says that all letters are frightful things and to be end

---

ABCDEFGHIJKLMNOPQRSTUVWXYZ 1234567890 abcdefghijklmnopqrstuvwxyz
ABCDEFGHIJKLMNOPQRSTUVWXYZ 1234567890 abcdefghijklmnopqrstuvwxyz
ABCDEFGHIJKLMNOPQRSTUVWXYZ 1234567890 abcdefghijklmnopqrstuvwxyz
ABCDEFGHIJKLMNOPQRSTUVWXYZ 1234567890 abcdefghijklmnopqrstuvwxyz

9/9

The main purpose of letters is the practical one of making t houghts visible. Ruskin says that all letters are frightful thi ngs and to be endured only on occasion, that is to say, in plac es where the sense of the inscription is of more importance than external ornament. This is a sweeping statement, fro m which we need not suffer unduly; yet it is doubtful wheth er there is art in individual letters. Letters in combination may be satisfying and in a well composed page even beautif
The main purpose of letters is the practical one of making t houghts visible. Ruskin says that all letters are frightful thi
The main purpose of letters is the practical one of making t houghts visible. Ruskin says that all letters are frightful thi

9/10

The main purpose of letters is the practical one of making t houghts visible. Ruskin says that all letters are frightful thi ngs and to be endured only on occasion, that is to say, in plac es where the sense of the inscription is of more importance than external ornament. This is a sweeping statement, fro m which we need not suffer unduly; yet it is doubtful wheth er there is art in individual letters. Letters in combination
The main purpose of letters is the practical one of making t houghts visible. Ruskin says that all letters are frightful thi
The main purpose of letters is the practical one of making t houghts visible. Ruskin says that all letters are frightful thi

9/11

The main purpose of letters is the practical one of making t houghts visible. Ruskin says that all letters are frightful thi ngs and to be endured only on occasion, that is to say, in plac es where the sense of the inscription is of more importance than external ornament. This is a sweeping statement, fro m which we need not suffer unduly; yet it is doubtful wheth er there is art in individual letters. Letters in combination
The main purpose of letters is the practical one of making t houghts visible. Ruskin says that all letters are frightful thi
The main purpose of letters is the practical one of making t houghts visible. Ruskin says that all letters are frightful thi

9/12

The main purpose of letters is the practical one of making t houghts visible. Ruskin says that all letters are frightful thi ngs and to be endured only on occasion, that is to say, in plac es where the sense of the inscription is of more importance than external ornament. This is a sweeping statement, fro m which we need not suffer unduly; yet it is doubtful wheth er there is art in individual letters. Letters in combination
The main purpose of letters is the practical one of making t houghts visible. Ruskin says that all letters are frightful thi
The main purpose of letters is the practical one of making t houghts visible. Ruskin says that all letters are frightful thi

TRUMP 10 POINT SET MINUS ½ UNIT

ROMAN, ITALIC, BOLD, BOLD ITALIC

abcdefghijklmnopqrstuvwxyz – 1 UNIT
abcdefghijklmnopqrstuvwxyz – ½ UNIT
abcdefghijklmnopqrstuvwxyz NORMAL

ABCDEFGHIJKLMNOPQRSTUVWXYZ 1234567890 abcdefghijklmnopqrstuvwxyz
ABCDEFGHIJKLMNOPQRSTUVWXYZ 1234567890 abcdefghijklmnopqrstuvwxyz
ABCDEFGHIJKLMNOPQRSTUVWXYZ 1234567890 abcdefghijklmnopqrstuvwxyz
ABCDEFGHIJKLMNOPQRSTUVWXYZ 1234567890 abcdefghijklmnopqrstuvwxyz

10/10

The main purpose of letters is the practical one of maki ng thoughts visible. Ruskin says that all letters are frigh tful things and to be endured only on occasion, that is to say, in places where the sense of the inscription is of mo re importance than external ornament. This is a sweepi ng statement, from which we need not suffer unduly; ye t it is doubtful whether there is art in individual letters. Letters in combination may be satisfying and in a well c omposed page even beautiful as a whole, but art in letter s consists rather in the art of arranging and composing t hem in a pleasing and appropriate manner. The main pu rpose of letters is the practical one of making thoughts v isible. Ruskin says that all letters are frightful things an d to be endured only on occasion, that is to say, in places where the sense of the inscription is of more importanc e than external ornament. This is a sweeping statement, from which we need not suffer unduly; yet it is doubtful whether there is art in individual letters. Letters in com bination may be satisfying and in a well composed page even beautiful as a whole, but art in letters consists rath er in the art of arranging and composing them in a pleasi ng and appropriate manner. The main purpose of letters
The main purpose of letters is the practical one of maki ng thoughts visible. Ruskin says that all letters are frigh
The main purpose of letters is the practical one of maki ng thoughts visible. Ruskin says that all letters are frigh

10/11

The main purpose of letters is the practical one of maki ng thoughts visible. Ruskin says that all letters are frigh tful things and to be endured only on occasion, that is to say, in places where the sense of the inscription is of mo re importance than external ornament. This is a sweepi ng statement, from which we need not suffer unduly; ye t it is doubtful whether there is art in individual letters. Letters in combination may be satisfying and in a well c omposed page even beautiful as a whole, but art in letter s consists rather in the art of arranging and composing t hem in a pleasing and appropriate manner. The main pu rpose of letters is the practical one of making thoughts v isible. Ruskin says that all letters are frightful things an d to be endured only on occasion, that is to say, in places where the sense of the inscription is of more importanc e than external ornament. This is a sweeping statement, from which we need not suffer unduly; yet it is doubtful whether there is art in individual letters. Letters in com bination may be satisfying and in a well composed page even beautiful as a whole, but art in letters consists rath
The main purpose of letters is the practical one of maki ng thoughts visible. Ruskin says that all letters are frigh
The main purpose of letters is the practical one of maki ng thoughts visible. Ruskin says that all letters are frigh

10/12

The main purpose of letters is the practical one of maki ng thoughts visible. Ruskin says that all letters are frigh tful things and to be endured only on occasion, that is to say, in places where the sense of the inscription is of mo re importance than external ornament. This is a sweepi ng statement, from which we need not suffer unduly; ye t it is doubtful whether there is art in individual letters. Letters in combination may be satisfying and in a well c omposed page even beautiful as a whole, but art in letter s consists rather in the art of arranging and composing t hem in a pleasing and appropriate manner. The main pu rpose of letters is the practical one of making thoughts v isible. Ruskin says that all letters are frightful things an d to be endured only on occasion, that is to say, in places where the sense of the inscription is of more importanc e than external ornament. This is a sweeping statement, from which we need not suffer unduly; yet it is doubtful whether there is art in individual letters. Letters in com
The main purpose of letters is the practical one of maki ng thoughts visible. Ruskin says that all letters are frigh
The main purpose of letters is the practical one of maki ng thoughts visible. Ruskin says that all letters are frigh

10/13

The main purpose of letters is the practical one of maki ng thoughts visible. Ruskin says that all letters are frigh tful things and to be endured only on occasion, that is to say, in places where the sense of the inscription is of mo re importance than external ornament. This is a sweepi ng statement, from which we need not suffer unduly; ye t it is doubtful whether there is art in individual letters. Letters in combination may be satisfying and in a well c omposed page even beautiful as a whole, but art in letter s consists rather in the art of arranging and composing t hem in a pleasing and appropriate manner. The main pu rpose of letters is the practical one of making thoughts v isible. Ruskin says that all letters are frightful things an d to be endured only on occasion, that is to say, in places where the sense of the inscription is of more importanc e than external ornament. This is a sweeping statement, from which we need not suffer unduly; yet it is doubtful
The main purpose of letters is the practical one of maki ng thoughts visible. Ruskin says that all letters are frigh
The main purpose of letters is the practical one of maki ng thoughts visible. Ruskin says that all letters are frigh

TRUMP 11 POINT SET MINUS ½ UNIT

ROMAN, ITALIC, BOLD, BOLD ITALIC

abcdefghijklmnopqrstuvwxyz – 1 UNIT
abcdefghijklmnopqrstuvwxyz – ½ UNIT
abcdefghijklmnopqrstuvwxyz NORMAL

ABCDEFGHIJKLMNOPQRSTUVWXYZ 1234567890 abcdefghijklmnopqrstuvwxyz
ABCDEFGHIJKLMNOPQRSTUVWXYZ 1234567890 abcdefghijklmnopqrstuvwxyz
ABCDEFGHIJKLMNOPQRSTUVWXYZ 1234567890 abcdefghijklmnopqrstuvwxyz
ABCDEFGHIJKLMNOPQRSTUVWXYZ 1234567890 abcdefghijklmnopqrstuvwxyz

11/11

The main purpose of letters is the practical one of making thoughts visible. Ruskin says that all lette rs are frightful things and to be endured only on oc casion, that is to say, in places where the sense of t he inscription is of more importance than external ornament. This is a sweeping statement, from whi ch we need not suffer unduly; yet it is doubtful wh ether there is art in individual letters. Letters in co mbination may be satisfying and in a well compos ed page even beautiful as a whole, but art in letters consists rather in the art of arranging and composi ng them in a pleasing and appropriate manner. The main purpose of letters is the practical one of maki ng thoughts visible. Ruskin says that all letters are frightful things and to be endured only on occasion, that is to say, in places where the sense of the insc ription is of more importance than external ornam ent. This is a sweeping statement, from which we need not suffer unduly; yet it is doubtful whether t
The main purpose of letters is the practical one of making thoughts visible. Ruskin says that all lett
The main purpose of letters is the practical one of making thoughts visible. Ruskin says that all lette

11/12

The main purpose of letters is the practical one of making thoughts visible. Ruskin says that all lette rs are frightful things and to be endured only on oc casion, that is to say, in places where the sense of t he inscription is of more importance than external ornament. This is a sweeping statement, from whi ch we need not suffer unduly; yet it is doubtful wh ether there is art in individual letters. Letters in co mbination may be satisfying and in a well compos ed page even beautiful as a whole, but art in letters consists rather in the art of arranging and composi ng them in a pleasing and appropriate manner. The main purpose of letters is the practical one of maki ng thoughts visible. Ruskin says that all letters are frightful things and to be endured only on occasion, that is to say, in places where the sense of the insc ription is of more importance than external ornam ent. This is a sweeping statement, from which we
The main purpose of letters is the practical one of making thoughts visible. Ruskin says that all lett
The main purpose of letters is the practical one of making thoughts visible. Ruskin says that all lette

11/13

The main purpose of letters is the practical one of making thoughts visible. Ruskin says that all lette rs are frightful things and to be endured only on oc casion, that is to say, in places where the sense of t he inscription is of more importance than external ornament. This is a sweeping statement, from whi ch we need not suffer unduly; yet it is doubtful wh ether there is art in individual letters. Letters in co mbination may be satisfying and in a well compos ed page even beautiful as a whole, but art in letters consists rather in the art of arranging and composi ng them in a pleasing and appropriate manner. The main purpose of letters is the practical one of maki ng thoughts visible. Ruskin says that all letters are frightful things and to be endured only on occasion, that is to say, in places where the sense of the insc ription is of more importance than external ornam
The main purpose of letters is the practical one of making thoughts visible. Ruskin says that all lett
The main purpose of letters is the practical one of making thoughts visible. Ruskin says that all lette

11/14

The main purpose of letters is the practical one of making thoughts visible. Ruskin says that all lette rs are frightful things and to be endured only on oc casion, that is to say, in places where the sense of t he inscription is of more importance than external ornament. This is a sweeping statement, from whi ch we need not suffer unduly; yet it is doubtful wh ether there is art in individual letters. Letters in co mbination may be satisfying and in a well compos ed page even beautiful as a whole, but art in letters consists rather in the art of arranging and composi ng them in a pleasing and appropriate manner. The main purpose of letters is the practical one of maki ng thoughts visible. Ruskin says that all letters are frightful things and to be endured only on occasion, that is to say, in places where the sense of the insc
The main purpose of letters is the practical one of making thoughts visible. Ruskin says that all lett
The main purpose of letters is the practical one of making thoughts visible. Ruskin says that all lette

TRUMP 12 POINT SET MINUS ½ UNIT

ROMAN, ITALIC, BOLD, BOLD ITALIC

abcdefghijklmnopqrstuvwxyz – 1 UNIT
abcdefghijklmnopqrstuvwxyz – ½ UNIT
abcdefghijklmnopqrstuvwxyz NORMAL

ABCDEFGHIJKLMNOPQRSTUVWXYZ 1234567890 abcdefghijklmnopqrstuvwxyz
ABCDEFGHIJKLMNOPQRSTUVWXYZ 1234567890 abcdefghijklmnopqrstuvwxyz
ABCDEFGHIJKLMNOPQRSTUVWXYZ 1234567890 abcdefghijklmnopqrstuvwxyz
ABCDEFGHIJKLMNOPQRSTUVWXYZ 1234567890 abcdefghijklmnopqrstuvwxyz

12/12

The main purpose of letters is the practical one of making thoughts visible. Ruskin says that al l letters are frightful things and to be endured o nly on occasion, that is to say, in places where t he sense of the inscription is of more importan ce than external ornament. This is a sweeping s tatement, from which we need not suffer undu ly; yet it is doubtful whether there is art in indi vidual letters. Letters in combination may be s atisfying and in a well composed page even bea utiful as a whole, but art in letters consists rath er in the art of arranging and composing them i n a pleasing and appropriate manner. The main purpose of letters is the practical one of making thoughts visible. Ruskin says that all letters are
The main purpose of letters is the practical one of making thoughts visible. Ruskin says that a
The main purpose of letters is the practical one of making thoughts visible. Ruskin says that al

12/13

The main purpose of letters is the practical one of making thoughts visible. Ruskin says that al l letters are frightful things and to be endured o nly on occasion, that is to say, in places where t he sense of the inscription is of more importan ce than external ornament. This is a sweeping s tatement, from which we need not suffer undu ly; yet it is doubtful whether there is art in indi vidual letters. Letters in combination may be s atisfying and in a well composed page even bea utiful as a whole, but art in letters consists rath er in the art of arranging and composing them i n a pleasing and appropriate manner. The main purpose of letters is the practical one of making
The main purpose of letters is the practical one of making thoughts visible. Ruskin says that a
The main purpose of letters is the practical one of making thoughts visible. Ruskin says that al

12/14

The main purpose of letters is the practical one of making thoughts visible. Ruskin says that al l letters are frightful things and to be endured o nly on occasion, that is to say, in places where t he sense of the inscription is of more importan ce than external ornament. This is a sweeping s tatement, from which we need not suffer undu ly; yet it is doubtful whether there is art in indi vidual letters. Letters in combination may be s atisfying and in a well composed page even bea utiful as a whole, but art in letters consists rath er in the art of arranging and composing them i n a pleasing and appropriate manner. The main purpose of letters is the practical one of making thoughts visible. Ruskin says that all letters are
The main purpose of letters is the practical one of making thoughts visible. Ruskin says that a
The main purpose of letters is the practical one of making thoughts visible. Ruskin says that al

12/15

The main purpose of letters is the practical one of making thoughts visible. Ruskin says that al l letters are frightful things and to be endured o nly on occasion, that is to say, in places where t he sense of the inscription is of more importan ce than external ornament. This is a sweeping s tatement, from which we need not suffer undu ly; yet it is doubtful whether there is art in indi vidual letters. Letters in combination may be s atisfying and in a well composed page even bea utiful as a whole, but art in letters consists rath er in the art of arranging and composing them i n a pleasing and appropriate manner. The main purpose of letters is the practical one of making
The main purpose of letters is the practical one of making thoughts visible. Ruskin says that a
The main purpose of letters is the practical one of making thoughts visible. Ruskin says that al

TRUMP 14 POINT SET MINUS ½ UNIT

ROMAN, ITALIC, BOLD, BOLD ITALIC

abcdefghijklmnopqrstuvwxyz – 1 UNIT
abcdefghijklmnopqrstuvwxyz – ½ UNIT
abcdefghijklmnopqrstuvwxyz NORMAL

ABCDEFGHIJKLMNOPQRSTUVWXYZ abcdefghijklmnopqrstuvwxyz
ABCDEFGHIJKLMNOPQRSTUVWXYZ abcdefghijklmnopqrstuvwxyz
ABCDEFGHIJKLMNOPQRSTUVWXYZ abcdefghijklmnopqrstuvwxyz
ABCDEFGHIJKLMNOPQRSTUVWXYZ abcdefghijklmnopqrstuvwxyz

14/14

The main purpose of letters is the practi cal one of making thoughts visible. Rus kin says that all letters are frightful thin gs and to be endured only on occasion, t hat is to say, in places where the sense of the inscription is of more importance th an external ornament. This is a sweepin g statement, from which we need not su ffer unduly; yet it is doubtful whether t here is art in individual letters. Letters i n combination may be satisfying and in a well composed page even beautiful as a whole, but art in letters consists rather
The main purpose of letters is the practi cal one of making thoughts visible. Rus
The main purpose of letters is the practi cal one of making thoughts visible. Rus

14/15

The main purpose of letters is the practi cal one of making thoughts visible. Rus kin says that all letters are frightful thin gs and to be endured only on occasion, t hat is to say, in places where the sense of the inscription is of more importance th an external ornament. This is a sweepin g statement, from which we need not su ffer unduly; yet it is doubtful whether t here is art in individual letters. Letters i n combination may be satisfying and in a well composed page even beautiful as
The main purpose of letters is the practi cal one of making thoughts visible. Rus
The main purpose of letters is the practi cal one of making thoughts visible. Rus

14/16

The main purpose of letters is the practi cal one of making thoughts visible. Rus kin says that all letters are frightful thin gs and to be endured only on occasion, t hat is to say, in places where the sense of the inscription is of more importance th an external ornament. This is a sweepin g statement, from which we need not su ffer unduly; yet it is doubtful whether t here is art in individual letters. Letters i n combination may be satisfying and in a well composed page even beautiful as a whole, but art in letters consists rather
The main purpose of letters is the practi cal one of making thoughts visible. Rus
The main purpose of letters is the practi cal one of making thoughts visible. Rus

14/17

The main purpose of letters is the practi cal one of making thoughts visible. Rus kin says that all letters are frightful thin gs and to be endured only on occasion, t hat is to say, in places where the sense of the inscription is of more importance th an external ornament. This is a sweepin g statement, from which we need not su ffer unduly; yet it is doubtful whether t here is art in individual letters. Letters i n combination may be satisfying and in a well composed page even beautiful as
The main purpose of letters is the practi cal one of making thoughts visible. Rus
The main purpose of letters is the practi cal one of making thoughts visible. Rus

UNIVERS 6 & 7 POINT SET NORMAL

LIGHT 45, ITALIC 46, BOLD 65, BOLD ITALIC 66

ABCDEFGHIJKLMNOPQRSTUVWXYZ 1234567890 abcdefghijklmnopqrstuvwxyz

ABCDEFGHIJKLMNOPQRSTUVWXYZ 1234567890 abcdefghijklmnopqrstuvwxyz

ABCDEFGHIJKLMNOPQRSTUVWXYZ 1234567890 abcdefghijklmnopqrstuvwxyz

ABCDEFGHIJKLMNOPQRSTUVWXYZ 1234567890 abcdefghijklmnopqrstuvwxyz

6/6

The main purpose of letters is the practical one of making thoughts visible. Ruskin says that al
l letters are frightful things and to be endured only on occasion, that is to say, in places where t
he sense of the inscription is of more importance than external ornament. This is a sweeping
statement, from which we need not suffer unduly; yet it is doubtful whether there is art in indi
vidual letters. Letters in combination may be satisfying and in a well composed page even be
autiful as a whole, but art in letters consists rather in the art of arranging and composing them
in a pleasing and appropriate manner. The main purpose of letters is the practical one of makin
g thoughts visible. Ruskin says that all letters are frightful things and to be endured only on oc
casion, that is to say, in places where the sense of the inscription is of more importance than e
xternal ornament. This is a sweeping statement, from which we need not suffer unduly; yet it
is doubtful whether there is art in individual letters. Letters in combination may be satisfying a
nd in a well composed page even beautiful as a whole, but art in letters consists rather in the a
rt of arranging and composing them in a pleasing and appropriate manner. The main purpose
The main purpose of letters is the practical one of making thoughts visible. Ruskin says that al
l letters are frightful things and to be endured only on occasion, that is to say, in places where t
The main purpose of letters is the practical one of making thoughts visible. Ruskin says
that all letters are frightful things and to be endured only on occasion, that is to say, in p

6/7

The main purpose of letters is the practical one of making thoughts visible. Ruskin says that al
l letters are frightful things and to be endured only on occasion, that is to say, in places where t
he sense of the inscription is of more importance than external ornament. This is a sweeping
statement, from which we need not suffer unduly; yet it is doubtful whether there is art in indi
vidual letters. Letters in combination may be satisfying and in a well composed page even be
autiful as a whole, but art in letters consists rather in the art of arranging and composing them
in a pleasing and appropriate manner. The main purpose of letters is the practical one of makin
g thoughts visible. Ruskin says that all letters are frightful things and to be endured only on oc
casion, that is to say, in places where the sense of the inscription is of more importance than e
xternal ornament. This is a sweeping statement, from which we need not suffer unduly; yet it
is doubtful whether there is art in individual letters. Letters in combination may be satisfying a
The main purpose of letters is the practical one of making thoughts visible. Ruskin says that al
l letters are frightful things and to be endured only on occasion, that is to say, in places where t
The main purpose of letters is the practical one of making thoughts visible. Ruskin says
that all letters are frightful things and to be endured only on occasion, that is to say, in p

6/8

The main purpose of letters is the practical one of making thoughts visible. Ruskin says that al
l letters are frightful things and to be endured only on occasion, that is to say, in places where t
he sense of the inscription is of more importance than external ornament. This is a sweeping
statement, from which we need not suffer unduly; yet it is doubtful whether there is art in indi
vidual letters. Letters in combination may be satisfying and in a well composed page even be
autiful as a whole, but art in letters consists rather in the art of arranging and composing them
in a pleasing and appropriate manner. The main purpose of letters is the practical one of makin
g thoughts visible. Ruskin says that all letters are frightful things and to be endured only on oc
casion, that is to say, in places where the sense of the inscription is of more importance than e
The main purpose of letters is the practical one of making thoughts visible. Ruskin says that al
l letters are frightful things and to be endured only on occasion, that is to say, in places where t
The main purpose of letters is the practical one of making thoughts visible. Ruskin says
that all letters are frightful things and to be endured only on occasion, that is to say, in p

6/9

The main purpose of letters is the practical one of making thoughts visible. Ruskin says that al
l letters are frightful things and to be endured only on occasion, that is to say, in places where t
he sense of the inscription is of more importance than external ornament. This is a sweeping
statement, from which we need not suffer unduly; yet it is doubtful whether there is art in indi
vidual letters. Letters in combination may be satisfying and in a well composed page even be
autiful as a whole, but art in letters consists rather in the art of arranging and composing them
in a pleasing and appropriate manner. The main purpose of letters is the practical one of makin
g thoughts visible. Ruskin says that all letters are frightful things and to be endured only on oc
The main purpose of letters is the practical one of making thoughts visible. Ruskin says that al
l letters are frightful things and to be endured only on occasion, that is to say, in places where t
The main purpose of letters is the practical one of making thoughts visible. Ruskin says
that all letters are frightful things and to be endured only on occasion, that is to say, in p

---

ABCDEFGHIJKLMNOPQRSTUVWXYZ 1234567890 abcdefghijklmnopqrstuvwxyz

ABCDEFGHIJKLMNOPQRSTUVWXYZ 1234567890 abcdefghijklmnopqrstuvwxyz

ABCDEFGHIJKLMNOPQRSTUVWXYZ 1234567890 abcdefghijklmnopqrstuvwxyz

ABCDEFGHIJKLMNOPQRSTUVWXYZ 1234567890 abcdefghijklmnopqrstuvwxyz

7/7

The main purpose of letters is the practical one of making thoughts visible. Rusk
in says that all letters are frightful things and to be endured only on occasion, tha
t is to say, in places where the sense of the inscription is of more importance tha
n external ornament. This is a sweeping statement, from which we need not suf
fer unduly; yet it is doubtful whether there is art in individual letters. Letters in c
ombination may be satisfying and in a well composed page even beautiful as a
whole, but art in letters consists rather in the art of arranging and composing the
m in a pleasing and appropriate manner. The main purpose of letters is the practi
cal one of making thoughts visible. Ruskin says that all letters are frightful things
and to be endured only on occasion, that is to say, in places where the sense of t
he inscription is of more importance than external ornament. This is a sweeping
The main purpose of letters is the practical one of making thoughts visible. Rusk
in says that all letters are frightful things and to be endured only on occasion, tha
The main purpose of letters is the practical one of making thoughts visible.
Ruskin says that all letters are frightful things and to be endured only on o

7/8

The main purpose of letters is the practical one of making thoughts visible. Rusk
in says that all letters are frightful things and to be endured only on occasion, tha
t is to say, in places where the sense of the inscription is of more importance tha
n external ornament. This is a sweeping statement, from which we need not suf
fer unduly; yet it is doubtful whether there is art in individual letters. Letters in c
ombination may be satisfying and in a well composed page even beautiful as a
whole, but art in letters consists rather in the art of arranging and composing the
m in a pleasing and appropriate manner. The main purpose of letters is the practi
cal one of making thoughts visible. Ruskin says that all letters are frightful things
and to be endured only on occasion, that is to say, in places where the sense of t
The main purpose of letters is the practical one of making thoughts visible. Rusk
in says that all letters are frightful things and to be endured only on occasion, tha
The main purpose of letters is the practical one of making thoughts visible.
Ruskin says that all letters are frightful things and to be endured only on o

7/9

The main purpose of letters is the practical one of making thoughts visible. Rusk
in says that all letters are frightful things and to be endured only on occasion, tha
t is to say, in places where the sense of the inscription is of more importance tha
n external ornament. This is a sweeping statement, from which we need not suf
fer unduly; yet it is doubtful whether there is art in individual letters. Letters in c
ombination may be satisfying and in a well composed page even beautiful as a
whole, but art in letters consists rather in the art of arranging and composing the
m in a pleasing and appropriate manner. The main purpose of letters is the practi
cal one of making thoughts visible. Ruskin says that all letters are frightful things
and to be endured only on occasion, that is to say, in places where the sense of t
The main purpose of letters is the practical one of making thoughts visible. Rusk
in says that all letters are frightful things and to be endured only on occasion, tha
The main purpose of letters is the practical one of making thoughts visible.
Ruskin says that all letters are frightful things and to be endured only on o

7/10

The main purpose of letters is the practical one of making thoughts visible. Rusk
in says that all letters are frightful things and to be endured only on occasion, tha
t is to say, in places where the sense of the inscription is of more importance tha
n external ornament. This is a sweeping statement, from which we need not suf
fer unduly; yet it is doubtful whether there is art in individual letters. Letters in c
ombination may be satisfying and in a well composed page even beautiful as a
whole, but art in letters consists rather in the art of arranging and composing the
m in a pleasing and appropriate manner. The main purpose of letters is the practi
cal one of making thoughts visible. Ruskin says that all letters are frightful things
The main purpose of letters is the practical one of making thoughts visible. Rusk
in says that all letters are frightful things and to be endured only on occasion, tha
The main purpose of letters is the practical one of making thoughts visible.
Ruskin says that all letters are frightful things and to be endured only on o

UNIVERS 8 & 9 POINT SET NORMAL

LIGHT 45, ITALIC 46, BOLD 65, BOLD ITALIC 66

ABCDEFGHIJKLMNOPQRSTUVWXYZ 1234567890 abcdefghijklmnopqrstuvwxyz

ABCDEFGHIJKLMNOPQRSTUVWXYZ 1234567890 abcdefghijklmnopqrstuvwxyz

ABCDEFGHIJKLMNOPQRSTUVWXYZ 1234567890 abcdefghijklmnopqrstuvwxyz

ABCDEFGHIJKLMNOPQRSTUVWXYZ 1234567890 abcdefghijklmnopqrstuvwxyz

8/8

The main purpose of letters is the practical one of making thoughts vis ible. Ruskin says that all letters are frightful things and to be endured o nly on occasion, that is to say, in places where the sense of the inscript ion is of more importance than external ornament. This is a sweeping statement, from which we need not suffer unduly; yet it is doubtful w hether there is art in individual letters. Letters in combination may be s atisfying and in a well composed page even beautiful as a whole, but a rt in letters consists rather in the art of arranging and composing them in a pleasing and appropriate manner. The main purpose of letters is th
The main purpose of letters is the practical one of making thoughts vis ible. Ruskin says that all letters are frightful things and to be endured o
The main purpose of letters is the practical one of making though ts visible. Ruskin says that all letters are frightful things and to be

8/9

The main purpose of letters is the practical one of making thoughts vis ible. Ruskin says that all letters are frightful things and to be endured o nly on occasion, that is to say, in places where the sense of the inscript ion is of more importance than external ornament. This is a sweeping statement, from which we need not suffer unduly; yet it is doubtful w hether there is art in individual letters. Letters in combination may be s atisfying and in a well composed page even beautiful as a whole, but a rt in letters consists rather in the art of arranging and composing them
The main purpose of letters is the practical one of making thoughts vis ible. Ruskin says that all letters are frightful things and to be endured o
The main purpose of letters is the practical one of making though ts visible. Ruskin says that all letters are frightful things and to be

8/10

The main purpose of letters is the practical one of making thoughts vis ible. Ruskin says that all letters are frightful things and to be endured o nly on occasion, that is to say, in places where the sense of the inscript ion is of more importance than external ornament. This is a sweeping statement, from which we need not suffer unduly; yet it is doubtful w hether there is art in individual letters. Letters in combination may be s atisfying and in a well composed page even beautiful as a whole, but a
The main purpose of letters is the practical one of making thoughts vis ible. Ruskin says that all letters are frightful things and to be endured o
The main purpose of letters is the practical one of making though ts visible. Ruskin says that all letters are frightful things and to be

8/11

The main purpose of letters is the practical one of making thoughts vis ible. Ruskin says that all letters are frightful things and to be endured o nly on occasion, that is to say, in places where the sense of the inscript ion is of more importance than external ornament. This is a sweeping statement, from which we need not suffer unduly; yet it is doubtful w hether there is art in individual letters. Letters in combination may be s atisfying and in a well composed page even beautiful as a whole, but a
The main purpose of letters is the practical one of making thoughts vis ible. Ruskin says that all letters are frightful things and to be endured o
The main purpose of letters is the practical one of making though ts visible. Ruskin says that all letters are frightful things and to be

---

ABCDEFGHIJKLMNOPQRSTUVWXYZ 1234567890 abcdefghijklmnopqrstuvwxyz

ABCDEFGHIJKLMNOPQRSTUVWXYZ 1234567890 abcdefghijklmnopqrstuvwxyz

ABCDEFGHIJKLMNOPQRSTUVWXYZ 1234567890 abcdefghijklmnopqrstuvwxyz

ABCDEFGHIJKLMNOPQRSTUVWXYZ 1234567890 abcdefghijklmnopqrstuvwxyz

9/9

The main purpose of letters is the practical one of making thou ghts visible. Ruskin says that all letters are frightful things and to be endured only on occasion, that is to say, in places where t he sense of the inscription is of more importance than externa l ornament. This is a sweeping statement, from which we nee d not suffer unduly; yet it is doubtful whether there is art in indi vidual letters. Letters in combination may be satisfying and in a well composed page even beautiful as a whole, but art in lett
The main purpose of letters is the practical one of making thou ghts visible. Ruskin says that all letters are frightful things and
The main purpose of letters is the practical one of making thoughts visible. Ruskin says that all letters are frightful t

9/10

The main purpose of letters is the practical one of making thou ghts visible. Ruskin says that all letters are frightful things and to be endured only on occasion, that is to say, in places where t he sense of the inscription is of more importance than externa l ornament. This is a sweeping statement, from which we nee d not suffer unduly; yet it is doubtful whether there is art in indi vidual letters. Letters in combination may be satisfying and in
The main purpose of letters is the practical one of making thou ghts visible. Ruskin says that all letters are frightful things and
The main purpose of letters is the practical one of making thoughts visible. Ruskin says that all letters are frightful t

9/11

The main purpose of letters is the practical one of making thou ghts visible. Ruskin says that all letters are frightful things and to be endured only on occasion, that is to say, in places where t he sense of the inscription is of more importance than externa l ornament. This is a sweeping statement, from which we nee d not suffer unduly; yet it is doubtful whether there is art in indi vidual letters. Letters in combination may be satisfying and in
The main purpose of letters is the practical one of making thou ghts visible. Ruskin says that all letters are frightful things and
The main purpose of letters is the practical one of making thoughts visible. Ruskin says that all letters are frightful t

9/12

The main purpose of letters is the practical one of making thou ghts visible. Ruskin says that all letters are frightful things and to be endured only on occasion, that is to say, in places where t he sense of the inscription is of more importance than externa l ornament. This is a sweeping statement, from which we nee d not suffer unduly; yet it is doubtful whether there is art in indi vidual letters. Letters in combination may be satisfying and in
The main purpose of letters is the practical one of making thou ghts visible. Ruskin says that all letters are frightful things and
The main purpose of letters is the practical one of making thoughts visible. Ruskin says that all letters are frightful t

UNIVERS 10 POINT SET MINUS ½ UNIT

LIGHT 45, ITALIC 46, BOLD 65, BOLD ITALIC 66

abcdefghijklmnopqrstuvwxyz – 1 UNIT
abcdefghijklmnopqrstuvwxyz – ½ UNIT
abcdefghijklmnopqrstuvwxyz NORMAL

ABCDEFGHIJKLMNOPQRSTUVWXYZ 1234567890 abcdefghijklmnopqrstuvwxyz
ABCDEFGHIJKLMNOPQRSTUVWXYZ 1234567890 abcdefghijklmnopqrstuvwxyz
ABCDEFGHIJKLMNOPQRSTUVWXYZ 1234567890 abcdefghijklmnopqrstuvwxyz
ABCDEFGHIJKLMNOPQRSTUVWXYZ 1234567890 abcdefghijklmnopqrstuvwxyz

10/10

The main purpose of letters is the practical one of making t houghts visible. Ruskin says that all letters are frightful thin gs and to be endured only on occasion, that is to say, in pla ces where the sense of the inscription is of more importan ce than external ornament. This is a sweeping statement, from which we need not suffer unduly; yet it is doubtful w hether there is art in individual letters. Letters in combinati on may be satisfying and in a well composed page even be autiful as a whole, but art in letters consists rather in the art of arranging and composing them in a pleasing and approp riate manner. The main purpose of letters is the practical o ne of making thoughts visible. Ruskin says that all letters a re frightful things and to be endured only on occasion, that is to say, in places where the sense of the inscription is of more importance than external ornament. This is a sweepi ng statement, from which we need not suffer unduly; yet i t is doubtful whether there is art in individual letters. Letter s in combination may be satisfying and in a well composed page even beautiful as a whole, but art in letters consists r ather in the art of arranging and composing them in a pleas ing and appropriate manner. The main purpose of letters is the practical one of making thoughts visible. Ruskin says t
The main purpose of letters is the practical one of making t houghts visible. Ruskin says that all letters are frightful thin
The main purpose of letters is the practical one of mak ing thoughts visible. Ruskin says that all letters are fri

10/11

The main purpose of letters is the practical one of making t houghts visible. Ruskin says that all letters are frightful thin gs and to be endured only on occasion, that is to say, in pla ces where the sense of the inscription is of more importan ce than external ornament. This is a sweeping statement, from which we need not suffer unduly; yet it is doubtful w hether there is art in individual letters. Letters in combinati on may be satisfying and in a well composed page even be autiful as a whole, but art in letters consists rather in the art of arranging and composing them in a pleasing and approp riate manner. The main purpose of letters is the practical o ne of making thoughts visible. Ruskin says that all letters a re frightful things and to be endured only on occasion, that is to say, in places where the sense of the inscription is of more importance than external ornament. This is a sweepi ng statement, from which we need not suffer unduly; yet i t is doubtful whether there is art in individual letters. Letter s in combination may be satisfying and in a well composed page even beautiful as a whole, but art in letters consists r ather in the art of arranging and composing them in a pleas
The main purpose of letters is the practical one of making t houghts visible. Ruskin says that all letters are frightful thin
The main purpose of letters is the practical one of mak ing thoughts visible. Ruskin says that all letters are fri

10/12

The main purpose of letters is the practical one of making t houghts visible. Ruskin says that all letters are frightful thin gs and to be endured only on occasion, that is to say, in pla ces where the sense of the inscription is of more importan ce than external ornament. This is a sweeping statement, from which we need not suffer unduly; yet it is doubtful w hether there is art in individual letters. Letters in combinati on may be satisfying and in a well composed page even be autiful as a whole, but art in letters consists rather in the art of arranging and composing them in a pleasing and approp riate manner. The main purpose of letters is the practical o ne of making thoughts visible. Ruskin says that all letters a re frightful things and to be endured only on occasion, that is to say, in places where the sense of the inscription is of more importance than external ornament. This is a sweepi ng statement, from which we need not suffer unduly; yet i t is doubtful whether there is art in individual letters. Letter s in combination may be satisfying and in a well composed
The main purpose of letters is the practical one of making t houghts visible. Ruskin says that all letters are frightful thin
The main purpose of letters is the practical one of mak ing thoughts visible. Ruskin says that all letters are fri

10/13

The main purpose of letters is the practical one of making t houghts visible. Ruskin says that all letters are frightful thin gs and to be endured only on occasion, that is to say, in pla ces where the sense of the inscription is of more importan ce than external ornament. This is a sweeping statement, from which we need not suffer unduly; yet it is doubtful w hether there is art in individual letters. Letters in combinati on may be satisfying and in a well composed page even be autiful as a whole, but art in letters consists rather in the art of arranging and composing them in a pleasing and approp riate manner. The main purpose of letters is the practical o ne of making thoughts visible. Ruskin says that all letters a re frightful things and to be endured only on occasion, that is to say, in places where the sense of the inscription is of more importance than external ornament. This is a sweepi ng statement, from which we need not suffer unduly; yet i t is doubtful whether there is art in individual letters. Letter
The main purpose of letters is the practical one of making t houghts visible. Ruskin says that all letters are frightful thin
The main purpose of letters is the practical one of mak ing thoughts visible. Ruskin says that all letters are fri

UNIVERS 11 POINT SET MINUS ½ UNIT

LIGHT 45, ITALIC 46, BOLD 65, BOLD ITALIC 66

abcdefghijklmnopqrstuvwxyz – 1 UNIT
abcdefghijklmnopqrstuvwxyz – ½ UNIT
abcdefghijklmnopqrstuvwxyz NORMAL

ABCDEFGHIJKLMNOPQRSTUVWXYZ 1234567890 abcdefghijklmnopqrstuvwxyz
ABCDEFGHIJKLMNOPQRSTUVWXYZ 1234567890 abcdefghijklmnopqrstuvwxyz
ABCDEFGHIJKLMNOPQRSTUVWXYZ 1234567890 abcdefghijklmnopqrstuvwxyz
ABCDEFGHIJKLMNOPQRSTUVWXYZ 1234567890 abcdefghijklmnopqrstuvwxyz

11/11

The main purpose of letters is the practical one of ma king thoughts visible. Ruskin says that all letters are f rightful things and to be endured only on occasion, th at is to say, in places where the sense of the inscripti on is of more importance than external ornament. Th is is a sweeping statement, from which we need not suffer unduly; yet it is doubtful whether there is art in individual letters. Letters in combination may be sati sfying and in a well composed page even beautiful as a whole, but art in letters consists rather in the art of arranging and composing them in a pleasing and app ropriate manner. The main purpose of letters is the pr actical one of making thoughts visible. Ruskin says th at all letters are frightful things and to be endured onl y on occasion, that is to say, in places where the sens e of the inscription is of more importance than extern al ornament. This is a sweeping statement, from whi ch we need not suffer unduly; yet it is doubtful whet her there is art in individual letters. Letters in combin
The main purpose of letters is the practical one of ma king thoughts visible. Ruskin says that all letters are f
The main purpose of letters is the practical one of making thoughts visible. Ruskin says that all lett

11/12

The main purpose of letters is the practical one of ma king thoughts visible. Ruskin says that all letters are f rightful things and to be endured only on occasion, th at is to say, in places where the sense of the inscripti on is of more importance than external ornament. Th is is a sweeping statement, from which we need not suffer unduly; yet it is doubtful whether there is art in individual letters. Letters in combination may be sati sfying and in a well composed page even beautiful as a whole, but art in letters consists rather in the art of arranging and composing them in a pleasing and app ropriate manner. The main purpose of letters is the pr actical one of making thoughts visible. Ruskin says th at all letters are frightful things and to be endured onl y on occasion, that is to say, in places where the sens e of the inscription is of more importance than extern al ornament. This is a sweeping statement, from whi ch we need not suffer unduly; yet it is doubtful whet
The main purpose of letters is the practical one of ma king thoughts visible. Ruskin says that all letters are f
The main purpose of letters is the practical one of making thoughts visible. Ruskin says that all lett

11/13

The main purpose of letters is the practical one of ma king thoughts visible. Ruskin says that all letters are f rightful things and to be endured only on occasion, th at is to say, in places where the sense of the inscripti on is of more importance than external ornament. Th is is a sweeping statement, from which we need not suffer unduly; yet it is doubtful whether there is art in individual letters. Letters in combination may be sati sfying and in a well composed page even beautiful as a whole, but art in letters consists rather in the art of arranging and composing them in a pleasing and app ropriate manner. The main purpose of letters is the pr actical one of making thoughts visible. Ruskin says th at all letters are frightful things and to be endured onl y on occasion, that is to say, in places where the sens e of the inscription is of more importance than extern al ornament. This is a sweeping statement, from whi
The main purpose of letters is the practical one of ma king thoughts visible. Ruskin says that all letters are f
The main purpose of letters is the practical one of making thoughts visible. Ruskin says that all lett

11/14

The main purpose of letters is the practical one of ma king thoughts visible. Ruskin says that all letters are f rightful things and to be endured only on occasion, th at is to say, in places where the sense of the inscripti on is of more importance than external ornament. Th is is a sweeping statement, from which we need not suffer unduly; yet it is doubtful whether there is art in individual letters. Letters in combination may be sati sfying and in a well composed page even beautiful as a whole, but art in letters consists rather in the art of arranging and composing them in a pleasing and app ropriate manner. The main purpose of letters is the pr actical one of making thoughts visible. Ruskin says th at all letters are frightful things and to be endured onl y on occasion, that is to say, in places where the sens e of the inscription is of more importance than extern
The main purpose of letters is the practical one of ma king thoughts visible. Ruskin says that all letters are f
The main purpose of letters is the practical one of making thoughts visible. Ruskin says that all lett

UNIVERS 12 POINT SET MINUS ½ UNIT

LIGHT 45, ITALIC 46, BOLD 65, BOLD ITALIC 66

abcdefghijklmnopqrstuvwxyz – 1 UNIT
abcdefghijklmnopqrstuvwxyz – ½ UNIT
abcdefghijklmnopqrstuvwxyz NORMAL

ABCDEFGHIJKLMNOPQRSTUVWXYZ 1234567890 abcdefghijklmnopqrstuvwxyz
ABCDEFGHIJKLMNOPQRSTUVWXYZ 1234567890 abcdefghijklmnopqrstuvwxyz
ABCDEFGHIJKLMNOPQRSTUVWXYZ 1234567890 abcdefghijklmnopqrstuvwxyz
ABCDEFGHIJKLMNOPQRSTUVWXYZ 1234567890 abcdefghijklmnopqrstuvwxyz

12/12

The main purpose of letters is the practical one of making thoughts visible. Ruskin says that all lette rs are frightful things and to be endured only on o ccasion, that is to say, in places where the sense of the inscription is of more importance than exte rnal ornament. This is a sweeping statement, fro m which we need not suffer unduly; yet it is doub tful whether there is art in individual letters. Lette rs in combination may be satisfying and in a well c omposed page even beautiful as a whole, but art in letters consists rather in the art of arranging an d composing them in a pleasing and appropriate manner. The main purpose of letters is the practic al one of making thoughts visible. Ruskin says th at all letters are frightful things and to be endured
The main purpose of letters is the practical one of making thoughts visible. Ruskin says that all lette
The main purpose of letters is the practical on e of making thoughts visible. Ruskin says tha

12/13

The main purpose of letters is the practical one of making thoughts visible. Ruskin says that all lette rs are frightful things and to be endured only on o ccasion, that is to say, in places where the sense of the inscription is of more importance than exte rnal ornament. This is a sweeping statement, fro m which we need not suffer unduly; yet it is doub tful whether there is art in individual letters. Lette rs in combination may be satisfying and in a well c omposed page even beautiful as a whole, but art in letters consists rather in the art of arranging an d composing them in a pleasing and appropriate manner. The main purpose of letters is the practic al one of making thoughts visible. Ruskin says th
The main purpose of letters is the practical one of making thoughts visible. Ruskin says that all lette
The main purpose of letters is the practical on e of making thoughts visible. Ruskin says tha

12/14

The main purpose of letters is the practical one of making thoughts visible. Ruskin says that all lette rs are frightful things and to be endured only on o ccasion, that is to say, in places where the sense of the inscription is of more importance than exte rnal ornament. This is a sweeping statement, fro m which we need not suffer unduly; yet it is doub tful whether there is art in individual letters. Lette rs in combination may be satisfying and in a well c omposed page even beautiful as a whole, but art in letters consists rather in the art of arranging an d composing them in a pleasing and appropriate manner. The main purpose of letters is the practic al one of making thoughts visible. Ruskin says th at all letters are frightful things and to be endured
The main purpose of letters is the practical one of making thoughts visible. Ruskin says that all lette
The main purpose of letters is the practical on e of making thoughts visible. Ruskin says tha

12/15

The main purpose of letters is the practical one of making thoughts visible. Ruskin says that all lette rs are frightful things and to be endured only on o ccasion, that is to say, in places where the sense of the inscription is of more importance than exte rnal ornament. This is a sweeping statement, fro m which we need not suffer unduly; yet it is doub tful whether there is art in individual letters. Lette rs in combination may be satisfying and in a well c omposed page even beautiful as a whole, but art in letters consists rather in the art of arranging an d composing them in a pleasing and appropriate manner. The main purpose of letters is the practic al one of making thoughts visible. Ruskin says th
The main purpose of letters is the practical one of making thoughts visible. Ruskin says that all lette
The main purpose of letters is the practical on e of making thoughts visible. Ruskin says tha

14 POINT SET MINUS ½ UNIT

LIGHT 45, ITALIC 46, BOLD 65, BOLD ITALIC 66

abcdefghijklmnopqrstuvwxyz – 1 UNIT
abcdefghijklmnopqrstuvwxyz – ½ UNIT
abcdefghijklmnopqrstuvwxyz NORMAL

ABCDEFGHIJKLMNOPQRSTUVWXYZ abcdefghijklmnopqrstuvwxyz
ABCDEFGHIJKLMNOPQRSTUVWXYZ abcdefghijklmnopqrstuvwxyz
ABCDEFGHIJKLMNOPQRSTUVWXYZ abcdefghijklmnopqrstuvwxyz
ABCDEFGHIJKLMNOPQRSTUVWXYZ abcdefghijklmnopqrstuvwxyz

14/14

The main purpose of letters is the practica
l one of making thoughts visible. Ruskin s
ays that all letters are frightful things and t
o be endured only on occasion, that is to s
ay, in places where the sense of the inscri
ption is of more importance than external
ornament. This is a sweeping statement,
from which we need not suffer unduly; ye
t it is doubtful whether there is art in indivi
dual letters. Letters in combination may b
e satisfying and in a well composed page
even beautiful as a whole, but art in letter
s consists rather in the art of arranging an
The main purpose of letters is the practica
l one of making thoughts visible. Ruskin s
The main purpose of letters is the prac
tical one of making thoughts visible. R

14/15

The main purpose of letters is the practica
l one of making thoughts visible. Ruskin s
ays that all letters are frightful things and t
o be endured only on occasion, that is to s
ay, in places where the sense of the inscri
ption is of more importance than external
ornament. This is a sweeping statement,
from which we need not suffer unduly; ye
t it is doubtful whether there is art in indivi
dual letters. Letters in combination may b
e satisfying and in a well composed page
even beautiful as a whole, but art in letter
The main purpose of letters is the practica
l one of making thoughts visible. Ruskin s
The main purpose of letters is the prac
tical one of making thoughts visible. R

14/16

The main purpose of letters is the practica
l one of making thoughts visible. Ruskin s
ays that all letters are frightful things and t
o be endured only on occasion, that is to s
ay, in places where the sense of the inscri
ption is of more importance than external
ornament. This is a sweeping statement,
from which we need not suffer unduly; ye
t it is doubtful whether there is art in indivi
dual letters. Letters in combination may b
e satisfying and in a well composed page
even beautiful as a whole, but art in letter
s consists rather in the art of arranging an
The main purpose of letters is the practica
l one of making thoughts visible. Ruskin s
The main purpose of letters is the prac
tical one of making thoughts visible. R

14/17

The main purpose of letters is the practica
l one of making thoughts visible. Ruskin s
ays that all letters are frightful things and t
o be endured only on occasion, that is to s
ay, in places where the sense of the inscri
ption is of more importance than external
ornament. This is a sweeping statement,
from which we need not suffer unduly; ye
t it is doubtful whether there is art in indivi
dual letters. Letters in combination may b
e satisfying and in a well composed page
even beautiful as a whole, but art in letter
The main purpose of letters is the practica
l one of making thoughts visible. Ruskin s
The main purpose of letters is the prac
tical one of making thoughts visible. R

UNIVERS 6 & 7 POINT SET NORMAL

ROMAN 55, ITALIC 56, BLACK 75, BLACK ITALIC 76

ABCDEFGHIJKLMNOPQRSTUVWXYZ 1234567890 abcdefghijklmnopqrstuvwxyz

ABCDEFGHIJKLMNOPQRSTUVWXYZ 1234567890 abcdefghijklmnopqrstuvwxyz

ABCDEFGHIJKLMNOPQRSTUVWXYZ 1234567890 abcdefghijklmnopqrstuvwxyz

ABCDEFGHIJKLMNOPQRSTUVWXYZ 1234567890 abcdefghijklmnopqrstuvwxyz

6/6

The main purpose of letters is the practical one of making thoughts visible. Ruskin says that all letters are frightful things and to be endured only on occasion, that is to say, in pl aces where the sense of the inscription is of more importance than external ornament. This is a sweeping statement, from which we need not suffer unduly; yet it is doubtful w hether there is art in individual letters. Letters in combination may be satisfying and in a well composed page even beautiful as a whole, but art in letters consists rather in the ar t of arranging and composing them in a pleasing and appropriate manner. The main pur pose of letters is the practical one of making thoughts visible. Ruskin says that all letters are frightful things and to be endured only on occasion, that is to say, in places where th e sense of the inscription is of more importance than external ornament. This is a swee ping statement, from which we need not suffer unduly; yet it is doubtful whether there i s art in individual letters. Letters in combination may be satisfying and in a well compos ed page even beautiful as a whole, but art in letters consists rather in the art of arrangin
The main purpose of letters is the practical one of making thoughts visible. Ruskin says that all letters are frightful things and to be endured only on occasion, that is to say, in pl
The main purpose of letters is the practical one of making thoughts visible. Ru skin says that all letters are frightful things and to be endured only on occasio

6/7

The main purpose of letters is the practical one of making thoughts visible. Ruskin says that all letters are frightful things and to be endured only on occasion, that is to say, in pl aces where the sense of the inscription is of more importance than external ornament. This is a sweeping statement, from which we need not suffer unduly; yet it is doubtful w hether there is art in individual letters. Letters in combination may be satisfying and in a well composed page even beautiful as a whole, but art in letters consists rather in the ar t of arranging and composing them in a pleasing and appropriate manner. The main pur pose of letters is the practical one of making thoughts visible. Ruskin says that all letters are frightful things and to be endured only on occasion, that is to say, in places where th e sense of the inscription is of more importance than external ornament. This is a swee ping statement, from which we need not suffer unduly; yet it is doubtful whether there i
The main purpose of letters is the practical one of making thoughts visible. Ruskin says that all letters are frightful things and to be endured only on occasion, that is to say, in pl
The main purpose of letters is the practical one of making thoughts visible. Ru skin says that all letters are frightful things and to be endured only on occasio

6/8

The main purpose of letters is the practical one of making thoughts visible. Ruskin says that all letters are frightful things and to be endured only on occasion, that is to say, in pl aces where the sense of the inscription is of more importance than external ornament. This is a sweeping statement, from which we need not suffer unduly; yet it is doubtful w hether there is art in individual letters. Letters in combination may be satisfying and in a well composed page even beautiful as a whole, but art in letters consists rather in the ar t of arranging and composing them in a pleasing and appropriate manner. The main pur pose of letters is the practical one of making thoughts visible. Ruskin says that all letters are frightful things and to be endured only on occasion, that is to say, in places where th
The main purpose of letters is the practical one of making thoughts visible. Ruskin says that all letters are frightful things and to be endured only on occasion, that is to say, in pl
The main purpose of letters is the practical one of making thoughts visible. Ru skin says that all letters are frightful things and to be endured only on occasio

6/9

The main purpose of letters is the practical one of making thoughts visible. Ruskin says that all letters are frightful things and to be endured only on occasion, that is to say, in pl aces where the sense of the inscription is of more importance than external ornament. This is a sweeping statement, from which we need not suffer unduly; yet it is doubtful w hether there is art in individual letters. Letters in combination may be satisfying and in a well composed page even beautiful as a whole, but art in letters consists rather in the ar t of arranging and composing them in a pleasing and appropriate manner. The main pur pose of letters is the practical one of making thoughts visible. Ruskin says that all letters
The main purpose of letters is the practical one of making thoughts visible. Ruskin says that all letters are frightful things and to be endured only on occasion, that is to say, in pl
The main purpose of letters is the practical one of making thoughts visible. Ru skin says that all letters are frightful things and to be endured only on occasio

---

ABCDEFGHIJKLMNOPQRSTUVWXYZ 1234567890 abcdefghijklmnopqrstuvwxyz

ABCDEFGHIJKLMNOPQRSTUVWXYZ 1234567890 abcdefghijklmnopqrstuvwxyz

ABCDEFGHIJKLMNOPQRSTUVWXYZ 1234567890 abcdefghijklmnopqrstuvwxyz

ABCDEFGHIJKLMNOPQRSTUVWXYZ 1234567890 abcdefghijklmnopqrstuvwxyz

7/7

The main purpose of letters is the practical one of making thoughts visible. Ruskin says that all letters are frightful things and to be endured only on oc casion, that is to say, in places where the sense of the inscription is of more i mportance than external ornament. This is a sweeping statement, from wh ich we need not suffer unduly; yet it is doubtful whether there is art in indivi dual letters. Letters in combination may be satisfying and in a well compos ed page even beautiful as a whole, but art in letters consists rather in the art of arranging and composing them in a pleasing and appropriate manner. T he main purpose of letters is the practical one of making thoughts visible. R uskin says that all letters are frightful things and to be endured only on occa sion, that is to say, in places where the sense of the inscription is of more im
The main purpose of letters is the practical one of making thoughts visible. Ruskin says that all letters are frightful things and to be endured only on oc
The main purpose of letters is the practical one of making thoughts visible. Ruskin says that all letters are frightful things and to be end

7/8

The main purpose of letters is the practical one of making thoughts visible. Ruskin says that all letters are frightful things and to be endured only on oc casion, that is to say, in places where the sense of the inscription is of more i mportance than external ornament. This is a sweeping statement, from wh ich we need not suffer unduly; yet it is doubtful whether there is art in indivi dual letters. Letters in combination may be satisfying and in a well compos ed page even beautiful as a whole, but art in letters consists rather in the art of arranging and composing them in a pleasing and appropriate manner. T he main purpose of letters is the practical one of making thoughts visible. R uskin says that all letters are frightful things and to be endured only on occa
The main purpose of letters is the practical one of making thoughts visible. Ruskin says that all letters are frightful things and to be endured only on oc
The main purpose of letters is the practical one of making thoughts visible. Ruskin says that all letters are frightful things and to be end

7/9

The main purpose of letters is the practical one of making thoughts visible. Ruskin says that all letters are frightful things and to be endured only on oc casion, that is to say, in places where the sense of the inscription is of more i mportance than external ornament. This is a sweeping statement, from wh ich we need not suffer unduly; yet it is doubtful whether there is art in indivi dual letters. Letters in combination may be satisfying and in a well compos ed page even beautiful as a whole, but art in letters consists rather in the art of arranging and composing them in a pleasing and appropriate manner. T he main purpose of letters is the practical one of making thoughts visible. R uskin says that all letters are frightful things and to be endured only on occa
The main purpose of letters is the practical one of making thoughts visible. Ruskin says that all letters are frightful things and to be endured only on oc
The main purpose of letters is the practical one of making thoughts visible. Ruskin says that all letters are frightful things and to be end

7/10

The main purpose of letters is the practical one of making thoughts visible. Ruskin says that all letters are frightful things and to be endured only on oc casion, that is to say, in places where the sense of the inscription is of more i mportance than external ornament. This is a sweeping statement, from wh ich we need not suffer unduly; yet it is doubtful whether there is art in indivi dual letters. Letters in combination may be satisfying and in a well compos ed page even beautiful as a whole, but art in letters consists rather in the art of arranging and composing them in a pleasing and appropriate manner. T he main purpose of letters is the practical one of making thoughts visible. R
The main purpose of letters is the practical one of making thoughts visible. Ruskin says that all letters are frightful things and to be endured only on oc
The main purpose of letters is the practical one of making thoughts visible. Ruskin says that all letters are frightful things and to be end

UNIVERS 8 & 9 POINT SET NORMAL

ROMAN 55, ITALIC 56, BLACK 75, BLACK ITALIC 76

ABCDEFGHIJKLMNOPQRSTUVWXYZ 1234567890 abcdefghijklmnopqrstuvwxyz

ABCDEFGHIJKLMNOPQRSTUVWXYZ 1234567890 abcdefghijklmnopqrstuvwxyz

ABCDEFGHIJKLMNOPQRSTUVWXYZ 1234567890 abcdefghijklmnopqrstuvwxyz

ABCDEFGHIJKLMNOPQRSTUVWXYZ 1234567890 abcdefghijklmnopqrstuvwxyz

8/8

The main purpose of letters is the practical one of making thought s visible. Ruskin says that all letters are frightful things and to be e ndured only on occasion, that is to say, in places where the sense of the inscription is of more importance than external ornament. This is a sweeping statement, from which we need not suffer und uly; yet it is doubtful whether there is art in individual letters. Lett ers in combination may be satisfying and in a well composed pag e even beautiful as a whole, but art in letters consists rather in the art of arranging and composing them in a pleasing and appropri

The main purpose of letters is the practical one of making thought s visible. Ruskin says that all letters are frightful things and to be e

The main purpose of letters is the practical one of making t houghts visible. Ruskin says that all letters are frightful thi

8/9

The main purpose of letters is the practical one of making thought s visible. Ruskin says that all letters are frightful things and to be e ndured only on occasion, that is to say, in places where the sense of the inscription is of more importance than external ornament. This is a sweeping statement, from which we need not suffer und uly; yet it is doubtful whether there is art in individual letters. Lett ers in combination may be satisfying and in a well composed pag e even beautiful as a whole, but art in letters consists rather in the

The main purpose of letters is the practical one of making thought s visible. Ruskin says that all letters are frightful things and to be e

The main purpose of letters is the practical one of making t houghts visible. Ruskin says that all letters are frightful thi

8/10

The main purpose of letters is the practical one of making thought s visible. Ruskin says that all letters are frightful things and to be e ndured only on occasion, that is to say, in places where the sense of the inscription is of more importance than external ornament. This is a sweeping statement, from which we need not suffer und uly; yet it is doubtful whether there is art in individual letters. Lett ers in combination may be satisfying and in a well composed pag

The main purpose of letters is the practical one of making thought s visible. Ruskin says that all letters are frightful things and to be e

The main purpose of letters is the practical one of making t houghts visible. Ruskin says that all letters are frightful thi

8/11

The main purpose of letters is the practical one of making thought s visible. Ruskin says that all letters are frightful things and to be e ndured only on occasion, that is to say, in places where the sense of the inscription is of more importance than external ornament. This is a sweeping statement, from which we need not suffer und uly; yet it is doubtful whether there is art in individual letters. Lett ers in combination may be satisfying and in a well composed pag

The main purpose of letters is the practical one of making thought s visible. Ruskin says that all letters are frightful things and to be e

The main purpose of letters is the practical one of making t houghts visible. Ruskin says that all letters are frightful thi

---

ABCDEFGHIJKLMNOPQRSTUVWXYZ 1234567890 abcdefghijklmnopqrstuvwxyz

ABCDEFGHIJKLMNOPQRSTUVWXYZ 1234567890 abcdefghijklmnopqrstuvwxyz

ABCDEFGHIJKLMNOPQRSTUVWXYZ 1234567890 abcdefghijklmnopqrstuvwxyz

ABCDEFGHIJKLMNOPQRSTUVWXYZ 1234567890 abcdefghijklmnopqrstuvwxyz

9/9

The main purpose of letters is the practical one of making t houghts visible. Ruskin says that all letters are frightful thi ngs and to be endured only on occasion, that is to say, in pl aces where the sense of the inscription is of more importa nce than external ornament. This is a sweeping statement, from which we need not suffer unduly; yet it is doubtful w hether there is art in individual letters. Letters in combinati on may be satisfying and in a well composed page even be

The main purpose of letters is the practical one of making t houghts visible. Ruskin says that all letters are frightful thi

The main purpose of letters is the practical one of m aking thoughts visible. Ruskin says that all letters ar

9/10

The main purpose of letters is the practical one of making t houghts visible. Ruskin says that all letters are frightful thi ngs and to be endured only on occasion, that is to say, in pl aces where the sense of the inscription is of more importa nce than external ornament. This is a sweeping statement, from which we need not suffer unduly; yet it is doubtful w hether there is art in individual letters. Letters in combinati

The main purpose of letters is the practical one of making t houghts visible. Ruskin says that all letters are frightful thi

The main purpose of letters is the practical one of m aking thoughts visible. Ruskin says that all letters ar

9/11

The main purpose of letters is the practical one of making t houghts visible. Ruskin says that all letters are frightful thi ngs and to be endured only on occasion, that is to say, in pl aces where the sense of the inscription is of more importa nce than external ornament. This is a sweeping statement, from which we need not suffer unduly; yet it is doubtful w hether there is art in individual letters. Letters in combinati

The main purpose of letters is the practical one of making t houghts visible. Ruskin says that all letters are frightful thi

The main purpose of letters is the practical one of m aking thoughts visible. Ruskin says that all letters ar

9/12

The main purpose of letters is the practical one of making t houghts visible. Ruskin says that all letters are frightful thi ngs and to be endured only on occasion, that is to say, in pl aces where the sense of the inscription is of more importa nce than external ornament. This is a sweeping statement, from which we need not suffer unduly; yet it is doubtful w hether there is art in individual letters. Letters in combinati

The main purpose of letters is the practical one of making t houghts visible. Ruskin says that all letters are frightful thi

The main purpose of letters is the practical one of m aking thoughts visible. Ruskin says that all letters ar

UNIVERS 10 POINT SET MINUS ½ UNIT

ROMAN 55, ITALIC 56, BLACK 75, BLACK ITALIC 76

abcdefghijklmnopqrstuvwxyz – 1 UNIT
abcdefghijklmnopqrstuvwxyz – ½ UNIT
abcdefghijklmnopqrstuvwxyz NORMAL

ABCDEFGHIJKLMNOPQRSTUVWXYZ 1234567890 abcdefghijklmnopqrstuvwxyz
ABCDEFGHIJKLMNOPQRSTUVWXYZ 1234567890 abcdefghijklmnopqrstuvwxyz
ABCDEFGHIJKLMNOPQRSTUVWXYZ 1234567890 abcdefghijklmnopqrstuvwxyz
ABCDEFGHIJKLMNOPQRSTUVWXYZ 1234567890 abcdefghijklmnopqrstuvwxyz

10/10

The main purpose of letters is the practical one of maki ng thoughts visible. Ruskin says that all letters are frig htful things and to be endured only on occasion, that is to say, in places where the sense of the inscription is of more importance than external ornament. This is a sw eeping statement, from which we need not suffer und uly; yet it is doubtful whether there is art in individual l etters. Letters in combination may be satisfying and in a well composed page even beautiful as a whole, but a rt in letters consists rather in the art of arranging and c omposing them in a pleasing and appropriate manner. The main purpose of letters is the practical one of maki ng thoughts visible. Ruskin says that all letters are frig htful things and to be endured only on occasion, that is to say, in places where the sense of the inscription is of more importance than external ornament. This is a sw eeping statement, from which we need not suffer und uly; yet it is doubtful whether there is art in individual l etters. Letters in combination may be satisfying and in a well composed page even beautiful as a whole, but a rt in letters consists rather in the art of arranging and c omposing them in a pleasing and appropriate manner.
The main purpose of letters is the practical one of maki ng thoughts visible. Ruskin says that all letters are frig
The main purpose of letters is the practical one o f making thoughts visible. Ruskin says that all le

10/11

The main purpose of letters is the practical one of maki ng thoughts visible. Ruskin says that all letters are frig htful things and to be endured only on occasion, that is to say, in places where the sense of the inscription is of more importance than external ornament. This is a sw eeping statement, from which we need not suffer und uly; yet it is doubtful whether there is art in individual l etters. Letters in combination may be satisfying and in a well composed page even beautiful as a whole, but a rt in letters consists rather in the art of arranging and c omposing them in a pleasing and appropriate manner. The main purpose of letters is the practical one of maki ng thoughts visible. Ruskin says that all letters are frig htful things and to be endured only on occasion, that is to say, in places where the sense of the inscription is of more importance than external ornament. This is a sw eeping statement, from which we need not suffer und uly; yet it is doubtful whether there is art in individual l etters. Letters in combination may be satisfying and in a well composed page even beautiful as a whole, but a
The main purpose of letters is the practical one of maki ng thoughts visible. Ruskin says that all letters are frig
The main purpose of letters is the practical one o f making thoughts visible. Ruskin says that all le

10/12

The main purpose of letters is the practical one of maki ng thoughts visible. Ruskin says that all letters are frig htful things and to be endured only on occasion, that is to say, in places where the sense of the inscription is of more importance than external ornament. This is a sw eeping statement, from which we need not suffer und uly; yet it is doubtful whether there is art in individual l etters. Letters in combination may be satisfying and in a well composed page even beautiful as a whole, but a rt in letters consists rather in the art of arranging and c omposing them in a pleasing and appropriate manner. The main purpose of letters is the practical one of maki ng thoughts visible. Ruskin says that all letters are frig htful things and to be endured only on occasion, that is to say, in places where the sense of the inscription is of more importance than external ornament. This is a sw eeping statement, from which we need not suffer und uly; yet it is doubtful whether there is art in individual l
The main purpose of letters is the practical one of maki ng thoughts visible. Ruskin says that all letters are frig
The main purpose of letters is the practical one o f making thoughts visible. Ruskin says that all le

10/13

The main purpose of letters is the practical one of maki ng thoughts visible. Ruskin says that all letters are frig htful things and to be endured only on occasion, that is to say, in places where the sense of the inscription is of more importance than external ornament. This is a sw eeping statement, from which we need not suffer und uly; yet it is doubtful whether there is art in individual l etters. Letters in combination may be satisfying and in a well composed page even beautiful as a whole, but a rt in letters consists rather in the art of arranging and c omposing them in a pleasing and appropriate manner. The main purpose of letters is the practical one of maki ng thoughts visible. Ruskin says that all letters are frig htful things and to be endured only on occasion, that is to say, in places where the sense of the inscription is of more importance than external ornament. This is a sw eeping statement, from which we need not suffer und
The main purpose of letters is the practical one of maki ng thoughts visible. Ruskin says that all letters are frig
The main purpose of letters is the practical one o f making thoughts visible. Ruskin says that all le

UNIVERS 11 POINT SET MINUS ½ UNIT

ROMAN 55, ITALIC 56, BLACK 75, BLACK ITALIC 76

abcdefghijklmnopqrstuvwxyz – 1 UNIT
abcdefghijklmnopqrstuvwxyz – ½ UNIT
abcdefghijklmnopqrstuvwxyz NORMAL

ABCDEFGHIJKLMNOPQRSTUVWXYZ 1234567890 abcdefghijklmnopqrstuvwxyz
ABCDEFGHIJKLMNOPQRSTUVWXYZ 1234567890 abcdefghijklmnopqrstuvwxyz
ABCDEFGHIJKLMNOPQRSTUVWXYZ 1234567890 abcdefghijklmnopqrstuvwxyz
ABCDEFGHIJKLMNOPQRSTUVWXYZ 1234567890 abcdefghijklmnopqrstuvwxyz

11/11

The main purpose of letters is the practical one of making thoughts visible. Ruskin says that all lette rs are frightful things and to be endured only on o ccasion, that is to say, in places where the sense o f the inscription is of more importance than exter nal ornament. This is a sweeping statement, from which we need not suffer unduly; yet it is doubtfu l whether there is art in individual letters. Letters i n combination may be satisfying and in a well co mposed page even beautiful as a whole, but art in letters consists rather in the art of arranging and c omposing them in a pleasing and appropriate ma nner. The main purpose of letters is the practical o ne of making thoughts visible. Ruskin says that all letters are frightful things and to be endured only on occasion, that is to say, in places where the sen se of the inscription is of more importance than e xternal ornament. This is a sweeping statement, f rom which we need not suffer unduly; yet it is do
The main purpose of letters is the practical one of making thoughts visible. Ruskin says that all lette
The main purpose of letters is the practical one of making thoughts visible. Ruskin says

11/12

The main purpose of letters is the practical one of making thoughts visible. Ruskin says that all lette rs are frightful things and to be endured only on o ccasion, that is to say, in places where the sense o f the inscription is of more importance than exter nal ornament. This is a sweeping statement, from which we need not suffer unduly; yet it is doubtfu l whether there is art in individual letters. Letters i n combination may be satisfying and in a well co mposed page even beautiful as a whole, but art in letters consists rather in the art of arranging and c omposing them in a pleasing and appropriate ma nner. The main purpose of letters is the practical o ne of making thoughts visible. Ruskin says that all letters are frightful things and to be endured only on occasion, that is to say, in places where the sen se of the inscription is of more importance than e xternal ornament. This is a sweeping statement, f
The main purpose of letters is the practical one of making thoughts visible. Ruskin says that all lette
The main purpose of letters is the practical one of making thoughts visible. Ruskin says

11/13

The main purpose of letters is the practical one of making thoughts visible. Ruskin says that all lette rs are frightful things and to be endured only on o ccasion, that is to say, in places where the sense o f the inscription is of more importance than exter nal ornament. This is a sweeping statement, from which we need not suffer unduly; yet it is doubtfu l whether there is art in individual letters. Letters i n combination may be satisfying and in a well co mposed page even beautiful as a whole, but art in letters consists rather in the art of arranging and c omposing them in a pleasing and appropriate ma nner. The main purpose of letters is the practical o ne of making thoughts visible. Ruskin says that all letters are frightful things and to be endured only on occasion, that is to say, in places where the sen se of the inscription is of more importance than e
The main purpose of letters is the practical one of making thoughts visible. Ruskin says that all lette
The main purpose of letters is the practical one of making thoughts visible. Ruskin says

11/14

The main purpose of letters is the practical one of making thoughts visible. Ruskin says that all lette rs are frightful things and to be endured only on o ccasion, that is to say, in places where the sense o f the inscription is of more importance than exter nal ornament. This is a sweeping statement, from which we need not suffer unduly; yet it is doubtfu l whether there is art in individual letters. Letters i n combination may be satisfying and in a well co mposed page even beautiful as a whole, but art in letters consists rather in the art of arranging and c omposing them in a pleasing and appropriate ma nner. The main purpose of letters is the practical o ne of making thoughts visible. Ruskin says that all letters are frightful things and to be endured only on occasion, that is to say, in places where the sen
The main purpose of letters is the practical one of making thoughts visible. Ruskin says that all lette
The main purpose of letters is the practical one of making thoughts visible. Ruskin says

UNIVERS 12 POINT SET MINUS ½ UNIT

ROMAN 55, ITALIC 56, BLACK 75, BLACK ITALIC 76

abcdefghijklmnopqrstuvwxyz – 1 UNIT
abcdefghijklmnopqrstuvwxyz – ½ UNIT
abcdefghijklmnopqrstuvwxyz NORMAL

ABCDEFGHIJKLMNOPQRSTUVWXYZ 1234567890 abcdefghijklmnopqrstuvwxyz
ABCDEFGHIJKLMNOPQRSTUVWXYZ 1234567890 abcdefghijklmnopqrstuvwxyz
ABCDEFGHIJKLMNOPQRSTUVWXYZ 1234567890 abcdefghijklmnopqrstuv
ABCDEFGHIJKLMNOPQRSTUVWXYZ 1234567890 abcdefghijklmnopqrstuv

12/12

The main purpose of letters is the practical on
e of making thoughts visible. Ruskin says that
all letters are frightful things and to be endure
d only on occasion, that is to say, in places wh
ere the sense of the inscription is of more imp
ortance than external ornament. This is a swe
eping statement, from which we need not suf
fer unduly; yet it is doubtful whether there is a
rt in individual letters. Letters in combination
may be satisfying and in a well composed pag
e even beautiful as a whole, but art in letters
consists rather in the art of arranging and co
mposing them in a pleasing and appropriate
manner. The main purpose of letters is the pr
actical one of making thoughts visible. Ruskin
The main purpose of letters is the practical on
e of making thoughts visible. Ruskin says that
The main purpose of letters is the practic
al one of making thoughts visible. Ruski

12/13

The main purpose of letters is the practical on
e of making thoughts visible. Ruskin says that
all letters are frightful things and to be endure
d only on occasion, that is to say, in places wh
ere the sense of the inscription is of more imp
ortance than external ornament. This is a swe
eping statement, from which we need not suf
fer unduly; yet it is doubtful whether there is a
rt in individual letters. Letters in combination
may be satisfying and in a well composed pag
e even beautiful as a whole, but art in letters
consists rather in the art of arranging and co
mposing them in a pleasing and appropriate
manner. The main purpose of letters is the pr
The main purpose of letters is the practical on
e of making thoughts visible. Ruskin says that
The main purpose of letters is the practic
al one of making thoughts visible. Ruski

12/14

The main purpose of letters is the practical on
e of making thoughts visible. Ruskin says that
all letters are frightful things and to be endure
d only on occasion, that is to say, in places wh
ere the sense of the inscription is of more imp
ortance than external ornament. This is a swe
eping statement, from which we need not suf
fer unduly; yet it is doubtful whether there is a
rt in individual letters. Letters in combination
may be satisfying and in a well composed pag
e even beautiful as a whole, but art in letters
consists rather in the art of arranging and co
mposing them in a pleasing and appropriate
manner. The main purpose of letters is the pr
actical one of making thoughts visible. Ruskin
The main purpose of letters is the practical on
e of making thoughts visible. Ruskin says that
The main purpose of letters is the practic
al one of making thoughts visible. Ruski

12/15

The main purpose of letters is the practical on
e of making thoughts visible. Ruskin says that
all letters are frightful things and to be endure
d only on occasion, that is to say, in places wh
ere the sense of the inscription is of more imp
ortance than external ornament. This is a swe
eping statement, from which we need not suf
fer unduly; yet it is doubtful whether there is a
rt in individual letters. Letters in combination
may be satisfying and in a well composed pag
e even beautiful as a whole, but art in letters
consists rather in the art of arranging and co
mposing them in a pleasing and appropriate
manner. The main purpose of letters is the pr
The main purpose of letters is the practical on
e of making thoughts visible. Ruskin says that
The main purpose of letters is the practic
al one of making thoughts visible. Ruski

UNIVERS 14 POINT SET MINUS ½ UNIT

ROMAN 55, ITALIC 56, BLACK 75, BLACK ITALIC 76

abcdefghijklmnopqrstuvwxyz – 1 UNIT
abcdefghijklmnopqrstuvwxyz – ½ UNIT
abcdefghijklmnopqrstuvwxyz NORMAL

ABCDEFGHIJKLMNOPQRSTUVWXYZ abcdefghijklmnopqrstuvwxyz
ABCDEFGHIJKLMNOPQRSTUVWXYZ abcdefghijklmnopqrstuvwxyz
ABCDEFGHIJKLMNOPQRSTUVWXYZ abcdefghijklmnopqrstuvwxyz
ABCDEFGHIJKLMNOPQRSTUVWXYZ abcdefghijklmnopqrstuvwxyz

14/14

The main purpose of letters is the pract ical one of making thoughts visible. Ru skin says that all letters are frightful thi ngs and to be endured only on occasio n, that is to say, in places where the sen se of the inscription is of more importa nce than external ornament. This is a s weeping statement, from which we ne ed not suffer unduly; yet it is doubtful whether there is art in individual letter s. Letters in combination may be satis fying and in a well composed page ev en beautiful as a whole, but art in lette
The main purpose of letters is the pract ical one of making thoughts visible. Ru
The main purpose of letters is the p ractical one of making thoughts vi

14/16

The main purpose of letters is the pract ical one of making thoughts visible. Ru skin says that all letters are frightful thi ngs and to be endured only on occasio n, that is to say, in places where the sen se of the inscription is of more importa nce than external ornament. This is a s weeping statement, from which we ne ed not suffer unduly; yet it is doubtful whether there is art in individual letter s. Letters in combination may be satis fying and in a well composed page ev en beautiful as a whole, but art in lette
The main purpose of letters is the pract ical one of making thoughts visible. Ru
The main purpose of letters is the p ractical one of making thoughts vi

14/15

The main purpose of letters is the pract ical one of making thoughts visible. Ru skin says that all letters are frightful thi ngs and to be endured only on occasio n, that is to say, in places where the sen se of the inscription is of more importa nce than external ornament. This is a s weeping statement, from which we ne ed not suffer unduly; yet it is doubtful whether there is art in individual letter s. Letters in combination may be satis fying and in a well composed page ev
The main purpose of letters is the pract ical one of making thoughts visible. Ru
The main purpose of letters is the p ractical one of making thoughts vi

14/17

The main purpose of letters is the pract ical one of making thoughts visible. Ru skin says that all letters are frightful thi ngs and to be endured only on occasio n, that is to say, in places where the sen se of the inscription is of more importa nce than external ornament. This is a s weeping statement, from which we ne ed not suffer unduly; yet it is doubtful whether there is art in individual letter s. Letters in combination may be satis fying and in a well composed page ev
The main purpose of letters is the pract ical one of making thoughts visible. Ru
The main purpose of letters is the p ractical one of making thoughts vi

WALBAUM 6 & 7 POINT SET NORMAL

ROMAN, ITALIC, BOLD, BOLD ITALIC

ABCDEFGHIJKLMNOPQRSTUVWXYZ 1234567890 abcdefghijklmnopqrstuvwxyz

ABCDEFGHIJKLMNOPQRSTUVWXYZ 1234567890 abcdefghijklmnopqrstuvwxyz

ABCDEFGHIJKLMNOPQRSTUVWXYZ 1234567890 abcdefghijklmnopqrstuvwxyz

ABCDEFGHIJKLMNOPQRSTUVWXYZ 1234567890 abcdefghijklmnopqrstuvwxyz

6/6

The main purpose of letters is the practical one of making thoughts visible. Ruskin says
that all letters are frightful things and to be endured only on occasion, that is to say, in pl
aces where the sense of the inscription is of more importance than external ornament.
This is a sweeping statement, from which we need not suffer unduly; yet it is doubtful
whether there is art in individual letters. Letters in combination may be satisfying and i
n a well composed page even beautiful as a whole, but art in letters consists rather in th
e art of arranging and composing them in a pleasing and appropriate manner. The mai
n purpose of letters is the practical one of making thoughts visible. Ruskin says that all l
etters are frightful things and to be endured only on occasion, that is to say, in places wh
ere the sense of the inscription is of more importance than external ornament. This is a
sweeping statement, from which we need not suffer unduly; yet it is doubtful whether t
here is art in individual letters. Letters in combination may be satisfying and in a well c
omposed page even beautiful as a whole, but art in letters consists rather in the art of ar
The main purpose of letters is the practical one of making thoughts visible. Ruskin says t
hat all letters are frightful things and to be endured only on occasion, that is to say, in pla
The main purpose of letters is the practical one of making thoughts visible. Ruskin
says that all letters are frightful things and to be endured only on occasion, that is t

6/7

The main purpose of letters is the practical one of making thoughts visible. Ruskin says
that all letters are frightful things and to be endured only on occasion, that is to say, in pl
aces where the sense of the inscription is of more importance than external ornament.
This is a sweeping statement, from which we need not suffer unduly; yet it is doubtful
whether there is art in individual letters. Letters in combination may be satisfying and i
n a well composed page even beautiful as a whole, but art in letters consists rather in th
e art of arranging and composing them in a pleasing and appropriate manner. The mai
n purpose of letters is the practical one of making thoughts visible. Ruskin says that all l
etters are frightful things and to be endured only on occasion, that is to say, in places wh
ere the sense of the inscription is of more importance than external ornament. This is a
sweeping statement, from which we need not suffer unduly; yet it is doubtful whether t
The main purpose of letters is the practical one of making thoughts visible. Ruskin says t
hat all letters are frightful things and to be endured only on occasion, that is to say, in pla
The main purpose of letters is the practical one of making thoughts visible. Ruskin
says that all letters are frightful things and to be endured only on occasion, that is t

6/8

The main purpose of letters is the practical one of making thoughts visible. Ruskin says
that all letters are frightful things and to be endured only on occasion, that is to say, in pl
aces where the sense of the inscription is of more importance than external ornament.
This is a sweeping statement, from which we need not suffer unduly; yet it is doubtful
whether there is art in individual letters. Letters in combination may be satisfying and i
n a well composed page even beautiful as a whole, but art in letters consists rather in th
e art of arranging and composing them in a pleasing and appropriate manner. The mai
n purpose of letters is the practical one of making thoughts visible. Ruskin says that all l
etters are frightful things and to be endured only on occasion, that is to say, in places wh
The main purpose of letters is the practical one of making thoughts visible. Ruskin says t
hat all letters are frightful things and to be endured only on occasion, that is to say, in pla
The main purpose of letters is the practical one of making thoughts visible. Ruskin
says that all letters are frightful things and to be endured only on occasion, that is t

6/9

The main purpose of letters is the practical one of making thoughts visible. Ruskin says
that all letters are frightful things and to be endured only on occasion, that is to say, in pl
aces where the sense of the inscription is of more importance than external ornament.
This is a sweeping statement, from which we need not suffer unduly; yet it is doubtful
whether there is art in individual letters. Letters in combination may be satisfying and i
n a well composed page even beautiful as a whole, but art in letters consists rather in th
e art of arranging and composing them in a pleasing and appropriate manner. The mai
n purpose of letters is the practical one of making thoughts visible. Ruskin says that all l
The main purpose of letters is the practical one of making thoughts visible. Ruskin says t
hat all letters are frightful things and to be endured only on occasion, that is to say, in pla
The main purpose of letters is the practical one of making thoughts visible. Ruskin
says that all letters are frightful things and to be endured only on occasion, that is t

---

ABCDEFGHIJKLMNOPQRSTUVWXYZ 1234567890 abcdefghijklmnopqrstuvwxyz

ABCDEFGHIJKLMNOPQRSTUVWXYZ 1234567890 abcdefghijklmnopqrstuvwxyz

ABCDEFGHIJKLMNOPQRSTUVWXYZ 1234567890 abcdefghijklmnopqrstuvwxyz

ABCDEFGHIJKLMNOPQRSTUVWXYZ 1234567890 abcdefghijklmnopqrstuvwxyz

7/7

The main purpose of letters is the practical one of making thoughts visible.
Ruskin says that all letters are frightful things and to be endured only on oc
casion, that is to say, in places where the sense of the inscription is of more
importance than external ornament. This is a sweeping statement, from w
hich we need not suffer unduly; yet it is doubtful whether there is art in ind
ividual letters. Letters in combination may be satisfying and in a well com
posed page even beautiful as a whole, but art in letters consists rather in th
e art of arranging and composing them in a pleasing and appropriate man
ner. The main purpose of letters is the practical one of making thoughts vis
ible. Ruskin says that all letters are frightful things and to be endured only
on occasion, that is to say, in places where the sense of the inscription is of
The main purpose of letters is the practical one of making thoughts visible. R
uskin says that all letters are frightful things and to be endured only on occa
The main purpose of letters is the practical one of making thoughts vis
ible. Ruskin says that all letters are frightful things and to be endured o

7/8

The main purpose of letters is the practical one of making thoughts visible.
Ruskin says that all letters are frightful things and to be endured only on oc
casion, that is to say, in places where the sense of the inscription is of more
importance than external ornament. This is a sweeping statement, from w
hich we need not suffer unduly; yet it is doubtful whether there is art in ind
ividual letters. Letters in combination may be satisfying and in a well com
posed page even beautiful as a whole, but art in letters consists rather in th
e art of arranging and composing them in a pleasing and appropriate man
ner. The main purpose of letters is the practical one of making thoughts vis
ible. Ruskin says that all letters are frightful things and to be endured only
The main purpose of letters is the practical one of making thoughts visible. R
uskin says that all letters are frightful things and to be endured only on occa
The main purpose of letters is the practical one of making thoughts vis
ible. Ruskin says that all letters are frightful things and to be endured o

7/9

The main purpose of letters is the practical one of making thoughts visible.
Ruskin says that all letters are frightful things and to be endured only on oc
casion, that is to say, in places where the sense of the inscription is of more
importance than external ornament. This is a sweeping statement, from w
hich we need not suffer unduly; yet it is doubtful whether there is art in ind
ividual letters. Letters in combination may be satisfying and in a well com
posed page even beautiful as a whole, but art in letters consists rather in th
e art of arranging and composing them in a pleasing and appropriate man
ner. The main purpose of letters is the practical one of making thoughts vis
ible. Ruskin says that all letters are frightful things and to be endured only
The main purpose of letters is the practical one of making thoughts visible. R
uskin says that all letters are frightful things and to be endured only on occa
The main purpose of letters is the practical one of making thoughts vis
ible. Ruskin says that all letters are frightful things and to be endured o

7/10

The main purpose of letters is the practical one of making thoughts visible.
Ruskin says that all letters are frightful things and to be endured only on oc
casion, that is to say, in places where the sense of the inscription is of more
importance than external ornament. This is a sweeping statement, from w
hich we need not suffer unduly; yet it is doubtful whether there is art in ind
ividual letters. Letters in combination may be satisfying and in a well com
posed page even beautiful as a whole, but art in letters consists rather in th
e art of arranging and composing them in a pleasing and appropriate man
ner. The main purpose of letters is the practical one of making thoughts vis
The main purpose of letters is the practical one of making thoughts visible. R
uskin says that all letters are frightful things and to be endured only on occa
The main purpose of letters is the practical one of making thoughts vis
ible. Ruskin says that all letters are frightful things and to be endured o

WALBAUM 8 & 9 POINT SET NORMAL

ROMAN, ITALIC, BOLD, BOLD ITALIC

ABCDEFGHIJKLMNOPQRSTUVWXYZ 1234567890 abcdefghijklmnopqrstuvwxyz
ABCDEFGHIJKLMNOPQRSTUVWXYZ 1234567890 abcdefghijklmnopqrstuvwxyz
ABCDEFGHIJKLMNOPQRSTUVWXYZ 1234567890 abcdefghijklmnopqrstuvwxyz
ABCDEFGHIJKLMNOPQRSTUVWXYZ 1234567890 abcdefghijklmnopqrstuvwxyz

8/8

The main purpose of letters is the practical one of making though ts visible. Ruskin says that all letters are frightful things and to be endured only on occasion, that is to say, in places where the sense of the inscription is of more importance than external ornament. This is a sweeping statement, from which we need not suffer und uly; yet it is doubtful whether there is art in individual letters. Let ters in combination may be satisfying and in a well composed pa ge even beautiful as a whole, but art in letters consists rather in t he art of arranging and composing them in a pleasing and appro
The main purpose of letters is the practical one of making thoughts visible. Ruskin says that all letters are frightful things and to be en
The main purpose of letters is the practical one of making tho ughts visible. Ruskin says that all letters are frightful things a

8/9

The main purpose of letters is the practical one of making though ts visible. Ruskin says that all letters are frightful things and to be endured only on occasion, that is to say, in places where the sense of the inscription is of more importance than external ornament. This is a sweeping statement, from which we need not suffer und uly; yet it is doubtful whether there is art in individual letters. Let ters in combination may be satisfying and in a well composed pa ge even beautiful as a whole, but art in letters consists rather in t
The main purpose of letters is the practical one of making thoughts visible. Ruskin says that all letters are frightful things and to be en
The main purpose of letters is the practical one of making tho ughts visible. Ruskin says that all letters are frightful things a

8/10

The main purpose of letters is the practical one of making though ts visible. Ruskin says that all letters are frightful things and to be endured only on occasion, that is to say, in places where the sense of the inscription is of more importance than external ornament. This is a sweeping statement, from which we need not suffer und uly; yet it is doubtful whether there is art in individual letters. Let ters in combination may be satisfying and in a well composed pa
The main purpose of letters is the practical one of making thoughts visible. Ruskin says that all letters are frightful things and to be en
The main purpose of letters is the practical one of making tho ughts visible. Ruskin says that all letters are frightful things a

8/11

The main purpose of letters is the practical one of making though ts visible. Ruskin says that all letters are frightful things and to be endured only on occasion, that is to say, in places where the sense of the inscription is of more importance than external ornament. This is a sweeping statement, from which we need not suffer und uly; yet it is doubtful whether there is art in individual letters. Let ters in combination may be satisfying and in a well composed pa
The main purpose of letters is the practical one of making thoughts visible. Ruskin says that all letters are frightful things and to be en
The main purpose of letters is the practical one of making tho ughts visible. Ruskin says that all letters are frightful things a

---

ABCDEFGHIJKLMNOPQRSTUVWXYZ 1234567890 abcdefghijklmnopqrstuvwxyz
ABCDEFGHIJKLMNOPQRSTUVWXYZ 1234567890 abcdefghijklmnopqrstuvwxyz
ABCDEFGHIJKLMNOPQRSTUVWXYZ 1234567890 abcdefghijklmnopqrstuvwxyz
ABCDEFGHIJKLMNOPQRSTUVWXYZ 1234567890 abcdefghijklmnopqrstuvwxyz

9/9

The main purpose of letters is the practical one of making thoughts visible. Ruskin says that all letters are frightful t hings and to be endured only on occasion, that is to say, in places where the sense of the inscription is of more impor tance than external ornament. This is a sweeping stateme nt, from which we need not suffer unduly; yet it is doubtfu l whether there is art in individual letters. Letters in comb ination may be satisfying and in a well composed page eve
The main purpose of letters is the practical one of making t houghts visible. Ruskin says that all letters are frightful thi
The main purpose of letters is the practical one of maki ng thoughts visible. Ruskin says that all letters are frig

9/10

The main purpose of letters is the practical one of making thoughts visible. Ruskin says that all letters are frightful t hings and to be endured only on occasion, that is to say, in places where the sense of the inscription is of more impor tance than external ornament. This is a sweeping stateme nt, from which we need not suffer unduly; yet it is doubtfu l whether there is art in individual letters. Letters in comb
The main purpose of letters is the practical one of making t houghts visible. Ruskin says that all letters are frightful thi
The main purpose of letters is the practical one of maki ng thoughts visible. Ruskin says that all letters are frig

9/11

The main purpose of letters is the practical one of making thoughts visible. Ruskin says that all letters are frightful t hings and to be endured only on occasion, that is to say, in places where the sense of the inscription is of more impor tance than external ornament. This is a sweeping stateme nt, from which we need not suffer unduly; yet it is doubtfu l whether there is art in individual letters. Letters in comb
The main purpose of letters is the practical one of making t houghts visible. Ruskin says that all letters are frightful thi
The main purpose of letters is the practical one of maki ng thoughts visible. Ruskin says that all letters are frig

9/12

The main purpose of letters is the practical one of making thoughts visible. Ruskin says that all letters are frightful t hings and to be endured only on occasion, that is to say, in places where the sense of the inscription is of more impor tance than external ornament. This is a sweeping stateme nt, from which we need not suffer unduly; yet it is doubtfu l whether there is art in individual letters. Letters in comb
The main purpose of letters is the practical one of making t houghts visible. Ruskin says that all letters are frightful thi
The main purpose of letters is the practical one of maki ng thoughts visible. Ruskin says that all letters are frig

WALBAUM 10 POINT SET MINUS ½ UNIT

ROMAN, ITALIC, BOLD, BOLD ITALIC

abcdefghijklmnopqrstuvwxyz – 1 UNIT
abcdefghijklmnopqrstuvwxyz – ½ UNIT
abcdefghijklmnopqrstuvwxyz NORMAL

ABCDEFGHIJKLMNOPQRSTUVWXYZ 1234567890 abcdefghijklmnopqrstuvwxyz
ABCDEFGHIJKLMNOPQRSTUVWXYZ 1234567890 abcdefghijklmnopqrstuvwxyz
ABCDEFGHIJKLMNOPQRSTUVWXYZ 1234567890 abcdefghijklmnopqrstuvwxyz
ABCDEFGHIJKLMNOPQRSTUVWXYZ 1234567890 abcdefghijklmnopqrstuvwxyz

10/10

The main purpose of letters is the practical one of mak ing thoughts visible. Ruskin says that all letters are frig htful things and to be endured only on occasion, that is to say, in places where the sense of the inscription is of more importance than external ornament. This is a s weeping statement, from which we need not suffer un duly; yet it is doubtful whether there is art in individua l letters. Letters in combination may be satisfying and in a well composed page even beautiful as a whole, bu t art in letters consists rather in the art of arranging an d composing them in a pleasing and appropriate man ner. The main purpose of letters is the practical one of making thoughts visible. Ruskin says that all letters ar e frightful things and to be endured only on occasion, t hat is to say, in places where the sense of the inscriptio n is of more importance than external ornament. This is a sweeping statement, from which we need not suff er unduly; yet it is doubtful whether there is art in indi vidual letters. Letters in combination may be satisfyin g and in a well composed page even beautiful as a who le, but art in letters consists rather in the art of arrangi ng and composing them in a pleasing and appropriate
The main purpose of letters is the practical one of maki ng thoughts visible. Ruskin says that all letters are frigh
The main purpose of letters is the practical one of making thoughts visible. Ruskin says that all letters

10/11

The main purpose of letters is the practical one of mak ing thoughts visible. Ruskin says that all letters are frig htful things and to be endured only on occasion, that is to say, in places where the sense of the inscription is of more importance than external ornament. This is a s weeping statement, from which we need not suffer un duly; yet it is doubtful whether there is art in individua l letters. Letters in combination may be satisfying and in a well composed page even beautiful as a whole, bu t art in letters consists rather in the art of arranging an d composing them in a pleasing and appropriate man ner. The main purpose of letters is the practical one of making thoughts visible. Ruskin says that all letters ar e frightful things and to be endured only on occasion, t hat is to say, in places where the sense of the inscriptio n is of more importance than external ornament. This is a sweeping statement, from which we need not suff er unduly; yet it is doubtful whether there is art in indi vidual letters. Letters in combination may be satisfyin g and in a well composed page even beautiful as a who
The main purpose of letters is the practical one of maki ng thoughts visible. Ruskin says that all letters are frigh
The main purpose of letters is the practical one of making thoughts visible. Ruskin says that all letters

10/12

The main purpose of letters is the practical one of mak ing thoughts visible. Ruskin says that all letters are frig htful things and to be endured only on occasion, that is to say, in places where the sense of the inscription is of more importance than external ornament. This is a s weeping statement, from which we need not suffer un duly; yet it is doubtful whether there is art in individua l letters. Letters in combination may be satisfying and in a well composed page even beautiful as a whole, bu t art in letters consists rather in the art of arranging an d composing them in a pleasing and appropriate man ner. The main purpose of letters is the practical one of making thoughts visible. Ruskin says that all letters ar e frightful things and to be endured only on occasion, t hat is to say, in places where the sense of the inscriptio n is of more importance than external ornament. This is a sweeping statement, from which we need not suff er unduly; yet it is doubtful whether there is art in indi
The main purpose of letters is the practical one of maki ng thoughts visible. Ruskin says that all letters are frigh
The main purpose of letters is the practical one of making thoughts visible. Ruskin says that all letters

10/13

The main purpose of letters is the practical one of mak ing thoughts visible. Ruskin says that all letters are frig htful things and to be endured only on occasion, that is to say, in places where the sense of the inscription is of more importance than external ornament. This is a s weeping statement, from which we need not suffer un duly; yet it is doubtful whether there is art in individua l letters. Letters in combination may be satisfying and in a well composed page even beautiful as a whole, bu t art in letters consists rather in the art of arranging an d composing them in a pleasing and appropriate man ner. The main purpose of letters is the practical one of making thoughts visible. Ruskin says that all letters ar e frightful things and to be endured only on occasion, t hat is to say, in places where the sense of the inscriptio n is of more importance than external ornament. This is a sweeping statement, from which we need not suff
The main purpose of letters is the practical one of maki ng thoughts visible. Ruskin says that all letters are frigh
The main purpose of letters is the practical one of making thoughts visible. Ruskin says that all letters

WALBAUM 11 POINT SET MINUS ½ UNIT

ROMAN, ITALIC, BOLD, BOLD ITALIC

abcdefghijklmnopqrstuvwxyz – 1 UNIT
abcdefghijklmnopqrstuvwxyz – ½ UNIT
abcdefghijklmnopqrstuvwxyz NORMAL

ABCDEFGHIJKLMNOPQRSTUVWXYZ 1234567890 abcdefghijklmnopqrstuvwxyz
ABCDEFGHIJKLMNOPQRSTUVWXYZ 1234567890 abcdefghijklmnopqrstuvwxyz
ABCDEFGHIJKLMNOPQRSTUVWXYZ 1234567890 abcdefghijklmnopqrstuvwxyz
ABCDEFGHIJKLMNOPQRSTUVWXYZ 1234567890 abcdefghijklmnopqrstuvwxyz

11/11

The main purpose of letters is the practical one o f making thoughts visible. Ruskin says that all lett ers are frightful things and to be endured only on occasion, that is to say, in places where the sense of the inscription is of more importance than ext ernal ornament. This is a sweeping statement, fr om which we need not suffer unduly; yet it is dou btful whether there is art in individual letters. Let ters in combination may be satisfying and in a we ll composed page even beautiful as a whole, but a rt in letters consists rather in the art of arranging and composing them in a pleasing and appropria te manner. The main purpose of letters is the pra ctical one of making thoughts visible. Ruskin say s that all letters are frightful things and to be end ured only on occasion, that is to say, in places wh ere the sense of the inscription is of more import ance than external ornament. This is a sweeping statement, from which we need not suffer undul

The main purpose of letters is the practical one of making thoughts visible. Ruskin says that all lette

The main purpose of letters is the practical on e of making thoughts visible. Ruskin says that

11/12

The main purpose of letters is the practical one o f making thoughts visible. Ruskin says that all lett ers are frightful things and to be endured only on occasion, that is to say, in places where the sense of the inscription is of more importance than ext ernal ornament. This is a sweeping statement, fr om which we need not suffer unduly; yet it is dou btful whether there is art in individual letters. Let ters in combination may be satisfying and in a we ll composed page even beautiful as a whole, but a rt in letters consists rather in the art of arranging and composing them in a pleasing and appropria te manner. The main purpose of letters is the pra ctical one of making thoughts visible. Ruskin say s that all letters are frightful things and to be end ured only on occasion, that is to say, in places wh ere the sense of the inscription is of more import ance than external ornament. This is a sweeping

The main purpose of letters is the practical one of making thoughts visible. Ruskin says that all lette

The main purpose of letters is the practical on e of making thoughts visible. Ruskin says that

11/13

The main purpose of letters is the practical one o f making thoughts visible. Ruskin says that all lett ers are frightful things and to be endured only on occasion, that is to say, in places where the sense of the inscription is of more importance than ext ernal ornament. This is a sweeping statement, fr om which we need not suffer unduly; yet it is dou btful whether there is art in individual letters. Let ters in combination may be satisfying and in a we ll composed page even beautiful as a whole, but a rt in letters consists rather in the art of arranging and composing them in a pleasing and appropria te manner. The main purpose of letters is the pra ctical one of making thoughts visible. Ruskin say s that all letters are frightful things and to be end ured only on occasion, that is to say, in places wh ere the sense of the inscription is of more import

The main purpose of letters is the practical one of making thoughts visible. Ruskin says that all lette

The main purpose of letters is the practical on e of making thoughts visible. Ruskin says that

11/14

The main purpose of letters is the practical one o f making thoughts visible. Ruskin says that all lett ers are frightful things and to be endured only on occasion, that is to say, in places where the sense of the inscription is of more importance than ext ernal ornament. This is a sweeping statement, fr om which we need not suffer unduly; yet it is dou btful whether there is art in individual letters. Let ters in combination may be satisfying and in a we ll composed page even beautiful as a whole, but a rt in letters consists rather in the art of arranging and composing them in a pleasing and appropria te manner. The main purpose of letters is the pra ctical one of making thoughts visible. Ruskin say s that all letters are frightful things and to be end ured only on occasion, that is to say, in places wh

The main purpose of letters is the practical one of making thoughts visible. Ruskin says that all lette

The main purpose of letters is the practical on e of making thoughts visible. Ruskin says that

WALBAUM 12 POINT SET MINUS ½ UNIT

ROMAN, ITALIC, BOLD, BOLD ITALIC

abcdefghijklmnopqrstuvwxyz – 1 UNIT
abcdefghijklmnopqrstuvwxyz – ½ UNIT
abcdefghijklmnopqrstuvwxyz NORMAL

ABCDEFGHIJKLMNOPQRSTUVWXYZ 1234567890 abcdefghijklmnopqrstuvwxyz
ABCDEFGHIJKLMNOPQRSTUVWXYZ 1234567890 abcdefghijklmnopqrstuvwxyz
ABCDEFGHIJKLMNOPQRSTUVWXYZ 1234567890 abcdefghijklmnopqrstuvwxyz
ABCDEFGHIJKLMNOPQRSTUVWXYZ 1234567890 abcdefghijklmnopqrstuvwxyz

12/12

The main purpose of letters is the practical on e of making thoughts visible. Ruskin says that all letters are frightful things and to be endure d only on occasion, that is to say, in places whe re the sense of the inscription is of more impo rtance than external ornament. This is a swe eping statement, from which we need not suf fer unduly; yet it is doubtful whether there is a rt in individual letters. Letters in combination may be satisfying and in a well composed pag e even beautiful as a whole, but art in letters c onsists rather in the art of arranging and com posing them in a pleasing and appropriate m anner. The main purpose of letters is the prac tical one of making thoughts visible. Ruskin s
The main purpose of letters is the practical one of making thoughts visible. Ruskin says that al
The main purpose of letters is the practical one of making thoughts visible. Ruskin say

12/13

The main purpose of letters is the practical on e of making thoughts visible. Ruskin says that all letters are frightful things and to be endure d only on occasion, that is to say, in places whe re the sense of the inscription is of more impo rtance than external ornament. This is a swe eping statement, from which we need not suf fer unduly; yet it is doubtful whether there is a rt in individual letters. Letters in combination may be satisfying and in a well composed pag e even beautiful as a whole, but art in letters c onsists rather in the art of arranging and com posing them in a pleasing and appropriate m anner. The main purpose of letters is the prac
The main purpose of letters is the practical one of making thoughts visible. Ruskin says that al
The main purpose of letters is the practical one of making thoughts visible. Ruskin say

12/14

The main purpose of letters is the practical on e of making thoughts visible. Ruskin says that all letters are frightful things and to be endure d only on occasion, that is to say, in places whe re the sense of the inscription is of more impo rtance than external ornament. This is a swe eping statement, from which we need not suf fer unduly; yet it is doubtful whether there is a rt in individual letters. Letters in combination may be satisfying and in a well composed pag e even beautiful as a whole, but art in letters c onsists rather in the art of arranging and com posing them in a pleasing and appropriate m anner. The main purpose of letters is the prac tical one of making thoughts visible. Ruskin s
The main purpose of letters is the practical one of making thoughts visible. Ruskin says that al
The main purpose of letters is the practical one of making thoughts visible. Ruskin say

12/15

The main purpose of letters is the practical on e of making thoughts visible. Ruskin says that all letters are frightful things and to be endure d only on occasion, that is to say, in places whe re the sense of the inscription is of more impo rtance than external ornament. This is a swe eping statement, from which we need not suf fer unduly; yet it is doubtful whether there is a rt in individual letters. Letters in combination may be satisfying and in a well composed pag e even beautiful as a whole, but art in letters c onsists rather in the art of arranging and com posing them in a pleasing and appropriate m anner. The main purpose of letters is the prac
The main purpose of letters is the practical one of making thoughts visible. Ruskin says that al
The main purpose of letters is the practical one of making thoughts visible. Ruskin say

WALBAUM 14 POINT SET MINUS ½ UNIT

ROMAN, ITALIC, BOLD, BOLD ITALIC

abcdefghijklmnopqrstuvwxyz – 1 UNIT
abcdefghijklmnopqrstuvwxyz – ½ UNIT
abcdefghijklmnopqrstuvwxyz NORMAL

ABCDEFGHIJKLMNOPQRSTUVWXYZ abcdefghijklmnopqrstuvwxyz
ABCDEFGHIJKLMNOPQRSTUVWXYZ abcdefghijklmnopqrstuvwxyz
ABCDEFGHIJKLMNOPQRSTUVWXYZ abcdefghijklmnopqrstuvwxyz
ABCDEFGHIJKLMNOPQRSTUVWXYZ abcdefghijklmnopqrstuvwxyz

14/14

The main purpose of letters is the prac
tical one of making thoughts visible. R
uskin says that all letters are frightful t
hings and to be endured only on occasi
on, that is to say, in places where the se
nse of the inscription is of more import
ance than external ornament. This is a
sweeping statement, from which we n
eed not suffer unduly; yet it is doubtful
whether there is art in individual letter
s. Letters in combination may be satisf
ying and in a well composed page even
beautiful as a whole, but art in letters c
The main purpose of letters is the practi
cal one of making thoughts visible. Rus
The main purpose of letters is the pr
actical one of making thoughts visib

14/15

The main purpose of letters is the prac
tical one of making thoughts visible. R
uskin says that all letters are frightful t
hings and to be endured only on occasi
on, that is to say, in places where the se
nse of the inscription is of more import
ance than external ornament. This is a
sweeping statement, from which we n
eed not suffer unduly; yet it is doubtful
whether there is art in individual letter
s. Letters in combination may be satisf
ying and in a well composed page even
The main purpose of letters is the practi
cal one of making thoughts visible. Rus
The main purpose of letters is the pr
actical one of making thoughts visib

14/16

The main purpose of letters is the prac
tical one of making thoughts visible. R
uskin says that all letters are frightful t
hings and to be endured only on occasi
on, that is to say, in places where the se
nse of the inscription is of more import
ance than external ornament. This is a
sweeping statement, from which we n
eed not suffer unduly; yet it is doubtful
whether there is art in individual letter
s. Letters in combination may be satisf
ying and in a well composed page even
beautiful as a whole, but art in letters c
The main purpose of letters is the practi
cal one of making thoughts visible. Rus
The main purpose of letters is the pr
actical one of making thoughts visib

14/17

The main purpose of letters is the prac
tical one of making thoughts visible. R
uskin says that all letters are frightful t
hings and to be endured only on occasi
on, that is to say, in places where the se
nse of the inscription is of more import
ance than external ornament. This is a
sweeping statement, from which we n
eed not suffer unduly; yet it is doubtful
whether there is art in individual letter
s. Letters in combination may be satisf
ying and in a well composed page even
The main purpose of letters is the practi
cal one of making thoughts visible. Rus
The main purpose of letters is the pr
actical one of making thoughts visib

WEISS 6 & 7 POINT SET NORMAL

ROMAN, ITALIC, BOLD, EXTRA BOLD

ABCDEFGHIJKLMNOPQRSTUVWXYZ 1234567890 abcdefghijklmnopqrstuvwxyz

ABCDEFGHIJKLMNOPQRSTUVWXYZ 1234567890 abcdefghijklmnopqrstuvwxyz

ABCDEFGHIJKLMNOPQRSTUVWXYZ 1234567890 abcdefghijklmnopqrstuvwxyz

ABCDEFGHIJKLMNOPQRSTUVWXYZ 1234567890 abcdefghijklmnopqrstuvwxyz

6/6

The main purpose of letters is the practical one of making thoughts visible. Ruskin says that all letters a re frightful things and to be endured only on occasion, that is to say, in places where the sense of the in scription is of more importance than external ornament. This is a sweeping statement, from which we need not suffer unduly; yet it is doubtful whether there is art in individual letters. Letters in combinati on may be satisfying and in a well composed page even beautiful as a whole, but art in letters consists r ather in the art of arranging and composing them in a pleasing and appropriate manner. The main purp ose of letters is the practical one of making thoughts visible. Ruskin says that all letters are frightful thi ngs and to be endured only on occasion, that is to say, in places where the sense of the inscription is of more importance than external ornament. This is a sweeping statement, from which we need not suffe r unduly; yet it is doubtful whether there is art in individual letters. Letters in combination may be sati sfying and in a well composed page even beautiful as a whole, but art in letters consists rather in the art of arranging and composing them in a pleasing and appropriate manner. The main purpose of letters is the practical one of making thoughts visible. Ruskin says that all letters are frightful things and to be en

The main purpose of letters is the practical one of making thoughts visible. Ruskin says that all letters are frightful things an d to be endured only on occasion, that is to say, in places where the sense of the inscription is of more importance than external

The main purpose of letters is the practical one of making thoughts visible. Ruskin says that all letter s are frightful things and to be endured only on occasion, that is to say, in places where th

6/7

The main purpose of letters is the practical one of making thoughts visible. Ruskin says that all letters a re frightful things and to be endured only on occasion, that is to say, in places where the sense of the in scription is of more importance than external ornament. This is a sweeping statement, from which we need not suffer unduly; yet it is doubtful whether there is art in individual letters. Letters in combinati on may be satisfying and in a well composed page even beautiful as a whole, but art in letters consists r ather in the art of arranging and composing them in a pleasing and appropriate manner. The main purp ose of letters is the practical one of making thoughts visible. Ruskin says that all letters are frightful thi ngs and to be endured only on occasion, that is to say, in places where the sense of the inscription is of more importance than external ornament. This is a sweeping statement, from which we need not suffe r unduly; yet it is doubtful whether there is art in individual letters. Letters in combination may be sati sfying and in a well composed page even beautiful as a whole, but art in letters consists rather in the art

The main purpose of letters is the practical one of making thoughts visible. Ruskin says that all letters are frightful things an d to be endured only on occasion, that is to say, in places where the sense of the inscription is of more importance than external

The main purpose of letters is the practical one of making thoughts visible. Ruskin says that all letter s are frightful things and to be endured only on occasion, that is to say, in places where th

6/8

The main purpose of letters is the practical one of making thoughts visible. Ruskin says that all letters a re frightful things and to be endured only on occasion, that is to say, in places where the sense of the in scription is of more importance than external ornament. This is a sweeping statement, from which we need not suffer unduly; yet it is doubtful whether there is art in individual letters. Letters in combinati on may be satisfying and in a well composed page even beautiful as a whole, but art in letters consists r ather in the art of arranging and composing them in a pleasing and appropriate manner. The main purp ose of letters is the practical one of making thoughts visible. Ruskin says that all letters are frightful thi ngs and to be endured only on occasion, that is to say, in places where the sense of the inscription is of more importance than external ornament. This is a sweeping statement, from which we need not suffe

The main purpose of letters is the practical one of making thoughts visible. Ruskin says that all letters are frightful things an d to be endured only on occasion, that is to say, in places where the sense of the inscription is of more importance than external

The main purpose of letters is the practical one of making thoughts visible. Ruskin says that all letter s are frightful things and to be endured only on occasion, that is to say, in places where th

6/9

The main purpose of letters is the practical one of making thoughts visible. Ruskin says that all letters a re frightful things and to be endured only on occasion, that is to say, in places where the sense of the in scription is of more importance than external ornament. This is a sweeping statement, from which we need not suffer unduly; yet it is doubtful whether there is art in individual letters. Letters in combinati on may be satisfying and in a well composed page even beautiful as a whole, but art in letters consists r ather in the art of arranging and composing them in a pleasing and appropriate manner. The main purp ose of letters is the practical one of making thoughts visible. Ruskin says that all letters are frightful thi ngs and to be endured only on occasion, that is to say, in places where the sense of the inscription is of

The main purpose of letters is the practical one of making thoughts visible. Ruskin says that all letters are frightful things an d to be endured only on occasion, that is to say, in places where the sense of the inscription is of more importance than external

The main purpose of letters is the practical one of making thoughts visible. Ruskin says that all letter s are frightful things and to be endured only on occasion, that is to say, in places where th

ABCDEFGHIJKLMNOPQRSTUVWXYZ 1234567890 abcdefghijklmnopqrstuvwxyz

ABCDEFGHIJKLMNOPQRSTUVWXYZ 1234567890 abcdefghijklmnopqrstuvwxyz

ABCDEFGHIJKLMNOPQRSTUVWXYZ 1234567890 abcdefghijklmnopqrstuvwxyz

ABCDEFGHIJKLMNOPQRSTUVWXYZ 1234567890 abcdefghijklmnopqrstuvwxyz

7/7

The main purpose of letters is the practical one of making thoughts visible. Ruskin says that all letters are frightful things and to be endured only on occasion, that is to say, in pl aces where the sense of the inscription is of more importance than external ornament. T his is a sweeping statement, from which we need not suffer unduly; yet it is doubtful wh ether there is art in individual letters. Letters in combination may be satisfying and in a well composed page even beautiful as a whole, but art in letters consists rather in the art of arranging and composing them in a pleasing and appropriate manner. The main purp ose of letters is the practical one of making thoughts visible. Ruskin says that all letters a re frightful things and to be endured only on occasion, that is to say, in places where the sense of the inscription is of more importance than external ornament. This is a sweepin g statement, from which we need not suffer unduly; yet it is doubtful whether there is ar

The main purpose of letters is the practical one of making thoughts visible. Ruskin says that all letters are fr ightful things and to be endured only on occasion, that is to say, in places where the sense of the inscription i

The main purpose of letters is the practical one of making thoughts visible. Ruskin say s that all letters are frightful things and to be endured only on occasion, that is to say, i

7/8

The main purpose of letters is the practical one of making thoughts visible. Ruskin says that all letters are frightful things and to be endured only on occasion, that is to say, in pl aces where the sense of the inscription is of more importance than external ornament. T his is a sweeping statement, from which we need not suffer unduly; yet it is doubtful wh ether there is art in individual letters. Letters in combination may be satisfying and in a well composed page even beautiful as a whole, but art in letters consists rather in the art of arranging and composing them in a pleasing and appropriate manner. The main purp ose of letters is the practical one of making thoughts visible. Ruskin says that all letters a re frightful things and to be endured only on occasion, that is to say, in places where the sense of the inscription is of more importance than external ornament. This is a sweepin

The main purpose of letters is the practical one of making thoughts visible. Ruskin says that all letters are fr ightful things and to be endured only on occasion, that is to say, in places where the sense of the inscription i

The main purpose of letters is the practical one of making thoughts visible. Ruskin say s that all letters are frightful things and to be endured only on occasion, that is to say, i

7/9

The main purpose of letters is the practical one of making thoughts visible. Ruskin says that all letters are frightful things and to be endured only on occasion, that is to say, in pl aces where the sense of the inscription is of more importance than external ornament. T his is a sweeping statement, from which we need not suffer unduly; yet it is doubtful wh ether there is art in individual letters. Letters in combination may be satisfying and in a well composed page even beautiful as a whole, but art in letters consists rather in the art of arranging and composing them in a pleasing and appropriate manner. The main purp ose of letters is the practical one of making thoughts visible. Ruskin says that all letters a re frightful things and to be endured only on occasion, that is to say, in places where the sense of the inscription is of more importance than external ornament. This is a sweepin

The main purpose of letters is the practical one of making thoughts visible. Ruskin says that all letters are fr ightful things and to be endured only on occasion, that is to say in places where the sense of the inscription i

The main purpose of letters is the practical one of making thoughts visible. Ruskin say s that all letters are frightful things and to be endured only on occasion, that is to say, i

7/10

The main purpose of letters is the practical one of making thoughts visible. Ruskin says that all letters are frightful things and to be endured only on occasion, that is to say, in pl aces where the sense of the inscription is of more importance than external ornament. T his is a sweeping statement, from which we need not suffer unduly; yet it is doubtful wh ether there is art in individual letters. Letters in combination may be satisfying and in a well composed page even beautiful as a whole, but art in letters consists rather in the art of arranging and composing them in a pleasing and appropriate manner. The main purp ose of letters is the practical one of making thoughts visible. Ruskin says that all letters a re frightful things and to be endured only on occasion, that is to say, in places where the

The main purpose of letters is the practical one of making thoughts visible. Ruskin says that all letters are fr ightful things and to be endured only on occasion, that is to say, in places where the sense of the inscription i

The main purpose of letters is the practical one of making thoughts visible. Ruskin say s that all letters are frightful things and to be endured only on occasion, that is to say, i

WEISS 8 & 9 POINT SET NORMAL

ROMAN, ITALIC, BOLD, EXTRA BOLD

ABCDEFGHIJKLMNOPQRSTUVWXYZ 1234567890 abcdefghijklmnopqrstuvwxyz

ABCDEFGHIJKLMNOPQRSTUVWXYZ 1234567890 abcdefghijklmnopqrstuvwxyz

ABCDEFGHIJKLMNOPQRSTUVWXYZ 1234567890 abcdefghijklmnopqrstuvwxyz

ABCDEFGHIJKLMNOPQRSTUVWXYZ 1234567890 abcdefghijklmnopqrstuvwxyz

8/8

The main purpose of letters is the practical one of making thoughts visible. R uskin says that all letters are frightful things and to be endured only on occasi on, that is to say, in places where the sense of the inscription is of more impor tance than external ornament. This is a sweeping statement, from which we need not suffer unduly; yet it is doubtful whether there is art in individual let ters. Letters in combination may be satisfying and in a well composed page e ven beautiful as a whole, but art in letters consists rather in the art of arrangin g and composing them in a pleasing and appropriate manner. The main purp ose of letters is the practical one of making thoughts visible. Ruskin says that
The main purpose of letters is the practical one of making thoughts visible. Ruskin says that a ll letters are frightful things and to be endured only on occasion, that is to say, in places where
The main purpose of letters is the practical one of making thoughts visible. Ruskin says that all letters are frightful things and to be endured only on oc

8/9

The main purpose of letters is the practical one of making thoughts visible. R uskin says that all letters are frightful things and to be endured only on occasi on, that is to say, in places where the sense of the inscription is of more impor tance than external ornament. This is a sweeping statement, from which we need not suffer unduly; yet it is doubtful whether there is art in individual let ters. Letters in combination may be satisfying and in a well composed page e ven beautiful as a whole, but art in letters consists rather in the art of arrangin g and composing them in a pleasing and appropriate manner. The main purp
The main purpose of letters is the practical one of making thoughts visible. Ruskin says that a ll letters are frightful things and to be endured only on occasion, that is to say, in places where
The main purpose of letters is the practical one of making thoughts visible. Ruskin says that all letters are frightful things and to be endured only on oc

8/10

The main purpose of letters is the practical one of making thoughts visible. R uskin says that all letters are frightful things and to be endured only on occasi on, that is to say, in places where the sense of the inscription is of more impor tance than external ornament. This is a sweeping statement, from which we need not suffer unduly; yet it is doubtful whether there is art in individual let ters. Letters in combination may be satisfying and in a well composed page e ven beautiful as a whole, but art in letters consists rather in the art of arrangin
The main purpose of letters is the practical one of making thoughts visible. Ruskin says that a ll letters are frightful things and to be endured only on occasion, that is to say, in places where
The main purpose of letters is the practical one of making thoughts visible. Ruskin says that all letters are frightful things and to be endured only on oc

8/11

The main purpose of letters is the practical one of making thoughts visible. R uskin says that all letters are frightful things and to be endured only on occasi on, that is to say, in places where the sense of the inscription is of more impor tance than external ornament. This is a sweeping statement, from which we need not suffer unduly; yet it is doubtful whether there is art in individual let ters. Letters in combination may be satisfying and in a well composed page e ven beautiful as a whole, but art in letters consists rather in the art of arrangin
The main purpose of letters is the practical one of making thoughts visible. Ruskin says that a ll letters are frightful things and to be endured only on occasion, that is to say, in places where
The main purpose of letters is the practical one of making thoughts visible. Ruskin says that all letters are frightful things and to be endured only on oc

---

ABCDEFGHIJKLMNOPQRSTUVWXYZ 1234567890 abcdefghijklmnopqrstuvwxyz

ABCDEFGHIJKLMNOPQRSTUVWXYZ 1234567890 abcdefghijklmnopqrstuvwxyz

ABCDEFGHIJKLMNOPQRSTUVWXYZ 1234567890 abcdefghijklmnopqrstuvwxyz

ABCDEFGHIJKLMNOPQRSTUVWXYZ 1234567890 abcdefghijklmnopqrstuvwxyz

9/9

The main purpose of letters is the practical one of making thoughts v isible. Ruskin says that all letters are frightful things and to be endur ed only on occasion, that is to say, in places where the sense of the in scription is of more importance than external ornament. This is a sw eeping statement, from which we need not suffer unduly; yet it is do ubtful whether there is art in individual letters. Letters in combinati on may be satisfying and in a well composed page even beautiful as a whole, but art in letters consists rather in the art of arranging and co
The main purpose of letters is the practical one of making thoughts visible. Ruskin s ays that all letters are frightful things and to be endured only on occasion, that is to
The main purpose of letters is the practical one of making thoughts visible. Ruskin says that all letters are frightful things and to be end

9/10

The main purpose of letters is the practical one of making thoughts v isible. Ruskin says that all letters are frightful things and to be endur ed only on occasion, that is to say, in places where the sense of the in scription is of more importance than external ornament. This is a sw eeping statement, from which we need not suffer unduly; yet it is do ubtful whether there is art in individual letters. Letters in combinati on may be satisfying and in a well composed page even beautiful as a
The main purpose of letters is the practical one of making thoughts visible. Ruskin s ays that all letters are frightful things and to be endured only on occasion, that is to
The main purpose of letters is the practical one of making thoughts visible. Ruskin says that all letters are frightful things and to be end

9/11

The main purpose of letters is the practical one of making thoughts v isible. Ruskin says that all letters are frightful things and to be endur ed only on occasion, that is to say, in places where the sense of the in scription is of more importance than external ornament. This is a sw eeping statement, from which we need not suffer unduly; yet it is do ubtful whether there is art in individual letters. Letters in combinati on may be satisfying and in a well composed page even beautiful as a
The main purpose of letters is the practical one of making thoughts visible. Ruskin s ays that all letters are frightful things and to be endured only on occasion, that is to
The main purpose of letters is the practical one of making thoughts visible. Ruskin says that all letters are frightful things and to be end

9/12

The main purpose of letters is the practical one of making thoughts v isible. Ruskin says that all letters are frightful things and to be endur ed only on occasion, that is to say, in places where the sense of the in scription is of more importance than external ornament. This is a sw eeping statement, from which we need not suffer unduly; yet it is do ubtful whether there is art in individual letters. Letters in combinati on may be satisfying and in a well composed page even beautiful as a
The main purpose of letters is the practical one of making thoughts visible. Ruskin s ays that all letters are frightful things and to be endured only on occasion, that is to
The main purpose of letters is the practical one of making thoughts visible. Ruskin says that all letters are frightful things and to be end

WEISS 10 POINT SET MINUS ½ UNIT

ROMAN, ITALIC, BOLD, EXTRA BOLD

abcdefghijklmnopqrstuvwxyz – 1 UNIT
abcdefghijklmnopqrstuvwxyz – ½ UNIT
abcdefghijklmnopqrstuvwxyz NORMAL

ABCDEFGHIJKLMNOPQRSTUVWXYZ 1234567890 abcdefghijklmnopqrstuvwxyz
ABCDEFGHIJKLMNOPQRSTUVWXYZ 1234567890 abcdefghijklmnopqrstuvwxyz
ABCDEFGHIJKLMNOPQRSTUVWXYZ 1234567890 abcdefghijklmnopqrstuvwxyz
ABCDEFGHIJKLMNOPQRSTUVWXYZ 1234567890 abcdefghijklmnopqrstuvwxyz

10/10

The main purpose of letters is the practical one of making thoug
hts visible. Ruskin says that all letters are frightful things and to b
e endured only on occasion, that is to say, in places where the se
nse of the inscription is of more importance than external ornam
ent. This is a sweeping statement, from which we need not suffer
unduly; yet it is doubtful whether there is art in individual letters.
Letters in combination may be satisfying and in a well compose
d page even beautiful as a whole, but art in letters consists rather
in the art of arranging and composing them in a pleasing and app
ropriate manner. The main purpose of letters is the practical one
of making thoughts visible. Ruskin says that all letters are frightf
ul things and to be endured only on occasion, that is to say, in pl
aces where the sense of the inscription is of more importance tha
n external ornament. This is a sweeping statement, from which
we need not suffer unduly; yet it is doubtful whether there is art i
n individual letters. Letters in combination may be satisfying an
d in a well composed page even beautiful as a whole, but art in le
tters consists rather in the art of arranging and composing them i
n a pleasing and appropriate manner. The main purpose of letter
s is the practical one of making thoughts visible. Ruskin says that
all letters are frightful things and to be endured only on occasion,
that is to say, in places where the sense of the inscription is of m
*The main purpose of letters is the practical one of making thoughts visible. Rusk
in says that all letters are frightful things and to be endured only on occasion, t*
**The main purpose of letters is the practical one of making thou
ghts visible. Ruskin says that all letters are frightful things and t**

10/11

The main purpose of letters is the practical one of making thoug
hts visible. Ruskin says that all letters are frightful things and to b
e endured only on occasion, that is to say, in places where the se
nse of the inscription is of more importance than external ornam
ent. This is a sweeping statement, from which we need not suffer
unduly; yet it is doubtful whether there is art in individual letters.
Letters in combination may be satisfying and in a well compose
d page even beautiful as a whole, but art in letters consists rather
in the art of arranging and composing them in a pleasing and app
ropriate manner. The main purpose of letters is the practical one
of making thoughts visible. Ruskin says that all letters are frightf
ul things and to be endured only on occasion, that is to say, in pl
aces where the sense of the inscription is of more importance tha
n external ornament. This is a sweeping statement, from which
we need not suffer unduly; yet it is doubtful whether there is art i
n individual letters. Letters in combination may be satisfying an
d in a well composed page even beautiful as a whole, but art in le
tters consists rather in the art of arranging and composing them i
n a pleasing and appropriate manner. The main purpose of letter
s is the practical one of making thoughts visible. Ruskin says that
*The main purpose of letters is the practical one of making thoughts visible. Rusk
in says that all letters are frightful things and to be endured only on occasion, t*
**The main purpose of letters is the practical one of making thou
ghts visible. Ruskin says that all letters are frightful things and t**

10/12

The main purpose of letters is the practical one of making thoug
hts visible. Ruskin says that all letters are frightful things and to b
e endured only on occasion, that is to say, in places where the se
nse of the inscription is of more importance than external ornam
ent. This is a sweeping statement, from which we need not suffer
unduly; yet it is doubtful whether there is art in individual letters.
Letters in combination may be satisfying and in a well compose
d page even beautiful as a whole, but art in letters consists rather
in the art of arranging and composing them in a pleasing and app
ropriate manner. The main purpose of letters is the practical one
of making thoughts visible. Ruskin says that all letters are frightf
ul things and to be endured only on occasion, that is to say, in pl
aces where the sense of the inscription is of more importance tha
n external ornament. This is a sweeping statement, from which
we need not suffer unduly; yet it is doubtful whether there is art i
n individual letters. Letters in combination may be satisfying an
d in a well composed page even beautiful as a whole, but art in le
tters consists rather in the art of arranging and composing them i
*The main purpose of letters is the practical one of making thoughts visible. Rusk
in says that all letters are frightful things and to be endured only on occasion, t*
**The main purpose of letters is the practical one of making thou
ghts visible. Ruskin says that all letters are frightful things and t**

10/13

The main purpose of letters is the practical one of making thoug
hts visible. Ruskin says that all letters are frightful things and to b
e endured only on occasion, that is to say, in places where the se
nse of the inscription is of more importance than external ornam
ent. This is a sweeping statement, from which we need not suffer
unduly; yet it is doubtful whether there is art in individual letters.
Letters in combination may be satisfying and in a well compose
d page even beautiful as a whole, but art in letters consists rather
in the art of arranging and composing them in a pleasing and app
ropriate manner. The main purpose of letters is the practical one
of making thoughts visible. Ruskin says that all letters are frightf
ul things and to be endured only on occasion, that is to say, in pl
aces where the sense of the inscription is of more importance tha
n external ornament. This is a sweeping statement, from which
we need not suffer unduly; yet it is doubtful whether there is art i
n individual letters. Letters in combination may be satisfying an
d in a well composed page even beautiful as a whole, but art in le
*The main purpose of letters is the practical one of making thoughts visible. Rusk
in says that all letters are frightful things and to be endured only on occasion, t*
**The main purpose of letters is the practical one of making thou
ghts visible. Ruskin says that all letters are frightful things and t**

WEISS 11 POINT SET MINUS ½ UNIT

ROMAN, ITALIC, BOLD, EXTRA BOLD

abcdefghijklmnopqrstuvwxyz – 1 UNIT
abcdefghijklmnopqrstuvwxyz – ½ UNIT
abcdefghijklmnopqrstuvwxyz NORMAL

ABCDEFGHIJKLMNOPQRSTUVWXYZ 1234567890 abcdefghijklmnopqrstuvwxyz
ABCDEFGHIJKLMNOPQRSTUVWXYZ 1234567890 abcdefghijklmnopqrstuvwxyz
ABCDEFGHIJKLMNOPQRSTUVWXYZ 1234567890 abcdefghijklmnopqrstuvwxyz
ABCDEFGHIJKLMNOPQRSTUVWXYZ 1234567890 abcdefghijklmnopqrstuvwxyz

11/11

The main purpose of letters is the practical one of making t houghts visible. Ruskin says that all letters are frightful thi ngs and to be endured only on occasion, that is to say, in p laces where the sense of the inscription is of more importa nce than external ornament. This is a sweeping statement, from which we need not suffer unduly; yet it is doubtful w hether there is art in individual letters. Letters in combinat ion may be satisfying and in a well composed page even be autiful as a whole, but art in letters consists rather in the ar t of arranging and composing them in a pleasing and appr opriate manner. The main purpose of letters is the practica l one of making thoughts visible. Ruskin says that all letter s are frightful things and to be endured only on occasion, t hat is to say, in places where the sense of the inscription is of more importance than external ornament. This is a swe eping statement, from which we need not suffer unduly; y et it is doubtful whether there is art in individual letters. Le tters in combination may be satisfying and in a well compo sed page even beautiful as a whole, but art in letters consis
The main purpose of letters is the practical one of making thoughts visib le. Ruskin says that all letters are frightful things and to be endured onl
The main purpose of letters is the practical one of making thoughts visible. Ruskin says that all letters are frightful t

11/12

The main purpose of letters is the practical one of making t houghts visible. Ruskin says that all letters are frightful thi ngs and to be endured only on occasion, that is to say, in p laces where the sense of the inscription is of more importa nce than external ornament. This is a sweeping statement, from which we need not suffer unduly; yet it is doubtful w hether there is art in individual letters. Letters in combinat ion may be satisfying and in a well composed page even be autiful as a whole, but art in letters consists rather in the ar t of arranging and composing them in a pleasing and appr opriate manner. The main purpose of letters is the practica l one of making thoughts visible. Ruskin says that all letter s are frightful things and to be endured only on occasion, t hat is to say, in places where the sense of the inscription is of more importance than external ornament. This is a swe eping statement, from which we need not suffer unduly; y et it is doubtful whether there is art in individual letters. Le tters in combination may be satisfying and in a well compo
The main purpose of letters is the practical one of making thoughts visib le. Ruskin says that all letters are frightful things and to be endured onl
The main purpose of letters is the practical one of making thoughts visible. Ruskin says that all letters are frightful t

11/13

The main purpose of letters is the practical one of making t houghts visible. Ruskin says that all letters are frightful thi ngs and to be endured only on occasion, that is to say, in p laces where the sense of the inscription is of more importa nce than external ornament. This is a sweeping statement, from which we need not suffer unduly; yet it is doubtful w hether there is art in individual letters. Letters in combinat ion may be satisfying and in a well composed page even be autiful as a whole, but art in letters consists rather in the ar t of arranging and composing them in a pleasing and appr opriate manner. The main purpose of letters is the practica l one of making thoughts visible. Ruskin says that all letter s are frightful things and to be endured only on occasion, t hat is to say, in places where the sense of the inscription is of more importance than external ornament. This is a swe eping statement, from which we need not suffer unduly; y et it is doubtful whether there is art in individual letters. Le
The main purpose of letters is the practical one of making thoughts visib le. Ruskin says that all letters are frightful things and to be endured onl
The main purpose of letters is the practical one of making thoughts visible. Ruskin says that all letters are frightful t

11/14

The main purpose of letters is the practical one of making t houghts visible. Ruskin says that all letters are frightful thi ngs and to be endured only on occasion, that is to say, in p laces where the sense of the inscription is of more importa nce than external ornament. This is a sweeping statement, from which we need not suffer unduly; yet it is doubtful w hether there is art in individual letters. Letters in combinat ion may be satisfying and in a well composed page even be autiful as a whole, but art in letters consists rather in the ar t of arranging and composing them in a pleasing and appr opriate manner. The main purpose of letters is the practica l one of making thoughts visible. Ruskin says that all letter s are frightful things and to be endured only on occasion, t hat is to say, in places where the sense of the inscription is of more importance than external ornament. This is a swe eping statement, from which we need not suffer unduly; y
The main purpose of letters is the practical one of making thoughts visib le. Ruskin says that all letters are frightful things and to be endured onl
The main purpose of letters is the practical one of making thoughts visible. Ruskin says that all letters are frightful t

WEISS 12 POINT SET MINUS ½ UNIT

ROMAN, ITALIC, BOLD, EXTRA BOLD

abcdefghijklmnopqrstuvwxyz – 1 UNIT
abcdefghijklmnopqrstuvwxyz – ½ UNIT
abcdefghijklmnopqrstuvwxyz NORMAL

ABCDEFGHIJKLMNOPQRSTUVWXYZ 1234567890 abcdefghijklmnopqrstuvwxyz
ABCDEFGHIJKLMNOPQRSTUVWXYZ 1234567890 abcdefghijklmnopqrstuvwxyz
ABCDEFGHIJKLMNOPQRSTUVWXYZ 1234567890 abcdefghijklmnopqrstuvwxyz
ABCDEFGHIJKLMNOPQRSTUVWXYZ 1234567890 abcdefghijklmnopqrstuvwxyz

12/12

The main purpose of letters is the practical one of maki ng thoughts visible. Ruskin says that all letters are frig htful things and to be endured only on occasion, that i s to say, in places where the sense of the inscription is o f more importance than external ornament. This is a s weeping statement, from which we need not suffer un duly; yet it is doubtful whether there is art in individua l letters. Letters in combination may be satisfying and i n a well composed page even beautiful as a whole, but art in letters consists rather in the art of arranging and composing them in a pleasing and appropriate manner. The main purpose of letters is the practical one of ma king thoughts visible. Ruskin says that all letters are fri ghtful things and to be endured only on occasion, that is to say, in places where the sense of the inscription is
The main purpose of letters is the practical one of making thoughts visible. Ruskin says that all letters are frightful things and to be end
The main purpose of letters is the practical one of ma king thoughts visible. Ruskin says that all letters are fr

12/13

The main purpose of letters is the practical one of maki ng thoughts visible. Ruskin says that all letters are frig htful things and to be endured only on occasion, that i s to say, in places where the sense of the inscription is o f more importance than external ornament. This is a s weeping statement, from which we need not suffer un duly; yet it is doubtful whether there is art in individua l letters. Letters in combination may be satisfying and i n a well composed page even beautiful as a whole, but art in letters consists rather in the art of arranging and composing them in a pleasing and appropriate manner. The main purpose of letters is the practical one of ma king thoughts visible. Ruskin says that all letters are fri ghtful things and to be endured only on occasion, that
The main purpose of letters is the practical one of making thoughts visible. Ruskin says that all letters are frightful things and to be end
The main purpose of letters is the practical one of ma king thoughts visible. Ruskin says that all letters are fr

12/14

The main purpose of letters is the practical one of maki ng thoughts visible. Ruskin says that all letters are frig htful things and to be endured only on occasion, that i s to say, in places where the sense of the inscription is o f more importance than external ornament. This is a s weeping statement, from which we need not suffer un duly; yet it is doubtful whether there is art in individua l letters. Letters in combination may be satisfying and i n a well composed page even beautiful as a whole, but art in letters consists rather in the art of arranging and composing them in a pleasing and appropriate manner. The main purpose of letters is the practical one of ma king thoughts visible. Ruskin says that all letters are fri ghtful things and to be endured only on occasion, that is to say, in places where the sense of the inscription is
The main purpose of letters is the practical one of making thoughts visible. Ruskin says that all letters are frightful things and to be end
The main purpose of letters is the practical one of ma king thoughts visible. Ruskin says that all letters are fr

12/15

The main purpose of letters is the practical one of maki ng thoughts visible. Ruskin says that all letters are frig htful things and to be endured only on occasion, that i s to say, in places where the sense of the inscription is o f more importance than external ornament. This is a s weeping statement, from which we need not suffer un duly; yet it is doubtful whether there is art in individua l letters. Letters in combination may be satisfying and i n a well composed page even beautiful as a whole, but art in letters consists rather in the art of arranging and composing them in a pleasing and appropriate manner. The main purpose of letters is the practical one of ma king thoughts visible. Ruskin says that all letters are fri ghtful things and to be endured only on occasion, that
The main purpose of letters is the practical one of making thoughts visible. Ruskin says that all letters are frightful things and to be end
The main purpose of letters is the practical one of ma king thoughts visible. Ruskin says that all letters are fr

WEISS 14 POINT SET MINUS ½ UNIT

ROMAN, ITALIC, BOLD, EXTRA BOLD

abcdefghijklmnopqrstuvwxyz – 1 UNIT

abcdefghijklmnopqrstuvwxyz – ½ UNIT

abcdefghijklmnopqrstuvwxyz NORMAL

ABCDEFGHIJKLMNOPQRSTUVWXYZ abcdefghijklmnopqrstuvwxyz

ABCDEFGHIJKLMNOPQRSTUVWXYZ abcdefghijklmnopqrstuvwxyz

ABCDEFGHIJKLMNOPQRSTUVWXYZ abcdefghijklmnopqrstuvwxyz

ABCDEFGHIJKLMNOPQRSTUVWXYZ abcdefghijklmnopqrstuvwxyz

14/14

The main purpose of letters is the practical on e of making thoughts visible. Ruskin says that all letters are frightful things and to be endure d only on occasion, that is to say, in places wh ere the sense of the inscription is of more impo rtance than external ornament. This is a swee ping statement, from which we need not suffe r unduly; yet it is doubtful whether there is art in individual letters. Letters in combination m ay be satisfying and in a well composed page e ven beautiful as a whole, but art in letters cons ists rather in the art of arranging and composi ng them in a pleasing and appropriate manner.

The main purpose of letters is the practical one of making thoughts visible. Ruskin says that all letters are frightful

The main purpose of letters is the practical o ne of making thoughts visible. Ruskin says th

14/15

The main purpose of letters is the practical on e of making thoughts visible. Ruskin says that all letters are frightful things and to be endure d only on occasion, that is to say, in places wh ere the sense of the inscription is of more impo rtance than external ornament. This is a swee ping statement, from which we need not suffe r unduly; yet it is doubtful whether there is art in individual letters. Letters in combination m ay be satisfying and in a well composed page e ven beautiful as a whole, but art in letters cons ists rather in the art of arranging and composi

The main purpose of letters is the practical one of making thoughts visible. Ruskin says that all letters are frightful

The main purpose of letters is the practical o ne of making thoughts visible. Ruskin says th

14/16

The main purpose of letters is the practical on e of making thoughts visible. Ruskin says that all letters are frightful things and to be endure d only on occasion, that is to say, in places wh ere the sense of the inscription is of more impo rtance than external ornament. This is a swee ping statement, from which we need not suffe r unduly; yet it is doubtful whether there is art in individual letters. Letters in combination m ay be satisfying and in a well composed page e ven beautiful as a whole, but art in letters cons ists rather in the art of arranging and composi ng them in a pleasing and appropriate manner.

The main purpose of letters is the practical one of making thoughts visible. Ruskin says that all letters are frightful

The main purpose of letters is the practical o ne of making thoughts visible. Ruskin says th

14/17

The main purpose of letters is the practical on e of making thoughts visible. Ruskin says that all letters are frightful things and to be endure d only on occasion, that is to say, in places wh ere the sense of the inscription is of more impo rtance than external ornament. This is a swee ping statement, from which we need not suffe r unduly; yet it is doubtful whether there is art in individual letters. Letters in combination m ay be satisfying and in a well composed page e ven beautiful as a whole, but art in letters cons ists rather in the art of arranging and composi

The main purpose of letters is the practical one of making thoughts visible. Ruskin says that all letters are frightful

The main purpose of letters is the practical o ne of making thoughts visible. Ruskin says th

ITC ZAPF INTERNATIONAL 6 & 7 POINT SET NORMAL

LIGHT, ITALIC, DEMI, DEMI ITALIC

ABCDEFGHIJKLMNOPQRSTUVWXYZ 1234567890 abcdefghijklmnopqrstuvwxyz

ABCDEFGHIJKLMNOPQRSTUVWXYZ 1234567890 abcdefghijklmnopqrstuvwxyz

ABCDEFGHIJKLMNOPQRSTUVWXYZ 1234567890 abcdefghijklmnopqrstuvwxyz

ABCDEFGHIJKLMNOPQRSTUVWXYZ 1234567890 abcdefghijklmnopqrstuvwxyz

6/6

The main purpose of letters is the practical one of making thoughts visible. Ruskin says that all let ters are frightful things and to be endured only on occasion, that is to say, in places where the sens e of the inscription is of more importance than external ornament. This is a sweeping statement, from which we need not suffer unduly; yet it is doubtful whether there is art in individual letters. Letters in combination may be satisfying and in a well composed page even beautiful as a whole, but art in letters consists rather in the art of arranging and composing them in a pleasing and app ropriate manner. The main purpose of letters is the practical one of making thoughts visible. Rusk in says that all letters are frightful things and to be endured only on occasion, that is to say, in plac es where the sense of the inscription is of more importance than external ornament. This is a swe eping statement, from which we need not suffer unduly; yet it is doubtful whether there is art in i ndividual letters. Letters in combination may be satisfying and in a well composed page even bea utiful as a whole, but art in letters consists rather in the art of arranging and composing them in a pleasing and appropriate manner. The main purpose of letters is the practical one of making thou
The main purpose of letters is the practical one of making thoughts visible. Ruskin says that all lett ers are frightful things and to be endured only on occasion, that is to say, in places where the sense of
The main purpose of letters is the practical one of making thoughts visible. Ruskin says t hat all letters are frightful things and to be endured only on occasion, that is to say, in plac

6/7

The main purpose of letters is the practical one of making thoughts visible. Ruskin says that all let ters are frightful things and to be endured only on occasion, that is to say, in places where the sens e of the inscription is of more importance than external ornament. This is a sweeping statement, from which we need not suffer unduly; yet it is doubtful whether there is art in individual letters. Letters in combination may be satisfying and in a well composed page even beautiful as a whole, but art in letters consists rather in the art of arranging and composing them in a pleasing and app ropriate manner. The main purpose of letters is the practical one of making thoughts visible. Rusk in says that all letters are frightful things and to be endured only on occasion, that is to say, in plac es where the sense of the inscription is of more importance than external ornament. This is a swe eping statement, from which we need not suffer unduly; yet it is doubtful whether there is art in i ndividual letters. Letters in combination may be satisfying and in a well composed page even bea
The main purpose of letters is the practical one of making thoughts visible. Ruskin says that all lett ers are frightful things and to be endured only on occasion, that is to say, in places where the sense of
The main purpose of letters is the practical one of making thoughts visible. Ruskin says t hat all letters are frightful things and to be endured only on occasion, that is to say, in plac

6/8

The main purpose of letters is the practical one of making thoughts visible. Ruskin says that all let ters are frightful things and to be endured only on occasion, that is to say, in places where the sens e of the inscription is of more importance than external ornament. This is a sweeping statement, from which we need not suffer unduly; yet it is doubtful whether there is art in individual letters. Letters in combination may be satisfying and in a well composed page even beautiful as a whole, but art in letters consists rather in the art of arranging and composing them in a pleasing and app ropriate manner. The main purpose of letters is the practical one of making thoughts visible. Rusk in says that all letters are frightful things and to be endured only on occasion, that is to say, in plac es where the sense of the inscription is of more importance than external ornament. This is a swe
The main purpose of letters is the practical one of making thoughts visible. Ruskin says that all lett ers are frightful things and to be endured only on occasion, that is to say, in places where the sense of
The main purpose of letters is the practical one of making thoughts visible. Ruskin says t hat all letters are frightful things and to be endured only on occasion, that is to say, in plac

6/9

The main purpose of letters is the practical one of making thoughts visible. Ruskin says that all let ters are frightful things and to be endured only on occasion, that is to say, in places where the sens e of the inscription is of more importance than external ornament. This is a sweeping statement, from which we need not suffer unduly; yet it is doubtful whether there is art in individual letters. Letters in combination may be satisfying and in a well composed page even beautiful as a whole, but art in letters consists rather in the art of arranging and composing them in a pleasing and app ropriate manner. The main purpose of letters is the practical one of making thoughts visible. Rusk in says that all letters are frightful things and to be endured only on occasion, that is to say, in plac
The main purpose of letters is the practical one of making thoughts visible. Ruskin says that all lett ers are frightful things and to be endured only on occasion, that is to say, in places where the sense of
The main purpose of letters is the practical one of making thoughts visible. Ruskin says t hat all letters are frightful things and to be endured only on occasion, that is to say, in plac

---

ABCDEFGHIJKLMNOPQRSTUVWXYZ 1234567890 abcdefghijklmnopqrstuvwxyz

ABCDEFGHIJKLMNOPQRSTUVWXYZ 1234567890 abcdefghijklmnopqrstuvwxyz

ABCDEFGHIJKLMNOPQRSTUVWXYZ 1234567890 abcdefghijklmnopqrstuvwxyz

ABCDEFGHIJKLMNOPQRSTUVWXYZ 1234567890 abcdefghijklmnopqrstuvwxyz

7/7

The main purpose of letters is the practical one of making thoughts visible. Ruskin s ays that all letters are frightful things and to be endured only on occasion, that is to s ay, in places where the sense of the inscription is of more importance than external ornament. This is a sweeping statement, from which we need not suffer unduly; yet it is doubtful whether there is art in individual letters. Letters in combination may be satisfying and in a well composed page even beautiful as a whole, but art in lette rs consists rather in the art of arranging and composing them in a pleasing and app ropriate manner. The main purpose of letters is the practical one of making thought s visible. Ruskin says that all letters are frightful things and to be endured only on oc casion, that is to say, in places where the sense of the inscription is of more importa nce than external ornament. This is a sweeping statement, from which we need not
The main purpose of letters is the practical one of making thoughts visible. Ruskin sa ys that all letters are frightful things and to be endured only on occasion, that is to sa
The main purpose of letters is the practical one of making thoughts visible. Ruskin says that all letters are frightful things and to be endured only on occ

7/8

The main purpose of letters is the practical one of making thoughts visible. Ruskin s ays that all letters are frightful things and to be endured only on occasion, that is to s ay, in places where the sense of the inscription is of more importance than external ornament. This is a sweeping statement, from which we need not suffer unduly; yet it is doubtful whether there is art in individual letters. Letters in combination may be satisfying and in a well composed page even beautiful as a whole, but art in lette rs consists rather in the art of arranging and composing them in a pleasing and app ropriate manner. The main purpose of letters is the practical one of making thought s visible. Ruskin says that all letters are frightful things and to be endured only on oc casion, that is to say, in places where the sense of the inscription is of more importa
The main purpose of letters is the practical one of making thoughts visible. Ruskin sa ys that all letters are frightful things and to be endured only on occasion, that is to sa
The main purpose of letters is the practical one of making thoughts visible. Ruskin says that all letters are frightful things and to be endured only on occ

7/9

The main purpose of letters is the practical one of making thoughts visible. Ruskin s ays that all letters are frightful things and to be endured only on occasion, that is to s ay, in places where the sense of the inscription is of more importance than external ornament. This is a sweeping statement, from which we need not suffer unduly; yet it is doubtful whether there is art in individual letters. Letters in combination may be satisfying and in a well composed page even beautiful as a whole, but art in lette rs consists rather in the art of arranging and composing them in a pleasing and app ropriate manner. The main purpose of letters is the practical one of making thought s visible. Ruskin says that all letters are frightful things and to be endured only on oc casion, that is to say, in places where the sense of the inscription is of more importa
The main purpose of letters is the practical one of making thoughts visible. Ruskin sa ys that all letters are frightful things and to be endured only on occasion, that is to sa
The main purpose of letters is the practical one of making thoughts visible. Ruskin says that all letters are frightful things and to be endured only on occ

7/10

The main purpose of letters is the practical one of making thoughts visible. Ruskin s ays that all letters are frightful things and to be endured only on occasion, that is to s ay, in places where the sense of the inscription is of more importance than external ornament. This is a sweeping statement, from which we need not suffer unduly; yet it is doubtful whether there is art in individual letters. Letters in combination may be satisfying and in a well composed page even beautiful as a whole, but art in lette rs consists rather in the art of arranging and composing them in a pleasing and app ropriate manner. The main purpose of letters is the practical one of making thought s visible. Ruskin says that all letters are frightful things and to be endured only on oc
The main purpose of letters is the practical one of making thoughts visible. Ruskin sa ys that all letters are frightful things and to be endured only on occasion, that is to sa
The main purpose of letters is the practical one of making thoughts visible. Ruskin says that all letters are frightful things and to be endured only on occ

ITC ZAPF INTERNATIONAL 8 & 9 POINT SET NORMAL

LIGHT, ITALIC, DEMI, DEMI ITALIC

ABCDEFGHIJKLMNOPQRSTUVWXYZ 1234567890 abcdefghijklmnopqrstuvwxyz

ABCDEFGHIJKLMNOPQRSTUVWXYZ 1234567890 abcdefghijklmnopqrstuvwxyz

ABCDEFGHIJKLMNOPQRSTUVWXYZ 1234567890 abcdefghijklmnopqrstuvwxyz

ABCDEFGHIJKLMNOPQRSTUVWXYZ 1234567890 abcdefghijklmnopqrstuvwxyz

8/8

The main purpose of letters is the practical one of making thoughts visibl e. Ruskin says that all letters are frightful things and to be endured only o n occasion, that is to say, in places where the sense of the inscription is of more importance than external ornament. This is a sweeping statement, from which we need not suffer unduly; yet it is doubtful whether there is art in individual letters. Letters in combination may be satisfying and in a well composed page even beautiful as a whole, but art in letters consist s rather in the art of arranging and composing them in a pleasing and ap propriate manner. The main purpose of letters is the practical one of mak
The main purpose of letters is the practical one of making thoughts visible. Ruskin says that all letters are frightful things and to be endured only on o
The main purpose of letters is the practical one of making thought s visible. Ruskin says that all letters are frightful things and to be e

8/9

The main purpose of letters is the practical one of making thoughts visibl e. Ruskin says that all letters are frightful things and to be endured only o n occasion, that is to say, in places where the sense of the inscription is of more importance than external ornament. This is a sweeping statement, from which we need not suffer unduly; yet it is doubtful whether there is art in individual letters. Letters in combination may be satisfying and in a well composed page even beautiful as a whole, but art in letters consist s rather in the art of arranging and composing them in a pleasing and ap
The main purpose of letters is the practical one of making thoughts visible. Ruskin says that all letters are frightful things and to be endured only on o
The main purpose of letters is the practical one of making thought s visible. Ruskin says that all letters are frightful things and to be e

8/10

The main purpose of letters is the practical one of making thoughts visibl e. Ruskin says that all letters are frightful things and to be endured only o n occasion, that is to say, in places where the sense of the inscription is of more importance than external ornament. This is a sweeping statement, from which we need not suffer unduly; yet it is doubtful whether there is art in individual letters. Letters in combination may be satisfying and in a well composed page even beautiful as a whole, but art in letters consist
The main purpose of letters is the practical one of making thoughts visible. Ruskin says that all letters are frightful things and to be endured only on o
The main purpose of letters is the practical one of making thought s visible. Ruskin says that all letters are frightful things and to be e

8/11

The main purpose of letters is the practical one of making thoughts visibl e. Ruskin says that all letters are frightful things and to be endured only o n occasion, that is to say, in places where the sense of the inscription is of more importance than external ornament. This is a sweeping statement, from which we need not suffer unduly; yet it is doubtful whether there is art in individual letters. Letters in combination may be satisfying and in a well composed page even beautiful as a whole, but art in letters consist
The main purpose of letters is the practical one of making thoughts visible. Ruskin says that all letters are frightful things and to be endured only on o
The main purpose of letters is the practical one of making thought s visible. Ruskin says that all letters are frightful things and to be e

---

ABCDEFGHIJKLMNOPQRSTUVWXYZ 1234567890 abcdefghijklmnopqrstuvwxyz

ABCDEFGHIJKLMNOPQRSTUVWXYZ 1234567890 abcdefghijklmnopqrstuvwxyz

ABCDEFGHIJKLMNOPQRSTUVWXYZ 1234567890 abcdefghijklmnopqrstuvwxyz

ABCDEFGHIJKLMNOPQRSTUVWXYZ 1234567890 abcdefghijklmnopqrstuvwxyz

9/9

The main purpose of letters is the practical one of making thoug hts visible. Ruskin says that all letters are frightful things and to b e endured only on occasion, that is to say, in places where the sens e of the inscription is of more importance than external ornamen t. This is a sweeping statement, from which we need not suffer u nduly; yet it is doubtful whether there is art in individual letters. Letters in combination may be satisfying and in a well composed page even beautiful as a whole, but art in letters consists rather i
The main purpose of letters is the practical one of making thought s visible. Ruskin says that all letters are frightful things and to be e
The main purpose of letters is the practical one of making t houghts visible. Ruskin says that all letters are frightful thi

9/10

The main purpose of letters is the practical one of making thoug hts visible. Ruskin says that all letters are frightful things and to b e endured only on occasion, that is to say, in places where the sens e of the inscription is of more importance than external ornamen t. This is a sweeping statement, from which we need not suffer u nduly; yet it is doubtful whether there is art in individual letters. Letters in combination may be satisfying and in a well composed
The main purpose of letters is the practical one of making thought s visible. Ruskin says that all letters are frightful things and to be e
The main purpose of letters is the practical one of making t houghts visible. Ruskin says that all letters are frightful thi

9/11

The main purpose of letters is the practical one of making thoug hts visible. Ruskin says that all letters are frightful things and to b e endured only on occasion, that is to say, in places where the sens e of the inscription is of more importance than external ornamen t. This is a sweeping statement, from which we need not suffer u nduly; yet it is doubtful whether there is art in individual letters. Letters in combination may be satisfying and in a well composed
The main purpose of letters is the practical one of making thought s visible. Ruskin says that all letters are frightful things and to be e
The main purpose of letters is the practical one of making t houghts visible. Ruskin says that all letters are frightful thi

9/12

The main purpose of letters is the practical one of making thoug hts visible. Ruskin says that all letters are frightful things and to b e endured only on occasion, that is to say, in places where the sens e of the inscription is of more importance than external ornamen t. This is a sweeping statement, from which we need not suffer u nduly; yet it is doubtful whether there is art in individual letters. Letters in combination may be satisfying and in a well composed
The main purpose of letters is the practical one of making thought s visible. Ruskin says that all letters are frightful things and to be e
The main purpose of letters is the practical one of making t houghts visible. Ruskin says that all letters are frightful thi

ITC ZAPF INTERNATIONAL 10 POINT SET MINUS ½ UNIT

LIGHT, ITALIC, DEMI, DEMI ITALIC

abcdefghijklmnopqrstuvwxyz – 1 UNIT
abcdefghijklmnopqrstuvwxyz – ½ UNIT
abcdefghijklmnopqrstuvwxyz NORMAL

ABCDEFGHIJKLMNOPQRSTUVWXYZ 1234567890 abcdefghijklmnopqrstuvwxyz
ABCDEFGHIJKLMNOPQRSTUVWXYZ 1234567890 abcdefghijklmnopqrstuvwxyz
ABCDEFGHIJKLMNOPQRSTUVWXYZ 1234567890 abcdefghijklmnopqrstuvwxyz
ABCDEFGHIJKLMNOPQRSTUVWXYZ 1234567890 abcdefghijklmnopqrstuvwxyz

10/10

The main purpose of letters is the practical one of making tho ughts visible. Ruskin says that all letters are frightful things a nd to be endured only on occasion, that is to say, in places wh ere the sense of the inscription is of more importance than ex ternal ornament. This is a sweeping statement, from which we need not suffer unduly; yet it is doubtful whether there is art in individual letters. Letters in combination may be satisf ying and in a well composed page even beautiful as a whole, but art in letters consists rather in the art of arranging and co mposing them in a pleasing and appropriate manner. The m ain purpose of letters is the practical one of making thoughts visible. Ruskin says that all letters are frightful things and to b e endured only on occasion, that is to say, in places where the sense of the inscription is of more importance than external o rnament. This is a sweeping statement, from which we need not suffer unduly; yet it is doubtful whether there is art in ind ividual letters. Letters in combination may be satisfying and i n a well composed page even beautiful as a whole, but art in l etters consists rather in the art of arranging and composing t hem in a pleasing and appropriate manner. The main purpo se of letters is the practical one of making thoughts visible. Ru skin says that all letters are frightful things and to be endured
The main purpose of letters is the practical one of making tho ughts visible. Ruskin says that all letters are frightful things an
The main purpose of letters is the practical one of maki ng thoughts visible. Ruskin says that all letters are frigh

10/11

The main purpose of letters is the practical one of making tho ughts visible. Ruskin says that all letters are frightful things a nd to be endured only on occasion, that is to say, in places wh ere the sense of the inscription is of more importance than ex ternal ornament. This is a sweeping statement, from which we need not suffer unduly; yet it is doubtful whether there is art in individual letters. Letters in combination may be satisf ying and in a well composed page even beautiful as a whole, but art in letters consists rather in the art of arranging and co mposing them in a pleasing and appropriate manner. The m ain purpose of letters is the practical one of making thoughts visible. Ruskin says that all letters are frightful things and to b e endured only on occasion, that is to say, in places where the sense of the inscription is of more importance than external o rnament. This is a sweeping statement, from which we need not suffer unduly; yet it is doubtful whether there is art in ind ividual letters. Letters in combination may be satisfying and i n a well composed page even beautiful as a whole, but art in l etters consists rather in the art of arranging and composing t hem in a pleasing and appropriate manner. The main purpo
The main purpose of letters is the practical one of making tho ughts visible. Ruskin says that all letters are frightful things an
The main purpose of letters is the practical one of maki ng thoughts visible. Ruskin says that all letters are frigh

10/12

The main purpose of letters is the practical one of making tho ughts visible. Ruskin says that all letters are frightful things a nd to be endured only on occasion, that is to say, in places wh ere the sense of the inscription is of more importance than ex ternal ornament. This is a sweeping statement, from which we need not suffer unduly; yet it is doubtful whether there is art in individual letters. Letters in combination may be satisf ying and in a well composed page even beautiful as a whole, but art in letters consists rather in the art of arranging and co mposing them in a pleasing and appropriate manner. The m ain purpose of letters is the practical one of making thoughts visible. Ruskin says that all letters are frightful things and to b e endured only on occasion, that is to say, in places where the sense of the inscription is of more importance than external o rnament. This is a sweeping statement, from which we need not suffer unduly; yet it is doubtful whether there is art in ind ividual letters. Letters in combination may be satisfying and i n a well composed page even beautiful as a whole, but art in l
The main purpose of letters is the practical one of making tho ughts visible. Ruskin says that all letters are frightful things an
The main purpose of letters is the practical one of maki ng thoughts visible. Ruskin says that all letters are frigh

10/13

The main purpose of letters is the practical one of making tho ughts visible. Ruskin says that all letters are frightful things a nd to be endured only on occasion, that is to say, in places wh ere the sense of the inscription is of more importance than ex ternal ornament. This is a sweeping statement, from which we need not suffer unduly; yet it is doubtful whether there is art in individual letters. Letters in combination may be satisf ying and in a well composed page even beautiful as a whole, but art in letters consists rather in the art of arranging and co mposing them in a pleasing and appropriate manner. The m ain purpose of letters is the practical one of making thoughts visible. Ruskin says that all letters are frightful things and to b e endured only on occasion, that is to say, in places where the sense of the inscription is of more importance than external o rnament. This is a sweeping statement, from which we need not suffer unduly; yet it is doubtful whether there is art in ind ividual letters. Letters in combination may be satisfying and i
The main purpose of letters is the practical one of making tho ughts visible. Ruskin says that all letters are frightful things an
The main purpose of letters is the practical one of maki ng thoughts visible. Ruskin says that all letters are frigh

ITC ZAPF INTERNATIONAL 11 POINT SET MINUS ½ UNIT

LIGHT, ITALIC, DEMI, DEMI ITALIC

abcdefghijklmnopqrstuvwxyz – 1 UNIT
abcdefghijklmnopqrstuvwxyz – ½ UNIT
abcdefghijklmnopqrstuvwxyz NORMAL

ABCDEFGHIJKLMNOPQRSTUVWXYZ 1234567890 abcdefghijklmnopqrstuvwxyz
ABCDEFGHIJKLMNOPQRSTUVWXYZ 1234567890 abcdefghijklmnopqrstuvwxyz
ABCDEFGHIJKLMNOPQRSTUVWXYZ 1234567890 abcdefghijklmnopqrstuvwxyz
ABCDEFGHIJKLMNOPQRSTUVWXYZ 1234567890 abcdefghijklmnopqrstuvwxyz

11/11

The main purpose of letters is the practical one of maki ng thoughts visible. Ruskin says that all letters are frigh tful things and to be endured only on occasion, that is t o say, in places where the sense of the inscription is of m ore importance than external ornament. This is a swee ping statement, from which we need not suffer unduly; yet it is doubtful whether there is art in individual letter s. Letters in combination may be satisfying and in a wel l composed page even beautiful as a whole, but art in le tters consists rather in the art of arranging and compos ing them in a pleasing and appropriate manner. The m ain purpose of letters is the practical one of making tho ughts visible. Ruskin says that all letters are frightful thi ngs and to be endured only on occasion, that is to say, in places where the sense of the inscription is of more imp ortance than external ornament. This is a sweeping sta tement, from which we need not suffer unduly; yet it is doubtful whether there is art in individual letters. Lette rs in combination may be satisfying and in a well comp
The main purpose of letters is the practical one of makin g thoughts visible. Ruskin says that all letters are frightf
The main purpose of letters is the practical one of making thoughts visible. Ruskin says that all lette

11/12

The main purpose of letters is the practical one of maki ng thoughts visible. Ruskin says that all letters are frigh tful things and to be endured only on occasion, that is t o say, in places where the sense of the inscription is of m ore importance than external ornament. This is a swee ping statement, from which we need not suffer unduly; yet it is doubtful whether there is art in individual letter s. Letters in combination may be satisfying and in a wel l composed page even beautiful as a whole, but art in le tters consists rather in the art of arranging and compos ing them in a pleasing and appropriate manner. The m ain purpose of letters is the practical one of making tho ughts visible. Ruskin says that all letters are frightful thi ngs and to be endured only on occasion, that is to say, in places where the sense of the inscription is of more imp ortance than external ornament. This is a sweeping sta tement, from which we need not suffer unduly; yet it is doubtful whether there is art in individual letters. Lette
The main purpose of letters is the practical one of makin g thoughts visible. Ruskin says that all letters are frightf
The main purpose of letters is the practical one of making thoughts visible. Ruskin says that all lette

11/13

The main purpose of letters is the practical one of maki ng thoughts visible. Ruskin says that all letters are frigh tful things and to be endured only on occasion, that is t o say, in places where the sense of the inscription is of m ore importance than external ornament. This is a swee ping statement, from which we need not suffer unduly; yet it is doubtful whether there is art in individual letter s. Letters in combination may be satisfying and in a wel l composed page even beautiful as a whole, but art in le tters consists rather in the art of arranging and compos ing them in a pleasing and appropriate manner. The m ain purpose of letters is the practical one of making tho ughts visible. Ruskin says that all letters are frightful thi ngs and to be endured only on occasion, that is to say, in places where the sense of the inscription is of more imp ortance than external ornament. This is a sweeping sta tement, from which we need not suffer unduly; yet it is
The main purpose of letters is the practical one of makin g thoughts visible. Ruskin says that all letters are frightf
The main purpose of letters is the practical one of making thoughts visible. Ruskin says that all lette

11/14

The main purpose of letters is the practical one of maki ng thoughts visible. Ruskin says that all letters are frigh tful things and to be endured only on occasion, that is t o say, in places where the sense of the inscription is of m ore importance than external ornament. This is a swee ping statement, from which we need not suffer unduly; yet it is doubtful whether there is art in individual letter s. Letters in combination may be satisfying and in a wel l composed page even beautiful as a whole, but art in le tters consists rather in the art of arranging and compos ing them in a pleasing and appropriate manner. The m ain purpose of letters is the practical one of making tho ughts visible. Ruskin says that all letters are frightful thi ngs and to be endured only on occasion, that is to say, in places where the sense of the inscription is of more imp ortance than external ornament. This is a sweeping sta
The main purpose of letters is the practical one of makin g thoughts visible. Ruskin says that all letters are frightf
The main purpose of letters is the practical one of making thoughts visible. Ruskin says that all lette

ITC ZAPF INTERNATIONAL 12 POINT SET MINUS ½ UNIT

LIGHT, ITALIC, DEMI, DEMI ITALIC

abcdefghijklmnopqrstuvwxyz – 1 UNIT
abcdefghijklmnopqrstuvwxyz – ½ UNIT
abcdefghijklmnopqrstuvwxyz NORMAL

ABCDEFGHIJKLMNOPQRSTUVWXYZ 1234567890 abcdefghijklmnopqrstuvwxyz
ABCDEFGHIJKLMNOPQRSTUVWXYZ 1234567890 abcdefghijklmnopqrstuvwxyz
ABCDEFGHIJKLMNOPQRSTUVWXYZ 1234567890 abcdefghijklmnopqrstuvwxyz
ABCDEFGHIJKLMNOPQRSTUVWXYZ 1234567890 abcdefghijklmnopqrstuvwxyz

12/12

The main purpose of letters is the practical one of making thoughts visible. Ruskin says that all letters are frightful things and to be endured only on occas ion, that is to say, in places where the sense of the in scription is of more importance than external orna ment. This is a sweeping statement, from which w e need not suffer unduly; yet it is doubtful whether t here is art in individual letters. Letters in combinati on may be satisfying and in a well composed page e ven beautiful as a whole, but art in letters consists r ather in the art of arranging and composing them i n a pleasing and appropriate manner. The main pu rpose of letters is the practical one of making thoug hts visible. Ruskin says that all letters are frightful t hings and to be endured only on occasion, that is to
The main purpose of letters is the practical one of m aking thoughts visible. Ruskin says that all letters ar
The main purpose of letters is the practical one of making thoughts visible. Ruskin says that al

12/13

The main purpose of letters is the practical one of making thoughts visible. Ruskin says that all letters are frightful things and to be endured only on occas ion, that is to say, in places where the sense of the in scription is of more importance than external orna ment. This is a sweeping statement, from which w e need not suffer unduly; yet it is doubtful whether t here is art in individual letters. Letters in combinati on may be satisfying and in a well composed page e ven beautiful as a whole, but art in letters consists r ather in the art of arranging and composing them i n a pleasing and appropriate manner. The main pu rpose of letters is the practical one of making thoug hts visible. Ruskin says that all letters are frightful t
The main purpose of letters is the practical one of m aking thoughts visible. Ruskin says that all letters ar
The main purpose of letters is the practical one of making thoughts visible. Ruskin says that al

12/14

The main purpose of letters is the practical one of making thoughts visible. Ruskin says that all letters are frightful things and to be endured only on occas ion, that is to say, in places where the sense of the in scription is of more importance than external orna ment. This is a sweeping statement, from which w e need not suffer unduly; yet it is doubtful whether t here is art in individual letters. Letters in combinati on may be satisfying and in a well composed page e ven beautiful as a whole, but art in letters consists r ather in the art of arranging and composing them i n a pleasing and appropriate manner. The main pu rpose of letters is the practical one of making thoug hts visible. Ruskin says that all letters are frightful t hings and to be endured only on occasion, that is to
The main purpose of letters is the practical one of m aking thoughts visible. Ruskin says that all letters ar
The main purpose of letters is the practical one of making thoughts visible. Ruskin says that al

12/15

The main purpose of letters is the practical one of making thoughts visible. Ruskin says that all letters are frightful things and to be endured only on occas ion, that is to say, in places where the sense of the in scription is of more importance than external orna ment. This is a sweeping statement, from which w e need not suffer unduly; yet it is doubtful whether t here is art in individual letters. Letters in combinati on may be satisfying and in a well composed page e ven beautiful as a whole, but art in letters consists r ather in the art of arranging and composing them i n a pleasing and appropriate manner. The main pu rpose of letters is the practical one of making thoug hts visible. Ruskin says that all letters are frightful t
The main purpose of letters is the practical one of m aking thoughts visible. Ruskin says that all letters ar
The main purpose of letters is the practical one of making thoughts visible. Ruskin says that al

ITC ZAPF INTERNATIONAL 14 POINT SET MINUS ½ UNIT

LIGHT, ITALIC, DEMI, DEMI ITALIC

abcdefghijklmnopqrstuvwxyz – 1 UNIT
abcdefghijklmnopqrstuvwxyz – ½ UNIT
abcdefghijklmnopqrstuvwxyz NORMAL

ABCDEFGHIJKLMNOPQRSTUVWXYZ abcdefghijklmnopqrstuvwxyz
ABCDEFGHIJKLMNOPQRSTUVWXYZ abcdefghijklmnopqrstuvwxyz
ABCDEFGHIJKLMNOPQRSTUVWXYZ abcdefghijklmnopqrstuvwxyz
ABCDEFGHIJKLMNOPQRSTUVWXYZ abcdefghijklmnopqrstuvwxyz

14/14

The main purpose of letters is the practical one of making thoughts visible. Ruskin says that all letters are frightful things and to be endured only on occasion, that is to say, in p laces where the sense of the inscription is of more importance than external ornament. This is a sweeping statement, from which we need not suffer unduly; yet it is doubtful whether there is art in individual letters. Let ters in combination may be satisfying and i n a well composed page even beautiful as a whole, but art in letters consists rather in th e art of arranging and composing them in a
The main purpose of letters is the practical o ne of making thoughts visible. Ruskin says t
The main purpose of letters is the practi cal one of making thoughts visible. Rus

14/15

The main purpose of letters is the practical one of making thoughts visible. Ruskin says that all letters are frightful things and to be endured only on occasion, that is to say, in p laces where the sense of the inscription is of more importance than external ornament. This is a sweeping statement, from which we need not suffer unduly; yet it is doubtful whether there is art in individual letters. Let ters in combination may be satisfying and i n a well composed page even beautiful as a whole, but art in letters consists rather in th
The main purpose of letters is the practical o ne of making thoughts visible. Ruskin says t
The main purpose of letters is the practi cal one of making thoughts visible. Rus

14/16

The main purpose of letters is the practical one of making thoughts visible. Ruskin says that all letters are frightful things and to be endured only on occasion, that is to say, in p laces where the sense of the inscription is of more importance than external ornament. This is a sweeping statement, from which we need not suffer unduly; yet it is doubtful whether there is art in individual letters. Let ters in combination may be satisfying and i n a well composed page even beautiful as a whole, but art in letters consists rather in th e art of arranging and composing them in a
The main purpose of letters is the practical o ne of making thoughts visible. Ruskin says t
The main purpose of letters is the practi cal one of making thoughts visible. Rus

14/17

The main purpose of letters is the practical one of making thoughts visible. Ruskin says that all letters are frightful things and to be endured only on occasion, that is to say, in p laces where the sense of the inscription is of more importance than external ornament. This is a sweeping statement, from which we need not suffer unduly; yet it is doubtful whether there is art in individual letters. Let ters in combination may be satisfying and i n a well composed page even beautiful as a whole, but art in letters consists rather in th
The main purpose of letters is the practical o ne of making thoughts visible. Ruskin says t
The main purpose of letters is the practi cal one of making thoughts visible. Rus

Designed by Jean Callan King and Tony Esposito.

Typography by Volk & Huxley, Inc., 228 East 45th Street, New York, New York.

Printed and bound by Halliday Lithograph Corporation, West Hanover, Massachusetts.